POETRY OF THE
SPANISH CIVIL WAR

The publication of this work has been aided by a grant
from the Andrew W. Mellon Foundation

POETRY OF THE
SPANISH CIVIL WAR

"Say that we saw Spain die."
Edna St. Vincent Millay

"Viva Franco! Arriba Espana!"
Roy Campbell

MARILYN ROSENTHAL
Virginia Polytechnic Institute and State University

NEW YORK · NEW YORK UNIVERSITY PRESS
1975

Copyright © 1975 by New York University
Library of Congress Catalog Card Number: 74-18952
ISBN: 0-8147-7356-7

Library of Congress Cataloging in Publication Data

Rosenthal, Marilyn
    Poetry of the Spanish Civil War.
    Bibliography: p.

    1. Spain—History—Civil War, 1936-1939—Literature
and the war. 2. Poetry, Modern—20th century—History
and criticism. I. Title.
PN1080.R65   809.1   74-18952
ISBN 0-8147-7356-7

Manufactured in the United States of America

In Memoriam

Norman J. Suski (1938-1975)

who deserved a better world

Preface

The Spanish Civil War deeply engaged the feelings and loyalties of poets of many countries—chiefly, of course, the poets of Spain and Latin America. I shall briefly survey here poets of six languages, undertaking a selective consideration of the involvement of, mainly, thirteen poets: two Spanish, one Peruvian, one Chilean, two English, one South African, one Scottish, one North American, one German, one French, one Russian, and one Italian. I have isolated a few poems by each as representative in order to make a close study of poems rather than survey, with less depth, many poems of the war. My purpose is to analyze and—to a certain extent—to compare poetic and political reactions to the war. The reason is, simply, that such research can throw light on the interplay between the poet's art and contemporary history.

The premise is that there is value to be derived from juxtaposing a historical event of considerable importance and of serious implications and the poetry of recognized poets. In undertaking this study of poems by significant poets on the same subject, I have tried to determine their differences, similarities, and relative importance. I have considered the war in all of its contexts to see what could be made of selected poems resulting from it. Poems, when studied comparatively, illuminate one another. Perhaps, too, human and historical truth is better understood through art than through politics. If we are to understand what happens in the world, not merely intellectually, but also emotionally, poetry can help us reach a higher sense of reality. As the Mexican poet Octavio Paz has said: there is no voice more faithful to a people than the voice of its poets.

My purpose is not to write a history of Spanish Civil War poetry, subdivided into styles and movements. It is to present a limited selection of poets, and also (in Appendix I) to look at the broad spectrum of contributors and their contributions. Because of the character of the conflict and reactions to it, the war extends a unique opportunity to study a number of poets whose artistic response might be considered representative of their varied nationality, background, temperament, talent, values.

An initial biographical sketch will be followed by the poems and individual analyses. My method has been to analyze, in depth and comparatively, one to three poems (rarely four) by each of these writers, drawing comparative conclusions. The works I have chosen are the following:

Spain: "La insignia" (1937) by León Felipe and "Vientos del pueblo me llevan" and "Recoged esta voz" (two parts), both included in *Viento del pueblo* (1937) by Miguel Hernández.

Peru: "Pequeño responso a un héroe de la República," "Masa," and "España, aparta de mí este cáliz," from *España, aparta de mí este cáliz* (1937) by César Vallejo.

Chile: "Explico algunas cosas," "Llegada a Madrid de la Brigada Internacional," and "Almería," collected in *España en el corazón* (1936-1937) by Pablo Neruda.

South Africa: Roy Campbell's *Flowering Rifle* (1939).

Scotland: Hugh MacDiarmid's *The Battle Continues* (1957).

England: W. H. Auden's *Spain* (1937) and Stephen Spender's "Ultima Ratio Regum," "Two Armies," and "To a Spanish Poet," included among his "Poems about the Spanish Civil War, 1936-1939."

North America: Muriel Rukeyser's "Mediterranean" (1937), published in *New Masses,* and "Third Elegy: Fear of Form" and "Nuns in the Wind," included in *A Turning Wind* (1939).

Germany: Johannes R. Becher's "General Mola: Aus dem spanischen Bürgerkrief," located in *Ausgewählte Dichtung aus der Zeit der Verbannung, 1933-1945,* and "Barcelona" and "Fliehende Mutter," from his *Gedichte 1936-1941.*

France: Paul Eluard's "Novembre 1936" and "La Victoire de Guernica," from *Cours naturel* (1938), and two short poems from *Poèmes politiques* (1948): "Espagne" and "En Espagne."

Russia: Níkolay Semyónovich Tíkhonov's "Ispantsi otstupili za Pirenyiei" (from the section "Gorï") and "Govorit fashist" and "Govorit antifashist" (from the section "Numancia"), located in his collection *Izbránnye proizvédenija v dvuch tómach* (1955).

Italy: Giorgio Braccialarghe's "Notti di Spagna," "Ai fratelli lontani . . . ," "Fratelli dell'Internazionale," and "Terra di Spagna . . . ," all four poems published by the Commissariat of the International Brigades in *Romancero de los voluntarios de la libertad* (1937).

I have translated all non-English poems into their English equivalents, which are found in Appendix II. I have included all the poems within the text except for W. H. Auden's *Spain,* for which permission is not available, and the very long poems by Roy Campbell (*Flowering Rifle*) and Hugh MacDiarmid (*The Battle Continues*), from which, instead, I have selected illustrative quotations of sufficient length.

The sequence of the poets and of the poems by each poet is roughly chronological within each grouping. Precision in this matter is impossible because some of the older poets outlived the younger ones, and some of the poets are contemporaneous. Besides, the dates of the individual poems are not always known. There are occasional gaps in biographical material, depending upon the sources, or lack thereof, available.

Auden wrote only one poem on the Spanish War. I have also included one poem each by Campbell, MacDiarmid, and Felipe, but only because of the length of their poems.

I have surveyed the corpus of each poet's work and alluded to additional poems to see what effect the war may have had on the poet's development. Biographical considerations are included to increase understanding of the poet and his poems.

Why have I chosen these particular poets and poems? They represent a varied selection of countries, backgrounds, politics, ages, and interests. These are major poets in their respective countries or, if not (as in the case of Braccialarghe), they offer something representative of war poetry and, specifically, of that war's poetry. The poems combine psychic, philosophical, and verbal elements. They reveal varying degrees of technical skill, intellectual achievement, and emotional quality. Some are more valid than others, whether poetically or politically. For the most part, these poems will survive the passage of time. Where the poems are not intrinsically valuable, they are, at least, of historical interest. Roy Campbell is the only Franco advocate among them because he was almost the only poet who supported Franco, and surely the most important poet on the Nationalist side. Among the thirteen poets, Auden, Becher, Eluard, MacDiarmid, Neruda, Spender, Tíkhonov, and Vallejo may be numbered among the communists, or their supporters, at least during the war.

I have made three main groupings: Chapter II combines Spanish and Latin poets because of the intimate connection between them; Chapter III isolates English-language poets, not only because of their cultural and linguistic affinity, but also because their reactions to the Spanish Civil War have elements in common. There are interesting distinctions and similarities to be derived from dividing the chapters in this way. Chapter IV focuses on four poets with a few poems by each in German, French, Russian, and Italian. Chapter V deals with more general conclusions concerning the poetry of the Spanish Civil War. This final chapter summarizes their approach, theme, language, tone, imagery, and general "experience" of the war. It also includes a consideration of war poetry in general. Appendix I includes a listing of many poets (other than my poets of concentration) who wrote in Spanish, English, German, French, Russian, and Italian. Appendix II offers my translations into English of all foreign poems that have been analyzed.

I do not value equally all of the poems included here, but each time I made a selection I had a particular reason. For the most part I find the poems in Spanish superior in quality to the others. Vallejo was my first choice, and the rest evolved from him.

I take this opportunity to thank Professor Gabriel H. Lovett, of the Spanish Department at Wellesley College, who introduced me to the Spanish Civil War. I am deeply indebted to Professor M. L. Rosenthal, of the English Department of New York University, who inspired, supported, and criticized this study. Professor Helene Anderson of New York University generously shared her understanding of the Hispanic poets with me through discussion and criticism. I also thank Professor Robert J. Clements, Chairman of the Comparative Literature Department at New York University, for encouragement and support from the very beginning. Among my translating assistants have been Professor Kenneth Negus of Rutgers University and Professors Segundo Cardona, Luis MacFie, Angie Noriega, and Michael Reck of the University of Puerto Rico, to all of whom I am grateful.

M.R.

Blacksburg, Virginia

Foreword

In the late Thirties poets were even busier than novelists converting the throes of the Spanish Republic into urgent words and
reminders. The novelists' concern for the human condition,
heightened by the Spanish Civil War, has been ably chronicled
in Frederick Benson's volume *Writers in Arms: The Literary
Impact of the Spanish Civil War* (N. Y. U. Press), the companion
volume to the present one. As Salvador de Madariaga wrote in his
introduction to Benson's book: "Those cities in ruins, those
trenches soaked in human blood, those cemeteries for not quite
dead human beings, which were the concentration camps, were to
act on the Western soul like a spiritual bombardment, and to
reduce it to shambles." Of the present book, whose contents page
was sent him, Madariaga found it most interesting, but wondered
why only the polarized poets of Left and Right were included,
leaving out such middle-of-the-road poets as himself. While it is
true that the great scholar Madariaga, spokesman for Spain in the
League of Nations during the Thirties, wrote a few poems less

directly concerned with the war, it is even more true that there
were almost no poetic chroniclers of the war who were not driven
to the Left or Right, as was every individual living within embattled Spain itself. Having been in Spain during the early phase
of the war, I had an opportunity to see how there was no option
for neutralism or washing of hands. Brothers within the same
family had to take sides, sometimes opposing sides, and the same
held true of poets. What is interesting and clearly demonstrated
by Marilyn Rosenthal in the following pages is that poets loyal to
the Republic—the majority—wrote the best poetry.

The poet in Spain has for centuries taken up his pen against
wars and oppression, ever since Cervantes in *Numancia* showed
how the will of the people could be pitted against that of the
legions of ancient Rome. Byron later joined the ranks of Spanish
poets decrying the one-sided struggles of the Spanish people, "without freedom's stranger-tree growing native of the soil." In a country which has enjoyed only six years of parliamentary government
during a two-thousand year history, poetry was always on the defensive. Larra, the poet who died one century before the Spanish
Civil War, predicted its outcome in the prophetic words: "here
lies half Spain, done to death by the other half." A young painter
told me one night in Madrid's Café Gijón that the history of
Spanish painting was the history of hunger. Reflecting on his
meaning, I eventually concluded that this comment applied as
well to poetry. Spanish poets in the Thirties were not like their
mesmerized counterparts in Italy, who believed like the Demokos
of Giraudoux that "la guerre exige un chant de guerre." Sadly
turning to the theme of war, they embraced rather the theme not
of fighting, but of fighting back. As if aware of their millennial
duty, the Spanish poets felt obliged to speak out with clarity. In
"La insignia," León Felipe observes that everyone has had his say
about the war except the one most likely to speak truth—the poet:

> Entonces falto yo solo.
> Porque el poeta no ha hablado todavía.

In "España, aparta de mí este cáliz" César Vallejo explains the
secular tragedy of Spain and instructs Spaniards how to cope with

the future in case of defeat. The same epic sweep of history is recalled by the "impassioned" voice of Miguel Hernández, even as he slips into the language of Vergilian heroic poetry:

Naciones, hombres, mundos, esto escribo.

The Hispanic poet, even if he witnessed only fleetingly the kaleidoscope of the war, wrote with posterity in mind. Neruda reveals his sense of duty to record what his eyes have seen: "Comrades, I have seen you, then, and my eyes are full of pride."

Just as the poets outside Spain—French, Chilean, Russian, or other—wish to remind the peninsular Spaniards that the outside world is empathizing with them, these same poets felt a great need to tell the outside world what was really going on in Spain. One of the most unreliable in his interpretations, as Marilyn Rosenthal documents, was Roy Campbell, whose single voice did damage to the forces in the Anglo-Saxon world who were trying to enlist more help for the Republic. Playing on racial and religious prejudices, he made of poetry, even more than the committed Marxists, an outright form of propaganda. If one must concede that his sentiments were sincerely felt, then one can only be gratified that the war bred few such poets. Campbell was clever enough to show that the Falangist side, too, had its moments of heroic courage to be commemorated, such as the defense of Toledo's Alcázar.

The insularity of Spain, the little real knowledge outside of the issues in conflict, the dual forces of propaganda sustained in Europe and America—these left much misunderstanding outside the peninsula. One side said nuns were raped; the other said peasants were being shot down. It is small wonder that poets inside and outside Spain felt it their mission to "explain." Thus, Neruda entitles one of his most cogent poems "Explico algunas cosas." From an explainer of Chile and Peru he has become that of Spain.

I am going to tell you all that happens to me . . .
You will ask why my poetry
Does not speak to you of the soil, of the leaves,
Of the great volcanoes of my native country.
Come see the blood in the streets.

Presenting the suitation in Spain to his Slavic comrades, Níkolaij Tíkhonov mocks the attitude of poet as teacher and explainer when this role is assumed by a Fascist poet: "Now let me explain to you why . . ."

The Spanish Civil War was not only a battle for survival of political institutions, but of prose and poetry as well. Stephen Spender makes this point in the following pages. And Auden hoped that the war would generate a land of great and prolific poetry: "Tomorrow for the young, the poets exploding like bombs." Their concern for the future was well-founded. Even if the pro-Communist group among the Republicans had wrested power after the war, the concern would have been justified. The exodus of writers from Spain, analogous to that of authors from Soviet Russia, was probably the greatest drain of talent that Spain ever experienced. Many tasted what Dante called the salty bread of exile. I have broken bread with many of them and enjoyed their friendship: Amado Alonso, Francisco Ayala, Arturo Barea, Ernesto DaCal, Jorge Guillën, Pedro Salinas, Ramón Sender, to mention a few. These writers were not middle-of-the-road. As I have suggested, the war polarized the writers to the extent that there were not enough middle-of-the-road poets to become a third element in Dr. Rosenthal's study. The greatest fluctuator toward the center of the road was Auden, who, as we learn below, after writing a splendid *légende des siècles* on Spain, denied his poem and claimed to have sacrificed doctrine to rhetoric. Auden made the same fastidious repudiation of his moving poem on the outbreak of the second World War, "September 1, 1939."

Middle-road poets would need a middle course to espouse. There was none. Even the novelists like Hemingway were rare who could assert that there were heroes and villains on both sides. The disunity of the free world was all too clear from the poets represented here. The weakness of the League of Nations left Republican Spain vulnerable. The Tory appeasement of Germany and Italy left the Falangists a free rein, and one indignant poet below will voice greater respect for the villains of Germany and Italy than for the weakling Britain. It became easy for the Communist Russians to appear as heroes in this tragic war, even though, as McDiarmid admits, he will be a Bolshevik only *before* the Revolution (here, war), for real literature cannot be written when communism "comes to rule the roost." Many poets, like Paul Eluard, saw Spain as a curtain-raiser for the polarization of the entire European continent. Its role as an experimental area for armaments and technology has no better poetic articulation than in Sender's poem on the dead child:

> Ask. Was so much expenditure justified
> On the death of one so young and so silly
> Lying under the olive trees, O world, o death?

The question has remained valid for all wars, a lament also for the little brown children of Viet Nam, napalmed and carpet-bombed so diligently.

Echoing the phrase of Malraux and Sender, the poets inside and outside Spain referred to the crisis of the human condition. It was an endemic crisis, threatening all times and all places. The struggle between Juan and Pedro was that of Hector and Achilles, Cain and Abel, Satan and Christ. Compare Maurice English's lines:

> Cain, Cain, Cain! Where is your brother Abel?
> Abel your brother—where is Abel, Cain?
> In bombed Guernica and Badajoz
> Calling among the ruin of the stones.

It occurs to me that the Spanish War was probably the first one which liberated poetry entirely from traditional Western forms of verse. Elegy loses metre, sonnets burst their bonds, odes defy syllable-counts. The forms of lyric poetry are cast aside as though the poet had discovered that there is no longer anything lyrical about war. Rhyme is more and more rejected, as though the poet no longer found rhyme or reason in war. Giorgio Braccialarghe, from a country which invented and codified many a lyrical form over the centuries, begins his poem to his Spanish brothers:

> Tonight I wish to sing for you
> without rhyme or meter.
> Poor palpitant words

as when after crying very much
one searches for one who is gone forever.

The best example of the explosion of metric rhythm and poetic structure is Paul Eluard's threnody on the bombing of Guernica (below). In total union with his friend Picasso's painting *Guernica,* Eluard not only expresses his thoughts in brief patches of words in Cubist fashion, but arranges these patches on the page as though they had been fractured by the detonation of a bomb from a disappearing Stuka.

The question of whether a poet writes best about what he has actually seen and experienced is probably an academic one. Or more likely, the disparate proofs on one side and the other make it impossible to draw a conclusion. We know that Muriel Rukeyser saw little but the first hours of the Civil War—and that from a departing ship—because she tells us so. Yet her poetry seems authentic and moving. In any case, there are certain dim indications from the poetry below that most poets lived through the agony of Spain, and not all these indications deal with cadavers and bursting shells. Let me choose just one evidence familiar to me.

The outbreak of the Civil War found me in Madrid as a vacationing student. During the months of July and August my brother and I traversed the peninsula from Irún to Algeciras, eyewitnesses to heightening hatreds and war. Barbarities and madnesses prevailed in this war, as Goya preached in his *Disasters of War* and his *The Sleep of Reason.* Or more simply, perhaps, Goya's *Saturn,* as Spain cannibalized its children. Yet there were long lulls and periods when daily life went on uneventfully and one wondered whether the country was really at war. These long interregna of calm and silence surprised us, even late in July, when we were jailed for two weeks in the little anarchical village of La Campana, in Andalucía Province. From the court of the jail we could enjoy the lovely moonlit skies over the *plaza mayor,* hear distant music, and see cranes listlessly flapping around their nest under the church steeple. Every afternoon the population observed the siesta hour, and later fell silently into bed around midnight. All this despite the fact that the Falangists took in turn Lora del Río, Carmona, and Ecija, all within an hour's drive from La Campana.

It was like the epic poetry of a Virgil or a Ronsard where the fighting is interrupted for long intervals of pastoral peace. Or more exactly, long periods of peace were interrupted only occasionally by war.

This curious sensation, this illusory armistice, is noted by Spender's lines:

> Clean silence drops at night, when a little walk
> Divides the sleeping armies . . .

An even clearer approximation to what I mean is found in Braccialarghe's "Nights of Spain," which must be read in full.

> Nights of Spain,
> the toads singing
> along the long ditches
> in the meadows . . .
> Nights of Spain,
> capes of peace thrown
> over tortured days
> returns of calm
> indefinite whispers
> quiet murmurs . . .

Then comes the finale to the poem, the gunshot in the starry night. This finale occurred during our stay in La Campana when army tanks raced through the sleepy Sunday siesta hour, shot and burned everything in sight, stacked the bodies like cordwood in the square, destroyed the water supply, ignited the late summer wheat, and raced out with us and the other prisoners. Spender visited wartime Spain on three occasions. Braccialarghe, having fought with the Garibaldi Battalion, also knew from experience these unreal periods of détente between assaults and air raids. Perhaps we may conclude that one does write most authentically about what one has lived through. Another generalization which may be permitted after a reading of this volume is that those poets who have not lived through an actual battle tend to paint more graphic, naturalistic scenes than those who have experienced these moments of truth.

A final word on Marilyn Rosenthal and her fine book. The author was hardly born when the Spanish Civil War began. Youth, as Burke put it, needs no apology, certainly not in this case, any more than for Hugh Thomas, author of one of the most used histories of the war, whose youth made his view of that event totally retrospective. Miss Rosenthal, whose doctorate is in Comparative Literature, found herself at an early age deeply preoccupied with this war. Her depth of feeling is as solid as her scholarship. It was remarkable that when she was ready for her book on this important theme, no one had yet worked this literary vein. The results, you will see, are useful and important. Not only does she supply the reader with ample biographical and historical material to understand the total meaning of the poetry (Spanish poems are translated totally and accurately, as are those from other languages), but as a literary scholar Marilyn Rosenthal has not neglected her function as literary critic and textual commentator, presenting the poems not only as historical documents, but as literary masterworks as well.

Robert J. Clements

Contents

CHAPTER I

Introduction

The Spanish Civil War, which ravaged Spain and reverberated around the world, had among its side effects a decisive impact upon literature and culture. It aroused the emotions of writers, artists, and intellectuals, affecting not just what they created as artists, but often how they behaved as human beings. It inspired much poetry of many kinds. In fact, seldom has a single socio-political event provoked so many poets to write so many poems.

The war, which erupted in 1936 and lasted thirty-three months, not only cost Spain "un millon de muertos" but also struck poets all over the world as a test of Western civilization. To many, the struggle threatened the very structure of society and the requisites of civilized life. Defending the role poets played in the war, Stephen Spender wrote:

> the struggle of the Republic . . . seemed a struggle for the conditions without which the writing and reading of poetry are almost impossible in modern society.[1]

1

Miguel Hernández also warned of the danger:

> Un porvenir de polvo se avecina,
> se avecina un suceso
> en que no quedará ninguna cosa:
> ni piedra sobre piedra ni hueso sobre hueso.[2]

> (A future of dust advances,
> a fate advances
> in which nothing will remain,
> neither stone on stone nor bone on bone.)

Since all the literature about the war was political (to a greater or lesser degree) and since it is impossible to comprehend the literary motivations and provocations without, at least, being acquainted with the major outlines of the conflict, I shall briefly survey the war, emphasizing its literary implications.

The Great Depression, the feeling that capitalism in its existing form was doomed, and the rise of the totalitarian dictators, reaching a climax in Hitler's assumption of power in January 1933, preceded and accompanied the Spanish Civil War. A long history of economic, social, and political problems within Spain precipitated it.[3] But the fighting actually began on July 17, 1936, when a group of generals led by Emilio Mola, Sanjurjo, Francisco Franco, and others started revolts in various cities in Spain and in Spanish Morocco against the weak but representative and liberal Spanish Republic (with Manuel Azaña as President). From the beginning, the rebels were supported by large elements of the clergy, nobility, and army. In addition, they quickly received supplies of materials and men from Germany and Italy, suggesting that they had received promises of foreign support in advance of the uprising.

The war brought devastation to many areas of Spain. It assumed an international character as men from twenty-odd nations came to Spain to take part. However, because of the efforts of Western democracies to prevent the Spanish conflict from extending beyond the Spanish borders, in a sense these great powers permitted the fascists to defeat Republican Spain. As many as 40,000 foreigners fought in the International Brigades on the Republican side, contrary to the policies of their individual countries and at great personal sacrifice. Of these, perhaps a third died in action in Spain. Many more later suffered political or professional ostracism because of their Spanish experiences. Many were executed in the purges of Eastern Europe of 1949 simply because they had been to Spain. So, most outside aid for the government of the Republic was shut off by the nonintervention policy of the big democratic powers; and, despite the support of most of the Spanish population, as well as of the moderate and Left-wing political parties—and despite the aid of Russian communists and International Brigades—the Republic fought a losing battle against the better-organized, better-supplied troops on Franco's side. By the spring of 1939, the organized Popular Front resistance had practically ceased, and General Franco became the dictator of a totalitarian state, while Hitler and Mussolini turned their attention, manpower, and matériel to World War II.

The Republic was unequivocally defeated by April of 1939. This result was predictable. There was intervention for Franco by Hitler's and Mussolini's forces. There was the tragically short-sighted aloofness of the Western democracies. There was the foreshortened intervention of Russia, supporting only what it approved, and only as long as it was useful to communism. Russia's duplicity, fascist support, democratic neutrality, and International Brigades made the war a tremendously complicated struggle.

On both sides the war was marked, especially in its early stages, by a ruthlessness which astounded the civilized world. Churches were burned or desecrated, and public religious observances forbidden throughout Republican Spain; ten bishops, many thousands of priests, and religious members of the laity were murdered in cold blood, for no political activity or crime. The Nationalists shot nonpolitical Federico García Lorca. They organized mass executions (e.g., in Badajoz) and subjected the Basque town of Guernica to terrorist air bombardment, while German ships vengefully attacked the town of Almería.

Participants and even survivors of a civil war, with its contingent postwar reprisals,[4] pay dearly. As André Malraux has Garcia muse: "Whichever way this war ends, what sort of peace can possibly prevail after such bitter hatred?"[5] Poor and limited supplies,

sketchy training, inefficiency, betrayals, and atrocities increased
despair and death. For the Loyalists to continue an increasingly
hopeless struggle demanded extreme bravery. Even spectators—
those who saw Spanish Loyalists as betrayed in a just cause—were
outraged. Such a combination of circumstances offered abundant
raw material as well as inspiration to writers. Faith in the Republican cause encouraged Hemingway to write:

> You felt, in spite of all bureaucracy and inefficiency and party
> strife something that was like the feeling you expected to have
> and did not have when you made your first communion. It was
> a feeling of consecration to a duty toward all the oppressed of
> the world which would be difficult and embarrassing to speak
> about as religious experience and yet it was authentic . . . It
> gave you a part in something that you could believe in wholly
> and completely and in which you felt an absolute brotherhood
> with the others who were engaged in it.[6]

The fact that the Insurgents were supported by Hitler's Germany and Mussolini's Italy, and that the military superiority was
clearly on their side, helps account for the challenge to humanitarian values felt by many authors and for the note of despair
common in their works. The war attracted writers of many nations
and elicited varied reactions. Viewpoints differed but, for the most
part, the literature reflects the idealism as well as the disillusionment of those who had seen it as a holy war. Albert Camus looked
back at the defeat of the Republic as a debacle:

> It is now nine years that men of my generation have had Spain
> within their hearts. Nine years that they have carried it with
> them like an evil wound. It was in Spain that men learned that
> one can be right and yet be beaten, that force can vanquish
> spirit, that there are times when courage is not its own recom-
> pense. It is this, doubtless, which explains why so many men,
> the world over, feel the Spanish drama as a personal tragedy.[7]

The fate of the Spaniards, combined with his high opinion of
them, influenced Arturo Barea's choice of the following epigraph
for the final section of his autobiography:

. . . honour eternal is due to the brave and noble people of Spain, worthy of better rulers and a better future! And now that the jobs and intrigues of their juntas, the misconduct and incapacity of their generals, are sinking into the deserved obscurity of oblivion, the national resistance rises nobly out of the ridiculous details . . . That resistance was indeed wild, disorganized, undisciplined and Algerine, but it held out to Europe an example which was not shown by the civilized Italian or intellectual German.[8]

Notes

1. Introduction to *Poems for Spain* (London: Hogarth Press, 1939), p. 7.

2. "Recoged esta voz," *Imagen de tu huella, el silbo vulnerado, el rayo que no cesa, otros poemas, viento del pueblo* (Buenos Aires: Editorial Losada, S. A., 1963), p. 110. (See pp. 49-52 for complete text.)

3. Sources for historical facts throughout this study are: Gabriel Jackson, *The Spanish Republic and the Civil War, 1931-1939* (Princeton: Princeton University Press, 1965); and Hugh Thomas, *The Spanish Civil War* (New York: Eyre, 1961).

4. Franco had 200,000 men executed after the war, according to an estimate from Jackson's *The Spanish Republic and the Civil War, 1931-1939*, pp. 538-39.

5. André Malraux, *Man's Hope* (New York: Random House, 1938), p. 252.

6. Ernest Hemingway, *For Whom the Bell Tolls* (New York: Scribner, 1940), p. 235.

7. Quoted as epigraph to Allen Guttmann's *The Wound in the Heart* (New York: Free Press of Glencoe, 1962).

8. The quotation from Richard Ford's *Handbook for Travellers in Spain and Readers at Home* appears as an epigraph to the third part of Arturo Barea's *The Forging of a Rebel* (New York: Reynal & Hitchcock, 1946), p. 420.

CHAPTER II

Civil War Poets of Spain and Latin America

The Spanish Civil War, fought on Spanish soil, affecting every level of Spanish society, culture, economy, and politics, complicated by strong international elements, had an enduring effect upon its population and sympathizers. For the Spaniards the war was an immediate and harrowing experience, resulting in radical changes. It had an effect still at the root of Spanish being and thinking. Spain and its people will never again be the same as before the war. This accounts for the fact that many literary works (prose as well as poetry) were published long after the war had ended, and that many of the writers went into exile. For Spanish poets, the war had ethnic as well as cosmic significance. They were caught up in it politically, poetically, personally, and emotionally. There is an intimate connection felt by Latin Americans for the Spanish people and a close affinity between their cultures. Even though Latin American-Spanish history has been characterized by love-hate ambivalence between an offspring and its mother country, there has

6

always been a deep awareness of common Hispanic origins and ties. The Spanish and Latin American poets shared an identification and involvement unavailable to non-Spaniards. There are noticeable differences between the Spanish/Latin view of Spain and the war and that of non-Spaniards.

For Spanish and Latin American poets, conception of the war had a distinctive quality—an added dimension. Their differences and similarities manifest themselves in their perspectives, poetic images, and tones. As an example, some deduction can surely be drawn from the frequent inclusion of blood imagery in their poetry.

Their common Roman Catholic background, even if later formally rejected, left an impact which frequent referral to God and religious symbols confirms. They had also been made aware, through Catholicism, of a resigned and fatalistic attitude about death. The nature of the Spanish language and culture influenced their poems. For example, Hernández, knowing his people, divided them by provinces and characteristics in his poem "Vientos del pueblo me llevan." Stephen Spender could characterize Spain by olive trees in his war poems; but Neruda went deeper in sensing the Spanish concept of death in "Llegada a Madrid de la Brigada Internacional." And Felipe clarified the nature of Spanish factiousness in "La insignia." The holocaust of Madrid and Neruda's personal world were inextricably connected in "Explico algunas cosas." Hernández could identify totally with the Spanish soldiers, having been one. The close association of these poets to what they wrote showed itself also in their preference for first-person narration of their poems. Their emotionality stems both from their relation to the subject matter and from the lack of reserve characteristically Latin (and not Anglo-Saxon). With the exception of Felipe, they had all written emotional, sometimes passionate, love poems prior to the Spanish Civil War. Felipe's "La insignia" is very Spanish, with its allusions to Don Quijote, patriotism, real understanding of the complexities of the situation, and deep feeling. The poems of all four poets offer authentic expressions of feeling.

Spain became a tormenting preoccupation for Vallejo, Neruda, Hernández, and Felipe. Felipe was deeply troubled by the divisions which rent his country. His view is cosmopolitan and transcends the national to an extent that one would not expect of a Spaniard. Hernández was both appalled and inspired by the situation. His idealism is attributable, in part, to his youth (twenty-six years) in 1936. Neruda found hope in the International Brigades but was poignantly discouraged by much else. He expressed the most bitterness (of the four) in his poem "Almería." Vallejo, with his "tragic sense of life," [1] apparent in all of his poetry ("Esta tarde llueve como nunca; y no/tengo ganas de vivir, corazón" [2]) felt a common suffering.

These four poets are representative of Spain and South America, and have written some of the finest poems on the subject of the Spanish Civil War. Vallejo and Neruda are major figures of twentieth-century Latin American poetry. Despite their affinities, they also had different preparations and preoccupations. They all had provincial backgrounds, although they were later attracted to urban centers of culture and literature. But Felipe had the least humble origin. Their rural backgrounds put them close to the land and nature, affecting their feeling for the land, their choice of images and sense of values. Vallejo and Neruda later turned to communism as a solution to the poverty and other inequities they had witnessed as children; penury was a state Vallejo endured as an adult as well. The Civil War and, hopefully, possible revolution were tied together. But while Neruda put his poetry at the service of his ideology, such ideology was not directly present in Vallejo's poems. Felipe was the most objective; he was also the oldest (fifty-two) at the time of the war. Hernández and Felipe were concerned with moral issues—in which politics seemed suddenly to deal with choices between life and death, civilization and barbarism. Felipe's background was the most academic. Any intellectual analysis of his poem "La insignia" testifies to this. Hernández had done the least traveling, and had the weakest international perspective. His poetry was the least academic and most idealistic, and his audience was the simplest. Also, he was the only one of the four who had actually fought in the war, although they had all been in wartime Spain and had firsthand experience of the war.

At the outbreak of the war in 1936 Felipe was fifty-two; Hernández was twenty-six; Vallejo, forty-four; and Neruda, thirty-two.

Felipe's life had been very much a part of everything that led up to the war. His exposure to the patterns of Spanish politics gave him a focus. Also, his presence in Mexico after its 1910 Revolution as well as during the political and cultural ferment of the 1920s molded his perspective. He had witnessed there the factions of the mid-1920s and the falling out among the groups that had overthrown the former dictatorship. The similar weakness of the Spanish Republican side was the main thrust of "La insignia." His background enabled him to be an objective commentator on the immediate circumstances and the entire period of the Spanish Civil War. Hernández was just emerging to consciousness as a man at the time he was catapulted into the war. His maturity and his death coincided. His youth helps account for his inflamed sense of injustice, his idealism, and the importance to him of the moment—of the here and now. His was a youthful idealism not solidified by formal ideological channeling. In the case of Vallejo, there are overtones of tiredness. He was weary of inequities, suffering, and injustice. Neruda, on the other hand, was more militant and accusing.

Biographical and literary sketches should provide further insight into their positions. After we have examined in detail the forces that shaped both the poets and their works, we shall be able to see in depth the nature of their individuality and collectivism, only touched upon in this introductory chapter. Beginning with the Spaniards, in the order of their birthdates, and then the South Americans, I am presenting brief histories of the four poets' lives and careers, followed by analyses of chosen poems.

León Felipe Camino y Galicia (1884-1963) used the pseudonym León Felipe so extensively that almost nobody remembers his real name.[3] He was born in Tabara, in the province of Zamora, Spain, on April 11, 1884. His father was a notary. From the age of two to nine years he lived in Sequeros, a village in the province of Salamanca. In 1893 his family moved to Santander, where León began his studies nearby at a school in Vallacarriedo; he later finished high school in Santander. Drawn to the theater, he directed a group of student actors in Santander at the age of eighteen. He also experienced the theater of Madrid, where he became acquainted with Shakespeare's plays. His interest in the theater helps account for the dramatic and rhetorical nature of his poetry. When his father died, Felipe finished his study of pharmacy, but from practical rather than deeply felt motivation. He practiced pharmacy in Santander and later in Balmaceda (Vizcaya), but a few years later left to join a theatrical troupe traveling around Spain and Portugal. During this time his interest in writing poetry increased. To facilitate his writing, he divided his year: winters in Madrid; and the other part practicing pharmacy in various Castilian towns, all the while composing his *Versos y oraciones de caminante.* This first work was published in 1920, when Felipe was nearly forty.

In Madrid he frequented the Universal Café in the Puerta del Sol, where literary people gathered. In 1920 he left for Africa, where he lived two years in Fernando Poo as an administrator of the hospitals of the Gulf of Guinea. Next he went to Mexico, where he met such intellectuals as Antonio Caso, the philosopher; Rivera, the painter; Pedro Henriquez Ureña; and Daniel Cosio Villegas. He worked for a time as a librarian. After meeting his wife-to-be in Mexico, he returned with her to Brooklyn, New York, where they were married. For a short period he taught Spanish at the Berlitz School. He studied for one year at Columbia University under Federico de Onis, then went to Cornell University to study Spanish language and literature. He stayed there from 1925 to 1929, his wife having joined its faculty. In collaboration, he and his wife translated Waldo Frank's *España virgen,* and Felipe composed the poems of the second volume of *Versos y oraciones de caminante,* which was published in 1929 by the Instituto de las Españas in New York.

Drop a Star was published in 1930 in Mexico. Felipe's nostalgia for his native country increased, and he returned for a few months. In 1933 he reinstated himself in North America, this time going to Las Vegas University in New Mexico. From there he proceeded to Mexico City, giving a course on Quijote to North American students at the Universidad Nacional and, at the same time, working for the Secretary of Education. He returned to Spain in 1934, occupying himself with translations. *Antología,* edited by friends in homage, appeared the following year in Madrid. He again crossed the Atlantic, this time going to Panama as professor at its university and, also, as Cultural Attaché at the Spanish Embassy.

It was in Panama in July of 1936 that he first received news of the rebellion in Spain. He quickly sided with what he saw as the justice of the Republican cause and embarked for Spain. In Madrid he suffered the cruel bombings of October and November. Afterward, in January of 1937, he went to Valencia, along with the intellectuals of the Casa de la Cultura.

From the tragic events of the Spanish Civil War, Felipe was able to write deeply motivated poetry. In 1937 he wrote "La insignia"; and in March of 1938, when the bombings of Barcelona worsened, he wrote "Oferta," which was combined in a book with "El payaso de las bofetadas y el pescador de caña." Both are tragic poems about the war. The latter work cynically considers the fate of Christ-like figures as this world goes:

—Pero . . . Don Quijote . . . ¿está loco y vencido?
¿No es un héroe?
¿No es un poeta prometeico?
¿No es un redentor?
—¡Silencio! ¿Quién ha dicho que sea un redentor?
Está loco y vencido y por ahora no es más que un
    clown . . .
un payaso . . .
Claro que todos los redentores del mundo han sido
    locos y derratados.
. . . Y payasos antes de convertirse en dioses.
También Cristo fue un payaso.

(—But . . . Don Quijote . . . is he crazy and
    defeated?
Is he not a hero?
Is he not a Promethean poet?
Is he not a redeemer?
—Silence! Who has said that he is a redeemer?
He is crazy and conquered and now is only a
    clown . . .
a payaso . . .

Surely all the redeemers of the world have been crazy
and defeated.
. . . And clowns before turning into gods.
Christ was also a clown.)

Restless and disillusioned over the outcome of the war, Felipe left
Spain and returned to Mexico City, joining other Spanish exiles
in the Casa de España set up by President Cardenas.

He stayed seven years in Mexico, during which he wrote and
read publicly a series of sad and critical poems: "El hacha: Elegía
española" (1939), "El español del éxodo y del llanto" (1939), "El
gran responsable" (1940), and "Ganarás la luz . . ." (1943). "El
hacha" expressed his hopeless view of Spain's massacre by a metaphorical axe:

¡Oh, este llanto de España,
que ya no es más que arruga y sequedad . . . !
¿Por qué habéis dicho todos
que en España hay dos bandos,
si aquí no hay mas que polvo? . . .
No hay más que un hacha amarilla
que ha afilado el rencor.
Un hacha que cae siempre,
siempre,
implacable y sin descanso . . .
Y el hacha es la que triunfa.

(Oh, this weeping of Spain,
that now is only frown and dryness! . . .
Why have you all said
that in Spain there are two bands (factions),
if here there is only dust? . . .
There is only a yellow axe
sharpened by animosity,
an axe that falls always,
always,
always,
implacable and without rest . . .
And it is the axe that triumphs.)

In 1945, he traveled throughout South America, reciting poetry and lecturing. In his later years he produced further works, including *Antología rota* in 1947 and *Llamadme publicano* in 1950. His 1947 poem "Variante" expressed disgust with the injustice of contemporary Spain: "La España de la tierra ya no me importa más que para sacar de allí a los que buscan la justicia." He died in Mexico in 1963 at the age of seventy-nine.

Felipe's poetry was strongly influenced by Walt Whitman, whose works he had translated, and by Antonio Machado, Cervantes, and the Bible. His religiosity was apparent as early as 1920 in *Versos y oraciones de caminante,* when he wrote about his verses with humility before God:

> ¡Oh pobres versos míos,
> hijos de mi corazón,
> que os vais ahora solos y a la ventura por el mundo . . .
> que os guíe Dios!

> (Oh my poor verses,
> children of my heart,
> that go through the world alone and at a risk . . .
> May God guide you!)

On February 11, 1937, after the fall of Málaga, Felipe wrote the first version of his first poem of the Spanish Civil War, "La insignia." He revised it a number of times, and read this poetic speech, as he called it, first in Valencia and, afterwards, in the Coliseum of Barcelona on March 28. Published in 1938, it is included for analysis here.

LA INSIGNIA [4]
Alocución Poemática (1937)

> Este poema de guerra se inició a raíz de la
> caída de Málaga y adquirió esta expresión después
> de la caída de Bilbao. Así como va aquí es la
> última variante, la más estructurada, la que

prefiere y suscribe el autor. Y anula todas las
otras anteriores que ha publicado la Prensa. No
se dice esto por razones ni intereses editoriales.
Aquí no hay Copyright. Se han impreso quinientos
ejemplares para tirarlos en el aire de Valencia y
que los multiplique el viento.

—León Felipe

¿Habéis hablado ya todos?
¿Habéis hablado ya todos los españoles?
Ha hablado el gran responsable revolucionario,
y los pequeños responsables;
ha hablado el alto comisario,
y los comisarios subalternos;
han hablado los partidos políticos,
han hablado los gremios,
los Comités
y los Sindicatos;
han hablado los obreros y los campesinos;
han hablado los menestrales;
ha hablado el peluquero,
el mozo de café
y el limpiabotas.
Y han hablado los eternos demagogos también.
Han hablado todos.
Creo que han hablado todos.
¿Falta alguno?
¿Hay algún español que no haya pronunciado su
 palabra? . . .
¿Nadie responde? . . . (Silencio).
Entonces falto yo sólo.
Porque el poeta no ha hablado todavía.

¿Quién ha dicho que ya no hay poetas en el mundo?
¿Quién ha dicho que ya no hay profetas?

Un día los reyes y los pueblos,
para olvidar su destino fatal y dramático

y para poder suplantar el sacrificio con el cinismo y con la
   pirueta,
sustituyeron al profeta por el bufón.
Pero el profeta no es más que la voz vernácula de un pueblo,
la voz legítima de su Historia,
el grito de la tierra primera que se levanta en el barullo del
   mercado, sobre el vocerío de los traficantes.
Nada de orgullos:
ni jerarquías divinas ni genealogías eclesiásticas.
La voz de los profetas—recordadla—
es la que tiene más sabor de barro.
De barro,
del barro que ha hecho al árbol—al naranjo y al pino—
del barro que ha formado
nuestro cuerpo también.
Yo no soy más que una voz—la tuya, la de todos—
la más genuina,
la más general,
la más aborigen ahora,
la más antigua de esta tierra.
La voz de España que hoy se articula en mi garganta como
   pudo articularse en otra cualquiera.
Mi voz no es más que la onda de la tierra,
de nuestra tierra,
que me coge a mí hoy como una antena propicia.
Escuchad,
escuchad, españoles revolucionarios,
escuchad de rodillas.
No os arrodilléis ante nadie.
Os arrodilléis ante vosotros mismos,
ante vuestra misma voz,
ante vuestra misma voz que casi habíais olvidado.
De rodillas. Escuchad.

Españoles,
españoles revolucionarios,
españoles de la España legítima,
que lleva en sus manos el mensaje genuino de la raza para

colocarle humildemente en el cuadros armonioso de la
Historia Universal de mañana, y junto al esfuerzo generoso
de todos los pueblos del mundo . . .
escuchad:
Ahí están—miradlos—
ahí están, los conocéis bien.
Andan por toda Valencia,
están en la retaguardia de Madrid
y en la retaguardia de Barcelona también.
Están en todas las retaguardias.
Son los Comités,
los partidillos,
las banderías,
los Sindicatos,
los guerrilleros criminales de la retaguardia ciudadana.
Ahí los tenéis.
Abrazados a su botín reciente,
guardándole,
defendiéndole,
con una avaricia que no tuvo nunca el más degradado
    burgués.
¡A su botín!
¡Abrazados a su botín!
Porque no tenéis más que botín.
No le llaméis ni incautación siquiera.
El botín se hace derecho legítimo cuando está sellado por una
    victoria última y heroica.

Se va de lo doméstico a lo histórico,
y de lo histórico a lo épico.
Este ha sido siempre el orden que ha llevado la conducta del
    español en la Historia,
en el ágora
y hasta en sus transacciones,
que por eso se ha dicho siempre que el español no aprende
    nunca bien el oficio de marcader.
Pero ahora,
en esta revolución,

el orden se ha invertido.
Habéis empezado por lo épico,
habéis pasado por lo histórico
y ahora aquí,
en la retaguardia de Valencia,
frente a todas las derrotas,
os habéis parado en la domesticidad.
Y aquí estáis anclados,
Sindicalistas,
Comunistas,
Anarquistas,
Socialistas,
Troskistas,
Republicanos de Izquierda . . .
Aquí estáis anclados,
custodiando la rapiña
para que no se la lleve vuestro hermano.
La curva histórica del aristócrata, desde su origen popular y
    heroico, hasta su última degeneración actual, cubre en
    España más de tres siglos.
La del burgués, setenta años.
Y la vuestra, tres semanas.
¿Dónde está el hombre?
¿Dónde está el español?
Que no he de ir a buscarle al otro lado.
El otro lado es la tierra maldita, la España maldita de Caín
    aunque la haya bendecido el Papa.
Si el español está en algún sitio, he de ser aquí.
Pero, ¿dónde, dónde? . . .
Porque vosotros os habéis parado ya
y no hacéis más que enarbolar todos los días nuevas banderas
    con las camisas rotas y con los trapos sucios de la cocina.
Y si entrasen los fascistas en Valencia mañana, os encontrarían
    a todos haciendo guardia ante las cajas de caudales.
Esto no es derrotismo, como decís vosotros.
Yo sé que mi línea no se quiebra,
que no la quiebran los hombres,
y que tengo que llegar hasta Dios para darle cuenta de algo

que puso en mis manos cuando nació la primera substancia española.

Eso es lógica inexorable.

Vencen y han vencido siempre en la Historia inmediata, el pueblo y el ejército que han tenido un punto de convergencia, aunque este punto sea tan endeble y tan absurdo como una medalla de aluminio bendecida por un cura sanguinario.

Es la insignia de los fascistas.

Esta medalla es la insignia de los fascistas.

Una medalla ensangrentada de la Virgen.

Muy poca cosa.

Pero, ¿qué tenéis vosotros ahora que os una más?

Pueblo español revolucionario,
¡estás solo!
¡Solo!
Sin un hombre y sin un símbolo.
Sin un emblema místico donde se condense el sacrificio y la disciplina.
Sin un emblema solo donde se hagan bloque macizo y único todos tus esfuerzos y todos tus sueños de redención.
Tus insignias,
tus insignias plurales y enemigas a veces, se las compras en el mercado caprichosamente al primer chamarilero de la Plaza de Castelar,
de la Puerta del Sol
o de las Ramblas de Barcelona.
Has agotado ya en mil combinaciones egoístas y heterodoxas todas las letras del alfabeto.
Y has puesto de mil maneras diferentes, en la gorra y en la zamarra
el rojo
y el negro,
la hoz,
el martillo
y la estrella.
Pero aún no tienes una estrella SOLA,
después de haber escupido y apagado la de Belén.

Españoles,
españoles que vivís el momento más trágico de toda nuestra
   Historia,
¡estáis solos!
¡Solos!
El mundo,
todo el mundo es nuestro enemigo, y la mitad de nuestra
   sangre—la sangre podrida y bastarda de Caín—se ha vuelto
   contra nosotros también.

¡Hay que encender una estrella!
¡Una sola, sí!
Hay que levantar una bandera.
¡Una sola, sí!
Y hay que quemar las naves.
De aquí no se va más que a la muerte o a la victoria.
Todo me hace pensar que a la muerte.
No porque nadie me defienda
sino porque nadie me entiende.
Nadie entiende en el mundo la palabra "justicia." Ni vosotros
   siquiera.
Y mi misión era estamparla en la frente del hombre
y clavarla después en la Tierra
como el estandarte de la última victoria.
Nadie me entiende.
Y habrá que irse a otro planeta
con esta mercancía inútil aquí,
con esta mercancía ibérica y quijotesca.
¡Vamos a la muerte!
Sin embargo,
aún no hemos perdido aquí la última batalla,
la que se gana siempre pensando que ya no hay más salida
   que la muerte.
¡Vamos a la muerte!
Este es nuestro lema.
¡A la muerte!
Este es nuestro lema.
Que se despierte Valencia y que se ponga la mortaja.

¡Gritad,
gritad todos!
Tú, el pregonero y el speaker
echad bandos,
encended las esquinas con letras rojas
que anuncien esta sola proclama:
¡Vamos a la muerte! .
Vosotros, los Comisarios, los capitanes de la Censura,
envainad vuestra espada,
guardad vuestro lápiz rojo
y abrid a este grito las puertas del viento:
¡Vamos a la muerte!
Que lo oigan todos. Todos.
Los que trafican con el silencio
y los que trafican con las insignias.
Chamarileros de la Plaza de Castelar,
chamarileros de la Puerta del Sol,
chamarileros de las Ramblas de Barcelona,
destrozad,
quemad vuestra mercancía.
Ya no hay insignias domésticas,
ya no hay insignias de latón.
Ni para los gorros
ni para las zamarras.
Ya no hay cédulas de identificación.
Ya no hay más cartas legalizadas
ni por los Comités
ni por los Sindicatos.
¡Que les quiten a todos los carnets!
Ya no hay más que un emblema.
Ya no hay más que una estrella,
una sola, SOLA y ROJA, sí,
pero de sangre y en la frente,
que todo español revolucionario ha de hacérsela
hoy mismo,
ahora mismo
y con sus propias manos.
Preparad los cuchillos,

aguzad las navajas,
calentad al rojo vivo los hierros.
Id a las fraguas.
Que os pongan en la frente el sello de la justicia.
Madres,
madres revolucionarias,
estampad este grito indeleble de justicia
en la frente de vuestros hijos.
Allí donde habéis puesto siempre vuestros besos más limpios.
(Esto no es una imagen retórica.
Yo no soy el poeta de la retórica.
Ya no hay retórica.
La revolución ha quemado
todas las retóricas.)

Que nadie os engañe más.
Que no haya pasaportes falsos
ni de papel
ni de cartón
ni de hojadelata.
Que no haya más disfraces
ni para el tímido
ni para el frívolo
ni para el hipócrita
ni para el clown
ni para el comediante.
Que no haya más disfraces
ni para el espía que se sienta a vuestro lado en el café,
ni para el emboscado que no sale de su madriguera.
Que no se escondan más en un indumento proletario esos que
aguardan a Franco con las últimas botellas de champán en
la bodega.
Todo aquel que no lleve mañana este emblema español revolucionario, este grito de ¡Justicia!, sangrando en la frente,
pertenece a la Quinta Columna.

Ninguna salida ya
a las posibles traiciones.
Que no piense ya nadie

en romper documentos comprometedores
ni en quemar ficheros
ni en tirar la gorra a la cuneta
en las huidas premeditadas.
Ya no hay huidas.
En España ya no hay más que dos posiciones fijas e inconmovibles.
Para hoy y para mañana.
La de los que alzan la mano para decir cínicamente: Yo soy un bastardo español,
y la de los que la cierran con ira para pedir justicia bajo los cielos implacables.
Pero ahora este juego de las manos ya no basta tampoco.
Hace falta más.
Hacen falta estrellas, sí, muchas estrellas
pero de sangre,
porque la retaguardia tiene que dar la suya también.

Una estrella de sangre roja,
de sangre roja española.
Que no haya ya quien diga:
esa estrella es de sangre extranjera.
Y que no sea obligatoria tampoco.
Que mañana no pueda hablar nadie de imposiciones,
que no pueda decir ninguno que se la puso una pistola en el pecho.
Es un tatuaje revolucionario, sí.
Yo soy revolucionario,
España es revolucionaria,
Don Quijote es revolucionario.
Lo somos todos. Todos.
Todos los que sienten este sabor de justicia que hay en nuestra sangre y que se nos hace hiel y ceniza cuando sopla el viento del Norte.
Es un tatuaje revolucionario,
pero español.
Y heroico también.
Y voluntario, además.

Es un tatuaje que buscamos sólo para definir nuestra fe.
No es más que una definición de fe.

Hay dos vientos hoy que sacuden furiosos a los hombres de
    España,
dos ráfagas que empujan a los hombres de Valencia.
El viento dramático de los grandes destinos, que arrastra a los
    héroes a la victoria o a la muerte,
y la ráfaga de pánicos incontrolables que se lleva la carne
    muerta y podrida de los naufragios a las playas de la co-
    bardía y del silencio.
Hay dos vientos, ¿no lo oís?
Hay dos vientos, españoles de Valencia.
El uno va a la Historia.
El otro va al silencio.
el uno va a la épica,
el otro a la vergüenza.

Responsables:
El gran responsable y los pequeños responsables:
Abrid las puertas,
derribad las vallas de los Pirineos.
Dale camino franco
a la ráfaga amarilla de los que tiemblan.
Una vez más veré el rebaño de los cobardes huir hacia el
    ludibrio.
Una vez más veré en piara la cobardía.
Os veré otra vez,
asaltando, con los ojos desorbitados, los autobuses de la evacu-
    ación.
Os veré otra vez
robándole el asiento
a los niños y a las madres.
Os veré otra vez.
Pero vosotros os estaréis viendo siempre.
Un día moriréis fuera de vuestra patria. En la cama tal vez.
    En una cama de sábanas blancas, con los pies desnudos (No
    con los zapatos puestos, como ahora se muere en España),
    con los pies desnudos y ungidos, acaso, con los óleos santos.

Porque moriréis muy santamente, y de seguro con un cruci-
fijo y con una oración de arrepentimiento en los labios.
Estaréis ya casi con la muerte, que llega siempre. Y os
acordaréis—¡claro que os acordaréis!—de esta vez que la
huisteis y la burlasteis, usurpándole el asiento a un niño
en un autobús de evacuación. Será vuestro último pensami-
ento. Y allá, al otro lado, cuando ya no seáis más que una
conciencia suelta, en el tiempo y en el espacio, y caigáis
precipitados al fin en los tormentos dantescos—porque yo
creo en el infierno también—no os veréis más que así,
siempre, siempre, siempre,
robándole el asiento a un niño en un autobus de evacuación.
El castigo del cobarde ya sin paz y sin salvación por toda la
eternidad.

No importa que no tengas un fusil,
quédate aquí con tu fe.
No oigas a los que dicen: la huida puede ser una política.
No hay más política en la Historia que la sangre.
A mí no me asusta la sangre que se vierta,
a mí me alegra la sangre que se vierta.
Hay una flor en el mundo que sólo puede crecer si se la riega
con sangre.
La sangre del hombre
está hecha no sólo para mover su corazón
sino para llenar los ríos de la Tierra,
las venas de la Tierra
y mover el corazón del mundo.

¡Cobardes: hacia los Pirineos, al destierro!
¡Héroes: a los frentes, a la muerte!

Responsables:
el grande y los pequeños responsables:
organizad el heroísmo,
unificad el sacrificio.
Un mando único, sí.
Pero para el última martirio.
¡Vamos a la muerte!

Que lo oiga todo el mundo.
Que lo oigan los espías.
¿Qué importa ya que lo oigan los espías?
Que lo oigan ellos, los bastardos.
¿Qué importa ya que lo oigan los bastardos?
¿Qué importan ya todas esas voces de allá abajo,
si empezamos a cabalgar sobre la épica?
A estas alturas de la Historia ya no se oye nada.
Se va hacia la muerte . . .
y abajo queda el mundo de las raposas,
y de los que pactan con las raposas.

Abajo quedas tú, Inglaterra,
vieja raposa avarienta,
que tienes parada la Historia de Occidente hace más de tres
    siglos,
y encadenado a Don Quijote.
Cuando acabe tu vida
y vengas ante la Historia grande
donde te aguardo yo,
¿qué vas a decir?
¿Qué astucia nueva vas a inventar entonces para engañar a
    Dios?
¡Raposa!
¡Hija de raposos!
Italia es más noble que tú.
Y Alemania también.
En su rapiña y en sus crímenes
hay un turbio hálito nietzscheano de heroísmo en el que no
    pueden respirar los mercaderes,
un gesto impetuoso y confuso de jugárselo todo a la última
    carta, que no pueden comprender los hombres pragmáticos.
Si abriesen sus puertas a los vientos del mundo,
si las abriesen de par en par
y pasasen por ellas la Justicia
y la Democracia heroica del hombre,
yo pactaría con las dos para echar sobre tu cara de vieja raposa
    sin dignidad y sin amor,

toda la saliva y todo el excremento del mundo.
¡Viejo raposa avarienta:
has escondido,
soterrado en el corral,
la llave milagrosa que abre la puerta diamantina de la
    Historia . . .
No sabes nada.
No entiendes nada y te metes en todas las casas
a cerrar las ventanas
y a cegar la luz de las estrellas!
Y los hombres te ven y te dejan.
Te dejan porque creen que ya se le han acabado los rayos a
    Júpiter.
Pero las estrellas no duermen.

No sabes nada.
Has amontonado tu rapiña detrás de la puerta, y tus hijos,
    ahora, no pueden abrirla para que entren los primeros
    rayos de la nueva aurora del mundo.
Vieja raposa avarienta,
eres un gran mercader.
Sabes llevar muy bien
las cuentas de la cocina
y piensas que yo no sé contar.
Sí sé contar.
He contado mis muertos.
Los he contado todos,
los he contado uno por uno.
Los he contado en Madrid,
los he contado en Oviedo,
los he contado en Málaga,
los he contado en Guernica,
los he contado en Bilbao . . .
Los he contado en todas las trincheras,
en los hospitales,
en los depósitos de los cementerios,
en las cunetas de las carreteras,
en los escombros de las casas bombardeadas.

Contando muertos este otoño por el Paseo de El Prado, creí
   una noche que caminaba sobre barro, y eran sesos humanos
   que tuve por mucho tiempo pegados a las suelas de mis
   zapatos.
El 18 de noviembre, sólo en un sótano de cadáveres, conté
   trescientos niños muertos . . .
Los he contado en los carros de las ambulancias,
en los hoteles,
en los tranvías,
en el Metro . . . ,
en las mañanas lívidas,
en las noches negras sin alumbrado y sin estrellas . . .
y en tu conciencia todos . . .
Y todos te los he cargado a tu cuenta.
¡Ya ves si sé contar!
Eres la vieja portera del mundo de Occidente,
tienes desde hace mucho tiempo las llaves de todos los postigos
   de Europa,
y puedes dejar entrar y salir a quien se te antoje.
Y ahora por cobardía,
por cobardía nada más,
porque quieres guardar tu despensa hasta el último día de la
   Historia,
has dejado meterse en mi solar
a los raposos y a los lobos confabulados del mundo
para que se sacien en mi sangre
y no pidan en seguida la tuya.
Pero ya la pedirán,
ya la pedirán las estrellas . . .

Y aquí otra vez,
aquí
en estas alturas solitarias
aquí
donde se oye si descanso la voz milenaria
de los vientos,
del agua
y de la arcilla

que nos ha ido formando a todos los hombres.
Aquí,
donde no llega el desgañitado vocerío de la propaganda mercenaria.
Aquí,
donde no tiene resuello ni vida el asma de los diplomáticos.
Aquí,
donde los comediantes de la Sociedad de Naciones no tienen papel.
Aquí, aquí,
ante la Historia,
ante la Historia grande
(la otra
la que vuestro orgullo de gusanos enseña a los niños de las escuelas
no es más que un registro de mentiras
y un índice de crímenes y vanidades).
Aquí, aquí,
bajo la luz de las estrellas,
sobre la tierra eterna y pristina del mundo
y en la presencia misma de Dios.
Aquí, aquí. Aquí
quiero decir ahora mi última palabra:

Españoles,
españoles revolucionarios:
¡El hombre se ha muerto!
Callad, callad.
Romped los altavoces
y las antenas,
arrancad de cuajo todos los carteles que anuncian vuestro drama en las esquinas del mundo.
¿Denuncias? ¿Ante quién?
Romped el Libro Blanco,
no volváis más vuestra boca con llamadas y lamentos hacia la tierra vacía.
¡El hombre se ha muerto!
Y sólo las estrellas pueden formar ya el coro de nuestro trágico destino.

No gritéis ya más vuestro martirio.
El martirio no se pregona,
se soporta
y se echa en los hombros como un legado y como un orgullo.

La tragedia es mía,
mía,
que no me la robe nadie.
Fuera,
fuera todos.
Todos.
Yo aquí sola.
Sola
bajo las estrellas y los Dioses.
¿Quiénes sois vosotros?
¿Cuál es vuestro nombre?
¿De qué vientre venís?
Fuera . . . Fuera . . . ¡Raposos!
Aquí,
yo sola. Sola,
con la Justicia ahorcada.
Sola,
con el cadáver de la Justicia entre mis manos.
Aquí
yo sola,
sola
con la conciencia humana,
quieta,
parada,
asesinada para siempre
en esta hora de la Historia
y en esta tierra de España,
por todos los raposos del mundo.
Por todos,
por todos.
¡Raposos!
¡Raposos!
El mundo no es más que una madriguera de raposos
y la Justicia una flor que ya no prende en ninguna latitud.

Españoles,
españoles revolucionarios.
¡Vamos a la muerte!
Que lo oigan los espías.
¿Qué importa ya que lo oigan los espías?
Que lo oigan ellos, los bastardos.
¿Qué importa ya que lo oigan los bastardos?
A estas alturas de la Historia
ya no se oye nada.
Se va hacia la muerte
y abajo queda el mundo irrespirable de los raposos y de los
    que pactan con los raposos.
¡Vamos a la muerte!
¡Que se despierte Valencia
y que se ponga la mortaja! . . .

Epílogo

Escuchad todavía . . .
Refrescad antes mis labios y mi frente . . . tengo sed . . .
Y quiero hablar con palabras de amor y de esperanza.
Oíd ahora:
La justicia vale más que un imperio, aunque este imperio
    abarque toda la curva del Sol.
Y cuando la Justicia, herida de muerte, nos llama a todos en
    agonía desesperada nadie puede decir:
"yo aún no estoy preparado."
La Justicia se defiende con una lanza rota y con una visera de
    papel.
Esto está escrito en mi Biblia,
en mi Historia,
en mi Historia infantil y grotesca
y mientras los hombres no lo aprendan el mundo no se salva.

Yo soy el grito primero, cárdeno y bermejo de las grandes
    auroras de Occidente.
Ayer sobre mi sangre mañanera el mundo burgués edificó en
    América todas sus factorías y mercados,

sobre mis muertos de hoy el mundo de mañana levantará la
  Primera Casa del Hombre.
Y yo volveré,
volveré porque aún hay lanzas y hiel sobre la Tierra.
Volveré,
volveré con mi pecho y con la Aurora otra vez.

The title, "La insignia," names the poem's central subject. It is essentially an exhortation to unify, to abandon plural insignias which multiply rapidly, and to have only one insignia that would sum up all insignias luminously: "¡Hay que encender una estrella! —una sola, sí!" For Felipe there is only one insignia—that of Justice. The multiple insignias represent the many factions comprising the Republican side: socialists, communists, working class, antifascists, etc. Felipe points out their multiplicity ironically, by listing them one to a line:

Sindicalistas,
Comunistas,
Anarquistas,
Socialistas,
Troskistas,
Republicanos de Izquierda . . .

Each organization or political group had its own letters and, as Felipe put it, "Has agotado ya en mil combinaciones egoístas y heterodoxas todas las letras del alfabeto." One thinks of such acronyms as CNT (Anarcho-Syndicalist Trade Union), FAI (Anarchist Secret Society), JSU (Socialist and Communist Youth group), POUM (Trotskyites), PSUC (United Catalan Socialist-Communist Party), UGT (Socialist Trade Union), and UMRA (Republican Officers group).

The poem begins by introducing the voice of its poet/prophet dramatically and rhetorically. It is addressed to Spaniards of every level of society as Felipe establishes that everyone has already had his say on the subject of the war, except himself—not as an individual person, but rather as the generic poet. His voice represents them all:

Yo no soy más que una voz—la tuya, la de todos—
la más genuina,
la más general,
la más aborigen ahora,
la más antigua de esta tierra.
La voz de España que hoy se articula en mi garganta como
    pudo articularse en otra cualquiera.

Despite his apparent diffidence, he sees himself as the poet-prophet
who towers above the crowd:

Pero el profeta no es más que la voz vernácula de un
    pueblo . . .
Nada de orgullos . . .
La voz de los profetas—recordadla—
es la que tiene más sabor de barro.
De barro,
del barro que ha hecho al árbol—al naranjo y al pino—
del barro que ha formado
nuestro cuerpo también.

Only he has the magnitude of vision, the insight, and the critical
evaluation to assume this role. Only he is capable of speaking for
them all. Detached from their pettiness, only he sees their predicament objectively. The tone of the poem belies his claim to be
only the vernacular voice, made of the same clay as the trees.

In the fourth and fifth stanzas he singles out "españoles revolucionarios" as his audience. They belong to "la España legítima"
and carry in their hands "el mensaje genuino de la raza." Felipe
carefully distinguishes between the "pueblo español" and those
who are leading them. He is proud of the Spanish people. What
he objects to is the in-fighting and selfish materialism of those who
are supposed to be supporting the Republican side but who are
losing sight of the main goal and creating divisiveness. He criticizes
their preoccupation with selfish, superficial values:

Abrazados a su botín reciente,
guardándole,

defendiéndole,
con una avaricia que no tuvo nunca el más delgado burgués.

The connotations of *botín* are strictly materialistic, reminding us
of theft and piracy, and *burgués* was undoubtedly a despicable
term in his lexicon. They forfeit epic and historic importance for
the sake of petty domesticity:

Habéis empezado por lo épico,
habéis pasado por lo histórico
y ahora aquí,
en la retaguardia de Valencia,
frente a todas las derrotas,
os habéis parado en la domesticidad.
Y aquí estáis anclados, . . .
custodiando la rapiña
para que no se la lleve vuestro hermano.

Instead of being suspicious and petty, they must combine forces
against the real enemy. They are alone in their divisiveness, and
final victory may allude them: "El botín se hace derecho legítimo
cuando está sellado por una victoria última y heroica." They are
struggling among themselves in the rearguard (as opposed to the
front line) of Valencia because they have the mentality of businessmen.

On the other hand, "el español no aprende nunca bien el oficio
de mercader." Felipe equates the revolutionary, fighting Spaniard
and Don Quijote. He feels that Spaniards have an innate sense of
justice: "este sabor de justicia que hay en nuestra sangre," and a
willingness to sacrifice themselves. The true Spaniard, whom Felipe
is searching for, is not to be found among the dissenting factions,
with their pragmatic intrigues and politics. And he is certainly not
to be found among the fascists, who have betrayed their fellow
Spaniards and represent "la España maldita de Caín." The real
Spaniard can only be on the Republican side, "Pero, ¿dónde,
dónde? . . . ¿Dónde está el hombre?/¿Dónde está el español?"

Felipe recognizes the tragic circumstances in which "todo el
mundo es nuestro enemigo, y la mitad de nuestra sangre—la sangre

podrida y bastarda de Caín—se ha vuelto contra nosotros también."
The Republican side is being weakened by internal strife while
enemy forces from inside and outside of Spain are attacking them.
They are being betrayed by the very forces who are supposed to be
helping them.

Felipe does not deal in the clichés of political propaganda. He
is critical of the Republican side because he wants them to overcome their dissension and win. At the same time he can give the
fascist side credit, at least, for having a single insignia and the
unification it implies. The fascist insignia is a religious one because
the enemy side, ironically, is like a Crusade united in Christ. Yet
Felipe is skeptical of their religious pretensions. His irony is unmistakable:

> El otro lado es la tierra maldita, la España maldita de Caín
>   aunque la haya bendecido el Papa.

Justice is at stake and no one understands it. It is the single
insignia of value. According to Felipe, justice is a very Spanish
concept. The attitude of Spain ("inútil . . . ibérica y quijotesca")
is different from that of the rest of the world. Spain does not have
a marketable quantity. She can be truly revolutionary, being un-
encumbered by the established concerns of business. The ideology
of justice is not foreign: it is Spanish:

> Una estrella de sangre roja,
> de sangre roja española.
> Que no haya ya quien diga:
> esa estrella es de sangre extranjera.

Spain is the embodiment of the fight for an ideal, such as Don
Quijote. The Spanish Civil War is the last in a series of quixotic
battles. Thus, Felipe has an idealized vision of the Spanish revolutionary and Spain. In the present conflict, Felipe believes that
"justice" is misunderstood by both sides:

> Y habrá que irse a otro planeta
> con esta mercancía inútil aquí,
> con esta mercancía ibérica y quijotesca.

He ironically and bitterly refers to "justicia" as "inútil . . . ibérica y quijotesca," appending the materialistic term "mercancía," with its disparaging overtones. However, he is not completely pessimistic, and that is probably the reason he can write a poem urging reform: "aún no hemos perdido aquí la última batalla." The poem, after all, was written in 1937, two years before the end of the war.

Felipe suggests that the revolutionary insignia of justice in the form of a star replace all others and be tattooed onto each person's forehead. In this way, those in the rear guard would shed their blood, he snidely adds. Those who do not wear the voluntary insignia would, thus, according to Felipe, belong to the Fifth Column.[5] Wearing this tattoo, his motto would be: "¡Vamos a la muerte!" Málaga had already fallen (the poem was begun February 11, 1937, the day after the Nationalists took over Málaga), and Felipe suspects that Valencia will be next. The poet is well aware of the frustrating and fatal circumstances that had surrounded the Republican fall in Málaga:

The situation in Málaga epitomized all the worst conditions existing in the Republican zone. In the second week of June (1937), labor violence had cost three lives through assassination. In the weeks after July 18 the city's shops were looted and the best residential quarters burned . . . . The sailors' committees in the fleet and the city administration were divided in mortal rivalry between CNT and Communist adherents. Valencian and Almerian truck drivers' syndicates could not agree on the division of labor between them for the delivery of supplies to Málaga, and one of the bridges on the main coastal road remained unrepaired for five months preceding the city's fall. Like all the Republican cities, it lacked antiaircraft defense. Its militiamen, mostly anarchists, built no trenches or road blocks. In January, the government assigned a dependable professional officer, Colonel Villaba, to organize the defense; but without ammunition to give his soldiers, and without the slightest possibility of controlling the bitter political rivalries within the city, there was virtually nothing he could do. . . . On February 6 about 100,-000 persons began a disorganized mass exodus along the coastal road to Almería.[6]

"¡Vamos a la muerte!" because only if Valencia awakens from its disunity and prepares for a last-ditch stand, can Justice perhaps survive. Felipe further suggests that "hay que quèmar las naves." The analogy is with Hernando Cortéz, the Spanish conqueror who, upon arrival in Mexico with his troops, had burned his ships and marched on Mexico City. In other words, there would be no escape: "De aquí no se va más que a la muerte o a la victoria." This is like "Vientos del pueblo me llevan," in which Hernández writes "vais de la vida a la muerte" and proceeds to glorify the manner in which he would die were he to die in such a cause ("Si me muero, que me muera con la cabeza muy alta . . . cantando espero a la muerte . . .").

We have seen that Felipe distinguishes between the brave, noble Spanish revolutionary and the disappointing, destructive leadership. He also points out the dichotomy between those who will fight bravely and perhaps die and those who will panic out of cowardice and flee on evacuation buses:

¡Cobardes: hacia los Pirineos, al destierro!
¡Héroes: a los frentes, a la muerte!

He urges them all to "keep the faith." Felipe writes as if inspired: "No importa que no tengas un fusil,/quédate aquí con tu fe." This reminds us of the conclusion of "Recoged esta voz": "fusil de nardos . . . espada de cera." And, then, from the Epilogue: "La Justicia se defiende con una lanza rota y con una visera de papel." The image is directly from Don Quijote; it is inspirational, impractical, and hopeless. He also juxtaposes two sets of values in the poem: those of Justice, Don Quijote, and Spain versus those of Spain's enemies, pragmatism, and cowardice.

Two-thirds of the way through the poem, Felipe begins his attack against England, "vieja raposa avarienta"; England is a very responsible party to the tragedy. The fox is an astute, flesh-eating animal, pragmatic about its own survival. He singles out England for vituperation for a number of reasons. Traditionally England was mercantile and had been the cradle of the Industrial Revolution. Spain and England had a long history of conflict, one of their most famous battles involving the Spanish Armada. And England's

Prime Minister at the time, Neville Chamberlain, gained a reputation for appeasement and, in a sense, the selling out of Republican Spain. England's neutrality affected the Republican side unfavorably. Felipe sees more nobility in Italy and Germany than in England. They, at least, by their inflated postures, did not reflect the petty world of merchants. They were capable of "jugárselo todo a la última carta," a flamboyant gesture beyond the conception of a practical bourgeois.

Felipe keeps count of the dead, mimicking the business accounts of England, and the poet holds up the specter of the bloody body of Spain. England had the power to help the Republicans: "tienes . . . las llaves de todos los postigos de Europa," and it is their reluctance to help, out of practical and cowardly concerns, that he condemns. He blames England for indirectly allowing Spain to be overrun by fascists and Nazis. Thus, there is a contemporary, political point to Felipe's focusing on England as an object of his bitterest scorn as well as a historical one.

Felipe personally identifies with the terrible course of events. At the end (as well as at the beginning) he assumes his role of poet/prophet along with its responsibilities: "La tragedia es mía." The poet/prophet who believes he is the sole custodian of Justice feels that the tragedy is his. "El mundo no es más que una madriguera de raposas y la Justicia una flor que ya no prende en ninguna latitud." For Felipe "¡El hombre se ha muerto!," that is, men who understand Justice have died. In the last two lines, awakening and death are part of the same process: "¡Que se despierte Valencia/y que se ponga la mortaja! . . ."

In the Epilogue Felipe reasserts the high value of Justice versus the triviality of material gain ("un imperio"). Like Christ, he is ready to rise again, to expose himself, and to triumph: "Y yo volveré" to combat the "lanzas y hiel sobre la Tierra" . . . with "una lanza rota y con una visera de papel."

Felipe has a declamatory, rhetorical style. When he claims he is not rhetorical, he means in the sense of not being complicated or artificial. Felipe frequently employs an enumerative technique. There are, also, many repetitions that emphasize through cumulative effects.

Even the beginning of the poem is framed by the reiteration of the compound past form of *hablar*. The use of "Responsables:/El gran responsable y los pequeños responsables" echoes from the first stanza. Obviously, Felipe has a strong point to make about those who are responsible, which reminds us of those dining on putrid food in Neruda's "Almería." The repetition emphasizes his scorn.

There is a highly dramatic effect produced as Felipe lists in repetitive form those among the dead whom he had counted. Blood was Hernández' metaphor for all the war dead, comparable in emotional impact with Felipe's counting of corpses. Vallejo's metaphor for the death of Spain in "Masa" was one dead soldier, an equally powerful image. Felipe, by counting cadavers, is metaphorically holding up the bloody body of Spain.

Felipe subtitled the poem "Alocución poemática," which suggests a combination of poetry and prose. Spain and South America in the nineteenth century had a tradition of oratory, which they considered a distinct genre, and from which Felipe may well have inherited his oratorical style. An example of his style which combines poetic and prosaic elements begins "Un día morireis fuera de vuestra patria. En la cama tal vez./En una cama de sábanas blancas, con los pies desnudos . . ." Felipe has illustrated here the poetic technique of concretizing experience in a graphic way. An individual on a white bed makes vivid Felipe's general disdain for cowards who run away to hygienic refuge. The sarcastic tone is unmistakable. Poetic qualities of the passage are the concrete imagery, repetition, condensation, informal grammar, emotional tone, and adjectival descriptions. Some of these qualities would also be true of rhetoric. The extension and logic of the narrative, the form in which the poet arranged it as if in a paragraph, and the lack of flowery speech are prosaic elements of Felipe's technique. His artistry derives not from the complexity of his metaphors but from the dramatic use he makes of his rhetorical technique. The poem is very stirring but its dramatic effect comes more from its structure than from its dramatic imagery. The structure could be considered architectural.

The poet often uses an irregular rhythm of short lines and short words. Some of the lines consist of only one word. He plays with length of line, gradation, and progressively lengthening (or short-

ening) repetition. Shrinking and expanding, his lines build up to
a crescendo (or decrease) in which the last line is the culmination
or diminution:

> La curva histórica del aristócrata, desde su origen popular
>   y heroico, hasta su última degeneración actual, cubre
>   en España más de tres siglos.
> La del burgués, setenta años.
> Y la vuestra, tres semanas.

The length of the lines offers an imaginative parallel to the historical curve, a technique used by Walt Whitman also.

The vocabulary is both simple and serious, less difficult than
that of Neruda or Vallejo. It is almost unpoetic in its everyday,
straightforward syntax. Felipe is an austere poet who has been
described by Luis Cernuda as avoiding the "halago de la palabra
y la magia del verso." Felipe matches his bare words with what he
hopes is a naked rhythm. The words, phrases, and framework are
often repetitive. There is also a humble simplicity to the form and
theme of "La insignia."

There is a development or progression of ideas in the poem as
the poet introduces his role and explains what is wrong with the
Republican side, which is precisely what he finds right about the
Nationalist side. The bloody body of Spain is present throughout
the poem. He distinguishes between the Spanish people and its
divided leadership, and condemns the traitorous Nationalists, the
fascists who side with them, and England, who remains neutral
and thus tips the scales in favor of the Nationalists. The single
insignia he recommends to the Republicans would represent Justice. He makes a clear distinction between the values of true Spain,
the Spanish revolutionary, Man, Don Quijote, and Justice, and
the values of their enemies—values of business and pragmatism.

"La insignia" is an intellectually critical poem as opposed to
the emotionally empathetic poems of Hernández and Vallejo.
While Neruda's poems are subjective, Felipe's vision is the most
historically realistic. He predicted the outcome, he predicted the
reasons for it, and he was right.

In sum, "La insignia" is a tremendous tour de force. It is not subtle and it is not especially metaphorical; the conception and technique of the poem are not so much poetic as rhetorical. It plays with repetition and cadence and has an architectural structure. The poem concretizes generalizations; for example, Felipe takes the fall of Málaga and the likely defeat of Valencia and makes them the metaphor for the larger death of Spain.

In his early works, Felipe was a human poet, a sad one, who saw human sorrows and society's evils. As he himself said, "no hay más que una causa: la del hombre." He later adopted a more belligerent tone, almost declamatory, but filled with both epic and lyric force which can be seen in "La insignia." He viewed what he felt was a disintegrating world where positive, constructive efforts were futile and where, perhaps, "nos salvaremos por el llanto." [7]

Miguel Hernández (1910-1942) was born in Orihuela, in the province of Alicante, in southeastern Spain.[8] His father was a goatherd and farm laborer, as was Miguel until the age of seven or eight. It is important to an understanding of his poetry that he had such direct contact with natural surroundings. Between the years 1920 and 1925 he studied near home at the Colegio de Santo Domingo, where he was educated by Jesuits. He received there a basic Christian education and was a good student. But he was hardly given a rigorous literary education, which he later achieved himself. He became familiar with poetic forms from Garcilaso through Góngora and, before the outbreak of the Spanish Civil War, published some Gongoristic poetry. In 1925 he left school to devote himself to the land, but wanting to broaden his literary horizons, he left for Madrid in 1931. He was given no immediate accolades, was unable to earn a living, and soon returned home. After the publication of a collection of his verse *Perito en lunas* in 1933, he went again to Madrid. This time he was well received and became friendly with such poets as Pablo Neruda and Vicente Aleixandre, to whom, out of appreciation, he later (1935-36) dedicated odes. He was also acquainted with Alberti, García Lorca (for whom he wrote an elegy), and Altolaguirre, and was encouraged by Antonio Machado and Juan Ramón Jiménez. His financial difficulties forced him to work in a notary's office in 1934. *El rayo que no cesa,* written in 1934, was published in 1936.

The Spanish Civil War found him in Madrid, where he immediately enlisted in the Republican army from a deep sense of social obligation and patriotism. He fought in the trenches, read his verses to fellow-soldiers, and escaped when he could to visit his fiancée, Josefina, in Orihuela. She inspired his passion, expressed in such lines as:

> . . . capaz de despertar calentura en la nieve . . .
> ¡Ay que ganas de amarte contra un árbol,
> ay qué afán de trillarte en una era . . . !
> > (from "Mi sangre es un camino"
> > —1935-36)

> (. . . capable of awakening fever in snow . . .
> Oh what wishes to love you against a tree,
> oh what desire to thrash you (like wheat) on the
> > ground . . . !)

In 1937, in the middle of the war, he married Josefina. In *Viento del pueblo,* published that same year, his style became graver and simpler.

In 1938 his first child was born but died a few months later. As part of his education and to study foreign theatre (Hernández wrote plays as well as verse) he traveled to Russia, Paris, London, and Stockholm. In 1939, close to the end of the war, another child was born, and another collection of his verse *El hombre acecha* was published. After the war, he was confined by the Franco Government in the Torrijos jail in Madrid and condemned to death for his political attitude during the war. Only at the intervention of some friends was his sentence commuted to thirty years' imprisonment.

In the long years of imprisonment, he wrote poems of great economy, simplicity, and feeling. He addressed many poems to his wife and to his son, whom he had never seen. When his wife wrote him that she had only bread and onions to feed their son, he composed one of his most moving poems "Nanas de la cebolla." His son's small life enhanced Hernández' unfortunate existence:

Tu risa me hace libre,
me pone alas.
Soledades me quita,
carcel me arranca.

                    (from "Nanas
                    de la cebolla")

(Your smile makes me free,
gives me wings.
It takes away loneliness,
wrenches the cell from me.)

He was moved to the prison of Palencia and later to Penal de Ocano, where he wrote *Cancionero y romancero de ausencia*. After Ocano he was confined in the prison of Alicante, where he arrived in July of 1941. He died in prison—early in 1942, at the age of thirty-one—of typhoid fever and tuberculosis. His premature death cut short one of the most promising poetic careers of his day. His poetry remained uncollected for ten years, at the end of which time a volume was published; it omitted, however, some of his finest pieces.

From 1936 on, his main themes were his country, love, and death. The war in Spain elicited from him a passionate response and a loyal dedication. Recognizing the tragedy, he was still able to sustain inspired hope throughout the war. Even up to his own last miserable days, his unquenchable spirit conflicted with the despair of his real situation, as in his poem "Vuelo":

Un ser ardiente, claro de deseos, alado,
quiso ascender, tener la libertad por nido.
Quiso olvidar que el hombre se aleja encadenado.
Donde faltaban plumas puso valor y olvido.

Iba tan alto a veces, que le resplandecía
sobre la piel el cielo, bajo la piel el ave.
Ser que te confundiste con una alondra un día,
te desplomaste otro como el granizo grave.

(An ardent being, clear of desires, winged,
wanted to ascend, to have liberty as a nest.

He wanted to forget that man goes away chained.
Where feathers were lacking he put bravery and
  forgetfulness.

He went so high at times, that the sky reflected
on his skin, the bird below his skin.
Being who thought yourself a lark one day,
another plummeted down like heavy hail.)

The two poems chosen for analysis here are from his collection *Viento del pueblo,* written and first published in 1937: "Vientos del pueblo me llevan" and "Recoged esta voz," which is in two parts. This is the order in which they appear among his collected works.

VIENTOS DEL PUEBLO ME LLEVAN [9]

<table>
<tr><td>1</td><td>Vientos del pueblo me llevan,
vientos del pueblo me arrastran,
me esparcen el corazón
y me aventan la garganta.</td></tr>
<tr><td>5</td><td>Los bueyes doblan la frente,
impotentemente mansa,
delante de los castigos:
los leones la levantan
y al mismo tiempo castigan</td></tr>
<tr><td>10</td><td>con su clamorosa zarpa.</td></tr>
<tr><td></td><td>No soy de un pueblo de bueyes,
que soy de un pueblo que embargan
yacimientos de leones,
desfiladeros de águilas</td></tr>
<tr><td>15</td><td>y cordilleras de toros
con el orgullo en el asta.
Nunca medraron los bueyes
en los páramos de España.</td></tr>
<tr><td>20</td><td>¿Quién habló de echar un yugo
sobre el cuello de esta raza?</td></tr>
</table>

¿Quién ha puesto al huracán
jamás ni yugos ni trabas,
ni quién al rayo detuvo
prisionero en una jaula?

25   Asturianos de braveza,
vascos de piedra blindada,
valencianos de alegría
y castellanos de alma,
labrados como la tierra
30   y airosos como las alas;
andaluces de relámpagos,
nacidos entre guitarras
y forjados en los yunques
torrenciales de las lágrimas;
35   extremeños de centeno,
gallegos de lluvia y calma,
catalanes de firmeza,
aragoneses de casta,
murcianos de dinamita
40   frutalmente propagada,
leoneses, navarros, dueños
del hambre, el sudor y el hacha,
reyes de la minería,
señores de la labranza,
45   hombres que entre las raíces,
como raíces gallardas,
vais de la vida a la muerte,
vais de la nada a la nada:
yugos os quieren poner
50   gentes de la hierba mala,
yugos que habréis de dejar
rotos sobre sus espaldas.

Crepúsculos de los bueyes
está despuntando el alba.

55   Los bueyes mueren vestidos
de humildad y olor de cuadra:
las águilas, los leones

y los toros de arrogancia,
y detrás de ellos, el cielo
60   ni se enturbia ni se acaba.
La agonía de los bueyes
tiene pequeña la cara,
la del animal varón
toda la creación agranda.

65   Si me muero, que me muera
con la cabeza muy alta.
Muerto y veinte veces muerto,
la boca contra la grama,
tendré apretados los dientes
70   y decidida la barba.

Cantando espero a la muerte,
que hay ruiseñores que cantan
encima de los fusiles
y en medio de las batallas.
                    —Miguel Hernández

Written in 1937, when the poet was only twenty-seven, "Vientos del pueblo me llevan" is an intensely emotional poem. In the title and first stanza, Hernández conceives of his people as "vientos del pueblo," a hurricane wind of pervasive and violent strength. Like the wind, his people are a strong, natural force—a force of nature unstoppable until death. Hernández is inspired by them:

Vientos del pueblo me llevan,
vientos del pueblo me arrastran,
me esparcen el corazón
y me aventan la garganta.

"Pueblo" means the common people who together share a country. Their dynamic quality is conveyed by such verbs as "llevan," "arrastran," "esparcen," and "aventan."

After the opening image of wind, Hernández turns to the physical and psychological posturing of oxen, lions, eagles, and bulls. He relates these images to the Spanish people. Oxen—domesticated, enslaved, and submissive—are unlike the Spaniards and are not even bred in Spain. Hernández sees the essence of Spain in certain animals. Bulls, of the same family as oxen, are completely different from them; they are immensely brave and strong and are even a national (Spanish) symbol. Spaniards also applaud wild lions that stand up to punishment with force, and eagles that swoop in disorder. Eagles, bulls, and lions are not easily dominated. Spaniards, too, fight with courage and dignity, even when challenging the unchallengeable. Spain's heritage is one of pride and bravery in the face of the impossible and of death. The poet conveys this quality of courage and determination through his metaphors.

The poem is presented from a first-person point of view, but this "I" represents a collective identity. There is identification between the poet and the people, making the "I" Spanish and proud of his people:

> Asturianos de braveza
> vascos de piedra blindada,
> valencianos de alegría
> y castellanos de alma . . .

There follows an enumeration of Spaniards from different provinces, with the characteristics of each. Hernández goes through all the provinces, evoking the way of life in each. This long list gives the impression of epic proportions. Fittingly, the reconquest of Spain after the Moorish invasion began with Asturias, whose people did, indeed, fight for the recovery of their pride there. Castilians, being in the heart of Spain, would represent its soul.

Hernández carefully weighs his metaphors, for example, in lines 33 and 34: "forjados en los yunques/torrenciales de las lágrimas." Anvils are the opposite of tears and the inconsistency helps create a striking image. Line 47 expresses the leitmotif of the poem, that of inevitability: "vais de la vida a la muerte."

The listed types are men of "hambre" and "sudor," rooted in Spain, and Spanish roots are proud. Hernández builds up in his poem to the climax of the surging forth of masses.

According to Hernández, the Spanish people are not to be subjugated. The comparison this time is with the impossible harnessing of a hurricane or imprisoning of a thunderbolt. The Spaniards are a force gathering like wind to throw off the yokes of enslavement.

At times the poet speaks about himself in particular (although always nationalistic in spirit) and, at times, he directly addresses his countrymen. He reminds them of their bravery and warns them not to acquiesce. He wants them to fight to the death rather than be conquered. He exhorts them to martyrdom. This poem is a far cry from Wordsworth's "emotion recollected in tranquillity." He wants them to break the yokes of their (unnamed) enemy across their enemies' backs:

> vais de la vida a la muerte
> vais de la nada a la nada:
> yugos os quieren poner
> gentes de la hierba mala,
> yugos que habréis de dejar
> rotos sobre sus espaldas.

Again the metaphor of the oxen is used. Oxen are bowed, subjugated, and degraded, and are yoked by their owners. Even the agony and death of oxen is of little consequence, while that of such virile animals as bulls, eagles, and lions can rock the universe. The poem has cosmic proportions like Vallejo's "España, aparta de mí este cáliz." The crepuscule is symbolic of the death of oxen.

The final stanzas are powerful and beautiful:

> Si me muero, que me muera
> con la cabeza muy alta.
> Muerto y veinte veces muerto,
> la boca contra la grama,
> tendré apretados los dientes
> y decidida la barba.

> Cantando espero a la muerte,
> que hay ruiseñores que cantan
> encima de los fusiles
> y en medio de las batallas.

To rephrase the ending of T. S. Eliot's "The Hollow Men," Hernández would die "not with a whimper but a bang."

The poet's voice is of the people, and speaks to and of them. Hernández is willing to die along with his people rather than be enslaved. Projecting himself into the struggle, he switches back to his first-person presentation with "Si me muero . . ." If he is to die, let it be proudly and decisively, the poet singing in the face of death. The metaphor here is sharp as he compares such a fateful circumstance to nightingales who sing hovering above rifles in the midst of battle. The incongruity between the beauty and life of the nightingale and its song, on the one hand, and the horror of war and death, on the other, is grotesque. It is reminiscent of the title of Roy Campbell's poem "Flowering Rifle."

The poem is sad because Hernández does not expect the Spaniards of whom he speaks to survive, but if death is the price of freedom, he advocates death, glorifying the reason for such a death. His people are not to be humbled; to die fighting is not a pessimistic prospect. What would be unforgivable would be to live on having given in and not having fought for freedom.

The contrast at the end is between oxen with bowed heads and free men "con la cabeza muy alta." They are all committed to the cause, not like slaves but free men.

To summarize, the poem is about people facing war. There is consistency in its imagery as Hernández characterizes the people of Spain. The natural force of hurricane winds points to the strength and determination of his people. They are a growing, surging force and the "llevar" of the title would mean "carry" or "push." They will stop when they have won either liberty or death. This is a martial poem, revealing a sense of fervor—the fervor of commitment—and dedication to something beyond oneself. It stresses the importance of collective freedom, not of individual death.

The poem is direct and straightforward, as Hernández faces the possibility of death with candor and says exactly what he thinks. The poem, a kind of ballad, could easily be memorized and recited to inspire soldiers. Hernández wished to encourage a people at war. He is able to write about the war without effort or affectation.

Being the son of a goatherd may not have been a disadvantage; it may have contributed to his natural and convincing poetry. The poem makes clear that Hernández felt close to the people and the land.

RECOGED ESTA VOZ [10]

1   Naciones de la tierra, patrias del mar, hermanos
del mundo y de la nada:
habitantes perdidos y lejanos,
más que del corazón, de la mirada.

5   Aquí tengo una voz enardecida,
aquí tengo una vida combatida y airada,
aquí tengo un rumor, aquí tengo una vida.

Abierto estoy, mirad, como una herida.
Hundido estoy, mirad, estoy hundido
10   en medio de mi pueblo y de sus males.
Herido voy, herido y malherido,
sangrando por trincheras y hospitales.

Hombres, mundos, naciones
atended, escuchad mi sangrante sonido,
15   recoged mis latidos de quebranto
en vuestros espaciosos corazones,
porque yo empuño el alma cuando canto.

Cantando me defiendo
y defiendo mi pueblo cuando en mi pueblo imprimen
20   su herradura de pólvora y estruendo
los bárbaros del crimen.

Esta es su obra, ésta:
pasan, arrasan como torbellinos,
y son ante su cólera funesta
25   armas los horizontes y muerte los caminos.

El llanto que por valles y balcones se vierte,
en las piedras diluvia y en las piedras trabaja,

y no hay espacio para tanta muerte,
y no hay madera para tanta caja.

30 Caravanas de cuerpos abatidos
Todo vendajes, penas y pañuelos:
todo camillas donde a los heridos
se les quiebran las fuerzas y los vuelos.

Sangre, sangre por árboles y suelos,
35 sangre por aguas, sangre por paredes
y un temor de que España se desplome
del peso de la sangre que moja entre sus redes
hasta el pan que se come.

Recoged este viento,
40 naciones, hombres, mundos,
que parte de las bocas de conmovido aliento
y de los hospitales moribundos.

Aplicad las orejas
a mi clamor de pueblo atropellado,
45 al ¡ay!, de tantas madres, a las quejas
de tanto ser luciente que el luto ha devorado.

Los pechos que empujaban y herían las montañas,
vedlos desfallecidos sin leche ni hermosura,
y ved las blancas novias y las negras pestañas
50 caídas y sumidas en una siesta oscura.

Aplicad la pasión de las entrañas
a este pueblo que muere con un gesto invencible
sembrado por los labios y la frente,
bajo los implacables aeroplanos
55 que arrebatan terrible,
terrible, ignominiosa, diariamente,
a las madres los hijos de las manos.

Ciudades de trabajo y de inocencia,
juventudes que brotan de la encina,
60 troncos de bronce, cuerpos de potencia
yacen precipitados en la ruina.

Un porvenir de polvo se avecina,
se avecina un suceso
en que no quedará ninguna cosa:
65   ni piedra sobre piedra ni hueso sobre hueso.

España no es España, que es una inmensa fosa,
que es un gran cementerio rojo y bombardeado:
los bárbaros la quieren de este modo.

Será la tierra un denso corazón desolado,
70   si vosotros, naciones, hombres, mundos,
con mi pueblo del todo
y vuestro pueblo encima del costado,
no quebráis los colmillos iracundos.

II

Pero no lo será: que un mar piafante;
75   triunfante siempre, siempre decidido,
hecho para la luz, para la hazaña,
agita su cabeza de rebelde diamante,
bate su pie calzado en el sonido
por todos los cadáveres de España.

80   Es una juventud: recoged este viento.
Su sangre es el cristal que no se empaña,
su sombrero el laurel y el pedernal su aliento.

Donde clava la fuerza de sus dientes
brota un volcán de diáfanas espadas,
85   y sus hombros batientes,
y sus talones guían llamaradas.

Está compuesta de hombres del trabajo:
de herreros rojos, de albos albañiles,
de yunteros con rostros de cosechas.
90   Oceánicamente transcurren por debajo
de un fragor de sirenas y herramientas fabriles
y de gigantes arcos alumbrados con flechas.

A pesar de la muerte, estos varones
con metal y relámpagos igual que los escudos,

95   hacen retroceder a los cañones
        acobardados, temblorosos, mudos.

        El polvo no los puede y hacen del polvo fuego,
        savia, explosión, verdura repentina:
        con su poder de abril apasionado
100   precipitan el alma del espliego,
        el parto de la mina,
        el fértil movimiento del arado.

        Ellos harán de cada ruina un prado,
        de cada pena un fruto de alegría,
105   de España un firmamento de hermosura.
        Vedlos agigantar el mediodía
        y hermosearlo todo con su joven bravura.

        Se merecen la espuma de los truenos,
        se merecen la vida y el olor del olivo,
110   los españoles amplios y serenos
        que mueven la mirada como un pájaro altivo.

        Naciones, hombres, mundos, esto escribo:
        la juventud de España saldrá de las trincheras
        de pie, invencible como la semilla,
115   pues tiene un alma llena de banderas
        que jamás se somete ni arrodilla.

        Allá van por los yermos de Castilla
        los cuerpos que parecen potros batalladores,
        toros de victorioso desenlace,
120   diciéndose en su sangre de generosas flores
        que morir es la cosa más grande que se hace.

        Quedarán en el tiempo vencedores,
        siempre de sol y majestad cubiertos,
        los guerreros de huesos tan gallardos
125   que si son muertos son gallardos muertos:
        la juventud que a España salvará, aunque tuviera
        que combatir con un fusil de nardos
        y una espada de cera.
                                    —Miguel Hernández

Highly emotional in tone and full of vivid hyperboles, "Recoged esta voz" may be classified as a wartime recruiting poem, its imagery derived from the passion of the battlefield. Discouraged by the course of the war (by 1937), Hernández asks for action by kindred spirits all over the world. He sees the war, then, not as a purely Spanish struggle. He feels the situation very intimately, as a Spaniard or Latin American would, and describes it from a firsthand point of view. Like Walt Whitman, he was there, but not just as a spectator—he had participated. His life was threatened and he, too, is being destroyed. It is a poem written out of the immediate circumstances of battle, revealing the poet's passionate, emotional involvement with no perspective of distance in time and space:

> Hundido estoy, mirad, estoy hundido
> en medio de mi pueblo y de sus males.

He is sunk in the midst of his people, as if in mire. Hernández notices bleeding wherever he goes—bleeding which is both physical and spiritual. There is an inundation of blood:

> Sangre, sangre por árboles y suelos,
> sangre por aguas, sangre por paredes
> y un temor de que España se desplome
> del peso de la sangre que moja entre sus redes
> hasta el pan que se come.

The vision of blood is vivid: "sangrando por trincheras y hospitales."

Hernández presents his people as violated and dying: the "¡ay! de tantas madres." These valiant people are being left "sin leche ni hermosura." Sweethearts find themselves alone, without hope or occupation. Cities are "de trabajo y de inocencia." Those who fight are snatched daily from the hands of their mothers, to fight with farm tools against powerful weapons and die bravely.

On the other hand, the enemy is described as barbaric, criminal, and unconscionable, wanting Spain to be nothing but a vast graveyard. The image of the enemy is that of an animal predator living off weaker animals. They have hooves and fangs and destroy "como torbellinos," while the poet's allies are like innocent children. Such a black-and-white vision shows the emotionality of the poet's commitment to the cause of the Republic. His poem shares with political cartoons an oversimplification and an intensity of the polarization between the two forces involved in the war, although political cartoons tend to be intellectualized while the poems of Hernández are not.

All around him Hernández sees chaos, mutilation, and death. Blood permeates everything, including the bread. There is a plethora of death images; Spain's life blood is being sapped, and Spain might collapse. The pervasive wind, like the ubiquitous blood, emanates from trenches and hospitals. It is the disturbed breath of a violated, desperate people losing a war.

The future that Hernández warns against would be a disaster:

> Un porvenir de polvo se avecina,
> se avecina un suceso
> en que no quedará ninguna cosa:
> ni piedra sobre piedra ni hueso sobre hueso.

The only way to avoid total holocaust is:

> si vosotros, naciones, hombres, mundos,
> con mi pueblo del todo
> y vuestro pueblo encima del costado,
> no quebráis los colmillos iracundos.

"Recoged esta voz" is a passionate poem. Hernández claims it for himself ("tengo una voz enardecida") and pleads for it from others ("aplicad la pasión de las entrañas"). Pulling no punches, he appeals to the strongest instincts and loyalties of his public. The audience he addresses is much simpler than that of Vallejo or Neruda (whose poems are less logical and more difficult to understand). The constant reminders of death ("muerte los caminos," "tanta muerte," "tanta caja," "caravanas de cuerpos abatidos") stress the urgent need for action. Hernández is addressing peasant soldiers so the imagery is rural and stated in terms understandable to the laborer: "herramientas fabriles," "la mina," "el arado," "un prado," etc. Hernández, being of humble origin himself, felt very close to the proletariat.

The first-person presentation makes the poem personal and direct in its appeal. The poet's voice is the voice of Spain, its force derived from the clamor of Spain. Hernández directs the poem to a collective "you": "atended," "escuchad," "recoged," "ved," "aplicad." He defines his audience in the first lines: "Naciones de la tierra, patrias del mar, hermanos/del mundo y de la nada," and redefines it similarly throughout the poem. His final plea is outright and unmistakable: "si vosotros . . . con mi pueblo del todo/y vuestro pueblo encima del costado,/no quebráis los colmillos iracundos." His feeling for collective humanity is like Vallejo's.

As in "Vientos del pueblo," he stresses that he is singing as he fights—his song is the poem: "sangrante sonido," "latidos de quebranto." And it is a cry to fight.

The second part of the poem continues informally with "Pero no lo será," which contradicts the total disaster ("Será la tierra un denso corazón desolado") that had been foreseen in Part I. Part II is much more affirmative, for despite the unevenness of the battle, he sees hope. Spain's hope, as in Vallejo's "España, aparta de mí este cáliz," lies in the future and with a youth who will restore and beautify Spain. Not just chronological youth, but peasant and working youth; these peasants, because of their commitment, bravery, and passion, will overcome cannons and fighter planes:

> la juventud que a España salvará, aunque tuviera
> que combatir con un fusil de nardos
> y una espada de cera.

In his poetic vision, Hernández sees the disinherited masses pitted against force, but the strength of the people "shall overcome."

There are many images in the poem. In the first stanza of Part II, youth is symbolized as a sea with the characteristics of a horse: "piafante" and "pie calzado." It is heroic, rebellious, and incorruptible. Hernández sees this vital force as composed of working men, and he eulogizes the common man with whom soldiers can easily identify.

In the second stanza, we have a variation of the title of the poem: "recoged este viento." This wind contains blood and breath —vital, essential ingredients. The title of the poem is significant as the voice and wind fill the atmosphere with a tremendous energy and force.

In the ninth stanza, the poet addresses the same audience as in Part I: "naciones, hombres, mundos." He looks on the war as offering some final hope—even if it brings temporary defeat and final death to some. He claims ultimate invincibility and victory for the brave youth of Spain, who are in perpetual and vigorous motion, communicating their dynamic qualities to everything they touch:

> El polvo no les puede y hacen del polvo fuego,
> savia, explosión, verdura repentina:
> con su poder de abril apasionado
> precipitan el alma del espliego,
> el parto de la mina,
> el fertil movimiento del arado.

A static element like "el polvo" contrasts dramatically with such dynamic elements as "fuego," "savia," "explosión," and "verdura repentina." Furthermore, the verb "precipitar"—and with respect to "verdura," the adjective "repentina"—implies abruptness to the aroma of the lavender plant, to the digging of the mine, and to the movement of the plow. Hernández sees the young Spaniards as colts, bulls, and flowers, and he and they believe that to die is the highest achievement. They will be victors, even if dead; they will die proudly, saviors of Spain no matter what the odds, even if fighting with flower guns and wax swords—metaphorical terms of futility rather than effectiveness. The poem ends on a note of inspiration and idealism. The ending reaffirms the martyrdom the poet sees as the necessary and only possible answer, and is very similar to the message of "Vientos del pueblo me llevan."

The poem is very visual:

30   Caravanas de cuerpos abatidos
34   sangre, sangre por árboles y suelos

66	España no es España, que es una inmensa fosa
67	que es un gran cementerio rojo y bombardeado.
87	Está compuesta de hombres del trabajo:
88	de herreros rojos, de albos albañiles,
89	de yunteros con rostros de cosechas.
90	Oceánicamente transcurren por debajo
91	de un fragor de sirenas y herramientas fabriles
92	y de gigantes arcos alumbrados con flechas.
113	la juventud de España saldrá de las trincheras
117	Allá van por los yermos de Castilla
118	los cuerpos que parecen potros batalladores,
119	toros de victorioso desenlace ; . .
122	Quedarán en el tiempo vencedores
123	siempre de sol y majestad cubiertos,
124	los guerreros de huesos tan gallardos
125	que si son muertos son gallardos muertos:
126	la juventud que a España salvará, aunque tuviera
127	que combatir con un fusil de nardos
128	y una espada de cera.

The movement of large masses, growing in force, offers almost a muralistic vision. The tone is exalted and heroic, and the heroic, victorious youth will be "siempre de sol y majestad cubiertos."

Including many repetitions, the vocabulary is not extensive, its repetition characteristic of an oral style. Hernández speaks to soldiers as another soldier might. He has intentionally kept the poem simple in all ways and melodic in rhythm, because he has directed it to the common people. Since Hernández meant it to be a song, since it tells a sad tale of Spain with only romantic notions of victory, and since it is directed to the people, the poem might be considered a ballad. The structure is well defined, a rhyme scheme continues throughout. Hernández plays on the natural rhythm of the Spanish language, which tends toward the predominant accentuation on the penultimate syllable of words.

There is much repetition of words as well as sounds, which makes it easier to memorize. In the second stanza, "aquí tengo" plus an indefinite article is repeated four times, the second and fourth being exact duplicates: "aquí tengo una vida."

In stanza three the alliteration and repetition create a particularly lyrical effect:

> Abierto estoy, mirad, como una herida.
> Hundido estoy, mirad, estoy hundido
> en medio de mi pueblo y de sus males.
> Herido voy, herido y malherido,
> sangrando por trincheras y hospitales.

The rhythm and repetition help to spell out the relentless message. There is some progression as Hernández makes his strongest plea at the end of Part I, and his most poetic claim for youth at the end of Part II.

There is a conflict in this poem between what is real and what is imagined or hoped—which is reminiscent of Vallejo's three poems.

"Recoged esta voz" is not polemical, nor is it especially narrative. Rather it is descriptive of a certain course of events through the presentation of a series of images. The poem is rhetorical and dramatic. Death is a major consideration. Hernández is emotionally committed to the Republican cause, and Hernández is highly subjective as he exaggerates his case in order to motivate and inspire his readers or listeners. The poet, coming from the working class, identifies with it, and directs his poem toward it. The poem was written by a soldier/poet very much involved in the war.

César Abraham Vallejo (1892-1938) was born in the town of Santiago de Chuco, in northern Peru, within sight of the Andes Mountains.[11] Santiago de Chuco is a small town with more than its fair share of disease, undernourishment, and cold weather. No doubt his background made Vallejo conscious of the meaning of hunger:

> . . . si no hubiera nacido,
> otro pobre tomara este café!
> Yo soy un mal ladrón . . . A dónde iré!
> (from "El pan nuestro,"
> *Los heraldos negros,* 1918)

(. . . If I had not been born,
another poor man could have drunk this
    coffee!
I feel like a dirty thief . . . where will I
    end!)

Both his grandmothers were full-blooded Indians. The youngest of eleven children, César was raised with strong Catholic training. As he grew older (by 1931 he was a communist) he renounced formal religion, but his poetry reveals his essential Christianity in its imagery and profound truth. Vallejo's poems frequently include God and Jesus:

Hay golpes en la vida, tan fuertes . . . Yo no sé!
Golpes como del odio de Dios.
                    (from "Los heraldos negros")

(There are blows in life, so hard . . . I don't
    know!
Blows as if from the hatred of God.)

Many of his poems depict the life of his native Andean town. Moving to Trujillo, he entered the University there and earned his Bachelor's degree two years later in 1915. He became involved in politics and was even imprisoned briefly. In Trujillo, too, he came into contact with and began to imitate the French poetic styles of the twenties, which he could not absorb.

By 1916 Vallejo was publishing poems in a small poetry magazine—poems that were collected in 1919 under the title, *Los heraldos negros*. One of these poems eulogizes his brother Miguel ("A mi hermano Miguel: in Memoriam"). His suffering for everyone and everything pervades all of his poetry. Vallejo could react to the plight of a spider with deep feeling:

. . . Y, al verla
atónita en tal trance,
hoy me ha dado qué pena esa viajera.
                    (from "La araña,"
                    Los heraldos negros)

(. . . And upon seeing it
confused in such danger,
what a strange pain that traveler has
given me today.)

Trilce, which contains surrealist poems, was published in 1923.
After *Trilce,* Vallejo left his country (he never returned to Peru)
for Europe, and for a while politics obsessed him to the exclusion
of poetry. In Europe he wrote short stories, novels, and dramas,
but lived mostly from his newspaper articles. He had frequent
financial difficulties, was often in a state of poverty and distress,
but had long-standing Spartan habits.

In 1930 he and his wife traveled to Spain, where he met such
writers as Salinas, Alberti, Unamuno, Gerardo Diego, and Lorca.
By 1931 he was a communist and his writing became Marxist
revolutionary propaganda. He became one of the founders of the
Spanish communist cells. After another trip to Russia, he returned to Spain, going from there to Paris in a destitute state.
He felt a deep nostalgia for Peru and his family and great indignation at the treatment of the Indian peasants.

The fascist uprising in Spain in July of 1936 disturbed him
profoundly. He soon left Paris for Barcelona and Madrid. Returning to Paris at the end of December, he was completely
absorbed in the Spanish cause. He left again for Spain in July
of 1937. It was after this final visit to Spain, and after nearly fifteen years of poetic silence, that he turned his energy toward
writing and revising the poems that comprise *Poemas humanos.*
As the title suggests, he had a strong sense of human compassion
and wished to extend his hand to anyone he felt needed it:

> Quiero ayudar al bueno a ser su poquillo de malo
> y me urge estar sentado
> a la diestra del zurdo, y responder al mudo,
> tratando de serle útil en
> lo que puedo, y también quiero muchísimo
> lavarle al cojo el pie,
> y ayudarle a dormir al tuerto próximo.
>   . . .

querría
ayudar a reír al que sonríe,
ponerle un pajarillo al malvado en plena nuca,
cuidar a los enfermos enfadándolos,
comprarle al vendedor,
ayudarle a matar al matador—cosa terrible—
y quisiera yo ser bueno conmigo
en todo.

(untitled poem from *Poemas humanos*)

(I want to help the good man to be a little bad
and I need to be seated to
the right of the lefthanded and respond to the mute,
trying to be useful to him in
some way, and also I want very
much to wash the cripple's foot,
and to help my one-eyed neighbor sleep.
. . .
I'd like
to help whoever smiles to laugh,
to put a little bird on the knave's neck,
to care for the sick exasperating them,
to buy from the salesman,
to help the killer to kill—terrible thing—
and to have been in everything
honest with myself.)

Either during this time or shortly afterwards, he wrote fifteen
poems inspired by the Republican cause, entitled *España, aparta
de mí este cáliz*. It was printed by Republican soldiers, but the
entire edition was lost in the disaster of Cataluña. These poems
and the poems that comprise *Poemas humanos* are much more
clearly expressed than the previous volume of poems, *Trilce*
(1923), whose obscurity attached it to the surrealist movement in
poetry. Perhaps, as in the case of Neruda, the brutal facts of the
war jolted him into an interest in having his poems communicate
a forthright message. On April 15, 1938, before the war came to
an end, Vallejo died in Paris. In 1940, almost three years after his
death, this same volume of poems was published in Mexico.

Of the three poems (from *España, aparta de mí este cáliz*) which I have chosen to analyze, the first, "Pequeño responso a un héroe de la República," is numbered IX in his collection. The second, "Masa," is XII; and the third, "España, aparta de mí este cáliz," is XIV. The themes of motherhood, death, and Man's isolation, suffering, and love are central to his poetry. It is clear that, although Vallejo cherished some inspired hope, he was skeptical and despairing over the outcome of the conflict. He had experienced at firsthand the horrors of Spain's Civil War, and was deeply concerned and involved. On his deathbed in Paris, in his final delirium, he said: "Voy a España . . . Quiero ir a España . . . ." [12]

PEQUEÑO RESPONSO A UN HÉROE DE LA REPÚBLICA [13]

1 Un libro quedó al borde de su cintura muerta,
   un libro retoñaba de su cadáver muerto.
   Se llevaron al héroe,
   y corpórea y aciaga entró su boca en nuestro
    aliento;
5 sudamos todos, el ombligo a cuestas;
   caminantes las lunas nos seguían;
   también sudaba de tristeza el muerto.

   Y un libro, en la batalla de Toledo,
   un libro, atrás un libro, arriba un libro, retoñaba
    del cadáver.

10 Poesía del pómulo morado, entre el decirlo
   y el callarlo,
   poesía en la carta moral que acompañara
   a su corazón.
   Quedóse el libro y nada más, que no hay
15 insectos en la tumba,
   y quedó al borde de su manga el aire remojándose
   y haciéndose gaseoso, infinito.

   Todos sudamos, el ombligo a cuestas,
   también sudaba de tristeza el muerto

20   y un libro, yo lo ví sentidamente,
        un libro, atrás un libro, arriba un libro
        retoñó del cadáver exabrupto.

                                        —César Vallejo

The "responso" of the title is a responsory, part of a church service sung in response to the reading of a text, but the poem itself hardly offers a formal religious context. There are, however, mystical circumstances, a religious occasion (a funeral), and a religious form to the poem. The poem concerns a small ritual (funeral) ceremony and offers a tribute to an unnamed, dead soldier of the Republic. The framework is localized and, basically, convincing. Vallejo's sentiments are clearly Republican; and the fateful battle at Toledo, where Republican forces failed to recapture the Alcázar, claimed many a hero.

The poem is not sequential. Rather, it is a succession of visual images that narrate an event. Many of the details emphasize physical and living aspects of the dead body and of those carrying it. Only remotely may it be considered a responsory: they go through the ritualistic motions of carrying the corpse during a funeral procession. Presumably, the body is buried. It may be supposed that some sort of anthem was sung on the same occasion—praising the enduring message of the "hero's" life and death, which is the main subject of the poem.

The hero is, in a sense, doubly dead: "cadáver muerto." His dead body is described in fragments: "cintura," "boca," "ombligo," and "mango." Fragmentation seems appropriate to the shattering of a life. His navel may symbolize part of the heritage that his poetry offered. From his sleeve his writing hand is missing. His mouth would have offered his word. His body is dead, but his words (his poetry, his message, and perhaps the meaning of his whole life) which he gave birth to live on—in this way, too, the umbilical cord is related. What remains is his book, his testament: "Quedóse el libro y nada más." What this book symbolizes is debatable. It may represent more than one man's lifetime. Since the poetic sequence (*España, aparta de mí este cáliz*) centers on the murder of Spain, the book may represent, in a broad sense, whatever value Spain may have which would survive were she destroyed.

Presumably, the body has been taken away, but the book which fell with the body on the battlefield insists on staying alive. It is already sending out sprouts to spread the meaning which had been within his heart: "poesía en la carta moral que acompañara a su corazón." If we limit the body to that of one individual, he died because he was a hero, but he will live on because of his poetry—a not unhappy idea for a fellow-poet to advance.

In lines two and nine the verb "retoñaba" has the force of continuing action, while in the last line the action has been accomplished: "retoñó." The finality is intensified by "exabrupto." But does this final word refer only to "retoñó," or to the book, or to the corpse? Or, does it mean all three?

The first stanza reports that a book remained at the side of the corpse, having emerged from it. The deceased shared the breath of those who carried his body. It is a strange corpse that still has breath and perspiration. Perhaps "sweating" is a sign of suffering. The derivation of "sudor" may be related to "sudario," which means a shroud. And it is a strange book that exudes from a body as if it, too, were a form of perspiration or, even more miraculously, of birth. The burden which they all feel is a burden of sadness, death, perhaps even mortality, as well as the burden of the body.

The first stanza is anguished, showing the passage of time through visual images. The two-line second stanza repeats that a book was sprouting from all over the corpse. A living book is thus deriving from the deceased. "Retoñaba" connotes quick development and budding, so that the extracted book is not only animate but also flourishing. The poetry is spreading, perhaps both in memory and influence. It multiplies in the sense that it becomes a greater part of the surrounding people.

The third stanza defines the book as poetry. The book reveals the dead man's very essence. The description here is condensed and suggestive rather than explicit. The body, decomposing, becomes infinite vapor as it enters into spirit.

The last stanza returns to the image of the first. "Todos sudamos" but this time a first-person narrator, who has evidently been giving us a firsthand report, interjects "yo lo ví sentidamente." The ending is sudden and definitive: "retoñó del cadáver exabrupto."

The responsory offers consolation to those who attend a funeral and reaffirms the power of his poetry. The word "responso" also denotes a service for the dead where a verse is repeated many times. Typical of religious chants and prayers, in general, is their repetitious and impressive drone. The poem contains many repetitions. "Libro" appears ten times; "cadáver," twice; "muerto," four times; and "retoñar," three. The phrase "el ombligo a cuestas" is repeated, the first time following "sudamos todos," the second time following its reverse, "todos sudamos." The seventh and ninth lines are exactly the same: "también sudaba de tristeza el muerto." This personification of the dead man magnifies his suffering whose source may be not only his death but also the pangs of creating (or giving birth). From everywhere the book asserts his message: "un libro, atrás un libro, arriba un libro." The repetition of the same occurrence in lines nine and twenty-one emphasizes the prevalence of the book and its message.

In line five, "el ombligo a cuestas" literally means "our navels on our shoulders, or back." Why navel? Is it because this anatomical part, through which the unborn child is nourished, is still central to us? Does the line then suggest that we bore away with us the very core and burden of our lives, after the hero's breath had entered our breath?

In lines ten through thirteen the poetry intended is halfway between telling and keeping silent:

> Poesía del pómulo morado, entre el decirlo
> y el callarlo,
> poesía en la carta moral que acompañara
> a su corazón.

It is the poetry that he was bearing in his heart when he performed his last act of sacrifice.

In lines fourteen and fifteen, "que no hay/insectos en la tumba" calls attention to the insects by negation. Their absence insures that the book will not be gnawed away by them; the poetry will endure.

There are many obscurities in this poem, for instance, the referent of "exabrupto" and the meaning of "pómulo morado."

Its relation to the sequence of poems among which it is included is also uncertain. Is it really just about a poet, or does it represent Spain, as do most of the fifteen poems of this Spanish Civil War collection? It is the most complex and difficult of the three poems of Vallejo to be analyzed.

MASA [14]

1	Al fin de la batalla,
	y muerto el combatiente, vino hacia él un hombre
	y le dijo: "¡No mueras; te amo tanto!"
	Pero el cadáver, ¡ay! siguió muriendo.
5	Se le acercaron dos y repitiéronle:
	"¡No nos dejes! ¡Valor! ¡Vuelve a la vida!"
	Pero el cadáver, ¡ay! siguió muriendo.
	Acudieron a él veinte, cien, mil, quinientos mil,
	clamando: "¡Tanto amor, y no poder nada contra la muerte!"
10	Pero el cadáver, ¡ay! siguió muriendo.
	Le rodearon millones de individuos,
	con un ruego común: "¡Quédate hermano!"
	Pero el cadáver, ¡ay! siguió muriendo.
	Entonces todos los hombres de la tierra
15	le rodearon; les vió el cadáver triste, emocionado;
	incorporóse lentamente,
	abrazó al primer hombre; echóse a andar . . .

—César Vallejo

"Masa" informs us immediately that the battle is over and the combatant dead. We know that the poem was the twelfth of fifteen written by Vallejo in his Spanish Civil War collection. It is obvious that when he wrote it (1937) he was in despair over the outcome of Spain's war.

The first man to approach says to the dead man, "¡No mueras," because "te amo tanto!" Two others approach and make the same

plea with the same result: "Pero el cadáver, ¡ay! siguió muriendo."
Then steadily increasing numbers surround the corpse, begging
it not to leave them. Finally, when everyone in the world is there,
with one common desire, the body resurrects, embraces the first
man, and begins to walk.

The narrative is simple but its symbolism has large dimensions.
A single dead soldier magnifies not just to the great body of all the
war dead, but even to Spain itself. Spain's fall is Spain's death, but
Spain, dead and dying (sic), resurrects (metaphorically, not literally). Spain in this poem symbolizes crucified humanity and, like
the traditional figure of Christ, died for mankind and rose from
the dead. The difference, however (and here lies the rub), is that
Christ, being God-like, always had within him the power to be immortal. Spain had no such option. The cadaver views all of mankind sadly and, moved by their solidarity in love, faith, and hope,
revives. It walks again as if out of pity for suffering humanity. But
could this miracle happen?

The title, "Masa," meaning "a mass of people," presents the
poignantly romantic notion that Spain could be revivified by the
love and hope of all the people in the world collectively. It is both
idealized in its hoping and despairing in its impossibility. It is in
its impossibility that it is so moving. It is the fantasy of a poet
yearning to believe. Vallejo poeticizes the dream romantically,
passionately, hopelessly.

But, from another viewpoint, an Hispanic poet could look at
the total image of Spain, of its cities, of its people, dying and being
destroyed, as the promise of a new Spain (this message underlay
"España, aparta de mí este cáliz" also). Vallejo agreed with Hernández that death is inevitable, and Vallejo could further regard
the war dead as not just dead and gone, but as part of a living
army, sharing in the struggle and in the future with the people
with whom and for whom they had fought.

The refrain, "Pero el cadáver, ¡ay! siguió muriendo," is a formal
part of the structure of the poem and produces a cumulative effect
of irony. It is like an undertow of fate and sadness. It is the last line
of every stanza until the end, when the trend is reversed with
"abrazó al primer hombre; echóse a andar . . . ." The reversal
would lead us to believe that the love and religious faith (in the

possibility of resurrection and in the individual Christ-figure) of all the people in the world (which is in itself impossible) could produce a miracle and save Spain. If this is what Spain's salvation depends upon, we are not much comforted.

The presentation of "Masa" is straightforward and relies on direct quotations. The structure of the brief poem is neat and simple. The vocabulary is limited to simple words and the dialogue is informal. There is a discrepancy between the mysterious, miraculous subject matter and the matter-of-fact tone.

It is curious that although Spain is "muerto" as of the second line, it continues dying in the refrain, as if it is in the process of becoming, and therefore retrievable, rather than an accomplished fact. The association of inanimate objects with animate qualities and vice versa is typical of Vallejo's (and Neruda's) poetry. In "Pequeño responso" the corpse sprouted and breathed ("retoñaba . . . entró su boca en nuestro aliento").

It is a very human poem, resulting from the personal anguish of Vallejo, registering his ironic protest against injustice: Spain deserves to be transformed. Vallejo obviously had a strong impulse for human solidarity, and this poem reveals his interest in man individually and collectively; after all, there is no landscape in the poem, only people and feelings. It is a sad, lyrical poem, expressing high idealism.

ESPAÑA, APARTA DE MÍ ESTE CÁLIZ [15]

1
Niños del mundo,
si cae España—digo, es un decir—
si cae
del cielo abajo su antebrazo que asen
5
en cabestro, dos láminas terrestres;
niños, ¡que edad la de las sienes cóncavas!
¡qué temprano en el sol lo que os decía!
¡qué pronto en vuestro pecho el ruido anciano!
¡qué viejo vuestro 2 en el cuaderno!

10
¡Niños del mundo, está
la madre España con su vientre a cuestas;

está nuestra maestra con sus férulas,
está madre y maestra,
cruz y madera, porque os dió la altura,
15   vertigo y división y suma, niños;
está con ella, padres procesales!

Si cae—digo, es un decir—si cae
España, de la tierra para abajo,
niños, ¡cómo váis a cesar de crecer!
20   ¡cómo va a castigar el año al mes!
¡cómo van a quedarse en diez los dientes,
en palote el diptongo, la medalla en llanto!
¡Cómo va el corderillo a continuar
atado por la pata al gran tintero!
25   ¡Cómo váis a bajar las gradas del alfabeto
hasta la letra en que nació la pena!

Niños,
hijos de los guerreros, entretanto,
bajad la voz, que España está ahora mismo
        repartiendo
30   la energía entre el reino animal,
las florecillas, los cometas y los hombres.
¡Bajad la voz, que está
con su rigor, que es grande, sin saber
qué hacer, y está en su mano
35   la calavera hablando y habla y habla,
la calavera, aquélla de la trenza,
la calavera, aquélla de la vida!

¡Bajad la voz, os digo;
bajad la voz, el canto de las sílabas, el llanto
40   de la materia y el rumor menor de las pirámides,
        y aún
el de las sienes que andan con dos piedras!
¡Bajad el aliento, y si
el antebrazo baja,
si las férulas suenan, si es la noche,
45   si el cielo cabe en dos limbos terrestres,

si hay ruido en el sonido de las puertas,
si tardo,
si no véis a nadie, si os asustan
los lápices, sin punta, si la madre
50   España cae—digo, es un decir—
salid, niños del mundo; id a buscarla! . . .

                                        —César Vallejo

The title (the same as that of the volume which contains the poem, along with fourteen others by Vallejo on the Spanish Civil War) is from the Bible. It is taken from Christ's words in the garden of Gethsemane: "O my Father, if it be possible, let this cup pass from me" (Matthew XXVI: 39; Mark XIV: 36; Luke XXII: 42). Vallejo changed it to "España, aparta de mí este cáliz," replacing Father with Mother Spain. The story behind the Biblical quotation is that Christ had had a premonition that he would be betrayed and that he would soon die. He had also prophesied that the next time he drank from the cup he would be beyond death, in the Kingdom of God. The chalice, then, symbolizes death. The night that Christ was apprehended, in a moment of weakness, as if he might change his fate, he asked that the cup be taken away. It was not and he went on to fulfill his divine destiny. A comparison is being made between his position—what he stood for, what he died for, carrying his own cross, being resurrected—and that of Spain, whose fate the poet is anguishing over, and would challenge if he could, Spain might be said to be dying for the sins of mankind, and Spain looks to its children as Christ might have looked to his disciples.

Vallejo addresses the poem to the future, to the "Niños del mundo." Spain's war has international implications. These children are "hijos de los guerreros" who represent multifarious nationalities. The war has cosmic overtones, also:

que España está ahora mismo repartiendo
la energía entre el reino animal,
las florecillas, los cometas y los hombres.

Vallejo means children who are children not only by age, development, activities, but in a sense, too, children of the Spanish world.

Latin American countries may be considered children of Mother Spain. As a Peruvian, Vallejo would have such a perspective.

The poem is a personification of Spain—in the first stanza as a huge image in the sky whose forearm is held in the grip of two earthly metal plates, which literally may refer to "armaments" or "engravings" that are opposing one another, and symbolically allude to the two distinct camps into which Spain, and the world, too, is divided. The poet then captures, by a series of images, some universal qualities of children:

> ¡qué edad la de las sienes cóncavas!
> ¡qué temprano en el sol lo que os decía!
> ¡qué pronto en vuestro pecho el ruido anciano!
> ¡qué viejo vuestro 2 en el cuaderno!

Whatever fate flesh is heir to is always part of us. The poet ascribes this mythical instinct to children: "el ruido anciano." One can visualize generations of school children laboriously forming the number "2" in their notebooks—a number difficult for them to draw.

Vallejo describes "la madre España" as most vulnerable and uncomfortable "con su vientre a cuestas," which recalls Christ's carrying his cross. She is mother and teacher, religious and secular. Again, there is grade-school terminology: "maestra con sus férulas . . . división y suma." This mother and teacher, "cruz y madera," reminding us again of Christ's cross and of Spain's being a source of religion, offers spiritual "altura" as well as physical "vertigo y división y suma." Spain, extended to represent the world, is divided and may or may not become united and whole again ("suma").

If Spain falls (and the repetition of this possibility makes it more likely), the consequences would be horrendous. In stanza three Vallejo lists some of the deleterious effects it would have upon the children. It would stunt their growth and the development of their teeth. All their learning would be arrested at the letter of the alphabet "en que nació la pena," which reminds us of line eight's ". . . en vuestro pecho el ruido anciano."

"¡Bajad la voz!" is perhaps a necessary admonition to boisterous children, but to hear what? Vallejo lists silent aspects of Spain's heritage and presents them in audible forms: ". . . el canto de las sílabas, el llanto/de la materia y el rumor menor de las pirámides . . . ." The comparison to the Pyramids suggests Spain's civilization. The fall of Spain brings with it the silent crumbling of centuries of history as well as its audible wreckage.

The poem personifies the image of Spain throughout. Spain represents to Vallejo not just the mother country, but the mother language, the source of civilization and religion as well. It is both a terrestrial image and a celestial one. Spain falls from above in the beginning, but from the earth in stanza three.

In the third stanza we return to the metaphor of stanza one: "si/el antebrazo baja," another way of hypothesizing Spain's fall, and if, thereby, the wooden rulers in the hand of this "madre-maestra" are lowered with a bang; and if it is night, a time particularly frightful for children; and if the sky is divided between two earthly states of limbo, where all are unbaptized and stagnating; and if doors slam on you as if you have been abandoned; and if "I" (the narrator) am late, a traumatic experience for children; and if you don't see anyone—which can be terrifying to children; and if your pencils without points scare you, then the scene is set for the final tragedy. Vallejo has led up to the climax in such a way, with the repetition of "if" this and "if" that, that the tragedy seems inevitable. It is as if a crescendo were created in which the climax is the death of the mother. This sequence of images has been carefully selected for its impact upon children. The final and ultimate loss is that of the mother. Vallejo ends the poem in the imperative. "Si la madre/España cae, . . . ¡salid niños del mundo; id a buscarla!" Not only will they look for "España," but, in a way, they will recreate her, for children recreate their parents by living on in their images.

Despite its tragic circumstances, there is hope in the poem that Spain can be saved. Reviewing the image of Spain, we may conclude that she extends up to the sky and down to the earth and that she is divided between two forces. Her fall is impending. She is in the clutch of the power of these opposing forces. She is both mother, familial and religious, and teacher of religion, language, culture. Mother connotes security, comfort, sustenance, nonabandonment. Teacher suggests learning, mental development, language, religion. In these two capacities, Spain would suggest to Spaniards and Latin Americans a long association of love, tradition, and civilization. Spain's energies are being drained, and in her hand is the skull of life. If she falls, life falls. The choice of children as part of the imagery in this poem is especially apt. Vallejo is able to play upon the powerful bond between children and their mother. Also, in their vulnerability and innocence, children and mothers evoke our emotions.

The poem is well unified in its imagery, the metaphors consistent with childhood. There is the pervasive, hovering image of Spain, and the reiteration of her possible fall. There is the focus of the poem toward the children, and the successions of images to represent the various aspects of Vallejo's vision. In the first stanza the children are presented. Spain, whose image has been suggested in stanza one, is further clarified in stanza two. In stanza three the fall of Spain is indicated by the effects it would have upon the children. Stanza four symbolizes the dimensions of the war. Here, for the first time, the "I" (the narrator and the poet himself, I presume) directs the children. Stanza five expresses other fatal implications of Spain's fall: "está en su mano/la calavera . . . aquélla de la vida." The final stanza offers the crux of his message to the children. The poet lists the contingencies upon which to base their (the children's) decision to take over. He exhorts that if the tragedy does occur, they should go forth and reclaim Spain, with all of its implications for the world. There is hope that the surviving children of the world will provide a better future.

The poem's five stanzas are of unequal length. The length of individual lines varies also, but with frequent repetition of words and sounds. There are numerous images in series, both visual and auditory, each with its own repetitive framework. Thus, we have, for example, "si cae" repeated five times and "si" alone introducing many instances; "que" precedes others.

There are many exclamatory sentences, the poem ending with an exclamation point. The tone of the poem is highly emotional; the personification of Spain as the mother figure and of those who are, in a sense, from her womb and under her influence as her children is effective and moving. The underlying assumption is that

Spain is in serious, terrible danger, but Vallejo places his hope upon the children and the future.

Neftali Ricardo Reyes y Basoalto, who was to assume the pseudonym Pablo Neruda, was born in Parral, a remote village in southern Chile, on July 12, 1904.[16] There he lived close to nature, an association especially apparent in his early poetry. His father was a railway employee, and Neruda knew what it was to be poor in a country noted for its poverty. In Parral he studied at the Liceo de Técnico, but at the age of sixteen he went to the capital, Santiago, to continue his studies at the Instituto Pedagógico of the University of Chile. In Santiago he spent most of his time in cafés talking about literature and writing poetry, and at the age of seventeen he won first prize in a poetry contest.

Neruda left Chile in 1927, proceeded to Europe, traveled in the Orient, where, between 1927 and 1932, he lived successively in Rangoon, Colombo, Singapore, and Batavia, visiting adjacent areas of Asia and Oceania, and was Chilean consul in Calcutta. On his return to Chile in 1933, Neruda was assigned first as consul to Buenos Aires (1932-1933) and then to Madrid (1933-1937), where he was received with admiration and acclaim by a generation of Spanish poets: Federico García Lorca, Rafael Alberti, Luis Cernuda, Miguel Hernández, and Manuel Altolaguirre. In Madrid, too, his first and second *Residencias* first appeared together, with enormous success, in 1935.

When the Civil War broke out in Spain in 1936, Neruda, heedless of diplomatic protocol, made no secret of his antifascist convictions. His active role in radical politics from 1936 on was to result in conflict with the Chilean government, expulsion, and, finally, exile. He was recalled to Chile in 1937, but a new President soon sent him off to Europe to expedite the emigration to America of Republican Spanish refugees. From 1939 to 1943, he served as Chilean consul to Mexico. He enrolled in the Communist Party of Chile in 1943, although his conversion to communism antedated this time.

The enumerative bibliography of his works is a long one, beginning with *La canción de la fiesta,* published in Chile in 1921, when he was seventeen years old. *Crepusculario,* consisting of poems written in 1919, was published in 1923. His romantic vein was most apparent in *Veinte poemas de amor y una canción desesperada,* published in 1924:

> Puedo escribir los versos más tristes esta noche. . . .
> Yo la quise, y a veces ella también me quiso.

> (I can write the saddest verses tonight.
> I loved her, and at times she also loved me.)

Tentativa del hombre infinito was published in 1933. *Residencia en la tierra,* Volume I, containing poetry from 1925 to 1931, in 1935. *Las furias y las penas,* written in 1934, was published in 1939. *Tercera residencia,* covering 1935 to 1945, appeared in 1945, and *Alturas de Macchu Picchu* in 1948.

At first he wrote in romantic and surrealist styles. After his war poetry in honor of the Spanish Republic, he began his lengthy and uneven *Canto general,* published in 1950. It was an attempt to portray his own country and continent in its place in time and political development. *Odas elementales, Estravagario,* and *Navegaciones y regresos* were published in 1954, 1958, and 1959, respectively. A volume of political verse, *Las uvas y el viento,* was published in 1954.

Neruda felt close to Vallejo and reacted to his death in a poem called "Pastoral":

> Sufro de aquel amigo que murió
> y que era como yo buen carpintero.
> Ibamos juntos por mesas y calles,
> por guerras, por dolores y por piedras.
> Cómo se le agrandaba la mirada
> conmigo, era un fulgor aquel huesudo,
> y su sonrisa me sirvió de pan,
> nos dejamos de ver y V. se fué enterrando
> hasta que lo obligaron a la tierra.
> (from Estravagario, 1958)

> (I mourn for that friend who died
> and who was, like myself, a good carpenter.

We walked together through plateaus and
  streets,
through wars, through sorrows, and
  through stones.
How he widened his gaze
with me, an intense fire was that boney
  man,
and his smile was my bread,
we parted and he was burying himself
until they forced him into the ground.)

In 1956 *Nuevas odas elementales* appeared; and the following year *Obras completas* and *Tercer libro de las odas* were published. In 1960 came *Cien sonetos de amor* and *Las piedras de Chile*. Neruda, considered Chile's major poet of the twentieth century, was awarded the Nobel Prize for Literature in 1971. He died September 23, 1973.

Throughout his poetic career, Neruda exhibited a variety of styles: symbolic, straightforward, lyrical, polemical, detached, sarcastic, fantastic, realistic, and surrealist.

The poems of my selection are contained in Neruda's collection *España en el corazón*, written between 1936 and 1937, when he was thirty-three. These hymns to the glories of the Spanish people during the Spanish Civil War form part of the third volume of *Residencia en la tierra*. The spectacle of death and injustice in the crushing of the Spanish Republic by the military awakened the political conscience of Neruda and forced him into a more engaged stance; his voice began to be heard less and less hermetically and more and more didactically. The poems analyzed here are "Explico algunas cosas," "Llegada a Madrid de la Brigada Internacional," and "Almería."

EXPLICO ALGUNAS COSAS [17]

1   Preguntaréis: Y dónde están las lilas?
         Y la metafísica cubierta de amapolas?
         Y la lluvia que a menudo golpeaba

5   sus palabras llenándolas
       de agujeros y pájaros?

       Os voy a contar todo lo que me pasa.

       Yo vivía en un barrio
       de Madrid, con campanas,
       con relojes, con árboles.
10   Desde allí se veía
       el rostro seco de Castilla
       como un océano de cuero.

                      Mi casa era llamada
       la casa de las flores, porque por todas partes
15   estallaban geranios: era
       una bella casa
       con perros y chiquillos.
                      Raúl, te acuerdas?
       Te acuerdas, Rafael?
20   Federico, te acuerdas
       debajo de la tierra,
       te acuerdas de mi casa con balcones en donde
       la luz de junio ahogaba flores en tu boca?

                      Hermano, hermano!
25   Todo
       era grandes voces, sal de mercaderías,
       aglomeraciones de pan palpitante,
       mercados de mi barrio de Argüelles con su estatua
       como un tintero pálido entre las merluzas:
30   el aceite llegaba a las cucharas,
       un profundo latido
       de pies y manos llenaba las calles,
       metros, litros, esencia
       aguda de la vida,
35   pescados hacinados,
       contextura de techos con sol frío en el cual
       la flecha se fatiga,
       delirante marfil fino de las patatas,
       tomates repetidos hasta el mar.

40   Y una mañana todo estaba ardiendo
       y una mañana las hogueras
       salían de la tierra
       devorando seres,
       y desde entonces fuego,
45   pólvora desde entonces,
       y desde entonces sangre.

       Bandidos con aviones y con moros,
       bandidos con sortijas y duquesas,
       bandidos con frailes negros bendiciendo
50   venían por el cielo a matar niños
       y por las calles la sangre de los niños
       corría simplemente, como sangre de niños.

       Chacales que el chacal rechazaría,
       piedras que el cardo seco mordería escupiendo,
55   víboras que las víboras odiarían!

       Frente a vosotros he visto la sangre
       de España levantarse
       para ahogaros en una sola ola
       de orgullo y de cuchillos!

60   Generales
       traidores:
       mirad mi casa muerta,
       mirad España rota:
       pero de cada casa muerta sale metal ardiendo
65   en vez de flores,
       pero de cada hueco de España
       sale España,
       pero de cada niño muerto sale un fusil con ojos,
       pero de cada crimen nacen balas
70   que os hallarán un día el sitio
       del corazón.

       Preguntaréis por qué su poesía
       no nos habla del suelo, de las hojas,
       de los grandes volcanes de su país natal?

75   Venid a ver la sangre por las calles,
         venid a ver
         la sangre por las calles,
         venid a ver la sangre
         por las calles!

                                        —Pablo Neruda

The title, "Explico algunas cosas," is intimate in the first person. Although one might expect the poem to be defensive, Neruda explains his change in poetic aesthetics aggressively and even bitterly. In part the poem represents a coming to terms with himself and his readers about his new aesthetics, and in part it offers a particular perspective on the war. Neruda was in Spain both as a poet and as a man, and the war had a profound effect upon him in both capacities. Neruda sees himself in the role of a poet in the war (Felipe does, too) and translates the Spanish catastrophe into a personal one. In this respect this poem is the most personal in tone and content of the three I shall deal with. Neruda begins on an intimate key, conversationally, with "preguntaréis," which is addressed to a familiar, collective "you." It is a confession to fellow poets and students since it is they who would read his poetry. "Os voy a contar todo lo que me pasa"—it is what is happening that is forcing him into a reappraisal of himself as a poet.

"Explico algunas cosas" is a poem transitional in his career from an earlier poetry ("las lilas," "la metafísica cubierta de amapolas," "la lluvia" filling his words with gullies and birds) which he echoes in the first stanza, only to reject in favor of a new poetic style. It is a re-examination of where he stands and where his poetry stands.

In his early poetry, before the *Residencias,* Neruda had demonstrated a lyric inclination, while concerned as a human being with problems of coping with love, death, abandonment, and loneliness. Elements of nature, very personal emotions, and artistic consciousness affected this poetry. His later experience aroused his political conscience. His commitment (to communism) was ideological, not artistic, but caused priorities within his verse to shift. His vision became less introspective and more outward-directed toward experience which involved him as a person and as a poet. Some critics have condemned the prosaic qualities they saw in his later works, for example, in *Canto general* (1950). Typical of his later development was his choice of such subjects in *Odas elementales* (1954-1957) as a lemon and an artichoke:

> La alcachofa
> de tierno corazón
> se vistió de guerrero,
> erecta, construyó
> una pequeña cupula . . .
> (beginning of
> "Oda a la alcachofa"
> from *Odas elementales*)

> (The artichoke
> of delicate heart,
> erect
> in its battle-dress, built
> a small cupola . . .)

But really Neruda has always been a poet. This particular poem is a critical point in the evolution of Neruda as a poet and as a social animal. And his decision is to put his poetry at the service of his commitment—which is clearly implied in his poem.

Typical of Neruda's poetry (as of Vallejo's) had been the juxtaposition of animate and inanimate objects, such as, from the first stanza: "la metafísica cubierta de amapolas." The fragrance, color, and life force of poppies contrast strikingly with the philosophical abstraction of metaphysics. Both Vallejo and Neruda had the knack of making disparate things live with each other, their logic often deriving from emotion rather than intellect.

In the third stanza, "Yo vivía en un barrio/de Madrid, con companas,/con relojes, con árboles" is near to conversation made rhythmic. While his description of Madrid as being arid and withered is not surprising, his use of simple analogies has a powerful effect, for instance: "el rostro de Castilla/como un océano de cuero." His quotidian experiences and the flowers are ordinary, but they make the impact of his later "Y una mañana" that much greater. The poem has religious, sacramental symbols, such as flowers and blood.

As in Auden's *Spain,* the poem is presented in three tenses: past, present, and future. In the past, Neruda's poetry had been metaphysical, with adornments from nature. In the past, too, the poet had lived in a beautiful house in Madrid in an idyllic situation. He reports in a conversational way that all was lovely and, then, asks intimately, in the present tense, if three particular friends who would have visited his house remember: Raúl (González Tuñón [18]), Rafael (Alberti), and Federico (García Lorca). He recollects the two living and one dead poet. (Lorca was shot at the outbreak of the Spanish Civil War in 1936 by adherents of Franco, although he had had no political interests.) Appropriately, lines 22 and 23 contain images like those of Lorca's poetry.

In line 24 Neruda addresses his audience "Hermano, hermano!" but more in the sense of brother poets than as comrades. He shared a fraternity with Lorca based on their mutual suffering because of the war—Neruda in the sense of uprooting his past life and poetry and Lorca in the total sense of giving his life. He may then have been asking if they remember the sense of life they shared. He continues in the past, telling how things were: business went on in the marketplace, a microcosm of prewar life in Madrid. The imagery is auditory and visual. There is the interchange of food and appropriate imagery related to food. The olive oil is integral to Spanish cuisine. He hears the movement of hands and feet like the throb of a heart. He captures the sheer sensuality of the feeling of life and a tremendous sense of movement and sound. This sense of physical force and dynamism is typical of Neruda's poetry. The hands and feet are performing daily tasks of life. Despite the ordinariness of the day, he is getting at the very essence of daily life and people: food sale and preparation, nourishment, and the palpitating sound of human beings. The configuration of rooftops and tiles is brought out in sharp, cold relief by an intense sun. Neruda makes the scene somewhat sacred by including the metaphor of a marble statue: "delirante marfil fino de la patatas." Included in this picture is the same disorder that pervades living: "aglomeraciones," "llegaba," "llenaba," "tomates repetidos hasta el mar." Despite the mundane subject, the imagery is far from common (much like Vallejo's): "su estatua/como un tintero pálido entre las merluzas." The rich imagery appeals to all of our senses.

One can taste, smell, hear, feel, and see what Madrid had been and meant to him.

And then there is a sudden reversal. "Y una mañana," still in the past, everything that has meant life is completely obliterated:

> Y una mañana todo estaba ardiendo
> y una mañana las hogueras
> salían de la tierra
> devorando seres,
> y desde entonces fuego,
> pólvora desde entonces,
> y desde entonces sangre.

The life/death contrast of the imagery of the poem is striking. It is as if someone came along and knocked over and leveled everything, leaving nothing. This image of destruction leads up to the total holocaust of the final stanza, consisting of the repetition three times of "venid a ver la sangre por las calles." Blood is a frequent image of Neruda's poetry as we see also in Almería" and "Llegada." The image is as terrifying as that of Hernández in "Recoged esta voz": "un porvenir de polvo se avecina,/se avecina un suceso/en que no quedará ninguna cosa:/ni piedra sobre piedra ni hueso sobre hueso." In contrast with the geometrical imagery of the market scene, this negation of life is generalized.

There follow political caricatures with characteristic imagery. He designates the enemy as "bandidos" with airplanes and names their accomplices: the Moors, the wealthy ("sortijas"), the aristocracy ("duquesas"), and the Church, represented by black (in dress and character) friars who go through the motions of their office perfunctorily. Neruda is alluding to the following facts: During the uprising that began the Spanish Civil War, General Franco declared war in Tenerife (Canary Islands) on July 17, 1936, flew to Casablanca (French Morocco), and then on to Spanish Morocco on July 19 to take command of the Army of Morocco. This army of Africa was transported to Spain across the Strait of Gibraltar, and became a formidable battalion for the Insurgent side.[19] Of the Franco forces in 1937, 100,000 were Moors, 70,000 were Italians, several thousand were Germans and Portuguese, and 250,000 were Spanish troops in Carlist and Falangist militia units. Thus, the Moors made the major contribution quantitatively.[20] In addition, the word "Moros" has negative connotations.

"Niños" are pitted against these forces and "por las calles la sangre de los niños/corría simplemente, como sangre de niños" is a powerful repetition. In this poem as well as in "Llegada" and "Almería," Neruda sees children as being particularly vulnerable (as had Vallejo in "España, aparta de mí este cáliz"): "chiquillos," "venían por el cielo a matar niños/y por las calles la sangre de los niños/corría simplemente, como sangre de niños."

The class struggle is emphasized in line 48: "bandidos con sortijas y duquesas." This ideological vision of the war as a product of particular economic interests is reminiscent of Spender's "Ultima Ratio Regum." In line 49 the Church is on the side of the rich. Neruda sees the rich versus the poor here as well as in "Almería."

Neruda calls the enemy by despicable names: he thinks in terms of things that feed on dead matter. Jackals are carnivorous and prey upon other animals. Vipers are venomous. Neruda challenges the enemy, "generales/traidores," to look upon the destruction they have wrought. Again he is aware of the historical fact that certain generals did revolt against the Republic to ignite the war. Lines 64 and 65, "pero de cada casa muerta sale metal ardiendo/en vez de flores," suggest line 15 of Spender's "Ultima Ratio Regum": "The unflowering wall sprouted with guns." But Neruda adds the twist that "de cada hueco de España sale España." Neruda had confidence in the ultimate retribution on the part of the victims:

> Frente a vosotros he visto la sangre
> de España levantarse
> para ahogaros en una sola ola
> de orgullo y de cuchillos!
> . . .
> pero de cada casa muerta sale metal ardiendo
> en vez de flores,
> pero de cada hueco de España
> sale España,
> pero de cada niño muerto sale un fusil con ojos,

> pero de cada crimen nacen balas
> que os hallarán un día el sitio
> del corazón.

It is as if all of Spain were arising to smother the jackals and traitors. This vow and cry for vengeance suggests in language and spirit the call to arms of Hernández.

Again Neruda speaks of his past poetry's having dealt with "el suelo . . . las hojas . . . los grandes volcanes . . . su país natal." Then he asks scornfully how they might have the audacity to wonder why his poetry does not speak of these trivialities (this is a most liberal transliteration), after the incalculable monstrosity, the overwhelming crime against children and against people with whom he has lived. The tone here is very different from before. He had begun the poem conversationally and with restraint. There had been a progressive gradation of emotional intensity, leading to his promise of revenge and his sense of outrage. His outrage and emotional reaction take precedence over the artist. The experience makes his new aesthetics unavoidable, and he answers his own question:

> mirad mi casa muerta
> mirad España rota:
> . . .
> Venid a ver la sangre por las calles,
> venid a ver
> la sangre por las calles,
> venid a ver la sangre
> por las calles!

In the final stanza, there is repeated play upon the same words, again as in Lorca's poetry (for example, "a las cinco de la tarde" and "verde . . . que te quiero verde"). Like the imagery of Hernández, the poem offers a growing crescendo of destruction.

Neruda is considering his own poetry in relation to what is happening (1937), but it is not an intellectual exercise. In the heat of a traumatic experience, the poem offers a re-evaluation of how the poet stands in relation to the large, collective experience outside himself. In view of the overwhelming facts, everything else becomes essentially academic. His style has changed from being obscure, metaphysical, and inner-directed to being a poetry of emotional, as well as ideological, commitment. Putting his poetry at the service of his beliefs, he wishes to present his doctrine clearly and simply. He uses fewer images, and there is an emphasis upon direct communication. Between 1936 and 1939, when the Spanish Civil War exploded upon the world of his tradition, culture, and language as well as upon the routine of his life in Madrid, Neruda offered to the world a changed heart and a new source of perception firmly aligned with suffering and embattled mankind. His communist affiliation engaged his political conscience and artistic talent on the side of the Republic.

There is poetic intensity in the choice of strong words to dichotomize the opposing factions (Nationalist vs. Republican), in the careful repetitions, bitter accusations, and acid declaration of Spain's tragedy as well as his own. There is artistic tension in terms of language and imagery.

Neruda chose to cast this most personal poem in the form of a soliloquy. It is as if he were thinking aloud in reordering his values and life. The poem includes a re-evaluation of his poetry in view of the Spanish tragedy and a nihilistic picture of devastated Spain. It indicates an ideological background and offers a battle cry of revenge.

The twelve stanzas, of varying length and form, condense his emotional and intellectual response, but also allow him a flexible framework in which to build up the intensity of the poem.

LLEGADA A MADRID DE LA BRIGADA INTERNACIONAL [21]

1   Una mañana de un mes frío,
        de un mes agonizante, manchado por el lodo y por
            el humo,
        un mes sin rodillas, un triste mes de sitio y
            desventura,

cuando a través de los cristales mojados de mi casa
se oían los chacales africanos
5   aullar con los rifles y los dientes llenos de sangre,
entonces,
cuando no teníamos más esperanza que un sueño
de pólvora, cuando ya creíamos
que el mundo estaba lleno sólo de monstruos
devoradores y de furias
entonces, quebrando la escarcha del mes de frío
de Madrid en la niebla
del alba
10   he visto con estos ojos que tengo, con este corazón
que mira,
he visto llegar a los claros, a los dominadores
combatientes
de la delgada y dura y madura y ardiente brigada
de piedra.
Era el acongojado tiempo en que las mujeres
llevaban una ausencia como un carbón terrible,
15   y la muerte española, más ácida y aguda que otras
muertes
llenaba los campos hasta entonces honrados por el
trigo.

Por las calles la sangre rota del hombre se juntaba
con el agua que sale del corazón destruído de las
casas:
los huesos de los niños deshechos, el desgarrador
20   enlutado silencio de las madres, los ojos
cerrados para siempre de los indefensos,
eran como la tristeza y la pérdida, eran como un
jardín escupido,
eran la fe y la flor asesinadas para siempre.

Camaradas,
25   entonces
os he visto,
y mis ojos están hasta ahora llenos de orgullo

porque os ví a través de la mañana de niebla llegar
   a la frente pura de Castilla
silenciosos y firmes
30   como campanas antes del alba,
llenos de solemnidad y de ojos azules venir de lejos
   y lejos,
venir de vuestros rincones, de vuestras patrias
   perdidas, de vuestros sueños
llenos de dulzura quemada y de fusiles
a defender la ciudad española en que la libertad
   acorralada
35   pudo caer y morir mordida por las bestias.
Hermanos, que desde ahora
vuestra pureza y vuestra fuerza, vuestra historia
   solemne
sea conocida del niño y del varón, de la mujer y
   del viejo,
llegue a todos los seres sin esperanza, baje a las
   minas corroídas por el aire sulfúrico,
40   suba a las escaleras inhumanas del esclavo,
que todas las estrellas, que todas las espigas de
   Castilla y del mundo
escriban vuestro nombre y vuestra áspera lucha
y vuestra victoria fuerte y terrestre como una
   encina roja.
Porque habéis hecho renacer con vuestro sacrificio
45   la fe perdida, el alma ausente, la confianza en la
   tierra,
y por vuestra abundancia, por vuestra nobleza, por
   vuestros muertos,
como por un valle de duras rocas de sangre
pasa un inmenso río con palomas de acero y de
   esperanza.

                                   —Pablo Neruda

   Neruda wrote "Llegada a Madrid de la Brigada Internacional"
about a particular event. On October 20, 1936, Franco issued
the general order for the capture of Madrid. On November 8

the first units of the International Brigades, formed at Albacete, arrived in Madrid. Some 3000 men, mostly Germans and Italians, many of them veterans of World War I and of fascist concentration camps, marching with absolute precision and singing revolutionary songs, paraded across the embattled capital. In total, there were to be twenty-odd nations represented in the International Brigades.[22] The poem enshrines a moment, and without that moment the poem would not live.

November would then be the cold month of the first line. It was a dying month because Madrid had by then been under siege for almost three weeks. It was a month without knees because its defenders would not acquiesce. The jackals are aptly "African" because Franco had come over from Africa, bringing the Moors. These African soldiers comprised the main force of the attack.

The enemy is called "chacales" (as in "Explico algunas cosas") in line 4, "monstruos devoradores y de furias" in line 7, and "bestias" in line 35. On the other hand, Neruda is so enthusiastic about the International Brigade that he cannot use enough adjectives: "la delgada y dura y madura y ardiente brigada de piedra." There is an interplay among the adjectives as the qualities of "fragility in numbers," "strength," "determination," and "burning commitment" are combined. The brigade is variously described. In line 11 the soldiers are "los claros" and "los dominadores." They are "camaradas" and "hermanos," "silenciosos y firmes," "llenos de solemnidad y de ojos azules." They come from all over the world, some having forfeited passports and, thus, their countries to do so. But they come not so much from country or group as from individual commitment to something in which they believe strongly. They come with "sueños" and out of true generosity of self ("abundancia").

In lines 13 and 14 "las mujeres/llevaban una ausencia como un carbón terrible." The simile suggests the intense burning within these solitary women left behind as they suffer frustration and unhappiness. In line 15 "la muerte española" is distinguished from other deaths. Death has often been the morbid preoccupation of Spaniards. Unamuno's "tragic sense of life" derives from a simultaneous awareness of mortality and yearning for eternal life. Death was all around—concretely manifested. It filled every corner: "llenaba los campos hasta entonces honrados por el trigo." It was amidst all this death that a vision of hope, in the form of the International Brigade, arrived.

In line 17 "la sangre rota" offers a mixed metaphor. It is as if the plumbing system of the human body had joined in broken chaos with that of the devastated houses.

Line 28's "la frente pura" of Castille alludes to Castille's location on high ground in relation to the rest of Spain, and its geographical centrality within the Iberian Peninsula.

The word "companas," in line 30, frequently used by Neruda, is one of beauty and clarity of sound, and Neruda plays upon it. The arrival of this Brigade was as stark and striking as the sound of bells in the otherwise utter silence before dawn. The analogy is further that the bells herald the coming of dawn as the Brigades herald the coming of a new day.

In the first stanza Neruda refers to the Brigade in the third person. Stanza two describes the destruction to the city and its inhabitants before their arrival. In stanzas three and four the poet calls them "camaradas" and "hermanos," expressing increasing gratitude. He is expressing a comradeship based on the commitment of one human life to another. In the final lines the soft quality of "un inmenso río con palomas" is juxtaposed with the hardness of "un valle de duras rocas" and "acero." This represents the very essence of hope: the illusion or ideal combined with the hard determination which gives it the ability to survive.

The poem expresses tremendous gratitude. It has an epic, larger-than-life quality and an ode-like tone. The whole vision of the Brigade filing into an embattled Madrid is panoramic and muralistic. Neruda describes the city prior to their arrival: the sense of apprehension and doom, the unhappy circumstances, the physical climate. Then he presents his proud feelings upon their arrival in glorified, idealistic terms. The Brigade's arrival is an inspiring experience, and one can almost hear martial music in the background.

The language is like that of a Spanish Civil War campaign song. The song/poem offers a hymn of gratitude to the volunteers who have come to help defend Spain. It is the intent which is of primary importance, and the language is the product of an intent both hyperbolic and glorifying. The combative elements of the language are like those of Hernández.

But the language is not especially original. The evocative details of Neruda's previous poetry are not present here. He is dealing in semantic generalities. The epithets are designed to evoke an emotional reaction not so much from their graphic suggestiveness as from the subjectivity of their connotations. Neruda has given us his highly emotional response to the ideological potential of the circumstances, and his canvas is huge. But the resulting poem is politically more stirring than poetically.

ALMERÍA [23]

1   Un plato para el obispo, un plato triturado y
                amargo,
           un plato con restos de hierro, con cenizas, con
                lágrimas,
           un plato sumergido, con sollozos y paredes
                caídas,
           un plato negro, un plato de sangre de Almería.

5   Un plato para el banquero, un plato con mejillas
           de niños del Sur feliz, un plato
           con detonaciones, con aguas locas y ruinas y
                espanto,
           un plato con ejes partidos y cabezas pisadas,
           un plato negro, un plato de sangre de Almería.

10   Cada mañana, cada mañana turbia de vuestra
                vida
           lo tendréis humeante y ardiente en vuestra mesa:
           lo apartaréis un poco con vuestras suaves manos
           para no verlo, para no digerirlo tantas veces:
           lo apartaréis un poco entre el pan y las uvas,
15   a este plato de sangre silenciosa
           que estará allí cada mañana, cada
           mañana.

Un plato para el Coronel y la esposa del
   Coronel,
en una fiesta de la guarnición, en cada fiesta,
20   sobre los juramentos y los escupos, con la luz de
   vino de la madrugada
para que lo veáis temblando y frío sobre el
   mundo.

Sí, un plato para todos vosotros, ricos de aquí
   y de allá,
embajadores, ministros, comensales atroces,
señoras de confortable té y asiento:
25   un plato destrozado, desbordado, sucio de sangre
   pobre,
para cada mañana, para cada semana, para
   siempre jamás,
un plato de sangre de Almería, ante vosotros,
   siempre.

                                —Pablo Neruda

On May 29, 1937, the German battleship *Deutschland* was attacked off Ibiza by two Republican aircraft. Thirty-one of the ship's company were killed and many others wounded. The Germans (especially Hitler) were furious, and at dawn on May 31 the Germans took their revenge. A cruiser and four destroyers appeared off Almería, on the southeastern coast of Spain, and fired 200 shots into the town, destroying thirty-five buildings and causing nineteen deaths. The Republic considered bombing the German fleet in the Mediterranean in retaliation, but there was too much pressure against it from fear of setting off world war. For reasons, then, mostly political, the incident of Almería was "forgotten." [24]

Pablo Neruda did not forget. The destruction to an innocent Almería, chosen as a convenient victim by such powerful adversaries, enraged the poet. Neruda metes out his particular retribution in an extravagantly ironic manner. He carefully sidesteps the German involvement and names the types of people he held responsible for the inception and maintenance of the war: "el

obispo," "el banquero," "el coronel y la esposa del coronel," "ricos
de aquí y de allá," "embajadores, ministros, conmensales atroces,/
señoras de confortable té y asiento" (the religious leaders, financial
controllers, army officials and their wives, the rich from all over
who lend support to the Nationalist side, and the political leaders
and idle aristocracy whose activity as well as neglect help to destroy
the Republic). Neruda emphasizes the class struggle underlying
the war, as Spender suggests it in "Ultima Ratio Regum." It is
the rich against the poor, the powerful minority with its material
and social advantages against the masses. In line 24 ("señoras de
confortable té y asiento"), Neruda is criticizing the bourgeoisie.
He is accusing the system—the Establishment. The poem is political and sounds socialistic in its criticism of the higher echelons of
the social hierarchy.

Neruda uses the metaphor of a variety of nauseating "edibles,"
such as garbage and suffering-thickened blood, to express his own
revulsion toward those he holds responsible for the tragedy. This
particular punishment suggests Cronos of Greek mythology, who
ate his own children, as well as Atreus, who killed Thyestes' young
children and had them served up at a banquet. Ironically, Neruda
is concentrating on those who might, ordinarily, take sensuous
pleasure in what they were eating. The food he introduces is calculated to curdle in their stomachs and to send a shiver through
their flesh. The blood he would offer them is hardly meant with
sacred and mysterious reverence, but with hate, contempt, and
horror. Neruda is telling the beneficiaries of his contribution to
their breakfast table (the first food of the day) that they will eat
the results of what they have created for the rest of their lives.
That particular philosophy is reminiscent of the Bible's "what
you sow, you shall reap" and "by their fruits shall ye know them,"
and also of the Mosaic law "an eye for an eye, a tooth for a tooth."

The imagery is visual and olfactory ("humeante y ardiente").
These potential gourmands will be made to smell, see, and swallow
the carrion of their making. The poem is unflinching in its viewpoint and unsparingly graphic in its cannibalism. The recipients
will sit there as mute victims of their own atrocities.

The ideological vision is of those with wealthy interests feeding
on the innocent bodies of children and other victims to sustain

themselves. This vision is Goyaesque (cf. his war sketches) in grotesqueness. Neruda transforms his ideological commitment into a plastic one which is overwhelming. It reminds me, also, of Jonathan Swift's "A Modest Proposal," in which instead of abstracting the problem of starving people, Swift suggests that the children of the poor be served up to their parents in a cannibalistic orgy.

In the first stanza, the "o" sound predominates like a sorrowful backdrop as Neruda insistently serves up a select menu for the chosen guests. There is much repetition not only of the "o" sound but of the word "plato," which appears six times in the brief quatrain. The refrain "un plato de sangre de Almería" concludes the first, second, and fifth stanzas.

It is obvious that Neruda meant the poem to be repetitious as well as inexorable. It is undoubtedly part of Neruda's irony that the poem should be stated with a variety of metaphors rich in adjectives, and frequent alliteration, assonance, and repetition. The sharp contradiction between the apparent generosity and the obvious bad faith of the giver is strengthened by the simplicity of the images. The poetic devices and lyrical qualities jarringly emphasize his bitterness. The poem's ironic vituperation is as strong as that of the Bible's Psalm 137.

"Almería" is epic in its larger-than-life imagery and Neruda speaks not of individuals but of broad categories of types. The imagery is much more graphic than that of "Llegada." There is a richness not only of emotional commitment, but also of language and imagery. The strength of its poetic language gives "Almería" a raison d'être that rises above its meaning, which is not true of "Llegada." "Llegada" is a poem of a particular time and place. "Almería" is more powerful and durable.

All four poets (Felipe, Hernández, Vallejo, and Neruda) sympathized with the Republican side, sharing deep reactions to the war. All of their poems analyzed here in depth were written, by coincidence, in 1937. Vallejo's presentation was in most personal terms. Neruda ("Llegada" and "Almería") wrote about specific events, as did Felipe in "La insignia" (the fall of Málaga and the threat to Valencia). Hernández had a more generalized approach, with insinuations about political background. He saw the need to

unite the nations of the world ("Recoged esta voz"). Vallejo included mention of Toledo in "Pequeño responso" but mostly
generalized. Felipe had the most transcendental view, but Neruda,
too, saw the war in international dimensions. Felipe was able to
criticize the Republican side for a lack of unity, while admiring
the cohesion of the Franco side. He bitterly condemned England
for her motives in failing to intervene on the side of justice. He
is the most historically realistic of the four. The Republican side
was, indeed, hopelessly divided, which weakened its effectiveness
and helped bring on its defeat. The prophetic ending of "La
insignia," however, intimates that Spain and Justice will somehow
resurrect. By 1939 Felipe's poems became completely pessimistic.

Felipe is more didactic than the other poets, having been a
teacher and a translator. He was understandably more concerned
with his message than with imagery, but all four made an effort to
create their war poems with a minimum of vague language and
obscure imagery ("Pequeño responso" is the most obscure). They
were trying to be understood. This came naturally to Hernández
whereas Vallejo and Neruda had to change their styles.

At the explosion of the war, Hernández enlisted immediately
to serve "la España de las pobrezas." He was attracted and drawn
by the "viento del pueblo" to the defense of their cause—the Republican cause. Like Vallejo he had a capacity for suffering—not
just for himself but for others—and a feeling for the solidarity of
his people. We can see his close identification with the common
man through his own first-person inclusion in the poems.

The poems are not strictly religious, but some of their elements
(the pervasive blood, for example) are true to the ritual of the
Catholic religion. They do not deal outrightly with politics or
economics, but they do show a class of peasants and workers fighting against enslavement. In "Vientos del pueblo me llevan" the
enemy is trying to put a yoke on the working and peasant class.
Hernández sees the conflict as the enslaved against the enslaver
more than as a civil war. His awareness of the economics and politics of the war is insinuated in a way that reminds us of the poems
of Stephen Spender. The two analyzed poems by Hernández are
not argumentative, but his patriotic and ideological commitment
is unmistakable. They are sometimes rhetorical and their purpose

is to move, encourage, and motivate the peasant soldiers and other forces for the Republic. He wrote for the common people who are most representative of the people of Spain. He spoke out directly, simply, and with understanding and empathy. He empathized from a deep sense of common humanity. Hernández and Neruda had in common this empathy for the people, but their perspective in time and space differed. Hernández was much closer to the people. But Neruda, also, had a definite sense of commitment to his theme and a sense of the responsibility and role of the poet.

Hernández put a personal and original stamp on his poems and was able to write vividly and vivaciously. His poetry is rich in images, virile passion, and humanity. The power of his poems derives from his strong emotional commitment. He wrote with the passion of immediate experience of the war. His poems reveal the inspiration and awareness of tragedy of the twenty-seven-year old poet whose courage and dedication cannot be doubted.

In comparison, Vallejo is a more academic poet who writes less vivacious, but more complex poems for more educated audiences. In Vallejo's poems there is no class confrontation. Rather he presents the trauma and death of Spain in war in intimate terms.

The three analyzed poems of Vallejo have religious elements, but they are not held in any orthodox way. They are dramatic and rely upon striking symbols and imagery. They are directly, simply, and forcefully expressed, disclosing a very vigorous hand. The poetry is sincere as well as passionate. Vallejo was deeply involved, and his poems about Spain are subjective, emotional, and inspiring.

Taken in the order in which they appeared in *España, aparta de mí este cáliz,* the first, "Pequeño responso," offers some hope (about poetry or, more broadly, about Spain) even during such a war. Its concept is romantic, although its imagery contains physical details—some of which are surrealistically expressed. The second poem, "Masa," is very lyrical, also romanticized, and, in its way, more despairing than "Pequeño responso." One can conceive of the enduring nature of a man's poetry, though Vallejo's imaginative conception of it is far from realistic. But to imagine a dead soldier, representative of Spain, resurrecting is both ironic and heart-breaking in its historical context. The third poem, "España, aparta de mí este cáliz," offers a more tangible hope than "Masa," although here again the imagery is very subjective. Vallejo looks to the children of all mankind for salvation. It is as if he had had the premonition that the fight would be prolonged and the hour of salvation delayed until the future. Vallejo was offering his prophetic words on the outcome.

"Pequeño responso" is expressed in brief images, abruptly (a word from the poem), and perhaps could be compared to the measured and abrupt steps of the funeral procession it depicts. "Masa" is beautiful both in sound and meaning, the miracle it concerns and the casual tone of its expression in contradiction to one another. It is the most ironic of the three poems. "España" is written in very long, periodic-type sentences, but also includes brief images. As in "Pequeño responso," some of its referents seem very obscure. "Masa" is the simplest of the poems.

Vallejo's tone is striking—firmly masculine despite his humility as a human being. His poems have an oral power (as do those of Hernández), and he uses common speech to lyrical advantage. His manipulation of language is both careful and original, with frequent repetition of sounds and words.

The poems are not doctrinaire, but deeply felt and forcefully, movingly expressed. Especially in "Masa" and "España" Vallejo exposes his desire for human solidarity, and one senses his feeling of brotherhood toward the oppressed and suffering. The hope of Vallejo was a hope for mankind—all those he acknowledged as brothers and with whom, along with Neruda, he took common cause.

It is most natural that the Spanish Civil War would have an impact on the poetry of Vallejo and Neruda because, from the start, they concerned themselves with the social realities with which they had lived. There was a common denominator between the tensions at home (Peru and Chile, respectively) and the Spanish Civil War. Vallejo could equate the Indians and miners of his homeland with the oppressed of Spain. This war was an extension of the confrontation between the disinherited and those who wield political, economic, and social power. The Spanish Civil War as a theme, therefore, occupied an understandable place in their vision.

Neruda's "Explico algunas cosas" is a personal poem, showing his close identification with the misfortunes of Madrid. At the same time he explains his new attitude about writing poetry, a change from inner- to outer-directedness, certainly in line with communist philosophy. The holocaust he describes is reminiscent of that which Hernández had predicted if the war went against the Republic. The poem is political; the method remains poetic. The enemy whom he does not hesitate to call derogatory names has the support in his conception, as well as in reality, of the Moors, the aristocracy, the Church, and moneyed interests. He calls the generals of the enemy side traitors.

"Llegada a Madrid de la Brigada Internacional" shows Neruda's awareness of the international context of the war. He is also aware of the dangers at the time (1936 in Madrid) but is suddenly hopeful, proud, and grateful because of the arrival of the first of the International Brigades.

"Almería" is the most ironic of the three poems, its form and rhythm the most regular. Its venom incriminates those he holds responsible for the war. The political implications of the poem are clear and have a factual basis. His nightmare-like punishment is for the Church, the economic leaders, the military, the rich, the aristocracy, and the political forces of the Nationalist side. He retaliates for the masses of Spanish Republicans, namely for the "niños del Sur feliz" and the poor. All three poems include bitter protest against a tragic course of events, but "Almería" has the sharpest answer.

Neruda's general condemnation (he has not named the offenders specifically) is very strong. There is no doubt about Neruda's strong convictions about the war and his deep involvement. He became politically minded at the time of the war, and we see the depiction of the class struggle clearly in his poems. The historical relevance of specific details is more apparent than in the poems of Hernández and Vallejo. There are some religious elements in his poems (the prevalence of blood and flowers) but also skepticism about the actual institution of the Church.

His close identification with the cause of the Spanish Republic comes not just because he was a Chilean with strong allegiance to Spain, but also because he was an antifascist (later to join the Com-

munist Party) and because he had lived in Madrid among Spaniards and was there during the first few years of the war.

Neruda wrote political poems conscious of class struggle. He
was aware of himself as a poet ("Explico algunas cosas") as Felipe
was conscious of his role at the beginning and end of "La insignia."
Vallejo's poems are of the tragedy of Spain in a personal, though
generalized, context. Felipe had a very independent slant on the
circumstances of the war, being critical of both sides and stub-
bornly demanding elimination of Republican dissension, materialism, and cowardice despite the course of events by 1937. Hernández
praised and inspired the Spanish soldiers and had a fatalistic idea
about death that Felipe held. Both encouraged martyrdom. Vallejo's poems contain emotional imagery and a sense of abandonment, desperation, and loneliness. Felipe intellectualized. His anguish came not so much from the military confrontation as from
the intrigues and rivalries within the Republican group. Unlike
Hernández and Vallejo, but in common with Neruda, Felipe is
declamatory. Hernández speaks as a soldier to other soldiers. Felipe
speaks as a poet/prophet, a gigantic figure astride the world, looking down at the people. Vallejo is more humble. Felipe is intellectually critical (as opposed to emotionally empathetic).

While Vallejo speaks in a muted, one-to-one dialogue, Neruda
may be said to declaim. While Vallejo scaled down an experience
(in tone, not in meaning), Neruda's voice has epic reverberations.
Neruda is always conscious of being a poet. Vallejo, on the other
hand, does not impose his own literary personality. Vallejo exposes
an anguished soul in a personal way. Hernández offers a battle cry
to fellow-soldiers, and at moments both he and Neruda present
nihilistic visions.

Being Latin American affected the imagery of Vallejo and
Neruda. Having a mother complex in relation to Spain, Vallejo
called Spain mother ("España, aparta de mí este cáliz"). Both fea-
tured children in their poems as being most vulnerable ("España,
aparta . . . ," "Almería," and "Explico algunas cosas")—which,
of course, they are.

For Felipe the war was a sobering experience which aroused a
more hostile and declamatory tone than he had adopted previously.
He went into permanent exile after the war and died in exile.

Hernández fought in the war, felt very close to his fellow-soldiers, and wrote tragic and inspired (as well as inspirational) poems. He died as a result of his prison experience after the war. At the time of the war, Vallejo had not written poetry for almost fifteen years. As meaning increased in importance to him, he abandoned the obscure surrealism of his earlier poems (*Trilce*, 1923) for more simplified expression in his last two (war) volumes. He died in Paris before the end of the war. Neruda changed considerably as a result of the war and, perhaps for the same reason as Vallejo, developed from obscurity toward didacticism. He never returned to Spain and remained a communist.

As to the durability of these war poems, we might ask whether they would survive outside their historical context. Although Felipe's poetic speech deals with particular circumstances, it is elevated to a transcendental plane. It derives its value from the fact that the poet does not speak through the mouths of certain men or names, but represents Man and is addressed to Man. Felipe is essentially concerned with Man. Felipe's poem goes beyond the Spanish Civil War to the hopelessness of all war. He is concerned with the ultimate brutality and horror of all war ("eran sesos humanos que tuve por mucho tiempo pegados a las suelas de mis zapatos."). He points to the grotesque discrepancy between the horrible carnage and the political in-fighting. His poetry has ideological survival value, being based on political truth, and his understanding of human nature (though cynical) rings true. The poem has artistic survival value in the form of its dramatic elements, architectural form, skillful repetition, vivid images, emotionally-suggestive language, and emotional impact. His concern for the Republicans can be compared to his feeling for the loneliness and anguish of the exile in "Español del éxodo y del llanto"; both have universal application.

Being completely caught up in the situation, Hernández wrote of the desperation and carnage of any war, with feelings of brotherhood, despair, and inspiration. His poems are exciting, full of energy and ideals, and have lyrical qualities which suggest they will last. The nature of Vallejo's poetic conception transcends the Spanish Civil War to include all of mankind. Besides, his poems are lyrical, intense, vivid, and beautiful in any context. His poems will survive because they are poetically conceived and because his message of compassion, feeling, and frustration-hope has universal meaning. His capacity for suffering reaches all humans. Of the three poems by Neruda considered here, "Explico" has the most artistic quality and "Llegada" the least. "Llegada" is the most limited of the three both in scope and artistry, but it does contain insights into human nature. Readers can identify with the bitterness and resentment of "Almería" with or without knowing the historical circumstances.

Notes

1. The phrase is Unamuno's.

2. Opening lines of "Heces," *Los heraldos negros* (Buenos Aires: Editorial Losada, 1918), p. 36.

3. Biographical material came mostly from the Prólogo by Guillermo de Torre to *Obras completas* by León Felipe (Buenos Aires: Editorial Losada, 1963); but also, in part, from the following: Angel del Río, *Historia de la literatura española,* Tomo II (New York: Holt, Rinehart and Winston, 1963) and Angel Valbuena Prat, *Historia de la literatura española,* Tomo II (Barcelona: Editorial Gustavo Gili, S. A., 1946).

4. León Felipe, *Obras completas* (Buenos Aires: Editorial Losada, 1963), pp. 927-44.

5. The Fifth Column refers to a clandestine subversive organization working within a given country to further an invading enemy's military and political aims. It was first applied in 1936 to the Franco supporters and sympathizers in Madrid by General Emilio Mola, who was leading four rebel columns of troops against that city.

6. Jackson, *The Spanish Republic and the Civil War, 1931-1939,* pp. 342-44.

7. This is the title of a poem in his collection "Español del éxodo y del llanto: Doctrina de un poeta español en 1939."

8. Biographical data was compiled from Juan Cano Ballesta: *La poesía de Miguel Hernández* (Madrid: Editorial Gredos, 1962); Juan Guerrero Zamora: *Miguel Hernández, poeta (1910-1942)* (Madrid:

Colección El Grifon, 1955); the Introduction (by José Luis Cano) to *Poemas: Miguel Hernández* (Barcelona: Editorial Gredos, 1964); and the Prologue (by María de Gracia Ifach) to *Obras completas: Miguel Hernández* (Buenos Aires: Editorial Losada, 1960).

9. Hernández, *Viento del pueblo,* pp. 95-97.

10. Hernández, *Viento del pueblo,* pp. 108-12.

11. Sources for biographical information were: Translator's Foreword to *Poemas humanos: Human Poems* by César Vallejo, translated by Clayton Eshleman (New York: Grove Press, 1969) and André Coyné, *César Vallejo* (Buenos Aires: Ediciones Nueva Visión, 1968).

12. Quotation appears on p. 311 of *César Vallejo* by André Coyné.

13. César Vallejo, *España, aparta de mí este cáliz* (Mexico: Editorial Séneca, 1940), pp. 69-70.

14. Vallejo, *España, aparta de mí este cáliz,* p. 81.

15. Vallejo, *España, aparta de mí este cáliz,* pp. 89-90.

16. Biographical details were obtained from: Introduction to his poems in *Antología de la poesia hispanoamericana,* Julio Caillet Bois, ed. (Madrid: Aguilar, 1958); and Amado Alonso, *Poesía y estilo de Pablo Neruda* (Buenos Aires: Editorial Sudamericana, 1966).

17. Pablo Neruda, *Poesía política* (Santiago de Chile: Editora Austral, 1953), I, 57-60.

18. Suggested in footnote 9, p. 354, of *Poesía y estilo de Pablo Neruda* by Amado Alonso.

19. Facts are from Jackson, *The Spanish Republic and the Civil War, 1931-1939,* pp. 231-33.

20. Jackson, p. 428.

21. Neruda, *Poesía política,* I, 66-68.

22. Jackson, pp. 327-28.

23. Neruda, *Poesía política,* I, 70-71.

24. Facts from Hugh Thomas, *The Spanish Civil War,* pp. 440-42.

CHAPTER III

Spanish Civil War Poets in the
English Language

The five poets in this grouping are linked not just by the English language but by their culture as well. These poets are representative of their various backgrounds and countries and, at the same time, have written poems resulting from the Spanish Civil War which may, in their own right, be considered important. There is only one poet to be discussed on the Nationalist side, Roy Campbell, because I could find no other who made a significant poetic contribution. That also accounts for there being only one woman, Muriel Rukeyser.

The focus of these non-Spanish, non-Latin poets is not the dead center of the Spanish Civil War. Their motivations and interests were, at least partially, elsewhere. None of them actually bore arms. Rukeyser was in Spain by chance at the opening of hostilities. W. H. Auden was there for only three months; and Stephen Spender made three brief visits in a literary capacity. Campbell, despite his claims, is said to have been evacuated in August of

1936 and to have returned only as a well-protected war correspondent. Hugh MacDiarmid did not go to Spain at all.

MacDiarmid was the oldest (forty-four in 1936) of the five poets at the time of the war, while Rukeyser was the youngest (twenty-three in 1936). MacDiarmid was a well-read intellectual, educated at Edinburgh University, who held radical socialistic views. He used his poetry as a weapon in his general political struggles and was able to assimilate the political thinker and the artist in himself. His background was not dissimilar to that of Neruda and Vallejo. He came from a working-class family and knew physical and economic hardship. His socialistic and communistic sympathies immediately sided him with the Republic. But the primary concern of his life was for Scottish unity and nationalism, so that he identified with the kindred nature of the struggle in Spain, not so much with its particular time, place, and circumstances.

Campbell was thirty-five in 1936. He had the least formal education of the five and was, probably, the most active physically. A convert to Roman Catholicism (in 1936), he staunchly supported the Nationalist side. He was anti-intellectual and antiliberal, and his lack of formal education perhaps influenced his subjectivity. His background was rural and his imagery favored nature over science and technology. His life and personality were entangled in his egocentric poetry and he harbored bitter grudges. Very emotional, his viewpoints were fanatically maintained.

The most similar backgrounds are those of Spender and Auden, who came from urban environments, were two years apart in age, went to the same college at Oxford, and had mutual friends. Both came from successful middle-class families of culture. Auden (the older) came from the industrial North, where he had witnessed economic depression. He was scientific in inclination and interests. Marx and Freud attracted his attention, and his political orientation gradually gave way to an interest in the psychology and sociology of man. His conversion to Anglo-Catholicism (1940) caused a more optimistic outlook and affected his thinking and writing.

Spender was twenty-seven in 1936. His poetry was personal, more subjective than Auden's, and removed from politics and propaganda. His attitude was humanitarian, antiwar, and antiromantic.

He joined the Communist Party but, like Auden, resented some of its practices and later disassociated himself. He was critical of the Party's regimentation ("Two Armies") and propagandistic deception ("Two Armies" and "Ultima Ratio Regum").

Rukeyser, American born, Jewish, urban, and liberal, was educated at Vassar. She had wide contemporary interests: social, political, and scientific. Her poetry suggests a passionate nature and there are frequent sexual allusions.

Her volume *A Turning Wind* was published in 1939 but only some of its poems refer to the Spanish Civil War. This was also the year of World War II's outbreak—which influenced her poetry. Her poem "Mediterranean" was published in 1937 in *New Masses* magazine.[1] Her antiwar attitude was a reaction to the times more than to one specific war. She was part of the group movement mobilized in America against militarism and fascism. Her viewpoint is humanitarian, and she includes many personal allusions in her poems, extending their focus beyond the war.

MacDiarmid's poem *The Battle Continues* is in reaction to Campbell's *Flowering Rifle*. Though Campbell and MacDiarmid have diametrically opposed philosophies, the two have much in common: vigor, egocentricity, strong views, verbosity. Campbell wrote eleven poems on the Spanish Civil War which, by far, comprise the largest poetic contribution by any of these five poets.

Auden's only poem on the war was *Spain*. His logical, objective approach to the subject reflects his scientific background. Spender included ten short poems in his *Collected Works* under the subtitle "Poems about the Spanish Civil War."

To repeat my main contention, not one of these poets was caught up in the war emotionally or intellectually to the extent that the Spanish-writing poets were. Campbell had many axes to grind. MacDiarmid retaliated against Campbell and was attracted to Republican Spain through its cause, kindred to that of Scotland. Each was working out personal feuds and personality idiosyncrasies. Rukeyser shared the pacifistic sentiments of many humanitarians of that time in history. Her poems are interwoven with personal considerations and there is only limited mention of Spain. Auden's contribution was a single poem in a detached, objective tone. Spender from a broad, humanitarian viewpoint extracted from the larger panorama individual, anonymous sufferers. While Auden's poem is political, Spender's are less obviously so. Campbell's and MacDiarmid's poems in their verbosity include many matters not germane to the war.

Since MacDiarmid's poem reacts to Campbell's, discussion of MacDiarmid follows that of Campbell. With that exception, the poets are discussed in chronological order, in accordance with their birthdates: Campbell, MacDiarmid, Auden, Spender, and Rukeyser. As in Chapter II, close analyses of selected poems follow each biographical-literary sketch.

While the Oxford poets (Auden, Day Lewis, MacNeice, Spender) were products of the old English university and of an urban and industrial milieu, Campbell (1901-1957) came from South Africa.[2] (Ignatius) Roy (Dunnachie) Campbell was born in Durban, Natal, a British colony in what became the Union of South Africa, in 1901, and left for England seventeen years later. The South Africa in which he grew up had not yet experienced its Industrial Revolution. His background had scarcely made him conscious of the problems of an urbanized society, post World War I economic problems, revolution (Russia, 1917), and social protest. The poetic images of his early poetry come from an ambience in which nature is close at hand (those of Auden, Day Lewis, MacNeice, and Spender allude much more often to the modern world, history, and science). Campbell's attitude toward life was optimistic, combative, direct, and simple. His vigorous, extroverted verse contrasted with the uneasy self-searching of the more socially conscious poets of the 1930s. Campbell was a romantic in the sense that he upheld the individual, the personal, and the value of imaginative and intuitive faculties, as opposed to technology, standardization, bureaucratization, and the anonymous millions. Politically he was a reactionary (antiliberal) and culturally he was an anti-intellectual.

His anti-intellectual attitude most likely stemmed from his having failed the entrance examinations for Oxford. In any case, he sustained a belief in the superiority of practical knowledge gained from action rather than from reading:

And reading without wisdom is to blame
For half the world destroyed with blood or flame—
By Left-wing reading incapacitated
Either to tolerate or be tolerated;
Experience better serves the most Unread
Who carry no Boloney home to bed.[3]

Campbell expressed contempt for nearly all leftist writers. He considered them too cerebral, too mincing and fussy, too fearful of the cruder elements of life, and, worst of all, too far removed from life itself.

In the Twenties Campbell took no interest in politics, social causes, or proletarian reforms, and stayed clear of leftist groups. Between 1928 and the outbreak of war in 1936, Campbell provided for his growing family by raising olives in Martigues, bullfighting in Provence, fishing off southern France, and steerthrowing and horsebreaking in Toledo. The intensity, excitement, and demands of this life did little to quicken an interest in politics, although his hostility toward the Bloomsbury group and their politics grew stronger, especially after he learned that a few of them had banned his poem "The Georgiad." [4] But his political detachment ended around 1935. As signs of unrest increased in Spain, Campbell, then living in Toledo, was forced to recognize the power of an ever more daring and hostile Left. To the frequent outbursts of lawlessness, he reacted vehemently, accusing the Spanish communists of deliberately creating disorder preparatory to launching an attack on the state. Their goal, he believed, was a communist-dominated Spain. He openly proclaimed his allegiance to the Church, which had already become a target of leftists. In June, 1936, Campbell and his wife were officially converted to Roman Catholicism, a defiant act in those times.

Campbell often expressed unpopular convictions. His combative, individualistic temperament kept him apart from literary movements of the day, and some of his lyrics express his sense of isolation and independence amidst the hostile forces of nature. His literary output was copious and uneven.

The best of Campbell is contained in his lyrics, epigrams, and translations. Of his verse, his reputation rests mainly on two early volumes "The Flaming Terrapin" (1924) and "Adamastor" (1930), both lyrical works. The former exalts the instinctive vital force that brings forth intelligent human effort out of apathy and disillusionment:

> . . . Old Ocean growls and tosses his grey mane.
> Pawing the rocks in all his old unrest . . .
> Then to my veins I feel new sap return,
> Strength tightens up my sinews long grown dull,
> And in the old charred crater of the skull
> Light strikes the slow somnambulistic mind
> And sweeps her forth to ride the rushing wind,
> And stamping on the hill-tops high in air,
> To shake the golden bonfire of her hair.

These poems were remarkable for energy, rhetorical power, and striking imagery. He followed these with many other volumes of verse. Among them are two long satires, "The Wayzgoose" (1928), which ridicules South African intellectuals, and "The Georgiad" (1931), which attacks the "Georgian" poets who were in vogue during the Twenties and anticipates the level of attack of *Flowering Rifle:*

> And in a Bloomsbury accent it could yodel . . .
> Unlike our modern homos, who are neither,
> He could be homosexual with either
> And heterosexual with either, too—
> A damn sight more than you or I could do!

He wrote poems of the Spanish Civil War, "Mithraic Emblems" (1936) and the long polemical satire *Flowering Rifle* (1939); and poems of the Second World War, "Talking Bronco" (1946), which attacks the literary figures of the Bloomsbury group. His *Collected Poems* (3 volumes) appeared 1949-1957. He published three autobiographical books, *Broken Record* (1934), *Light on a Dark Horse* (1951), and *Portugal* (1957).

Campbell translated St. John of the Cross (1951), Lorca (1952), Baudelaire, and other Spanish, French, and Portuguese writers. He also wrote five or six prose books, including the above-mentioned autobiographies and critical studies of Burns, Taurine Provence, and Lorca.

Campbell wrote only eleven poems based on the Spanish Civil War, but, in all, they offer perhaps the most extensive treatment of the war by a single poet. Campbell was almost the only poet writing in English who was on the fascist side, and I have chosen to analyze *Flowering Rifle,* a 157-page poem which he subtitled "from the Battlefield of Spain."

Repeatedly, Campbell tried to give the impression that he had fought in the front ranks of Franco's army, and in one footnote to *Flowering Rifle* he actually stated as much (p. 224 of Volume 2 of *Collected Works,* London: The Bodley Head, 1957). There is, however, some evidence that Campbell was not the front-line combat soldier he claimed to be. Robert Graves wrote that Roy Campbell "was evacuated from Spain early in August, 1936 . . . and returned there only as a well-protected war correspondent." [5]

Since he had just become a Roman Catholic, and since the Nationalist rebels proclaimed themselves anticommunists and saviors of the Catholic Church, it was not surprising that Campbell chose the side of the "Christian Crusade against Communism." The Thirties had been a decade of unemployment and hunger marches, of the rise of fascist tyrannies; to almost all writers and intellectuals the only hope at the time seemed to lie with the forces of socialism and even communism. The emotional partisanship generated by the Spanish Civil War was intense. When in the middle of all this, Campbell produced *Flowering Rifle,* a fanatical view of the Spanish Civil War in which he jeered at those "pinks" and "wowsers" who supported the "Reds," he was fiercely attacked and his books boycotted.

This was a continuation of Campbell's famous feud with the young Thirties poets, Auden, Spender, MacNeice, and Day Lewis. Cliques, groups, and movements in poetry were anathema to Campbell, quite apart from his disagreement with the left-wing political attitudes held by these four, whom he later satirized under the acronym of MacSpaunday in "Talking Bronco," which is no more than an epigraph to *Flowering Rifle.*

Campbell's bias probably derived, in part, from his South African birth and half-pastoral upbringing. He accounts for other sources of his prejudice in the Author's Note to the 1939 edition of *Flowering Rifle:* "Like all English writers on Spain I am biassed, but . . . I am biassed, unlike any of the others, by a thorough first-hand experience of life under both regimes as one of the working population." While it is probably true that Campbell was more familiar with the workaday world of Spain than most other English-speaking poets who became involved in the war, religion also motivated his Spanish Civil War poetry. Campbell, especially as a new convert, was sensitive to attacks on the institution for which he obviously held an intensely emotional respect.

During World War II he (paradoxically) fought against fascism with the British Army in Africa. In the post World War II years, Campbell wrote less original poetry. The injuries he sustained during World War II forced him to lead a more sedentary life. Action, with Campbell, was accessory to poetry; the one stimulated the other. He died in a car accident near Setubal, Portugal, on April 22, 1957.

The fruit of Campbell's experience in the war, his aversion to the communist ideology, his contempt for British Intellectualism of the Left, and his loyalty to the Church were combined in *Flowering Rifle,* which was first published at the end of the Spanish Civil War. What provoked Campbell's sizable reaction to the Spanish Civil War was the poet's firm belief that the Nationalist cause embodied most of the values and ideas which he as a man and poet profoundly agreed with or, at least, respected; and that, on the other hand, the Loyalist cause of "freedom and democracy" was nothing but camouflage to conceal the ambitions of a ruthless group of communists to seize control of Spain. Furthermore, he believed the Republican leaders had attracted nearly every enemy he had ever made, including particular left-wing poets.

Campbell found his values, disbeliefs, friends, and enemies felicitously arranged into opposing camps. To divide the combatants into groups representing right and wrong was probably an easier task for him than it had been for most poets. His personal designations for the combatants expose his prejudice: "Wowsers" and "Reds" for the Republicans and the simple but ennobling epithet

"Men" for the Nationalists. At the beginning of Part II Campbell clarifies his bias:

> A hundred years of strife with warring vans
> Had winnowed Spain in two distinctive clans
> Upon the left, inflammable, the chaff,
> Corn to the right, the vulnerable half,
> And thus in Spanish history began
> The war between the Wowser and the Man—
>   (p. 31)

His admiration for the Carmelite fathers of Toledo, who had heard his confession and received him into the Church, is suggested in his description of the part they played in defending the Alcázar:

> With iron valour vascoing their ship,
> The Carmelites rose up to show the way:
> For martyrdom their eagle spirits burned
> As fierce as angry captains for the fight—
>   (Part III, p. 85)

Campbell attributed determination and courage to the Church that warred against the "godless horde" (p. 50) of Republicans. He conceived of the Church as a church-militant, forced to fight for its own survival and determined to resurrect a new Spain out of the ashes of war. He fashioned the heroic defense of the Alcázar into a symbol of "Resurrected Spain" (p. 87). He saw the Nationalist cause as a great crusade to expel the heretics whose "dogmatized Utopias" (p. 36) threatened to destroy the religious as well as social and political traditions of the country. The Church alone gave purpose and symbolic value to the cause:

> The Army of the Peoples of the World,
> The hoarse blaspheming of the godless hoard
> Against the Cross and Crescent of the Lord,
> The Cross, our Hammer, and the Quarter Moon
> Our Sickle, and Hosanna for our tune!
>   (Part II, p. 50)

Campbell often stated that when Spain would again be ruled by the Right, it would experience an unprecedented economic revival. Under the Nationalists, he foresaw a much improved standard of living for everyone, an abundance of food, more work, and even greater international prominence. In fact, he declared that the economic transformation had already begun wherever Franco's soldiers had won victories—wherever, that is, the influence of the Church had been restored—for he believed that a fruitful economy simply could not exist under the Left. The wealth of Spain flowed only where "Christ is King" (p. 28), but:

> Where the Red Curse is, there will Hunger be!
> . . .
> They gasp to see our half-ton bullocks bleed
> Whom wealth of mighty nations failed to feed,
> To see the flocks of fat merinos spring
> From some poor provinces where Christ is King,
> Where loaves are multiplied from scanty grain
> And fishes seem deserters from the main.
>
> (Part I, p. 28)

Not only would the starved survivors of "Red" domination be taught the science of agriculture, but having seen the prosperity of their former enemies, they would themselves set about laboring to improve their conditions:

> Now through the Nation as our legions spread
> The richer by the poorer half is fed:
> Beside the lewd inscription, where they sprawl,
> From loafing idly charcoaled on the wall
> Hammer and Sickle to their labour fall.
> Storks to the steeples, rollers to the wires
> Return, and swallows to the broken spires—
> And men to the religion of their Sires!
>
> (Part I, p. 28)

Such was the restorative power of the Church that it would effect not only a religious but an economic recovery. Campbell viewed the whole Nationalist effort as an "extraordinary awakening of a national consciousness in a ruined and prostrate country" (Author's Note). It represented the needs and desires of the majority of the Spanish people, including most of the workers; only the "literate lounging class . . . that first conceived this Rabies of the brain" (p. 41), or communism, tried to obstruct this demonstration of the people's will. But the help this class received from alien "Reds" or "Wowsers" amounted to almost nothing. When they did not run away from battle, they either surrendered or defected; their very presence in Spain, Campbell contended, augured the defeat of the Republic:

> Vultures and crows so rally to the field
> And where they "group" you know the doom
>   is sealed,
> Before it hits our nostrils ripe and hot
> They've long ago divined the inward rot,
> And as by sympathy I sense the rose
> Of Victory before its buds unclose,
> So they (before it trumpets to the nose)
> Anticipate the maggot on its way,
> With it co-operate in swift decay,
> And so with one more carcass strew the way:.
>   (Part I, p. 20)

The occurrence in *Flowering Rifle* which Campbell claimed he foresaw was the capture of 300 British volunteers at San Mateo (it did happen in 1938). Campbell refers to the incident repeatedly throughout *Flowering Rifle*, always in a snickering and vindictive manner. He evidently believed that they were captured because Campbell had willed it. He believed that his prophetic words had somehow directed the volunteers to their ignominious fate:

> But let these prisoners speak for my precision
> And answer for my range and drive of Vision,
> Who promised this before the war begun,
> And drilled them with my pen before my gun
>   . . .

Surrendering without a single blow
For nothing, save that I foretold it so—
. . .
The British International Brigade,
And twice predicted clearly in advance . . .
(Part I, pp. 22-23)

Claiming nature as a colleague, he maintained that nature also contrived to frustrate the labor of the Republicans by refusing to allow grass and corn to grow in their territory:

But nature's elements, except for gold,
Will shun the Yiddisher's convulsive hold,
And it's an axiom that mere eyesight yields—
Grass hates to grow on communist fields!
(Part I, p. 15)

Corn, out of shame, refused for them to grow . . .
(Part II, p. 34)

For still where Marx's influence is least,
Red fields with vestiges of grass are fleeced,
But where his lore we trample and oppose
Reviving Nature thanks us with the rose . . .
Part III, p. 79)

(The former is also one of many examples of Campbell's derisive equating of Jews and Communists.) Matter in Campbell's animistic universe does its part, too, to defeat the enemy, by showing a sort of natural hostility toward those whose insensitivity to order would force it into incongruous forms:

In its behavior, Matter proved no dolt,
And that it has opinions of its own—
. . .
Whether it's guns to fire, or bricks to pile,
Matter is always sensitive to style
(Which is the breathing rhythm of the soul)

And shows itself Devout from pole to pole:
. . .
But when democracy begins to soar
To whom the jail, the brothel, and the store,
Stand for the Church, and tries for like proportions
Matter complies with sorrowful distortions,
And rather as a slave than an ally
"Co-operates" to raise them to the sky,
                                        (Part II, p. 58)

Even the sun is made a fascist ally, and on one occasion literally bakes Russian tank crews into surrendering:

We needed tanks: as if they knew the road,
They came like bakers' vans to orders booked,
When the fierce sun their crews of Russians cooked
Who have to be like convicts bolted in—
Surrender being their one besetting sin:
And with the Centigrade at sixty-seven
Their brains were baked and yeasted in their leaven,
And what the sun began, the iron heated,
The Fahrenheit and Centigrade completed,
To save us any need of work more fiery,
As they came nosing to our mazed inquiry,
For the good sun, our ally and physician,
Had kept those dread-vans in the best condition,
                                        (Part II, p. 57)

As if it were not enough to have the natural universe take sides, Campbell declares that even the Loyalists' war machinery rebelled: "For even their machinery rebelled/And as by miracles, our armouries swelled:/Till we could almost pray for what we wanted/ And take the answer to the prayer for granted," (p. 56).

This all-out effort to consecrate the Nationalists by claiming that nature, matter, and even God actively intervened on their behalf to defeat the Republicans exposes Campbell's fanatical determination to win support for his side. *Flowering Rifle* really develops no argument that might conceivably persuade anyone that the Nationalists had a better cause. For Campbell cannot conceive that any logical argument about logistics, for example, could outweigh the fact (and for him it was a fact) that the Nationalists had been blessed with holy sanction. To dispute about politics, land reform, social rights, or about the respective merits of the belligerents was irrelevant: the Nationalists were "holy crusaders," the Loyalists were "godless marauders," and this distinction, in Campbell's opinion, not only superseded debate but also made all the difference between Right and Wrong.

What is objectionable about Campbell is not just his boasting, which frequently sounds hollow, but also the tediousness of the ex-cathedra tone in which his predictions and views are uttered. And the monotony is intensified by the regularity with which these prophecies are recited or defended. Campbell's determination to impress us with "the constant certitude of his pen" (p. 26) has led to a tedious tirade in his own defense, which all but overshadows his primary purpose, which was to herald the supremacy of the Nationalist cause. Repetition is one of the propagandist's most effective tools, but it is fatal to poetry when it is used as a means of self-glorification, having little to do with the principal subject of the poem. Prejudicial is not just the absence of political neutrality (although this would be unacceptable to the impartial reader) but also the personal and spiteful tone which sparks so much of his satire. *Flowering Rifle* is uncontrolled in form and emotion.

Campbell wished to give the impression that the substance of his verse was authentic, that it was the work of one who, having lived in Spain ("As I who've lived beneath the two regimes," Part II, p. 40), had thoughtfully chosen to defend the side that was fighting to preserve Spain's best traditions. *Flowering Rifle* has the subtitle "A Poem from the Battlefield of Spain" and contains myriad details about the war and the poet. The poem has scanty explanatory notes (and those appear only in the *Collected Poems* edition of 1957). What this mass of details (including names, nicknames, places, events, etc.) does is to give it the appearance of a trustworthy document where all the information has been meticulously gathered. However, beneath the apparent factuality are extravagant claims, some of which contradict objective evidence and most of which would be difficult to corroborate: [6]

1. that the Republicans, besides having foreign aid before Franco, received alien soldiers who outnumbered foreign enlistees on Franco's side four to one:

> Such foreign aid as, later, we were lent,
> The Reds already to the front had sent,
> Out-numbering still, to-day, by four to one,
> And antedating with four months to run:
> (Part II, p. 39)

2. that whatever aid Franco received—less substantial than on the Loyalist side—"was proffered, not entreated":

> Although in foreign aid by one to four
> Outnumbered as preceded months before,
> Which on our side was proffered, not entreated
> (Part II, p. 50)

3. that the Moors, first solicited by Azaña, preferred to serve as mercenaries with Franco, even at lower pay:

> As to the Moors, whom they were first to bribe
> With their Autonomy—that Spanish tribe
> Whom they invited first . . .
> To swell the People's Army on the plain.
> Azaña's ten pesetas to refuse
> And fight for five—the Moors were free to choose
> And be called "Mercenaries" as are we
> Who in the Legion are content with three,
> . . .
> Without Autonomy, without more pay,
> They chose with us the clean equestrian way,
> (Part II, pp. 50-51)

4. that the Nationalists, by nature peace-loving, were forced to fight in order to preserve Spain from the "Red Curse" (p. 91), often only having arms captured from the Reds themselves:

Upon the Right his would-be victim stood,
Armed chiefly with a sense of Bad and Good,
(Part II, p. 32)

When with our cities blown about our ears
We bore in silence what they bawl in tears
Before we had a bomber fledged to fly,
And months before we ventured to reply;
(Part II, p. 34)

Many besides myself have touched no gun
Or cutlery, but what from them was won.
(Part II, p. 37)

5. that Mussolini's invasion of Ethiopia was simply a matter of settling an account with an old enemy:

Now thanking old allies for rendered aid
He bombs the Arabs, whom his Jews invade,
Yet turns on Mussolini censures venomous
Because he does the same to his old enemies.
(Part IV, p. 117)

6. that the Left, inclined toward "filth and famine," was completely devoid of morality, but that the "clean hands" of the Nationalists would purify the "filth and dirt" of these sham reformers:

Invariably they side with filth and famine,
Morality for them has never mattered,
(Part I, p. 21)

Our own clean hands accept the filth and dirt,
(Part III, p. 74)

7. that the Left was guilty of the most callous sort of aerial bombing and of killing their own forces:

Who bombing their best allies to their shame,
(Part II, p. 51)

It was natural that it (Humanitarianism) should side with the party that, at the very beginning, had slaughtered more unarmed victims than the whole war has yet slain . . .

(Author's Note, p. 8)

8. that the destruction of Guernica was the work of Loyalists who tried to blame the Nationalists for the tragedy:

> To blame us for the Reds' Subhuman crimes,
> Guernica dynamited from within
> He lays to Franco's aeroplanes the sin,
> And with humanitarian fuss makes bold
> To "save Bilbao's children" (and its gold!)
>
> (Part IV, pp. 114-15)

9. that, in contrast to the heroic defense of the outnumbered Nationalists, the Reds were not only uncommonly cowardly but afraid even to save their own wounded:

> And at the sight (of aurora borealis), the foe half-
>   dead with fright,
> Fled howling in their Gadarene stampede,
> Nor stop to help their comrades when they bléed
> But downwards to the ocean hurl their flight,
> And shed their arms, in mountains, on the plain,
>
> (Part VI, p. 156)

10. and, finally, that Franco clearly foreshadowed his greatness by bidding "the epic years begin" (p. 44), while the Red leaders revealed their cowardice by escaping Spain before the war ended.

The first edition of 1939 *Flowering Rifle* extends for 157 pages and contains six parts including more than 5000 lines. Part I is a satire of British intellectuals of that period, of their leftist tendencies and their conduct in war. Campbell criticizes the sympathies of the English generally toward Red Spain. He satirizes the contradictions of their reasoning and attacks certain individuals (Day Lewis, Auden, Spender), ending with a lyrical meditation of political and religious character.

Part II ridicules some of the established values in British society of 1920 to 1940—institutions, customs, concept of life—in the light of Spain and the Spanish war. He alludes to some traditional misconceptions of the English and eulogizes the heroic Nationalists for singlehandedly sweeping away Reds and Jews. He extracts social and moral consequences from the differing payments that the red militia and the Nationalist soldiers receive.

Part III begins with a juxtaposition of the beliefs that were conflicting in the Spanish Civil War, frequently blaming Marx and Freud. He describes the burning of the Carmelite convent of Toledo, alluding to the massacres and searches of the days of terror, and comments on the death of García Lorca, whom he considers his poetic inferior (cf. footnote on p. 199 of the 1957 edition), and of José Antonio Primo de Rivera, whom he reveres.

Part IV returns to the charge against certain personalities who have helped corrupt modern British thinking. He satirizes capitalism as much as communism and criticizes what he considers British hypocrisy and cowardice in misconstruing such incidents as Guernica and the Basque children.

Part V describes the disruption of social life induced by the Left to gain their objectives of power, and satirizes "liberty" as it is understood by them. It praises the discipline, order, and hard work of the Nationalists while deriding the stagnation, confusion, and materialism of the Republicans.

The last part begins with a description of a bloody battle that symbolizes the clash between Nationalist and Red Spain, and is suggestive of *Gulliver's Travels:* the tanks become black beetles and the men become ants. Campbell ends his poem with a description of the symbolic phenomenon of the aurora borealis that took place at the end of the war.

In its first edition (1939) *Flowering Rifle* was in six parts, prefaced by an Author's Note. Its length and heroic conception of the Nationalists are epic. The poem extends to more than 5000 four-beat lines of rhymed (heroic) couplets. There is an almost total lack of form except for the division into six parts. The poem suffers from extreme repetitiveness, even in one or two instances repeating the same lines without representing some artistic design:

> In its behavior, Matter proved no dolt,
> And that it has opinions of its own—
> As any one who's worked in wood and stone
> Can tell you . . .
>
> (Part II, p. 58)

> For Matter has opinions of its own
> As any one who's worked with wood and stone
> Can tell you . . .
>
> (Part VI, p. 154)

It appears that Campbell simply piled one contention on top of another indiscriminately, without any careful consideration to the shape of the finished poem. For instance, an argument favoring the Nationalists suddenly ends, a passage of autobiographical boasting begins (shifting to the first person), which, in turn, stops, and a section of satire on British intellectuals commences—all perhaps within a page or two, and without transition.

Like his contentions, Campbell's images are presented one upon the other, the accumulation massive. Like his ideas, many of his images are repetitive, the fat bourgeois representing the self-indulgent Republicans and gold representing their acquisitiveness. Charlie is his name for the typical left-winger. He speaks frequently of right and left hands to distinguish between the sides. But there are no encompassing images to unite the expansive poem, which suffers from diffuseness. Many of its metaphors are clichés, for example, "kill-joy parents" (p. 105), or downright antipoetic, like "banana peel" (p. 76) and "baloney" (p. 41), but such wording is perhaps appropriate to his purpose.

The poem is very uneven in thought and quality due both to its extreme length and to Campbell's lack of restraint and talent. Campbell does not achieve, nor does he aim for, sustained narration, description, or logic. The flow of thought is choppy, and the emotion fluctuates—indeed it would be impossible to sustain a sometimes hysterical tone.

While Campbell had force and humor, produced original and often witty rhymes, and while his diction could be racy and colloquial and nearly always vivid and alive, he did not have the subtlety of ear which the manipulation of the heroic couplet requires, nor could he manage the delicate variations of pace and beat with which Dryden and Pope were able to avoid the monotony which is the chief peril of the form. Worse, writing in heroic couplets encouraged Campbell's great weakness, a tendency to the prolix; and it may be said that all his poems in this meter suffer from monotony and go on far too long.

Verse is, perhaps, the worst vehicle for argument, and, in particular, political argument. *Flowering Rifle* is more tedious than most political poems because of its enormous length, its interminable tirades, and its savage vituperation, in which Campbell, in political and emotional isolation (from everyone else I have read on the subject), often seemed to lose all sense of proportion.

His battle scenes, especially those describing the siege of the Alcázar, are brilliant pageantry and reveal his attitude about war as a glorious contest. He felt an overwhelming ecstasy marching into battle:

> How thrilling sweet, as in the dawn of Time,
> Under our horses smokes the pounded thyme
> As we go forward; streaming into battle
> Down on the road the crowded lorries rattle
> Wherein the gay blue-shirted boys are singing,
> As to a football match the rowdies bringing—
> But of this match the wide earth is the ball
> And by its end shall Europe stand or fall:
>
> (Part VI, p. 138)

Considered one of Scotland's greatest modern poets, Hugh MacDiarmid (the pseudonym of Christopher Murray Grieve) was born in Langholm, Dumfriesshire, near the Scottish-English border, in 1892.[7] His native language was Scots. His father was a rural postman whose people had been mill workers. His mother's people had been agricultural workers, but Christopher's faith lay with the industrial, not the rural, and in the growth of the third factor between Man and Nature—the Machine. His development owed a great deal to his growing up in a working-class family. He spent his childhood in the Scottish Border country, where he came into contact with a life which, in his own words, was "raw, vigorous, rich, bawdy, and simply bursting with life and gusto." He was later to bring his broad awareness of natural phenomena and love of color into his poems.

The Langholm Public Library was housed in the same building as the Grieve family, and he had free access to a collection of "upwards of twelve thousand books." By his own account he had "certainly read almost every one of them" by the time he left home for Edinburgh at the age of fourteen.[8] He was an omnivorous reader and note-taker, as the eclecticism of his works testifies. Nothing was wasted upon the boy—his nearness to neither the land, working people, nor books.

Such difficulties as came about between the adolescent boy and his family seem to have centered on the "ambitious gentility" of his mother and the opposition of both parents to his early decision to become a poet. His break with their devout religion appears to have been accomplished with a minimum of recrimination, perhaps because he retained a deep awareness of religious issues while rejecting all the orthodoxies.

He was educated at Langholm Academy, Broughton Junior Student Centre (Edinburgh), and Edinburgh University. When his father died in 1911, Grieve had already joined various local socialist societies. His political nationalism grew out of his reading of Scottish history and literature, and the search for Scottish unity became one of the main concerns of his life. In 1912 he turned to journalism and worked until 1920 as editor-reporter of *The Montrose Review.* When World War I erupted, he served as a member of the Royal Army Medical Corps. Again in Montrose, he edited three issues of the first postwar Scottish verse anthology, *Northern Numbers* (1921-1923). In 1922 he founded the monthly *Scottish Chapbook,* in which he advocated a Scottish literary revival (or "Renaissance") and published the lyrics of "Hugh MacDiarmid," later collected as *Sangschaw* (1925) and *Penny Wheep* (1926). Grieve's first book, entirely of his own work, was *Annals of the Five Senses* (1923), in which poems alternate with prose pieces. Rejecting English as a medium for Scottish poetry, Grieve wrote in "synthetic" Scots, an amalgam of elements from various dialects and literary sources, and he achieved notable success both in his lyrics and in *A Drunk Man Looks at the Thistle* (1926), a long, semiphilosophical poem, ranging from investigation of his own personality to exploration of the mysteries of time and space. Later, as he became increasingly involved in metaphysical speculation and accepted the philosophy of dialectical materialism, he found it difficult to express his themes adequately in modern Scots, which had lost most of its intellectual terminology. After writing Scotticized English in *To Circumjack Cencrastus* (1930) and archaic Scots in *Scots Unbound* (1932), he returned to "King's English" and sought to produce a "poetry of fact" in *Stony Limits* (1934) and *Second Hymn to Lenin* (1935), where his treatment of Scottish scenes and social circumstances has all the verve and penetration, though less of the ironic humor and the formal dexterity, of his earlier work in Scots. He realized the frustration of readers because of his alternation between Scots and English: "I write now in English, and now in Scots/To the despair of friends who plead/ For consistency: sometimes achieve the true lyric cry,/Next but chopped up prose . . ."

In 1929 he went to London to become London editor of *Vox*, a radio critical journal. He then spent a year in Liverpool as publicity officer, returning to London a little later to join a publishing firm. His domestic affairs were in a bad state and led to divorce in 1931. He married again shortly thereafter, but with little money or income. His determination early in life was to avoid the acquisition of money, a principle on which he seems not to have compromised. He and his family endured extreme physical hardship and poverty, and his physical and psychological suffering resulted in a serious, general breakdown in 1935.

He thought of communism as the hope of downtrodden humanity, and by the end of 1932, he was describing himself in print as a communist, though he did not join the Party until 1934. After much trouble with the Scottish Nationalists because of his communism, and with the communists because of his nationalism, he was expelled from the Communist Party in 1938, the reason ascribed to his nationalistic deviation in regard to the Spanish Civil War. He did not rejoin until 1957, precisely when so many members were leaving the Party because of the Hungarian uprising.

The reason for his timing is unclear considering the nature of the Hungarian suppression, but MacDiarmid has written in his prose work *The Uncanny Scot* (London, 1968, p. 170) that only a convinced communist would have remained loyal at such a time.

He moved from London to Whalsay (Shetland) in 1933 and remained until 1941. There he wrote *The Golden Treasury of Scottish Poetry, Lucky Poet,* and *The Islands of Scotland.* After the outbreak of World War II, he returned to Scotland to work first for a large engineering firm and then entered the Merchant Service as a First Engineer. He was fifty-three years old at the war's end.

After the war he lived on dole, and only after about twenty years of struggle did his life assume some comfort and security. He was awarded an honorary LL.D. from Edinburgh University in 1957, but it was in 1962 that the real breakthrough came, the occasion being his seventieth birthday, celebrated all over the world.

In almost all MacDiarmid's thought and work, two or three interrelated themes have been constant: Scottish Nationalism (which includes anti-Englishism), the literary revival of Scots and Gaelic, and communism. His work falls into three main categories—lyrical poetry, nonlyrical poetry, and prose criticism and polemical writing. His lyrical poetry is MacDiarmid's richest and most permanent contribution to literature. There is a directness of statement in both the longer and shorter works that is both moving and unusual, revolutionary, yet deeply traditional.

His poetry was political from the outset, though he is outside the Auden-Spender-Day Lewis group. In "Lo! A Child is Born" (from *Second Hymn to Lenin*) the marvel of the birth of a child is stated against a political background of the unemployed and hungry:

> Then I thought of the whole world . . .
> There is a monstrous din of the sterile who con-
>   tribute nothing
> To the great end in view, and the future fumbles,
> A bad birth, not like the child in that gracious home.

While such poets on the Left as Auden, Spender, and Lewis left barely one unquestionably outstanding piece of Marxist writing, there are among Hugh MacDiarmid's poems twenty pieces in which his Marxism or communism found a style, an imagery, and a rhythm, that drew upon the very fabric of that movement. MacDiarmid's poems combined a truly Marxist intellectual content and a truly vernacular speech-idiom. He was the first important communist poet in Britain (his *First Hymn to Lenin* preceded any of the so-called communist poetry of the Auden group). Passionate admirer of Lenin though he was, his communism is not doctrinaire and he is no man for a party line. Rather it is the expression of his revolt against modern capitalist civilization and what it has done to Scotland:

> For I am like Zamyatin. I must be a Bolshevik
> Before the Revolution, but I'll cease to be one quick
> When Communism comes to rule the roost,
> For real literature can exist only where it's produced
> By madmen, hermits, heretics,
> Dreamers, rebels, sceptics,
> —And such a door of utterance has been given me
> As none may close whosoever they be.[9]

It would have been surprising if a man who despised mere logical consistency in every other respect were to be a party-liner in his politics; and, in fact, he interpreted communist doctrine in his own highly individualistic way: "I am a poet; our fools ask me for logic not life." [10]

Between 1935 and the appearance of his *Collected Poems* in 1962, very little poetry by MacDiarmid was published in book form, and nearly all of it is fragmentary. *The Battle Continues,* published in 1957 in Edinburgh, was an exception and seems something of an anomaly, appearing almost twenty years after the event which inspired it, the Spanish Civil War. He kept voluminous notes for his works over the years, and it seems likely that he had written *The Battle Continues* long before getting back to it and having it published. MacDiarmid had not been in Spain prior to or during the war. His long, polemical poem was a reaction mainly against Campbell's *Flowering Rifle,* fascism, and capitalism. The book went unnoticed and unreviewed in the United States. There is much that corresponds between his poem and Campbell's, making its inclusion here essential.

His *Collected Poems,* brought out first in America, was published belatedly in Scotland, where Edwin Morgan wrote in the *Glasgow Herald:*

> . . . What he may lose to T. S. Eliot in fastidious precision of language or to Ezra Pound in music and cadence, he gains in the greater interest of his subject-matter . . . what he loses to Wallace Stevens in brilliance of metaphor and symbol he gains by command of simile and analogy. Why then has he not achieved the estimation these poets have achieved? [11]

The Battle Continues, inspired by the Spanish Civil War and impelled glaringly by a negative, hostile reaction to Roy Campbell and his *Flowering Rifle,* is 107 pages long. It is lengthy in keeping with its "impetus," the even longer *Flowering Rifle.* MacDiarmid has written a devastating denunciation, putting an enormous amount of energy into this work and displaying an excess of vituperation.

There is in the nature of the man a suitability to the type of poem he chose to write. Although their beliefs were diametrically opposed, MacDiarmid and Campbell shared certain tendencies which encouraged them to produce similar poems. They were both passionate, talkative, strongly opinionated, outspoken, energetic, and practically fanatical. Their egos seem immense. But although they both wrote long, subjective, denunciatory poems, there are fundamental, important differences.

The Battle Continues is a major reaction in 1957 (publication date) to Campbell's stand in *Flowering Rifle.* It may be a parody of Campbell's poem, which would account for its similarity in form and structure. But it has an additional twist, philosophically, against everything Campbell represented. If MacDiarmid wrote the poem prior to 1957, it is not clear why he waited so long to publish it. Epistolary inquiry produced no answer from the poet.

MacDiarmid is basically an idealist with a philosophical bent toward polemics. Though he clings to communism as man's hope, his belief in man's justice has frequently been shattered—which accounts for his bitterness and disillusionment, though never pessimism. The epigraphs to the book are, not surprisingly, cynical: ". . . O God, giver of Light, hater of Darkness, of Hypocrisy and Cowardice, how long, how long!" and "Chrétiens d'Espagne, vous êtes abandonnés." MacDiarmid was a Scottish nationalist with a deep feeling and affinity for the common, working man. He could, therefore, identify with the masses of Spaniards in their fight against oppression, greed, crime, cant, and possible extinction. He looked at Spain from the overview of a Scottish nationalist and, in a sense, took Spain out of its time and place, seeing the universality of the fight.

The poem begins with a direct, caustic attack upon Campbell:

> Anti-Fascism is a bit out of date, isn't it?
> All just yesterday's pancakes now?
> And all the Spanish War newspaper clippings
> Dried out like the lives of so many of my friends?
> Forgotten—that's the way you would like it,
> Calf-fighter Campbell, I have no doubt,
> But there's an operation to do first
> —To remove the haemorrhoids you call your poems
> With a white-hot poker for cautery,
> Shoved right up through to your tonsils!
>
> (p. 1)

The attack is ad hominem, with insult heaped upon insult with little reasonable development of ideas: "Campbell, they call him —'crooked mouth,' that is—" (p. 1). The attack on Franco is equally personal:

> A lock of lank hair falls over an insignificant
> And slightly retreating forehead. The back head is
> shallow.
> The nose is large but badly shaped and without
> character.
> His movements are awkward, almost undignified.
> There is no trace in his face of any inner conflict

Or self-discipline. Fit generalissimo, Campbell,
    For conscript armies armed with flowering
        rifles!

(p. 52)

The language is abusive, unrelenting, and can be scatological: "speaking with a voice not only banal/But absolutely anal" (p. 1). MacDiarmid manipulates gross, unpoetic language to convey the nature of his emotion. According to MacDiarmid, Campbell has brutally betrayed "Everything noble and disinterested,/Everything that elevates the life of man" (p. 6) and MacDiarmid attacks him:

The same dislocation affects, it's clear,
His eyes and brain and so-called soul as well,
While if his rifle flowers it only bears
Such roses as in syphilis a penis wears.

(p. 6)

His picking up of such terms as "penis" and "syphilis" is a direct retort to Campbell's overbearing assertion of *machismo,* and MacDiarmid plays on Campbell's virility problem.

The quotations to support the poet's views are well chosen and appropriately inserted. A "Mickiewicz" has somewhere stated what MacDiarmid considers true of Campbell:

Sunk in tyranny—he who once was human,
Abandoned by the Lord to slow corruption,
He has driven from him like an evil thing
His last resource of conscience.

(pp. 1-2)

MacDiarmid presents analogies and disparities by direct statement or in the form of metaphors, anecdotes, and quotations. For example, MacDiarmid compares the massacre of a vulnerable Spanish people to the sport of a bullfight, with Campbell fulfilling a "degrading thirst after outrageous stimulation":

To have an indomitable great pain-blinded people
To torture in your bloody bull-ring for a change!
. . .

For who can add insult to injury more deftly than
  you
Or salt an open wound to please the afficionados
  better?

(p. 3)

MacDiarmid sustains a sarcastic tone: "You (Campbell) are indeed an honourable man" (p. 3). He further jibes:

And I am perfectly entranced for my part
Not only with your expertise but even more
With your genial courtesy and largeness of heart,

(pp. 3-4)

There is no doubting that Campbell is anathema, for MacDiarmid keeps the words in proper perspective. When he quotes Edmund Blunden's praise of *Flowering Rifle*, "Nobody else could have struck such a blow in verse," the irony of his pun is unmistakable. The first line of the poem questions rhetorically a situation which MacDiarmid would not have admitted nor permitted to be true: "Anti-Fascism is a bit out of date . . ." (p. 1). But there are other times when the poet is less coy and gives full vent to his bitterly ironic attack: "All that's diseased, malformed, obscene,/Mankind accepts and guards" (p. 11) and "Rien que la mediocrité est bon./ C'est sortir de l'humanité/Que de sortir du milieu." (p. 11).

Among the images of the poem is one of light and darkness. With the darkness-decay of Campbell, MacDiarmid juxtaposes the light-life of Lenin: ". . . Ah, Lenin,/Life and that more abundantly, thou Fire of Freedom!" (p. 10).

It is at first disconcerting that MacDiarmid should write in a poem published in 1957 on the subject of the Spanish Civil War: "The forces of 'life and that/More abundantly' will triumph in the end" (p. 10). And further:

It is impossible that Franco can win
Since his victory would represent
The abandonment of all human hope, . . .

(p. 11)

It is not until the third of the three parts of the poem that the
reader understands upon what MacDiarmid's hope is sustained.
And, furthermore, in the sense of his broad historical view, the
success or defeat of fascism is still a pregnant question.

MacDiarmid transfers his insults from Campbell the bullfighter
to Campbell the poet he claims to be. "Hitler the painter, Campbell the poet!" (p. 12). The analogy is pungent. He expands his
comparison to Republican and fascist poetry: "Poetry versus Animal Noises,/Our cause versus yours!" (p. 13). He denigrates Campbell's poetry by declaring that fascism can breed no true poets:
"You are no true poet that they (fascists) tolerate you./No poet
worth a damn is on your side." (p. 14), and "you, Campbell, stand
for all/The hypocrisy, falsity, and callousness of the Law, . . ."
(p. 14). This is not a developed argument, but the implication is
that poetry demands a commitment to life whereas Hitlerism leads
to death.

He considers Campbell the "Nadir of English Literature" (p. 16)
and includes Lorca as a dynamic contrast to Campbell: "Lorca
dead lives forever./Campbell, living, is dead and rots." (p. 15).

MacDiarmid attempts to define poetry:

Men of work! We want our poetry from you,
From men who will dare to live
A brave and true life.

(p. 19)

Again taking a broad view, MacDiarmid equates culture, poetry,
and people, stressing that Spanish art and culture have always been
close to the people. Of the two poetries, that of the Republic and
that of the fascists, he reaffirms that poetry can only be on the side
of the people—on the liberal Left.

The Battle Continues is largely political and didactic, and Mac-
Diarmid explains that the military insurgents of Spain are fascists,

"Supported by foreign states and marching hand in hand/With the catholic church and the capitalists" (p. 20). He prophesies the death of the bourgeoisie and the supremacy of communism and democracy over capitalism. He denounces the Moorish mercenaries and curses all fascists:

> It were better that you all should rot in your vices
> In the bottomless filth of damnation,
> And that they (Spanish comrades) should live!
>
> (p. 17)

He takes a final swipe against Campbell's manhood and poetry: "He's poor shakes as a soldier and poorer as a poet!" (p. 24).

Part II begins with the admonition that we should "endlessly boycott" the forces of evil that caused this Spanish tragedy and that among these forces Campbell is but an insignificant tool. Campbell had lived among the Spaniards and been proud of it. MacDiarmid relegates his relation to Spain to that of a tourist and aficionado. And as to Campbell's ability to make judgments, MacDiarmid contends that he had no intimate insights to offer and toyed with Spanish anguish in a superficial way. He continues his denunciation by contrast: "Lorca, not Campbell!/Christ, not Barabbas!" (p. 34).

Reminiscent of the open-mindedness of Felipe's *La insignia*, in which he criticized the factions of his fellow Spaniards, Mac-Diarmid here turns against the English and puts them on an even lower level than the Nazis and fascists:

> There is nothing the Nazis and Fascists have done
> That the English haven't done again and again
> In the name of very different ideals, of course,
> And are not repeating or trying to repeat
> Continually. The horrors of Czechoslovakia
> And China and Spain are the very stuff
> Our Empire is founded upon. We have nothing to
>   learn
> From Hitler or Mussolini. We've forgotten more
>   than they know . . .
>
> (p. 34)

But then we realize that MacDiarmid is for the Spanish masses, the Spanish Republic, all working people of the world, communism, nationalism (Scottish, especially), and that his bias is indeed consistent and is dead-set against fascism, Nazism, capitalism, colonialism, and oppression anywhere.

He pits his faith in the Spanish Republic ("I sing of the Spanish Republic,/Of men who went to their deaths not with the hope of victory," (p. 36)—which shows MacDiarmid had learned something from Walt Whitman) against his disdain for the fascists and, also, for the British: "Struggling to think and feel as little as possible" (p. 39). As for the Queen, he profanes her name, too:

> a great bloated watery mass,
> Safe in a dark cavity for underground,
> With nevertheless a power so all-pervading
>   (pp. 39-40)

MacDiarmid expresses his pride over being Scottish and claims that 90 per cent of the Scottish had supported the Republican cause.

His next classification of Campbell is that of "Cheer-Leader of World Fascism" (p. 46). He sees Campbell as an active spectator, a sideliner with fervor and zeal at best, and not as an important participant. Athletic Campbell is for MacDiarmid a kind of world cheerleader/tourist/aficionado. He despises those who might applaud Campbell, such as Hitler, Mussolini, Franco, and Chamberlain. Chamberlain's gross capitulation is summed up by a brutal anecdote attributed to Tolstoy. MacDiarmid's anecdotes are potent weapons of abuse.

Again the poet asks a curious question for 1957: "if Fascism wins —who would wish to live?" (p. 56). He is not talking about only Spain now, but looking at fascism in a broad historical perspective and condemning it to extinction. MacDiarmid is applying his considerations to a contemporary, universal setting. The thrust of the poem is not to give a sense of time and place, but to present a broader perspective essential to both his title and his theme.

His extended criticism of bourgeois capitalism is based on its lack of creativity, spirit, spine, and substance. It is practical (a sin to an idealist), self-indulgent, and without culture, morals, or religion (in its ethical ramifications, presumably).

The end of Part II contrasts Campbell with Heine. Heine chose communism out of a "generosity of despair" because "every man has the right to eat" (p. 60). Like Heine, MacDiarmid believes:

> . . . the future belongs to Communism
> And that the present system is rotten from top
>   to bottom
>
> (p. 61)

He concludes, "But there is no generosity of despair in you, Campbell, . . ." and besides "Heine's a poet," the insinuation being clear.

Part III is the most ideological, idealistic, and hopeful of the three parts. It is also the part based most on reasonable arguments, and gives us a good indication of the political, economic, and social background of the Spanish Civil War, as well as of the poet's hope for the future. He generalizes about the human will and the cause for which the Spanish Republicans fought and died. But out of the defeat of the temporal battle, he praises their spiritual victory:

> I thank you, my Spanish comrades, for this most
>   timely
> And invaluable reassurance—
> For vouchsafing me so wonderful a spectacle
> Of the movement of individual will
> Towards a common beckoning good,
> Always distant, yet always implicit
> In love and in understanding,
> And the only alternative to callousness and
>   despair,
> And for all the glimpses you have given me of
>   the incredible beauty
> Of those who give themselves while they are yet
>   young
> Selflessly, to a noble Cause.
>
> (p. 63)

The imagery is abstracted, idealistic, and lyrical. The trajectory of the poem begins at the level of the sewer, with its anal cavities, and moves upwards, reaching the idealism of the Spanish people. Their sacrifice is juxtaposed with the hypocritical self-interest of Franco. The language alternates between coarse, gutter, street language and abstract, lyrical, idealistic language.

MacDiarmid prides himself on the Marxist philosophy Campbell had detested. MacDiarmid blames Franco for Guernica, the shelling of civilian Madrid, and "pointless wholesale cruelties" (p. 70).

Their lack of ethical values is disguised by the lip service the Nationalists give to religion: "Where is the humanitarian heart of the millions/Who go to Church and pray to God . . ." (p. 70). They are superstitious and lack understanding. Dictators are vile as evidenced by the ruthlessness with which Franco "handled" even fellow-Spaniards.

MacDiarmid glorifies the International Brigade ("Ideals of duty and sacrifice"—p. 77) and writes some of his most lyrical lines to commemorate them.

According to MacDiarmid, Franco, like Campbell, has no real significance, and will be forgotten by history. But he sees the Spanish people themselves as admirable and wishes that the British resembled them.

MacDiarmid distinguishes the Left from the Right, the Republicans from the Nationalists/fascists. He asserts romantically and idealistically that it is better to fail on the side of humanity than to win with Hitler, Mussolini, Franco, Chamberlain. The side of mankind is unlimited in potentiality and vitality while the other side is rotten or dead.

MacDiarmid also expresses strong anti-Bloomsbury sentiment:

> And Auden, Spender, Allott, Grigson,
> The Woolfs, the *New Statesman* clique,
> All Left Fascists, so very pointedly unrevolutionary,
> Writing nothing any "intelligent" Fascist
> Might not equally well write.
>
>   (p. 85)

MacDiarmid felt that the work of Auden and Spender was completely antipopular and anti-Scottish as well. They do not belong to the working class while MacDiarmid does. He had no use for them or any of the English Literary Left. Their grasp of socialist theory was always inadequate—which characterized the English movement in general. Besides, the English Left is an incongruity since it arises in an oppressor-country.

Much like Felipe in *La insignia* and for the same reasons, Mac-Diarmid denounces in a definite order:

> I prefer the forthright brutality and aggression
>   of Hitler
> To the smug double-crossing and sanctimonious
>   hypocrisy
> Of Britain's umbrella-bearer.
>
> (p. 85)

MacDiarmid presents his political values most clearly in this third and final part of the poem. The ideology of democracy encompasses social change and a search for truth. These values will survive "though my comrades themselves are slain" (p. 86). He shares their belief "in the philosophy/Of equality of opportunity" (p. 86). He understands "that the revolution had its roots/In the social life of Spain" (p. 88) and that "the Republic was justified in seeking/A drastic transformation of Spain's economic life" (p. 87).

In Britain, where all the Institutions work against the people, MacDiarmid predicts:

> I confidently believe that the day is near
> When Capitalism will be abolished here
> And Labour will rule the British Isles
> But . . . it won't come without a fight,
> And a bitter one!
>
> (p. 89)

He fears the British proletariat could be betrayed, as the Spanish people had been.

After accusing Campbell of nursing an inferiority complex, he goes on, like Dante, to arrange people in Hell; he would place

Mussolini's supporters ("Hateful to God and to the enemies of God!"—p. 94) even below Mussolini.

He accepts the tragic past of Manchuria, Ethiopia, Spain, China, Austria, and Czechoslovakia, only because they are established facts. But he is optimistic about the future, because deliverance can come through wisdom and courage. According to him, we must demand truth. We must redouble our efforts for peace (*The Battle Continues*). And we must choose democracy, because "Democracy is the best form of government" (p. 96) and dictatorship is the worst.

He repeats some of his previous contentions: ". . . criminal and stupid murder/Of García Lorca who took no part in politics" (p. 98). The Spaniards were without illusions and "knew what they were fighting for." (p. 99).

The end of the poem offers an ecstatic eulogy to the Spanish workers who fought ("one against ten/Against World Fascism"—p. 105) and were killed. Their spirit transcends the temporal disaster and pervades the world (cf. poem's title).

He closes his poem with a renewed attack on Campbell's poetry:

> And your poetry is the sort of stuff one expects
> From a mouth living close to a sewer
> And smelling like a legacy from Himmler.
>
> (p. 106)

His final analogy by means of an anecdote is abrasive and unforgiving as he buries *Flowering Rifle* along with Campbell.

The poem is divided into three main parts and into many stanzas. Some of the stanzas are titled; others are simply quotations from other writers. The poem bristles with so many quotations from others that it looks like an anthology if one simply thumbs through the pages. Yet the diverse nature of the quotations—an indication of the astonishing range of MacDiarmid's reading and retention—and their order and arrangement in relation to the poet's presentation of his own ideas, gives the book some of its power and uniqueness. MacDiarmid makes eclectic use of widespread material. The poem combines quotations from other writers, expressions from foreign languages, dialogue, and references and allusions to worldwide figures—literary, political, and others.

MacDiarmid relies at times upon rhyme. His language varies from the clichés of pamphleteering to flights of beautiful expression. Some of his imagery is poetic; other images are purposely repulsive; and some of his lines lack images altogether. Some of his unpoetic language may parody Campbell's poem. But, when he chooses, MacDiarmid can manage a rich technique, deriving from emotional impetus, imagery, and lyric quality.

He abandoned traditional meter and allowed himself great rhythmic freedom. His tendency is to drop into prosaic rhythms— prosaic in the sense that our ear tells us they belong to prose contexts of a comparatively unimaginative order—for example:

> No man or group of men has any right
> To force another man or other groups of men
> To do anything he or they do not wish to do.
> There is no right to govern without
> The consent of the governed. Consent is not only
> Important in itself, and as a nidus for freedom
> And its attendant spontaneity, (clearly valuable
> As the opposed sense of frustration is detrimental),
>   but the sole
> Basis of political obligation. . . .
>
>   (p. 5)

Freed from traditional discipline, MacDiarmid lets the poem run on for too long. But some of its lyricism is striking, for example:

> Ah, Spain, already your tragic landscapes
> And the agony of your War to my mind appear
> As tears may come into the eyes of a woman very
>   slowly,
> So slowly as to leave them clear!
>
> Spain! The International Brigade! At the moment
>   it seems
> As though the pressure of a loving hand had gone,
> (Till the next proletarian upsurge!)

> The touch under which my close-pressed fingers
>   seemed to thrill,
> And the skin to divide up into little zones
> Of heat and cold whose position continually
>   changed,
> So that the whole of my hand, held in that clasp,
> Was in a state of internal movement.
> My eyes that were full of pride,
> My hands that were full of love,
> Are empty again . . . for a while.
>   For a little while!
>   (pp. 85-86)

There is more repetition and playing upon sound in this passage than in the previously quoted one. The first four lines contain a number of soft vowel sounds, mostly "a" and "o." There is skillful parallelism of presentation as he repeats Spain and other words ("hand," "that were full of," etc.). Here beauty and meaning are blended.

The support and illustrations for MacDiarmid's points include statistics although, as with Campbell's "facts," these are strongly stated and would be difficult to support:

> One out of every 25 Spaniards dead,
> And another one wounded;
> A million lives lost in all,
> A quarter of them civilians,
> At a cost of 22 hundred million pounds
> —(Enough to have given the whole population
>   of Spain
> Abundance in perpetuity
> Instead of the terrible distress
> That is all it has purchased).
>   (p. 2)

His facts are oversimplified: ". . . in Spain the arms were on one side" (p. 28). The exaggeration here appeals for an emotional reaction. However, much of his argument relies upon a reasonable, ideological basis. He names places, people, and events; he quotes others (though out of context). Such evidence lends credence to his views. He is certainly partisan, and he deviates from neutrality in the direction of liberalism, Marxism, and democracy, and, most importantly, toward humanitarianism. He believes in mankind. He is an idealist interested in changing the world. But, at the same time, he was very emotionally antagonized by Campbell and his fascist cohorts. Some of MacDiarmid's attack is as subjective as Campbell's, but as the poem progresses the poet relies more upon a reasonable argument.

His poem is often passionate. His abuse is sometimes humorous. He makes effective use of puns and includes powerful illustrative material.

The Battle Continues is an unforgiving, injustice-collecting effort. It is a long, bitter, accusing indictment, but with hope sustained through the enduring spirit of the working class. MacDiarmid addressed all of his works in the first place to his fellow countrymen. However, within the poem he verbally addresses Campbell, Blunden, his Spanish comrades, profascists, International Brigades, Spain, among others, depending upon his focus or point.

He juxtaposes his material, is somewhat repetitious of ideas, stoops to namecalling at times, uses nouns to categorize his opponents rather than more temporary adjectives, but manages, especially in Part III, to develop an argument that convinces and shows a broad basis of knowledge and understanding of the complexities of the Spanish Civil War.

Wystan Hugh Auden, Anglo-American poet, dramatist, and literary critic, was born on February 21, 1907, in York, England.[12] The son of refined, enlightened parents, he had what Campbell would have called a bourgeois upbringing. His father was a surgeon, his mother a cultured woman of Anglican learning. His grandfathers and four uncles were Anglican clergymen. His name was Nordic, and his background, affinities, and tastes Northern. He lived in the Midlands, where he came in contact with Britain's industrial area. From York his family moved to Birmingham, where he had firsthand experience of economic depression. Growing up during the

Great Depression, when unemployment was at a peak in England, Auden and his contemporaries, in sympathy with the problems of the working class, looked to Marxism as a possible solution to social conditions and to Sigmund Freud for answers to the spiritual barrenness resulting from these conditions. He received his education at Gresham's School and Christ Church, Oxford (1925-1928). His earliest interests were scientific (geology, machinery, and mining), and his specialty was biology. While at Oxford he developed an interest in psychology. Afterwards, from 1928 to 1929, he visited pre-Hitler Germany. When he returned to England, he became a schoolmaster.

Auden was fully conscious of the disintegration of values and the forces which were to produce Hitler and the Spanish Civil War. He visited Spain from January to March, 1937, from a desire at least "to do something" (cf. "Conversation with Claud Cockburn," *The Review,* No. 11/12, July, 1964, p. 51). *Spain,* the only poem he overtly wrote about the Spanish Civil War and his most famous political poem, resulted from his brief trip and was first published as a pamphlet in May of 1937, the proceeds being donated to the British Medical Unit in Spain.

But Auden's social and political concern was subordinate to his interest in the nature of man and in the roots of his social and individual problems (metaphysics). Several related themes run throughout Auden's work. He sees man as an individual isolated in society. "Musée des Beaux Arts" emphasizes this separation; suffering, says Auden, "takes place while someone else is eating or opening a window or just walking dully along":

> In Brueghel's *Icarus,* for instance: how everything
>   turns away
> Quite leisurely from the disaster; the ploughman
>   may
> Have heard the splash, the forsaken cry,
> But for him it was not an important failure . . .

As early as his undergraduate days, Auden had told Spender that the "poet must have no opinions, no decided views which he seeks to put across in his poetry" and that "poetry must in no way be concerned with politics." [13] Probably disgusted with the condition of Europe, Auden immigrated to America in 1939, with no intention of returning. In America he exchanged his inclination toward Marxism for a commitment to Christianity, becoming an Anglo-Catholic about 1940. This conversion to Christianity provided him with a conceptual and emotional framework.

In both his pre-Christian and Christian poems Auden wrote of love as the salvation of mankind, but both humanistic and Christian love in his poetry are extremely impersonal. Even the so-called love lyric "Lay Your Sleeping Head My Love" is strangely abstract:

> Beauty, midnight, vision dies.
> Let the winds of down that blow
> Softly round your dreaming head
> Such a day of sweetness show
> Eye and knocking heart may bless,
> Find the mortal world enough;
> Noons of dryness see you fed
> By the involuntary powers,
> Night of insult let you pass
> Watched by every human love.

Auden also wrote of the necessity for human relationships and mutual concern. His view is well expressed in these lines from *For the Time Being* (1944):

> Space is the Whom our loves are needed by,
> Time is our choice of How to love and Why.

While Marx and Freud were anathema to Campbell, Auden found in them a psychological approach to social evils and a philosophical conception of the condition of man which anticipated his later approach to existentialism. Based on the firm foundation of Marx and Freud, Auden had a keen, objective, reporter's sense of scientific observation.

His first volume of *Poems* (1930) combined ideas from Marx, Darwin, Freud, and Homer Lane, and celebrated in conversational rhythms the decay of middle-class society and his hopes for a new order. It showed Auden's versatile style and originality.

His next work, *The Orators—An English Study* (1932), dedicated to Stephen Spender, gave a rather immature picture of the twentieth-century "hero" as a young airman. The book offered a prophetic picture of the idealists who were to fight in the Spanish Civil War, and it showed a country in crisis. By this time, Auden, though not a professed communist, was commonly considered one; at least, he was one of the group of so-called leftist writers, including Spender, Christopher Isherwood, Louis MacNeice, and C. Day Lewis, who directed their writing toward a search for meaning in a world which seemed to them empty and mechanical.

The social criticism implicit in *The Orators* became explicit in his most Marxist poetic play, *The Dance of Death* (1933), and in the three dramatic works he composed with Isherwood, the most notable being *The Dog Beneath the Skin* (1935) and *The Ascent of F. 6* (1936). The gist of *The Dance of Death* is summed up in the Announcer's opening words: "We present to you this evening a picture of the decline of a class, of how its members dream of a new life, but secretly desire the old, for there is death inside them. . . ." The play was a satire on the decadence of the bourgeoisie in the 1930s. *The Dog Beneath the Skin,* a satirical parody of ecclesiastical eloquence employed in the interest of political propaganda, denounced upper-class hypocrisy, while *The Ascent of F. 6* showed its hero, driven by the ambitious and false values of his parents and their bourgeois social milieu, undertaking the ascent of Mt. Everest. In *On the Frontier* (1938) Auden passed from the concept of the individual versus society to the plane of international catastrophe through a conflict of ideologies.

With Isherwood again, he wrote *Journey to a War* (1939), an account of their visit to China. Gradually Auden's idiom became less private and his technique more sure. *Look, Stranger!* (1936) and in 1940 *Another Time* (which included a reissue of the poem "Spain 1937," first published in 1937 as *Spain* and the text of which varied slightly from the original edition) [14] encompass the period covering the Spanish Civil War and the events leading up to the Second World War.

After coming to the United States, Auden lectured at a number of universities and, in 1946, became a U.S. citizen. Auden published over a dozen collections of poems after coming to America, including *Nones* in 1951, *The Shield of Achilles* in 1955, and *The Old Man's Road* in 1956. He won the 1948 Pulitzer Prize for *The Age of Anxiety* (1947) and the 1953 Bollingen Prize in Poetry. From 1956 to 1961, he was Professor of Poetry at Oxford University, although his home remained the United States until 1972, when he returned to Oxford. He died in Vienna in 1973.

Auden was, from first to last, a moralist who wanted his poems to arouse his audience into critical self-awareness and to incite them to reform (at first politically and then religiously). His poems are characteristically ironic, indirect, impersonal, and largely "anti-poetic." They are composed of a bewildering mixture of flippancies and profundities. He can be witty, as in the following verse from "Law Like Love" (from Part III, 1939-1947, of his *Collected Shorter Poems, 1927-1957*):

> Law, says the judge as he looks down his nose,
> Speaking clearly and most severely,
> Law is as I've told you before,
> Law is as you know I suppose,
> Law is but let me explain it once more,
> Law is The Law.

And he can be gloomy, as in "Journey to Iceland" (from Part II, 1933-1938, of the *Collected Shorter Poems, 1927-1957*):

> Where is the homage? When
> Shall justice be done? O who is against me?
> Why am I always alone?

After the relatively free early poems, Auden's mature verse, starting in the middle 1930s, embodies a deep commitment to the precision of formal control as a means of controlling and stimulating the imagination.

According to Spender, "The effect of the turmoil of the 1930s on Auden's poetry was a tremendous inflow of new impressions, influences, and ideas, which he met with an ever-increasing virtuosity. Auden belonged more with his conscience than either with head or heart to the antifascist movement of this time. He felt, as others did, that fascism was wicked, political persecution a crime, and the Spanish Republic the best cause of the first half of the twentieth century." [15]

In *Spain* (1937) Auden revealed his reforming enthusiasm. By 1939 his poetry had gone a long way toward accepting life with all its imperfections. Auden's interest in changing the world faded and then disappeared entirely, while his emphasis on accepting life appeared in nearly every poem. This transition, already faintly noticeable in a few poems published between 1936 and 1939, was almost certainly speeded up by his discovery of Kierkegaard (who gave philosophical reasons for accepting life and a theology insisting that it must be accepted). Auden's cynical distrust of civilization gave way, then, to his religious hope for it. Also, by 1939 he showed a new interest in light verse and, as his form became more conventional, his meanings became more transparent.

Spain is Auden's one poem on the subject of the Spanish Civil War and it is analyzed here because of its high poetic quality and its illuminating viewpoint. Unfortunately, because of Auden's subsequent doubts about the value of the poem (discussed later), he extracted it from the final (in his lifetime) edition of his collected works, and it is not available for reproduction in toto. The quotations from *Spain* that follow are from the 1938 edition, published in London by Faber and Faber.

Spain resulted from Auden's visit to that country from January to March, 1937. Whatever merits it has as a poetic statement, afterward he neither wrote nor spoke publicly about Spain. It is one of his few poems to include communism conspicuously.

The poem's title pinpoints its subject matter as does Auden's brief description of the country's typography: "that arid square, that fragment nipped off from hot/Africa, soldered so crudely to inventive Europe;/On that tableland scored by rivers." The poem has three basic divisions: past, present, and future, with the refrain, "but to-day the struggle," infringing upon both the past and the future. Around the vision of past, present, and future, with the moment of struggle the highest achievement of the present, Auden molded his analysis of the Spanish problem. The poem's purpose is to call to arms Republican sympathizers to defend Spain against the fascist insurrection.

The poem consists of twenty-six quatrains of free verse, in each case the third line briefer than the other three. The beginning of the poem shows the pattern:

> Yesterday all the past. The language of size
> Spreading to China along the trade-routes; the diffusion
>   Of the counting-frame and the cromlech;
> Yesterday the shadow-reckoning in the sunny climates.
>
> Yesterday the assessment of insurance by cards,
> The divination of water; yesterday the invention
>   Of cartwheels and clocks, the taming of
> Horses. Yesterday the bustling world of navigation.

It opens with a rapid survey, in six stanzas, of the past civilization of Europe. Yesterday was sensible and exorcised superstition ("abolition of fairies and giants"). The past age of believing folk-lore was completely gone. This new age turned to science, based its knowledge on empiricism, and provided many of our basic inventions, explorations, and discoveries. Religion was still important enough to be discussed, and there were miracles. God was alive and well and so were heroes. Greek values were inviolate— standards were classical and there was restraint ("the taming of/ Horses").

We have the ending of an age. All the past, with its structures and its tensions, is gone and would be an anachronism "today." The poem's present (1937) epitomizes the struggle of the Spanish Civil War and the impossibility of a normal life without the triumph of the Republican cause. If the Republic wins, the future would rebound to a normality free from terror ("To-morrow, perhaps the future"), and there would be a return to romantic love, poetry, research, exploration, and reassuring trivial pursuits.

After building up tension with the repeated "But to-day the struggle," the poet, the scientist, and finally the nations of the world are shown raising their cry of protest and of prayer. They are averse to accept an unfavorable outcome and, at the same time, expect some deus ex machina to come to their rescue. The stricken nations appeal to the Life-force:

And the nations combine every cry, invoking the life
That shapes the individual belly and orders
     The private nocturnal terror:
"Did you not found the city state of the sponge,

"Raise the vast military empires of the shark
And the tiger, establish the robin's plucky canton?
     Intervene. O descend as a dove or
A furious papa or a mild engineer, but descend."

Although the poem aligns itself with the cause of the Spanish
Republicans, the speaker talks less of Spanish politics than of matters of general human nature, specifically the subject of freedom-
necessity-choice. He shows that in the middle of agonizing circumstances, when men are desperate for a change, they hope some god
will turn up fortuitously, thus relieving them of choice and responsibility: Christ, or a Freudian father figure, or an omnipotent god
("O descend as a dove or/A furious papa or a mild engineer").

   Instead of coming, "Life" replies, in the guise of Spain, that life
can be whatever the nations choose to make of it, and that what
they make of it will depend on what they make of Spain. Each
man is responsible for what happens. Men make their own fate
and their own world ("I am whatever you do . . . I am your
choice"). Choices must be made, actions taken, and freedom won.
In the Spain of 1937, choices and actions were particularly painful:
"To-day the inevitable increase in the chances of death;/The conscious acceptance of guilt in the necessary murder . . . ."

          "O no, I am not the mover;
     Not to-day; not to you. To you, I'm the

     "Yes-man, the bar-companion, the easily-duped;
     I am whatever you do. I am your vow to be
          Good, your humorous story.
     I am your business voice. I am your marriage.

     "What's your proposal? To build the just city? I will.
     I agree. Or is it the suicide pact, the romantic
          Death? Very well, I accept, for
     I am your choice, your decision. Yes, I am Spain."

The point is that a crisis has been reached and the human species has a political will to exercise. Men can become committed and critically involved. Without this, the Just City, the whole premise of civilized society, is an impossible dream. If the struggle fails (through the implied failure of the political will), then "History to the defeated/May say Alas but cannot help nor pardon." "History," the poem dramatically explains, means nothing without responsible, individual decisions.

Some understood the stakes and stood up to be counted, risking their lives in the fight against fascism ("but to-day the struggle"). These men of conviction and idealism comprised the international brigades and came from various parts of the world:

> . . . remote peninsulas,
> On sleepy plains, in the aberrant fisherman's islands
> Or the corrupt heart of the city,
> Have heard and migrated like gulls or the seeds of
> a flower.
>
> They clung like birds to the long expresses that lurch
> Through the unjust lands, through the night,
> through the alpine tunnel;
> They floated over the oceans;
> They walked the passes. All presented their lives.

While asserting the urgency of the Spanish struggle, Auden also fears that if the battle is lost in Spain the struggle will thereupon terminate ("History to the defeated/May say Alas but cannot help nor pardon."). The true Marxist would never agree that defeat in Spain meant the end of the struggle. Auden implies that history cannot be altered. This conclusion, while not exactly defeatist, is far from optimistic.

In stanzas twenty to twenty-three the poem passes to a consideration of the future, a return to normal life, only to revert relentlessly to the urgent problems of here and now in the final three stanzas:

> To-day the deliberate increase in the chances of death,
> The conscious acceptance of guilt in the necessary
> murder;

> To-day the expending of powers
> On the flat ephemeral pamphlet and the boring
>   meeting.
>
> To-day the makeshift consolations: the shared
>   cigarette,
> The cards in the candlelit barn, and the scraping
>   concert,
>   The masculine jokes; to-day the
> Fumbled and unsatisfactory embrace before hurting.
>
> The stars are dead. The animals will not look.
> We are left alone with our day, and the time is
>   short . . .

Although the poem offers a kind of projection of what a successful socialist revolution might accomplish, there is, too, the condemnation of an ideology whose ends justify the means ("the conscious acceptance of guilt in the necessary murder"). And there is
the derision implied about communist, bureaucratic procedures:
"To-day the expending of powers/On the flat ephemeral pamphlet
and the boring meeting." From the poem, Auden could not be
confused with a doctrinaire Marxist, but rather shows himself to
be disenchanted and aware of what the practical outcome of bureaucracy is. Also, Auden has soberly demythicized the idealism
of the present struggle in his projected, mundane, commonplace
future.

The poem's large rhetorical structure, contrasting past and future, necessity and political will, helps establish the poem's call to
action. There is frequent repetition of the refrain, "But to-day the
struggle." The words "yesterday" and "to-morrow" are also used
repetitively. Auden sets up rhetorical patterns; for example, he
begins abruptly "Yesterday all the past." There is no verb though
the meaning is vividly clear. This pattern recurs in each of the first
six stanzas: "Yesterday the assessment of insurance by cards . . .
Yesterday the abolition of fairies and giants," etc. Then, there is
the pattern established by "And the investigator peers through his
instruments," continuing with "And the poor in their fireless lodg-

ings . . . And the nations combine every cry," each critical of fascism.

Auden raised the discussion of the Spanish struggle to an objective level. The tone of the poem is impersonal. The language contains none of the slogans or cant so frequently used to exhort sympathy for the Republic. The poem is depersonalized in the same way that a philosophical analysis or report in the newspapers exists as an impersonal argument or as information:

> To-morrow, perhaps the future. The research on
>   fatigue
> And the movements of packers; the gradual explor-
>   ing of all the
>   Octaves of radiation;
> To-morrow the enlarging of consciousness by diet
>   and breathing.

The poet is outside these lines. There are no signs of Auden's emotional or physical involvement in the struggle, nor is there identification of the viewpoint of the poem—beyond its survey of conditions past, present, and future. Detachment makes the presentation more objective, but in excluding the personal element, Auden may have deprived the poem of the vital force needed to bring to life the rather lengthy rhetorical analysis, or, at least, Louis MacNeice might have concluded as much:

> His (poet's) object is not merely to record a fact but to record a fact plus and therefore modified by his own emotional reaction to it.[16]

Auden utilizes dialogue to make his points more dramatic. The best example is when Life/Spain speaks out, disclaiming creation and leadership: "I am not the mover," etc. (stanzas 12 through 14).

Auden's imagery suggests the essence and diversity of past and present societies. As man triumphed over ignorance and superstition or merely substituted new superstitions for old ones, he learned to use mechanized power, made discoveries about his origin, and gradually grew less dependent upon antiquity's "inviolate" example. He presents this panoramic view along with the values at stake and the possibilities for the future through a series of short, clipped images.

The logical development of the thought, advancing from yesterday through today to tomorrow, gives the poem clear definition and a firm structure. For example, Auden introduces the idea of struggle ("But to-day the struggle") to prepare for its actual demands in the final stanzas. The balance of the various aspects of the theme is careful. The intensity and high seriousness of the theme and its treatment are well sustained, and despite the fact that the poem is built entirely upon a series of choppy assertions, the rhythm moves smoothly. Auden has relied on long lines (and even longer sentences), packed with images and elevated diction. But he is also deft with conversational style:

> . . . I am not the mover;
> Not to-day; not to you. To you, I'm the
>
> "Yes-man, the bar-companion, the easily-duped;
> I am whatever you do. . . .

Through his regular peppering of assertions, verbs in the present tense, and condensed wording, Auden has achieved for the poem a sense of immediacy and urgency.

The poem states an argument in favor of the Loyalist cause, but it is not an oversimplification or a romantic idealization of the war. On the contrary, the less pleasant demands of the struggle are clearly shown in the last three stanzas. But somehow "To-day the deliberate increase in the chances of death" is unconvincing. It is a ponderous and abstract way to express death in wartime. Add to this the unemotional tone of the entire piece and the reader can conclude that Auden was not involved in the war or the cause in a profoundly emotional way and that the poem was written far from the battlefield. However, the notion that Auden was clinically detached, diagnosing the ills of society, is not limited to this poem. His antiromantic and scientific attitude predominates in most of his poetry before as well as after *Spain*.

Auden seems never to have been seriously troubled by the temptation to confuse art and propaganda. His poetic view, expressed in the Introduction to *The Poet's Tongue*,[17] is almost a statement of the central thesis of *Spain:*

> Poetry is not concerned with telling people what to do, but with extending our knowledge of good and evil, perhaps making the necessity for action more urgent and its nature more clear, but only leading us to the point where it is possible for us to make a rational and moral choice.

Spain represents a theoretical (not experiential) analysis of the values at stake in Spain, past, present, and future, with Spain the key to the direction history will follow. His consideration of Marxism, on the other hand, is practical ("boring meeting").

The audience he aimed at was that of the educated middle class with left-wing or revolutionary sympathies. Auden's relation to his reader is not one-to-one with a fellow human being, but as if he were presenting the reader with a verbal mirror to reflect some aspect of his human nature. Also, the elegant form of the poem would inhibit the reader's identification with it. However, Auden extracted from the occasion of the poem a universal significance. Although *Spain* is fundamentally political, it is also predominantly lyrical.

Auden disowned *Spain* years later, dismissing it as dishonest and having sacrificed doctrine for the sake of rhetoric. However, he was forever denigrating certain of his poems as unworthy or unripe.

Stephen Spender came from an educated and cultured family, with liberal views, of mixed German, Jewish, and English origins.[18] His father was a well-known journalist. Stephen was born in London on February 28, 1909. He was educated at the University College School and the University College, Oxford, where Auden was his slightly older friend and mentor. At Oxford he associated with Auden, Isherwood, Cecil Day Lewis, and MacNeice. He first attracted notice with *Poems* (1933); several pieces in this volume derive technically from Walt Whitman and D. H. Lawrence. Praising labor and denouncing capital, they are more political and more violent than most of the works of Spender's friends. Other poems in the volume concerning, for example, pylons ("those pillars/Bare like nude giant girls that have no secret"—from "The Pylons"), trains, and aerodromes, reveal Spender's lyric power. He was interested in contemporary material, and wrote about aspects, functions, and images of modern machinery:

> More beautiful and soft than any moth
> With burring furred antennae feeling its huge path
> Through dusk, the air-liner with shut-off engines
> Glides over suburbs and the sleeves set trailing tall
> To point the wind. Gently, broadly, she falls
> Scarcely disturbing charted currents of air.
>
> > (first stanza of "The Land-
> > scape near an Aerodrome")

Vienna (1934), a long poem, celebrates the abortive revolution of Viennese socialists in 1934 against the Dollfuss government. In *The Destructive Element* (1936) Spender implied that the Russian government occasionally suppressed or opposed freedom and truth. In 1938 he published *Trial of a Judge,* an antifascist verse play in the manner of Auden.

At the suggestion of Harry Pollitt, Communist Party Secretary in London, Spender joined the Party, because it was the only group in England during the Spanish Civil War supporting the Loyalists. Spender accepted Pollitt's proposition on condition that he be permitted to state his reasons for joining in an article to appear in the *Daily Worker.* However, he rejected Pollitt's suggestion to go to Spain as a member of the International Brigade, maintaining that he was unqualified for soldiering, but that he would go in any "useful capacity."

He made three trips to Spain. His first visit grew out of an assignment from the *Daily Worker* to investigate the fate of the crew of a Russian ship which Italians had sunk in the Mediterranean.

The primary purpose of his second visit to Spain was to take a position as head of English broadcasting for the radio station of the Socialist Party in Valencia. When the position failed to materialize, he decided to remain in Spain. The experiences during the next few weeks provided most of the material for his Spanish War poetry and undermined his communist ties. Spender objected to party functionaries for enlisting men in the brigades without telling them they were communist-controlled and he resented their regimentation. This sentiment comes out somewhat in his poems "Ultima Ratio Regum" and "Two Armies."

Spender's third and final visit to Spain during the war occurred in July, 1937, when he joined a small band of British party writers at an International Congress in Madrid and Valencia. For ten days, intellectuals and writers from several European countries and Russia discussed their attitude toward the Spanish Civil War. The principal purpose of the Congress was to show the world that intellectuals supported the Spanish Republic. At the International Congress Spender came into contact with Rafael Alberti, Gide, Hemingway, Malraux, and Neruda, among many other distinguished writers. Manuel Altolaguirre became one of his best friends in Spain and served as catalyst for one of his war poems, "To a Spanish Poet."

In *Forward from Liberalism* (1937) he had maintained the individualism of the artist against Marxist demands, although he also revealed his commitment to communism. But after the German-Soviet pact of 1939, like most English leftists, he recognized the moral and intellectual failure of Marxism, and modified his political sympathies. He chronicled his repudiation of communism in his autobiographical *The God That Failed* (1950). He co-edited, with John Lehmann, an anthology occasioned by the Spanish Civil War, entitled *Poems for Spain* (1939).

Spender's subsequent volumes of poetry, *The Still Centre* (1939), *Ruins and Visions* (1942), and *Poems of Dedication* (1946), more self-centered than his earlier works, lack their conviction and power. Spender has also written critical essays, and published an analytical autobiography, *World Within World*, in 1951. In recent years he has been Professor of English at the University of Connecticut.

His *Collected Poems* (1928-1953), published in London in 1955, has eleven parts. The fourth, entitled "Poems about the Spanish Civil War (1936-1939)," contains ten poems from which I have chosen three for analysis: "Two Armies," "Ultima Ratio Regum," and "To a Spanish Poet." Of the three, only "Ultima" was included in his anthology *Poems for Spain*.

Spender's antiwar attitude was intensified by his visits to Spain and by his disenchantment with communism. Only occasionally in his poems does Spender allude to the themes of freedom and liberty, to the democratic nature of the war, or to the humanitarian feelings it evoked, all of which he had articulated at Loyalist rallies and in numerous articles published between 1936 and 1939, defending the legitimacy and morality of the Madrid government.

The depth of Spender's moral convictions antedated the Spanish Civil War and was sounded in an untitled poem beginning "I think continually of those who were truly great," in which the poet praises the unsung heroes and visionaries who never allowed "the traffic to smother/with noise and fog, the flowering of the Spirit":

> those who in their lives fought for life,
> who wore at their hearts the fire's centre.
> Born of the sun they traveled a short while toward
>   the sun,
> and left the vivid air signed with their honour.
>   (from "Preludes"—1930-1933)

He celebrated the heroism of the international volunteers, praised the meticulous care with which the Republic had handled Spain's art masterpieces, and confirmed the agony of Spain which Picasso had epitomized in *Guernica*. In writing alone, Spender did more than either Day Lewis or Auden to advance the Loyalist cause.

But Spender's philosophy of artistic creation was to maintain some separation between it and political commitment, and in his war poetry he excluded explicit political ideology. In this sense, Spender subordinated the war to his personal view and avoided mention of humane and political ideals of the period.

Spender included an apologia in *The Still Centre* (1939) to explain his restraint from a propagandistic stance or heroic vision:

As I have decidedly supported one side—the Republican—in that conflict, perhaps I should explain why I do not strike a more heroic note. My reason is that a poet can only write about what is true to his own experience, not about what he would like to be true to his experience.

Poetry does not state truth, it states the conditions within which something felt is true. Even while he is writing about the little portion of reality which is part of his experience, the poet may be conscious of a different reality outside.[19]

He preferred to treat this most political of wars in a personal, non-political, and traditional manner. Instead of fundamental ideals about freedom and liberty, his poems touch upon death, suffering, fear, and concern over the fate of the innocent and cowardly. His poems are the antithesis of poetry which fuses "public policy and poetry."

ULTIMA RATIO REGUM [20]

1   The guns spell money's ultimate reason
In letters of lead on the Spring hillside.
But the boy lying dead under the olive trees
Was too young and too silly
5   To have been notable to their important eye.
He was a better target for a kiss.

When he lived, tall factory hooters never
    summoned him
Nor did restaurant plate-glass doors revolve to
    wave him in
His name never appeared in the papers.
10   The world maintained its traditional wall
Round the dead with their gold sunk deep as
    a well,
Whilst his life, intangible as a Stock Exchange
    rumour, drifted outside.

Oh too lightly he threw down his cap
One day when the breeze threw petals from the
    trees.

15   The unflowering wall sprouted with guns,
            Machine-gun anger quickly scythed the grasses;
            Flags and leaves fell from hands and branches;
            The tweed cap rotted in the nettles.

            Consider his life which was valueless
20   In terms of employment, hotel ledgers, news
               files.
            Consider. One bullet in ten thousand kills a
               man.
            Ask. Was so much expenditure justified
            On the death of one so young and so silly
            Lying under the olive trees, O world, O death?
                                        —Stephen Spender

Spender titled his poem with a Latin phrase meaning the last resort of kings, presumably the resort to arms or war. Its contemporary translation to "money's ultimate reason" suggests that behind the war were the interests of the wealthy and the powerful. If extended further, the metaphor of the title concerns itself with the mystique of a terrible experience which is the ultimate reality of modern life. The Spanish Civil War crystallized this feeling that the final reality of fascism, capitalism, and finally of Stalinism—was as tragic as the death of the boy in Spender's poem.

   The plot line is very simple: obscure boy killed in battle, ultimately, perhaps, the victim of an economic system. While guns focused lethally on "the Spring hillside," an anonymous soldier was killed. The disparity between "Spring hill" and all considerations of war is huge, but at least the guns, lead, and money can be considered compatible. The boy, introduced by "but" to emphasize his contrariety to the situation in which he is found, was "too young and too silly" to have been worth killing. To the extent that they are lethal the guns take on importance. Spender's irony is sharp as he adds "He was a better target for a kiss." He was not only young, but harmless, and his fate under these olive trees, representative of Spain, was so unlikely.

   To add to our sympathy for the boy, Spender gives us such details as: he had been too young to be employed; he had never been inside a fine restaurant, nor been written up in the newspaper. Spender implies that those with business success, with "gold sunk

deep as a well," in the sense of being invested, were dead spiritu-
ally, if not physically, in contrast to our vital hero. (The idea of
living dead people has often been considered by poets.) But while
they were protected, he, being outside the mainstream, was vulnerable. The simile, "intangible as . . . rumour," suggests his vague-
ness and unimportance in their materialistic world. The "rumour"
of the simile, although suitable to the comparison and meaningful,
strikes me as being somewhat inconsistent with the other images
of the poem.

In the third stanza, "lightly" has two implications, one physical
and the other psychological. The day he made his decision was,
in contrast to its repercussions, beautiful: "when the breeze threw
petals from the trees." The repetition of "t" sounds adds to the
delicacy of the phrase. The wall which would not have flowered
in any other way "sprouted with guns," as if it were a natural
development. Meanwhile, nature itself was being destroyed by the
fighting: "machine-gun anger quickly scythed the grasses." "Flags
and leaves fell from hands and branches" as humans and trees were
destroyed simultaneously and confusedly. As time passed, "The
tweed cap" of civilian life "rotted in the nettles."

In the last stanza, Spender asks the reader to consider the boy's
life as "valueless" in ordinary economic terms and obscure by accepted social standards. The poem is bitter and ironic as Spender
compares the unformed boy's trivial life with the enormous expenditure required to destroy him: "One bullet in ten thousand
kills a man." It is ironic that that one bullet found him. The
poem ends with Spender's rhetorical question to the reader: "Was
so much expenditure justified/On the death of one so young
and so silly/Lying under the olive trees, O world, O death?"
His repetition of "so young and so silly" makes a final appeal for
an outraged sense of justice. The enormity of the fact of this boy's
death, played down by language, statement, and (ironic) tone, is
nevertheless effectively communicated.

The last phrase contains a compound apostrophe, which Spender
personifies into listening creatures, "O world, O death." Perhaps
he is not so much directing his question to "world" and "death"
as crying out to them. He couches his last statement in an inter-
rogative form, because he wishes to point out ironically the absurdity of what happened.

The first stanza gives a close-up of the battle and the dead boy and introduces the essential fact of his death. The middle two stanzas describe some of the background information on the boy and what happened to him; the second stanza stresses his unimportance in the world of important people, and the third stanza presents the casual effect of the character of his death. The last stanza analyzes why it happened and asserts the pointlessness of it all. The title, exaltedly in Latin, further emphasizes the remoteness of the course of events from this innocent, kissable boy.

The vocabulary is popular and the images are, at times, rural: "scythed . . . grasses," "tweed cap." The metaphors are predictable: money and gold to represent the business interests supporting the cost of the war; factory, restaurant, hotel to represent the social system; olive trees and spring hill-side to indicate Spain; guns and lead, the fallen tweed cap, the mowing down of grass, flags, and leaves, and the boy's death to show aspects of the war. Ironically, Spender uses investment terminology of gain and loss to express what happened to this young soldier: "money's ultimate reason," "gold sunk deep as a well," "valueless," "was so much expenditure justified." Such terms are a far cry from his uncomplicated life. There are no clues to the identity of the boy; he is just another innocent victim. We are not told which war or when, although "olive trees" clearly suggest Spain and the poem appears in his "Poems about the Spanish Civil War—1936-1939." On the contrary, Spender presents it as a personal tragedy. It is a rhetorical and subjective poem depending mostly on Spender's attitude. The abstraction of the poem suggests that the poet was not physically involved in the war.

The tone of the poem is important. Not much happens quantitatively, but Spender sustains a relentless mood of irony.

TWO ARMIES [21]

1   Deep in the winter plain, two armies
      Dig their machinery, to destroy each other.
      Men freeze and hunger. No one is given leave
      On either side, except the dead, and wounded.

5   These have their leave; while new battalions wait
    On time at last to bring them violent peace.

    All have become so nervous and so cold
    That each man hates the cause and distant words
    That brought him here, more terribly than bullets.
10 Once a boy hummed a popular marching song,
    Once a novice hand flapped their salute;
    The voice was choked, the lifted hand fell,
    Shot through the wrist by those of his own side.

    From their numb harvest, all would flee, except
15 For discipline drilled once in an iron school
    Which holds them at the point of the revolver.
    Yet when they sleep, the images of home
    Ride wishing horses of escape
    Which herd the plain in a mass unspoken poem.

20 Finally, they cease to hate: for although hate
    Bursts from the air and whips the earth with hail
    Or shoots it up in fountains to marvel at,
    And although hundreds fall, who can connect
    The inexhaustible anger of the guns
25 With the dumb patience of those tormented
        animals?

    Clean silence drops at night, when a little walk
    Divides the sleeping armies, each
    Huddled in linen woven by remote hands.
    When the machines are stilled, a common suffering
30 Whitens the air with breath and makes both one
    As though these enemies slept in each other's arms.

    Only the lucid friend to aerial raiders
    The brilliant pilot moon, stares down
    Upon this plain she makes a shining bone
35 Cut by the shadows of many thousand bones.
    Where amber clouds scatter on No-Man's-Land
    She regards death and time throw up
    The furious words and minerals which destroy.
                                    —Stephen Spender

Written in an even more somber tone than "Ultima Ratio Regum," though similarly ironic, "Two Armies" is a sobering poem about two opposing armies during wartime. It breaks down romantic illusions. It is not just against the Spanish Civil War but against all war; the same general condemnation of war was present in "Ultima Ratio Regum."

There is an unusual number of monosyllabic words in the poem, which accelerate the beat. It is simply expressed, clear, and direct, but its war dissent is hardly simplistic.

To analyze the poem systematically: it takes place in winter. The two armies are there "to destroy each other," "destroy" having strong emotional connotations. The discomfort of war is stressed, "men freeze and hunger." Ironically, Spender notes: "No one is given leave/. . . except the dead, and wounded." He adds, bitterly, that new battalions will replace them, providing "violent peace" for recently-removed souls.

In stanza two the men are still uncomfortable and tense. Curiously and unfairly, those who caused and planned the war are not the same as those who fight it. Those distant manipulators with their political propaganda have become anathema. The victims sound so innocent: one who "hummed a marching song" and another who saluted. Being shot by happenstance by those of his side (politically) is one of the hazards of war. There is, perhaps, another explanation. Spender has objected to the ruthless methods communists used to maintain superiority and to force men to stay in the line, among which firing on a "comrade" was not unknown. The poem may refer to deliberate firing upon a fellow-soldier who wished to desert.

In stanza three the metaphor for war is "numb harvest," numb both psychologically because war is an ordeal, and physically because the weather is cold. This so-called harvest produces not crops, except in the minds of the perverted, but discomfort, suffering, and death. The soldiers do not run and go AWOL, because they are trained and guarded by severe taskmasters. Only during sleep do they give vent to their real desires for escape—which, in their waking moments, remain "a mass unspoken poem." Finally, they become senseless of their hate for their enemy as well as for the cause in which they must fight. They are "tormented animals" and their numbness and servility (as opposed to the tyranny of their leaders and discipline) reveal themselves in a "dumb patience."

At night nothing less ethereal than silence and sleep separates the enemy armies. They seem small and dependent, "huddled in linen woven by remote hands." The affectionate concern of others for them is far removed.

Stanza five describes enemy forces resting at night only a few yards apart:

> When the machines are stilled, a common suffering
> Whitens the air with breath and makes both one
> As though these enemies slept in each other's arms.

Wartime enemies are practically indistinguishable in their "common suffering." The exigencies of war act as a kind of neutralizing agent, or common enemy, and create a bond between combatants on both sides. These men "cease to hate" and like "tormented animals" practice a "dumb patience" while waiting for the fighting to end. This is the sadness which men at war share.

The final stanza introduces the moon as illuminator and spectator. She (the moon) is personified as watching while "death and time," those ubiquitous, omnipotent forces, emit "the furious words and minerals which destroy." Here we have repetition of the word, "destroy," used with the same strong effect as in the second line except that it reverberates in its final position. We may assume that minerals in the right combination comprise the "machinery" of destruction used in war. And the poem ends on that note.

Spender is antiromantic on the subject of war and sees none of its heroism. Here again (as in "Ultima Ratio Regum") the armies and individuals are anonymous. His points are all negative. His sense of the irretrievable loss during war is universal, rather than limited to a specific war. He has deep pity for the victims of war, the weak and unheroic, and sympathizes here with the dispirited volunteers. Spender considers the ironic notion that it is a struggle they would gladly abandon if they could. His concern for innocent and common people extends to a feeling for all men who become involved in a war without realizing all the implications and contingencies, and who would get out of it if they possibly could. The defeatist sentiments are probably thinly veiled references to what Spender considered the communist strangle hold on the Republican army, although they are applicable to any war.

TO A SPANISH POET [22]
(To Manuel Altolaguirre)

1   You stared out of the window on the emptiness
       Of a world exploding;
       Stones and rubble thrown upwards in a fountain
       Blown to one side by the wind.
5   Every sensation except being alone
       Drained out of your mind.
       There was no fixed object for the eye to fix on.
       You became a child again
       Who sees for the first time how the worst things
          happen.

10   Then, stupidly, the stucco pigeon
       On the gable roof that was your ceiling,
       Parabolized before the window
       Uttering (you told me later!) a loud coo.
       Alone to your listening self, you told the joke.
15   Everything in the room broke.
       But you remained whole,
       Your own image unbroken in your glass soul.

       Having heard this all from you, I see now
       —White astonishment haloing irises
20   Which still retain in their centres
       Black laughter of black eyes.
       Laughter reverberant through stories
       Of an aristocrat lost in the hills near Malaga
       Where he had got out of his carriage
25   And, for a whole week, followed, on foot, a
          partridge.

Stories of that general, broken-hearted
Because he'd failed to breed a green-eyed bull.

But reading the news, my imagination breeds
The penny-dreadful fear that you are dead.

30   Well, what of this journalistic dread?

Perhaps it is we—the living—who are dead
We of a world that revolves and dissolves
While we set the steadfast corpse under the earth's
    lid.
The eyes push irises above the grave
35   Reaching to the stars, which draw down nearer,
Staring through a rectangle of night like black
    glass,
Beyond these daylight comedies of falling plaster.

Your heart looks through the breaking ribs—
Oiled axle through revolving spokes.
40   Unbroken blood of the swift wheel,
You stare through centrifugal bones
Of the revolving and dissolving world.
                      —Stephen Spender

This third poem by Spender is more objective than the other two in the sense that it deals with its subject more specifically. It is localized in its dedication to the Spanish poet Manuel Altolaguirre, to whom the "you" of the poem refers.

In the first stanza Altolaguirre is looking out his window during wartime. The metaphor which compares his sensitivity to that of a child "Who sees for the first time how the worst things happen" is apt. War is exaggeratedly dreadful and as remote to the uninitiated as evil is to the innocent.

In stanza two the stucco pigeon that fell from the roof uttered "a loud coo." Spender injects parenthetically that the Spanish poet had told him so, lending support to the validity of the anecdote.[23] His soul of glass suggests the fragility of life and of all things in such an environment, though he had managed to survive that particular holocaust. Prior to the massive bombings of World

War II, the attacks on Spanish cities were the largest and deadliest the world had yet seen.

Spender claims to have described the situation as the Spaniard had explained it to him, and then proceeds to describe the man himself:

> —White astonishment haloing irises
> Which still retain in their centres
> Black laughter of black eyes.

The laughter originates from several more anecdotes allegedly told in his presence: one concerns "an aristocrat lost in the hills near Malaga" during an unlikely mission in pursuit of a partridge. The other mocks a general, saddened by his failure to breed a green-eyed bull. Both of these absurd quests appear grotesque amid the real trials and contingencies of war.

Spender now reverts to the present, the three prior stanzas having referred to the past. This two-line stanza followed by a single line stanza adds a certain immediacy to the poem. Spender has been reading newspapers, most likely tabloids. These would have dramatized events and cost about a penny each in the 1930s. Their sensationalism would exploit the dangers of the war scene and remind Spender of the likelihood of his friend's death.

It is at this point that Spender becomes more philosophical: "Well, what of this journalistic dread?"—journalistic in the sense that it resulted from a newspaper.

In the penultimate stanza, the notion that it is the living who are dead recalls those living dead, laden with money, in "Ultima Ratio Regum." He qualifies the death by characterizing a disintegrating world, reminiscent of Yeats' prediction in "The Second Coming." The imagery in this stanza is extended and complex. Spender suggests our responsibility for the present crisis: "we set the steadfast corpse under the earth's lid." The world resurrects to the level of its irises. "Irises" offers a double entendre, being the colored portion of the eye surrounding the pupil, as well as the name of a plant and flower. The stars gaze through the "rectangle of night like black glass" to meet the staring eyes. "Rectangle" suggests the shape of a coffin and, otherwise, seems an unlikely choice for the description of night. There is something sinister in characterizing the holocaust of war as "daylight comedies of falling plaster." Perhaps the hope lies in the possible recovery of a world not completely underground. Its "steadfast corpse" indicates durability.

The final stanza is rather anatomical. The heart is literally encased beneath the ribs. It is Altolaguirre's heart that "looks through the breaking ribs." Spender envisions this as "oiled axle through revolving spokes." "Unbroken" in reference to blood seems a mixed image since blood is liquid and not to be broken. It likely implies that the flow of blood is uninterrupted. The wheel is analogous to the rib cage and comprised of the axle and spokes. Again Altolaguirre is staring. In the first line of the poem he stares through a window, and this time through his ribs, "centrifugal bones." "The revolving and dissolving world" is an expansion upon the body/wheel imagery and a further indication of Spender's penchant for machine terminology. The poem appeals mostly to the sense of sight.

The incident on which the poem was based was not particularly significant to Altolaguirre, who had played it down ("I have been too ashamed to tell about the air raid"—p. 263 of *World Within World*). But the story captured Spender's imagination or, at least, appealed to him as a vehicle through which to honor his friend, about whom he obviously cared (". . . my imagination breeds/ The penny-dreadful fear that you are dead").

Muriel Rukeyser was born in New York City in 1913, at the beginning of World War I.[24] She entered Vassar College in the fall of 1930, and before she left in 1932 had written what has been called a "painfully mature" poem, "Effort at Speech Between Two People." In December of 1932 she became literary editor of the *Student Review*, a left-wing publication aimed toward undergraduate consumption.

She was urban-oriented, aware of what was happening, liberal, revolutionary (in spirit), strong minded, and Jewish. She associated with no group of radical poets like that of Auden, Lewis, Spender, and others in England. Her poetic interests and moods, often highly subjective, extended to social, political, and scientific themes. Besides being a poet of the proletariat, she has been a journalist, translator, prose writer (biographies, short stories, children's books, essays), and teacher.

In the spring of 1935, she became associate editor of *New Theatre* magazine, leaving this post the following summer. That same year her first volume of poetry, *Theory of Flight,* was chosen for the Yale Series of Younger Poets, an annual contest sponsored by Yale University Press. The poetry shows her power of expression, strong technique, and rebellious nature. Some critics accused her of "striving for effect" but they were agreed that the twenty-one-year-old had real inventiveness and wisdom to speak her politics "like a poet." [25] In *Theory of Flight,* she portrayed youth as rebelling against the older generation and its tradition. The meaning may be obscure, but the language is unadorned and often simplified to the rhythm of actual speech:

> One day we voted on whether he was Hamlet
> or whether he was himself and yesterday
> I cast the deciding vote to renounce our mouths.
> > (from II. "The Committee-
> > Room," *Theory of Flight*)

The style is swift, abrupt, and syncopated, in keeping with the disrupted world of the thirties and its technological progress:

> Master in the plane shouts "Contact"   :
> master on the ground: "Contact!"
> > he looks up : "Now?" whispering : "Now."
> > "Yes," she says. "Do."
> > Say yes, people.
> > Say yes.
> > YES
> >
> > > (ending of "Theory of
> > > Flight," *Theory of Flight*)

The force and intensity of flight (of an airplane) symbolizes the energy of all powerful machines. The impression of the work is emotional and affirmative.

Rukeyser, who had undergone the disappointments and tor-

tured doubts of the 1930s, including the Depression, had succeeded
in enlarging her strength of purpose and the scope of her poetry.
Having glimpsed the collapsed prosperity of the Depression generation, she enlisted in the cultural movement of the Left.

Life and Letters Today, the London magazine, sent her in the
fall of 1936 to Spain to cover the first People's Olympiad, proposed
as an anti-Nazi celebration of workers' sports clubs of Europe and
America and an active retort to Hitler's Olympics. She arrived by
train with a group of antifascist Olympic participants at the outbreak of the Spanish Civil War, and was evacuated on July 25,
1936. Of her Spanish visit, she later wrote: "I crossed the frontier
into Spain on the first day of the war, and stayed long enough to
see Catalonia win its own war and make peace, a peace that could
not be held." [26] Before her return to the States, she worked with
the Spanish Medical Bureau. She, later, described the Spanish
Loyalists as being "weaponless against what must have seemed
like the thunder and steel of the whole world." [27]

After Spain, she explored U.S. Highway 1 from Maine southward. The title of her second book of poems, *U.S. 1,* was derived
from the federal highway that runs from Maine to Florida. Its first
section, "Book of the Dead," appeared in the late spring of 1938.
It was originally conceived as part of a long, poetical evaluation
of the Atlantic Coast, from Maine to Key West. Having been
criticized for too much intensity, emotionality, and even melodrama, here she tended to objectify her feelings.

U.S. 1 reveals her assimilation of such influences as Hart Crane
and W. H. Auden. Her diction is condensed, and her presentation
of factual data somewhat dramatic.

A Turning Wind, her third volume, revealed further progress
in her intentness and originality. Written between her twenty-
third and twenty-fifth years, the book indicates continuing growth
and complexity. From the simple form of declaration in the common phrases of urban speech of her earlier poetry, she developed
a gnarled, intellectual, almost private observation. In her earlier
verse, the poetic images were few and simple; in her later works,
images became those of a psychologist or a surrealist—ubiquitous,
charged with meaning, and increasingly complicated. Some critics
complained of the complexities of *A Turning Wind:* abrupt

changes of tense and action, overcrowded lines, fragmentary phrases and half-sentences, inexactness of pronominal references, too swiftly juxtaposed images, and allusive symbols. They criticized her "baffling style" and the uncertainties of her "metaphysical soul-searching," stressing that communication is essential for the social poet. However, Rukeyser's poetry clearly shows strength of conviction and power of communication.

There are five long poems at the end of the volume, offering a kind of metaphysical soul-searching of a painter, a poet, a mathematician, a musician, and an agitator.

Rukeyser finished *A Turning Wind* on September 1, 1939, at a time when world peace was a far-off possibility. She said of the poems that they projected "some of the valid sources of power which have come down to us." [28]

Instinctively pacifistic, she was against everything in any organization which represented the brutal life of enforced regimentation and national slavery. She was against war, conscription, and the forcing of others into war. "M-Day's Child is Fair of Face" (from *A Turning Wind*) contains the particular theme of the menaced child within a broader denunciation of military horror in general:

> M-Day's child is fair of face,
> Drill-day's child is full of grace,
> Gun-day's child is breastless and blind,
> Shell-day's child is out of its mind,
> Bomb-day's child will always be dumb,
> Cannon-day's child can never quite come,
> but the child that's born on the Battle-day
> is blithe and bonny and rotted away.

Her attitude was antiwar, but she knew what she had to fight; she was unconditionally pledged to oppose Hitlerism and preserve civil liberties. She remembered the poet Lorca, who could have been murdered by both sides—who figuratively was, since neither could protect him.

In the midst of desperate remedies and clamoring negatives, she affirmed the life of people and the life of poetry—the life of the spirit which makes possible the creative life which was at once an answer to the problem of living slavery and to the wish for quick escape, comforting death. She asserted:

> that climax when the brain acknowledges the world,
> all values extended into the blood awake.
>> (from "Reading Time: 1 minute 26
>> seconds," *A Turning Wind*, p. 43)

Having been criticized for the objectification of social data in the poem *U.S. 1*, she made the symbols in *A Turning Wind* strong and evocative, when, for example, expressing the concept of death:

> This was their art: a wall daubed like a face,
> a penis or finger dipped in a red pigment.
>> (from "Third Elegy. The Fear of
>> Form," *A Turning Wind*, p. 24)

It became evident in the late Thirties that the "revolution" was a lost cause. While the movement slackened and its influence diminished, its partisans were thrown into even greater despair by the spectacle of an appeasement policy on the part of great nations that violated every tenet of progress. In the face of this, Rukeyser achieved perhaps her finest sequence of poems—the five elegies that begin the volume *A Turning Wind*. These poems showed an authority superior to all that she had done before. She had come to terms with tragedy:

> Rejecting the subtle and contemplative minds
> as being too thin in the bone; and the gross thighs
> and unevocative hands fail also. But the poet
> and his wife, those who say Survive, remain;
> and those two who were with me on the ship
> leading me to the sum of the years, in Spain.
>
> When you have left the river you will hear the war.
> In the mountains, with tourists, in the insanest groves
> the sound of kill, the precious face of peace.
> And the sad frightened child, continual minor,
> returns, nearer whole circle, O and nearer

all that was loved, the lake, the naked river,
what must be crossed and cut out of your heart,
what must be stood beside and straightly seen.

> (from "First Elegy. Rotten
> Lake," *A Turning Wind*, p. 16)

The Soul and Body of John Brown was published in 1941. A biography of the scientist Willard Gibbs was published a year later. *Beast in View* came out in 1944, and *The Green Wave*, a year later. This last work represented a change toward impersonality. She presented herself and love affairs in unusually abstract terms:

The motive of all of it was loneliness,
All the panic encounters and despair
Were bred in fear of the lost night, apart,
Outlined by pain, alone. Promiscuous
As mercy. Fear-led and led again to fear
At evening toward the cave where part fire, part
Pity lived in that voluptuousness
To end one and begin another loneliness.

> (from "The motive of all
> of it," *The Green Wave*, 1948)

In 1949 came *Orpheus*. If the *Elegies* (1957) stresses outrage, *Orpheus* affirms possibility:

To live and begin again.
The body alive and offering,
whole, up and alive,
and to all men, man and woman,
and to all the unborn,
the mouth shall sing
music past wounding
and the song begin:
. . . sing/creation not yet come.

> (ending of *Orpheus*)

This is an allegory of poetic love; the poet is a prototype of humanity. The death of Orpheus is creative in effect, for from this death comes the birth of the god.

The Life of Poetry (1949) is an essay speaking for the interrelations of poetry and other disciplines, including science, and for the linkings of imagination. *Body of Waking* (1949) includes the long poem, "Suite for Lord Timothy Dexter," a ballad celebrating the life and fortune of a famous New England eccentric. It also includes translations from the Spanish of Octavio Paz. Translations of his poems were published further in *Selected Poems of Octavio Paz* and in *Sun Stone*. The poems in *Elegies* (1957) are general and cosmic in their reference, brooding upon the confusion and bitterness of human fate, attempting finally to arrive at some affirmation of hope within despair. Other of her writings include *Selected Poems* (1951) and *One Life* (1957), a biography, dealing with the American conflict as seen in the life of Wendell Willkie. That same year she also published a biography of Houdini.

In 1960 *The Speed of Darkness* was published, followed the next year by three works: *Colors of the Day* (a play), *The Speaking Tree*, and *Poems Selected and New*. *Waterlily Fire* came out in 1962. Rukeyser collaborated with Leif Sjoberg in translating poems of Gunnar Ekelöf. *The Orgy*, a voyage of discovery by a few people on the west coast of Ireland, was published in 1965. She has also written children's books: *Come Back, Paul* (1955), and *I Go Out* (1961).

I have chosen for analysis the following three poems in which Rukeyser alludes to the Spanish Civil War: "Mediterranean," published in *New Masses* magazine in 1937, celebrated her timely arrival in Barcelona; "Third Elegy. The Fear of Form"; and "Nuns in the Wind," the last two published in *A Turning Wind* (1939).

MEDITERRANEAN [29]

On the evening of July 25, 1936, five days after the outbreak of the Spanish Civil War, the Americans with the antifascist Olympic games were evacuated from Barcelona at the order of the Catalonian government. In a small Spanish boat, the

Ciudad di Ibiza, which the Belgians had chartered, they and a group of five hundred, including the Hungarian and Belgian teams as well as the American, sailed overnight to Sete, the first port in France. The only men who remained were those who had volunteered in the loyalist forces: the core of the future International Brigades.

I

1   At the end of July, exile. We watched the
          gangplank go
      cutting the boat away, indicating: sea.
      Barcelona, the sun, the fire-bright harbor, war.
      Five days.

5   Here at the rail, foreign and refugee,
      we saw the city, remembered that zero of attack,
      chase in the groves, snares through the olive hills,
      rebel defeat: leaders, two regiments,
      broadcasts of victory, tango, surrender.
10   The truckride to the city, barricades,
      bricks pried at corners, rifle-shot in street,
      car-burning, bombs, blank warnings, fists up, guns
      busy sniping, the torn walls, towers of smoke.
      And order making, committees taking charge,
          foreigners
15   commanded out by boat.

      I saw the city, sunwhite flew on glass,
      trucewhite from window, the personal lighting
          found
      eyes on the dock, sunset-lit faces of singers,
      eyes, goodbye into exile. Saw where Columbus rides
20   black-pillared: discovery, turn back, explore
      a new-found Spain, coast-province, city-harbor.
      Saw our parades ended, the last marchers on board
      listed by nation.

      I saw first of those faces going home into war
25   the brave man, Otto Boch, the German exile,
          knowing

he quieted tourists during machine-gun battle,
he kept his life straight as a single issue—
left at that dock we left, his gazing Breughel face,
square forehead and eyes, strong square breast
    fading,
30   the narrow runner's hips diminishing dark.
I see this man, dock, war, a latent image.

The boat *Ciudad di Ibiza,* built for two hundred,
loaded with five hundred, manned by loyal sailors,
chartered by Belgians when consulates were
    helpless,
35   through a garden of gunboats, margin of the port,
entered: Mediterranean.

II

Frontier of Europe, the tideless sea, a field of power
touching desirable coasts, rocking in time
   conquests,
fertile, the moving water maintains its boundaries,
40   layer on layer, Troy-seven civilized worlds,
Egypt, Greece, Rome, jewel Jerusalem,
giant feudal Spain, giant England, this last war.

The boat pulled into evening, underglaze blue
flared instant fire, blackened towards Africa.
45   Over the city alternate light occurred;
                    and pale
in the pale sky emerging stars.
No city now, a besieged line of light
masking the darkness where the country lay,
but we knew guns
50   bright through mimosa
singe of powder
and reconnoitering plane
flying anonymous
scanning the Pyrenees
55   tall black above the Catalonian sea.

Boat of escape, dark on the water, hastening, safe,
holding non-combatants, the athlete, the child,
the printer, the boy from Antwerp, the black boxer,
lawyer and Communist.

60   The games had not been held.

A week of games, theater and festival;
world anti-fascist week. Pistol starts race.
Machine-gun marks the war. Answered unarmed,
charged the Embarcadero, met those guns.

65   And charging through the province, joined that
                  army.
Boys from the hills, the unmatched guns,
the clumsy armored cars.
Drilled in the bullring. Radio cries:
To Saragossa! And this boat.

70   Escape, dark on the water, an overloaded ship.
Crowded the deck. Spoke little. Down to dinner.
Quiet on sea: no guns.
The printer said, In Paris there is time,
but where's its place now; where is poetry?

75   This is the sea of war; the first frontier
blank on the maps, blank sea; Minoan boats
maybe achieved this shore;
mountains whose slope divides
one race, old insurrections, Narbo, now

80   moves at the colored beach
destroyer, wardog. "Do not burn the church,
companeros, it is beautiful. Besides,
it brings tourists." They smashed only the image
madness and persecution.

85   Exterminating wish; they forced the door,
lifted the rifle, broke the garden window,
removed only the drawings: cross and wrath.
Whenever we think of these, the poem is,
that week, the beginning, exile

90   remembered in continual poetry.

Voyage and exile, a midnight cold return,
dark to our left mountains begin the sky.
There, pointed the Belgian, I heard a pulse of war,
sharp guns while I ate grapes in the Pyrenees.
95   Alone, walking to Spain, the five o'clock of war.
In those cliffs run the sashed and sandaled men,
capture the car, arrest the priest, kill captain,
fight our war.
The poem is the fact, memory falls
100   under and seething lifts and will not pass.

Here is home-country, who fights our war.
Street-meeting speaker to us:

                       ". . . came for games,
    you stay for victory; foreign? your job is:
    go tell your countries what you saw in Spain."
105   The dark unguarded army left all night.
M. de Paiche said, "We can learn from Spain."
The face on the dock that turned to find the war.

III

Seething, and falling black, a sea of stars,
black marked with virile silver. Peace all night,
110   over that land, planes
death-lists—a frantic bandage
the rubber tires burning—monuments,
sandbag, overturned wagon, barricade
girl's hand with gun—food failing, water failing
115   the epidemic threat
the date in a diary—a blank page opposite
no entry—
however, met
the visible enemy heroes: madness, infatuation
120   the cache in the crypt, the breadline shelled,
the yachtclub arsenal, the foreign check.
History racing from an assumed name, peace,
a time used to perfect weapons.

If we had not seen fighting
125   if we had not looked there
            the plane flew low
            the plaster ripped by shot
            the peasant's house
        if we had stayed in our world
130   between the table and the desk
        between the town and the suburb
        slow disintegration
        male and female
        If we had lived in our cities
135   sixty years might not prove
            the power this week
            the overthrown past
            tourist and refugee
        Emeric in the bow speaking his life
140   and the night on this ship
        and the night over Spain
        quick recognition
        male and female

        And the war in peace, the war in war, the peace,
145   the face on the dock
        the faces in those hills.

        IV

        Near the end now, morning. Sleepers cover the
            decks,
        cabins full, corridors full of sleep. But the light
        vitreous, crosses water; analyzed darkness
150   crosshatched in silver, passes up the shore,
        touching limestone massif, deserted tableland,
        bends with the down-warp of the coastal plain.

        The colored sun stands on the route to Spain,
        builds on the waves a series of mirrors
155   and on the scorched land rises hot.
        Coasts change their names as the boat goes to

France, Costa Brava softens to Cote Vermeil,
Spain's a horizon ghost behind the shapeless sea.

160   Blue praising black, a wind above the waves
moves pursuing a jewel, this hieroglyph
boat passing under the sun to lose it on the
attractive sea, habitable and old.
A barber sun, razing three races; met
from the north with a neurotic eagerness.

165   They rush to the solar attraction; local daybreak
         finds
them on the red earth of the colored cliffs; the
         little islands
tempt worshipers, gulf-purple, pointed bay;
we crowd the deck,
welcome the islands with a sense of loss.

V

170   The wheel in the water, green, behind my head.
Turns with its light-spokes. Deep. And the
         drowning eyes
find under the water figures near
in their true picture, moving true,
the picture of that war enlarging clarified
175   as the boat perseveres away, always enlarging,
to become clear.

Boat of escape, your water-photograph.
I see this man, dock, war, a latent image.
And at my back speaking the black boxer,
180   telling his education: porter, fighter, no school,
no travel but this, the trade union sent a team.
I saw Europe break apart
and artifice or martyr's will
cannot anneal this war, nor make
185   the loud triumphant future start
shouting from its tragic heart.

Deep in the water the Spanish shadows turn,
assume their brightness past a cruel lens,
quick vision of loss. The pastoral lighting takes
190   the boat, deck, passengers, the pumice cliffs,
the winedark sweatshirt at my shoulder.
Cover away the fighting cities
but still your death-afflicted eyes
must hold the print of flowering guns,
195   bombs whose insanity craves size,
the lethal breath, the iron prize.

The clouds upon the water-barrier pass,
the boat may turn to land; these shapes endure,
rise up into our eyes, to bind
200   us back; an accident of time
set it upon us, exile burns it in.
Once the fanatic image shown,
enemy to enemy,
past and historic peace wear thin;
205   hypocrite sovereignties go down
before this war the age must win.

VI

The sea produced that town: Sète, which the boat
     turns to,
at peace. Its breakwater, casino, vermouth factory,
     beach.
They searched us for weapons. No currency went
     out.
210   The sign of war was the search for cameras,
pesetas and photographs go back to Spain,
the money for the army. Otto is fighting now, the
     lawyer said.
No highlight hero. Love's not a trick of light.
But.—The town lay outside, peace, France.
215   And in the harbor the Russian boat Schachter;
sharp paint-smell, the bruise-colored shadow swung
under its side. Signaling to our decks

sailors with fists up, greeting us, asking news,
making the harbor real.
Barcelona.

220   Slow-motion splash. Anchor. Small from the beach
the boy paddles to meet us, legs hidden in canoe,
curve of his blade that drips.
Now gangplank falls to dock.
Barcelona

everywhere, Spain everywhere, the cry of planes for
    Spain.

225   The picture at our eyes, past memory, poems,
to carry and spread and daily justify.
The single issue, the live man standing tall,
on the hill, the dock, the city, all the war.
Exile and refugee, we land, we take

230   nothing negotiable out of the new world;
we believe, we remember, we saw.
Mediterranean gave
image and peace, tideless for memory.

For that beginning

235   make of us each
a continent and inner sea
Atlantis buried outside
to be won.

"Mediterranean," divided into six sections of free verse, considers the Spanish Civil War from a rather special point of view.
It is presented in the first person and autobiographically. As the
prose narrative preceding the poem explains, Rukeyser was evacuated from Barcelona and Spain along with other Americans
connected with the antifascist Olympic games by order of the
Catalonian government. The poem vivifies that departure. Barcelona was five days into the war. Rukeyser reviews the excitement
and other emotions of those first chaotic days: ". . . barricades,/
bricks pried at corners, rifle-shot in street,/ car-burning, bombs,
blank warnings, fists up, guns/busy sniping, the torn walls, towers
of smoke." The first part ends with the boarding by 500 escaping

foreigners onto a boat built to contain 200 passengers, *Ciudad di Ibiza*. Ironically, it was not the consulates who were able to arrange and execute the departure, but the Belgians. The poet speaks feelingly of Otto Boch: "I see this man, dock, war, a latent image." The poet looks upon the recent past nostalgically.

The second section describes the Mediterranean by reviewing its past. She provides information about the circumstances of the ordered departure, the passengers, and the "world anti-fascist week," which had been canceled:

> . . . of escape, dark on the water, hastening, safe,
> holding non-combatants, the athlete, the child,
> the printer, the boy from Antwerp, the black boxer,
> lawyer and Communist.
>   The games had not been held.

In contrast to a pistol shot which announces the beginning of a race, machine-gun fire attended the war. With gunfire in the distance, those to leave the country were advised: "go tell your countries what you saw in Spain."

Part III again evokes the fighting. The five days had been world-shaking: "the power this week/the overthrown past/ tourist and refugee."

The ship, having left Barcelona around midnight, the scene the following morning was: "Sleepers cover the decks,/cabins full, corridors full of sleep." The Costa Brava becomes the Cote Vermeil: "Spain's a horizon ghost behind the shapeless sea." As they approach some little islands, emotions are ambivalent: "welcome the islands with a sense of loss." As distance from Spain increases, the war can be focused more clearly.

In Part VI the boat is ready to dock at the peaceful French city of Sete. The passengers are searched for cameras, pesetas, and photographs—to be confiscated and sent back to Spain. With nostalgic memories of Spain, they go forth, taking with them nothing that might prove useful to the Republic:

> For that beginning
> make of us each

a continent and inner sea
Atlantis buried outside
to be won.

Atlantis, the mythical island or continent located in the Atlantic Ocean, west of Gibraltar, was purported to have sunk. A free Spain, the Republic of the Loyalists, was something to be sought, won, and prized. The lines are reminiscent of Donne's "no man is an island unto itself," with very similar implications.

Rukeyser is sensitive to the lighting of the sea and harbor under both sun and moonlight. She notices the light reflected off people as well:

I saw the city, sunwhite flew on glass,
trucewhite from window, the personal lighting found
eyes on the dock, sunset-lit faces of singers,
eyes, goodbye into exile.

She also notices the smoke above the city.

She emphasizes with metaphors the contrast between her safe retreat to the Pyrenees and the war below: "I heard a pulse of war,/ sharp guns while I ate grapes in the Pyrenees."

Part II begins with a description of stars. In Part IV the lighting again is paramount in her observation:

But the light
vitreous, crosses water; analyzed darkness
crosshatched in silver, passes up the shore,
touching limestone massif, deserted tableland,
bends with the down-warp of the coastal plain.

Sights and sounds converge in poetic expression of her Spanish experience. The colored sun stands on the route to Spain, builds on the waves a series of mirrors, and rises on the scorched land.

She frequently brings in color: "Blue praising black, a wind . . ." and "local daybreak finds/them on the red earth of the colored cliffs."

In the final stanza of the poem, Atlantis is the metaphor for Spain, offering a remote repository of hope.

Grammatically, there is a frequent absence of verbs. An example of her telegraphic style occurs in Part III:

> . . . Peace all night,
> over that land, planes
> death-lists—a frantic bandage
> the rubber tires burning—monuments,
> sandbag, overturned wagon, barricade
> girl's hand with gun—food failing, water failing,
> the epidemic threat
> the data in a diary—a blank page opposite
> no entry—

Such sounds as those of broadcasts, music, rifle shots, bombs, and guns sniping abound. The machine-gun fire of war replaces the pistol shot initiating peacetime races. In Part II, "I heard a pulse of war." Later, as the anchor is thrown overboard, there is a "slow-motion splash." And, as they disembark, there is the "cry of planes for Spain," a plea repeated in her "Third Elegy." The unpreparedness of the Loyalists for war is stressed in the following imagery:

> Boys from the hills, the unmatched guns,
> the clumsy armored cars.
> Drilled in the bullring.

In wartime, poetry does not have top priority, and the poet asks: "Where is poetry?"

The tone of the poet is revealed somewhat in her calling herself an "exile and refugee." She had identified with the struggle and cause during her brief stay. The inclination of the Republic toward liberal reform would have matched her own. She was moved and felt somewhat guilty about eating grapes in the Pyrenees, simultaneously with the war below. Her description of Sete, "its break-water casino, vermouth factory, beach," also suggests her guilty conscience. She does not delude herself about its being an easy "escape." She was emotionally and philosophically, if not physically, involved: "we believe, we remember, we saw."

THIRD ELEGY. THE FEAR OF FORM [30]

Tyranny of method! The outrageous smile
seals the museums, pours a mob skidding
up to the formal staircase, stopped, mouths open.
And do they stare? They do.
At what? A sunset?

Blackness, obscurity, bravado were the three colors;
wit-play, movement, and wartime the three moments;
formal groups, fire, facility, the three hounds.

This was their art: a wall daubed like a face,
a penis or finger dipped in a red pigment.
The sentimental frown gave them their praise,
prized the wry color, the twisted definition,
and said, "You are right to copy."

But the car full of Communists put out hands and
    guns,
blew 1—2—3 on the horn before the
surrealist house, a spiral in Cataluña.

New combinations: set out materials now,
combine them again! the existence is the test.
What do you want? Lincoln blacking his lessons
in charcoal on an Indiana shovel?
or the dilettante, the impresario's beautiful skull
choosing the tulip crimson satin, the yellow satin
as the ballet dances its tenth time to the mirror?
Or the general's nephew, epaulets from birth,
run down the concourse, shouting Planes for Spain?

New methods, the staring circle given again
force, a phoenix of power, another Ancient
sits in his circle, while the plaster model
of an equation slowly rotates beneath him,
and all his golden compass leans.
Create an anti-sentimental : Sing!

"For children's art is not asylum art,
"there are these formal plays in living, for
"the equal triangle does not spell youth,
"the cube nor age, the sphere nor ever soul.
"Asylum art is never children's art.
"They cut the bones down, but the line remained.
"They cut the line for good, and reached the point
"blazing at the bottom of its night."

*

A man is walking, wearing the world, swearing
saying You damn fools come out into the open.
Whose dislocated wish? Whose terrors whine?
I'll fuse him straight.
The usable present starts my calendar.
Chorus of bootblacks, printers, collectors of shit.
Your witwork works, your artwork shatters, die.
Hammer up your abstractions. Divide, O zoo.
—He's a queer bird, a hero, a kangaroo.
What is he going to do?

He calls Rise out of cities, you memorable ghosts
scraps of an age whose choice is seen
to lie between evils. Dazzle-paint the rest,
it burns my eyes with its acetylene.
Look through the wounds, mystic and human fly,
you spiritual unicorn, you clew of eyes.

Ghosts to approach the blood in fifteen cities.
Did you walk through the walls of the Comtesse de
     Noailles?
Was there a horror in Chicago?
Or ocean? Or ditches at the road. Or France,
while bearing guarding shadowing painting in Paris,
Picasso like an ass Picasso like a dragon Picasso like a
romantic movement
and immediately after, stations of swastikas
Prague and a thousand boys swing circles clean
girls by the thousand curve their arms together

geometries of wire
the barbed, starred
Heil

Will you have capitals with their tarnished countesses
their varnished cemetery life
vanished Picassos
or clean acceptable Copenhagen
or by God a pure high monument
white yellow and red
up against Minnesota?

Does the sea permit its dead to wear jewels?

Flame, fusion, defiance are your three guards,
the sphere, the circle, the cluster your three guides,
the bare, the blond and the bland are your three
    goads.

Adam, Godfinger, only these contacts function:
light and the high accompanied design,
contact of points   the fusion say of sex
the atombuster too along these laws.
Put in a sphere, here, at the focal joint,
he said, put it in. The moment is arrangement.
Currents washed through it, spun, blew white,
fused.   For!   the sphere!   proving!

This was the nightmare of a room alone,
the posture of grave figure, finger on other head,
he puts the finger of power on him,
optic of grandiose delusion.
All you adjacent and contagious points,
make room for fusion; fall,
you monuments, snow on your heads,
your power, your pockets, your dead parts.

Standing at midnight corners under corner-lamps
we wear the coat and the shadow of the coat.
The mind sailing over a scene lets light arrive
conspicuous sunrise, the knotted smoke rising,

the world with all its signatures visible.
Play of materials in balance,
carrying the strain of a new process.
Of the white root, the nature of the base,
contacts, making an index.
And do they stare? They do.
Our needs, our violences.
At what? Contortion of body and spirit.
To fuse it straight.

—Muriel Rukeyser

"Third Elegy. The Fear of Form" is the third in a series of five elegies found in *A Turning Wind* (1939), probably modeled on Rilke's *Duino Elegies*. It is an elegy in the sense that it commemorates the war dead, presumably the Spanish Civil War dead in 1939, and in the broader sense of being a lyric-contemplative poem of deeply serious cast. Its title states that there is something to be feared in form. The form in question is symbolically represented as that of artworks but suggests further the state or shape of the world as the poet sees it. The art symbolizes reality, and the real world of 1939, as Rukeyser sees it, is dehumanized and horrible. As we are abruptly informed, the method of going about making the form is authoritarian and overbearing ("Tyranny of method!"). It suggests the attitude of dictators or storm troopers. The contemporary (1939) vista is presented symbolically as nightmare horror in a museum of art.

Rukeyser gives ironic emphasis to the fact that the viewers are not exposed to an ordinary sunset, but to: "Blackness, obscurity, bravado . . ./witplay, movement, and wartime . . ./formal groups, fire, facility," alliterations being common to the stanza. Each aspect of its "art" is expressed by a trinity of words. The spectators are impressionistically described in a state of flow and shock. The "outrageous smile" would belong, perhaps, to the guide of this exhibition; his expression is grossly inappropriate because there should be no pleasure amid the wreckage of war.

The art itself is strongly expressed: "a penis or finger dipped in a red pigment," the coloring matter being the blood of war. Again the "sentimental frown" refers to the tour leader's face which spouts praise for the show and encourages the artistically-inclined to imitate the works ("you are right to copy"). This has to be cynical and bitter. The poet elsewhere urges creativity: "new combinations," "new methods," "create an anti-sentimental : Sing!" And the poem itself is a living example of the destruction of traditional form in poetry and an assertion of individualism.

The art is genuine. One picture shows communists shooting their way through Cataluña. Like the poem, the house in the painting is transformed into a spiral surrealistically. The poem is most experimental (revolutionary for its time) in technique.

The poet or narrator asks what subject matter one might want if not this. The sentimentality of "Lincoln blacking his lessons in charcoal on an Indiana shovel"? That would be edifying but irrelevant. An even more superficial subject is suggested: "the dilettante, the impresario's beautiful skull," and others. These examples remind us of the aristocrat chasing a partridge and the general trying to breed a green-eyed bull in Spender's "To a Spanish Poet." They are far removed from the present tragedy and the tone of presentation is disdainful. The imagery is superficial and unreal with the showy, cheap satin in bright colors and the ballet arranged before a mirror. Even the shouts for "Planes for Spain" ring hollow when we learn that the shouter is running, hardly a dignified, serious, or effective framework for his request, and that he has gained his high position through nepotism.

What are needed are "new combinations," "new methods." "Anti-sentimental" plays upon its similarity to "anti-Semitism," a concept not foreign to the perpetrators of the Spanish Civil War. The song in quotes speaks grotesquely of the art at hand: asylum art in contrast to children's art. The art is appropriately antisentimental; the extremity of the subject matter could not be dealt with otherwise. The new methods are dehumanized, abstract, and geometrical: "They cut the bone down, but the line remained."

The theme is life and death. The death imagery is often black: "Blackness, obscurity," while the imagery of life refers to art and suggests flux and change.

The second part begins with a man, burdened by the world, but who has some perspective. The world is a shambles but he is ready to begin again with what is left: "The usable present starts my calendar." The so-called artists of the holocaust are defamed: "Chorus of bootblacks, printers, collectors of shit" and cursed ("die"). A jingle follows:

> Divide, O zoo.
> —He's a queer bird, a hero, a kangaroo.
> What is he going to do?

They are like wild animals and represent a kind of zoo in their colossal and diverse inhumanity. On the other hand, he is a type of savior, a hero. The vision out of which he commands the ghosts to rise is warlike in its facets: chaos ("clew"), destruction ("scraps"), "evils," "burns my eyes with its acetylene," and "wounds." The blood pervades a wide area ("the blood in fifteen cities"). The ghosts of those who died in the war are told "to approach" the destruction and to explain where they have been and what they have seen.

There is a predominantly "o" sound in this consideration of ghosts. Picasso, a staunch upholder of the Republic, is included. The Nazi "swastikas" and large numbers of disciplined youngsters crowd the forceful scene of war:

> geometries of wire
> the barbed, starred
> Heil.

The capitals of the world endure while their inhabitants are "tarnished," surely an ironic euphemism for what can happen. On the other hand, cemeteries are crowded and "varnished."

The irrelevance of the question, "Does the sea permit its dead to wear jewels?" is striking. A materialistic concern about the dead can only be bitter. Again we have triads of words:

> Flame, fusion, defiance are your three guards,
> the sphere, the circle, the cluster your three guides,
> the bare, the blond and the bland are your three
>   goads.

There is alliteration in each of these lines and the last words alliterate also. There is force in the laconic style.

The concepts are again abstract considerations of design: contacts, function, points, fusion, and arrangement. There is an analogy of these concepts to sex: "the fusion say of sex":

> Put in a sphere, here, at the focal joint,
> he said, put it in. The moment is arrangement.
> Currents washed through it, spun, blew white,
> fused. For! the sphere! proving!

The "say" is an attempt to be casual about something which obviously preoccupies Rukeyser. The masculine command in this sexual act proves his assertiveness, authority, force, and strength. These characteristics are those of activists in any sense and are not unrelated to wartime. Fusion at certain points suggests art work as well.

The last stanza describes destruction:

> . . . fall,
> you monuments, snow on your heads,
> your power, your pockets, your dead parts.

The viewers of this destruction ("Our needs, our violence./. . . contortion of body and spirit") try to make some sense out of it all ("To fuse it straight") The poet wants the relation of life (sex, art) to be clear and out in the open. She is for art that faces issues honestly. Realizing the meaningless violence—the death that pervades the world—we need to confront the antihuman terror. Her title is, therefore, ironic, since she wishes us *not* to fear form.

This is a thoughtful poem that frequently asks questions and demands rereadings. The dominant symbol is that of a kind of tour (journey) through the landscape of a museum, the subject matter of whose art results from the realities of war and the present state of ruin in the world. Life and death mingle in this highly serious poem. The poem represents, through the pretense of viewing paintings on the subject, a negative, depressing situation.

This surrealist poem is a conscious denial of objective reality (a kind of nihilism) through Rukeyser's extreme individualism. It is as if the poet were looking with contempt upon the exterior world, refusing to follow the contours of objects and the succession of events. Logical language proves inadequate to express alienation of sensations. As a result, there is disorder in the poem and the referents of the symbols are not always limited and clear. Rukeyser has deliberately destroyed traditional form in the poem. She is urging against "the fear of form." Form is a living, organic, dynamic principle, not a set of conventions or static achievements.

The poem is preoccupied with life and death and there is an effort to distort our focus upon the dehumanized figures involved. The poet blends the concrete with the abstract. The conciseness of the language lends itself to the emptiness and ruin of the landscape. It is a pessimistic poem, oriented toward the past, not the future.

The pervasive blood over the landscape recalls Hernández' "Recoged esta voz"; Hernández was twenty-seven and Rukeyser was twenty-six when they wrote their respective poems.

NUNS IN THE WIND [31]

As I came out of the New York Public Library
you said your influence on my style would be noticed
and from now on there would be happy poems.
              It was at that moment
the street was assaulted by a covey of nuns
going directly toward the physics textbooks.
Tragic fiascos shadowed that whole spring.
The children sang streetfuls, and I thought:
O to be the King in the carol
kissed and at peace; but recalling Costa Brava
the little blossoms in the mimosa tree
and later, the orange cliff, after they sent me out,
I knew there was no peace.
              You smiled, saying: Take it easy.

That was the year of the five-day fall of cities.
        First day, no writers. Second, no telephones.
        Third, no venereal diseases. Fourth, no income
        tax. And on the fifth, at noon.

The nuns blocked the intersections, reading.
I used to go walking in the triangle of park,
seeing that locked face, the coarse enemy skin,
the eyes with all the virtues of a good child,
but no child was there, even when I thought, Child!
The 4 a.m. cop could never understand.
You said, not smiling, You are the future for me,
but you were the present and immediate moment
and I am empty-armed without, until to me is given
two lights to carry: my life and the light of my death.

If the wind would rise, those black throbbing umbrellas
fly downstreet, the flapping robes unfolding,
my dream would be over, poisons cannot linger
when the wind rises. . . .

All that year, the classical declaration of war was lacking.
There was a lot of lechery and disorder.
And I am queen on that island.

Well, I said suddenly in the tall and abstract room,
time to wake up.
Now make believe you can help yourself alone.
And there it was, the busy crosstown noontime
crossing, peopled with nuns.
        Now, bragging now,
the flatfoot slambang victory,
           thanks to a trick of wind
will you see faces blow, and though their bodies
by God's grace will never blow,
cities shake in the wind, the year's over,
calendars tear, and their clothes blow. O yes!
                —Muriel Rukeyser

Rukeyser has looked at the Spanish Civil War in the way a North American poet can, and perhaps must—from a distance. What she has done in "Nuns in the Wind" is to combine memories of her personal life with civilian impressions about the war, and her free-verse poem is complex in symbolism. The scene opens at the New York Public Library. Curiously, the nuns "assault" the street before their visit to the library to secure physics books. Nuns travel in groups, "covey of nuns," and are a kind of dark manifestation associated with the church and alien to the life of the speaker (poet). Rukeyser can find escape in a library. Also, love and religion might help her create a dream world, but, nevertheless, she yearns for peace—her own and the world's—while absorbed by the dreadful reality of war: "O to be the King in the carol/kissed and at peace"; this King would be Jesus Christ, and her wish is wistful. This is wartime, and its contrast to peacetime is striking:

> but recalling Costa Brava
> the little blossoms in the mimosa tree
> and later, the orange cliff, after they sent me out,
> I knew there was no peace.

She had seen the difference in Spain at the time of her evacuation (1936) as well as later in New York, where she encountered "that locked face, the coarse enemy skin."

She is clearly against war. Her metaphor for the disruptive influence of war is understatedly sarcastic:

> That was the year of the five-day fall of cities.
> > First day, no writers. Second, no telephones.
> > Third, no venereal diseases. Fourth, no income
> > tax. And on the fifth, at noon.
> The nuns blocked the intersection, reading.

The "five-day fall of cities" refers to Spain, particularly. The abrupt shift to the nuns blends the not-so-remote war and the library experience. Reading may seem doubly impractical in the context of traffic and wartime, but they did succeed in interfering with the activity around them. Besides, it is physics that they choose to study—not anything emotional or idealistic. The nuns are both definite and vague and manage to block the speaker's desire. This is analogous to the balking of life by war. In a sense, the speaker's pleasure and happiness are part of this complex image. And they are being stymied by the accidental presence of nuns. It is a sort of nightmare vision.

The poet's male companion and lover had claimed he would have a happy influence upon her and her poetry, but the pessimistic times would not permit his effect to last. War pervades all as does the wind. Her lover could think in terms of their future, but Rukeyser was skeptical and, as it turned out, more realistic. There was only the here and the now and, in fact, she is without him and alone in the immediate present of (the writing of) the poem.

"All that year, the classical declaration of war was lacking," because although Germany and Italy were involved in the Spanish Civil War, no formal announcement was given.

The poet's sex life has been amplified by the war tension—perhaps through promiscuity, lack of inhibition, and experimentation:

> There was a lot of lechery and disorder.
> And I am queen on that island.

This queen is quite a switch from the previous King. The lack of classical declaration is related to the sense of disorder in her own life. Her being "queen on that island" on a personal level suggests further the disorder in the world. She reminds herself to awaken from the dream-like escape of sex.

The end of the poem with its wind imagery presents the revolutionary potential of the time. It has been a nightmarish vision which the wind could affect. The wind, transforming everything, could make a difference. Rukeyser names the poem after the vague nuns who are studious and gregarious. If the nuns could brag over a victory, they may represent the religious power that rooted Franco so firmly. The curious affirmation at the end of "O yes!" is surely another example of sarcasm. As time passes, the wind affects everything except (the bodies of) these sturdy nuns who are staunchly protected by God and whose repressed bodies are not

alive and would not be moved. But, still, there may be hope symbolized through the wind. The wind suggests, also, the passage of
time which may help: "cities shake in the wind, the year's over,/
calendars tear, and their clothes blow. O yes!"

Of the five English-writing poets under consideration, four supported the Republican side (to varying degrees), while one (Campbell) was firmly aligned with Franco, Roman Catholicism, and the
Nationalists. We would expect foreign poets to have a more international perspective on the war than Spanish and Latin-American
poets. At the same time, a dimension of intimate experience open
to Spaniards would not likely impress foreigners. Campbell had a
romantic love affair with the Spain of his choice during the Spanish
Civil War. He eulogized the Nationalists and defamed the Republicans. He took this extreme stand for the propagandistic purpose
of converting his readers to the fascist/Franco camp and of gloat-
ing over their victory. He also used the opportunity to harangue
about his own personal, poetic, and prophetic prowess, while chas-
tising such poets as Spender and Auden and the social basis of their
point of view. His involvement in the struggle probably came
about more because of a wish to defend himself and the Catholic
faith, and to castigate his literary enemies, than from his desire to
propound the merits of fascism (especially since he later fought
against the fascists in World War II). He saw the situation in absolute terms of Right and Wrong and expressed his view with confidence. While Campbell criticized the Republican side for false-
hoods ("For them the Lie, false Lenin's 'powerful arm,' "—p. 82),
Flowering Rifle would seem to be full of his own deliberate distortions and untruths. Campbell's style is grandiose with vigorous and
flamboyant rhetoric in keeping with his exaggerated thinking. In
view of the fascist victory (at least by the 1939 publication date),
it is not surprising to find his epic written in an attitude of opti-
mism and exuberance.

Of the poets discussed, Neruda, Felipe, MacDiarmid, and Campbell would appear to have the greatest egos, with Rukeyser a
close second. Like Neruda, Felipe, and MacDiarmid, Campbell
wrote in a stentorian voice. He, too, saw his role as poet-prophet,
but although their egos seem sturdy, Campbell's arrogance looms;

he pontificates. All poets writing about the Spanish Civil War were partisan, but Campbell presents the most absolute value judgments. While Neruda calls the Nationalists derogatory names like "jackals," Felipe, considering his partiality for the Republican side, is remarkably objective. Campbell is most vehement in downgrading the side he opposed. Neruda's "Almería" is a bitter attack but the facts alluded to, although dramatized, are valid.[32] Also, unlike *Flowering Rifle,* "Almería" has intrinsic artistic merit. Neruda uses the artistic means at his command as a poet, which Campbell does not. Neruda's motivation is political too, but he applies a poet's graphic ability by making visual, auditory images come to life. Campbell does not.

Campbell expressed no feelings that were subtle (in the sense that Vallejo could), only extravagant ones. Most of Campbell's shouting seems to verge on hysteria, while Felipe's polemic is rational. It could be argued that the poem was not meant to be subtle, but to elicit an ideological response on a nonreflective basis. Who, then, would his audience have been?—the lowest common denominator of prejudice.

While Hernández is recruiting in his poem, Campbell is pamphleteering and haranguing at the pettiest, name-calling level. He uses the typical clichés of fascist propaganda; for example, Jews are avaricious and equated with communists. He employs the language of propaganda in a verbal, political, cartoon context. He labels people. He evokes no visual or auditive response—only an emotional, instant reaction to Jews and communists, among others. In the manner of cartoonists and caricaturists, he capitalizes stereotypes, exaggerates, and deforms.

Vallejo and Hernández identify with the common people. Campbell prides himself with having shared the common life of Spain, but there seems to be no feeling of shared experience. He is antiintellectual but somehow much more intellectual than a peasant. Perhaps this same objection could be brought against Vallejo, but Vallejo expressed a great sense of and feeling for humanity, while Campbell is even contemptuous of humanitarianism.

Campbell is very defensive, and his relation with the rest of the literary world at the time is so negative that he may be considered to be outside his contemporaneous literary current, rejecting the whole English literary Establishment.

The appeal or interest of *Flowering Rifle* would be very limited outside the context of the Spanish Civil War. The poem is difficult to understand and follow, since he wrote from an extremely personal perspective and relied upon his own particular hang-ups to focus his attack. Nor does the aesthetic quality of the poem save it from oblivion. Only as an historical curiosity is the poem fascinating, if not grotesque.

Like Campbell, MacDiarmid has a weak sense of architectonics and form. He has written far too much (for a polemical poem), quoted too much, and discriminated too little. Both expend their energy in tearing down, but MacDiarmid depends more upon reason (especially in Part III of *The Battle Continues*) to lead us to a forward-looking challenge. Campbell, on the other hand, relies upon diatribe without offering any constructive message. Besides, one can follow a logical argument in MacDiarmid's poem which is absent in Campbell's. Because of this, *The Battle Continues* has more shape and is easier to follow and analyze.

MacDiarmid has the positive outlook of a true believer in an ideology. He has faith in communism and democracy. Neruda and Vallejo were also communists, and for communists and Scottish Nationalists Spain offered a giant metaphor. MacDiarmid's idealism derives, in part, from the fact that he was so far removed from the scene of the battle and, in part, from his being convinced of the right (and wrong) of the battle. MacDiarmid glorifies the International Brigades (as Neruda had) and the Spanish Republicans.

Both Scots and Spaniards are noted for their individuality. It is this fierce individuality that made it impossible to organize their forces—of which factions Felipe was critical—and which would have appealed to MacDiarmid. MacDiarmid is first, last, and always a Scotsman. As a Scottish nationalist, he saw the lack of support for the Republic as a sacrifice of "morality" in favor of political self-interest.

At the same time MacDiarmid has a strong, enduring interest in justice for the common people. The Spanish Civil War appealed to his humanitarian instincts because he believes in man—whatever the nationality. He speaks of other tragedies of the nature of Spain's. Having never gone to Spain during or before the war, his involvement was necessarily limited. Also the catalyst for his poem (at a publication distance of twenty years!) was Campbell's poem, although its inspiration derives from the war itself. While the poem is very sincere and was written by someone who knows how to harbor hatred, for MacDiarmid it might have been any other war. Not so for Hernández, Felipe, Neruda, and Vallejo. For the Spaniards and Latins it was personal; it was an assault upon their very being. For MacDiarmid it was ideological and humanitarian, although the stakes are a continued preoccupation ("the battle continues") and source of anguish. Those who were closer to the events would perhaps be more passionately committed, but, as in the case of someone who goes from passionate involvement to bitter reflection, MacDiarmid has reached that later stage. In a way, MacDiarmid was addressing himself to a double defeat: to the irrevocable defeat of the Republican cause in Spain at that time; and to the loss of the living memory of the struggle for those to whom this period has become meaningless history.

His perspective on the war is international and very knowledgeable. He seems to understand its complexities in an objective way, while at the same time to feel its emotional impact.

Auden and Spender were very different from Campbell in background, tastes, values, interpretations of the Spanish Civil War, poetic talent, and touch. Whereas Campbell expended considerable poetic energy blaspheming Auden and his so-called group, Auden remained emotionally detached. While *Flowering Rifle* lacks economy and form, "Spain" is concise and orderly, and its thesis is clear and cogent.

Of the poets considered, Auden is the least present in his poem and the most impersonal. *Spain* surveys rather than participates in the battle. It is also true that, among Hernández, Felipe, Neruda, Vallejo, and Campbell, Auden was the least familiar with Spain at firsthand. Felipe was objective, too, but was an integral part of "La insignia" in the role of poet/prophet. Auden's poem is somewhat prophetic, but the narrator of the third-person presentation is lacking—which adds a certain abstraction to the poem.

Auden does not impose his identity, or that of any other persona, upon his poem. Being outside his lines gives him an air of authority. His imagery is not especially emotional, but reveals scientific-technological leanings. Neruda wrote political poems; "Llegada a Madrid de la Brigada Internacional" showed awareness of the international brigades, and "Almería" showed awareness of the class struggle. Felipe, too, had written of the participation of foreign powers in the war. Such considerations were not present in Auden's poem, although a vision of the class struggle is shown indirectly in Spender's "Ultima Ratio Regum."

Both Felipe and Auden relied upon logical argument. Auden has a detached, objective, and impersonal view as perhaps only a non-Spaniard and noncombatant could. Since he was in Spain for so short a time (three months) and was involved so superficially, his poetic effort was not infringed upon by the demands of participation. Not overly concerned about the fate of Spain, he gave it nominal support. He wrote only one Spanish Civil War poem, and it was also his last poem to include communism significantly. That Auden could thereafter neglect Spain poetically and later denounce his poem suggests that he remained unscathed psychologically or otherwise by that upheaval. His detachment eventually led him to withdraw from politics altogether.

His attitude about death was not that of a combatant: "To-day the deliberate increase in the chances of death." Anyone who had actually seen people shot would have been less glib and less detached about the occurrence.

Although *Spain* is more about war politics than the personal emotion of the poet, Auden offers insights that are universal and avoids mere political propaganda (unlike Campbell). Auden's poem transcends the immediate issues of the war to consider the fundamental values at stake. His perspective is broad enough to permit a deep understanding. When he speaks of "the conscious acceptance of guilt in the necessary murder," he is conscious of something beyond the Spanish Civil War. Besides, *Spain* is an accomplished, visionary poem—one of the best in the English language about the war. Auden successfully separates his poem from political propaganda.

In Auden's poem we do not find the suffering and personal

involvement of Vallejo and Hernández, nor the emotional outrage of Neruda, Campbell, and even Felipe (in his attack against the British). But, like the level-headed Felipe (with the aforementioned qualification), Auden was objective. Auden succeeded in appealing more to the intellectual conscience than to the heart of his readers—which was his intention.

In his derision of the bureaucratic procedures (presumably, those of communism), Auden approaches the objective skepticism of Felipe, who symbolized the divisions on the Republican side by the use of the metaphor of multiple insignias. Such objectivity suggests that the motivation for these poems was not primarily partisan. Also the rhetorical analysis of *Spain* is like that of Felipe's poem. Auden attempted in *Spain* to present a theoretical as well as practical application of the hypothesis of Marxism.

The consciousness of a larger perspective from which to view the war is reasonably a non-Spanish ability. Auden, for example, could look at it in the context of an ideological, modern, new age. Of the poets writing in Spanish, Felipe comes closest in sophistication and perspective to Auden.

The abstraction of such a poem as "Ultima Ratio Regum" suggests Spender's lack of involvement in the war, that is, in the fighting itself. It reflects Spender's left-wing politics, but Spender believed that personal experience and private emotion were the real basis of poetry, and for that reason direct reference to his politics seldom occurred in his verse. "Two Armies" reveals Spender's traditional (in the manner of Thomas Hardy, for example) attitude against war. Of the three poems by Spender, "To a Spanish Poet" is the least abstract and most personal. In this poem Spender considers that, even if his friend is dead, perhaps it is the living who are most dead, rationalizing about an unhappy state of affairs. These three poems are a form of protest against the Spanish Civil War. They are antiromantic but, at the same time, emotional. Spender is full of pity for the victims of war: for the weak and unheroic. He is obsessed with the incalculable loss felt by all humanity. He is concerned with man in relation to his fellow man and believes in the love of one man for another.

Spender wrote two kinds of war poems: those that depict the impact of war upon his sensibility and are defeatist, like "Ultima

Ratio Regum," "Two Armies," "The Room Above the Square," and "Thoughts During an Air Raid"; and those that render wartime events objectively, with a few oblique references to the struggle's tragic implications, for example, "Fall of a City," "At Castellon," and "To a Spanish Poet." "Port Bou" combines both kinds, as the poet is a first-person spectator at a definite time and place on the periphery of the war.

Spender has a fine poetic ear and often employs subtle combinations of sound effects. For that reason as well as for the truth of his insights into human nature and genuine emotion, his poems reach beyond the Spanish Civil War.

Rukeyser's language is provocative and strong, but she is not always a perfectionist about language (in the sense that T. S. Eliot was). Her poems are sometimes rhetorical and sometimes untidy (especially the earlier ones). She has a rich nature, with strong convictions and feelings; her liberal attitudes have been consistent throughout the years.

Her antiwar vigor is shown in "M-Day's Child" via the shocking nature of an innocent child's destruction by war. Her language is much stronger but her perspective is similar to that of Spender in "Ultima Ratio Regum." "M-Day's Child" is as bitter as Neruda's "Almería," but she is looking beyond the Spanish Civil War to the oncoming World War II and to all war.

Like Neruda in "Explico algunas cosas," Rukeyser sees children as vulnerable. But, while Neruda's wrath is vindictively turned against the enemy (the Nationalists), Rukeyser's is more universally applied to all warmongers, whatever their politics. At least, there are no direct references in "M-Day's Child" except to a generalized war situation.

She can be as nihilistic as Neruda, and her nightmarish vision in "Third Elegy" compares with some of the landscapes inundated by blood evoked by Hernández. But Hernández could look optimistically (perhaps romantically) to the future, while Rukeyser makes no favorable affirmations. Her first Spanish Civil War poem, "Mediterranean," was written about her 1936 experience and left some room for hope. It is largely narrative, with lyric expressions of changing impressions. It is straightforward (journalistic), perceptive, sensitive (to implications in the objective events as well as to sensory data), and poetic. "M-Day's Child" is devastating and completely negative. It is condensed and strongly expressed. Its being included in a 1939 collection of poems helps account for its expression of disillusionment. The "Third Elegy" makes no hopeful predictions. The picture is honestly reported as bad. But her technique here is impressionistic and highly symbolic.

Rukeyser's philosophical and political inclinations were always liberal, and she would have rooted for the Republicans in any case, but her physical presence at that time was a coincidence. As a result, she was able to write "Mediterranean." Her strong antiwar stand in "M-Day's Child" is vaguely focused, making her criticism universally applicable. "Third Elegy" makes vague reference to Spain and the war, but its surrealistic presentation further blurs assignation. The main purpose of surrealist poetry is not to communicate ideas. It presents disordered images and impressions, not well-defined concepts. It seems to me that a Spaniard deeply involved in the cause of the Spanish Civil War would not choose to put a smoke screen in front of his message. Vallejo's poem "Pequeño responso a un héroe de la República" has surrealist elements but its framework is unmistakably clear.

Rukeyser's perspective is more general than that of Hernández, Felipe, Neruda, and Vallejo, and she does not prove through her poems that she understands the politics of the war as does Felipe. Rukeyser is very serious, honest, and intense, but her focus is not purely Spanish. What she is is a humanitarian (most like Spender) with strong convictions, poetic talent, liberal views, and an accidental arrival in Spain at the outbreak of the war. Although Campbell and MacDiarmid are more extreme in their viewpoints, she shares something of their emotional nature and exposes herself (at times) as they do. Her preoccupation with sex, for example, is evident in her poems. Neruda, Vallejo, and Hernández could write about sex but not in their Spanish Civil War poems. A similar example would be that of Campbell. In denouncing him, MacDiarmid picks up his fatuous masculinity, because Campbell so often flaunted his manhood in *Flowering Rifle*. This concern with extraneous and most personal aspects was much more frequent in the poems of those poets not deeply involved in Spain and its war.

Notes

1. Muriel Rukeyser, "Mediterranean," *New Masses,* XXIV (Sept. 14, 1937), 18-20.

2. Sources for biographical information on Campbell were the following works: David Wright, "Roy Campbell," *Writers and Their Work,* No. 137 (London: Longmans, Green & Co., 1961); *Encyclopaedia Britannica: Micropaedia* (Chicago: Encyclopaedia Britannica, Inc., 1974), II, 490; Hugh D. Ford, *A Poets' War: British Poets and the Spanish Civil War* (Philadelphia: University of Pennsylvania Press, 1965), pp. 177-201; and Esteban Pujals, *España y la guerra de 1936 en la poesia de Roy Campbell* (Madrid: Ateneo, 1959).

3. Roy Campbell, *Flowering Rifle: A Poem from the Battlefield of Spain,* Part II (London: Longmans, Green & Co., 1939), p. 41.

4. Ford, *A Poets' War,* p. 178.

5. Robert Graves, "A Life Bang Full of Kicks and Shocks," *N.Y. Times Book Review* (Jan. 5, 1958), p. 6.

6. My analysis of *Flowering Rifle* is largely derivative from an original and excellent interpretation by Doug Ford, "Roy Campbell, the Voice of the Insurgents," *A Poets' War,* Ch. 7, pp. 177-201. Here, for example, I have expanded upon Professor Ford's breakdown of Campbell's glaring exaggerations and distortions.

7. Information about MacDiarmid came from the following sources: Kenneth Buthlay: "Hugh MacDiarmid (C. M. Grieve)," *Writers and Critics Series,* eds. A. Norman Jeffares, David Daiches, and C. P. Snow (Edinburgh and London: Oliver and Boyd, 1964); David Daiches, "MacDiarmid and Scottish Poetry," *Poetry Magazine,* vol. 72, no. 4 (July 1948); K. D. Duval and Sydney Goodsir, eds., *Hugh MacDiarmid: a festschrift* (Edinburgh: Duval, 1962); *Encyclopaedia Britannica: Micropaedia,* VI, 437; Hugh MacDiarmid, *The Battle Continues* (Edinburgh: Castle Wynd Printers Limited, 1957); and MacDiarmid, *Lucky Poet—A Self-Study* (London: Methuen & Co., Ltd., 1943).

8. *Lucky Poet,* pp. 8-9.

9. "Talking with Five Thousand People in Edinburgh," *Poetry—Scotland,* 2nd collection, p. 50.

10. Hugh MacDiarmid, *Stony Limits and Other Poems* (London: V. Gollance, Ltd., 1934), p. 53.

11. "Hugh MacDiarmid: The Poet at Seventy," *Glasgow Herald,* 11 August 1962.

12. I referred to the following works while researching Auden's background: Joseph Warren Beach, *The Making of the Auden Canon* (Minneapolis: University of Minnesota Press, 1957); John Blair, *The Poetic Art of W. H. Auden* (Princeton: Princeton University Press, 1965); *Colliers Encyclopedia* (New York: Collier Publishing Co., 1965), III, 211-12; *Encyclopedia Britannica:* Micropaedia, I, 642; John Fuller, *A Reader's Guide to W. H. Auden* (New York: Farrar, Straus & Giroux, 1970); Herbert Greenberg, *Quest for the Necessary: W. H. Auden and the Dilemma of Divided Consciousness* (Cambridge, Mass.: Harvard University Press, 1968); Justin Replogle, *Auden's Poetry* (Seattle: University of Washington Press, 1969); Francis Scarfe, "W. H. Auden," *Contemporary British Poets* series (Monaco: The Lyrebird Press, 1949); Monroe K. Spears, ed., *Auden: A Collection of Critical Essays* (*Twentieth Century Series*) (Englewood Cliffs, N.J.: Prentice-Hall, 1964); and Spears, *The Poetry of W. H. Auden: The Disenchanted Island* (New York: Oxford University Press, 1963).

13. Stephen Spender, "W. H. Auden and His Poetry," *Twentieth Century Views* (Englewood Cliffs, N.J.: Prentice-Hall, 1964), p. 27.

14. The later version of the poem, with slight revisions, was also contained in *The Collected Poetry of W. H. Auden* (New York: Random House, 1945) on pp. 181 ff. as "Spain 1937"; the text I chose for my analysis was that of the first edition in 1937.

15. Spender, "W. H. Auden and His Poetry," p. 32.

16. Louis MacNeice, *Modern Poetry* (Oxford: Oxford University Press, 1938), p. 197.

17. *The Poet's Tongue* is an anthology of poems edited by Auden in collaboration with John Garrett (London: Bell, 1935). The quotation appears on p. ix.

18. Sources for biographical information on Spender were: biography by William Y. Tindall, *Collier's Encyclopedia;* Ford's *A Poets' War;* and *World Within World: the Autobiography of Stephen Spender* (London: Hamilton, 1951).

19. *The Still Centre* (London: Faber and Faber, Ltd., 1939), p. 10.

20. Stephen Spender, "Poems about the Spanish Civil War (1936-1939)," *Collected Poems 1928-1953* (London: Faber and Faber, Ltd., 1965), p. 99.

21. Spender, *Collected Poems 1928-1953*, pp. 97-98.

22. Spender, *Collected Poems 1928-1953*, pp. 108-09.

23. Spender wrote of the air raid which Altolaguirre recounted to him in his autobiography *World Within World* (1951), pp. 262-63. Their original meeting and something of their friendship ("one of my best friends in Spain") is related on p. 231.

24. Information about Rukeyser was culled from the following sources: B. Alsterlund, biographical sketch, *Wilson Library Bulletin,* no. 15 (Oct. 1940), 110; J. M. Brinnin, "Social Poet and the Problem of Communication," *Poetry,* no. 61 (Jan. 1943), 554-75; T. Parkinson, "Some Recent Pacific Coast Poetry," *Pac. Spec.,* IV, no. 3 (1950), 300-02; Muriel Rukeyser, autobiographical essay, "Under forty," *Contemporary Jewish Rec.,* no. 7 (Feb. 1944), 4-9; and L. Untermeyer, "Language of Muriel Rukeyser," *Sat. R. Lit.,* no. 22 (Aug. 10, 1940), 11-13.

25. Stephen Vincent Benet, Foreword, *Theory of Flight* (New Haven: Yale University Press, 1935).

26. From autobiographical essay, *Contemporary Jewish Record,* p. 7.

27. From *Contemporary Jewish Record,* p. 8.

28. From the Author's Note which precedes *A Turning Wind* (New York: The Viking Press, 1939).

29. Muriel Rukeyser, "Mediterranean," *New Masses,* XXIV, New York, Sept. 14, 1937, pp. 18-20.

30. Muriel Rukeyser, *A Turning Wind,* pp. 24-28.

31. Rukeyser, *A Turning Wind,* pp. 55-56.

32. My standard for factuality is based upon my understanding of two histories of the war, one by Hugh Thomas, the other by Gabriel Jackson.

CHAPTER IV

Concentration on Poets in German, French, Russian, and Italian

The extraordinary reaction in poetry to the Spanish Civil War was not limited just to the Spanish and English languages. The contribution of continental European poets in German, French, Russian, and Italian attests to the literary and human history resulting from that war. The poems by foreigners to Spain proved that the Spaniards were not alone in their opposition. Despite the discrepancies among these poets, there exists a profound common denominator: upon dealing with a Spanish theme, they Europeanize and universalize it. An interest solely in Spain would not have motivated this literature. What happened in that war was that it aroused the most vivid themes of that epoch, to which few writers could feel foreign. The war helped awaken their social consciences. In the literature of the war in Spain were planted the great themes of the twentieth century: the value of liberty and the sense of democracy; the criticism of fascist and Nazi totalitarianism as an enemy of democracy and liberty; the criticism of

205

the society of capitalism and the search for a humanitarian socialism; the protest against the disillusionment provoked by communism; and, also, the desire to establish better equality among the
social classes, by means of distribution of wealth, in order to
extend to all the benefits of modern civilization. Somewhere
among these values a great quantity and quality of writers found
an identity.

Among the major powers, it was only in the Soviet Union that
popular feeling and government policy coincided in favoring the
cause of the Republic. The dictators of Italy and Germany were
committed on the side of the Nationalists.

The conflict in Spain, which had started as a military insurrection against an established regime, soon degenerated into a laboratory experiment where fascists and communists tested out themselves and each other. Italian and German ground and air detach-
ments were rushed to General Franco's Nationalist side while
Soviet planes and generals under assumed names fought for the
Republic. The Luftwaffe tried out tactics and the Russians tried
out aircraft. Communist leadership assumed a strong voice in the
government while outright fascism succeeded the rebels' conventional military rule. The democratic powers opted out of the
struggle.

As many as 40,000 foreigners fought in the International Brigades, though the Brigades never exceeded 18,000 at any time.
Most of them were volunteers, a fraction of them being mercenaries, who fought in five brigades, numbered 11 through 15,
whose strength varied between 2000 or 3000 to 10,000 to 15,000
men. The majority of Internationals acted as fellow travelers,
regarding the communists as the most efficient organizers of the
antifascist resistance in Europe.

The poets from Germany, France, Russia, and Italy were interested in antifascist revolutionary movements in general and some
fought in their own country, Spain, or elsewhere, either prior to,
during, or subsequent to the Spanish Civil War, for greater freedom and humanitarian reforms.

Johannes Robert Becher was born in Munich in 1891 and died
in Berlin in 1958. The son of a magistrate, he early broke with

the *bürgerliche klasse* of his origin, like many of his generation. He became a poet, dramatist, critic, editor, and political activist. As a government official he was among the most important advocates of revolutionary social reform in Germany during the 1920s.

Becher studied medicine, literature, and philosophy, and, in 1918, at a time when the Russian Revolution was an inspiration to many German leftist intellectuals, he joined the German Communist Party (KPD). He shared Brecht's faith in and action for the Party. Becher was already an established commentator on the social and artistic scene and a leader of the movement to transform German society through a revolution of the proletariat. Involved in the Expressionist school that dominated German writing in the period 1910-1920, he wrote romantic, emotionally complex poetry that mirrored both his personal turmoil and his visions of a new social order. His earliest verse *Der Ringende* (1911) and his novel *Erde* (1912) prefigure the collision in his Expressionist verse of religious and (in broadest sense) political emotions.

Becher's work shows a clear development: from religiously motivated antibourgeois aggression (with its emotional disorder), to communist *Kulturpolitik* and doctrinaire popular verse. His verse of the former phase was later recanted by him in favor of his later work.

Though elected to the German Reichstag in 1933, he was forced into exile with the advent of Nazi power and went to Moscow. Like Brecht again, Becher wrote in exile. In Moscow he edited a German language newspaper (1935-1945). Life in Moscow disillusioned him about Joseph Stalin's communism but not about the ideology.

The class struggle, the Spanish Civil War, life in the Soviet Union, and exile in general gain in emotional impact by the factualness of their presentation in his poems. Banned from Germany, he rediscovered through his poetry the land, the villages and the cities, the people, its history and its culture; the old fatherland became a "gescholossene Realitat" which the poet interwove with a decade of experience in Russia. Love of homeland and gratitude for the country of his refuge were, along with class and party loyalty, activating elements of Becher's poetry.

Returning to Germany in 1945, he was made President of the

Association for the Democratic Rebirth of Germany (*Kultur-bund*). In 1954 he returned to Berlin and subsequently became a leading figure in the literary life of the German Democratic Republic, and was appointed East German Minister of Culture.

Many of his works are political and of a revolutionary tone: *Verbruderung* (1916), *Paean gegen die Zeit* (1918), *Ewig im Aufruhr* (1920), *Am Grabe Lenins* (1925), *Arbeiter, Bauern, Soldaten* (1925), and *Der Glucksucher und die sieben Lasten* (1938). Of the three poems included for analysis, "General Mola" is from *Ausgewahlte Dichtung aus der Zeit der Verbannung, 1933-1945,* while "Barcelona" and "Fliehende Mutter" are from *Gedichte 1936-1941.*

BARCELONA [1]

1   Unsere Stadt, am Meere hochgebaut,
        Und das Meer hat lichtvoll sie durchblaut,
        Und das Meer schaut träumend zu ihr her,
        Denn dort, wo sie steht, war einst das Meer—

5   Weite Stadt der Säulen und der Hallen.
        Seht, es glänzt wie Muscheln und Korallen,
        Und versunkene Glocken tönen nah,
        Santa Anna, Santa Monica . . .

        Freundenklänge und ein Lied voll Klagen
10   Hast du fernhin bis zu uns getragen.
        Barcelona! Oh, dein Name hat
        Uns verzaubert. In uns lag die Stadt.

        Bargen dich wie einen heiligen Schatz.
        Deine Plätze nahmen in uns Platz
15   Und in meinem Herzen kreuzten sich
        Deine Strassen und belebten mich.

        Wir—wir haben uns mit dir empört,
        Und die ganze Welt hat dich gehört,
        Als du sprachst mit Volkes Stimme—deine
20   Stimme machte stark und fest die meine.

Mir auch stand der Himmel grausam offen,
Und ich sah, du sankst, zu Tod getroffen,
Und ich richtete in mir ein Feuer
Gegen jene feigen Ungeheuer . . .

25   Barcelona, Trümmer. Blutige Pfützen.
Henker in den roten Baskenmutzen.
Fremder Söldnerknecht als Mordgeselle.
Francos Fahne auf der Zitadelle.

Schlechter Rat spricht tückisch auf mich ein:
30   "Schweige still und lass dein Fragen sein!"
Nein, ich werde nach der Wahrheit fragen,
Muss ich mir doch selbst die Wahrheit sagen.

Wie geschah es? Wie war's möglich, dass—
Frag ich, frage ohne Unterlass,
35   Und ich fürcht auch diese Wahrheit nicht:
Scheiterhaufen, Folter, Blutgericht.

Was niemals gelang der Übermacht,
Hat Verrat, hat der Verrat vollbracht,
Und ich frag in London und Paris,
40   Wer ist's, der die Feste fallen liess? . . .

Barcelona. Opferreiche Stadt.
Stadt, die auch für mich geblutet hat.
Unsere Gräber aber öffnen sich.
Barcelona—das bist du und ich—

45   Und das Meer schaut träumend zu dir her,
Denn dort, wo du stehst, war einst das Meer,
Und das Meer hat lichtvoll dich durchblaut;
Unsere Stadt, am Meer hochgebaut!
                    —Johannes R. Becher

Barcelona, the capital of Catalonia, played a strategic role in the Spanish Civil War. A port on the Mediterranean, Barcelona was built as a fortress and its original site was walled, as Becher suggests.

There were a few days of civil war within the city in early 1937.

Ever since July 18, 1936, Barcelona had been the mecca of un-orthodox revolutionary groups. French Proudhonians, English utopian socialists, Italian and Balkan anarchists, Russian menshe-vik intellectuals—all saw in the Catalan revolution the beginnings of a non-Stalinist, "pure" revolution. The communists did not have the prestige in Barcelona that they had in Madrid. Becher's disillusionment with Stalinist communism may have attracted him to the plight of Barcelona.

At the request of Prime Minister Negrin, France (under Leon Blum) opened its border and long-held Russian supplies began rapidly to pass to Barcelona. Mussolini replied to the French with a series of mass bombing raids on the city of Barcelona, beginning on the full-moon night of March 16, 1938. The military damage accomplished was very minor, but coming after twenty months of war, and striking at a slowly starving city, the raids contributed to the steadily sinking morale of the general population. As in the cases of Madrid and Guernica, the Western powers protested the fate of this civilian population in wartime.

On January 22, 1939, General Yajui's troops began to occupy the city of Barcelona, virtually without firing a shot. The battle had already been fought within the city. One-half million refugees from Catalonia began trudging toward the French border. Both Tíkhonov and Eluard consider this exodus and its aftermath in their poems. The majority of the population, and most of the municipal officials, passively awaited the arrival of the Nationalists. The Moors entered vacated apartments and looted heavily. By January 26 the occupation of Barcelona was accomplished.

Becher identifies with the natives, "unsere Stadt," and the city has appealed greatly to his sensibilities. Becher knew the lovely city well and describes it perceptively. Much of the description of the city is lyrical and contains rhymed couplets. He describes the city and angrily despairs over its ruin. He considers its wreck-age and defeat a betrayal by all those powers who might have helped and didn't. The cry for help from Barcelona, a metaphor for the pride and potential of all of Republican Spain, was neg-lected by such capitals as London and Paris. It takes an interna-tional perspective (of a foreigner to Spain) to put the blame clearly outside of Spain.

There is repetition of lines: 45 and 3; 46 and 4; 47 and 2; and line 48, in echoing line 1, allows the poem to end neatly with the same line with which it began.

GENERAL MOLA [2]
Aus dem spanischen Bürgerkrieg

1   Wenn er so dasass, ohne aufzuschauen,
Ein Urteil nach dem andern unterschrieb:
Nichts Menschliches sass da—ein hagres Grauen,
Daran allein der Rock noch menschlich blieb.

5   Als könnte er auch weinen oder lachen,
So menschlich war der Rock, aus feinem Tuch,
Von Menschenhand gemacht, wie der Versuch,
Ein Menschenbild aus einem Rock zu
      machen . . .

Als eines Tags ein Flugzeug unbekannt
10   Abstürzte im Gebirge und verbrannte,
Aus nichts war eine Herkunft ablesbar:

Bis man ein Stück von einem Rocke fand,
Woran man ihn, den General erkannte—
Das einzige, was menschlich an ihm war.
            —Johannes R. Becher

General Emilio Mola Vidal was the last Director General of Security under the monarchy. Early in 1932 it looked as though the government would retire him to the reserve; however, he appeared to be one of the more loyal to the governmnt of the senior generals. In the spring of 1936 he was moved from command of the Moroccan army to that of the Pamplona military district. Mola's new assignment was a stroke of luck for the plotters against the Republic. While the General was no monarchist, he had developed a violent hatred for Azaña because of the latter's military reforms. And now he was military commander in the heart of the Carlist country, the one portion of Spain where the conspirators could count on a degree of public support.

One of the original junta of military men to rise against the Republic, in the months of August and September 1936, Mola shared the military power of the Nationalists with Queipo de Llano and Franco. He was a shrewd man of great intelligence and energy. Among his peers he had a reputation as a policeman rather than as a soldier and, generally speaking, authoritarians of both the Right and the Left have never wished to hand over supreme power to the head of the police.

To indicate his character, as commander of the North (Navarre-Castille), Mola once told assembled mayors of Navarre that he would not hesitate to shoot anyone caught sheltering "Reds" for any reason whatever. As commander of "four columns" marching on Madrid, Mola claimed to have a "fifth column" of partisans waiting within the city. Also, in March of 1937, General Mola concentrated roughly 40,000 troops in Guipuzcoa and Alava with Navarrese and Moroccans in the lead and Italians in reserve.

Flying to Burgos on June 3, 1937, General Mola crashed on the hill of Buitrago. Inevitably, a question mark surrounds the manner of Mola's death. Was there, perhaps, a time bomb in the airplane? Certainly there were many who might have desired the death of Mola—Franco among them.

Very sarcastic and bitterly denunciatory, Becher views General Mola. He is seen as a scarecrow without humanness or humanity. Becher offers the poetic conceit of two highly dissimilar objects, General Mola, portrayed as a nonsubstantive, complete nonentity, and his richly made and bedecked military jacket. The man himself was nothing—only an authoritarian robot-like military-political figure, responsible for many decisions and many deaths, leading up to and during the war. The jacket, in contrast, is much closer to being human than the man.

Mola was killed without fanfare, in an anonymous plane in an obscure region. Even in death he was unrecognizable. He was identified only through a piece of his jacket—not even the whole jacket —all that was left of this anonymous, insignificant "thing." Becher here sharply ridicules and indicts everything that Mola stood for. The poem indicates a degree of hatred also seen, for example, in Neruda's "Almería."

The sonnet has aspects of both Petrarchan and Shakespearian

sonnets. It has the blank verse of the Shakespearian and the octave and sestet of the Petrarchan. Besides, there is the generalization about the man in the octave and the specific comment about him in the sestet, common to Petrarchan sonnets. Its tone is highly ironic, full of hate and contempt for General Mola.

Becher tells of a fascist general in Spain who in a machine-like fashion had signed one death sentence after another and who, when he crashed in a plane in the mountains, could not be identified until "man ein Stück von einem Rocke fand,/Woran man ihn, den General erkannte—/Das einzige, was menschlich an ihm war."

FLIEHENDE MUTTER [3]

1   "Ich weiss ja nicht, ob ich willkommen bin
      In Ihrem Land . . . Ich bin so weit vertrieben . . .
      In diesem Bündel? . . . Waffen? . . . 's ist darin
      Was Liebes, Herr . . . Sonst ist mir nichts
        geblieben . . .

5   Das kam nun so . . . Das Dorf war lang schon leer,
      Die Männer fort im Krieg . . . nur Kinder,
        Frauen . . .
      Da kam ein Donnern, Herr, vom Ebro her . . .
      Wir liefen auf das Feld um auszuschauen . . .

      Kein Stückchen Brot. Nichts—viele Tage lang . . .
10   Und da, da kamen sie . . . So schnell von oben . . .
      Und einer, der sich tief herunterschwang . . .
      Kein Schrein . . . Ich hab mein Kindlein
        aufgehoben—

      Und plötzlich war die Strasse nicht mehr da.
      War eine Schlucht. War Eis. Ein Felsen meinte
15   Es gut mit mir . . . Sie kamen wieder nah . . .
      Der Felsen barg mich. Auch der Felsen weinte . . .

      Ich weiss ja nicht, bin ich noch irgendwo?! . . .
      Darf ich es jetzt in Ihre Erde betten? . . .

Verzeihen Sie, mein Herr . . . Das kam nun so . . .
20   Man muss die Toten . . . auch die Toten
         retten . . ."

—Johannes R. Becher

Since Becher has also written a poem commemorating Barcelona, it is likely that he had the general exodus from Catalonia in mind. The emigrants would cross the French border to seek escape from the intolerable present conditions and the darkly foreshadowed future in Spain. Away from home, they would be disoriented aliens, having lost, perhaps, everything, including loved ones.

On July 24, 1938, the Republicans crossed the Ebro heading southward. The Nationalists opened the dams along the Pyrenean tributaries of the Ebro, flooding the area. Meanwhile, General Franco rushed reinforcements to the area with the result that by August 1 the Republican advance had been stopped just short of the towns of Gandesa and Villalba de los Arcos. Nationalist artillery kept the Republican troops pinned to the ground during daylight hours and destroyed all land communication. It was a losing battle and, when they saw the writing on the wall, many began to evacuate across the French border. The "fliehende mutter" would have been among these.

This mother who, as she says, had lost everything else was carrying her dead baby: "auch die Toten retten," hoping to bury him away from the battlefield, having kept him with her as long as possible. He had died without cries, shot down by airplane fire, within hearing distance of the Battle of the Ebro.

The ellipses suggest the groping in the woman's mind concerning what happened and where she is going. The weeping of the boulder suggests the flow of blood from the wounded, dying, and dead. In fragmented glimpses Becher presents a brief, narrative, suggesting the utter rootlessness, defenselessness, and desperation of this solitary woman who carries her treasure-tragedy along with her. No home. No family. No solace. No future. Nothing but being alive with a tortured memory. And, even in her nothingness, she must supplicate, in asking permission to bury her treasured dead.

Of the generation of French poets who came to maturity between the two world wars, Eluard is one of the few whose work
has enduring value. Paul Eluard, the pseudonym of Eugene Grin-
del, was born in Saint-Denis, Paris in 1895. After fighting a lung
disease in his youth, for which he spent two years in a Swiss sanato-
rium, and being gassed during World War I, Eluard turned to
Dadaism as to a bitter refuge against the absurdity of wars and of
a literature which had stooped to carrying nationalistic propaganda.

He lived almost exclusively in Paris and frequented avant-garde
literary and artistic groups. In 1919 he met the poets André Breton,
Philippe Soupault, and Louis Aragon, with whom he participated
in the foundation of surrealism, and remained in close association
with them until 1938.

Many of his early poems were formless and obscure, and nearly
always attempt to translate into verse his vision of a world beyond
reality. Much of his best-loved poetry was written in the 1920s but
he continued to publish a good deal of verse throughout his lifetime. At its best his work has a direct tone and a concrete simplicity.

In 1926 he joined the Communist Party, which he abandoned
in 1933. The Spanish Civil War and the crisis of Munich made
him, along with his friend Picasso, approach communism again.
He rejoined the Party in 1942.

His works emerge from his life experiences: World Wars I and
II, the Spanish Civil War (he visited Spain during that war),
German occupation, Resistance, struggles of the Communist Party,
the women he loved, daily tide of events, encounters, friendships,
and dreams.

He wrote some political poetry for the communist movement
which is not among his best. His best verses are lyrical and have
the clarity of classical French poetry. After the Spanish Civil War,
he abandoned surrealist experimentation as being too rigidly
doctrinaire. In reaction to the war he simplified his verse, aiming
for broad understanding, very much what Neruda and Vallejo
had done for the same reason. His late work reflects his political
militance and a deepening of his underlying attitudes: rejection

of tyranny and search for happiness. During World War II, he was
one of the Resistance writers. He died in 1952.

Among his volumes of verse are: *Le Devoir et l'inquietude*
(1917), *Poèmes pour la paix* (1918), *Mourir de ne pas mourir*
(1924), *Capitale de la douleur* (1926), *Defense de savoir* (1928), *La
Vie immediate* (1932), *Les Yeux fertiles* (1936), *Cours naturel*
(1938), *Chanson complete* (1939), *Le Livre ouvert* (1940), *Poesie et
verite* (1942), *Le Malheurs des immortels* (1945), *Au Rendezvous
allemand* (1945), *Poesie ininterrompue* (1946), *Poèmes politiques*
(1948), and *Le Phoenix: Poesie ininterrompue* (2ᵉ edition, 1953).

Of the poems chosen for analysis, two are from *Cours naturel*,
published in 1938; the other two, one of which is very brief, were
published in *Poèmes politiques*, 1948.

NOVEMBRE 1936 [4]

1   Regardez travailler les bâtisseurs de ruines
       Ils sont riches patients ordonnés noirs et bêtes
       Mais ils font de leur mieux pour être seuls sur
           terre
       Ils sont au bord de l'homme et le comblent
           d'ordures
5   Ils plient au ras du sol des palais sans cervelle.

       On s'habitue à tout
       Sauf à ces oiseaux de plomb
       Sauf à leur haine de ce qui brille
       Sauf à leur céder la place.

10   Parlez du ciel le ciel se vide
       L'automne nous importe peu
       Nos maîtres ont tapé du pied
       Nous avons oublié l'automne
       Et nous oublierons nos maîtres.

15   Ville en baisse océan fait d'une goutte d'eau
           sauvée
       D'un seul diamant cultivé au grand jour

Madrid ville habituelle à ceux qui ont souffert
De cet épouvantable bien qui nie être en
   exemple
Qui ont souffert
20   De la misère indispensable à l'éclat de ce bien.

Que la bouche remonte vers sa vérité
Souffle rare sourire comme une chaîne brisée
Que l'homme délivré de son passé absurde
Dresse devant son frère un visage semblable
25   Et donne à la raison des ailes vagabondes.

                        —Paul Eluard

LA VICTOIRE DE GUERNICA [5]

1

1   Beau monde des masures
De la mine et des champs

2

Visages bons au feu visages bons au froid
Aux refus à la nuit aux injures aux coups

3

5   Visages bons à tout
Voici le vide qui vous fixe
Votre mort va servir d'exemple

4

La mort coeur renversé

5

Ils vous ont fait payer le pain
10   Le ciel la terre l'eau le sommeil
Et la misère
De votre vie

6

Ils disaient désirer la bonne intelligence
Ils rationnaient les forts jugeaient les fous

15 Faisaient l'aumône partageaient un sou en
deux
Ils saluaient les cadavres
Ils s'accablaient de politesses

7

Ils persévèrent ils exagèrent ils ne sont pas
de notre monde

8

Les femmes les enfants ont le même trésor
20 De feuilles vertes de printemps et de lait pur
Et de durée
Dans leurs yeux purs

9

Les femmes les enfants ont le même trésor
Dans les yeux
25 Les hommes le défendent comme ils peuvent

10

Les femmes les enfants ont les mêmes roses
rouges
Dans les yeux
Chacun montre son sang

11

La peur et le courage de vivre et de mourir
30 La mort si difficile et si facile

12

Hommes pour qui ce trésor fut chanté
Hommes pour qui ce trésor fut gâché

13

Hommes réels pour qui le désespoir
Alimente le feu dévorant de l'espoir
35 Ouvrons ensemble le dernier bourgeon de
l'avenir

14
Parias la mort la terre et la hideur
De nos ennemis ont la couleur
Monotone de notre nuit
Nous en aurons raison.

—Paul Eluard

"Novembre 1936" and "La Victoire de Guernica" have in common that they reflect Eluard's outrage over the injustice and inhumanity of the attacks on Madrid and Guernica. Both poems are obscure, reflecting surrealist tendencies in their visions outside reality, but also suggesting the brutal truth of what happened to these two places.

In November of 1936 Madrid was, indeed, under siege. General Mola commanded 25,000 troops and attempted to terrorize the city into surrender by indiscriminate bombing. There were air raids every day, and on November 17 the Nationalists made a supreme effort at bombardment. Two thousand shells an hour landed in the center of Madrid, which had no air-raid shelters and almost no antiaircraft artillery. Although approximately five hundred persons were killed that night, Madrid Republicans held their own so that from late November 1936 until the end of the Civil War, the areas of the city held by Nationalists and Republicans remained about the same.

The poem evokes the ferocious resistance of Madrid in the autumn of 1936. The enemies are "bâtisseurs de ruines." They overwhelm Madrid by their creation of garbage, but the capital ("ville habituelle à ceux qui ont souffert") is strongly determined not to give an inch ("Sauf à leur céder la place"). The hope of liberty and equality lives despite the terrifying impact of the land and air attacks.

This same hope inspires the poet in "La Victoire de Guernica." The bombardment of the ancient capital of the Basque country becomes under his pen a "victoire" for the men who endured it because they were conscious of their power and their despair: "Alimente le feu dévorant de l'espoir." The harassed people, enduring so many military reversals affecting their existence, have learned to know their masters and have determined to face up to the future and fight:

> Parias la mort la terre et la hideur
> De nos ennemis ont la couleur
> Monotone de notre nuit
> Nous en aurons raison.

In these poems of 1938 Eluard's poetry has become more accessible through simplified expression. The lines are, in general, short, having been reduced to the essential. But, for that same reason, the style is telegraphic, leaving out transitions that would clarify obscure ideas.

"La Victoire de Guernica" suggests its meaning through a fragmentary series of brief images from the unexpected perspective of Guernica's having been a victory. Guernica, a small town in the Basque province of Vizcaya, had a population of 7000. On April 26, 1937, a Monday (and, therefore, like all Mondays in Guernica, a market day), the small farmers from nearby were bringing into the main square the fruits of the week's toil. At this time Guernica lay about eighteen miles from the front. At half-past four in the afternoon, a single peal of church bells announced an air raid. There had been some raids in the area before, but Guernica had not been bombed. At twenty minutes to five, German Heinkels (flown by Condor aviators) began to appear, first bombing the town and then machine-gunning its streets. The Heinkels were followed by Junkers 52. People began running from the town; they were machine-gunned. Incendiary bombs, weighing up to one thousand pounds, and also high explosives, were dropped by waves of aircraft arriving every twenty minutes until a quarter to eight. The center of the town was, by that time, destroyed and burning. 1654 people were dead; 889 wounded. These facts have been attested to by eye witnesses. This became one of history's most famous premeditated experiments in terror. It symbolized the Nationalist intention to destroy Basque autonomy, and Hitler made it possible.

In no way would Eluard view this disaster area as "beau monde." The people massacred were civilians, among them women and children. "La mort si difficile et si facile" suggests the suddenness and swiftness of their tragic finality. If one were to extract victory from such a debacle, it would be in the dedicated purpose of the lives of those who remain: "Nous en aurons raisons."

Eluard paints a picture so horrible and unjust that the final exhortation ("Nous en aurons raison") has to be true if civilization is to survive. The wish is desperate and romantic, perhaps more despairing than idealistic, but strongly felt and strongly expressed. Eluard, illustrating the affinity between Frenchmen and Spaniards, closely identifies with the Spanish tragedy in general, and with Guernica and Madrid in particular.

EN ESPAGNE [6]

S'il y a en Espagne un arbre teint da sang
C'est l'arbre de la liberté

S'il y a en Espagne une bouche bavarde
Elle parle de liberté

S'il y a en Espagne un verre de vin pur
C'est le peuple qui le boira.

—Paul Eluard

ESPAGNE [7]

1   Les plus beaux yeux du monde
   Se sont mis à chanter
   Qu'ils veulent voir plus loin
   Que les murs des prisons
5   Plus loin que leurs paupières
   Meurtries par le chagrin

   Les barreaux de la cage
   Chantent la liberté
   Un air qui prend le large
10   Sur les routes humaines

Sous un soleil furieux
Un grand soleil d'orage

Vie perdue retrouvée
Nuit et jour de la vie
15   Exilés prisonniers
Vous nourrissez dans l'ombre
Un feu qui porte l'aube
La fraîcheur la rosée

La victoire

20   Et le plaisir de la victoire.
                    —Paul Eluard

In 1948, in his *Poèmes politiques,* Eluard resumed his theme of Spain. "En Espagne" is a strong, brief poem. Anaphora, repetitions, simple words, density collaborate to express the ardent desire of Eluard for the liberty of the Spanish people. The vision being after the war, the tree stained with blood suggests the fighting and bloodshed that should have earned Spain its liberty. Eluard further implies that if there is anything in Spain worth talking about, it is liberty. And, finally, if there is to be wine drunk (so typically Spanish) and toasts made, the wine will be pure (because Spanish) and it is the people who will drink it. The masses of the people, then, are still for liberty and, therefore, opposed to Franco and everything his succession to power represents.

"Espagne" does not refer directly to the Spanish Civil War but to Spanish resistance to the French regime afterwards. The exiles and prisoners become in "Espagne" "les plus beaux yeux du monde" (Spaniards frequently have large, striking, brown eyes) that sing of their obsession with light and freedom. Despite their confinement (in relocation centers behind barbed wire or, actually, in prisons, they haven't lost their courage. Meanwhile the air ("Chantent la liberté") escapes and these prisoners will end by triumphing. The long phrases of this poem are produced by run-on lines and, separated by one or two lines which mark time, allowing for reflection, they present a look of firm marching toward a definite goal: victory. These exiles, already having lost their homeland, want their freedom.

Eluard's viewpoint as a Frenchman had naturally been attracted to the situation and condition of the Spaniards in France.

Like other surrealists, Eluard was fundamentally an optimist; he was confident that ways could be found or devised to alter man's fate and to accomplish miracles challenging the misery of the world. But, like all men, he knew moments of dejection. These ups and downs are reflected in his poems both during and after his surrealist period.

Eluard was a poet with a moral conscience who repudiated poetry of complacent self-contemplation, which bemoaned the writer's solitude. He also abhorred all that was ornamental and rhetorical in poetry; he wished to be understood even by common people, for which purpose he chose simple language and evocative imagery.

Nikoláy Semyónovich Tíkhonov was born in St. Petersburg (now Leningrad) in 1896. Born into a lower-middle-class family, he attended a commercial high school and received a rather poor formal education. He fought in a hussar regiment during World War I, later joining the Red Army and participating in the Revolution and Civil War in Russia from 1918-1922. Having helped to defend Leningrad from the Whites, he later (still in the early 1920s) settled there.

Spirited and fond of adventure, in the 1920s and 1930s, he traveled in the outlying parts of the Soviet Union, Asia, and Europe, and tried several occupations, acting among them, before he turned to literature, which to him then meant poetry. His first collection of poems appeared in 1922. Other books of verse, as well as of prose, followed, and of translations, chiefly of Georgian poetry. In the early 1920s he belonged to the Serapion Brothers, a literary group who in the midst of the Russian Revolution were bold enough to champion political neutrality. Tíkhonov confessed publicly to a weakness for anarchy. This fraternity of writers admired the romanticism of the German writer E. T. A. Hoffmann and was strongly influenced by Gumilev, who glorified courage, virility, and loyalty in his terse poems of civil war and revolution.

In his first two collections of poetry *Orda* (1922) and *Braga* (1923), Tíkhonov sought to express the sensations of his years of war and adventure. He extolled the revolutionary romanticism of civil war and individual acts of bravery. In these and other early poems, the influence of Acmeism (a literary doctrine that advocated concrete, individualistic realism, stressing clarity, emotional intensity, and verbal freshness) is evidenced by his use of concrete images, pictorial detail, and semantic precision. These poems also showed the influence of Gumilev and of the English romantics, especially in Tíkhonov's predilection for the ballad. Tíkhonov had a positive attitude toward the 1917 Revolution, which he saw as a release of tremendous energy and as an event from which to learn and exhibit courage.

In the mid-1920s under the influence of the poets Velemir Khlebnikov and Boris Pasternak, Tíkhonov experimented in his poetry. He traveled to the East and to Central Asia, gaining new materials, tones, and colors for poetic use.

By the early 1930s Tíkhonov began to concern himself in his poetry more and more with broad social issues. His prose works, however, continued to be romantic in style and in spirit, as in his short stories of marvels and mysteries. He changed his mind about anarchy and became a staunch supporter of the Soviet regime and an ardent patriot. He stressed in his writings during World War II the same ideals of duty and courage he had in his earlier writings.

From 1944 until the purge in the field of the arts which took place in the summer of 1946, Tíkhonov held the important post of chairman of the board of the Union of Soviet Writers. Tíkhonov's literary and political work (he served as cultural ambassador on several occasions and also wrote propaganda) earned him the Order of Lenin. During World War II he wrote many patriotic poems, one of which won him the Stalin Prize, and essays, including *Leningrad Tales* (1943), a series of stories in which he celebrated the heroism of the seige of Leningrad. He won Stalin Prizes in 1942, 1949, and 1952.

During the late 1950s Tíkhonov alienated many other Soviet writers because of his part in a critical campaign against Pasternak.

In his poetic career, Tíkhonov, after 1922, left the misty symbolism of the Cosmists Movement and developed toward greater concretization and toward realism, romantic and otherwise. Tíkhonov had an intensely private vision of the world. He was a poet of the Russian Revolution whose devotion to the cause went beyond idealized allegiance. His highly individualistic, lyrical verse found its inspiration in the cause of communism. His ballads on the Russian Civil War were both romantic and realistic. Their lyrical tone was that of heroic romanticism. For his poems he preferred sharp, definite outlines and bright colors.

Tíkhonov, although Pasternak's principal rival for top honors in Soviet poetry, possessed neither the sheer poetic power nor the originality of Pasternak. On the other hand, his poems are relatively free of the difficult language and complicated handling of themes that prevented Pasternak's poems from winning wide popularity.

It is difficult to place Tíkhonov in any particular poetic school, for from his early narrative verse tales (*Orda* and *Braga*) to his later ballads on civil war themes and his recent poems, he has consistently and independently developed his art largely as a medium for treating romantic themes of revolution in a clear, realistic manner. At times, Tíkhonov seems more like a novelist in verse. His simple, unrestrained realism has influenced later Russian poets.

Among his poems are "David" (1919), "Orda" (1922), "Ballada o sinem pakete" (1922), "Ballada o gvozdyakh" (1919-1922), "Braga" (1923), "Litsom k litsu," "Doroga," "Shakhmaty" (1920s). Among his collections of verse are: *Poeski geroya* (1927), *Yurga* (1926-1930), *Stikhi o kakhetii* (1935), the last two concerning contemporary life in Turkmenia and in Georgia. His collection *Tien' drouga* (1936) was based on his Western impressions and contains a passionate condemnation of fascism, declaring the poet's loyalty to the antifascist forces. The poems in this grouping present impressionistic perspectives of the upheavals wrought in Western Europe by World War I, as well as premonitions of the coming of new battles. *Chudesnaya trevoga* was written from 1937 to 1940 and *Gori* from 1938 to 1940. Among his patriotic verse and poems are "Kirov s nami" (1941), "Leningrad prinimaet bay" and "Ognenny god" (both in 1942). Among his verse cycles are: "Stikhi o Yugoslavii" (1947), "Gruzinskaya vesna" (1949), "Dva potoka" (1951), and "Na vtorom vsemirnom kongresse storonnikov mira"

(1951). He wrote the poem "Mys dondra" in 1960. *Mayskoe utro* (1961) is a collection of verse and stories.

Although Tíkhonov did not fight in Spain or even go to Spain, he had fought in Russia in a popular revolution and could identify intellectually with such a movement in Spain. Besides, he was a communist at the time of the war and still is. The three poems for analysis are: "Ispantsi otstupili za Pirenyiei," "Govorit fashist," and "Govorit antifashist." The first is in the section of Tíkhonov's collected poems titled "Gorï" (1938-1940). The other two appear under the heading "Numancia" (1938).

ИСПАНЦЫ
ОТСТУПИЛИ ЗА ПИРЕНЕИ[8]

1   Не могу прикоснуться к перу,
       Словно полны чернила заклятий,
       А в глухом иностранном бору
       Лишь о войнах выстукивал дятел.

5   Только видятся женщины мне
       Среди зимней дороги скалистой,
       Только дети, упавшие в снег,
       Только рощ обгоревшие листья.

       И о пепельных, полных седин,
10   Так пронизанных порохом рощах,
       И о людях, молящих воды
       За колючею проволкой ночью, —

       Что ни скажешь о жизни такой,
       Все не так, и не то, и все мало, —
15   Все уж сказано детской рукой,
       Из-под снега торчащей на скалах.
       —Níkolay Semyónovich Tíkhonov

In this neatly arranged lyrical poem, Tíkhonov evokes the aftermath of the Spanish Civil War. It is very powerful, the final disturbing image being a child's hand projecting from the snow. Over the hushed terrain, devastated, destroyed, ruined a woodpecker hammers as if via the Morse code. Women and children, among others unmentioned by Tíkhonov, have trekked from Catalonia, across the Pyrenees, to France in search of refuge. Their march was long, harassing, and brutal, sometimes terminating in death. There is also a glimpse of those who reached their destination and were interned behind barbed wire fences. They are now thirsty beggars in this hapless solution to the problem of the large influx into France. The poet admits his inadequacy to the task of writing down such a scene; however, unlike that of Braccialarghe, Tíkhonov's modesty belies his skillful, poignant poem. Tíkhonov claims that the vision he wishes to evoke has already been far more eloquently expressed by the isolated hand of the dead child and other remnants of the war—which does give one pause for thought.

The poem appeals to the emotions, expressing compassion for the suffering of the women and children, the most innocent victims of war. It also makes a strong visual appeal. This might have been an antiwar poem about any war except for the title which clearly depicts the final retreat from Spain beyond the Pyrenees and the barbed wire which denotes the French internment camps thereafter.

Говорит Фашист:[9]

1
    Вот говорят: фашистская держава
    Не знает человеческого права,
    Что мы глядим на вещи слишком просто,
    Что любим мы лишь тишину погоста.

5
    Сейчас я объясню вам, отчего:
    Народ — дитя, мы — фюреры его.
    Ребенка вы, чтоб вырос он титаном,
    С младенчества кормите барабаном.

    Парадов факелом слепите по ночам,
10
    Привейте вкус к воинственным речам.
    Довольно книг — в костер обложек глянец!
    Вокруг костра устраивайте танец,
    Какой плясал в медвежьей шкуре предок,
    И песню затяните напоследок,
15
    Что всей земли народов вы грозней
    И призваны господствовать над ней.

    Но так как ваш народ не до конца
    Покорен воле фюрера-отца
    И хочет жить, трудиться, веселиться,
20
    И предками не хочет он гордиться,
    И с ним вы не справляетесь добром, —
    Вооружитесь добрым топором.

И вот, когда по мере власти роста
Во всей стране величие погоста,
25   И введены военные харчи,
И есть приказ: работай и молчи! —
Тогда, чтоб не нагрянула разруха,
Возьмитесь вы за воспитанье духа:

Верните женщин кухне и перине,
30   Утехой воинов будут пусть отныне.
Усильте рев газетных батарей:
Виной всех бед марксист или еврей,
И что подчас они одно и то же —
Пускай наш гром скорей их уничтожит!
35   Нас вовсе сжали жалкие соседи,
В военной мы нуждаемся победе!

Твердите всем: обижены судьбою,
Отныне приступаем мы к разбою!
Чтобы за вами выла вся страна:
40   «Война! Война! Да здравствует война!»

Да здравствует война всегда и всюду,
И городов пылающие груды,
И вопли женщин, и оружья грохот,
Победы гул и побежденных ропот.
45   Покой и труд — марксистская гримаса,
Все расы — прах, есть только наша раса!

Так в пепел все — над пеплом знамя наше,
Пусть вражьи черепа идут на чаши.
Дохнем из них дыхание вина —
50   И все до дна: да здравствует война!
                    —Níkolay Semyónovich Tíkhonov

Tíkhonov wrote a Prefatory Note to the two poems, "Govorit fashist" and "Govorit antifashist," among others, explaining that the play *Numancia* by Cervantes depicts an episode of the battle between ancient Rome and Spain. The tragic details of the attack on the city of Numancia by the Romans show us the unceasing struggle for freedom of the Spanish people, their courage and contempt for death. The Roman world became aware of the Spaniards' sacrificial acceptance of death through the defense of their ally, the city of Saguntum, against the Carthaginians, and by the long fight of their enemy, the Celtiberian stronghold of Numancia, climaxed by the destruction of the city and the collective suicide of its inhabitants—who thus deprived Scipio of his victory over them. The bravery and love of liberty of Spain's ancestors compares with the heroism of the defenders of Republican Spain, 1936-1939.

In Cervantes' tragedy, comprised of four days' journeys, he introduced an intermezzo in verse. In the scene were presented allegorical figures: Spain, War, the River Duero, Hunger, and Glory (this listing is Tíkhonov's and differs somewhat from Cervantes' original). These allegorical figures deliver speeches about Spain during the time of Cervantes, and each figure speaks according to his viewpoint. The heroic tragedy, *Numancia,* was performed with great effect during the Spanish Civil War as an antifascist play.

Tíkhonov translated the intermezzo to *Numancia* and added new figures, the Fascist and the Antifascist, each speaking from his particular role's philosophy. He also changed the River Duero to the River Ebro.

"Dovorit fashist" is politically motivated and offers hard line Party rhetoric. The true fascist, according to Tíkhonov's scathing view, wishes to subjugate the world, while destroying it at the same time:

> Tak v pyépyel vsye—nad pyéplom známya náshe,
> Pust'vrázhyi chyeryepá idut na cháshi.
> Dokhnyóm iz nikh dĭkhániye viná—
> I vsyo do gna: da zdrávstvuyet voyná!

It is a completely military, anticultural viewpoint: "Dovól'no knyig—v kostyór oblózhek glyányets!" Women would be objects, exploited in the kitchen and bedroom. The enemy is the familiar .Marxist-Jewish scapegoat. The defensive claim is that the fascists have been oppressed by miserable neighbors, thus explaining their self-righteous prerogative to dominate and seize everyone and everything.

The devastation they will cause is a source of pride and is vividly depicted by violent, audio-visual-olfactory images of lines 41 through 50.

It is a patronizing perspective in which: "Naród—dityá, mĭ—fyúreri yevó." The masses are to be trained from childhood by military drums, martial speeches, torch parades, bonfires, songs, the specter of the war mentality pervading.

This is a highly ironic poem, with an exaggerated depiction of the fascist stand. The vocabulary is strong and energetic, as are the images. Death imagery is a motif. There is a pun on the word "pogosta" in line 4. Silence would prevail in a cemetery, but also, implicitly, there would be many graves. Again he speaks of enemy skulls and of complete ruination.

Considering the content, the traditionally pleasant rhyme scheme (aabb) is striking. The vocabulary is adapted to the theme and the poem and its implications are very strong, providing a merciless, violent attack upon fascism.

Its general condemnation rather than specific one against fascism in Spain (although the Spanish tie-in was clearly stated in Tíkhonov's Prefatory Note) suggests Tíkhonov's ideological aversion to fascism wherever it occurs, and lack of particular identity with Spain.

Говорит Антифашист:[10]

1   Чтоб надо мной стояла ночь и день
     Тюремщика вихляющая тень,
     Чтоб каждой мысли вольное движенье
     Немедленно бралось под подозренье,
5   Чтобы страницы мной любимых книг
     Костер фашистский уничтожил вмиг,
     Чтоб вместо слов простых и человечных
     Рев фюреров я слышал бесконечный,
     Чтобы всю жизнь под диких песен вой
10   Шагал с лопатой в лагерь трудовой,
     Чтобы, презренной жизнью дорожа,
     К народам пленным шел я в сторожа,
     Участвовал в разбойничьих походах,
     Чтобы убийц я славил в рабских одах,
15   Чтоб стал, как труп, безмолвен и, как труп,
     Гнил заживо между заводских труб,
     Одной войне дымящих славословье,
     Моих друзей обрызганное кровью,
     Чтоб я забыл, что есть на свете разум.
20   Косясь на мир налитым злобой глазом,—

Нет! Будет мир стоять неколебим!
Он помнит все, что пережито им:
Пожары, казни, бедствия, сраженья,
Века позора, рабства, униженья,
25 Где б ни свистел кнутами новый Рим —
Мы ничего ему не отдадим!

Ни наших нив, шумящих морем хлеба,
Ни наших гор, вонзивших пики в небо,
Ни наших рек, струящихся в тиши,
30 Ни начатых народами работ,
Ни городов, где улиц гул веселый,
Ни тех полей, где расцветают села;
И соловей не должен умереть,
О нашей славе будет он греметь,
35 И ястреба, что над холмов горбами,
Пускай парят простыми ястребами,
И ни тропинки розовой, весенней,
И ни морей, что нету многопенней,
И ни костра, чей вьется рыжий дым
40 В лесу осеннем, — мы не отдадим.
Не отдадим улыбок наших смелых,
Ни парусов на лодках наших белых,
Ни воздуха, которым дышим мы,
Ни блеска дня, ни теплой ночи тьмы,
45 Последней ветви яблони румяной,
Луча зари над спящею поляной,
Ни гордости самим собою быть,
Ни права завоеванной судьбы.
Фашизм найдет лишь гибель впереди —
50 Мы ничего ему не отдадим!

Пусть северный иль южный встанет Рим —
Смертельно с ним в бою поговорим!
—Níkolay Semyónovich Tíkhonov

This poem, written from an antifascist viewpoint, begins in
the first person as a German (or Russian) soldier ponders his conscription into an army under a führer (or führers) against his will.
He feels himself and even his innermost thoughts imprisoned and
judged. Fascism destroyed a culture that he loved and he worked
in a labor camp where he was forced to listen to nothing but the
loudest incantations of the führer and indoctrination songs.

He has been forced to serve as a soldier with those whom he
despised, and forced to repeat poems glorifying soldiers who were
no more than pirates. He worked in factories, serving the war

effort, and could not speak up without risk of his life. His friends were dying from overwork in these factories, and he was numbed into forgetting that there might be a reasonable world somewhere outside and beyond.

This antifascist hates what he has seen and protests against what he has had to do. The first stanza offers a lament for what has happened and what is happening. In the second part he is awakened out of his stupor and doubting into a strong assertion of his convictions. Rome's imperialism is equated with that of Nazi-fascism. The stanza ends with his declaration never to surrender what freedom offers and what fascism would, most assuredly, destroy.

The third stanza lists magnificently, beautifully, and lyrically what it is he is unwilling to part with and surrender to Nazi-fascism. And it is a lovely vision of peacetime, nature, and what is best in the world.

Finally, he shouts that whether Northern or Southern Rome (Germany, that is) rises up, he and his antifascist, fellow-soldiers will meet them in a battle to the death. It expresses a stand as well as a threat. There is a point beyond which men will not submit even if it costs them their lives.

The poem reveals its message in a stentorian voice. It is a strongly-felt, strongly-stated, didactic poem preaching antifascism, condemning Nazi-fascism. Although rhetorical, the words are not empty; the verse expresses a militancy, hostility, and vitality that must derive from an energetic, absolutely dedicated antifascist.

Giorgio Braccialarghe was the son of a better-known writer than himself, Comunardo Braccialarghe (who wrote under the pseudonym Folco Testena). Despite Giorgio's obscurity, he had the distinction of having fought in the Spanish Civil War as vice-commander of the Garibaldi Battalion, composed of idealistic young Italians, numbering 3350, and of having written at least four poems about the war. Two of the poems eulogize his International Brigade; and the other two, also, speak directly from his war experience. He signed his poems, collected in an anthology of International Brigade poetry, *Romancero de los voluntarios de la libertad,* published in Madrid in 1937, only with his last name. It was only in his father's biography in *Dizionario bio-grafico degli italiani* that Giorgio is not only mentioned, but definitely connected with the Spanish Civil War. After the war, he continued to fight against Nazi-fascism in Europe, where he was arrested and imprisoned on Ventotene, an island in the Gulf of Naples. His ultimate fate remains unknown.

TERRA DI SPAGNA . . .[11]

1   Terra di Spagna quando annotta. Freme
     per gli uliveti e sopra l'arsa terra
     la nuova voce di chi più non teme
     l'immane vergogna della guerra.

5   Per quelli che verranno un'altra sorte
     la voce canta, e noi che l'ascoltiamo
     in essa la consegna ritroviamo:
     Non v'è resurrezione senza morte.

     Terra di Spagna quando annotta. Voi
10   col sublime linguaggio degli eroi
     questa consegna tramandaste a noi
     ed ai venturi che verran da noi.

     Voi moriste, o compagni, ma la morte
     v'illuminò la vita. Noi vivremo
15   perchè la vita illumini la morte
     di chi prescelse il sacrificio estremo.
                              —Giorgio Braccialarghe

This is a very idealistic, lyrical poem written with youthful vigor and faith by a soldier-poet who desperately wants and needs to believe that the many deaths in his own battalion have not been in vain. In order to carry on one must believe that the sacrifice has meaning, purpose, and possibilities beyond itself ("resurrezione," "illuminò la vita").

The voice that roars above the subdued landscape of nighttime Spain ("per gli uliveti e sopra l'arsa terra") comes from those

heroes (with whom the poet closely identifies) who have died—
who are beyond fear—but are still present in spirit. The voice
commands that those still left in the fight know that death for
their cause has positive value with great rewards. Such a philosophy offers consolation, hope, courage, and faith in the difficult
trials of war that lie ahead. Braccialarghe meant to inspire his
fellow-men in a continuing struggle. He considers the language
of these dead heroes "sublime." Braccialarghe addressed his poem
to his fellow soldiers with simple and repetitious praise.

Reminiscent of "Notti di Spagna" when the lull at nighttime
makes such thoughts possible, "Terra di Spagna . . ." glorifies
death in this battle to achieve some meaning from life. It is
through death in such a struggle that life might have some meaning in the future. Identification with the aims of the war, as well
as hope and faith, align this soldier-poet with the Hispanic poets
we have discussed.

NOTTI DI SPAGNA [12]

1
 V'è tanta biacca nel cielo
 che sembra che una sposa
 abbia dimenticato il suo velo
 appeso ad una rosa.

5
 E il velo sventoli nella campagna
 come un filtro pieno d'incantamento
 che lasci passare
 il chiarore lunare
 tra i fremiti del vento.

10
 Notti di Spagna,
 cantando le raganelle
 lungo i fossati
 tra i prati.

 V'è un bisbiglio assonnato
15
 come se le belle
 ascoltassero i segreti
 dei loro innamorati.

20

Notti di Spagna,
mantelli di pace gettati
sui martoriati giorni
ritorni di calma
sussurri indefinite
rumori azzittiti.

25

Le seninelle immobili nell'ombra;
sembrano statue sperse
nei sentieri d'un parco.

30

Notti di Spagna
nelle trincee serpeggiano
ingenue confidenze
qualcuno parla della fidanzata
qualcuno narra l'ultima avanzata.

35

E nei brevi silenzi
che punteggiano le frasi
voci lontane
di compagni scomparsi
sussurrano parole strane.

Intanto, nella notte stellata
risuona qualche fucilata.
—Giorgio Braccialarghe

As a soldier Braccialarghe would have known the dreamlike nights of Spain, as well as the days of desperate, determined destruction. He looks at the dark sky with its clouds and moon and sees them metaphorically in terms of a bride's veil hanging upon a rose. The nights are so quiet that the toads can be heard. The trenches, ironically, are located in meadows which were once peaceful and beautiful. The silence is, for the poet, like the atmosphere when lovers whisper secrets.

The peaceful nights belie the horror-filled days that have preceded and will follow. Even the sentry on guard, ready to shoot at a moment's notice, seems like a statue in a peacetime park. Again, because of the stillness, innocent conversations about loved ones or past battles are heard in the trenches.

It seems, between sounds, when the hush is total, that even the strange, remote dialogue of dead comrades can be heard, as in "Terra di Spagna . . . ." Meanwhile, from time to time, in the night full of stars, a gunshot shatters the calm, reverberates, and reminds us of what the situation really is.

This is a laconic poem that leaves out more than it includes. Full of brief glimpses and sounds in the night, the poem offers a romantic and oblique perspective during the respite between battles. It is what is suggested, but not mentioned, that makes an impact. The gunshot in the final line provokes sober, somber reflection from the reader. This is a lyrical, eulogistic poem whose mood is nostalgic for peacetime behavior, attitudes, and environment.

AI FRATELLI LONTANI . . .[13]

1   Stanotte voglio cantare per voi
        senza rima né metro.
        Povere parole balbettate
        come quando dopo aver pianto tanto,
5   uno ricerca chi sparì per sempre.
        E gli parla. E non sa cosa dice
        né che vorrebbe dire.
        Voglio parlarvi, O fratelli lontani
        come quando m'eravate vicini
10   e sembravate titani.
        Titani nella lotta, fanciulli nella pace.
        Non posso pensare che qualcuno giace
        sbiancato, in un bianco letto
        col suo sembiante di giovinetto
15   che non vuol morire.
        Non posso pensare che non debba venire
        il giorno della resurrezione
        per il nostro battaglione.

Il terzo: il più forte!
20 Primo all' attacco e primo alla vittoria.
Scriveva le pagine più belle della storia
tra una canzone e l'altra.
Colonna gagliarda di gagliardi eroi.
Poco meno di mille,
25 mille anime in ognuno.
Avanti, avanti, avanti.
Sopportando fatiche e digiuno
sonno e sete ma avanti
come tanti giganti
30 che s'alimentano d'ideali
e che non chiedono che ali
per il volo trionfale
verso la meta finale.
Poco meno di mille,
35 ma quanta, quanta fede!
Sui colli martoriati del Jarama
nei boschi dell'Alcarria
tutto un inno di gloria
scritto col vostro sangue
40 immortalato dal vostro sacrificio.
—Madrid intanto
sopportava il lugubre canto
dei cannoni nemici.
E su nella Viscaglia
45 l'eterna canaglia
distruggeva ogni cosa.—
Che importa? Nei lettini
degli ospedali da campo
sorgeva una rosa
50 di sangue, sorgeva un sorriso
nel vostro viso di giovani eroi
Avevate fiducia in noi.
In noi che restando alla lotta
occupavamo, fieri, il vostro posto

55   o scomparsi di ieri
            o destinati a vivere domani.
            Domani, quando dai campi liberati
            dalle officine redente
            s'eleverà solennemente in coro
60   l'inno della pace e del lavoro.
                              —Giorgio Braccialarghe

Similar to "Fratelli dell'Internazionale," "Ai fratelli lontani . . ."
deals with the International Brigade. Randolfo Pacciardi, an
Italian Republican émigré (never a communist) had approached
the Spanish government and had gotten its approval for his idea
of forming an Italian Legion in Spain, independent of political
parties, to be recruited at first in Paris out of Italian political
exiles.

The first groups of International Brigades arrived in Spain in
October of 1936. They were nearly all Frenchmen, with some
Polish and German exiles from Paris. There were also some White
Russians. These were shortly joined by many of the foreign vol-
unteers who had fought in Aragon and in the Tagus valley, in-
cluding the German Thaelmann Centuria, the Italian Gastone-
Sozzi Centuria, and the French Paris Battalion.

The Garibaldi Battalion was formed in November of 1936 as
the Italian trainees took over the village of Madrigueras. On
November 12 the new XIIth International Brigade, comprised
of the Thaelmann, André Marty, and Garibaldi Battalions of
Germans, French, and Italians, was sent to the sector of the front
at the Madrid-Valencia highway. Braccialarghe's calling his battalion the third is, therefore, confusing.

Pacciardi, who proved himself from the start an outstanding
leader, led the Garibaldi Battalion. Giorgio Braccialarghe was
a vice-commander.

When the Brigade first entered battle, commands were confused
because of the language problem in giving orders. Besides, having
marched almost nine miles that day, the Brigade was tired before
it started to fight. Artillery support was inadequate, and certain
companies got lost. Fighting went on for the rest of the day, but

the object of the attack, the hill in the geographical center of Spain known as Cerro de los Angeles, remained impregnable. The Brigade then withdrew and was transferred to the Madrid front. The Brigade was also later involved in the attack against Huesca on the Aragon front, in an attempt to draw Nationalist fire away from Bilbao.

It can be assumed that Braccialarghe was painfully aware that the fighting of the Brigade was very rough going and that a third of the Brigade died in action in Spain.

"Ai fratelli lontani . . ." is full of the clichés of war and peace and of enemies and allies. It glorifies the memory of those soldiers who are now far away in Death. He explains his technique: no rhyme, no meter. And he addresses himself directly to the war dead.

Although Braccialarghe is a part of the military force, he has not lost his humanity. He feels obliged to write, wishing to express what he has inside himself. Yet he recognizes his poetic limitations. Like Hernández, he is a young idealist who fights and writes poems on behalf of his convictions.

He yearns to believe in the resurrection of the war dead. Again, as in "Fratelli dell'Internazionale," the soldiers through their deeds, figuratively, write beautiful pages of history. From lines 19 to 22, he speaks of the soldiers and the poems they have within them. Their idealism, youth, hope, bravery, hardships, and final sacrifice are eloquent. Braccialarghe numbers the battalion at a thousand and mentions various locations of their battles: Jarama, Alcarria, Viscaglia. He uses the rose, a common metaphor, here as in "Notti di Spagna." Turning to those still left to fight, he means to urge them on by reminding them of their obligation to their dead brothers. He dreams of liberty and imagines the future, after victory is achieved: "della pace e del lavoro." The poem is nostalgic in tone as it romanticizes the soldiers, the war, and the future.

The poem begins lyrically and becomes epic and martial toward the end as it lists some of the battlegrounds. Of lyrical origin in its desire for peace, it is a political poem, socialistic in its notion of brotherhood.

FRATELLI DELL'INTERNAZIONALE [14]

1

I primi sei mesi di lotta sono passati: avanti, fratelli
dell'Internazionale.

2

La vittoria ancora non è stata raggiunta: avanti,
fratelli dell'Internazionale.

3

A palmo, a palmo, e con al fianco il sacrificio che
è bello, e con il ricordo dei nostri caduti nel
cuore: avanti, fratelli dell'Internazionale.

4

Voi siete i seminatori dei domani. Già l'alba si è
affacciata nel cielo rosso della rivoluzione, già la
terra di Spagna conosce la vostra seminagione:
avanti, fratelli dell'Internazionale.

5

La lotta dell'oggi reca le promesse di pace del
domani, la sementa di ieri, i frutti dell'avvenire:
avanti, fratelli dell'Internazionale.

6

Tra tutte le vostre canzoni manca quella della
Spagna liberata. Voi ne sarete gli epici poeti, voi
la creerete con le vostre gesta, giorno per giorno,
ora per ora: avanti, fratelli dell'Internazionale.

7

Vi conosco uno per uno, ma se conoscessi uno solo
di voi, vi conoscerei tutti. Per il patrimonio di
fede, di disciplina e di volontà che vi rende
uguali, per la semplicita che veste ogni vostra
azione sublime.

8

Dopo sei mesi vi riconosco uno per uno. Siete
ancora gli stessi, ancora portate in voi il fermo
desiderio di vittoria che baciò la fronte chiara
dei nostri Caduti.

9

Avanti, fratelli dell'Internazionale. Per altre lotte,
per altri trionfi; uniti; per la Spagna accogliente,
nel suo grembo sanguinante, i destini del mondo:
invincibili.

10

Avanti, fratelli dell'Internazionale. Con voi la
giustizia, contro di voi la rabbia del falsi potenti.

11

Ognuno di voi che cade è una goccia d'olio nella
lampada votiva della Libertà. Ogni nemico che
abbattete e una maglia infranta della catena che
tiene avvinta l'Umanità.

12

Avanti, fratelli dell'Internazionale. Avanti, avanti,
avanti. Per il domani di Spagna. Per l'avvenire
di tutto il mondo. Avanti!

—Giorgio Braccialarghe

Braccialarghe presents his poem, "Fratelli dell'Internazionale,"
from a first-person-singular viewpoint and addresses it to the
Brigade in the second person plural: "Voi siete i seminatori dei
domani." He knows them "uno per uno," and identifies with
their cause of world freedom, at the same time that he has a perspective above them that a commander would have.

He dates the poem January 1937 in the first line. This early
in the war the outcome could still have been mistaken. Although
there have been heavy losses, he justifies the price of present glory
and future victory. The poem is reminiscent of those by Hernández, who glorified death in such a movement.

Until the Nationalist and Red Revolutionary (he sounds like a fellow traveler) side wins, Spain cannot be free. In this sense, it is a political poem. The side of the Republic is just; the enemy is "falsi." He knows not only whom they fight against, but what they fight for.

He honors the soldiers, calls them, figuratively, epic poets, glorifies their cause, and emphasizes the difficult epic struggle ahead. He considers that Spain herself, transformed into the metaphor of a bleeding bosom, awaits them.

The poem serves the purpose of a marching song, especially with its refrain, calling his fellow soldiers to arms, urging them forward toward final victory. It is youthfully optimistic, idealistic, encouraging, and inspirational. Their task is noble and will affect the whole world.

The poem is lyrical and has a limited vocabulary. It is energetic both in content and form. There is much repetition as well as internal and external rhyme, which takes advantage of the frequent vowel endings in Italian.

Since it was anthologized among poems by volunteers in a dangerous struggle, an anthology hastily put together without biographical information on the poets, dates, or even first names, the poems included were probably written hastily near the battlefield.

Braccialarghe has written straightforward, simple poems based on his firsthand experience of the war. He was young, idealistic, and caught up in a movement capable of changing the world for the better, as he saw it. His imagery relies on familiar symbols: blood, veil, and the rose, but has a vital simplicity. These poems are significant in terms of their time and place in the history of the war. Braccialarghe's vision is understandable in view of his youth and idealism, the year in which they were written (early 1937), the many efforts and sacrifices from himself and his countrymen in a cause to which, as a foreign volunteer, one had to be totally dedicated. The poems are subjective, appealing to emotions rather than to intellect, and humbly offered ("senza rima né metro./Povere parole balbettate").

Notes

1. Johannes R. Becher, *Gedichte 1936-1941* (Berlin: Aufbau-Verlag, 1966), pp. 411-12.

2. Becher, *Ausgewählte Dichtung aus der Zeit der Verbannung, 1933-1945* (Berlin: Aufbau-Verlag, 1945), pp. 119-20.

3. Becher, *Gedichte 1936-1941*, p. 413.

4. Paul Eluard, *Cours naturel* (Paris: Editions du Sagittaire, 1938), pp. 13-15.

5. Eluard, *Cours naturel*, pp. 48-52.

6. Eluard, *Poèmes politiques* (Paris: Gallimard, 1948), p. 31.

7. Eluard, *Poèmes politiques*, p. 35.

8. Níkolay Semyónovich Tíkhonov, *Izbránnye proizvédenija v dvuch tómach* (Moscow: State Publishing Co. of Literature of Art, 1955), p. 246.

9. Tíkhonov, *Izbránnye proizvédenija v dvuch tómach*, pp. 263-65.

10. Tíkhonov, *Izbránnye proizvédenija v dvuch tómach*, pp. 265-66.

11. "Nuestros héroes," *Romancero de los voluntarios de la libertad* (Madrid: Ediciones del Comisariado de las Brigadas Internacionales, 1937), p. 58.

12. "La hora de ensueños," *Romancero de los voluntarios de la libertad*, p. 61.

13. *Romancero de los voluntarios de la libertad*, pp. 70-72.

14. Section 5, "¡Adelante!," *Romancero de los voluntarios de la libertad*, pp. 88-89.

CHAPTER V

General Comparative Conclusions

All the poems discussed here have in common that they were written on the occasion of, or in memory of, the Spanish Civil War. Is there a valid basis for comparing and contrasting them? Limiting the selection of poems to those deriving from the broad impetus of a particular set of events allows us to concentrate on other variables. Many comparative factors affecting the poems were considered in Chapters II, III, and IV. It was shown, for example, that there are differences between the Spanish/Latin view of Spain and the war, and that of non-Spaniards. Countless other variables affected the war poetry: age of poet, environment, class, education, upbringing, personality, religion, political convictions, personal involvement (in war), knowledge and understanding (of war), moral conscience, objectivity, focus, style, talent, intellect, literary influences, purpose, when and where written (proximity to war). Each brought to the occasion of the war his own nature and uniqueness as a poet and as a human being.

The Spanish Civil War was contended on many levels. Men

were deeply moved to voluntary service, sacrifice, and death. Soldiers, civilians, peasants, aristocrats, politicians, businessmen, clergy, political activists, and many others took sides. Literary men, too. It was a truly ideological conflict and the issues were very clear. All literature about it is political to some extent. There were two writers' factions: one of the Left and one of the Right. There were no neutral writers. These poets were not all committed to the same ideals nor were their commitments equally strong. There were many forms their resistance took.

Although disapproving of extremism on both sides, most of the intellectuals were antifascist and sympathetic to the cause of the Republic. This is not surprising, since the socially conscious are traditionally on the Left. From both sides of the Atlantic, support came for Franco, especially from Roman Catholic writers.

While the war had multiple meanings outside Spain, to many Spaniards it was the latest episode in a long and tragic domestic conflict. The Spanish writers emphasized the internal strife of the country—the socioeconomic and political conditions that left the people dissatisfied and divided.

Foreign writers were often ignorant of the deadly struggle between the Spanish Right and the parties of the Left (anarchists, socialists, communists) which had precipitated the uprising. Foreign writers have been criticized for being narrow-minded about the total situation. They have been accused of propagandizing.

To the foreigners the war seemed less concerned with issues indigenous to Spain than with worldwide problems. When it became known that Italy and Germany had intervened on the side of the Nationalists and that Russia had begun to supply the Loyalists, little doubt remained that Spain had become the international battleground of opposing ideologies. Foreigners, then, tended to view the war as it happened (1936-1939) and in an international context.

Spaniards, on the other hand, looked back to the evolution of Spanish discord. They searched within Spain and its people for the deep roots of their misfortune and discontent. But Spanish writers, too, have their limitation. The Spanish could recall their history, knew the Spanish character as native, and concentrated on the origins of the conflict in Spain. But the war grew beyond

Spain. It developed beyond domestic strife and discontent. It assumed the proportions of big-power politics and modern warfare, so that "Spanish Civil War" became, decidedly, a misnomer.

Roy Campbell was violently pro-Franco. MacDiarmid was an ardent Scottish nationalist and saw the Spanish struggle in terms of his own people. The same is true of Tíkhonov, who looked at the struggle in relation to Russia; he would have been opposed to fascism wherever he found it, as would Braccialarghe. Auden, Becher, Eluard, MacDiarmid, Neruda, Spender, and Tíkhonov were, at one time or another, communists or, at least, fellow travelers. Members of the "Auden generation" tended to be fellow travelers partly for personal reasons to do with their background but mainly because they had already formed in their own minds sets of values which were not compatible with communist ideology. Spender and Rukeyser held general antiwar attitudes. Their diverse backgrounds and experience fostered divergent perspectives and some contradictory viewpoints. There are also parallels among their works: often they corroborate or supplement one another.

Believing wholly in an ideology (communism, Christianity, fascism, nationalism, or whatever) can give one a more confident, positive, and heroic outlook on events. The belief in a total enemy—such as is implied by religious or ideological conviction—encourages the idea of total commitment, whereas halfhearted belief can lead to questions, doubts, and soul-searching. When poets were moved enough or when they considered the message they wished to impart and the response they hoped to elicit important enough, there was always the possibility of over-simplifying or exaggerating reality. Besides, it is difficult under any circumstances to maintain objectivity, and especially so in a war as emotionally charged as this one. And, finally, objectivity is not a prerequisite of poems—the way it should be of journalism, for example.

Felipe understood the demands of his Republican cause and was deeply troubled by the divisions on his side as well as antagonistic toward powers that could have helped but, opportunistically, ignored the plight of the Republic. His religious faith, however, provided him with an idealistic hope which he embraced at the end of "La insignia." But it was a romantic notion much like Vallejo's. MacDiarmid was temporarily disillusioned but maintained hope through his faith in the final justice of communism and democracy. The note of disaffection with communism was apparent in Auden's *Spain* and Spender's "Two Armies" and "Ultima Ratio Regum." Auden criticized communist bureaucracy, Spender its duplicity. Campbell could be exultant and exuberant because he fiercely maintained that the side that had won he totally believed in. His religion, also, buoyed his spirits. Hernández fought for Spain poetically as if he were writing for his life. It was an all-out, idealistic commitment, partly attributable to his youth. Rukeyser and Spender were staunchly humanitarian and pacifistic, and critical disillusionment over the means and outcome (of war in general) crept into their poems. Becher, MacDiarmid, and Tíkhonov did not travel to Spain physically but supported the ideological cause of antifascism in Spain intellectually. They identified it as a struggle against tyranny.

Eventually the poets had to make a choice between poetry and physical participation in the events. Sometimes they did not have a choice (some poets were killed). Of all the poets who wrote about the war, a dozen or so volunteered to fight and all of them with the Loyalists (I think it's clear that fascism is not likely to inspire soldier/poets or poets at all). Sometimes they had to write under conditions inimical to poetry writing. There was apt to be a gap between conception and achievement of war poems. It is difficult, near a battlefield, to achieve the composure and concentration necessary for creating poetry. Hernández and Braccialarghe fought. The poet/soldiers had to snatch what moments they could from other, tyrannical duties. Vallejo was dead before the war was over.

Auden was able to separate his political poem from mere propaganda because of his disciplined sensibility and technique. Spender's intention was to separate his politics from his poetry, and therefore he expressed a personal reaction to the war, with ideology entering only as a vague backdrop. Rukeyser's poems had political overtones but were mainly, like Spender's, personal. Neruda was politically oriented and his poems were political, but in "Explico" he transformed the public tragedy into a personal one. Both MacDiarmid and Campbell wrote political poems, with little restraint of their propagandistic proselytizing; Tíkhonov would be of this school. Campbell squandered his energy in tearing down his enemies, while MacDiarmid spent much of his effort in destroying Campbell. Tíkhonov exaggerated the fascist and antifascist stands. Vallejo's political ideology, although an integral part of his thinking and being, was not brought out directly in his poems.

The Spanish Civil War was a vast and amorphous theme of which the poets could make what they wished. What matters in poetry on such a public subject is the vision which the poet has of it, his insight into its essential character, and its relevance to the human state. Perhaps the truth of human understanding can be found more in art than in politics. Personal emotion is perhaps a more enduring subject for poetry than war politics.

The poetic vision of these poets allowed them to know not only what they were fighting against, but also what they were fighting for. Broad patriotism, love of life, and faith in a better future combined with intense hatred, prompted by equally intense moral indignation.

There are things that cannot and should not be forgiven, things which it would be nothing but moral cowardice and callousness to forgive. It is with love—and hate—that some of these poems were written. Poems can help to overcome a moral crisis. The poems offered sympathy and encouragement as well as condemnation. Poems can be like ammunition to be used against an enemy that must be stopped.

The struggle for existence in the Spanish Civil War coincided, right from the start, with a gigantic struggle for fundamental human rights and decencies, united by a single purpose for whose achievement no effort, no sacrifice, seemed too great. Men were dying in order that future generations might lead a life worthy of human beings. That's why the war attracted so many idealists.

Some of the poems dealt with are more valid than others. My own bias is that the best war poems are not limited to war, but transcend it, leading to the deepest speculations about man. Good poems communicate experience, not propaganda. The most successful war poets are probably those who have no disposition to propagandize or to prophesy and write about their personal sensations in new ways or by adapting old ways. The best war poetry achieves a universality transcending the particular. It expresses the poet's attitude to something beyond the immediacy of war, encompassing a variety of interpenetrating meanings.

Which subjects other than the war did these poets consider in their poems? Auden wrote of human values and politics, and surveyed the past, present, and future in *Spain*. Vallejo considered death, love, man's aloneness, the arbitrariness of authority and fate, and the values at stake in Spain. The map of the peninsula of Spain played on the imagination of Hernández. He urged action, love, and even the sacrifice of one's life in his poems. Neruda and Rukeyser wrote of their personal lives as well as of the war, but Neruda's life was more integral to that of Spain ("Explico"). Neruda chose satire to express "Almería." He considered the effect of the war on his poetry in "Explico." Felipe, too, considered his role in view of the events. He emphasized unity, manhood, and justice. The poems of MacDiarmid and Campbell concerned multifarious aspects of their lives and philosophies while centering on the war. Braccialarghe concentrated on the perspective of a soldier and on the International Brigade to which he belonged.

Do the poems transcend politics and the immediate issues of war to consider the fundamental values of man? Auden's poem especially does. Felipe's comprehensive view allowed him to consider what ultimately counts. Neruda was concerned about the welfare of the Republicans. Vallejo and Hernández empathized with mankind. Rukeyser and Spender felt deeply for those who suffer in any war. Vallejo's feeling encompassed all of mankind. Spender, too, expressed the loss felt by all humanity. Neruda could see the tragedy both as personal ("Explico") and in broader ("Almería"), more panoramic ("Llegada") terms. There are international implications in the poems of Neruda ("Llegada"), Felipe, Hernández ("Recoged esta voz"), MacDiarmid, and Campbell. Auden's, Spender's, Rukeyser's considerations transcend the immediate war situation. Neruda and Eluard were outraged that a civilian population was ruthlessly attacked at Almería or anywhere. Eluard was concerned for the most innocent victims:

women and children; we see a similar focus in Tíkhonov's "Ispantsi otstupili za Pirenyiei."

What was the effect of the Spanish Civil War on their poetry? Once they had found a cause to communicate, Eluard, Neruda, and Vallejo changed from previously obscure styles to more clarity and simplicity. Neruda developed from subjectivism and multiple images to objectivity and fewer images. Vallejo left surrealism in favor of greater simplicity and realism ("Pequeño responso" is an exception). As for Vallejo, he was jolted into poetic creativity after a silence of fifteen years. Vallejo was depressed, while Neruda had energy for a sarcastic and militant stand ("Almería"). Eluard abandoned surrealism and simplified his verse, also. Becher ("General Mola") and Eluard ("La Victoire de Guernica") were caustic, while Tíkhonov ironically spouted his venom against fascism ("Govorit fashist"). Felipe became embittered, belligerent, and declamatory. The conditions of war create in many readers or listeners a state of mind which makes them more hungry for poetry and more responsive to it than ordinarily. Hernández met such a need; he was inspired and inspiring. Campbell and MacDiarmid gave free rein to their emotional, political, and talkative extremism. Auden maintained a measured calm, part of his essential nature and technique; Spender was more emotional. Rukeyser was bitterly against war in "M-Day's Child" and "Third Elegy." Braccialarghe was provoked into poetic expression by the war but admitted his inadequacy to the task. Tíkhonov, though far superior to Braccialarghe as a poet, also expressed that the war spoke much more eloquently for itself than any poem could.

How did the war, and their individual natures, affect the tones they assumed? A mature Vallejo, desperately disappointed, understated his poems (in tone). Neruda declaimed and asserted a strong, militant stand ("Almería"). Hernández and Braccialarghe, young, idealistic, and passionate, emotionally advocated martyrdom in the face of such a tragic future. Felipe was mature, objective, and knowledgeable in his rhetorical, dramatic analysis of the situation. He was also emotional and despairing, but offered a rather fanciful glimmer of hope at the end. Tíkhonov followed his Party line in "Govorit fashist" and "Govorit antifashist," assuming a pontifical tone, while "Ispantsi otstupili za Pirenyiei" is muted and lyrical.

Becher unmercifully and sarcastically attacked General Mola, while Eluard made a strong statement in "La Victoire de Guernica" through the use of sarcasm.

Campbell ranted and raved, flaunting his *machismo* and the absolute rightness of his causes while denouncing his foes. He defiantly proclaimed a new heroic age. MacDiarmid answered in kind, but with more of a relevant argument. Auden was detached and impersonal. Spender felt the tragedy personally and expressed it with measured emotionality. Rukeyser was strongly opinionated and passionate in her poems. Their natures accommodated, but did not change basically, to the perspectives from which they viewed the struggle and outcome. None of the tones in the war poetry was comic. Profound distaste and gravity do not lend themselves to comedy. You can't laugh about something unless you are detached and feel secure about it.

War, like love and justice, has had constant attention from poets and other writers. In a sense, all war literature is similar. War makes people come to grips with questions of values. The immediacy of death in war makes one question the value of life when weighed against such intangible stakes as freedom, justice, loyalty, honor, and courage. Scanning a threatening, hopeless present, León Felipe exhorted "Vamos a la muerte!" ("La insignia"). Not death for its own sake, but an heroic death in a fight against evil forces. For similar reasons, Hernández wrote "Cantando espero a la muerte" ("Vientos del pueblo me llevan"). It was to be a death that represented a brave fight and a refusal to submit to tyranny.

A difference in ways of looking at death in the war separated Hispanic poets, aligned with those poets who fought, from those who neither were Hispanic nor fought. Vallejo, Hernández, and Braccialarghe saw death itself as inevitable, while Auden, viewing death less directly, saw the inevitability of the "increase in the chances" of it. The Hispanic poets had faith in the fruitfulness of the sacrifice in bringing about a new life; this faith, perhaps desperate and romantic, was devoid of the bitterness apparent, for example, in Spender's "Ultima Ratio Regum" about the dead soldier on a Spanish field. Neruda employed bitter irony in "Almería," but it was not directed at war deaths. Among the Hispanic war poets, there were wrath, anger, imprecation as well as hope and pity, but rarely irony about the death. When Spender wrote "Consider. One bullet in ten thousand kills a man./Ask. Was so much expenditure justified/On the death of one so young and so silly . . . ," he expressed a bitter sense of the futility of the death of a boy. The Hispanic poets had more faith. The image of Spain, of its cities, of its people, dying and destroyed, but becoming the seed of a New Spain, appears time and again among Hispanic poems. They regarded the war dead not as dead but as a part of a living army, not as absent and finished but as sharing in the continuing struggle and in the future with the people with whom and for whom they had fought. The Hispanic poets abandoned themselves more to their fight and felt closer to the feelings of the people.

For Vallejo these men could be immortal, but not in the usual sense of immortality by fame and glory through people's memory, but immortal in being alive through the totality of their living comrades and of the ideals behind their cause. It would not, then, be survival in the traditional Christian sense of life after death of individual souls. Even in 1937, when the war was already lost, there was hope for a better future, if not immediately, then ultimately.

Overcoming death by resurrecting, after having died in battle, is not in the Hispanic poets of the 1936-1939 war a personal and individual survival. It was, on the contrary, a survival embodied in the prevailing ideals and cause in which the dead men believed and for which they accepted the need to sacrifice themselves, usefully and fruitfully. Even among pain, destruction, and death, the Hispanic and soldier/poets could be hopeful and joyful (Vallejo's "Masa" and "España, aparta de mí este cáliz"; Felipe's "La insignia"; Hernández' "Vientos del pueblo me llevan" and "Recoged esta voz"; Neruda's "Llegada a Madrid de la Brigada Internacional"; Braccialarghe's "Ai fratelli lontani . . ." and "Fratelli dell'Internazionale"). Spender and Rukeyser are more prone to personal despondency and despair.

If one might not (because Death rudely interrupts) enjoy a better future himself, at least, one's surviving comrades and one's children would, and a man could—through them—feel rewarded and justified. Vallejo ("España, aparta de mí este cáliz") and

Braccialarghe in his two poems about the Italian Brigade express this. For the Hispanic poet, then, the general, ultimate welfare took priority over personal salvation.

There is a difference between the treatment of death by combatants and noncombatants. Those who are not in constant contact with death might be deeply affected by it, glamorize it, or deal with it abstractly and remotely. They not only might express their grief freely but also might see in death much more than its immediate presence (for example, comradeship and glory). The average soldier is fatalistic, making speculation superfluous. It is useless to lament or do anything except remain silent and hide one's feelings. There is dignity in silence in the face of something about which there is nothing to say. Where death comes all the time, it hardly calls for special remark. The open expression of horror in the fairly abstract "M-Day's Child" suggests that Rukeyser's knowledge of combat was not firsthand. Spender's anonymous victim ("a better target for a kiss" than a bullet) in "Ultima Ratio Regum" suggests a similar distance from the fighting. Auden's poem, too, was far from the scene of battle: "All presented their lives." Braccialarghe, however, was able to reconcile himself to the abundant death surrounding him in battle by idealizing the cause, viewing the dead as martyrs, and thus justifying it.

Anyone who had actually seen children shot would have been less glib about the occurrence than Auden in *Spain* and less abstract than Spender in "Ultima Ratio Regum." The cold logic of Auden's phrases, "To-day the deliberate increase in the chances of death" and ". . . to-day the/Fumbled and unsatisfactory embrace before hurting" rings hollow. Attempts to grasp the war as a whole and to see it as a natural or cosmic process were made largely by men who were far from the front or, at least, took no active part in the fighting. They had the advantage of detachment and the freedom to look at things in a wide context without the distracting urgency of the battlefield. The perspective of MacDiarmid and Auden suggests this, as does Felipe's. Felipe's objectivity intimates a perspective of distance and maturity not available to Hernández, for example.

Living in his own isolated world of the trenches, the soldier may feel that the enemy is closer to him than many of his own countrymen, and especially than the invisible commanders who, from a remote security, order multitudes to a senseless death. Spender saw it this way and brought it out ironically in "Ultima Ratio Regum" and "Two Armies." Braccialarghe, looking around during the respite between battles, wrote from a soldier's perspective.

Those who stayed at home in England, America, Russia, or wherever and wrote were driven not by personal danger, but by abstract beliefs which probably meant a great deal to them. Their poems suffered from not being immediately engaged in the events of which they wrote. Their vision was generally unconfined by the borders of Spain. Tíkhonov saw the Spanish War in terms of the Russian Revolution and Civil War. Becher, too, saw it as another class struggle. They shared an intellectual affinity with the Republican side because of the ideology involved. Becher, MacDiarmid, and Tíkhonov were the only foreign poets (out of the thirteen discussed) not to have set foot on Spanish soil during the war years. Of the non-Spanish poets, only Braccialarghe actually fought and would later fight against Nazi-fascism in World War II. Among the Spanish poets, only Hernández was a soldier, but these poets had spent longer periods in Spain and were more intimately part of it. There is a desperation and understanding (especially in the poem by Felipe) and even an authenticity about the Spanish poems not to be found among the non-Spanish ones.

When poetry began to come from those who had a firsthand knowledge of battle and war, it took on a new character. It showed that war was not at all what romantic convention assumed (starting as far back as *The Iliad*), and it emphasized aspects of it which were commonplaces to fighting men but disturbing anomalies to those who stayed at home. It is from such moments that we can get the most revealing and most authentic poetry of war, based on a perceptive acquaintance with its real nature and an unpremeditated response to its unforeseen demands. It illustrates how wrong established notions of war may turn out to be when they are tested by hard facts. For the men who did the fighting, or knew of it at close range, it was a war like any other: lice, betrayals, death, and all. Unpleasant aspects of the war were expressed by all these poets. Campbell's notions were the most glorified, but then he was the only poet on the winning side. The other poets put aside illusions, at least at times, to face the realities of war.

But those deeply involved were also able to transcend the reality they knew so well. Braccialarghe ("Ai fratelli lontani" and "Fratelli dell'Internazionale"), Eluard ("La Victoire de Guernica"), Felipe, Neruda ("Llegada"), and Vallejo ("Masa") expressed a hope that derived from desperation and, perhaps, from their religious backgrounds. Not one of them could have expected the Republic to win after 1937. Auden could write of a possible future because that future lay outside of Spain. MacDiarmid's notions of future success also lay beyond Spain. Felipe's and Vallejo's hopes were fantasies.

It is important to consider when, in relation to the war, the poems were written. During the first year, it was still possible to think that the Loyalists could win. By 1937 the battle was already uneven. Sommerfield wrote of exciting victories of 1936; Neruda spoke glowingly of the arrival of foreign volunteers in Madrid in 1936, while Alvah Bessie wrote of their evacuation in 1939. Campbell's poem was published after the Franco victory. None of the poems discussed was written early enough to be very hopeful about the Republic.

In difficult, chaotic times with strong opinions rampant, there are commonly poets so occupied with their theme or message that their mode of presentation is not of paramount concern to them. This would especially be true of young poets undeveloped poetically at the time of the crisis (e.g., Braccialarghe). Certainly, this is also true of Campbell and MacDiarmid, where quantity outweighs quality. Felipe, too, seems more interested in his views than in his aesthetics. Rukeyser would seem to be insistent about her ideas while sometimes hasty in expressing them. For them the urgent, immediate task was to transform their preoccupations or sorrow into poetry, and in some cases they had not the technique to make the most of their themes. Tíkhonov's "Ispantsi otstupili za Pirenyiei" is much more aesthetically conceived than his poems on fascism and antifascism. In the latter two he was more concerned with propaganda.

How did the war affect their imagery? The images, after all, are the logical products of the poet's vision of the war. Felipe's themes were justice, martyrdom, and unity (a form of patriotism). To achieve these goals, an insignia served both as the poem's title and as its unifying symbol. The proposed symbol to offset divisiveness would be cut out of blood in the form of a star. Another frequent symbol was that of Man—who believes in justice and the Republican cause. Whereas Felipe counted cadavers, representing the war dead, Hernández saw a landscape flooded with blood. Vallejo saw Spain through the metaphor of a dead combatant in "Masa" and a corpse sprouting poetry in "Pequeño responso." She was Mother Spain, an anthropomorphic figure, in "España, aparta de mí este cáliz." Neruda saw the dead as decaying garbage to be consumed by those who caused their murder in "Almería" and as blood in the streets in "Explico." As in Rukeyser's poems (and, to a lesser extent, in Felipe's), the wind was a pervasive force in the poems of Hernández. In "Vientos del pueblo me llevan" Hernández compared brave Spaniards to bulls, the antithesis of yoked oxen. In "Recoged esta voz" the imagery derives from the passion of the battlefield: bandages, bleeding, and blood. Vallejo's poems were included in his collection *España, aparta de mí este cáliz.* The encompassing image of this title is that of a cup or chalice representing suffering, anguish, and death. The request for its removal is as futile as Christ's in the Bible. The book of poetry which survived the destruction of the soldier's body in "Pequeño responso" may symbolize the art and culture of a Spanish people that will survive their limited mortality. Vallejo's mourners are joined in a brotherhood of perspiration rather than blood. In "Explico" Neruda contrasted the beautiful life prior to the war, symbolized by his house full of flowers, children, dogs, friends, with the image of blood: "Venid a ver la sangre por las calles." Does the anguish of the Spanish poets affect their images? Their morbid outlooks are revealed in their death imagery concretized, for example, through a predominance of blood. But the Catholic background of the Hispanic poets would make them fatalistic and resigned to death when it comes. Perhaps this allows them to consider death more openly than most people.

There is no comprehensive image to counterbalance the diffuseness of Campbell's poem. MacDiarmid set up some dichotomies that he sustained, for example, the light/life of communism versus the darkness/decay of Campbell.

Auden's imagery suggests the essence and variety of past, present, and future values and societies. The images reveal Auden's broad knowledge and intellect. Spender's images are drawn both from rural and technological spheres. In "Third Elegy" Rukeyser set up a tour/journey through the landscape of a museum's artworks, with sustained life and death (blood) imagery. In "Nuns in the Wind" the wind and nuns symbolize the war. It is a sophisticated poem whose imagery derives from an intellectual source.

Some of the poems were meant as agents of moral clarification with value judgments about the right and wrong of the situation (those of Auden, Becher, Campbell, Felipe, MacDiarmid, Neruda, Rukeyser, Spender, and Tíkhonov). The poems of Braccialarghe, Felipe, and Hernández offered calls to action and urged martyrdom. All but Campbell and Auden suffered and lamented. Campbell rejoiced. Auden calibrated the situation. Spender and Rukeyser denounced (all) war. Tíkhonov shouted the horrendous implications of fascism ("Govorit fashism"), which would be impossible to live under. Felipe's poetry was essentially didactic. Addressed to a specific audience, it was intended to teach the audience specific truths, both moral and practical.

For the most part the aesthetic quality of the selected poems in Spanish exceeds that of the poems in other languages. The poems written about the war are frequently more important to the corpus of an Hispanic poet's works than those of a non-Spanish poet in relation to his total poetic accomplishment. Not that my selection of other poets is unimpressive. There are major poets included here (Braccialarghe, most obscure, is an exception), but the contribution of non-Spanish poets in respect to the war was not often among their best or most important poetry.

The events of the Thirties are sufficiently remote to be "historic," but also offer parallels with contemporary political-moral issues—such issues as racism and manipulation of society by vast military and industrial interests. Too much government influence over political, social, moral, or aesthetic lives, and too much centralization of power within the head of the government, remind one of the dictatorships which many tried to avoid in the 1930s and 1940s. What happened in Spain could happen anywhere.

W. B. Yeats, T. S. Eliot, and Wyndham Lewis were Rightist

(though Eliot announced during the Spanish Civil War that he "preferred to remain isolated, and take no part in these collective activities"). Although Eliot did not write poems on the Spanish Civil War, he had an insight into the decadence of bourgeois Western civilization (e.g., in "The Love Song of J. Alfred Prufrock" and *The Waste Land*) but did not carry the situation further to revolution. For anyone with strong political convictions, Yeats was a reactionary.

In their youth many poets can be unpolitical, indeed antipolitical, and above all completely opposed to the idea that there is any connection between politics and literature. This was true of Auden, Day Lewis, MacNeice, and Spender, among others. Their generation inherited attitudes which were the aftermath of World War I. Important among these was a profound contempt for politics. The politicians were the cynical old men who had sent the young men into the trenches of the Eastern front (cf. Pound's "Hugh Selwyn Mauberley"). The rise of Hitler, rampant murders and vandalism, and suppression of liberal freedoms, forced the nonpolitical Thirties' generation into politics (delayed political consciousness would not be true in the Soviet Union). The slightly younger generation (e.g., John Cornford) had a different attitude, often more spontaneously passionate.

Ever since that grim July day in 1936 in Spain when modern ideological warfare began, the world has never been the same. The poets involved, also, were not to be the same. Some died; some went to prison or into exile. Some continued to write postwar poetry about Spain, but these were mostly Spanish poets in exile (since poems are apt to be spontaneous and emotional, most of the poems were written during the war years or shortly thereafter). Some poets radically changed their styles as a result or felt compelled into creativity. For some the Spanish Civil War has not ended.

The result was fascist victory followed by a global encounter in which the reluctant democrats and embarrassed communists managed to save themselves only by alliance against a, by then, vastly swollen Nazi danger. And, as Auden eloquently, but pessimistically, put it: "History to the defeated/May say Alas but cannot help nor pardon."

APPENDIX I

Survey of Spanish Civil War Poets Other Than Poets of Concentration

Among those poets who wrote in Spanish were: Rafael Alberti, Vicente Aleixandre, Dámaso Alonso, Manuel Altolaguirre ("Ultima muerte"), Felix Antonio, Antonio Aparicio, Luis Cernuda, Pedro Garfias, Jorge Guillén, Nicolás Guillén, José Herrera Petere, Antonio Machado, José Moreno Villa, Emilio Prados, Arturo Serrano Plaja, and Lorenzo Varela.

Rafael Alberti (b. 1902) wrote from Moscow, Paris, and Madrid about the International Brigades, about Madrid under siege, and finally sought exile in Argentina. Various of his collections contain Spanish Civil War poems: *De un momento a otro* (1937); *Poesías* (1940); and *Entre el clavel y la espada* (1941).

Vicente Aleixandre (b. 1898) had a collection of poems published in 1960, *Poesías completas,* which contained some Spanish Civil War poems. Manuel Altolaguirre (1905-1959) wrote a few poems on the subject in 1937.

In *Hijos de la ira,* published in 1944, Dámaso Alonso (b. 1898) mentioned nothing specific, but the poem, expressing anguish at human suffering, obviously resulted from the Spanish Civil War. Antonio Aparicio (b. 1912) wrote a few poems. Felix Antonio wrote a volume titled *Arriba las cruces.*

Luis Cernuda (1902-1963) left Spain after the war. He wrote "Elegía española" and "Elegía a la luna de España," included in the volume *La realidad y el deseo* (1936).

Pedro Garfias (1901-1967) went into exile in Mexico, having left Spain in 1939. His works *Poesía de la guerra* (1937) and *Héroes del Sur* (1938) deal with the war. Juan Gil-Albert wrote related poems in *Siete romances de guerra, Cancionero revolucionario internacional,* and *Candente horror.*

A relatively conservative group of poets who participated actively in the Spanish Civil War were: Leopoldo Panero (1909-1963), Luis Rosales (b. 1910), and Dionisio Ridruejo (1912-1975), who supported Franco. If a poet chose to remain in Spain after the war, he either had to support Franco, write subtly and ambiguously, or remain silent. Ridruejo later broke with Franco and went into exile.

Jorge Guillén (b. 1893) escaped to Massachusetts. He wrote *Guirnalda civil,* which was published in 1970. Nicolás Guillén (b. 1902), born in Cuba, went to Spain during the Spanish Civil War. Committed to social justice and human solidarity, he fought on the side of the Republic in the war. His *Cantos para soldados y sones para turistas* was published in 1937. *España, poema en cuatro angustias y una esperanza* (1937) expressed his admiration for Spain's history and despair at its imminent self-destruction. After the defeat of the Republic, he returned to Cuba.

José Herrera Petere (b. 1910) was a volunteer in the 5th regiment. His collections *Acero de Madrid* and *Guerra viva,* both published in 1938, contain some Spanish war poems.

Antonio Machado (1875-1939), born in Sevilla, died in exile. *Poesías completas* (1936) and *Poesías de guerra* (1961) contain Spanish Civil War poems.

José Moreno Villa (1887-1955) left Spain in 1937 on a cultural mission and, at the end of the war, sought refuge in Mexico. *Salon sin muros* (1936) and *Puerta severa* (1941) contain pertinent poems.

Blas de Otero (b. 1916) was born in Bilbao. A lyric poet he wrote about the war from a distance in time in *Pido la paz y la palabra* (1955) and *Que trata de España* (1965).

Emilio Prados (1899-1962) was born in Málaga. *Llanto subterráneo* (1936), *Llanto en la sangre* (1937), *Mínima muerte* (1939), and *Penumbras* (1942) contain relevant poems.

Pedro Salinas (1891-1951) included his war poems in *Poesías completas* (1955). After the war he went into exile, living in Baltimore.

Lorenzo Varela (b. 1917) emigrated to France after 1939 and then to South America (Buenos Aires). *Elegías españoles* (1941) has poems touching on the war.

Max Aub (1903-1972) mostly wrote prose, but composed the poem "Me acuerdo hoy de Aranjuez" in 1941 from the concentration camp at Djelfa, Algeria.

Many of these poets on the Republican side, grateful for international support, extolled the International Brigades: Rafael Alberti, Manuel Altolaguirre, Pedro Garfias, Juan Gil-Albert, José Herrera Petere, Juan Paredes, Perez Infante, Emilio Prados, Arturo Serrano Plaja, Lorenzo Varela. After 1939, all anti-Franco poets would have written in exile.

Among the poets who wrote in English were some who sacrificed their lives (and writing) for the physical struggle and died in Spain: Julian Bell, John Cornford ("Poem," "Full Moon at Tierz: Before the Storming of Huesca," and "Heart of Heartless World"), Christopher Caudwell, Ralph Fox, James Lardner, Sam Levinger. They were all volunteers in the International Brigades and wrote a few poems each. Some British communist poets were Caudwell, Charles Donnelly, Cornford, and Fox.

Edwin Rolfe (1909-1954), born in Philadelphia, had three volumes published: *To my Contemporaries* (1936), *Lincoln Battalion* (1939), *First Love* (1951). His "Elegy for Our Dead" was published in 1938. A volunteer in Spain, he fought with the International Brigades.

Langston Hughes (1902-1967), born in Missouri, traveled to Spain, where he preoccupied himself with the Negro soldiers among the Internationals. He wrote "Air Raid: Barcelona,"

"Madrid," "October 16th," "Post Card from Spain," as well as the collection *A New Song,* all published in 1938.

Genevieve Taggard (1894-1948), born in Washington, had three volumes with relevant poems: *Calling Western Union* (1936), *Collected Poems* (1938), and *Long View* (1942).

Louis MacNeice (1907-1963), born in Belfast, Ireland, went to Spain in 1936. Three volumes resulted: *Out of the Picture* (1937), *The Earth Compels* (1938), and *Autumn Journal* (1939). While MacNeice found inspiration in the human values at stake, his involvement with the Spanish people never went beyond a vague general sympathy. For example, he never supported the Republic in any political sense, probably because he was as aware as Spender of the hazards of mixing propaganda and poetry.

C. Day Lewis (1904-1972), a communist, was one of the leading British poets of the 1930s. The following are some of his Spanish war poems: "Noah and the Waters" (1936) and published in 1938: "Child of Misfortune," "Overtures to Death and Other Poems," "The Nabara," "Starting Point," "Bombers."

There were many other poets in English writing on the war, most of whom wrote single poems: John Malcolm Brinnin ("For a Young Poet dead in Spain"); Richard Church; Kenneth Fearing ("The Program"); Redmayne Fitzgerald; S. Funaroff ("To Federico García Lorca"); Brian Howard; Rolfe Humphries; John Lepper; Jack Lindsay; Edna St. Vincent Millay ("Say that we saw Spain die"); Geoffrey Parsons; Herbert Read ("Bombing Casualties" and "A Song for the Spanish Antichrists" from his volume *Thirty-Five Poems* (1940); Kenneth Rexroth ("Two Poems"); Edgell Rickword; Norman Rosten ("The March"); Vincent Sheean ("Puigcerdà"); Rex Warner; Sylvia Townsend Warner ("Waiting at Cerbere" and "Benicasim"); Tom Winringham ("Granien" and "The Splint"); and David Wolff ("The Defenses").

Among the German contributors, all writing in exile from Germany, Bertolt Brecht (1898-1956), whose original name was Eugen Berthold Friedrich Brecht, was the best known among them. Born in Ausburg, Bavaria (now in West Germany), he died in East Germany. He was a poet, playwright, and theatrical reformer, whose epic theater departed from the conventions of theatrical illusion and developed the drama as a social and ideological forum. His "epic" theater kept his audience at an objective distance from the dramatic artifice.

He abandoned medical studies for the theater. His military service in World War I made him a pacifist for the rest of his life. In the late 1920s his antipathy to middle-class society took the form of Marxism. His first major success, *Dreigroschenoper* (1928), gained him an international reputation.

After the rise of Hitler in Germany, Brecht lived in Denmark (1933-1939), Sweden, Finland, and the U.S. (1941-1947). Among his important mature plays are: *Leben des Galilei, Der gute Mensch von Sezuan, Mutter Courage und ihre Kinder,* and *Der Kaukasische Kreidekreis.* He returned to Europe in 1947 and, in his last years (from 1949 on), directed the Berliner Ensemble, a company of actors in East Berlin. More than forty plays and operas have established Brecht as one of our century's most provocative playwrights.

Themes of death, decay, and drowning reappear constantly in Brecht's poetry, especially in verses written in the 1920s, before his radical nihilism was replaced by Marxist ideology. Although he wrote a play that touches on the war, *Die Gewehre der Frau Carrar,* I could find only one poem written by Brecht on the Spanish Civil War, "Mein Bruder War ein Flieger," for which music was later composed by Paul Dessau:

> Mein Bruder war ein Flieger
> Eines Tags bekam er eine Kart
> Er hat seine Kiste eingpackt
> Und sudwarts ging die Fahrt.
>
> Mein Bruder ist ein Eroberer
> Unserm Volke fehlt's an Raum
> Und Grund und Boden zu kriegen, ist
> Bei uns ein alter Traum.
>
> Der Raum, den mein Bruder eroberte
> Liegt in Guadarramamassiv.
> Er ist lang einen Meter achtzig
> Und einen Meter fünfzig tief.[1]

(My brother was a pilot
One day he received his orders
He packed his bags
And made his journey southward.

My brother is a conqueror
Our people lack space
To conquer land is
For us an old dream

The space which my brother
    conquered
Lies in the Guadarrama mass of
    mountains
It is 8 feet long
And 6 feet deep.)

Brecht's figurative brother lies in a coffin in the Guadarrama mountain range, his plane having crashed during the Spanish Civil War. The insinuation that his brother was looking for more land to conquer, his homeland never having been enough for the Germans, is ironic and bitter in tone. This criticizes German expansionism in general and surely doesn't do justice to this dead pilot who volunteered and gave his life for the cause in Spain. This second point is intentionally made obliquely.

Erich Fried (b. 1921), born in Vienna, fled to England in 1938 after the German occupation of Austria and has lived in London since 1946. He wrote "Schulkinder," a generally antiwar poem which clearly includes the Spanish Civil War.

Louis Fürnberg wrote "Die Spanishe Hochzeit," which was published in 1948.

Rudolf Leonhard extolled the revolutionary struggle and its international aspects in his Spanish war poems; he showed how in the Spanish Civil War were pitched: "Deutsche gegen Deutsche vor Madrid in der Schlacht,/die Freiheit gegen die Niedertracht," and in so doing he anticipated a struggle in Germany in which Germans would be lined up on opposite sides. In a "Londoner Ballade," England's aloofness from the Spanish people's struggle is scorned; the British "gehen geruhig in ihrem sehr hübschen Garten/und wollen warten" until their realm also would be brutally violated.

Erich Weinert (1890-1953), a popular communist poet, wrote two poems, "Kinderspiel in Madrid" and "Internationale Brigade," that were published in *Romancero de los voluntarios de la libertad* (1937).

Among the French poets who focused attention on the war were: Louis Aragon (b. 1897), who began as a surrealist and became a spokesman for communism; Eugene Guillevic (b. 1907), who wrote *Requiem* in 1938; and Paul Claudel (1868-1955), whose mystical crisis led him into Catholicism and the Nationalist side.

There were a number of Russian poets. Evgenii Aronovitch Dolmatovski (b. 1915) wrote *Stikhi i pesni* (1952), which included "Pis'mo k Rafael Alberti."

Ilya Grigorievitch Ehrenburg (1891-1967) was a correspondent in Spain in 1936 and mostly wrote journalism. One of his poems, "Kino," touched on the war.

Semion Isaakovitch Kirsanov (b. 1906), born in Odessa, wrote *Vojna Tchume* (1936), *Tvojá Poema* (1937), and *Sočinenija v dvuch tómach* (1954). Among his poems was "Vy iz Madrid."

Born in Milan, Italy, Giuliano Carta (b. 1914) wrote *Madrid, Vega, Santa Margherita Ligure* (1938), which included "Madrid."

Note

1. Bertolt Brecht, *Gedichte 1934-1941* (Frankfurt: Suhrkamp Verlag, 1961), p. 31.

APPENDIX II

Translations into English
of Analyzed Poems

"La insignia" by León Felipe

THE INSIGNIA
Poetic Speech (Address) (1937)

This war poem was begun right after the fall of Málaga and
acquired this expression after the fall of Bilbao. So the way
it is here is the last variation (of the text), the most
structured, that which the author prefers and subscribes to.
And it annuls all the other anterior editions that the press
has published. This is not said for editorial reasons or
interests. Here there is no Copyright. Five hundred copies
have been printed to throw in the air of Valencia and so that
the wind may multiply them.

—León Felipe

Have you all spoken already?
Have all you Spaniards spoken already?
Has the great responsible revolutionary spoken
and the small responsible ones;
has the high commissary spoken,
and the subordinate commissaries;
have the political parties spoken,
have the corporations spoken,
the Committees
and the Syndicates;
have the workers and the peasants spoken;
have the mechanics spoken;
has the barker spoken
the waiter in the café
and the bootblacks.
And have the eternal demagogues spoken also.
Has everyone spoken.
I believe that everyone has spoken.
Is anyone missing?
Is there some Spaniard that might not have pronounced his
    word? . . .
No one answers? . . . (Silence).
Then only I am missing.
Because the poet has not yet spoken.

Who has said that now there are not poets in the world?
Who has said that now there are not prophets?

One day the kings and the people
to forget their fatal and dramatic destiny
and to be able to replace the sacrifice with cynicism and the
    pirouette
substituted the clown for the prophet.
But the prophet is no more than the native voice of a people,
the legitimate voice of its History,
the cry of the first soil that is raised in the confusion of the
    market, above the clamor of the dealers.
Nothing of prides:
neither divine hierarchies nor ecclesiastical genealogies.

The voice of the prophets—remember it—
it is that which has more flavor of clay.
Of clay,
of the clay that has made the tree—the orange tree and the
    pine—
of the clay that has formed
our body also.
I am not more than a voice—yours, that of everyone—
the most genuine,
the most general,
the most indigenous now,
the most ancient of this earth.
The voice of Spain that today is united in my throat as it
    could unite itself in any other.
My voice is no more than the wave of the land,
of our land,
that seizes me today like a favorable antenna.
Listen,
listen, revolutionary Spaniards,
listen on your knees.
Don't kneel down before anyone.
Kneel down before yourselves,
before your own voice,
before your own voice that you had almost forgotten.
On your knees. Listen.

Spaniards,
revolutionary Spaniards.
Spaniards of the legitimate Spain,
that carries in its hands the genuine message of the race to
    place it humbly in the harmonious pictures of the
    Universal History of tomorrow, and together with the
    generous effort of all the peoples of the world . . .
listen:
There they are—look at them—
there they are, you know them well.
They walk in all of Valencia,
they are in the rear guard of Madrid

and in the rear guard of Barcelona also.
They are in all the rear guards.
They are the Committees,
the small parties,
the factions,
the Syndicates,
the criminal guerrillas of the city rear guard
There you have them.
Embraced with their recent booty,
guarding it,
defending it,
with an avarice that the most degraded bourgeois never had.
Their booty!
Embracing their booty!
Because they have nothing more than booty.
Don't even call it attachment to property.
Booty is made a lawful privilege when it is sealed by an
    ultimate and heroic victory.

One goes from the domestic to the historic,
and from the historic to the epic.
This has always been the order that has guided the conduct
    of the Spaniard in History,
in the plaza
and even in their transactions,
that it has always been said therefore that the Spaniard never
    learns well the merchant trade.
But now
in this revolution,
the order has been reversed.
You have started with the epic,
you have passed through the historic
and now here,
in the rear guard of Valencia,
facing all the defeats
you have stopped yourselves in domesticity.
And here you are anchored.
Syndicalists,

Communists,
Anarchists,
Socialists,
Trotskyites,
Republicans of the Left . . .
Here you are anchored,
guarding the plunder
so that your brother might not take it away.
The historical curve of the aristocrat, since his popular and
    heroic origin, until his final present degeneration, covers
    in Spain more than three centuries.
That of the bourgeoisie, seventy years.
And yours, three weeks.
Where is man?
Where is the Spanish man?
Do not go to seek him on the other side.
The other side is the cursed land, the cursed Spain of Cain
    although the Pope might have blessed it.
If the Spaniard is in some place, it has to be here.
But, where, where? . . .
Because you have already stopped yourselves
and all you do every day is hoist new banners with the ripped
    shirts and dirty rags of the kitchen.
And if the fascists were to enter Valencia tomorrow, they
    would find everyone standing guard before the strong boxes.
This is not defeatism, as you say.
I know that my prophetic line is not broken,
that the men do not break it,
and that I have to arrive before God to give him an account
    of something that he put in my hands when the First
    Spanish substance was born.
That is inexorable logic.
The ones who conquer and have always conquered in
    immediate History are the people and the army that have
    had a point of convergence, although this point may be as
    weak and as absurd as an aluminum medal blessed by a
    bloodthirsty priest.
It is the insignia of the fascists.

This medal is the insignia of the fascists.

A medal stained with the blood of the Virgin.

Very little thing.

But, what do you have now that unites you more?

Revolutionary Spanish people,

you are alone!

Alone!

Without a man and without a symbol.

Without a mystical emblem where sacrifice and discipline are crystallized.

Without a single symbol that captures in a solid and unique block all your forces and all your dreams of redemption.

Your insignias,

your plural and sometimes enemy insignias, you buy them in the market capriciously from the first (second hand) dealer of the Plaza de Castelar,

of the Puerta del Sol

of the Ramblas de Barcelona.

You have exhausted already in a thousand egotistical and heterodox combinations all the letters of the alphabet.

And you have put in a thousand different manners, on the cap and on the sheepskin jacket

the red

and the black,

the sickle,

the hammer

and the star.

But you do not even have a star ALONE,

after having spit out and extinguished that of Bethlehem.

Spaniards,

Spaniards who live the most tragic moment of all our History,

You are alone!

Alone!

The world,

all the world is our enemy, and half of our blood—the rotted and bastard blood of Cain—has turned against us also.

We have to light a star!
One alone, yes!
We have to raise a banner.
One alone, yes!
And we have to burn the ships.
From here one goes only to death or victory.
Everything makes me think to death.
Not because no one defends me
but because no one understands me.
No one in the world understands the word "justicia." Not
    even you.
And my mission was to imprint it on the forehead of man
and to hammer it after on the earth
like the flag of the final victory.
No one understands me.
And we will have to go to another planet
with these useless goods here,
with these Iberian and quixotic goods.
Let us go to our death!
However,
we have not yet lost here the last battle,
that which is always won thinking that there is no longer any
    exit but death
Let us go to death!
This is our motto.
To death!
This is our motto.
Let Valencia wake up and put on the shroud.

Shout!
all shout!
You, the town crier and the speaker
produce edicts,
light the corners with red letters
that announce this proclamation alone:
Let us go to our death!
You, the Commissars, the captains of Censureship,
sheath your swords

guard your red pen
and open to this shout the doors of the wind:
Let us go to our death!
Let all hear it. All.
Those who deal in silence
and those who deal in insignias.
Dealers of the Plaza de Castelar,
dealers of the Puerta del Sol,
dealers of the Ramblas de Barcelona,
destroy,
burn your goods.
There are no longer domestic insignias,
there are no longer insignias of brass.
Neither for the caps
nor for the sheepskin jackets.
There are no longer identification cards.
There are no longer legal letters
neither by the Committees
nor by the Syndicates.
Let them take away all identification cards!
Now there is only one emblem.
Now there is only one star,
one alone, ALONE and RED, yes,
but of blood and on the forehead,
let every Spanish revolutionary do it for himself
just today
right now
and with their own hands.
Prepare the knives,
sharpen the blades,
heat the irons to live red.
Go to the forges.
Let there be put on your forehead the stamp of justice.
Mothers, revolutionary mothers,
stamp this indelible shout of justice
on the forehead of your children.
There where you have always put your cleanest kisses.
(This is not a rhetorical image.

I am not the poet of rhetoric.
Now there is no rhetoric.
The revolution has burned
all the rhetorics.)

Let no one deceive you any more.
Let there be no false passports
neither of paper
nor of cardboard
nor of tin plate.
Let there be no more disguises
neither for the timid
nor for the frivolous
nor for the hypocrite
nor for the clown
nor for the actor.
Let there be no more disguises
neither for the spy who sits at your side in the café,
nor for the ambusher who does not leave his hole.
Let not those who wait for Franco with the last bottles of
   champagne in the wine cellar hide any more in a
   proletarian garment.
All those who do not wear tomorrow this Spanish
   revolutionary emblem, this shout of justice, bleeding on
   their forehead, belong to the Fifth Column.

No outlet now
to possible treacheries.
Let no one finally think
of ripping compromising documents
nor of burning boxes of official cards
nor of throwing the cap in the trench
in premeditated flights.
There are no longer flights.
In Spain now there are only two fixed and immovable
   positions.
For today and for tomorrow.
That of those who raise their hand to say cynically: I am a
   Spanish bastard,

and that of those who shut it with ire to ask justice under
  the implacable skies.
But now this play of hands finally is not enough.
More is necessary.
Stars are missing, yes, many stars
but of blood
because the rear guard has to give theirs also.

A star of red blood,
of red Spanish blood.
Let there no longer be someone who might say:
that star is of foreign blood.
And let it not be obligatory either.
Tomorrow let no one speak of impositions,
let no one say that a pistol was put in his chest.
It is a revolutionary tattoo, yes.
I am a revolutionary,
Spain is revolutionary,
Don Quijote is revolutionary.
We all are. All.
All who feel this taste of justice that there is in our blood
  and that makes for us bitterness and dust when the North
  wind blows.
It is a revolutionary tattoo,
but Spanish.
And heroic also.
And voluntary, besides.
It is a tattoo that we seek only to define our faith.
It is only a definition of faith.
There are two furious winds today that shake at the men of
  Spain,
two gusts of wind that push the men of Valencia.
The dramatic wind of the great destinies, that moves the
  heroes to victory or death,
and the gust of wind of incontrollable panics that carries dead
  and rotted flesh of shipwrecks to the beaches of cowardice
  and silence.
There are two winds, do you not hear it?

There are two winds, Spaniards of Valencia.
One goes to History.
The other goes to silence.
the one goes to the epic,
the other to shame.

Responsible ones:
the great responsible one and the small responsible ones:
Open the doors,
overthrow the barricades of the Pyrenees.
Give open road
to the yellow gust of wind of those who tremble.
Once more I shall see the flock of cowards flee toward scorn.
Once more I shall see cowardice in herd.
I shall see you again,
assaulting with bulging eyes, the buses of evacuation.
I shall see you again
robbing the seat
from children and mothers.
I shall see you again.
But you will be seeing yourselves always.
One day you will die outside of your country. In bed perhaps.
   In a bed of white sheets, with naked feet (not with shoes
   put on, as one now dies in Spain), with naked and anointed
   feet, maybe with sacred oils. Because you will die very
   simply, and securely with a crucifix and with an oration
   of repentance on your lips. You will be already almost with
   death, which always arrives. And you will remember—
   clearly you will remember—that this time you fled and
   ridiculed, usurping the seat of a child in an evacuation bus.
   It will be your last thought. And there, on the other side,
   when finally you are only a disembodied conscience, in
   time and space, and you plunge swiftly to the depth of
   Dantesque torments—because I believe in the inferno also
   —you will only see yourselves in this manner,
always, always, always,
robbing the seat from a child in an evacuation bus.
The punishment of the coward finally without peace and
   without salvation for all eternity.

It does not matter that you do not have a gun,
remain here with your faith.
Do not listen to those who say: the flight can be a political
    one.
There is no more politics in History than blood.
Blood that flows does not scare me,
blood that flows makes me happy.
There is a flower in the world that can only grow if it is
    irrigated with blood.
The blood of man
is made not only to move his heart
but to fill the rivers of the Earth,
the veins of the Earth
and to move the heart of the world.

Cowards: towards the Pyrenees, to exile!
Heroes: to the fronts, to death!

Responsible ones:
the great and small responsible ones:
organize the heroism,
unify the sacrifice.
A unique command, yes.
But for the final martyrdom.
Let us go to death!
Let all the world hear it.
Let the spies hear it.
What does it matter now that the spies hear it?
Let them hear it, the bastards.
What does it matter now that the bastards hear it?
What do all those voices there below matter now
if we begin to ride (on horseback) above the epic?
At these heights of History one no longer hears anything.
One goes towards death . . .
and below remains the world of the foxes,
and of those who make a pact with foxes.

Below you remain, England,
old greedy fox,

you halted the History of the West more than three centuries
    ago,
and enchained Don Quijote.
When your life finishes
and you come before the great History
where I wait for you,
what are you going to say?
What new cunning are you going to invent then to deceive
    God?
Fox!
Daughter of foxes!
Italy is more noble than you.
And Germany also.
In their plundering and in their crimes
there is an obscure Nietzschean breath of heroism in which
    merchants cannot breathe,
an impetuous and confused gesture of gambling everything
    on the last card, that practical men cannot understand.
If they were to open their doors to the winds of the world,
if they were to open them wide
and if Justice
and the heroic Democracy of man were to pass through them,
I would make a pact with the two to throw in your face of an
    old fox without dignity or love,
all the saliva and all the excrement of the world.
Old greedy fox:
you have hidden,
buried in the yard,
the miraculous key that opens the diamantine door of
    History . . .
You know nothing.
You understand nothing and you enter all the houses
to close the windows
and to blind the light of the stars!
And the men see you and leave you.
They leave you because they believe that the beams to
    Jupiter have already been exhausted.
But the stars do not sleep.

You know nothing.

You have heaped your plunder behind the door, and your children, now, cannot open it so that the first rays of the new dawn may enter.

Old greedy fox,

you are a great merchant.

You know very well how to keep

the accounts of the kitchen

and you think that I do not know how to count.

Yes I know how to count.

I have counted my dead.

I have counted them all,

I have counted them one by one.

I have counted them in Madrid,

I have counted them in Oviedo,

I have counted them in Málaga,

I have counted them in Guernica,

I have counted them in Bilbao . . .

I have counted them in all the trenches,

in the hospitals,

in the deposits of the cemeteries,

in the gutters of the highways,

in the rubbish of the bombarded houses.

Counting dead people this fall by the Paseo de El Prado, I believed one night that I was walking on mud, and there were human brains that for a long time were stuck to the soles of my shoes.

The 18th of November, only in one cellar of cadavers, I counted three hundred dead children . . .

I have counted them in the cars of the ambulances,

in the hotels,

in the street cars,

in the subway . . . ,

on livid mornings,

on black nights without illumination and without stars . . .

and in your conscience all of them . . .

And all of them I have charged to your account.

Now you see if I know how to count!

You are the old porter of the Western world,
since long ago you have the keys of all the ports of Europe,
and you can let enter and leave whomever you take a fancy to.
And now through cowardice,
through nothing more than cowardice,
because you wish to guard your pantry until the last day of
    History,
you have let intrude in my ancestral mansion
the foxes and the conspiring wolves of the world
so that they might be satiated in my blood
and might not ask at once for yours.
But finally they will ask for it,
finally the stars will ask for it . . .

And here again,
here
in these solitary altitudes
here
where one hears if I relax the millenary voice
of the winds,
of the water
and of the clay
that has been forming all of us men.
Here,
where the shrieked clamor of mercenary propaganda does not
    arrive.
Here,
where the asthma of diplomats has not breathing nor life.
Here,
where the comedians of the Society of Nations do not have a
    part.
Here, here,
in the presence of History,
in the presence of great History
(the other
the one which your worm-like pride teaches to school
    children
is only a record of lies

and an index of crimes and vanities).
Here, here,
under the light of the stars,
above the eternal and pristine earth of the world
and in the very presence of God.
Here, here. Here
I wish to say now my final word:

Spaniards
revolutionary Spaniards:
Man has died!
Quiet, quiet.
Break the loudspeakers
and the antennas,
tear up by the roots all the posters that announce your drama
    in the corners of the world.
Denunciations? Before whom?
Rip the White Book,
no longer turn your mouth with calls and laments toward the
    vacant.
Man has died!
And only the stars can form now the choir of our tragic
    destiny.
No longer shout your martyrdom.
Martyrdom is not proclaimed,
it is endured
and casts itself on the shoulders like a legacy and a pride.

The tragedy is mine,
mine,
let no one rob me of it.
Get out,
get out all of you.
All of you.
I here alone.
Alone
under the stars and the Gods.
Who are you?
What is your name?

From what womb do you come?
Outside . . . Outside . . . Foxes!
Here,
I alone. Alone,
with Justice killed by hanging.
Alone,
with the corpse of Justice between my hands.
Here,
I alone,
alone
with human conscience,
quiet,
stopped,
assassinated for always
in this hour of History
and in this land of Spain,
for all the foxes of the world.
For all,
for all.
Foxes!
Foxes!
Foxes!
The world is only a den of foxes
and Justice a flower that now does not grow in any latitude.

Spaniards,
revolutionary Spaniards.
Let us go to death!
Let the spies hear it.
What does it matter now that the spies hear it?
Let them hear it, the bastards.
What does it matter now that the bastards hear it?
At these heights of History
now nothing is heard.
One goes toward death
and below remains the unbreathable world of the foxes and
    of those who make a pact with foxes.
Let us go to death!

Let Valencia awaken
and put on the shroud! . . .

Epilogue

Listen still . . .
Beforehand, refresh my lips and my forehead . . . I am
  thirsty . . .
And I want to speak with words of love and hope.
Listen now:
Justice is worth more than an empire, although this empire
  were to include all the curve of the Sun.
And when Justice, fatally hurt, calls to all of us in desperate
  agony no one can say:
"I am still not prepared."
Justice is defended with a broken spear and with a paper
  visor.
This is written in my Bible,
in my History,
in my infantile and grotesque History
and as long as men do not learn it, the world will not be
  saved.

I am the first, livid and cardinal shout of the great sunrises
  of the West.
Yesterday upon my early risen blood the bourgeois world
  built in America all its factories and markets,
upon my dead ones of today the world of tomorrow will raise
  the First House of Man.
And I shall return,
I shall return because there are still spears and bitterness on
  Earth.
I shall return,
I shall return with my chest (figuratively: heart) and with the
  Dawn again.

"Vientos del pueblo me llevan" by Miguel Hernández

THE WINDS OF MY PEOPLE CARRY ME

1 The winds of my people carry me,
  the winds of my people move me,
  they scatter my heart,
  and inflate my throat.

5 Oxen bow their forehead (figuratively:
   head)
  impotently tame,
  before punishments:
  lions lift theirs
  and at the same time punish
10 with their strident claw.

  I am not from a people of oxen,
  I am from a people that impede
  the grazing of lions,
  single flights of eagles,
15 and mountain ranges of bulls
  with pride in their horn.
  They never breed oxen
  on the bleak highlands of Spain.

  Who spoke of setting a yoke
20 on the neck of this race?
  Who has ever put
  yokes or braces on the hurricane,
  or detained a thunderbolt
  prisoner in a cage?

25 Asturians of bravery,
  Basques of armored stone,
  Valencians of happiness
  and Castilians of soul,
  worked over like the soil
30 and airy as wings;
  Andalusians of lightning,

born amidst guitars
and forged in torrential
anvils of tears;
35   Estremadurans of rye
Galicians of rain and tranquillity,
Catalans of firmness,
Aragonese of caste,
Murcians of dynamite
40   fruitfully propagated,
men of Leon and Navarre, masters
of hunger, of sweat, and of the axe,
kings of mining
gentlemen of farming,
45   men who among roots,
like brave roots yourselves,
you go from life to death,
you go from nothing to nothing:
they wish to put yokes on you
50   people of bad grasslands,
yokes that you have to leave
broken across their backs.
Dawn is indicating
the twilight of the oxen.

55   Oxen die clad
in humility and the odor of stables:
the eagles, the lions
and the bulls of arrogance,
and behind them, the sky
60   neither disturbs itself nor ends.
The agony of the oxen
is of little countenance,
that of the virile animal
enlarges all of creation.

65   If I must die, let me die
with my head very high.
Dead and twenty times dead,
my mouth against the grass,

I shall have my teeth clenched
70   and my chin firm.

Singing I await death,
for there are nightingales that sing
above the rifles
and in the midst of battles.

"Recoged esta voz" by Miguel Hernández

HEAR THIS VOICE

1   Nations of the earth, countries of the sea,
            brothers
of the world and of nothing:
lost inhabitants—more distant
from sight than from the heart.

5   Here I have an impassioned voice,
here I have a life attacked and angered,
here I have a message, here I have a life.

Open I am, look, like a wound
Sunk I am, look, I am sunk
10   amidst my people and its ills.
Wounded I go, wounded and badly wounded,
bleeding through trenches and hospitals.

Men, worlds, nations,
pay attention, listen to my bleeding sound,
15   gather up my beats of affliction
in your spacious hearts,
because I clutch the soul when I sing.

Singing I defend myself
and I defend my people when
20   the barbarians of crime imprint
their hooves of powder and clatter on my
            people.

This is their work, this:
They pass, they destroy like whirlwinds,
and before their funereal choler
25   the horizons are arms, and the roads, death.

The lament that pours through valleys and
    balconies,
deluges the stones and works in the stones,
and there is no space for so much death,
and there is no wood for so many coffins.

30   Caravans of beaten-down bodies.
All is bandages, pains, and handkerchiefs:
all is stretchers on which the wounded
have broken their strength and their wings.

Blood, blood through the trees and the soil,
35   blood in the waters, blood on the walls,
and a fear that Spain will collapse
from the weight of the blood which soaks
    through her networks
right to the bread that is eaten.

Gather together this wind,
40   nations, men, worlds,
that proceeds from the mouths of disturbed
    breath
and from the hospitals of the dying.

Apply your ears
to my clamor of a violated people,
45   to the "ay!" of so many mothers, to the
    complaints
of so many a bright being whom grief has
    devoured.

The chests that pushed and hurt the
    mountains,
see them weakened without milk or beauty,

and see the white sweethearts and the black
    eyelashes
50   fallen and depressed in an obscure siesta.

Apply the passion of your entrails
to this people who die with an invincible
    gesture
scattered by the lips and the brow
beneath the implacable airplanes
55   that snatch terribly,
terribly, ignominiously, every day
sons from the hands of their mothers.

Cities of work and innocence,
youths that blossom from the oak,
60   trunks of bronze, bodies of power
lie down rushed into ruin.

A future of dust advances,
a fate advances
in which nothing will remain:
65   neither stone on stone nor bone on bone.

Spain is not Spain, it is an immense grave,
it is a vast cemetery red and bombarded:
the barbarians want it this way.

The earth will be a dense heart laid waste,
70   if you, nations, men, worlds,
with the whole of my people
and your people on their side,
do not break the ferocious fangs.

II

But it will not be: that a pawing sea
75   always triumphant, always decided,
made for the light, for the heroic deed,
stirs its head of unmanageable diamond,
pounds its shoed foot amidst the noise
of all the cadavers of Spain.

80   It is youth: gather up this wind.
         Its blood is the crystal that does not tarnish,
         its hat the laurel wreath and its breath the
             flint.
         Where the force of its teeth holds on fast
         buds a volcano of transparent swords,
85   and its beating shoulders,
         and its heels open up sudden blazes.

         It is composed of working men:
         of red blacksmiths, of snow-white masons,
         of plowboys with faces of harvesting.
90   They pass oceanically beneath
         a clamor of sirens and manufacturing tools
         and of gigantic arcs illuminated with arrows.

         Despite death, these men
         with metal and lightning equal to shields,
95   make cannons draw back
         Intimidated, trembling, mute.

         The powder cannot harm them and they
             make fire from powder
         sap, explosion, sudden greenness:
         with their power of impassioned youth
100   they precipitate the soul of the lavender
             plant,
         the creation of the mine,
         the fertile movement of the plow.

         They make of each ruin a pasture,
         of each pain a fruit of happiness,
105   of Spain a sky of beauty.
         See them make gigantic the midday
         and beautify everything with their young
             bravery.

         They deserve the foam of the thunder,
         they deserve life and the odor of the olive
             tree,

110   the Spaniards—extensive and serene
who move their glance like a proud bird.

Nations, men, worlds, this I write:
the youth of Spain will leave the trenches
on foot, invincible like the seed,
115   because it has a soul full of flags
that never surrenders or kneels down.

There go through the deserts of Castille
the bodies that seem struggling colts,
bulls of victorious conclusion,
120   telling in their blood of generous flowers
that to die is the greatest thing that one does.

They will remain, in time, victors,
always covered by sun and majesty,
the fighters of bones so brave
125   that if they are dead they are brave dead:
the youth that will save Spain, although it
      had to
fight with a gun of nards
and a sword of wax.

"Pequeño responso a un héroe de la República" by César Vallejo

A BRIEF FUNERAL LITURGY FOR A HERO
OF THE REPUBLIC

1   A book remained at the edge of his dead waist,
a book was sprouting from his dead corpse.
They carried away the hero,
and carnal and sad his mouth shared our
      breath;
5   all of us sweated, our navels a burden;
the wandering moons were following us;
the dead man from grief was sweating too.

And a book, in the battle of Toledo,
a book, behind a book, above a book, was
    sprouting from the corpse.

10   Poetry of the purple cheek bone, between
        saying
    and keeping silent,
    poetry in the moral message that might have
        accompanied
    his heart.
    The book remained and nothing more, for
        there are no
15   insects in the tomb,
    and there remained at the edge of his sleeve
        the air soaking itself
    and making itself vaporous, infinite.

    We all sweated, our navels a burden,
    the dead man also sweated from grief
20   and a book, I saw it feelingly,
    a book, behind a book, above a book
    sprouted from the corpse abruptly.

"Masa" by César Vallejo

MASSES

1   At the end of the battle,
    and the combatant dead, a man came toward
        him
    and said to him: "Do not die; I love you so
        much!"
    But the cadaver, alas! went on dying.

5   Two approached him and repeated to him:
    "Don't leave us! Courage! Return to life!"
    But the corpse, alas! went on dying.

Twenty arrived, one hundred, one thousand,
    five hundred thousand,
shouting: "So much love, and not to be able
    to do anything against death!"
10   But the corpse, alas! went on dying.

Millions of individuals surrounded him,
with a common plea: "Remain brother!"
But the corpse, alas! went on dying.

Then all the men of the earth
15   surrounded him; the corpse looked at them
    sadly, deeply moved;
he sat up slowly,
he embraced the first man; he began to
    walk . . .

"España, aparta de mí este cáliz" by César Vallejo

SPAIN, REMOVE FROM ME THIS CHALICE

1   Children of the world,
if Spain falls—I say, it's merely conjectural—
if its forearm falls
from the sky down, that two terrestrial segments
5   would grip in a halter;
children, how aged are her concave temples!
how early in the (history of the) sun what I was
    telling you!
how soon in your chest (figuratively, heart) the
    ancient sound!
how old the "2" in your copybook!

10   Children of the world, it is
mother Spain with her womb on her shoulders;
it is our teacher with her rulers,
it is mother and teacher,
cross and wood, because it gave you height,

15   dizziness and division and sum, children;
      she is doing her duty, while men tend to legal
          matters!

      If she falls—I say, it's just a way of speaking—if
          Spain
      falls, from the earth down,
      children, how you are going to stop growing!
20   how the year is going to punish the month!
      how your teeth are going to remain at 10,
      in outline the diphthong, the medal in tears!
      How the lambskin is going to continue
      tied by the foot to the great inkwell!
25   How you are going to lower the grades of the
          alphabet
      until the letter in which pain was born!

      Children,
      sons of fighters, among so many,
      lower your voice, for Spain
30   is now dividing its energy among the
      animal kingdom, little flowers, comets, and men.
      Lower your voice, for it is
      with its rigor, which is great, without knowing
      what to do, and in its hand is
35   the speaking skull and it speaks and speaks
      the skull, that of braids,
      the skull, that of life!
      Lower your voice, I tell you
      lower your voice, the canto of syllables, the
          weeping
40   of the material and the murmur less than the
          pyramids, and even
      that of the temples (anatomical) that walk with
          two stones!
      Lower your breath, and if
      its forearm comes down,
      if the rulers make noise, if it is night,
45   if the sky fits in two earthly limbos,

if there is noise in the sound of doors,
if I am late,
if you don't see anyone, if your pencils
without point scare you, if mother
50   Spain falls—I say, it's merely supposing—
go forth children of the world; go to find her! . . .

"Explico algunas cosas" by Pablo Neruda

I EXPLAIN SOME THINGS

1   You will ask: And where are the lilacs?
And the metaphysics covered with poppies?
And the rain which often was pounding
his words filling them
5   with gullies and birds?

I am going to tell you all that happens to me.

I was living in a suburb
of Madrid, with bells,
with clocks, with trees,
10   From there could be seen
the dry face of Castille
like an ocean of leather.

My house was called
the house of the flowers, because everywhere
15   geraniums were exploding: it was
a beautiful house
with dogs and little children.
Raúl, do you remember?
Do you remember, Rafael?
20   Federico, do you remember
under the ground,
do you remember my house with balconies where
the light of June was drowning flowers in your
mouth?

Brother, brother!

25 All
  was big voices, the salt of the merchandise,
  agglomerations of vibrating bread,
  markets of my suburb of Arguelles with its statue
  like a pale inkwell among the hake:
30 oil was arriving to the spoons,
  a profound throb
  of feet and hands was filling the street,
  meters, liters, the active essence
  of life,
35   heaped fish,
  texture of roofs with cold sun in which
  the deflection tires itself
  delirious fine ivory of the potatoes,
  tomatoes repeated until the sea.
40 And one morning all was burning
  and one morning the bonfires
  sprang from the earth
  devouring the living,
  and since then fire,
45 gunpowder since then,
  and since then blood.

  Bandits with airplanes and with Moors,
  bandits with rings and duchesses,
  bandits with black, blessing friars
50 were coming via the sky to kill children
  and in the streets the blood of the children
  was flowing plainly, like the blood of children.

  Jackals that the jackal rejected,
  stones that the dry thistle would eat spitting out,
55 vipers that vipers would hate!

  Facing you I have seen the blood
  of Spain uplift itself
  to drown you in a single wave
  of pride and of knives!

60   Generals
          traitors:
          look at my dead house,
          look at broken Spain:
          from each dead house sprouts burning metal
65   in place of flowers,
          from each ditch of Spain
          Spain emerges,
          from each dead child sprouts a gun with eyes,
          from each crime bullets are born
70   that will discover one day the place
          of your hearts.

          Will you ask why his poetry
          does not speak to us of the soil, of the leaves,
          of the great volcanoes of his native country?

75   Come see the blood in the streets,
          come see
          the blood in the streets,
          come see the blood
          in the streets!

"Llegada a Madrid de la Brigada Internacional" by Pablo Neruda

ARRIVAL IN MADRID OF THE
INTERNATIONAL BRIGADE

1   One morning in a cold month,
          in a dying month, stained with mud and smoke,
          a month without knees, a sad month of siege and
              misery,
          when through the wet window panes of my house
              African jackals were heard
5   to howl with the rifles and their teeth full of blood,
              then
          when we were having no more hope than a dream
              of gunpowder, when we were already believing

that the world was full of only ravenous monsters
    and rages
then, crushing the white frost of the cold month in
    Madrid in the fog
of the dawn

10   I have seen with these eyes that I have, with this
    heart that looks,
I have seen arrive the clear, the dominating soldiers
of the thin and hard and mature and ardent brigade
    of stone.
It was the afflicted time in which women
were sustaining an absence like a terrible coal,

15   and Spanish death, more acid and sharp than other
    deaths
filled the fields until then honored by wheat.
In the streets the broken blood of man was joining
the water that leaves the destroyed heart of the
    houses:
the bones of undone children, the heartbreaking

20   mourning silence of mothers, the eyes
of the defenseless closed for always,
were like the sadness and the loss, were like a garden
    spit upon,
were faith and flower assassinated for always.

Comrades,
25   then,
I have seen you,
and my eyes are until now full of pride
because I saw you through the foggy morning arrive
    at the pure forehead of Castille
silent and firm

30   like bells before the dawn,
full of solemnity and blue eyes coming from far away
    and even farther,
coming from your corners, from your lost countries,
    from your dreams
full of burned sweetness and of guns

to defend the Spanish city in which entrapped
    freedom
35 could fall and die eaten by beasts.
Brothers, from now on may
your purity and your force, your solemn history
be known by the child and by the man, by the
    woman and by the old man,
may it come to all the beings without hope, that
    might go down to the mines corroded by the
    sulfuric air,
40 may it rise to the inhuman staircases of the slave,
may all the stars, all the wheat of Castille and of the
    world
write your name and your rough fight
and your strong and terrestrial victory like a red oak
    tree.
Because you have made to be born again with your
    sacrifice
45 the lost faith, the absent soul, the confidence in the
    land,
and by your abundance, by your nobleness, by your
    dead,
as through a valley of hard rocks of blood
passes an immense river with doves of steel and hope.

"Almería" by Pablo Neruda

ALMERÍA

1   A dish for the Bishop, a dish that is chewed and
        bitter,
    a dish made of iron-ends, ashes, tears,
    a dish submerged with sobs and fallen walls,
    a black dish, a dish of blood of Almería.

5   A dish for the banker, a dish with cheeks
    ot children of the happy South, a dish of
    explosions, crazed waters and ruins and terror,

a dish of smashed axles and trampled heads,
a black dish, a dish of blood of Almería.

10   Each morning, each turbid morning of your lives
you will have it smoking and burning on your table:
you will push it away with your delicate hands
in order not to see it, in order not to digest it so
      many times:
you will remove it a little between the bread and
      the grapes,
15   to this plate of silent blood
that will be there each morning, every
morning.

A dish for the Colonel and the wife of the Colonel,
at a party in the barracks, at every party
20   above the oaths and the spit, with the light of wine
      of the morning
so that you might see it trembling and cold over
      the world.

Yes, a dish for all of you, rich from here and there,
ambassadors, ministers, atrocious table companions,
ladies of comfortable tea and sofa seat:
25   a dish wasted, overflowing, dirty with poor blood,
for every morning, for every week, for ever and ever,
a dish of blood of Almería, before you, always.

"Barcelona" by Johannes R. Becher

BARCELONA

1   Our city built high by the sea,
And the sea has imbued her with blue light,
And the sea looks dreamily at her,
For there, where she stands, was once the sea—

5   City of columns and forums.
Look, it glows like muscles and corals,

And lowered bells resound from nearby,
Saint Anna, Saint Monica . . .

Sounds of friends and a song full of lament
10   Were carried by you to us from afar.
Barcelona! Oh, your name has
Enchanted us. The city has become a part of us.

They contained you like a holy treasure.
Your squares found their place in us
15   And in my heart your streets
Crossed each other and enlivened me.

We—we along with you were outraged,
And the whole world heard you,
As you spoke with the voice of the people—your
20   Voice made my voice strong and firm.

Also for me the sky stood horribly open,
And I saw how you sank mortally wounded,
And I ignited a fire in myself
Against those cowardly monsters . . .

25   Barcelona, Ruins. Bloody puddles.
Henchmen in the Red Basque caps.
Foreign mercenary is a murderous fellow.
Franco's flag on the citadel.

Bad advice speaks within me treacherously:
30   "Be quiet and stop the questioning!"
No, I'm going to ask about the truth,
And I myself must speak the truth to myself.

How did it happen? How is it possible that—
I'm asking, I'm asking incessantly,
35   And I'm not afraid of this truth:
Stakes, torture, death court (court that sentences
    to death).

That which the authorities never succeeded in
    doing,
Was accomplished by treachery, by treachery,

And I ask in London and Paris,

40   Who is it who allowed the fortresses to fall? . . .

Barcelona. City rich in sacrifices.
City which also bled for me.
Our graves however are opening.
Barcelona—that's you and I—

45   And the sea looks dreamily at you,
For there where you stand was once the sea,
And the sea has imbued you with blue light.
Our city built high above the sea!

"General Mola: Aus dem spanischen Bürgerkrieg" by Johannes R. Becher

GENERAL MOLA
from the Spanish Civil War

1   When he sat there, without looking up,
Signing one judgment after another:
Nothing human sat there—an emaciated horror,
On which only his jacket still remained human.

5   As if it could weep or laugh,
So human was the jacket made of fine cloth,
By a human hand, as if it were an attempt,
To make the picture of a human being from a
    jacket . . .

When one day an unknown airplane
10   Crashed in the mountain range and burned up,
From nothing was his origin discernible:

Until a piece of a jacket was found,
From which one could recognize him, the
    General—
The only thing that was still human about him.

"Fliehende Mutter" by Johannes R. Becher

FLEEING MOTHER

1   "I don't really know if I'm welcome
           In your land . . . I have been banished from
               so far away . . .
           In this bundle? . . . Weapons? . . . in it
           Is something dear to me, Sir . . . I lost
               everything else . . .

5   Here's how it happened . . . The village had
               been empty for a long time,
           The men gone to war . . . only children,
               women . . .
           Then came a thundering, Sir, from the direction
               of the Ebro . . .
           We ran out on the field to look around . . .

           Not a morsel of bread. Nothing—for many
               days . . .
10   And then, then they came . . . so quickly from
               above . . .
           And one of them, who swooped down low . . .
           No cries . . . I picked up my child—

           And suddenly the road was no longer there.
           It was a chasm. It was ice. A boulder
15   Offered me support . . . They came back
               again . . .
           The boulder protected me. Also the boulder
               wept . . .

           I don't know, am I anywhere? . . .
           May I bed him down in your earth? . . .
           Forgive me, Sir . . . I was overwhelmed . . .
20   The dead . . . the dead must be rescued . . ."

"Novembre 1936" by Paul Eluard

NOVEMBER 1936

1   Look at the builders of ruins at work
      They are rich, patient, orderly, black and stupid
      But they do their best to be the only ones on
        earth
      They are at the extreme edge of being men and
        are full of trash
5   They construct on the bare ground palaces
        without brains.

      One gets used to everything
      Except to these leaden birds
      Except to the hatred of that which is shining
      Except to yielding space to them.

10   Talk of the sky the sky empties itself
      The autumn matters little to us
      Our masters stamped their feet
      We have forgotten autumn
      And we will forget our masters.

15   City as if at the base of the ocean made of only
        one saved drop of water
      From only one diamond cultivated in plain day
      Madrid city accustomed to those who suffered
      From this terrible good which denied being an
        example
      Of those who suffered
20   From the indispensable misery to the glare of
        this good.

      That the mouth rises towards its truth
      Blows a rare smile like a broken chain
      Which man delivered from his absurd past

Raises before his brother a similar face
25   And gives reality to vagabond wings.

"La Victoire de Guernica" by Paul Eluard

THE VICTORY OF GUERNICA

1

1   Beautiful world of hovels
Of mine and of fields

2

Faces good in the fire faces in the cold
In the denials of night of insults of blows

3

5   Faces good for everything
Here is the void which stares at you
Your death will serve as an example

4

Death a heart overturned

5

They make you pay for bread
10   For sky for earth water sleep
And the misery
Of your life

6

They said to desire good intelligence
They rationed the strong judged the fools
15   Gave charity split a halfpenny in two
They greeted the cadavers
They overburdened themselves with politeness

7

They persevere they exaggerate they are not of
    our world

8

The women the children have the same treasure
20   Of green leaves of spring and of pure milk
And of endurance
In their pure eyes

9

The women the children have the same treasure
In their eyes
25   The men defend as they can

10

The women the children have the same red roses
In their eyes
Each one shows its blood

11

Fear and the courage to live and to die
30   Death so difficult and so easy

12

Men for whom this treasure was sung
Men for whom this treasure was spoiled

13

Real men for whom despair
Feeds the devouring fire of hope
35   Let us open the last bud of the future together

14

Pariahs death earth and hideousness
Of our enemies have
The monotonous color of our night
We shall overcome.

"En Espagne" by Paul Eluard

IN SPAIN

1   If there is in Spain one tree stained with blood
It is the tree of liberty

If there is in Spain one talkative mouth
It talks of liberty

5   If there is in Spain one glass of pure wine
It is the people who will drink it.

"Espagne" by Paul Eluard

SPAIN

1   The most beautiful eyes in the world
Began to sing
That they want to see further
Than the walls of prisons
5   Further than their eyelids
Made black and blue by grief

The bars of the cage
Sing of liberty
An air that escapes
10   Over human roads
Under a furious sun
A huge sun of tempest

Life lost regained
Night and day of life
15   Exiles prisoners
You feed in the shade
A fire that brings dawn
Freshness dew

Victory

20   And the pleasure of victory.

"Ispantsi otstupili za Pirenyiei" by Níkolay Semyónovich
Tíkhonov

THE SPANIARDS HAVE RETREATED
BEYOND THE PYRENEES

1   As if the ink were full of incantations
I am not able to touch the pen,
In a thick strange forest
A woodpecker hammered only about the war.

5   Women only are seen by me
On the rocky winter road,
Only infants fallen in the snow,
Only scorched leaves of the thicket.

And about the thicket full of ashy hair,
10   So pierced through with powder,
About the people begging for water
At night behind the barbed wire,—

Whatever you say of such a life
All is inadequate,—
15   All has already been said by the child's hand
Sticking out from the snow on the cliff.

"Govorit fashist" by Níkolay Semyónovich Tíkhonov

THE FASCIST SPEAKS:

1   This they say: the Fascist power
Ignores human rights
That we look on things too simply
That we love only the graveyard stillness.

5   Now let me explain to you why:
The people are children, we are their Führer

The child, so that he grows into a titan
You nourish him from infancy with the drum.

Dazzle them nightly with torches of parades,
10   Encourage their taste for martial speech.
Enough of books—instead let the bonfire gleam
Round the bonfire hold a dance
Such as our ancestors performed in bearskins,
And strike up a song at the end
15   So that you threaten the whole world of people
And are called upon to dominate them.

But since your people do not till the end
Obey the will of our Führer-father
And want to live, work, rejoice
20   And do not want to be proud of their ancestors
And you cannot make them obey
Arm yourselves with a good axe.

And now, when according to the power of growth
Throughout the country there is the greatness of
          the graveyards,
25   And the war supplies are provided,
There is a command: work and keep silent!—
Then, so that disorder does not break out,
You, take care of the education of the spirit:

Return women to the kitchen and feather bed,
30   Let them be the joy of the soldiers hereafter,
Strengthen the roar of batteries of newspapers:
The Marxist and the Jew are to blame for all evils
And they are at times one and the same—
Let our thunder destroy them quickly!
35   We were oppressed by miserable neighbors,
We need victory in war!

Repeat this to all: feeling injured by fate,
Henceforth let us set ourselves to banditry!
So that the whole country howls behind you:
40   "War! War! Long live war!"
Long live war always and everywhere,

And the flaming bosoms of cities,
And women's wails, and the din of weapons,
The boom of victories and the grumble of the
    conquered,
45   Peace and work is the Marxist grimace,
All races are dust, there is only our race!

When all is in ashes, on the ashes our banner,
Let the enemies' skulls be bowls for us
Let us inhale from them the aroma of wine,—
50   To the dregs: then long live war!

"Govorit antifashist" by Níkolay Semyónovich Tíkhonov

THE ANTI-FASCIST SPEAKS:

1   That over me stood day and night
The dangling shadow of the jailer,
That the free motion of each thought
Immediately came under suspicion,
5   That the Fascist bonfire destroyed in a flash
The pages of my beloved books,
That instead of simple human words
I heard the endless roar of the Führers,
That all my life under the wild howl of songs
10   I strode with a shovel in the labor camp,
That giving value to a contemptible life,
I went as sentry to imprisoned peoples
And took part in piratic raids,
That I glorified the assassins in servile odes,
15   That I stood like a corpse silent and, like a
        corpse,
Rotted alive among factory pipes
Emitting smoke only for the glory of war
Spattered with the blood of my friends,
So that I might forget reason exists in the world,
20   I squinting at the world with hateful eye.

No! The world will remain unshaken!
It remembers all that was suffered by it
Fires, executions, disasters, battles,
Ages of shame, of servitude, of degradation,

25   Wherever the new Rome should whistle with
            its whip,
We shall not surrender anything to it!

Neither our wheatfields, rustling with a sea of
            bread,
Nor our mountains, thrusting their peaks to
            heaven,
Nor our rivers, streaming in tranquillity,

30   Nor our songs of heart and soul,
Nor our songs of love or of friendship or of
            worries
Nor the works begun by the people
Nor our cities where the streets rumble merrily,
Nor those fields where villages blossom;

35   And the nightingale should not die,
He will roar out our glory,
And the hawks above the humps of the hills
Let them soar like simple hawks,
And not the little path of spring roses,

40   Nor the highly foaming seas
Nor the bonfire that whirls off reddish smoke
In the autumn forest—we shall not surrender
            them.
We shall not surrender the smiles of our daring
            ones,
Nor the sails on our white boats,

45   Nor the air that we breathe,
Nor brightness of day, nor darkness of warm
            night,
The last boughs of rosy apple trees,
The rays of dawn on a sleeping glade,
Nor the pride of being ourselves

50   Nor the rights of a conquered destiny.

Fascism will find only ruin ahead—
We will never surrender anything!

Let a northern or a southern Rome arise—
We will have a fatal conversation in battle!

"Terra di Spagna . . ." by Giorgio Braccialarghe

LAND OF SPAIN

1   Land of Spain when night falls. Roars
through the olive groves and over the burned
    land
the new voice of one who is no longer afraid
the imminent shame of war.

5   For those to whom another destiny will come
the voice sings, and we who listen to it
find in it the command:
There is no resurrection without death.

Land of Spain when night falls. You
10   with the sublime language of heroes
this command you transmitted to us
and to those adventurers who will come after us.

You died, oh comrades, but death
illuminated life. We will live
15   because life illuminates the death
of those who choose the ultimate sacrifice.

"Notti di Spagna" by Giorgio Braccialarghe

NIGHTS OF SPAIN

1   There is so much white in the sky
that it seems that a bride

has forgotten her veil
attached to a rose.

5   And the floating veil in the country
        like a filter full of enchantment
        permits the brightness of the moon
        to pass
        through the roaring of the wind.

10   Nights of Spain,
        the toads singing
        along the long ditches
        in the meadows.

        There is a drowsy murmur
15   as if beautiful women
        were listening to the secrets
        of their lovers.

        Nights of Spain,
        capes of peace thrown
20   over tortured days
        returns of calm
        indefinite whispers
        quiet murmurs.

        The immobile sentry in the shadow
25   seems like a lost statue
        on the paths of a park.

        Nights of Spain
        in the winding trenches
        innocent confidences
30   one speaks of his fiancée
        one speaks of the last advance.

        And in the brief silences
        that punctuate the phrases
        distant voices
35   of comrades gone away
        murmur strange words.

Meanwhile, in the starry night
resounds a gunshot.

"Ai fratelli lontani . . ." by Giorgio Braccialarghe:

TO DISTANT BROTHERS . . .

1 Tonight I wish to sing for you
  without rhyme or meter.
  Poor palpitant words
  as when after having cried very much
5 one searches for one who is gone forever.
  And speaks to him. And knows not what he says
  nor what he would say.
  I wish to speak to you, Oh distant brothers
  as when you were nearby
10 and seemed titans.
  Titans in war, young boys in peace.
  I can't believe that anyone lies down
  pale, on a white bed
  with his youthful appearance
15 who does not wish to die.
  I can't believe that
  the day of resurrection may not come
  for our battalion.
  The third: the strongest!
20 First in attack and first in victory.
  Wrote the most beautiful pages of history
  between one song and another.
  Gallant colony of gallant heroes.
  Fewer than a thousand,
25 a thousand souls in each one.
  Onward, onward, onward.
  Enduring fatigue and hunger
  sleep and thirst but onward
  like so many giants
30 who nourish themselves on ideals

and who ask no more than wings
for the triumphant flight
towards the final goal.
Fewer than a thousand,
35   but how much, how much faith!
On the tortured hills of Jarama
in the woods of Alcarria
nothing but a hymn of glory
written with your blood
40   immortalized by your sacrifice.
—Madrid, meanwhile
endured the gloomy song
of the enemy cannons.
And up there in Viscaglia
45   the eternal scoundrel
was destroying everything.—
What does it matter? On the beds
of the field hospitals
grew a rose
50   of blood, grew a smile
on your faces of young heroes
You had faith in us.
In us who remaining at the battlefront
occupied, fiercely, your posts
55   oh disappeared of yesterday
oh destined to live tomorrow.
Tomorrow, when from the liberated camps
of restored offices
shall rise solemnly in chorus
60   the hymn of peace and work.

"Fratelli dell'Internazionale" by Giorgio Braccialarghe

BROTHERS OF THE INTERNATIONAL

1

The first six months of war have passed: onward, brothers
of the International.

2

The victory is not yet attained: onward, brothers of the International.

3

Inch by inch and on our side the sacrifice which is beautiful, and with the memory of our fallen ones in our heart: onward, brothers of the International.

4

You are the sowers of tomorrow. Already the dawn has shown itself in the sky, red from the revolution, already the land of Spain knows about your sowing: onward, brothers of the International.

5

Today's struggle brings the promise of peace tomorrow, the sowing of yesterday, the fruits of the future: onward, brothers of the International.

6

Among all your songs is missing that of a liberated Spain. You would be the epic poets of it, you would create it with your deeds, day by day, hour by hour: onward, brothers of the International.

7

I know you one by one, but if I knew only one of you, I would know all of you. By the heritage of faith, discipline, and willpower that makes you all equal, by the simplicity that endows each of your splendid actions.

8

After six months I recognize you one by one. You are still the same, still you carry within you the constant desire for victory that kissed the white forehead of our fallen ones.

9

Onward, brothers of the International. To other battles, other triumphs; united; by receptive Spain, to her bleeding bosom, the destinies of the world: invincible.

10

Onward, brothers of the International. With you justice, against you the rage of false powers.

11

Each one of you who falls is a drop of oil in the votive lamp of Liberty. Every enemy whom you bring down is a violated net from among the chain that has Humanity tied.

12

Onward, brothers of the International. Onward, onward, onward. For the tomorrow of Spain. For the future of all the world. Onward!

BIBLIOGRAPHY

Poetry:

Alberti, Rafael, ed. *Romancero de la guerra española*. Buenos Aires: Patronato Hispano Argentino de Cultura, 1944.

Auden, W. H. *Collected Poetry*. New York: Random House, 1945.

———. *Spain*. London: Faber & Faber, 1938.

Becher, Johannes R. *Ausgewählte Dichtung aus der Zeit der Verbannung, 1933-1945*. Berlin: Aufbau-Verlag, 1945.

———. *Gedichte 1936-1941*. Berlin: Aufbau-Verlag, 1966.

Caillet Bois, Julio, ed. *Antología de la poesía hispanoamericana*. Madrid: Aguilar, 1958.

Campbell, Roy. *Collected Poems*. London: The Bodley Head, 1957.

———. *Flowering Rifle. A Poem from the Battlefield of Spain*. London: Longmans, Green and Co., 1939.

Eluard, Paul. *Cours naturel*. Paris: Editions du Sagittaire, 1938.

———. *Poèmes politiques*. Paris: Gallimard, 1948.

Felipe, León. *Obras completas*. Buenos Aires: Editorial Losada, 1963.

Hernández, Miguel. *Imagen de tu huella, el silbo vulnerado, el rayo que no cesa, otros poemas, viento del pueblo.* Buenos Aires: Editorial Losada, S.A., 1963.

———. *Obras completas.* Buenos Aires: Editorial Losada, 1960.

———. *Poemas.* Barcelona: Plaza & Janes, S.A., Editores, 1964.

MacDiarmid, Hugh. *The Battle Continues.* Edinburgh: Castle Wynd Printers Limited, 1957.

———. *Stony Limits and Other Poems.* London: V. Gollancz, Ltd., 1934.

Neruda, Pablo. *Poesía política.* Santiago (Chile): Editora Austral, 1953.

Puccini, Dario. *Romancero della resistenza spagnola, 1936-1965,* 2. Rome: Editori Riuniti, 1965.

Romancero de los voluntarios de la libertad. Madrid: Ediciones de Comisariado de las Brigadas Internacionales, 1937.

Rukeyser, Muriel. "Mediterranean." New York: *New Masses,* XXIV, September 14, 1937.

———. *Theory of Flight.* New Haven: Yale University Press, 1935.

———. *A Turning Wind.* New York: The Viking Press, 1939.

Spender, Stephen. *Collected Poems, 1928-1953.* London: Faber and Faber, 1965.

Spender, Stephen, and John Lehmann, eds. *Poems for Spain.* London: The Hogarth Press, 1939.

Tíkhonov, Níkolay Semyónovich. *Izbránnye proizvédenija v dvuch tómach.* Moscow: State Publishing Co. of Literature of Art, 1955.

Vallejo, César. *España, aparta de mí este cáliz.* Mexico: Editorial Séneca, 1940.

———. *Poemas Humanos.* New York: Grove Press, 1968.

Prose:

Alonso, Amado. *Poesía y estilo de Pablo Neruda.* Buenos Aires: Editorial Sudamericana, 1966.

Alsterlund, B. "Biographical Sketch." New York: *Wilson Library Bulletin,* 15:110, October, 1940.

Ayala, Francisco. *Histrionismo y representación*. Buenos Aires: Editorial Sudamericana, 1944.

Barea, Arturo. *The Forging of a Rebel*. New York: Reynal & Hitchcock, 1946.

Beach, Joseph Warren. *The Making of the Auden Canon*. Minneapolis: University of Minnesota Press, 1957.

Benson, Frederick R. *Writers in Arms*. New York: New York University Press, 1967.

Blair, John. *The Poetic Art of W. H. Auden*. Princeton: Princeton University Press, 1965.

Bowra, Sir Cecil Maurice. *In General and Particular*. London: Weidenfeld and Nicolson, 1964.

————. Poetry & Politics. Cambridge (England): Cambridge University Press, 1966.

Brinnin, J. M. "Social Poet and the Problem of Communication." *Poetry,* no. 61 (January 1943), 554-75.

Buthlay, Kenneth. "Hugh MacDiarmid." *Writers and Critics Series*. Edinburgh, 1964.

Calvo Serer, Rafael. *La literatura universal sobre la guerra de España*. Madrid: Ateneo, 1962.

Cano Ballesta, Juan. *La poesía de Miguel Hernández*. Madrid: Gredos, 1971.

Collier's Encyclopedia. New York: Crowell-Collier Publishing Co., 1965.

Coyné, André. *César Vallejo*. Buenos Aires: Ediciones Nueva Visión, 1968.

del Río, Angel. *Historia de la literatura española,* Tomo II. New York: Holt, Rinehart and Winston, 1963.

Dizionario biografico degli italiani. Rome: Istituto della Enciclopedia Italiana, 1971.

Duval, K. D., and S. G. Smith, eds. *Hugh MacDiarmid: a Festschrift*. Edinburgh: Duval, 1962.

Eberhart, Richard, and Selden Rodman, eds. *War and the Poet*. New York: The Devin-Adair Co., 1945.

Encyclopaedia Britannica. Chicago: Encyclopaedia Britannica, Inc., 1967.

Ford, Hugh D. *A Poets' War: British Poets and the Spanish Civil War*. Philadelphia: University of Pennsylvania Press, 1965.

Fuller, John. *A Reader's Guide to W. H. Auden*. New York: Farrar, Straus & Giroux, 1970.

Greenberg, Herbert. *Quest for the Necessary: W. H. Auden and the Divided Consciousness*. Cambridge (Mass.): Harvard University Press, 1968.

Guerrero Zamora, Juan. *Miguel Hernández, poeta (1910-1942)*. Madrid: Colección El Grifon, 1955.

Guttmann, Allen. *The Wound in the Heart*. New York: The Free Press of Glencoe, 1962.

Hemingway, Ernest. *For Whom the Bell Tolls*. New York: Scribner, 1940.

Jackson, Gabriel. *The Spanish Republic and the Civil War, 1931-1939*. Princeton: Princeton University Press, 1967.

MacDiarmid, Hugh. *Lucky Poet. A Self-Study*. London: Methuen & Co., Ltd., 1943.

Malraux, André. *Man's Hope*. New York: Random House, 1938.

Muste, John M. *Say That We Saw Spain Die*. Seattle: University of Washington Press, 1966.

Parkinson, T. "Some Recent Pacific Coast Poetry." *Pacific Spectator* 4, no. 3 (1950), 300-02.

Pujals, Esteban. *España y la guerra de 1936 en la poesía de Roy Campbell*. Madrid: Ateneo, 1959.

Replogle, Justin. *Auden's Poetry*. Seattle: University of Washington Press, 1969.

Rukeyser, Muriel. "Under Forty." *Contemporary Jewish Record*. Vol. VII, no. 1. February, 1944.

Scarfe, Francis. "W. H. Auden." *Contemporary British Poets*. Monaco: The Lyrebird Press, 1949.

Spears, Monroe K., ed. *Auden: A Collection of Critical Essays*.
————. *The Poetry of W. H. Auden: The Disenchanted Island*. New York: Oxford University Press, 1963.

Spender, Stephen. *The Still Centre*. London: Faber and Faber, Ltd., 1939.
————. "W. H. Auden and His Poetry." *Twentieth Century Views*. Englewood Cliffs (N.J.): Prentice-Hall, 1964.
————. *World Within World. The Autobiography of Stephen Spender*. London: Hamilton, 1951.

Thomas, Hugh. *The Spanish Civil War*. New York: Eyre, 1961.

Valbuena Prat, Angel. *Historia de la literatura española*. Tomo II. Barcelona: Editorial Gustavo Gili, S.A., 1946.

Weintraub, Stanley. *The Last Great Cause*. New York: Weybright and Talley, 1968.

Wright, David. "Roy Campbell." *Writers and Their Work*. No. 137. London: Longmans, Green & Co., 1961.

THE PACIFIC COAST RANGES

THE PACIFIC COAST RANGES

EDITED BY RODERICK PEATTIE

THE CONTRIBUTORS: Archie Binns, John Walton Caughey, Lois Crisler, Aubrey Drury, Idwal Jones, Donald Culross Peattie, Thomas Emerson Ripley, Richard Joel Russell, Judy Van der Veer, Daniel E. Willard

THE VANGUARD PRESS · NEW YORK

TITLE PAGE PHOTOGRAPH: The Channel Islands from hills above Santa Barbara — by infra-red photography. (Courtesy of Josef Muench.)

CONTENTS

v

CONTENTS

ILLUSTRATIONS

Acknowledgment: Photographs number 1, 3, 11, 16, 19, and 29 are printed by courtesy of Josef Muench; numbers 2, 4, 23, courtesy of the Redwood Empire Association; number 5, courtesy of Gabriel Moulin, and numbers 13, 14, and 17, courtesy of Gabriel Moulin and the Save-the-Redwoods League; numbers 6 and 8, courtesy of the Los Angeles County Chamber of Commerce; number 7, courtesy of Everett F. Chandler; numbers 9, 10, and 12, courtesy of William and Irene Finley; numbers 15 and 28, courtesy of Edward Weston; numbers 18, 25, and 26, courtesy of Wilkes and the Santa Barbara Chamber of Commerce; numbers 20 and 21, courtesy of the National Park Service; number 22, courtesy of Frank Woodfield and the Astoria Chamber of Commerce; number 24, courtesy of the Palm Springs Chamber of Commerce; number 27, courtesy of the Northern Pacific Railway.

INTRODUCTION

BY RODERICK PEATTIE

My wife was driving along a Coast Range Highway, sitting beside a very small nephew. The lad watched the wonderful scenery unrolling beneath the so-blue California sky and asked, "Why do people live in the East?" Frankly, after editing this volume, I have not the answer. Herein are recorded the enthusiasms of a group of experts in the appreciation of one of the most charming and, at times, dramatically splendid of American landscapes.

We should not speak in the singular of the western Coast Range landscapes. You should know that our western coast extends over sixteen degrees of latitude, which is to say, a distance of better than eleven hundred miles. Moreover, the reach of the coast runs at right angles to the climatic belts. About San Diego one has subtropical climate. North of San Francisco the control of weather is by the westerly winds, and as latitude increases, altitude on the mountain slopes becomes more and more significant. Donald Culross Peattie, one of the contributors, came to Santa Barbara from the Riviera and found to his delight that the southern California coast surpasses that of France in beauty. Quite unlike the beflowered south, the coasts of Oregon and Washington have dark grandeur or, under the drifting sea fogs, all the mysticism of impressionistic art. One feature the Coast Ranges possess which is unique among the ranges of our country: This is the sea. Headlands and mountain spurs stand boldly into the sea, and elsewhere there are long beaches. I remember my delight at the "lost" coves along the sea

south of Carmel. In places the coast road, carved from the mountain sides, almost impends above the water.

There is not one Coast Range, but many. In places the mountains extend east to the Sierra Nevada and the Cascades. The Coast Ranges are not easy of definition. To accomplish that definition a section from Dr. Willard's chapter on the geologic story has been placed here.

"The North American continent, on its western side, is marked by one of the world's outstanding mountain systems, the Coast Ranges. The mountains are not the highest in the world and not the oldest, but, standing close upon the Pacific Ocean, they rise from near sea level and present a majestic wall against the attacking waves of the ocean. Few mountain ranges in the world, rising from near sea level, stand so boldly against the sea and command so wide a view of the ocean on one hand and of a sweeping valley landscape, but little above sea level, on the other hand.

"The system of ranges extends from the tip of Lower California (Baja California) to the St. Elias Range in Alaska, approximately one fourth the distance from the North Pole to the South Pole. The system includes no fewer than thirty-nine ranges of mountains to which specific names have been given. Far north the high mountains are perennially snow-capped. At the extreme south, eight hundred miles south of the United States-Mexican boundary, the Peninsular Range terminates at the tip of Baja California in Mount Lazaro, eight thousand feet above the sea, an arid, uninhabitable region, storm-swept in torrid heat.

"The western margin of the continent is thus fortified by a great mountain wall against which the waves and tides of the Pacific Ocean beat and lash. In many places the mountains stand out in bold promontories, offering a resistant wall against the ever-aggressive ocean waves. The view westward from these mountain heights is awe-inspiring. The last rays of the setting sun kiss these heights (when the weather is clear) in a golden splendor that no other part of the continent enjoys.

"It is impossible to go any farther west by land, and indeed this is far enough! Look to the east from out on the blue expanse and behold! Here is a wall of rock that seems to say to the rolling waves and the inswelling tides 'thus far and no farther.' The heart of the seafaring man is bound to beat faster as he approaches the rugged shore wall. It may be bathed in fog, but he knows it is there.

"The mountain wall however is not unrelenting. At the Golden Gate the wall seems to open the portcullis and bid the sea come in—to safe harbor. Ships enter the harbor of San Francisco Bay across the axis or backbone of the Coast Range mountains, and far north at the strait of Juan de Fuca the great harbor of Puget Sound invites the seafaring traffic of the world. The wall relents and allows the sea to enter on friendly and peaceful terms. No other great harbor exists for three thousand miles. Monterey Bay and Mission Bay at San Diego—alas for the glory of the land that has disappeared! The mountain wall gave way and let the sea come in. These are drowned valleys. And off the Santa Barbara coast the mountain wall has been conquered, and only the tops of what were towering mountains now rise above the waves. The Farallones, far off from the Golden Gate, tell of a land that was and is not. Still the great mountain wall of the Coast Ranges courageously holds its unquestioned sway. If it yields in a few places it is only to be neighborly. It remains the rampart of the western continental coast.

"The Coast Ranges of the Far West represent a different type of mountains from the Appalachians of the eastern United States. The Appalachians are older. They were formed when it is thought the outer crust of the globe was less rigid than now, and hence upheaval resulted in folding and wrinkling of the rocks, whereas the mountains of the Far West are mainly block mountains, bounded by faults or fractures, the great forces of earth's interior causing the more rigid crust to break or fracture rather than bend. The mountains of the western coast are mainly uplifted fault blocks. The great Sierra Nevada Range, near neighbor of the Coast Ranges, is a vast uplifted block, bounded on the east by great faults, and the block as a whole rotated toward the west, the eastern side of the block uplifted and the western side depressed.

"There is no book of family records from which the 'ages' of the mountain ranges can be ascertained. The pages of the geological family Bible are the rock formations, and the Acts are the geologic processes involved. The record of the rocks shows that the 'beginning' of the Coast Ranges was much later than the upheaval of the ancestral Sierra Nevada Range, and many millions of years after the uplifting of the Appalachian Mountains. The beginning of the Coast Ranges goes back an estimated 140 million years. While geologically young compared with the old mountains of the East, the Coast Ranges rank high among the mountain

ranges of the world in the complexity of their formation and in the effect they have had upon the history of the human race and in shaping the trends of civilization."

To define the variety and charm of life and landscape of these ranges is more difficult. Certainly no mere paragraphs here would be adequate. Indeed, no single writer has the necessary experience. To that end this volume is a symposium of experts and artists. Who the contributors are, who have a right to speak for these delights, is in itself interesting.

Donald Culross Peattie contributes two chapters. Part of both chapters are the property of the *Reader's Digest* and are reprinted here by their permission. As outlined, the tour of the missions is recommended as one of the most interesting auto voyages in America. If the chapter on the flora seems inadequate to bespeak the variety and beauty of the flowers and forests, the reader is referred to *Flowering Earth* and *Road of a Naturalist* to make up this lack, both by Donald Peattie. It was Donald Peattie who, with great enthusiasm, collected the photographs which we so proudly present.

Dr. John Caughey writes the story of the Indians of the mountains. He is Associate Professor of History in the University of California at Los Angeles. Like most Midwesterners who have migrated to California, he has a passionate attachment to the land of his choice. Among his half dozen scholarly volumes is a history of California, published in 1940. His picturesque narrative of Indian and Spanish days in this volume is the result of extensive study. California's literature stands out splendidly, like its mountains, Dr. Caughey says, and he contributes a chapter on California writing, going back to its Indian and Spanish beginnings and continuing to its well-known present.

Officially Aubrey Drury is Administrative Secretary of the Save-The-Redwoods League. Thus he is an almost ecclesiastical official of those cathedral groves. His *California, An Intimate Guide* is now in its fourth edition. His passionate enthusiasm and varied unselfish interests make him one of the leading citizens of his State. Here he writes on animal life.

With delight, we offer Judy Van der Veer's chapter on foothills. Miss Van der Veer was born in San Diego County which she describes. Her volumes *The River Pasture* and *Brown Hills* are well known. To best appreciate her intimate attachment to the foothills of which she writes,

I quote from her last letter: "If Red Anderson had not offered to bring in the cows every morning, I would not have had my daily hour for writing. This ought to be the best book of the 'American Mountain Series' because these are the best mountains."

Idwal Jones is a specialist in human nature. He has been a newspaperman, distinguished novelist, and is currently in publicity work for Paramount Pictures. His latest novel, *The Vineyard,* is a symbolic tale of a wine farm in Napa Valley. His "China Boy," a short story appearing first in *The American Mercury,* has been many times reprinted. As a specialist in California folklore, he is a professional haunter of the Coast Ranges from Trinity River to San Benito and back.

With Lois Crisler's chapter on the Wilderness Mountains, we have entered the wild, dark realm of the Olympics. Mrs. Crisler knows her mountains. As wife of the well-known rancher and woodsman, "Herb" Crisler, she lives in the forest eleven miles from a mailbox, with mail twice a month. As a former teacher of English at the University of Washington, she has done the writing of this chapter, but we strongly suspect a collaboration with her husband. Her last letter tells of an adventurous trip into the mountains, before the snows were gone, to plant a food cache for later expeditions.

Thomas Ripley is an old tyee of the lumber business of the Northwest. His lusty account of "rigginslingers," and "highballing the big sticks" is an epic and is a "must" for publication before his generation passes on. Author of a delightful book of reminiscences, *A Vermont Boyhood,* Mr. Ripley is also a painter and lives in Santa Barbara. In his own words, his reasons for seeking out the Northwest were "the alluring names of Puget Sound, the Stilaguamish, the Snohomish and the Skykomish; the illimitable forests and the illimitable wealth, the salmon so thick they crowded themselves onto the river banks, the sailing, the fishing, and the town lots that multiplied while you sailed and fished."

Archie Binns is associated with the Northwest in the minds of a large reading public through his novels, *Lightship* and *The Laurels Are Cut Down.* The latter was a Literary Guild choice and a prize winner. *The Land Is Bright* is now a standard work on the Oregon Trail. Our volume would indeed be incomplete without his authoritative contribution. Mr. Binns does not write as an outsider. He knows his country and is becoming the Homer of the Northwest.

Professor Willard wrote the geological story. He is one of those rare geologists who can write popularly on his subject. He has written largely in this vein for he has published *Adventures in Scenery—A Popular Reader of California*. His chapter answers a legion of questions which the intelligent voyager is sure to ask himself.

Professor Richard Joel Russell is a distinguished American geographer. His chapter is a model for climatologists in the art of popularization. Packed with facts and detail, it not only answers queries but reads like a piece of creative writing. More than that, Dr. Russell is a diplomat. Few persons could have handled so artfully a study of the elements about which the coast peoples are so sensitively proud.

These then are the contributors to the latest volume of the "American Mountain Series."

Lying on the Coast Ranges are many beautiful towns and cities. It is these towns and cities that, every week end and for longer vacations, furnish sojourners who are among the greatest enthusiasts of the mountains. Indeed they feel their cities, in which they take more than usual pride, to be integral parts of the mountain territory. Why then are not the towns and cities described in this volume? If it is not enough to say that this series is particularly about mountain life and mountain folk; the city dwellers will agree that to do justice to their cities would occupy a large volume. Rather than do them the injustice of brevity, they are omitted.

"FATHER SERRA'S ROSARY"

BY DONALD CULROSS PEATTIE

It was, of course, the Spaniards who were first among the Europeans to venture into the Coast Ranges. That they had a passion for their new-found land is evident from their journals. But their tasks were dedicated to God, and yet the missions they built are in part so charming because they were adapted to the environment. The missionaries had imagination and poetry in their religion. None of the austerity of the Reformation defeated their appreciation of the beauties of the surroundings. The early fathers were the first lovers of the Coast Ranges. (R. P.)

Strung like precious beads upon the thread of the old *Camino Real,* the nineteen original missions of California, founded by the Spanish Franciscans, were all located in the Coast Ranges, either at their feet or in valleys amongst our mountains or actually upon their gentler slopes. Of all the works of man in these mountains of ours, the missions are the oldest, the loveliest, the richest in history. Though time has dealt so harshly with them, by earthquake and torrential rains, it has mellowed them too, like old ivory, old meerschaum, or old violins. Though history has desecrated them, with neglect, with secularization, with active and intentional destruction and profanation, it is a matter of recent history that the people of California have carefully and lovingly restored their missions, preserving as many of them as they could. Of all that the visitor comes to the Coast Ranges to see, the missions are the most popular. This may make them seem trite or banal—to those who have seen them only on picture postcards. To those who live within the sound of their tolling bells, within the sight of their softly glowing colors and softly flowing lines, the missions grow increasingly beloved and significant. In the end there is no resisting their sweet charm.

True, the California missions are far from being the oldest buildings in America. For the actual structures that we see today (which replace in most cases those earlier primitive shelters from which historians date the *founding* of each church) are none of them older than 1780, and many of them were built in the earliest years of the nineteenth century. But the missions have taken the patina of time in a way that the uncompromising meetinghouses of New England, for instance, have never

3

done, and, unless we except the log cabin, I know of no other American buildings which blend so harmoniously with the soil from which they spring and seem so native a growth of the landscape.

Yet, by the standards of the eastern visitor, the allure of the missions lies in their very foreign quality. They seem like a piece of Europe set down amidst the chaparral—the largest piece of Europe, indeed, and the most striking, in all our architectural heritage. They bring the southern Coast Ranges closer, in culture and "feel," to the mountains of Spain, than they are to the not-far-off Sierra. If to the missions themselves we add the presidios which became the nuclei of San Diego, Santa Barbara, Monterey, and San Francisco, and the spacious adobe dwellings that were the homes of the great ranch-owning families all the way from the Mexican border to San Francisco Bay, we realize that in the southern Coast Ranges there has, for a century and more, been a way of life here that was far from primitive. It would be appropriate to compare the southern Coast Ranges to the Riviera, where a pleasure coast of resorts and modern hotels has for its background a hill country long inhabited by a people of old and distinctive traditions. Of these traditions, the fairest expression is the chain of missions.

Theirs is a story of the noblest intentions of mankind, as exemplified in the selfless devotion, the true spirit of the Christian missionary, which the Franciscan founders exhibited. It is the story, too, of the thwarting of that high intent by the lowest motives of greed and exploitation on the part of the secular power, though the men who wielded it professed the Catholic creed. And in the end redemption came, largely through the efforts not of Spanish-speaking Catholics but of Americans, both Protestant and Roman. But I run ahead of my story, which begins while George Washington was still a loyal subject of King George, and Dan Boone was oiling his rifle for his first trip into Kentucky. At that date another pioneer, three thousand miles further west, was exploring the remotest corner of the future United States. Father Junípero Serra, in his gray Franciscan robes, was no less daring and resourceful, no less visionary of the future greatness of a new land, than the English-speaking pioneers. And he was just as much an American as the Mayflower settlers. For, like them, he had been born in the Old World and had come a painful way to build in the New a better home. Again, like them, Serra had no intention of returning: at the age of fifty-five he had

cast in his lot for life with the fate of the wild, wide North American continent.

THE STORY OF PADRE SERRA

It was on July 16, 1769, that Serra, Father-President of the California missions, first said Mass at the foot of a cross overlooking the fine harbor that is today San Diego's. There and then he dedicated the first of the twenty-one famous missions of California—"Father Serra's Rosary" as today it is affectionately called. But the little band of men—fellow Franciscans, a handful of soldiers, and some Indians from Lower California—were witnessing more than the beginnings of the great "mission system." They were actually present at the founding of California itself, neglected as inaccessible for two hundred years after being first sighted by rare vessels.

Better perhaps than even the military commander of the expedition, Gaspar de Portolá, Serra foresaw the great consequences of the new venture. He dared to dream, there in that arid, sun-scorched wilderness, amid hostile Indians, with men dying of scurvy, of a land glowing with the orange and rippling with grain, inhabited by peaceful Christian people. Back in Mexico City, some of the wise-of-earth had their grave misgivings or they scoffed openly. Yet in his wildest imaginings Serra could not have visioned a State with almost eight million population, richer than all the fabled wealth of the Incas and Aztecs. And could he return today, he would find that probably half a million visitors, in years of peace, come to the carven doors of the gracious old missions, some to worship, all to admire.

Father Serra, born in 1713 on the island of Majorca, was not the type of man one would pick for a pioneer. He was a scholar, a doctor of theology and professor of philosophy. He was a frail man who suffered from chronic bronchitis. He had received an injury to one of his legs that made walking an agony. Yet with sandaled feet he was to trudge six thousand sore and dusty miles on his apostolic labors. When nothing better offered, he hardened himself to sleep on the ground and live on roots and seeds. While the soldiers and the Indians were fighting and killing each other, Serra passed unharmed among "the gentiles," his "pagan children" as he called them, for even savages often loved him upon sight.

Not primarily for the saving of pagan souls had the government of King Carlos III sent Portolá on a two-pronged expedition by land and sea for the exploration and defense of Alta (Upper) California, but in order to forestall any further advance down the Pacific Coast by the Russian bear which was reaching a paw down from Alaska toward California. But the Crown recognized the value of the Franciscan missionaries in pacifying the Indians. Momentarily Spain intended to use the mission system, but it planned in its own time to secularize the converted red men and transfer them to civil administration. But to honest Father Serra all this new land was still the Indians'. Even the mission buildings were to be theirs, and all the cattle and sheep, all the farms and the produce of the mission system were to be held in trust by the Franciscans who, themselves, owned nothing of this world's goods.

Fired with the love of God and the fellowship of man, the brave father within a year had founded another mission almost four hundred miles further into the wilderness, on the shores of Monterey Bay, the Mission of San Carlos Borromeo, known as Carmel Mission. The next year saw Serra and two other Franciscans trudging into the wilderness. In an oak-studded valley of the Santa Lucia Mountains, blazing with July heat, the dauntless Serra slung his bell from a gnarled old tree. Bravely he tolled it to the unresponding silence. "Come, gentiles, come to the Holy Church; come and receive the faith of Jesus Christ!" he cried.

One of his companions remarked that he might save his breath and labor, for not a pagan was in sight. Yet the cry of the bell had sped through the forest. It had been heard by savage ears. Presently an Indian appeared and looked on with awe as Serra was saying Mass under the cross he had raised. Given presents, the Indian returned with others of his tribe, who brought pine seeds and acorns. All were friendly, all loved Serra, who set about learning their language. Together the men in gray robes and the men in their bronze nakedness raised the first crude structure that was the Mission San Antonio de Padua.

For the mission "churches" of these first, brave, struggling years were not at all the solid and shapely structures we see now, with their six-foot walls, their carven doors and painted ceiling beams, their stone floors, their gardens and fountains, their bells and cool cloisters. Such structures would require the work of years and of hundreds of neophytes

7

or Indian converts; they are what blessed old Serra dreamed of, and seldom saw completed. No, the first "missions" he knew were but rude shelters of boughs and bulrushes. None the less were they houses of God.

Yet, with trifling changes, the missions of today stand pretty much where Serra and his successors first planted the Cross. Not whimsically were their sites selected. Serra was fixing, he realized, the seat of future settlements. Carefully he searched for abundant water, good soil, healthful climate, timber, and a location on the coastwise highway of which he dreamed. How well he chose is shown by the fact that on the sites he selected grew up San Diego, Los Angeles, Monterey, and San Francisco. Of the nine missions Serra started, only San Antonio today has no city, or at least a town, around it.

When Serra had founded four missions and had been in California three years, troubles that had been brewing in the perilous colony came to a crisis. The new country had not yielded any quick returns either in revenue or converts. Puny as the first colonies look now, they had already cost more than was bargained for. Every item of equipment and almost all the food still had to be brought an immense distance by irregular small sailing vessels. The Indians, indignant at the treatment given their women by the soldiers, retaliated with arrows and firebrands. San Diego Mission was burned, its padre killed. All the others were in danger.

The missions weren't succeeding much better than the forts or presidios. Complex language difficulties and lack of enough presents slowed down intercourse with the Indians. At first almost the only heathen the Franciscans had been able to baptize were children, often brought in a dying condition in some desperate hope that blessed water was big medicine. If it failed, the missionaries were blamed. The new governor, Fages, opposed the founding of more missions, as he would have to protect them with his total of sixty-one soldiers.

Thus caution counseled a retreat. Or so suspected both the Viceroy of New Spain (Mexico) and the Father Superior of the Franciscans back in Mexico City.

So Serra set out for the capital—a round trip of twenty-four hundred miles—to save the great California venture. For talking points he had

no material gains so far, and few spiritual. He had only his shining vision and the conviction of absolute truth his words seemed to carry.

And he got all he asked for: the dismissal of Fages; the right to found more missions; more money both for the missions and for the military; the establishment of an overland road to California; and the immigration of more settlers, especially of families and of women to provide wives for the soldiers. In short, instead of retreating, the Viceroy and the Father Superior were persuaded by Serra to advance, to pour fresh blood and treasure into California.

Stronger in health than when he set out, Serra returned to found six more missions: Dolores (San Francisco), beautiful San Juan Capistrano in the hills near San Diego, San Luís Obispo, and San Buenaventura (Ventura for short) on the Santa Barbara channel coast. In the seventieth year of his age, having confirmed over five thousand heathen converts, noble old Padre Serra felt his last reserves of strength fast ebbing. On foot he trod the round of his nine missions, from San Diego to San Francisco. At each he bade a sorrowful farewell to his brother Franciscans and the weeping Indians. Death found him at Carmel Mission in 1784. The double tolling of its bells brought the grief-stricken Indians, who came with wild flowers to lay upon the redwood coffin of the Apostle of California.

Today the Catholics of his State have taken the first steps toward the canonization of *Fray* Junípero Serra. For this, the existence of miracles due to his intercession must be proved. A postulator has been appointed by the Vatican to collect and sift evidence of miracles that may have occurred in Serra's lifetime. Many Protestants express a tender interest in the canonization of noble old Junípero Serra. For all Americans can understand a pioneer.

THE GOLDEN AGE OF THE MISSIONS

The successor of Serra as Father-President of the missions of Alta California was a man of no less ability. For, like Serra, Father Fermin Francisco Lasuén founded nine missions, including Santa Barbara. In 1787 he built Purísima in the hills to the north; four years after that he began Soledad (Solitude) near Carmel. But 1797 was the year of Lasuén's glory, though he was then seventy-four years old, for in it he consecrated the ground of four missions: San José near San Francisco

Bay, San Juan Bautista near Carmel, San Miguel in central California, and San Fernando in the valley of that name.

Only three missions were added after Lasuén had ceased his work: Santa Inés near Santa Barbara, San Rafael in the healthful climate across the bay from San Francisco, and Solano in what is now the "wine country" of the sunny inner Coast Ranges. To the surprise of all, the Russians over in the fog belt sent gifts and good wishes to the founding of these last two, the padres' "farthest north."

Father Lasuén was an even greater administrator than Serra, more tactful with the civil authority, and quite as sweet in nature, and as tireless and strong. He brought the mission system to its highest peak of influence, efficiency, and prosperity. It was his ambition to make the missions self-sufficient. At them the Indians learned more than fifty trades, so that a mission could employ carpenters, tilemakers, stonecutters, bricklayers, shoemakers, tanners, wheelwrights, cowboys, and sheepherders. The Indian women were taught to spin, weave, and make clothes. Tallow, hides, pottery, baskets, blankets, saddles, soap, candles, and wine were produced. The missions grew potatoes, turnips, squash, beans, peas, and lentils; oranges and lemons were planted, and so too were olives, almonds, walnuts, figs, dates, apples, pomegranates, apricots, and grapes. With Indian labor the fathers plowed and planted great fields of wheat, barley, corn, and oats. In fact, between 1783 and 1832 the twenty-one missions produced 4,137,625 bushels of food for the Indians and struggling colonies. Among them the missions may have had as much as 150,000 head of cattle and perhaps as many sheep grazing on the hills.

Great irrigation works were started by the Franciscans. They dammed streams, built reservoirs, constructed aqueducts. Beautiful fountains came to adorn many of the gardens. The water turned, too, grain and olive mills. In many cases these hydraulic systems are still partly in use by the towns and ranches of California.

The fruit of all the mission labors was given first to the Indians who came to live around the missions, and surpluses were then placed at the disposal of settlers, soldiers, and travelers. Indeed, the chain of missions, spaced at approximately a day's ride apart, became the inns of the voyagers of those days. Clean, quiet, cool, secure from Indian hostility, they must have looked like heaven to the weary folk who came

to their doors. And when refreshed in body, the traveler could converse with men of breeding and education, or read in the mission libraries.

The very location of the missions largely determined the route of the *Camino Real* or King's Highway, first worn smooth by the toiling Franciscans, later broadened to accommodate the trains of *carretas* or wagons from Mexico. On the *Camino* traveled officers and officials, immigrants and their families. When the United States entered on the conquest of California, it found the footsteps of Serra almost the only line of military communication. Today U.S. Highway 101 and the coast route of the Southern Pacific Railway follow approximately the old *Camino Real*, and during World War II millions of American soldiers and untold quantities of guns, tanks, and supplies were moved along the track first broken by the old fathers.

In Father Lasuén's day almost all the mission churches began to take on much the appearance that the best preserved of them have now. Without being trained architects, the Franciscans had to solve their own structural and artistic problems. From bitter experience they learned that nothing is so likely to fall down in an earthquake as a wall of stone blocks or of adobe—that is, bricks of sunbaked clay. So walls as much as six feet thick, often supported by buttresses, came to give the missions their air of strength. Frequent fires taught the fathers that roofs of thatch were impractical, and so they taught the Indians to make tiles, and now that colorful and harmonious type of roofing is characteristic.

The bell tower, or at least a bell frame, was a prominent feature of the missions. Serra usually began with cross and bell, and all the padres were addicted to the sound and use of bells, while the Indians venerated and delighted in them too, for the language of bells can be understood by all. So bells have come to be the very symbol of the California missions. And time has only mellowed their tone. Even to a Protestant like myself, the tolling of the mission bells, to which I wake each morning, chimes its way into the rhythm of living.

Within the mission churches—usually dark and distinctly cool, in adaptation to the often hot and brilliant climate—the native art of the Indian was given sway, for he had a natural, strong sense of color and design. Most of the original mission doors are deeply carven with parallel

waving lines—the Indian's symbolic "river of life." The wise Franciscans permitted Indian artists to make their own form of offering to God.

So friar and neophyte worked out together a distinctive style in architecture and decoration. That architecture is functional—that is, it is economically adapted to the intended uses of the buildings. With their softly flowing lines and delicately tinted surfaces, the missions are deeply harmonious with their natural setting. They look kind—tranquil, hospitable, and strong. They have served as the inspiration and model for a whole California style, expressed in many modern churches, civic buildings, houses, and even shops, and if not all of this is equally good, that is no fault of the originals.

DECLINE AND RESTORATION

Just when the missions had reached the height of their usefulness and beauty, when they had become the one civilizing force holding the frontier communities together, a deadly blow was directed at them, first by the Government of Spain and, a little later and even more viciously, by independent Mexico. The missions were secularized, that is, reduced to parish churches with a single priest, and stripped of everything except the immediate buildings themselves. First, many of the pioneering padres, who had been men of education and high ideals, were supplanted by inferior friars, some of them none too intelligent or holy. Such men often mishandled the neophytes and muddled the accounts. Then the lands, which the fathers held in trust for the Indians and had brought to high productivity, were taken over and given in immense feudal tracts to settlers from Mexico, the rancheros or ranchmen. The Indians, who had given up their native life for the white man's way, were stripped of both at once, and so driven to beggary or to acts of violence for which they could be punished. One greedy ranchero took the clothes from the backs of hundreds of them. As the missions, deprived of sustenance, fell into despair and were abandoned, the governor, Pio Pico, sold them off at auction, enriching himself with commissions.

So that by the time the American armies came in 1847, the missions were already in a sad state of neglect. Some were serving as stables and liquor cellars and other profane uses. Many Americans stood amazed, shocked, and sorrowful at such desecration. True, Uncle Sam soon de-

clared the sale of the mission property illegal, and much of it was restored to the Church. For the old gentleman has always respected church property of any denomination. Abraham Lincoln signed some of the documents that restored mission property to the Catholic Church.

Mission Santa Barbara was unique in that it was never absolutely abandoned by the religious and has never passed out of the control of the Franciscans. True, their number dwindled till at last only two were left, their order all but powerless to support them; still they clung on in the neglected shell of the once-great church and cloisters, guarding the precious records of the whole mission movement. Only at Santa Barbara has the altar flame never gone out.

By 1888 the people of southern California had become so conscious of the heritage of beauty in the missions, and so indignant at their neglect, that they formed the Association for the Preservation of the Missions, under the leadership of Charles F. Lummis, the enthusiastic writer and historian. First they leased San Juan Capistrano, in order to save it from further decay, and then set to work to rescue San Diego and San Fernando. At San Luís Rey, one of the noblest of the southern missions, Father O'Keefe was struggling heroically to restore the church, and the Association came forward with funds to help him.

Largely to save the northern missions, the California Landmarks League was organized at San Francisco in 1902, and soon the societies of the "Native Sons" and "Native Daughters" joined in a state-wide campaign to pick up the scattered pearls of Father Serra's rosary, the jewel-like string of missions.

Walls again were raised, and roofless altars covered again from rain and dust. Profane objects were swept away, both within the missions and, where possible, in the immediate surroundings. Sacred objects, once mission property, were rediscovered where they had fallen into private hands and many of them were bought or donated and restored to their places. Some of the missions which had not actually suffered neglect or outright theft had suffered from excessive attention. Local congregations and parish priests, in the tasteless period of American life, had sometimes tried to disguise the mission origins: wooden steeples had been added; walls had been breached to admit sickly stained glass; beautiful old Indian murals had been smeared over with whitewash; just about every conceivable atrocity had been committed with the best of

intentions. It was a task to get this undone, and it is not all put to rights yet.

San Rafael Mission has totally disappeared; Soledad is a hopeless adobe rubble, fast melting away; Sonoma is turned into a local museum full of Civil War and pioneer relics. In some of the missions the church building itself has disappeared, leaving only the cloisters or other appurtenant structures, but these in themselves have been well worth preserving. In other cases, especially in some of the now-large cities, the church is still there but all else is gone, and the churches are closely pressed upon by the thriving town.

Not all the work of restoration was done by large societies. Sometimes the local priest and his congregation would undertake the work alone. Usually the Protestants of the community joined in heartily; some who could not give money came and gave their labor. At Santa Inés a band of wandering hoboes saw the struggles of restoration and worked for weeks to help. The church at Santa Cruz was completely restored as the gift of one person, Mrs. Gladys Sullivan Doyle. When a child, she suffered an injury to her leg and was taken to Lourdes in the hope of a miraculous cure. Some years later the lameness disappeared, and as a thank offering she had a complete replica of the old mission built; it was finished in 1931.

Even more recent and more remarkable is the restoration of Purísima. It was a crumbling ruin up in California's oil-bearing coast hills when the land on which it stands was bought by the Union Oil Company. The local superintendent became interested in the old mission, with its tragic history of Indian sieges and repeated earthquakes, and he talked until he got the company to offer the land to the county of Santa Barbara, or the State, on condition that the mission be restored. Nothing happened for eleven years, till Father Raley of near-by Lompoc began to agitate for the rescuing of the mission. In 1935 county and State at last took action. The National Park Service, a tireless guardian of historical monuments, came forward with offers of assistance, and the labor of the CCC boys was placed at the disposal of the restoration. Excavations revealed numberless valuable articles, and, bit by bit, the fine old structures were restored, and the garden most tastefully re-created. If Purísima is now a monument rather than a real mission, it is a monument to that appreciation of olden beauty which, contrary to much

opinion, is quick in the veins of many an American, and of the Government too. Here is a case where government, business, and local community united to preserve a noble and lovely thing.

All the way from San Diego, the first of the missions, to Sonoma, the last of them, north of San Francisco Bay, the Mission Trail, as it is called, is marked for those who wish to follow it. The visitor will find that all the missions can be reached by U.S. Highway 101, or a short detour will bring him to their carven doors. It is unnecessary here to tell anyone how to follow Highway 101, for it corresponds to U.S. Highway 1 on the Atlantic seaboard, though the western counterpart is infinitely more beautiful. Nor have I space to tell here about all the missions in detail—all that have survived, that is. Each mission is rich in historical associations. Here I purpose but to speak of a few of them which have been spared, or restored to something like their original beauty and completeness. These are "going concerns" with spacious settings around them, as in the old days, with gardens, cloisters, monasteries, libraries, and, in many cases, with Franciscans still or again in charge, going about their duties on sandaled feet, though their robes have changed in color from gray to brown, and in inclement weather some of them wear Homburg hats! Such missions are more than parish churches and burying grounds, more than modern duplications of what once was; they are like giant redwoods which have sprouted from the stump and grown again, green and tall and noble. So, though it is delightful to visit all the missions if one has time, the following, to me at least, are "musts."

THE TOUR—STARTING SOUTH FROM SAN FRANCISCO

Suppose, then, that you are starting south from San Francisco, by car, to see the greatest of the missions. Follow Highway 101 if you like, or must; for myself, I never take a highway if I can take a byway, and I make it a deliberate point to loiter and explore. So, if you're of my frame of mind, start south on California State Highway 1, following the coast in great loops, now high up on the cliffs of the Santa Clara Mountains, now sweeping down to the wild beaches, now in the ghostly vales of mist, now in the sun-steeped canyons heavy with the scent of sage, till you come to Watsonville. Turn east here through hills, golden in sum-

mer with sun-bleached grass, and studded with live oaks, to San Juan
Bautista, planning on a wonderful lunch or dinner of bubble and squeak
or *olla podrida* at the Casa Rosa. For San Juan, even without its mission,
must not be missed. Here Time, the old tramp, seems to have been resting his dusty feet, his pack in the flowering weeds, ever since the stagecoach days of the 1870's, when Tiburcio Vasquez, the highwayman,
was hanged here. In those days eleven stage lines converged at the
doors of the Plaza Hotel, a fine old adobe in the beautiful indigenous
Monterey style, built about 1792. It had its rivals in other buildings,
Castro House next door, once a mansion belonging to the *commandante*
of all this region, and the Zanetti house, scene of gay balls in the great
second-story room. All of them face upon the dusty plaza, with its old
fountain and its locust trees still with hitching rings in their boles. And
so does the mission, founded in 1797 by good Father Lasuén.

The old monastery rooms can still be visited, filled with churchly
treasures. The church itself is rather stern, but the redwood beams in
the ceiling still bear the strange designs, traced with vegetable dyes,
with which the Indians glorified God. Poor Indians—who took such delight in singing in *Fray* Tapis' choir and listening to *Fray* de la Cuesta
preach in thirteen Amerind dialects—the church was built large enough
to hold one thousand red worshipers, but four thousand of them are
said to lie in a great trench outside the walls.

For by 1812 deaths exceeded births in most of the missions. There
was a continual procession from the sinful, healthy life of the naked
savage through the mission doors—to death, with salvation. Theo-
logically this may be the supreme privilege; biologically it was suicidal.
Such Indians as heeded their normal instincts and fled to the hills were
brought back by force, soundly whipped, and again confined to a life
of toil and prayers and white men's diseases. This of course was the
padre's great failure—one which they did not foresee and could not
understand. Before we blame them too much, it is well to remember that Americans of English descent cannot point to any course of
action taken by them which was conducive to the highest good of the
aborigines.

Mission Carmel is next upon your list—San Carlos de Borromeo, to give
it its true name—and you will reach it by following 101 to Salinas (John
Steinbeck's home town). Then, leaving the noisy highway, take a road

that jogs sweetly through the Carmel Valley to Monterey. At this historic spot Father Serra originally planted his mission, and you'll want to spend a lot of time in the little city which has more that is genuinely old than any other spot west of the Appalachians. And don't fail to eat at Fishermen's Wharf, when the sun sets and the gulls come crying home after the fishing smacks.

But the mission was moved by Serra himself to a little hill, just outside the present-day town of Carmel (beloved by the artists), and there it stands, a little apart, its soft sandstone weathered by the sea winds, overlooking Carmel Bay and cedar-crowned Point Lobos, with a distant view of the Santa Lucias plunging from their perpetual cloudcap into the perpetual ocean. No other mission has so beautiful a setting, and no other was so dear to Serra. True, the lovely church is not the one he knew, poor man, pioneering in a wilderness. But they can show you in the little monastery the very cell he slept in, with its bed of leather thongs, and his crucifix and Bible, the stone he laid on his chest while praying, and the iron chains with which he flagellated himself.

If you are more esthetic than ascetic, you will be happier in the shade of the great cork oak whose ancestors must have grown in Spain, looking at the utterly satisfying proportions of the façade. As Hildegarde Hawthorne says, "You can look a long while at that combination of line and surface, arch and square, and feel better every moment." When the old bells toll, they are answered by the clang of buoys on the sea rocks. When the priests chant, the crickets answer them from the wild flowers that crowd to the mission walls. When the choir boys swing their incense, the boughs of the Monterey pines breathe fragrance as the wind from the bay passes softly through them. Of all the missions this is the most beautifully situated; here Serra chose to live, making it what would have been his cathedral church had he been bishop of Alta California in name as he was in effect. And here he died and is buried. Once again its library is filled with rare volumes, and once again the spot is holy, after the dark ages that followed Mexican misrule.

If you go south on 101 you can stop at San Miguel Mission, and turn aside for lonely San Antonio, in the Santa Lucias, deserted now except for a caretaker and an annual celebration of Mass. But if you are for avoiding the highway with its gasoline fumes and traffic cops and roadside stands and billboards, leave Carmel by State Highway 1, for a

breath-taking one hundred miles of the great San Simeon Highway (often closed in the rainy season on account of landslides). In all America there is no such magnificent stretch as this. The Corniche road of the French Riviera is child's play compared with it, and if you aren't too timorous a motorist, you will count those hours that you traversed it among the most glorious of your life, with the sea far beneath you down a dizzying slope, and wild flowers all about you, drugging you with their perfume and color.

At Morro Bay, with its bold rock, the road turns inland, and you leave the crying of the gulls for the rapture of meadow-lark song and the wistful notes of the white-crowned sparrows tearing at the petals of the golden poppies. At Santa Maria, keep on State Highway 1, avoiding U.S. 101, and cross the pine-covered hills until, just before you reach Lompoc, you turn aside, at a sign, for the Mission Purísima Concepción. How this was restored I have already told. It is not in any sense a church today, much less a mission, being, rather, a secular monument. But it has the advantage that one may climb into the pulpit, or tramp through the old monastery cells without fear of sacrilege and without the ubiquitous guide. The garden is the finest thing about Purísima, for my taste, for unlike most of the mission gardens, which represent a hodgepodge of showy modern exotics, this scholarly bit of horticultural restoration has admitted no plantings except such trees, shrubs, and herbs as the old fathers would have brought from Spain and Mexico, or might have adopted out of the aromatic native vegetation.

Inquire for the byway that takes you cross-country to Buellton; there cross U.S. 101 again with an aristocratic hauteur that refuses to notice such things, and jog into Solvang, a comfortable Danish settlement where is located the Santa Inés Mission (so spelled by Church authority, in good Spanish). The mission is *not* at the near-by town of Santa Ynez (so spelled by authority of the U.S. Post Office Department).

Santa Inés is a lonely mission, a place of tragic memories of an Indian uprising, which looks out across a valley once plowed by hundreds of neophytes, toward the Santa Ynez Range, clothed in a magnificent forest of broad-leaved evergreens. Because the community is almost wholly Protestant (there's a fine example of Danish fourteenth-century church architecture at Solvang) few communicants come to the mission of departed glories, presided over by a priest with a strong Irish brogue.

As an epitome of the isolation of Santa Inés, my friend Mr. Ripley, who writes of northwest timber in this book, tells how the predecessor of the present priest confessed his predicament. "How am I doing? Well, Mr. Ripley, me pants is wearing out. I wrote to the bishop asking if there wasn't some fund to cover them, but he said there was none. But—glory be to God!—the seat of them is still holding!"

Take State Highway 150 up the valley, famed for its golden Palomino horses and Tennessee trotters, over the San Marcos Pass, and down by swoops like a sailing buzzard's, through the flowering chaparral, into Santa Barbara.

AT SANTA BARBARA

Santa Barbara Mission stands at the edge of the little city, backed by the mighty wall of the Santa Ynez Mountains, and surrounded by open fields in front, and the cloister gardens behind. Of all the missions, it has the greatest stir of life within it, for it is the seat of an important theological seminary, with sandaled monks forever coming and going about it, and visitors from all over the country thronging to its doors from dawn to dark. And after dark, how serene it looks, its noble stones bathed in moonlight! How fair it shines from amid its sycamores, as I see it each morning from my hilltop when I walk down for my mail! Well has it been called the Queen of the Missions—a lovely lady of churches, of which the most beautiful view, amongst the many one may catch, is that in the reflecting pool of the old fountain underneath the pepper trees.

Within there are two gardens. One is shown to all the visitors, a small but very mossy cemetery garden reminding one, in its antiquity and mellowness, of some of the churchyards of New Orleans or Charleston. The other, reserved for the meditation of the Franciscans, is shown only to male visitors who are known to the brothers. No woman, except a reigning monarch or the wife of a nation's head, has ever seen this sacred plot. But, ladies of the garden clubs of America, do not feel too put out. My brown-robed friends have shown it to me and I assure you that, horticulturally, you are not missing a great deal; the planting is neither old and rich in historic traditions nor superb in modern exotic effects. Could I wave my wand and have my way, I would replant the garden with the flowers of the Holy Land and healing herbs and fruits

Bell Tower of the Spanish chapel at Pala.

Old Russian church at Fort Ross (1812).

This overshot mill near St. Helena was built in 1846.

Santa Barbara Mission has kept alive her altar fires since 1876.

of the Bible—which would find the climate perfectly agreeable—or at least with the traditional garden plants of Spain, Mexico, and California. But the minds of the good men who pace there with their breviaries are upon still higher things, we know.

Of all the missions, Santa Barbara is richest in historic records. In the darkest hours of neglect, these were not quite abandoned to the tooth of Time, and today they are precious beyond price. Here Father Zephyrin Engelhardt wrote his great history, or rather his histories—one for each of the missions.

At early Mass, one summer morning in 1925, the floor of the noble old mission was heaved with a frightful earthquake shock. And while the citizens leaped from their beds, and the shops of State Street were collapsing, the good Franciscans knelt in a prayer that might have been the last of their lives—and probably saved them, as it kept them from hastening out the entrance where stones fell in a sudden landslide. The brave Superior, Augustine Hobrecht, dashed into the apartment of Father Engelhardt, now an aged cripple, and carried him to safety on his shoulders.

The massive buttresses—a lesson learned from the great tremor of 1812—saved the church from complete destruction. The restoration and reinforcing of the church was participated in by the entire community. For the Protestants of Santa Barbara love their mission as much as the Catholics.

For a mile and more above the mission there are still visible the signs of its builders' dreams and schemes. Mission Creek, for instance, was dammed with a stout wall, as strong today as ever, where the precious water in this semi-arid land was impounded. It was then led away in aqueducts of which there are traces all over the canyon below my house, and these made fertile the fields plowed by the neophytes and, after them, the robed padres. At its height, Santa Barbara Mission constituted a whole civilization, self-contained and self-supporting, with all that man could want from bread to salvation.

ON TO SAN DIEGO

You'll have to take 101 to Ventura, where you may stop for a glimpse of the Mission of San Buenaventura. And you may continue into Los Angeles on the same highway, choosing the alternate that takes you by

the coast, at the base of the rugged Santa Monicas. But if you would keep to country byways, leave Ventura by State Highway 118, cross over the flowery Santa Susana Pass and so down into the famed San Fernando Valley. Little enough is left of San Fernando's mission, but the valley is as fair as it is vaunted, and, by joining U.S. 99, you can glide into Los Angeles and stop at the Mission San Gabriel Arcángel, now sadly crowded by the boisterous city, but rich in historic memories of the time when, to the weary travelers of old California, this mission looked like a bit of heaven upon earth.

Try Alternate 101, as you leave the city—the branch that takes you through Whittier and the old German colony of Anaheim. For this leads you over the Santa Ana hills, tramped by the padres' feet so long ago, and brings you, down a long canyon, upon San Juan Capistrano. Capistrano, once the most ambitiously conceived of all the missions, is now a ruin. Yet, preserved by loving hands from further decay, it is still the most impressive ruin in the United States, to judge by the numbers of its visitors. Everywhere there are arches, fountains, bells, flowers, birds. They make of it one of earth's sweetest spots, a place like one long-breathed prayer of which every *Ave* is now inaudible, and there is left of it nothing except a breath like that of God's upon the mouth of Adam.

Millions who know nothing else about Capistrano know from their newspapers, and more particularly the Sunday supplements, of the swallows of San Juan. Tradition has it that every year they return upon the selfsame date, the nineteenth of March. As this is St. Joseph's Day, the birds are supposed to show their piety by this punctual return, and on that day batteries of camera men assemble. Radio announcers have even been known to broadcast the return of the birds, and crowds gather from San Diego, Los Angeles, and points east all the way to Maine, to exclaim and shout and bellow maudlin songs. If the swallows frequently arrive the next day, or the day before, can anyone blame them?

Several times a year I receive defiant letters (because, I suppose, I am a naturalist who is not a mystic) suggesting that I explain how it is that the swallows know St. Joseph's Day when it dawns, and always plan to return to their nests at this date. The answer is that they must have been coming to this region since before St. Joseph was born. And that all the old buildings, and many a new one, in California, have their

colonies of swallows. At Santa Barbara they would nest on the façade if the fathers did not knock their nests with long poles. (One wonders what St. Francis would have to say to that, or what he would make of the explanation that the birds are a risk to ladies' Easter bonnets!)

When all is said, though, the swallows of Capistrano, forever flashing and turning, crying and sailing between the ruined arches, and building their mud nests in the coigns of the ancient masonry, are indeed among its greatest charms, in a place that is all charm.

There is nothing for it but to take 101 south from Capistrano, but it is at its fairest here, as it goes bowling along beside the sea, with grand views of the Coast Ranges rolling way in the east up to the mists, and it will take you to the Mission of San Luís Rey de Francia, just a little inland from the village of Oceanside. If Santa Barbara is the Queen of Missions, San Luís claims to be their king, though less than fifty years ago it was a pathetic ruin of its former greatness. Today it is restored in all its grandeur—perhaps the most pretentious and spacious of the missions.

Many of the missions had branches or *asistencias,* chapels as we might say. Of them all only the Asistencia de Pala, an appanage of San Luís, is still standing, as shown in the photograph in this book, with its background of the Santa Rosa Mountains. To reach it from San Luís Rey, take the road to Elsinore, turn south on U.S. 396 to Temecula, and then take the road that will be pointed out to you through Pechanga Canyon to the Pala Indian Reservation. Long neglected, its tiles and carvings stolen, its bright Indian murals smeared with whitewash, Pala is now restored. Again its murals shine, again the Indians come to worship, and carefully tend the flowers between the visits of the priest. The tiles have been brought back, the precious carvings recovered, and the Palatingwa Indians have learned to ring the bells hung from the stout sycamore beams.

The road south from Pala mounts the grand desertic Santa Rosa Range, then plunges into oak-shaded canyons, from Santa Ysabel, where you must turn west for Ramona, and so on down into San Diego, with its poignant memories of the first prayers of Serra upon the soil of the future United States. Here is the oldest of all the missions, in date of founding, San Diego de Alcalá, founded in 1769, though the present building dates from a cornerstone laid in 1808. Tragic are its memories,

with the great Indian uprising of 1775 when fire swept it, and Father Jayme was brutally beaten to death. San Diego Mission was never able to sustain itself as well as most of the others; it was an expense, rather than an asset, and owed its continuation to its strategic importance as a gateway from Mexico. The Indians were a miserable, treacherous lot, thieving, unchaste, and murderous, and for their faults recourse was had to the whip and the stocks as well as excommunication.

No one would think, though, of these unpleasant memories, to look at the façade of San Diego Mission, perhaps the most flowing and gracious of them all, with its exquisite flanking campanile and five olden bells.

So I have come to the end of my unorthodox mission trail, conscious that I have passed by a number of missions with scant mention, and some with none at all. By no means does this imply that the others, too, are not fair and rich in interest. If you would see them all, you must find your own way to their hospitable doors. If you would read the story of each, there is a rich literature at your command. And, if such is your temperament, be as thorough as you will. I have essayed no more than a swallow's flight through the California missions, alighting where fancy pleased, and chattering nothing of any great importance.

THE FIRST INHABITANTS
OF THE COAST RANGES

BY JOHN WALTON CAUGHEY

What of the Indians among whom the missions were established? For the eastern half of our population the word Indian brings to mind a pre-Columbian New York State culture or something very similar. The Indians of the west coast were altogether different, and here is told their story. (R. P.)

In the Summary Journal of the expedition of Juan Rodríguez Cabrillo in 1542 an entry runs as follows: "All the coast passed this day is very bold; there is a great swell and the land is very high. There are mountains which seem to reach the heavens, and the sea beats on them; sailing along close to land, it appears as though they would fall on the ships." Because their summits were snow-covered, Cabrillo called these mountains the Sierras Nevadas, or Snowy Ranges. In the singular that name has now migrated eastward to a mightier rampart, and the mountains Cabrillo saw are called the Santa Lucias.

On its eastern side the United States begins with a broad coastal plain, cut by many estuaries, and only slightly raised above sea level. On the west coast the mountains come right down to the sea; there are bold headlands, and almost everywhere the approaching seafarer finds a sharply uplifted shore. The Coast Ranges make this difference. They fill most of the belt that might otherwise have been a Pacific coastal plain.

Beginning with the Olympics of western Washington, the Coast Ranges extend in less regular alignment through Oregon, reach wild confusion in the Klamaths, and then straighten out to march in echelon formation down the coast. The parallel ranges of this latter part of the system are long and narrow; they point eastward a bit more than does the coastline; and they embrace a series of long narrow valleys. With altitudes of 8,150 at Mount Olympus, 9,345 in the Klamaths, 9,214 at Mount Pinos, and 11,485 at San Gorgonio, they far outreach the highest

peaks in the Appalachians. In area and in mass they also exceed this eastern system, yet as mountains they have gone largely unnoticed.

They are, of course, overshadowed by their neighbors, the loftier Sierra Nevada and the Cascades, Mount Shasta and Mount Rainier. They are even eclipsed by their own valleys, for it is in these valleys and on the small fragments of coastal plain that the vast majority of Pacific Coast residents have their homes. The southernmost range, as if in despair, has allowed itself to be partially drowned. It survives only as the chain of offshore islands in the Santa Barbara-Santa Catalina group.

Piecemeal and individually the Coast Ranges do get some attention. San Francisco, for example, not only confronts Mount Tamalpais but is built on the lower hills of one of the ranges. Berkeley and Oakland lean back against another. Santa Barbara and the foothill cities of the Pasadena chain are set against dramatic mountain backdrops, while San Diego and Monterey nestle more comfortably against gentler slopes. Seattle and the other cities of western Washington, it is true, face the Sound rather than their mountains, and Portland, Sacramento, and the rest of the interior valley cities, though in the lee of the Coast Ranges and climatically much indebted to them, have little consciousness of these western bulwarks. Los Angeles, likewise, though its mountains are in clear view, seems to sprawl away from, rather than toward them, thereby symbolizing the general tendency to minimize these far western ranges.

Fortunately, the Coast Ranges are not one unbroken rampart, but, as their name implies, are plural. The Columbia has cut one unmistakable gateway for east-west communications. There are others, notably San Francisco's magnificent Golden Gate. Fortunately also, the system lends itself to north-south travel. Besides California's Great Central Valley, the Puget Sound depression, and the Willamette Valley, in which the Coast Ranges have a half interest, there is a whole series of north-south valleys interleaved between the ranges. These include the Umpqua, the Rogue, the Klamath-Trinity, the Mad, the Eel, the Russian, the Napa-Livermore, the Santa Rosa-Santa Clara, the Salinas, the Santa Maria, the Santa Clara of the south, the Los Angeles, and the Santa Ana. These valleys are not only where most Far Westerners live and work, they are also the channels for the principal communications up and down the coast. The relative ease of getting through the Coast Ranges doubtless

impels Westerners to take them more casually than the more massive
Sierra and Cascades, and is a factor in the comparative disregard that
has been their lot.

CHILDREN OF NATURE

Originally the Coast Ranges and their valleys and the fragmented
coastal plain belonged to the Indians. Then as now, there were more
persons living in this particular belt than in any other vertical slice for
a long way to the eastward. Then as now, the people living here were
distinctive or, as others might say, peculiar. Both the Californians
and the Indians on up the coast were a far cry from our generalized and
somewhat inaccurate picture of the Indian, as outlined by Cooper and
Parkman, touched up by Beadle and Buffalo Bill, and revitalized in our
day by the Hollywood western and radio's redskins. These far western
natives were not great hunters or horsemen; they did not live in Iro-
quoian long houses or in hide-covered tepees; they had no birchbark
canoes, no tomahawks, no scalp dances; they planted no Indian corn,
made no pottery, wore no feathered headgear; and in many other respects were unlike the composite of their eastern brethren. Because of
the simplicity of their ways the Californians in particular were regarded
by the American pioneers as the lowest of the low, yet when discriminat-
ing whites took time to get better acquainted they often found much
to admire in ingenious adjustment to environment and in the evolvement
of a philosophy of life.

The Californians long since had discovered that they did not need
elaborate housing or clothing. The dwellings they constructed were
the flimsiest of huts, of sticks and wattle and mud, casually put together.
Some were cone-shaped, others, as Father Crespi described them, "like
half an orange." Insinuation has been made that this original California
architecture was unpretentious out of respect to earthquake dangers:
the real reason seems to be that out-of-door life was more inviting, and
interest in housing almost at the vanishing point.

In attire, likewise, sun and air were unimpeded. There were woven
rabbit-skin robes, in the south there were sandals, and in the north
basketry hats were affected by deep-sea fishermen, but the manly way
was to go naked, and the standard garment for the gentler sex was a
two-piece apron, usually of shredded bark, one flap at the back and a

smaller one in front. False modesty did not bother these Californians, yet the customs of the land were as inexorable as in our civilization, and girl infants were promptly garbed with the badge of their sex.

Going naked doubtless had its drawbacks, but the reminiscent view upon it, as reported unanimously by the old-timers interviewed by anthropologist Mark R. Harrington, is entirely favorable. These oldsters averred the practice to be a most pleasurable thing for one brought up to it. Constant exposure to sun, wind, and water toughened the skin so that flies merely tickled, and the sting of the harvesting ant was an agreeable sensation. It made, they said, for fleetness of foot, stamina, and athletic prowess, for erect figure and good posture. Colds were rare and tuberculosis unknown, nor was there any trouble with piles, cancer, or venereal disease. Furthermore, it "made the individual entirely free from body-lice and fleas during the daytime"; it helped ensure a long life and "a life with lots of fun all the time."

ARTS AND CHORES

In their food habits these Californians were almost equally children of nature. In the semi-arid southern interior they lived none too well on grass seeds, herbs, cactus, grasshoppers, rabbits, and other small game. Along the coast, especially at the Santa Barbara channel, where the natives made excellent plank boats, fish enriched the diet. Here the Indians were more numerous as well as better fed. From this point northward the acorn was the staff of life. Some early and forgotten genius had devised a method of grinding and leaching, whereby the tannic acid could be extracted. He may well have been after this juice for a dye, mordant, or drug, but he got, at any rate, sweet acorn meal, palatable and nutritious. The cooking was in baskets by stone-boiling, and the resulting gruel, sometimes of one-finger, sometimes of two-finger consistency, could be eaten plain or flavored with nuts, herbs, rabbit meat or grasshoppers. Acorn grinding, leaching, and cooking were woman's work, and, because the leached meal would not keep, it was never done. Yet the acorn crop almost never failed, acorns were easy to store, and this food habit gained such hold that the Californians, until the padres put them to work, were not interested in the opportunity to become tillers of the soil.

As acorn fanciers they clustered around the oak groves on the floors of the valleys and followed them up the lower slopes. Their villages were approximately, though not precisely, where they would have been in an agricultural society. Few Indians lived on the actual mountain tops, which today have almost no population. Rather more were in the acorn and pine-nut belt of the upper valleys than is the case today, which helps to explain how a deserted region like the San Antonio Valley happened to have enough Indians to justify a mission.

For all its ingeniousness, the acorn process was a chore rather than an art. There was an art, however, in which the California women were highly expert, that of basketry. Using a variety of fibers and several different techniques of weaving, they made baskets for all conceivable purposes: large hampers in which to store acorns, smaller baskets for baby-carrying, flat trays for winnowing the acorn kernels, watertight baskets in which to boil water for the leaching process and for cooking, and thimble-sized miniatures to demonstrate their virtuosity. The most common relic of California Indian days is the stone mortar in which acorn grinding was done, but the best displays of skilled workmanship are in collections of Pomo basketry.

Characteristically, the Californians dwelt in villages of a few score or a few hundred souls. They burdened themselves with a minimum of government. Except for occasional brief forays they lived at peace with one another, and when they did fight it was without discipline, under impromptu leadership, and with the tools of their hunting and fishing, or by letting fly any stones that lay conveniently at hand. Relatively speaking, however, it was a land of peace.

SOCIAL CUSTOMS

Their social institution of greatest prominence was the *temescal,* or sweathouse, a hut more solidly constructed than their average. In it a fire was kindled. Bathers lay around on the floor to avoid the worst of the smoke, and then, when the sweat really ran, they dashed out to plunge in a near-by lake or stream. Such treatments were cleansing, and for certain complaints had therapeutic value. More often, however, the treatment was taken for the fun of it. The *temescal* customarily was a sort of men's club where gossip was exchanged, and in some villages the men habitually slept at the club rather than at home.

Other curious customs abounded. Both Cabrillo and Drake were harangued, loudly and at length, Cabrillo by an old and libidinous Indian who paddled out from the Santa Barbara coast, and Drake by the great Hi-oh, whose words, shouts, and gestures were interpreted as offering the entire land to the English. While he spoke, a number of Indian women stood in the background, scratching themselves until the blood ran, holding their hands above their heads, and dashing themselves to the ground, doubtless with the idea of propitiating their strange visitors.

Another distinguishing feature of the Californians was their passion for games. They played shinny, a variety of lacrosse, and a ball game that was essentially a football race. As late as 1852 Indian agent B. D. Wilson reported that the addiction to these games cut seriously into his wards' usefulness as laborers, and that he had known young men to play so strenuously as to die from overexertion.

These athletic contests were always used as the basis for wagering, but the more favored mode of gambling was upon the guessing games. The most popular was merely to guess in which hand a small stick was concealed. The Indians played it four on a side, with singers paid so much a game, and an umpire "who kept count, held the stakes, settled disputes, and prevented cheating. He was paid so much a night, and had to provide the firewood." The players at this game not uncommonly made a night of it. Considering their poverty, the stakes were high. Clothing and other personal belongings changed hands frequently, and even wives were lost to the superior luck or skill of an opponent.

To the glories of the acorn process and basketry, the *temescal* and gaming, the California civilization added another, a remarkable accumulation of mythological tales. The characters were mostly animal—Coyote, Hare, Eagle, and the like—and their psychology was as human as Br'er Rabbit's. The stories abounded in folk history and cosmic explanations—for example, how fire was discovered, and what caused earthquakes. One such, recorded by Stephen Powers among the Yokuts, a long lifetime ago, will illustrate.

Once there was a time when there was nothing in the world but water. About the place where Tulare Lake is now, there was a pole standing far up out of the water, and on this pole perched a hawk and a crow. First one of them would sit on the pole awhile, then the other would knock him off and sit

on it himself. Thus they sat on top of the pole above the waters for many ages. At length they wearied of the lonesomeness, and they created the birds which prey on fish such as the kingfisher, eagle, pelican, and others. Among them was a very small duck, which dived down to the bottom of the water, picked its beak full of mud, came up, died, and lay floating on the water. The hawk and the crow then fell to work and gathered from the duck's beak the earth which it had brought up, and commenced making the mountains. They began at the place now known as Ta-hi-cha-pa Pass, and the hawk made the east range, while the crow made the west one. Little by little, as they dropped in the earth, these great mountains grew athwart the face of the water, pushing north. It was a work of many years, but finally they met together at Mount Shasta, and their labors were ended. But, behold, when they compared their mountains, it was found that the crow's was a great deal the larger. Then the hawk said to the crow, "How did this happen, you rascal? I warrant you have been stealing some of the earth from my bill, and that is why your mountains are the biggest." It was a fact, and the crow laughed in his claws. Then the hawk went and got some Indian tobacco and chewed it, and it made him exceedingly wise. So he took hold of the mountains and turned them round in a circle, putting his range in place of the crow's; and that is why the Sierra Nevada is larger than the Coast Range.

Other stories probed deeper philosophical mysteries, such as the problem of good and evil and the question of life after death. This whole philosophy was considerably more advanced than one would expect on the basis of the primitive simplicity of the material culture. Indeed, the whole life of the Californians was more successful than has usually been credited. Today we talk of the Four Freedoms, which for many mortals are still only aspirations. The Californians had substantial enjoyment of freedom from war, freedom from oppression, freedom from want, and, to top it all, freedom from exertion.

FISHERMEN AND WOODWORKERS

Farther north, approximately at the Oregon line, began another culture province, likewise nonagricultural, but in most other respects sharply contrasting with California. These Indians were primarily fishermen. With hook and line, with nets, with traps and weirs, with fishing spears and harpoons, they worked the streams and the coastal waters. A stranded whale was the signal for an orgy of feasting. They also ventured out to sea on whale hunts, a post of particular honor among

them being that of chief harpooner. More important was the harvest at the annual runs of salmon and candlefish. Dried salmon was their year-round staple, and the candlefish yielded an oil essential to the rounding out of their diet. At the time of the runs everyone worked feverishly, raking out the fish, scaling and cleaning, smoking and drying the fillets, or heating the candlefish and squeezing out the oil. During the run they ate only entrails, heads, and trimmings. The catch might or might not be enough to tide them through the year. In any case, it was supplemented with additional catches of fish and with herbs and berries and game. Often these Indians lived farther up in the mountains than the stress on fish might indicate.

Although they had no better tools than horn and bone chisels and stone adzes, these Indians were highly expert woodworkers, by far the best in America. They could split out planks, which they applied over heavy frames of posts and beams to make large several-family dwellings. By judicious application of fire they could hollow out a log for a canoe bottom. By application of steam they could spread the middle of such a canoe. The sides then were raised by sewing on plank sideboards, and prow and stern superstructures were similarly attached. The outcome might be a seaworthy craft some sixty feet in length and with room for fifty or sixty men. By bending and sewing they constructed boxes for all sorts of household purposes, including cooking.

Canoes, boxes, and doorposts were given a decorative going-over in the style best known to us through the totem pole. Human faces, conventionally animalized, were the basic element. They were chosen and arranged to convey a particular meaning; a totem pole, for example, is literally some Indian's family tree, or at least a representation of his ancestry. On blankets, also, an art peculiar to the Northwest found expression. Here a design was presented dissected: a bear, for example, with eyes, teeth, claws, snout, ears, and his other component parts, but arranged in an arbitrary pattern rather than the customary assemblage.

Climate, diet, disposition, or some other factor made these Indians much more warlike than the Californians. Jedediah Smith found this out to his sorrow in 1828 when the Umpquas practically annihilated his band of stalwart beaver trappers. The settlers of southern Oregon were hard pressed in the Rogue River War in the early fifties. And Seattle was

saved from destruction only because of a warning from Chief Sealth's daughter and because the U.S.S. "Decatur" stood in toward shore and bombarded the hostile Indians.

POTLATCH DANCES

Yet, despite the valor and the ferocity of these Northerners, the most curious (and modern) feature of their customs was the stress that they put on wealth, or, more accurately, on the display of wealth. They accumulated property in houses, in planks, in canoes, in "coppers"—plaque-like disks made of the free copper occasionally found in this area—in dried salmon, in stores of fish oil, and even in slaves. With suitable excuse, such as a name-changing ceremony, a man of wealth would invite in guests whom he wished to impress. A lavish feast would be spread and the guests urged to gorge themselves. For their further delectation a copper might be broken, a valuable canoe hacked to pieces, a slave killed, or fish oil poured on the fire until the house itself was ignited. Etiquette demanded obeisances of approval from the guests, even in this last extremity, until the host gave the signal to extinguish the flames. Contemplating the practices of these Indians of the northwest coast, a pre-Columbian Veblen would have found illustrations of "conspicuous expenditure" and "willful waste" as apt as those that modern society supplies.

THE COMING OF THE TRADERS

This northwestern edge of what is now the United States was one of the many parts of America not discovered in 1492. Columbus came nowhere near these shores, and, for another three hundred years, another twelve or fifteen generations, the Indians had the region to themselves, unmolested by any whites and sheltered from the impact of a foreign culture.

Then, late in the eighteenth century, the European rivals for empire in America began to reach out toward this area. The Russians, having carried a fur trade across Siberia, extended it into the Aleutians and developed designs on the North American mainland. The British, after absorbing the greater part of French America, sought to push their fur trade across to the Pacific and, through Captain James Cook's most ambitious voyage, approached by sea as well as by land. These actions

prompted Spain, long the sole claimant of western America, to send out
expeditions to reassert her title and to ward off any encroachments. And
when Cook reported a wealth of furs at Nootka, on present Vancouver
Island, and a ready market for them in China, New England merchants
and seafarers made the United States a party to the rivalry for control
of the northwest coast.

According to Indian tradition there had been occasional chance landings somewhat earlier. At Nehalem, Oregon, for example, twenty-five
or thirty men are said to have got ashore after a shipwreck. For a time
the natives accepted them in peace, but because of too much attention
to the Indian women, they were set upon, their resistance, with improvised slingshots, was beaten down, and they were killed. Another
more lurid report describes a ship coming to anchor south of Neahkahnie.
From it a small boat came ashore. With a treasure chest and several
bags, the boat crew climbed the mountainside, dug a hole, drew lots,
killed one of their number, and buried him with the treasure as a protection against its being looted by the Indians. This pirate story is only
partially spoiled by the fact that searches for the buried treasure have not
succeeded. Other reports of shipwrecked mariners being washed ashore
and leaving red-haired or pale-skinned progeny may have basis in fact,
for all anyone can prove to the contrary. At Nehalem also, at various
times, some ten tons of beeswax has been discovered, circumstantial
evidence of the stranding of a Manila galleon.

Not until 1774, however, was there an actually recorded visit. In that
year the Spaniard Juan Pérez came up the coast on orders from the viceroy at Mexico City. His farthest north was near fifty-four forty, and so,
by a tenuous connection, he had something to do with Polk's campaign
for the presidency in 1844. Returning south, he sighted Mount Olympus,
or, as he chose to call it, the Sierra Nevada de Santa Rosalia, but he
made no landings in present Washington or Oregon, and the Indians of
this area were unaffected by his sailing past. Something of the same
may be said of Bruno Heceta, under whose leadership the Spaniards returned the next year. He found a great river, the Columbia, and called
it the San Roque. From the second ship in his expedition, a boat crew
went ashore near the mouth of the Moclips River and was promptly
massacred by the Indians. Aside from this melancholy adventure, Heceta
had no contact with the natives of Washington or Oregon.

Early in 1778 Captain James Cook sighted the Oregon coast at a spot which he was inspired to name Foulweather. His only landings were at Nootka and points farther north, but his visit had epochal importance for the entire northwest coast, for his voyage, or, more accurately, the book that described it, produced a rush of trading vessels to gather up the sea-otter pelts so abundant all up and down this coast. British traders crossed from India or came out from home by the Cape Horn route. Americans, led by Gray and Kendrick, likewise hurried out. And Spain sent a whole series of navigators to see what was going on and to stand up for Spanish rights. Most of the trading, and likewise the famous Nootka controversy which soon developed, centered a bit farther to the north, but from the late eighties on, the Indian monopoly of all this area was clearly over.

In the following decades a number of prominent persons engaged in spectacular deeds along this coast. Robert Gray returned to make his discovery of the Columbia River in 1792. George Vancouver of the British Navy was on hand at the same time, upholding his nation's interest, mapping the region, and bestowing dozens of place names as perpetual reminders of his companions and compatriots—Puget, Baker, Rainier, Hood, Townsend, Whidbey, and Vashon. Not many years later, Lewis and Clark made winter camp near the mouth of the Columbia, and they were followed by the employees of John Jacob Astor, who chose this same vicinity for their Oregon headquarters.

To most readers of history, Gray and Vancouver, Lewis and Clark, and Astor are the names that impress. To the northwestern natives the fur trade was what really counted. Explorers might come and go, but the important thing was the frequenting of the coast by trading schooners. There, if we may assume the Indian viewpoint, a pittance in furs could be bartered for glass beads, steel knives, fishhooks, copper pots, blankets, guns, and, most alluring, for fiery drink. Property-minded though these natives were, it appears that on the whole they were no match for the shrewd Yankee traders. Yet the persistence of the trade is proof of a sort that it was regarded as mutually advantageous. Out of it the New Englanders got a good fraction of the commodities for the China trade that was to be such an important element in bringing the infant United States its first period of prosperity. They continued to come to the coast as long as the sea otter and the seals held out. Out of it

the northwestern Indians likewise got the wherewithal for a more abundant life, a higher and more elaborate standard of living. At times they rose in wrath against dishonest or overbearing traders, as at Clayoquot Sound in 1811 when they seized and pillaged Astor's ship, the "Tonquin," but in general they welcomed the coming of the traders.

DEMORALIZATION AND DECLINE

For the Indians, however, the immediate benefits were more than counterbalanced by demoralizing influences. With the acquisition of new gadgets, some of the old skills tended to disappear. New appetites and the newly acquired thirst threatened the sway of the old standards of conduct, while the sailors' contribution of measles, smallpox, and the social diseases cut severely into the physical vigor of the tribes.

The decline in spirit and robustness is easy to chart. In 1791, when Gray was wintering at Clayoquot Sound and was in the midst of graving his ship, he narrowly averted an Indian attack that almost certainly would have overwhelmed his party. Near Point Higgins the Indians killed his second mate and two seamen who had gone shoreward to fish. Upon entering the Columbia, he was also approached by a number of war canoes, and to keep them off he had to unlimber a nine-pounder and destroy one of the larger canoes with its complement of twenty warriors. By the time Lewis and Clark came along, the Chinooks on the lower Columbia were in possession of brass kettles, frying pans, articles of sailor garb, muskets, pistols, and powder flasks, but their minds seemed to be set on thievery and prostitution, which the American leaders regarded as the more deplorable because of the prevalence of venereal disease. By the 1820's, when John McLoughlin came to Oregon as the Hudson's Bay Company factor, the degradation of the coastal Indians had gone even further. It justified his transfer of the company headquarters to a new site farther inland.

The techniques of trade, demoralization, and infection may seem like a casual way of softening the native stock and wearing it down. It may be questioned, however, whether an earlier descent on the region by columns of settlers would have been any better. The Indians had no chance to vote on it, but in all probability would have preferred to be undermined and debilitated by commercial contacts, many of which had a pleasant side, rather than to be overwhelmed and ousted by an

avalanche of settlers. For at least three score years and ten after the appearance of Pérez, Heceta, and Cook, they were practically free from pressure by prospective settlers. When it did come, these Indians were not the stalwarts they once had been, but they knew considerably more of the white man's ways, and they put up a fairly effective resistance. The land is long since civilized, and few of their descendants are to be seen, yet in place names, trails, legends, and pioneer history, their imprint on the land is not entirely lost.

THE CALIFORNIANS AS MISSION INDIANS

Meanwhile, white strangers also broke in upon the solitude of the Indians of coastal California. The early visitors included such famous men as Juan Rodríguez Cabrillo, discoverer of the coast of southern California; Francis Drake, freebooter and circumnavigator; Sebastián Rodríguez Cermeño, who lost a Manila galleon, cargo and all, in his efforts to explore California; and Sebastián Vizcaíno, merchant adventurer, a prodigious namer of places, and the creator of the legend of the Port of Monterey. These men brought back the descriptions that shaped the world's picture of California from the sixteenth century until late in the eighteenth. Their visits, however, had only the most transitory effect upon the California natives. They accomplished nothing toward dispossessing these original inhabitants and they appear to have produced no change in the patterns of life in the region.

The real culture-bearers of a new civilization were the Spaniards of the late eighteenth century, who came not just to explore, but to lay hold upon the region for imperial Spain. The motives for this expansion were strategic and missionary, and the whole procedure was Government-directed and Government-financed. It was part of the protective expansion whereby the Spaniards sought to build "defenses in depth" for their threatened older holdings, and it was carried out with practiced economy of manpower and matériel. Three main agencies were employed: small army posts (presidios), small civilian settlements (pueblos), and, better publicized and probably more important, the missions. Through the latter, in particular, the California natives were introduced to the ways of the civilized world and were remolded into useful subjects of the Spanish Crown.

To begin with, only four missions were established, but in a decade

and a half Father-President Junípero Serra increased the number to nine, and in a slightly longer period his successor added as many more. Three others were subsequently established. Even with twenty-one missions functioning, the chain was still a slender one, yet it managed to bring under its influence practically all the natives of the Coast Ranges from San Diego on the south to the northern shores of San Francisco Bay, a stretch of more than five hundred miles.

What it meant to the Indians to be shepherded into the missions has never been adequately set forth. Our accounts are from the missionaries, from Spanish officials who took the system for granted, or from foreign visitors who commented on its bizarre features. The Indians themselves were neither literate nor vocal. Most of them, furthermore, entered the missions at such a tender age—in the latter stages practically all were mission-born—that they were not in a position to make valid comparison with life outside.

It is clear enough that the Spaniards sought to attract Indians to the missions rather than to force them in. They chose likely spots, strategically located, with arable land and wood and water, and with a sufficient Indian population near by. Then, by presents of baubles, by gifts of food, by entertaining with the pageantry of the Catholic rituals, they won the interest of the natives.

THE MISSION OF THE MOUNTAINS

Such, for example, were the circumstances of the founding of San Antonio de Padua, often called the mission of the mountains. Its approximate site, in the valley of the San Miguel, a western tributary of the Salinas, had been discovered by the Portolá expedition in September, 1769, as it labored northward in search of the fabulous Port of Monterey. So pleasant was the prospect of oak-studded valley enfolded by pine-covered slopes that Portolá named the place La Hoya (Jewel) de la Sierra de Santa Lucía. Two summers later, after a beginning had been made at Monterey, Serra came with two Franciscans, a corporal and six soldiers, three sailors, and several Christian Indians from Lower California to establish St. Anthony's mission. Arrived at the spot, he was quite overcome with enthusiasm. He ordered a hasty unpacking, had the bells suspended from a spreading liveoak, and forthwith began to ring them vigorously. Father Miguel remonstrated that it was a waste

of effort, that no Indian was within hearing distance, and that he was tiring himself needlessly. Serra, however, was not discouraged. A large cross was built, blessed, and erected, an arbor constructed, with a table to serve as the altar, and Serra began to celebrate holy mass. At the point in the ritual when he turned to read the gospel and to preach, he was overjoyed to see that an Indian had approached and was intently watching the curious proceedings. This sight, unprecedented at the opening of the earlier missions, Serra interpreted as an omen of special blessings for the mission of San Antonio. Caressing this savage, and bestowing upon him various presents, Serra sought to win his friendship and that of his fellows. This overture brought in a number of other Indians with presents of pine-nuts and acorns, for which the friars returned glass beads, corn meal, and beans.

Although gentle persuasion was the technique for attracting the natives, once an Indian had cast his lot with the mission, he was not allowed to change his mind. Thenceforth he submitted to the friars' teachings, worked under their direction, slept at the mission, ate the mission fare, and was subject to mission discipline twenty-four hours a day and three hundred and sixty-five days a year. At first relatively few Indians—and these mostly women and children, the aged, and the decrepit—cared to surrender their freedom for this regimentation and discipline. Yet in the kindness of the friars, the novelties of the mission program, the pleasures of the religious performances, the creature comforts of food and clothing and shelter, and the social security that the system guaranteed, the missions had much to offer. The going was often hard, but in the long run the missions prevailed.

In its first year Mission San Antonio was nothing but a rude shack to house the friars, a house of comparable construction for the guard, and an unpretentious room to serve as the church. By the close of 1773 an adobe church with a flat roof of beams and mortar had been built. Similar rooms housed the friars and the workshops. There were smaller houses of wood and mud for the three soldiers who had acquired Indian wives, and a village of huts of poles and tules for the assembled natives. Baptisms had numbered one hundred and fifty-eight, marriages fifteen, and deaths eight. The mission had four mares, one stallion, four riding horses, two riding mules, nine pack mules with the necessary harness, thirty-eight head of cattle, and thirty pigs. An irrigation ditch

had been constructed, and a plot of ground cleared for wheat sowing, but as yet neither stock-raising nor crop-production had gone far enough to support the Spaniards, let alone feed all the neophytes. Some stuff was packed in from Monterey, but the Indians still had to live on the native foods: pine-nuts, acorns, wild seeds, rabbit meat, and squirrels.

By 1776, according to Father Pedro Font, who visited San Antonio with the Anza expedition, the adherents of the mission numbered some five hundred souls. The resident fathers were having a good deal of trouble persuading many of these natives to wear the clothing recommended to them; they were also struggling with the language, which abounded in "guttural, barbaric, and ridiculous" sounds. Indeed, in Father Sitjar's laboriously compiled vocabulary he had to make use of "K" and numerous accents and signs not needed in Castilian. Yet with workmen no further removed from the primitive, the fathers contrived, in 1779, to erect an adobe church measuring one hundred and thirty-three feet by twenty-six. The following year they roofed it with tile and built a tile-roofed dormitory two hundred and twenty-six feet in length.

A heavy frost at Easter time in 1780 apparently ruined the wheat planting, which might have meant that the Indians would have had to revert to hunting and seed gathering, much to the detriment of mission discipline. The fathers, however, decided on a special effort in prayer and irrigating. They summoned the natives to make a *novena*, nine days of concentrated praying for the intervention of the mission's patron saint, and they flooded the fields with all the water the ditches would carry. As the novena ended, the wheat turned green again, harvest time brought a bumper crop, and friars and neophytes alike experienced a redoubled faith in the goodness of God and the power of his saints.

THE DECLINE OF INDIAN CULTURE

A full generation later, in 1814, Fathers Pedro Cabot and Juan Bautista Sancho made an elaborate and illuminating report upon Mission San Antonio. They noted that practically all their Indians understood Spanish and spoke it with sufficient fluency, and that those who had had instruction were fond of reading and writing in Spanish. The fathers complained that the Indians were too indulgent toward their children and did not give them much training. But, they added, this was to be

expected because the missionaries still had to give the adult Indians instructions in such ordinary things as sweeping, washing, sleeping high off the ground, and eating with cleanliness. They had to supervise things corporeal as well as spiritual, to see that their charges cultivated the soil, sowed and harvested, guarded the herds of cattle and sheep, labored at weaving and tanning, and made harness and saddles and shoes.

Superstitions unfortunately persisted: the fathers reported, for instance, that one man produced infirmities, that another had the power to make it rain, that a dreamer would find something of value, that by fasting one could make sure of winning at games, and that fasting would increase a man's potency. The fathers rejoiced that the Indians were no longer shameless about going "with their nakedness uncovered," and that their manner of eating was considerably improved though still not "dainty."

Somewhat contradictorily the fathers described their charges as honorable in the keeping of bargains and promises, but as natural liars to whom it was a hardship to tell the truth. Impurity was their dominant vice, and although they knew its ill effects, especially since the race had been contaminated through contact with the soldiers and others, self-restraint and continence seemed to be beyond them. Likewise, they were hopelessly addicted to gambling. Yet they lived peaceably and obediently at the mission, they did all the work that needed doing, they were passable farmers, gardeners, cowboys, irrigators, builders, weavers, cooks, carpenters, masons, etc. And they were particularly adept at music, their voices clear and sonorous and their sense of pitch excellent. Part singing and plain chants were well within their capacity. The men wore cotton overalls; the women, cotton chemises and skirts; and when the weather called for it both sexes added blankets. All partook of a morning meal of atole (a whole-wheat gruel), a noon meal of meat and pozole (a dish based on wheat, corn, or peas), and an evening ration of atole. Between meals the Indians nibbled away at pine-nuts and seeds or partook of their old favorite, the acorn. All who were old enough made confession once a year; those who were sufficiently instructed took communion; and the sick sent for the priest and received the sacraments "with as much devotion as could be expected."

For the other California missions somewhat similar reports were being made. Some were more prosperous than San Antonio; others,

especially those more recently founded, had made less progress. In general, however, it was true that the Indians of the coastal district had been partially made over in the Spanish pattern. In dress and housing, in food habits, in gardening and farming and stock raising, in the manual arts, in artisanry, in social practices, in religion, in artistic and cultural expression, they conformed more and more closely to the Spanish standard, and because of these spiritual as well as material changes they were increasingly useful to the Spanish province and empire.

AFTER SECULARIZATION

Another two decades and the mission system came to its end. California by that time was republicanized, in consequence of Mexico's becoming an independent nation, and the mission with its monarchical and medieval flavor had come to be regarded as an anachronism. Besides, the missions had the principal wealth of the province, owned the best lands, and monopolized the labor market. The missions, therefore, were secularized. As religious institutions they were transformed into parish churches. The Indians were released from the friars' paternal care and were put on their own. From the property that had been accumulated and held in trust for the Indians, each released neophyte was allotted a reasonable amount. Secular administrators controlled the oftentimes considerable residue, and the surplus lands reverted to the state, which was ready to parcel it out generously to prospective rancheros.

Some of the liberated Indians went inland, found kinsmen or friends, and reverted to aboriginal ways. A few became landed proprietors on small tracts and succeeded in what now would be called subsistence farming or ranching. The majority, however, were at loose ends. The mission system had not yet prepared them to be their own masters. They hung about the old sites, or about the towns and presidios. The property allotted them soon slipped away for drink and other extravagances, and they were reduced to beggary, petty thievery, and whatever honest work they could get. As alcalde at Monterey in 1846, Walter Colton noted the rhythmic reappearance before his court of Indians charged with drunkenness and other minor offenses. These were sentenced to necessary work about the town or to fines that they worked out under some individual. At Los Angeles in the fifties the same system was in vogue. The Indians regularly had a spree on Saturday

night, spent Sunday night in jail, appeared before the magistrate on Monday morning, and were allotted to ranchmen or other employers to work out their fines and earn enough for another Saturday-night spree.

That this was deplorable was freely conceded by thoughtful Californians. As part of his report in 1852, B. D. Wilson suggested that the ideal solution, and one that would have strong appeal to the Indians, would be to reassemble them at the missions and to reinstitute the old system. Since that, for various reasons, was out of the question, he advocated instead a gathering of the Indians on reservations, where under the supervision of Government agents they could reproduce the material, though not the religious, features of the old regime.

Something of the sort was put into practice at Fort Tejon, and then at other centers. Difficulties included dishonest administrators, lobbying to keep the United States Senate from ratifying treaties already accepted by most of the California Indians, and increased pressure upon the Indians because of the overnight influx of thousands of gold-seekers. The California reservations were in most respects a failure, but they provided a model which the United States soon standardized as its Indian program, and they helped ward off what might have been the complete extermination of these Indians.

Indian population had declined under the impact of the Spaniards. With secularization it dropped more rapidly. American pioneers, forty-niners, and early settlers contributed to a further decline in numbers, as they took over Indian lands, chopped down oak and pine trees, fouled the fishing waters, and—some of them at least—took pot shots at stray Indians. The fifties saw a whole series of Indian "wars" in which hundreds of more or less innocent tribesmen were slaughtered, and the unsatisfactoriness of the reservation system gave Helen Hunt Jackson ammunition for her *Century of Dishonor* and her crusading novel *Ramona*. A few thousand California Indians still survive. The majority are from the less desirable interior that the Spaniards had not penetrated. Whole tribes that once were missionized are now extinct, and only a few relicts are left descended from the thousands of Coast Range Indians who once swarmed at the twenty-one stations along *El Camino Real* between San Diego de Alcalá and San Francisco Solano.

FOOTSTEPS OF SPRING—
A WILD FLOWER TRAIL

BY DONALD CULROSS PEATTIE

We should ourselves discover these mountains. No introduction to these delectable hills and peaks could be more charming than a springtime adventure following the opening of the blossoms from south to north. (R. P.)

"If I ever had plenty of money, and all my debts were paid" (as a wistful poet put it), I should start in February at California's southern border and slowly follow northward a little flower the hue of pale sunshine, which Westerners call footsteps-of-spring. At least I should follow it symbolically, if not literally, through its whole extent from Mexico to Canada. I should travel through the Coast Ranges, as valley and mesa, peak and forest lighted up with blooms of every color. I should begin with those lonely canyons of the San Jacinto Range that look toward the desert and the morning, where the fan palm of California grows wild and native. I should pick my way north through the inner Coast Ranges to Mint Canyon (well-named) where the beekeepers or beemasters dwell, and their golden slaves haunt the flowering sage. I should ask to be on the Lompoc hills in time for the lupine. Then I should jog slowly up the San Simeon Highway where the Santa Lucia Mountains plunge into the Pacific without a beach, drugged in the wealth of golden lupine and vermilion paintbrush and the tilting cups of farewell-to-spring.

Then, instead of saying farewell to it, I should pursue it north through the redwood belt. And after that—green Oregon, clothed in a rich forest and laced with waterfalls. Until, at last, in July I should stand at the foot of eternal snows on the Olympic Mountains of northern Washington, and pluck from the glacier's lip that little arctic-alpine, the purple campion on its mossy clump.

Actually I have never taken such a continuous six months' trip, devoted exclusively to botanizing. But I have, at one time and another,

47

seen much of the Coast Ranges throughout their great length of twelve hundred miles, and seen them as a man who refused to pass by any species new to him, or even an "old" one which, breathing abroad all its little charms, demanded of his naturalist's piety a moment of worship.

I do not know that anyone has ever computed just how many species there are in the Coast Ranges proper, from Mexico to the strait of Juan de Fuca, but they run into the thousands. If our Coast Ranges were moved to the eastern side of the United States, they would stretch from the latitude of Savannah in Georgia to that of Mount Katahdin in Maine. Unlike the Appalachians, with which they might be compared in length and height (though the comparison favors the Coast Ranges), these mountains, in the south, dip deep into a subtropical desert, and, in the north, reach the zone of perpetual snow. Some of the Coast Ranges are composed of limestone, and their soils are on the alkaline side; others are granitic, with acid soils. So the one is rich in the members of the brilliant pea family, the other in adherents of the heath family. Altogether, the Coast Ranges bear upon their flanks such a wealth of plants that in these few pages I can but speak of a few of the chief floral treasures. I cannot mention more than one species in hundreds, much less can I tell you how to identify the plants as you go.

"WHERE ARE THE FLOWERS?"

The visitor to southern California is frequently heard to ask, "Where are all these glorious wild flowers I have been told about? I see nothing but withered wild oats!" And he looks about at the barren tawny hills and feels, not unnaturally, that he has been "sold." Indeed, some of the naturalists who touched upon our coast in the earliest days of exploring expeditions of the eighteenth century, speak of southern California as if the desert came right down to the sea. For, as ill luck would have it, too many arrived in summer, which is, biologically, southern California's winter, or in autumn which, as a separate season, hardly exists for the vegetation of this province. When David Douglas, the great plant explorer, came to California to find new garden beauties for the Royal Horticultural Society, he wrote, at first, of California in terms of disappointment, after having seen the great forests and perpetually running streams of Oregon and Washington. But all that changed swiftly when spring came.

The fact is that just as southern California has a rainy season, it has a wild flower season, as is the case wherever the Mediterranean type of climate is found. From such a climate come those lines of poetry as keen in their scientific observation as rich in rhythm:

> For lo, the rains are over and gone
> And the flowers appear on the earth.

But here, as in Solomon's kingdom, the flowers, too, after their season, are presently over and gone. And when gone, they are very gone, just like the creeks which run in winter and spring only. Southern California has but a diminished summer flora, while in winter the rains return and greenness greets the hungry eyes again. Only a few wild plants, many of them coarse or trivial weeds, bloom the year around. The conception of California as ever-blooming is correct chiefly as applied to garden vegetation which is made up largely of exotics selected to produce that effect. Similarly, the idea that California has no seasons is based upon the fact that most of the native trees, too, are evergreen, and also upon the fact that the seasons are less extreme, and do not behave as they do in the eastern States. It is certainly not true that California has no springtide. No spring—when you walk an Elysian carpet of flowers, rolling down to the blue Pacific's shores, and the whistle of the western meadowlarks, the most joyful voice in all the world of birds, rises up all about you? I have heard a lady from New England object that she liked snow on her wild flowers. Another of the same race protested that California wild flowers are "*too* beautiful" and they "have no fragrance"; and a third, that this part of the world "doesn't seem like America." I shall not argue with any of them.

Indeed I shall freely admit (contradicting the careless rapture of many Californians) that there are not, usually, more species in any one spot in California than elsewhere. On the contrary, botanical statistics would show that there is perhaps less sheer variety. So that any boasting must rest upon the quality of our wild flowers, and on that score I am willing to accept challenge. I must confess, too, that if you stand still here, instead of following spring northward, the height of the flower season may last as little as three weeks and the entire floral procession is likely to pass you by in about two months,

though sometimes it lingers longer on cool, misty slopes, dipping toward the ocean.

THE CALIFORNIA FLOWER BASKET

But what a glorious two months! Not even the most oblivious, the most earth-bound and beauty-blind and hurried, miss the display of southern California wild flowers. Even on crowded Highway 101, there is a place south of Santa Maria where lupine and poppies spill over the crest of each hill and down to the roadside in a way to make the most furious motorist draw to a stop. Travelers on the "Daylight," the express between San Francisco and Los Angeles, crane from their windows, as the train swings round Point Conception, to see that magic carpet of bloom unrolled to the very beach. When they go in to lunch, they find the design of the California poppy on their table service, for it is the State flower, the first State flower to be adopted and still, perhaps, the most completely natural and inevitable choice made by any State. England her rose, France her lilies, and California its poppy.

For Californians are more conscious of their heritage of wild flowers and of the uniqueness of it than any other people among whom I have lived. As the Japanese are said to go out in families to admire their cherry blossoms, so the Californian thinks nothing of getting in his car, be it ever so humble, and going a hundred or two hundred miles upon the mere rumor that some lonely canyon or some arid slope has burst into bloom. The whole family comes, and for a day they revel in a feast of color and scent. There is a gaminess about the hunt, too. The intensity of blooming depends upon the rainfall, and that is "spotty"— good here and poor there in the same year. So that the newspapers carry items about the places where good hunting is to be had. And even the service stations put up signs: "Wild flower information here." Yet so vast is the field that one can always be alone if one wishes. For myself, I do not object to the sight of children gamboling, tripping, and rolling in the waves of blossom.

Californians of today have strong principles, as well as some stringent laws, about wild-flower protection. Whatever their past sins, they now frown upon the grabber and the exploiter as pariah. But it is not the fingers of children which are the real enemies of our wild flowers. Rather is it the growth of cities and suburbs, excessive drainage, and overgraz-

California poppies and the yucca.

Joshua trees of the so-called forest just over the range from Los Angeles.

Each individual blossom of the rhododendron is a joy in itself. These are Oregon flowers.

Our Lord's Candle or yucca bloom

ing, with attendant drought and erosion. Ever since the days of the first Spanish settlements, untold numbers of cattle and sheep have been pastured on these lands. With them came in such foreign weeds as wild oats, mustard, and filaree, which too often supplant the abused native flora. Some people extravagantly admire the mustard when in bloom. To my taste no such cold brassy yellow can ever compensate for the rich, soft-glowing orange of the poppy's sun-filled cup.

So, to see the native flora in its Eden innocence, you must go far away from cities, ignore the splendor of gardens, and even avoid the hospitality of ranches, and get off by yourself in the mountains, in the steep canyons, on the sea cliffs, or on the lonely arid slopes tipping toward the Great Central Valley. And there you may fill your soul with wild flowers as you have always dreamed of them, as they might be in Heaven.

There is usually a dominant color in any given landscape of our flowers—blue, purple, rose, yellow, orange, or white, depending on which species happens in that spot to be most plentiful that year, or at that moment the tallest in the field. But through each dominant color there are likely to be streaks or patches of some contrasting hue. Perhaps the commonest, certainly the most famous and most satisfactory, is that flower carpet, seen to perfection in Santa Barbara and San Luis Obispo Counties, of a sky-blue lupine and a complementary mixture of orange poppies, dancing over the mesas and filling the glades between the wide-spaced oaks.

Lupines California has without end. In fact, it is richer in this glorious genus, of which the northeastern States have but one species, than any area of the same size in the world. It boasts all three of the primary colors, but most commonly the lupines here are purple, sometimes wondrously deep and dark. Some are lilac, and the form of their flowers reminds one then of wisteria; others are pure white, and one kind, called bluebonnet, is rich blue. But the loveliest of all is the thick but tiny species that looks as if the April sky had fallen on the hills. A fleck of white upon the banner petal blending with the blue softens, at a distance, the ethereal shade to something milky, as if the most delicate sea mist had crossed the heavens.

Its constant partner, the California poppy, is too well known in gardens all over the world to need description. It was perhaps the

first plant collected by the poet-botanist Chamisso when he stepped upon the botanically-unexplored strand of California, and the first California wild flower to be figured in a drawing; certainly it was the first to attain popularity in the gardens of Europe. Yet in no garden plot does it ever look so fair as in the spring fields of its native land. Softened by the green grass blades springing around it, caught in the greater lupine sea of blue, dappled with the passing clouds and the leaning oak trees' pools of shade, set dancing in the sea wind, or the warm breath from the panting Great Central Valley, California poppies glow with a radiance that, once seen, you can see forever behind your eyelids when you close your eyes.

But there are other effects quite as glorious. A whole hillside may be tinged with a soft rose-purple by that quaint little plant, the owl's-clover. And with reckless brush Nature may lay on it streaks of gorgeous vermilion paintbrush. But, more than likely, this Bulgarian embroidery will be softened by those white forget-me-nots which children aptly call popcorn flowers and the Spanish Californians named *nievetas* or "little snows."

As one travels from one lonely ridge or wild valley to another, fresh combinations come to view. For reasons best known to Nature, different little floras are found, each in their nooks, especially if one travels across the Coast Ranges, to or from the sea on the one side and the steppe-like Central Valley on the other. So one may come upon various landscapes dominated by quite different assemblages of plants. Here it may be the California bluebells (Phacelia to the botanist) that fill up the field. There it may be that baby blue-eyes cover the ground. Again, a field is barren under the sun, but toward night the evening-snow may suddenly wink open, whitening the hill with living moonlight. In some localities beardtongue or pentstemon is abundant, sometimes white or, in the flower called scarlet-bugler, cardinal red; but most of our pentstemons are of an intense radiant blue. Or the whole sod may be covered with a fall of shooting stars, our New-World cyclamens, that leap away from earth on fine stems as if they spurned it, only to point to it on nodding stalks, with their twisted petals flaring up behind them.

The sages or salvias of California are many, and all are beautiful and intensely fragrant. On them, and on the orange blossom, is founded

the great honey industry of the California beemasters. White sage, black sage, and purple sage all yield fine honeys. But most beautiful of all is the thistle sage, its long, narrow, lilac corolla arching aristocratically out of an exquisite great puff of silvery cottony hairs around the calyx, and the silvery foliage giving off a delicious odor commingling lemon with mint.

One could go on to speak of those flowers whose names suggest the days of the forty-niners—miner's lettuce and gold-fields. Or of dainty creamcups and tidytips, of little Johnny-tuck, and, keeping pace with him over the hills, one Johnny-nip.

But the out-of-state reader will get the bewildered impression of a lot of names with which he is not familiar, and flowers which he knows not where to place. If this is his impression, it is the correct one, for that is just what he will feel when for the first time he tumbles out the lovely content of southern California's flower basket.

SPANISH MEMORIES

Curious to know the impression that a southern Californian spring must have made on its first European beholders, I once turned confidently to the narratives of early exploration. I was much disappointed. The Spanish conquistadores and padres had, I suppose, more pressing things on their minds, in a grizzly-ridden wilderness, with starvation, thirst, and flying arrows all around them. One of the earliest diarists, Father Juan Crespi, did make many notes on the vegetation. He was a native of Majorca, and there is much resemblance between the vegetation of the Mediterranean lands and that of California. So he was able to recognize and distinguish live oaks (*encinas*) and deciduous oaks (*robles*), alders (*alisos*), the ash tree (*fresno*) and poplar (*alamo*) and the strawberry tree (*madroño*), walnuts (*nogales*) and pines (*piños*); and such words persist today in California as names of canyons, peaks, promontories, streets, towns, and suburbs.

But here Crespi's little store of botanical knowledge almost ended, and even in the height of the flowering season he can only speak, over and over, of "many flowers whose names I did not know," and "various shrubs which we do not recognize." Indeed, in 1769, when Crespi wrote, probably no one would have known his way in this unexplored flora unless Linnaeus himself could have been set down here. Sixteen years be-

fore, Linnaeus had completed his great *Species Plantarum*; he would have had to enlarge it could he have collected the first specimens from this new land, then the remotest part of the temperate zone.

One flower alone poor Crespi could recognize, the rose. He cannot contain his rapture over the wild rose of California, though it does not seem to our eyes especially showy. Every time he comes to a rose bush he has to tell us about it; he counts the number of opened and unopened buds on the branch he plucked. He calls it "the rose of Castile." And therein, perhaps, lies the explanation of his enthusiasm. He took it, not unforgivably, to be identical with the wild rose of Spain; here in this heathen land was one familiar flower face, a flower, moreover, intimately bound up with Christian mythology and symbolism. Thus do we all tend to fall with homesick gladness, in far-off exotic places, upon the dearly familiar.

With time, of course, the Spanish settlers came to be familiar with the flora of their adopted country. Unfortunately they produced no poets or native naturalists, and were not at all a literary people. So we have left only some fragments, surviving by tradition, of their rich plant lore. We know that they drank a tea made from yerba buena, a little pennyroyal from whose pervading fragrance was once named the city that is now San Francisco. That they used the amole, a plant something like asphodel, for making soap. That they decorated the churches with malva rosa, the tree mallow; and they esteemed the sage, chia, for curing gunshot wounds. Perhaps a hundred Spanish Californian plant names have survived, some of them truly Spanish, others really from Nahuatl or other Indian languages, slightly Hispaniolized and perhaps best called Mexican. Added to the English and Latin names, they enrich our plants with a surprising amount of human and historical associations in a flora so new to the world as this.

CHAPARRAL IN BLOOM

Not all the wild flowers of southern California are found in the open fields. There are in the Coast Ranges beautiful canyons shaded by live oaks, white-limbed sycamores, and alders of tree size, which look rather like slim beech trees with their smooth trunks and emerald shade. Here is the place to look for a small but attractive flora of herbaceous

perennials like the hummingbird sage with its superb scarlet flowers, and Humboldt's lilies—true members of the genus Lilium, and specifically named for the great explorer. Here you find those dainty flowers called milkmaids (from their dairy complexion) and a particularly dark purple lupine with beautifully clean bright leaves. To come on the canyon sunflower, blooming here in early spring, is startling to the Easterner, who does not expect such flowers before autumn.

But the dominant woody vegetation of much of southern California is not trees but intricate, impenetrable shrubbery called chaparral, closely corresponding in type to the celebrated maquis or macchia of the Mediterranean, though not at all made up of the same species. The "chaps" of the cowboy's costume—flapping leather guards for the shin bone—are the protection he wears against the sharp twigs of the chaparral, which gives you an idea of about how high chaparral rises around a mounted man. The word chaparral is derived from the Spanish *chaparro,* for an evergreen oak. In California the meaning is often extended to denominate the whole plant complex, largely evergreen and permanently of dwarf stature, which covers the intermediate altitudes of the Coast Ranges of southern California with a compact growth of what some claim are really trees, or as much of trees as conditions allow, even though they look like shrubs to you. So chaparral is sometimes referred to as elfin forest—which, as Herodotus would say, is "the invention of some poet or other." As to whether the chaparral is forest or shrubbery I can only add the personal testimony that it is too low to give shade and too high to see over. But to give it its due: chaparral is a soil cover in an almost treeless region of torrential rains.

It is true that many species which are trees in central California become dwarfs when growing among the chaparral. Such forest kings as the black oak, the tanbark oak, the giant chinquapin, the coast and interior live oaks, even the noble canyon live oak and the aristocratic California laurel, demean themselves, as it were, with stunted replicas in the chaparral.

But the most characteristic chaparral plants are the gnarled tree-shrubs, numberless in species and variously called wild or California lilac or blue blossom when their flowers are blue or lavender, and white-thorn or snowbush when they are white, and sometimes redheart and

redroot, in allusion to the color of their wood. Collectively they are reckoned as Ceanothus, which is really their botanical name, though Californians use it as vernacular. The woodcutter calls all Ceanothus simply "chaparral," and by any name it smells as sweet. For we all like, in southern California, to burn its burls and branches on our hearths for the sake of their aroma and the threads of dancing, vanishing sparks they send up the chimney.

Promiscuous as some of the company in the chaparral may seem, it has some distinct beauties in it. There are, for instance, the flaunting prickly phlox, and the toyon, whose white blooms, like strawberry flowers, are followed by bright red berries, used like holly for Christmas decoration; from it Hollywood takes its name. Then there are the frosty-flowered manzanitas, relatives of eastern bearberry, with twisted red stems, looking like the arms of Indians in struggle. And when all this has faded, the yucca, just before it dies, sends up enormous spires ten and fifteen feet high, of creamy white flowers that light up the mountainsides for miles. Chamiso, too, is a shrub of the chaparral, having flowers like meadowsweet but needle-like leaves, which also whitens the hillsides in late spring, and may in places tolerate almost no rivals.

One of the unforgettable features of the chaparral is its blended aroma. Napoleon is said to have stated that were he set down blindfold in the maquis of his native Corsica he would know it by the odor. Without comparing my nose to Napoleon's (which is said to have been hypersensitive!) I can say that I would know the chaparral blindfold, too, though I am sure I could not describe it to one who did *not* know it. I would not call it sweet—not nearly as sweet, at least, as the Mediterranean maquis. But strong it is, rather like wormwood, from the sagebrush and the gray-leaved "old man"; rather turpentiny, too, on account of squawbush and sugarbush and laurel sumac; and minty withal, because of the many sages. The whole gives off a sneezy sort of aroma, a bit of Nature's snuff, which I find, to my own surprise, I am glad to take again when I have been long away from it.

CONSIDERING THE LILIES

One may overtake spring again, as the height of the wild flower display begins to fade in the south, either by going northward or by ascend-

ing the high mountains of southern California, where spring comes only when the snows have melted. Peaks in the San Bernardino Mountains, and in the San Gabriel Range, which shuts the north winds away from Pasadena, rise up ten thousand feet and more. So that you can see a fine flora blooming full tilt in June and July around Bear Lake, for instance, in the San Bernardinos, or on Mount Pinos in Ventura county. There is much kinship between these so-called montane floras in the south and that of the subalpine zone of the Sierra Nevada.

However, this trip which I am projecting is intended to end up in northern Washington, so I shall have to be on my way. And indeed I can see at moderate elevations in the north many of the same flowers which are to be found in the south only at the highest altitudes.

So I shall be quitting southern California by about the second half of May, quite aware that there are many delights of all sorts still on the calendar down there, but hastening northward to keep a series of appointments.

In central-western California will be the first of these. Perhaps I cannot define such a province but I can loosely indicate it as running south to the "Robinson Jeffers country" of Big Sur (about latitude 36°) and north along the coast to the "Russian country" where the Muscovites, coming down from Alaska in 1812, built a fort at about latitude 39°; and inland, of course, the region extends as far as the sunny, half-arid inner Coast Ranges, when they sink away into the floor of the Great Central Valley. Thus the region includes San Francisco and all its bay region, Monterey Bay, and the "wine country" of the Napa hills. In many ways central California "has everything"—seacoast and mountains, fields of wild flowers and chaparral like the south, coniferous forests like northern California, and fine park-like woodlands of evergreen hardwoods or broad-leaved trees.

Thus the San Franciscan is a lucky dog who has only to start out to be sure of coming soon to some beautiful and interesting place, and he has the widest variety of trips to take. He may make an excursion up Mount Tamalpais, or strike inland for isolated Mount Diablo, a classic collecting ground since the days of David Douglas—a whole book has recently been written on its vegetation. Or he can go to Muir Woods and see the majestic redwoods, or meet them down in the Santa Clara Moun-

tains. Or he can visit Monterey for its pines and contorted cypresses, or climb the Santa Lucias for their little-known firs.

If I lived in central California I should make a speciality of the lily family, amongst all the wild flowers of that region. For there and in the northern part of the State, this tribe of exquisites reaches its highest development on the continent of North America. Of the lily genus itself there are eight fine species here, and an equal number of fritillaries, those strange little blooms, sometimes yellow or white, sometimes scarlet or purple or even brown (one of the rarest of flower colors), which pass by such a variety of names as checkered lily, mission-bells, brownbells, and chocolate lily. Numbering no less than eighteen species are those lovely little flowers generically called Brodiaea. They are perhaps the analogue of the squills of the Mediterranean flora—mostly blue or lavender or purple, sometimes white, or even yellow (as in the golden star) and in one notable species, the firecracker-flower, scarlet. You find them everywhere—in the open fields, in woodlands, in deep forest, by the roadside, on the mountainsides—a lovely throng. Perhaps they made a deep impression on me because the first Californian wild flower I ever gathered was one of these, the harvest-bell that I found burning bluely in the stubble, of a golden blazing June afternoon near Woodside. I thought I had never seen so fair a flower in so casual a role. I seemed to have come to a land where the very weeds had something ethereal about them! Not wholly true, alas, but a case of love at first sight.

But fairest of all the lily family must be reckoned the many kinds of Calochortus. It is the western representative, perhaps, of the Old World tulip, but far more delicate in form and color. How many forms it takes may be judged from the names for the different species: fairylantern, star tulip, pussy-ears, lily bell, satinbells, sego lily, Mormon lily, and Mariposa ("butterfly," of course, in Spanish). There are Mariposas or Calochortus all over the West, but northern and central California is their favorite home, and each valley or mountain range may have its own enchanting species.

Truly there is no finer place one can go for wild flowers than the region about San Francisco Bay. A delightful account of the amenities of collecting thereabout will be found in the *Scientific Monthly* for October, 1929, in an article by Frederic Bioletti on amateur botanizing.

One may well read this for its humor and for its pictures of famous California scientists of a generation ago.

THE REDWOOD EMPIRE

Now we quit the world of fields and field flowers, of sunny open valleys and bare sun-bitten crags, and for the first time we enter a forest—such a forest indeed that it stretches for more than a thousand miles in a north-and-south direction, one of the greatest stands of merchantable timber in the world. And we begin with the coast redwoods, Sequoia sempervirens, the ever-living sequoia. For redwoods are a whole world in themselves, and they reach further south than any of the other great forest formations of the northwest coast.

As the so-called Big Trees (Sequoia gigantea) belong to the Sierra Nevada, even so do the coast redwoods—*the* redwoods, strictly speaking—belong to the Coast Range. Indeed they are its greatest pride and glory, its most notable single botanical feature.

Redwoods range all the way from extreme southwestern Oregon southward for four hundred and fifty miles. Their narrow belt averages only twenty miles in width, and is sometimes close to the sea, but, again, it may be thirty or forty miles inland as it follows the wandering crest of the Coast Ranges. Redwoods ascend to some three thousand feet in the mountains.

From San Francisco to the Oregon line the main belt is almost unbroken, though inland there is a parallel chain of redwood "islands" wherever there are fog pockets. Indeed the redwood is not found anywhere outside the reach of the summer sea fogs which, by saturating the atmosphere in the dry season, cut down the loss of water from the leaves and are thus the equivalent of a larger rainfall supplied to the roots.

The redwood reappears on the San Francisco peninsula in a scattered way and there, indeed, is located the southernmost grove of gigantic specimens, near Santa Cruz. Redwoods in the south make a final stand in the Santa Lucia Mountains and may be seen in the precipitous gorges that plunge toward the sea along the San Simeon Highway. But they take on odd shapes there, with broad flat tops and wide branches. There are no redwoods growing outside of cultivation south of Monterey County.

The great redwood belt from San Francisco to the Oregon line has been called the Redwood Empire, and it merits the name. The readily workable wood is smooth and even of grain, producing boards with handsome color and fine luster. Preserved from decay by the tannin in it, redwood is, moreover, not subject to attack by termites and is valued for this reason in the far-off tropics. The first railroads of California were laid on redwood ties. In redwood cradles were rocked the pioneers' babies. Redwood telephone poles carry the Californian's voice. Redwood boxes enclose the agricultural products of California. California's famous wines are kept in redwood vats because this wood imparts no flavor of its own to the wine, to spoil it. Redwood has built many of the homes and towns of California. Probably the first man to be buried in a redwood coffin—certainly the first famous one—was saintly old Padre Junípero Serra, in 1784, founder of the initial nine of California's missions. The sorrowing Indians, it is said, gathered wild flowers from the fields about Carmel and laid them on the redwood casket.

THOUSAND-YEAR-OLD GROVES

This is a chapter about wild flowers and not about trees, but when trees reach the size of redwoods they cease to be merely trees; they correspond to mountains in their profound modification of the climate beneath them; they are, practically, a natural force or a whole environment in themselves, and the little wild flowers blooming so palely and fragilely beneath the redwoods and having, many of them, affinities with the flora of Alaska, have little in common with the riot of color in the open sunny fields whose floral kinship is likely to be with the Mediterranean.

Of all the trees on the Pacific coast, the most world-renowned are the redwoods. With their close relatives the Big Trees (which are not found here but up in the Sierra Nevada), these sequoias constitute a unique phenomenon among the wonders of the earth. Nothing else that lives dares compare itself with the titan proportions and staggering antiquity of these trees. Even a man, with all his self-esteem, cannot nod his head at a sequoia and say, "I am greater than that."

For redwoods can boast diameters of from twelve to sixteen feet (that is, a girth of more than twenty-five feet). They are the tallest trees in the world. commonly reaching three hundred feet and sometimes

three hundred and sixty. No other trees with valuable wood can regularly produce so many board feet of fine timber to the acre. Though they are not so long-lived as the big trees, the coast redwoods are known to live a thousand years and perhaps some attain twice ten centuries.

Bret Harte once said that the coast redwoods were the "poor relations" of the big trees. Let us yield the crown to the Big Trees for craggy grandeur. But if it is beauty we are discussing, the Big Trees are only the kings of trees—the coast redwoods are queens!

With their richly red bark, the mighty boles give an air of cheer and warmth to the interior of a sequoia grove not equaled by any other forest type I have ever seen. The ferny, flat sprays of redwood foliage, rather like that of hemlock or yew, are softly gleaming. The airy, benignant, down-sweeping of the boughs is unexpectedly graceful in so colossal a tree. And I know of no other members of the vegetable kingdom which, to humans, seem so living, individual, and oracularly inhabited. It is interesting to watch a group of people entering a grove of ancient redwoods and to see how everyone—not only children, who might be expected to have such intuitions, but even adults—will knock on the resounding armor of the ruddy bark and then turn their faces up to the crowned heads of the trees, as if expecting a deep voice of answer, or at least a nod. But millennial redwoods, though just as living as we, take no cognizance of our May-fly existences. They do not look down at us; they may look back—only a mystic could say.

Of all God's great out-of-doors, the groves of thousand-year-old redwoods are most like something man might have dreamed of making. It is inevitable to compare them to temples, with their clean and level floors, their straight and close-ranked columns, their long aisles. Or to cathedrals, with their narrowed Gothic windows to the sky, the pointed arches of their vault, the darkness and hush of their interiors, and the wandering puffs of fog, like incense, through which the sun sends down shafts of holy light. But never was nave so long, nor clerestory so lofty, never spire so near the heaven to which it points; never were columns so great, so many, so ancient, or so ruddy.

To step out of the brilliant California sunlight, where birds and men call loudly and speed brightly, into the astounding dimness and silence of one of these mighty groves is like entering a room—infinitely lofty —and closing a door behind you. The sheer overwhelming vertical

strength and the sense of sanctity in this place lay two fingers on the restless pulses and bid them be quiet. The impression of hoary antiquity is quaintly enhanced by the spider webs that, like a fluttering gray napery, enshroud the crevices of the red bark.

Here your footfalls make no noise upon the century-old carpet of needles. Yet some few sounds there are—the gossip of a stream on its stones, the note, like a blurred whistle, of the black-throated gray warbler and the slow, passing sigh of the great canopy itself, as the sea wind moves rememberingly among the boughs.

So lofty are the groves that the tops of the trees may actually emerge from the fog into sunlight while the cloud, ghostly silent, flows on the forest floor. Again, the fog may cling to the upper levels of the forest, and the foliage may collect, mechanically, the moist particles and precipitate them in the form of a delicate rain which bedews the mosses and ferns two hundred feet and more below.

This, then, is one case where forests actually do attract or cause rainfall. It has been denied that trees can do this, but it is certainly true in the case of redwoods. In other ways, too, redwoods create a climate and regulate weather. For the interior of a great redwood grove may be stirred by breezes but it is seldom actually windy. The amount of humidity may change considerably and quite visibly when the sea fog rolls in, but, even so, the change is doubtless much less than in many places, and changes of temperature are surprisingly slight. Spring is late in the redwoods, but then so is winter. In fact the seasons seem never to come quite, and never quite to go. But for the autumnal coloration of the maples, shining like golden windows down the dim architraves of the redwood cathedral, one could have little knowledge that fall was at hand.

The very quality of the daylight seems altered in the redwood groves. They are not actually dark except where, among young redwoods, still growing close, there is a crowding in of somber trees like Douglas fir and California laurel. (Then you really do get a black-out, entirely too dim and stuffy for *my* taste!) But the light in which the leaves of the forest plants must function is remarkably subdued as, in long, smoky shafts, it falls from the top of the forest canopy to some great altar-like log overlaid with the most exquisite lacework of mosses I have ever seen. It is as if the sunlight had changed more as to quality and quantity

in passing through the redwood canopy, two hundred feet or more over-head, and through the errant drifts of vapor from the never-distant ocean than in all its flight from the sun star to the planet and the tree-tops. And this, indeed, is probably the case.

Finally, it should be said that among the redwoods the creeks never cease from running—in sharp distinction from the water systems of the part of California called sunny. Here (and hereafter all through the rest of this chapter) the stream flow must be thought of as constant and, on the whole, remarkably regular. This implies not only abundant rain-fall but a deep carpet of humus and moss acting like a great sponge or an infinitely porous reservoir.

So in all respects the redwood habitat is exquisitely tempered, per-haps the most truly "temperate" environment in the world, outside of a cold frame or a cave or a sea grotto—a world as nearly changeless as one could expect.

The venerable age of the redwoods leaves one with the impression that they have been growing where we find them from the beginning of time. Actually, as geologic time is reckoned, they are comparative new-comers in their present site. The botanical genus Sequoia, once number-ing perhaps ten or more species, goes back to the Tertiary and even to the Cretaceous, well back in the Middle Ages of plant life on earth. The ancestors or relatives of our two sequoias were scattered far and wide in the north temperate zone; some lived in Alaska, some in Labrador, some in Siberia, some in western Europe, and some in what is now the desert of Turkestan. But fifty million years ago there were none in California. For here, in far-off times, flourished a forest whose relatives today are best represented in the moist tropics.

Then the Ice Age, which drove the tropical forest out of California, likewise exterminated all but the two extant sequoias, and these found asylum where we know them today: the big trees in the Sierra Nevada of eastern California, and the redwoods in the Coast Ranges. With the redwoods, it is reasonable to suppose, came all the wild flowers, ferns, and mosses that still grow at their feet—a band of refugees from a once-widespread flora found generally around the north temperate zone.

So they all existed here together—giant trees and delicate herbs—in secret as it were, or at least unknown to Europeans and to science until on Tuesday, March 26, 1776, Friar Pedro Font, Franciscan chronicler

of d'Anza's exploration party to San Francisco Bay, records that he beheld "a few spruce trees which they call red wood (*palo colorado*), a tree that is very beautiful; and I believe it is very useful for its timber, for it is very straight and tall." On March 29 the explorers descried near San Francisquito Creek a redwood "rising like a great tower," and next day came to its foot. The good father calculated the tree to be fifty varas high (137 feet and 6 inches). This tree still stands at Palo Alto; indeed the name of the locality in Spanish signifies "tall tree."

GREAT TREES, MINUTE FLOWERS

In this softened, emerald light, in this mild temperature, and this frequent fine rain, there flourishes a little flora of much charm. It is little in more than one sense. First, the number of species is quite surprisingly small, as if this were a closed and choice society, unwilling to tolerate any intrusions of a crasser or less pedigreed sort. And, at the same time, it completely fills up the limited environment, with a plant of some sort—be it lichen, moss, fern, or flower—to fit every niche. In short, there is a constant redwood flora, always present wherever the great tree is predominant. However, the wild flowers of the redwoods are not, on the whole, peculiar to this habitat. Many range far north to British Columbia and Alaska, and they even show their kinship with the forest flowers of Siberia and northern Europe.

Again, the redwood wild flowers are, many of them, little in stature as well as variety, as if the colossal trees had used up all the bigness allotted by Nature. Tiny flowers, tiny stature are almost the rule; even the cones of the redwood are astonishingly small for the mammoth tree. The wild flower cover on the forest floor, when one looks down at it after gazing up at the titanic proportions of the trees, appears to be seen through the wrong end of a telescope. The ferns are the only really big herbaceous plants. The sword fern, perching on every fallen redwood log and every hummock, is very nearly tropical in luxuriance. The chain fern grows lushly, too, and summer glades are often brimming with big bracken.

Perhaps the commonest of all the flowering plants is the redwood sorrel, the Oregon oxalis, that often carpets every foot of ground, far as eye can see, with its bright green shamrock leaves. To make a path in the redwoods all you have to do is tramp down this sorrel with its

dainty, veined flowers. The path seems to remain forever, the obliging plant carpeting all else but leaving you your way.

Almost as common as the oxalis is the inside-out-flower, with leaves like maidenhair fern, and a fleck of tiny blooms like a dash of sea spray. Everywhere you remark, too, the sugarscoop and the deerfoot—named for the shapes of their leaves, but alike in the airy, misty bits of bloom they produce—mere will-o'-the-wisps drifting away under the somber trees. In common most of these plants have white or nearly white petals. Color is a rarity found in the bleeding heart, the redwood rose, and the redwood lily. And there are other flowers you see and yet only half believe in—the phantom orchid, the coralroot, the windflower dancing down the canyons, the wild ginger with its little jug-shaped flowers half hidden in the very earth.

Where there is a growth of shrubs beneath the trees, life is less ethereal. There are sudden superb banks of rose-bay (a purple-flowering rhododendron) and of an intensely fragrant azalea, both of which re-mind one of the Carolina wild flowers. In fact one cannot fail to see, in azalea, rhododendron, sweet shrub (Calycanthus), trillium, wild ginger and a beautiful, starry white dogwood, something distinctly Appalachian about the redwoods' associates.

OREGON VERDURE

For all the grandeur of California's redwood groves, to travel north-ward up the Oregon coast in June brings no disappointment. The south-western part of Oregon has what is possibly the richest flora in the State. Thus Josephine County boasts seventeen species of conifers (cone-bearing trees of the pine family) and southwestern Oregon generally can show twenty-three species of these kingly trees—a record, if I am not mistaken, unequaled by any part of the world of comparable size. And what trees! Besides occasional groves of redwood, there are vast forests of Douglas fir, second only to the sequoias in height; and of western hemlocks, the largest of all their tribe; of the enormous Sitka spruce, the grand fir, the giant or canoe cedar, and the rare weeping spruce. And you may be so lucky as to find a few of the Port Orford cedars, whose white wood, having a fragrance of roses, used to be in such demand for coffins in the Orient that there is, one might fancy, as much of it underground in China as above it in Oregon. Destructive

fires have almost completed the reduction of this most exquisite cabinet wood in America—of which most Americans have never even heard.

In addition to the conifers, Oregon has a number of broad-leaved trees or hardwoods; some evergreens like the laurel and the madroña; and others such as the Oregon blue oak, the ash, and, above all, the Oregon maple, which are deciduous and display beautiful tints in autumn. Most of the hardwoods are in the canyons or close to water, or on burned-over land. The conifers occupy the mountain ridges, far as the eye can see.

The whole makes a marvelous forest cover, mixed hardwoods and conifers, somewhat as in the Appalachians but far grander and wilder and more lushly green. In fact I do not know a spot on earth more delightfully forested than the Coast Ranges of Oregon. The big timber of the Olympic Peninsula is in some places much denser, and the California redwoods are more awe-inspiring. But both are almost crushing in their grandeur. The Oregon coast woods, on the other hand, are livable and lovable. Everywhere there are rushing streams, sometimes cascades, always cool glades, and the most delicious mingling of mountain air, sea air, and forest air in all the world.

After the trees themselves, the dominant vegetation is not flowering plants but ferns and mosses. So that it is of a green world, rather than a flowery one, that the traveler returned from coastal Oregon brings back memories. Learning to know the mosses properly is, I confess, one part of my botany lesson I have shirked, though I can recognize some of them generically, calling their names that sound like those of elves: Grimmia, Sphagnum, Mnium, Hypnum, and Bryum; but I should think Oregon would be a bryologist's happy hunting ground. Certainly it is a prime place for ferns. Sword fern and deer fern, big bracken and an Oregon selaginella of almost tropical luxuriance cover the ground everywhere and mount upon the fallen logs.

In these woods one sees banks of an immense leaf that everyone asks about—the umbrella plant. It seems to have no more flowers than a fern. That is because the flowers appear in earliest spring and then wither away before the leaves come out. Everyone asks, too, about the shrub with pleasing red berries. But it is not pleasant to get into this briery bush, for it is the devil's-club, whose thorns deal painful wounds. It is all very well when you can see the shrub, but at night the wood-

wanderer may soon have his clothes and flesh torn to ribbons by devil's-club.

According to a legend of certain Oregon Indians, a hero, in escaping the wrath of an evil spirit or giant, hurled behind him a thicket of devil's-club, in which his pursuer became grievously entangled. The story of "The Magic Flight," involving not only briery bushes but mountains and lakes and other obstacles the hero hurls behind him, is an ancient and a widespread legend which, something like certain of Oregon's wild flowers, is circumpolar, and is diffused from Siberia all the way to South America, passing through geographical, language, race, and culture barriers, as if they were no obstacle to a good story, no matter how old.

Indeed, Oregon plants of all sorts are thickly encrusted with Indian legends and Indian names. Many of these were adopted by the pioneers who came to a new flora with no nomenclature of their own for it. So people still use such names as ookow (for a brodiaea), wapatoo (for arrowhead), sego (pronounced *seego,* from *pah-see-go,* a name for Mormon lily), camass or quamash (for a hyacinthine marsh flower), wokas (for a cow lily or spatterdock), and yampa (for a sort of wild caraway whose roots, discovered and grubbed up by the faithful Indian girl, Sacajawea, often fed the Lewis and Clark Expedition, when all else failed).

Though these names come from various Indian languages, the plants have much in common, for they are all edible, all valuable food plants around which centered much religion, dance, song, and magic of the aborigines. Those food resources were so good that they created here exceptionally stable instead of nomadic Indian societies. Although there was game in the woods and the menfolk did hunt it, there was surprisingly little, according to Lewis and Clark, who can certainly be said to have seen aboriginal conditions. Rather did the large Indian populations depend on vegetable diet, notably the roots, tubers, and bulbs of the plants just mentioned. They did not cultivate them, or not usually, but the womenfolk did harvest a great number of native foods, far more indeed than I could enumerate. At any rate, the native flora is either remarkably edible, or else these Indian women were remarkably experimental and persistent herbalists.

One of their discoveries, at least, has not been neglected—that of the

bark of the cascara tree, used medicinally all over the world. The Spanish padres learned at an early date to appreciate a related species, and it was they who named it *cáscara sagrada,* or "sacred bark." Cascara trees (really a kind of buckthorn) are still stripped, in summer, by seasonal labor, as quinine and cinnamon bark are stripped in tropic lands, and you see signs in the woods, advertising for cascara barkers, at the peak of the employment period.

FOREST SPRITES

It must not be thought that there is only greenery and no fair flowering in the coastal mountains of Oregon. True, there are fewer massed effects. There are not the riotous colors and pert forms of southern California flowers. These and the brilliant families that produce them have to be foregone by our forest blooms, which draw so many of their numbers from the saxifrage, ranunculus, rose, and heath families. White is the usual color; the deep rose-purple of the salmonberry is exceptional. Fragrance instead of color becomes the prevalent mode of seduction. The very foliage of the deerleaf is fragrant in drying, for it is rich in the chemical coumarin, found in sweet grass and vanilla. So the pioneers named it sweet-after-death and hung its herbage from their rafters.

But though these flowers rest their charms upon their air of innocence, most of them are not so utterly meek nor so unearthly fragile as the flora that fairly cringes at the redwoods' feet. The heavier rainfall but much less fog and more sun of southwestern Oregon make for a vigorous growth—herbs often tall and lush, flowering branches flinging wide their arms. To typify them I would choose that abundant, refreshing flower so well named ocean spray. You find it flung up all through the woods or breaking over a lichened boulder or seething down a bank, a foam-castle of bloom, a drift of spume on the forest wind.

For the first time on this journey, orchids become frequent. For orchids, if they can't have the wet tropics, prefer the north woods. Certainly there is nothing fairer in the world than the lady's-slipper of Oregon or the pink cytherea, justly named for the Cytherean Venus.

Still I have said nothing of Oregon's State flower, the Oregon grape, so-called. It may be known to you already in eastern or European gardens, where, under the nurseryman's name of mahonia, it is a favorite

plant of the formal suburban driveway on account of its lacquered-looking evergreen leaves, precocious bright gold flowers, and handsome, heavy, dark blue berries. In its native state, however, the leaves of this evergreen barberry are picked like holly by the country people and sold at Christmas. Mountain people make an excellent grape-flavored jelly from the berries, and the yellow roots are sought by the pharmaceutical collectors for their medicinal value.

The gardener from the East may exclaim, as at sight of a truant child, to see the foxglove leaning tall along the roadsides of Oregon. This seems far from home for this favorite of the perennial border, Digitalis purpurea, well-known to the pharmacist, oft mentioned by Shakespeare, and sacred to the fairies (for "foxglove" is a corruption of "folks' glove," that is, the wee folk). Foxglove is perfectly naturalized here, mile upon mile of it seeming to melt against the forest background, though actually you never find it except along the roads. It is a native, of course, of Europe, at home in the Norwegian forest, in England and Denmark, in the Thuringian Forest, and far-off Transylvania. Here it has become self-sown from northern California to Washington, and northward now we shall follow it.

OLYMPIC MAJESTY

On the Fourth of July, 1788, the mists of the strait of Juan de Fuca rolled away, and Captain John Meares from the deck of his exploring vessel beheld a vision of congested peaks rising out of the sea, above a dark green band of forest, mantled in the purest snow. Old salt that he was, and probably by no means poetic or given to hyperbole, he cried that they were mountains fit for the abode of gods. And he slapped them down on his chart as the Olympic Mountains. Thus, fittingly, have they been called ever since.

On the roster of altitudes the Olympics are not high among the mountains of this world. Mount Olympus, the tallest of them, just tops eight thousand feet. But every bit of its eight thousand one hundred and fifty feet is mountain. I mean that Mount Olympus, like the whole Olympic Range, rises up from sea level, in soaring majesty. So it stands nearly as high above the observer at the shore as does Pikes Peak above Colorado Springs which is already six thousand feet high on the Great Plains. A mountain may be said to be as high as it looks, and by that standard

the Olympics need not bow their white heads to every upstart range that seems to challenge them.

The beauty of the Olympics is a thing of many parts and circumstances. First there is the magnificence of their situation on a great peninsula, in base area about as large as Massachusetts, surrounded by the open ocean, by the strait of Juan de Fuca and Puget Sound and, everywhere, winding inlets and fiords, bays and sounds.

Then there is the deep clothing of forest, the greatest stand of coniferous timber in the world, most of the trees conifers other than pine. Nothing can express the density or the unbroken extent of primeval grandeur of these Sitka spruces, western hemlocks, giant canoe cedars, grand or tideland spruce, and, most titanic of all, the Douglas firs, second only to the sequoias. This forest, at once very dark and glittering, every serrated lance point of it gleaming, completely swathes the bases of the mountains and seems almost to besiege them, scaling their flanks in solid masses and sending long sallies up the ridges. They make a rich contrast with the caps of perpetual ice and snow that surmount the higher peaks. When the gods up there do not wrap themselves in clouds, these snows shine with a dreamy purity—not sharply as on the Rockies, but through a softer air, forever heavy with moisture from the Pacific close at hand.

Although Mount Washington in New Hampshire is only a little further south, and quite as high as some of the Olympics which wear perpetual snows, it has snow only in winter. In summer its summit shows bald rocks. The reason for the Olympic snowcaps is that the prevailing westerlies, sweeping in from the north Pacific, surcharged with moisture, drop upon this, the first high mountain range they come to, a tremendous precipitation—up to 140 inches. At high altitudes most of this comes down in the form of snow. So more snow falls in winter than can be melted in summer. Under these conditions glaciers form in some spots, and there are more than fifty of these glittering ice rivers still lurking in the recesses of the Olympics.

I say "still" because in the Glacial period there were undoubtedly many more. Furthermore, a tremendous ice field sweeping down from the Cascades crossed what is now Puget Sound and shoved its snout, like a cold monster, far up on the eastern flanks of the Olympics. All the upper levels of the Olympic Ranges are deeply ice-carved and scoured,

resulting in true alpine scenery, and setting the stage for an arctic-alpine flora—the only such to be found in the Coast Ranges within the borders of the United States.

Only hastily here can we pass through the great forest zone. The wild flowers found within it are very much the same as those described for the mountains of Oregon. Others are identical with certain ones in the north woods of New England and the Adirondacks, and still more are found at tide level far up the Alaskan coast. One can but speak in passing of the rose-purple blooms of the great fireweed and the banked masses of Washington's State flower, the purple rhododendron, which brings thousands out, in season, from the towns and cities to admire it. Everywhere in these lower woods you see shallon or salal, a fine shrub whose berries were a chief vegetable in the diet of many of the Indian tribes, and are made by white settlers into pies, much as blueberries are, "back East." Salal is closely related to the eastern wintergreen.

On we go, through the so-called Canadian zone, with its mountain hemlock and western white pine, up to the Hudsonian zone, where the trees, all of them conifers now, become smaller and smaller. However, as they go on living just as long as other trees, though their stems are so stunted, their growth is ingrowing, that is, they go in for intricacy and twigginess. In the Alps this sort of a formation is called the *Krummholz* or dwarfed wood, and perhaps knowledgeable alpinists use that word for it here—if they don't use a much worse word for it. Though the *Krummholz* is all very picturesque if someone has laboriously cut a trail through it, it is a cruel experience to try to wriggle or crush your own unbroken way, as I can testify.

PARNASSIAN PASTURES

But the reward of passing through such a Sleeping-Beauty tangle is to come out upon the enchantment of the subalpine meadows which bloom at their height in July and August. The day when you step out in the thin mountain air upon such bright little parterres, thick enameled with their close society of bloom, each plant in its little station so intent on its brief but supreme purpose—such a day, I say, the plantsman lives for, and he never forgets it. I could sit down today and write out a list of the plants I saw on the "alpine gardens" of Mount Washington,

twenty-six years ago, though I have never been back since. Indeed I can remember the hour and date—about three in the afternoon of the first of August, 1919. I can recall all the flowers I gathered in the Col du Lauteret in the Savoy Alps, in the summer of 1929. I am not saying there is anything unusual about my memory; it is the flowers that are unusual. Any plantsman worth his salt would appreciate his opportunities if he found himself in the Tuolomne Meadows of Yosemite or Logan Pass in Glacier Park. And he would remember every floral detail.

Orthodox botany requires us to make a distinction between the subalpine zone, which is found in the Olympics between thirty-five hundred and five thousand feet, where the flowers are thick-spangled and are found growing in a fairly deep, well-watered soil, and the zone of the true arctic-alpines which lies above five thousand feet, where plants frequently grow on desolate crags with almost no visible soil at all. Not only are the two floras composed, largely, of different species, but the whole look and feel of the two places is different. The flora of the subalpine meadows, such as I have been describing, is far richer. There are not only the meadows but the forest and the *Krummholz,* and there are many tiny glacial lakes or cirques around which flowers are found, and even little bogs and swamps.

In these meadows the most conspicuous plant is likely to be the bear grass, whose great white heads of bloom are a favorite subject with western mountain photographers. It is no true grass, of course, but a member of the lily family, with strangely grassy leaves that, very tough and enduring, used to be woven into watertight baskets by the Indian women, whence the alternative name of squaw grass, though the squaws called it *quip-quip.* It is said, too, though I do not know it to be so, that in early spring bears are fond of pawing up the roots for food. Chipmunks and squirrels cut down the young shoots; elk are said to eat the mature leaves. And certain tourists pick the great flowering stalks, since such a mass of bloom even the most oblivious cannot miss. So bear grass gets more than its share of attention as it lights up the mountain meadow with its white candelabra.

Next in showiness, but quite surpassing in loveliness, are the avalanche lilies that burst from their bulbs at the very edge of the melting snow banks, and go dancing down to timber line. They are kin to the trout lily or dogtooth violet of the eastern States. In such wild gardens you

may come, too, on shooting stars and pentstemons and lupine, all of which will remind you of the fields of southern California. Here you will find larkspur and paintbrush, to recall to you high days on the mountains of Colorado. And, to make you think of the Alps, fragile anemones and tremulous white stars of saxifrage.

True, none of the species is strictly the same as those found in the Alps, for absolute identity is characteristic of the zone above this, but not of the subalpine. Yet out of ninety-five genera growing in this zone, fifty-eight are also found in the Alps.

Indeed the subalpine world, wherever you find it, is much the same. For it is a world in itself, one literally removed to a higher level and out of our ordinary reach. Always there is the same sense of the intensity and brevity of flowering, the sharp contrast between the short alpine summer and the long alpine day. It is long both because these mountains are situated so far north, and because the sun does not set so soon when observed from a high altitude. And then there is the marvelous alpine afterglow, the *Gegenschein*, that wells up from one can't say where and is reflected back and forth between glacier and bare rock cliff.

And always there are the flowers themselves, in the steeply pitched garden, all leaning one way, or many of them winking shut at the passing of a cloud, for alpine wild flowers are frequently photosensitive. Or you may see them all winnowing and rippling before the Tartar sword of the wind. Or when the wind is still, you may see them individually ducking and bobbing as the bees, that come from no one ever knows where, on blue days, tumble them or pry open their lips in satisfying themselves at the nectaries and performing pollination upon the stigmas.

The large size of alpine and subalpine flowers gives one the impression, indeed, that the whole plant lives only for this hour. Not all alpine flowers are actually outsize, but many of them appear so by a contrast between the unreduced corolla and the greatly diminished stature of the plant as a whole. Leaves are often very small, or narrow and grassy, or inrolled; stems are frequently prostrate, or very short, or subterranean, or even nonexistent so that all the leaves lie flat on the ground, in a basal rosette, while the flower stalk serves like a little, short, annual stem.

A familiar example of the rosette type is the common dandelion weed. You will say that is no alpine. However, most of the dandelions of the world are alpines, the vulgar and ubiquitous species being but a lowland outcast and tramp of this highland clan. The Olympic Mountains, indeed, have an alpine dandelion of their own, quite peculiar to their high altitudes. Such plants, known only from a given environment or range, are called endemics. The Olympics, though much poorer in species than Mount Rainier or the Cascades generally, are fairly rich in endemics, at least at high altitudes.

In the true alpine zone another form of adaptation in plant forms becomes common. That is the "pincushion" type of plant (as one might describe it), a dense, usually rounded, and very twiggy growth—sometimes a colony of plants—usually with evergreen, and sometimes very woolly leaves, which probably furnish the maximum of protection for the buds in a region that has also the maximum of snowfall. From the top of these cushions, in the brief alpine summer, bloom the little flowers, lifted so insouciantly aloft to such high winds and such rare visitants.

Conditions in the highest zone of all, where true arctic-alpine plants are found, are so severe that only a chosen few can endure them, and those few seem to have a way of turning up all around the world in similar spots. Up here on the arid crags, plants find any niche they can. Occasionally there are small patches of turf, alpine grasses, and sedges that whistle thinly in the breeze that never seems to stop up there, as if it were the wind of the planet's turning. Most of the flowers belong to the family of the Compositæ; edelweiss is the most famous Alpine example of it, though it does not grow here.

Often these arctic-alpines are found *above* the snow and ice—that is, on declivities too steep to hold ice and snow. In such places conditions are unsurpassed even by the severity and low temperatures of the arctic zone, as to high wind velocities, excessive aridity, and lack of soil. Here the best adapted of all plants are probably certain mosses such as Grimmia and Andreaea.

Setting, certainly, has much to do with the surpassing charm of alpine wild flowers. The miles—hundreds or even thousands—that you may have come before you ever reach the base of the mountain, the weeks of preparation and anticipation, the study of contour maps and the location of ascent trails, the exertion of the climb itself, the passage through

the deep forest, the emergence at last, breathless and weary, on some flowering slope, in the empyrean noon—these are all part of the price you pay for the flowers themselves, when at last you fling yourself down upon them. And when you pluck from its stem the little corolla, so cunningly twisted to its purpose, so innocent in its complete seduction, so brief in its desperate tenure upon the hours, the very minutes, of the alpine day, you realize that you, too, in a few hours, or a few minutes, must depart. You must leave all these to the winding sheet of snows so soon to come. You must go back to tide level or approximately that, where Nature evidently fitted the human animal to live. And you cannot know when, if ever, you will tread again the grass of Parnassus.

GLIMPSES OF WILD LIFE

BY AUBREY DRURY

Glimpses are all that one gets of wild life, but that very fact makes the subject intriguing. It is comforting to know that the last grizzly died more than a decade ago and that lesser bears are hard to discover. Yet this chapter warns us that two types of skunks may be met with. The chapter is full of animal secrets. (R. P.)

Where the redwood forests sweep away southward from Del Norte through Humboldt and Mendocino, covering the lower mountains and riverside flats with a mantle ever green, a vast redwood belt with outlying fragments such as Muir Woods upon the seaward flank of Tamalpais and the Big Basin in the Santa Cruz Mountains; where, above those delectable mountains, lifts the crest of dark Loma Prieta; where the Little Sur River splashes down its canyon around Pico Blanco's base, and the Big Sur out of the heart of the Sierra Santa Lucia; where Junipero Serra Peak spires mile-high, and, fronting the Pacific, the mountain wall rises almost sheer above the resounding surf line; where the pinnacles are upthrust amid grotesque badlands; along south in the Sierra Santa Ynez, back of Santa Barbara; in the Sierra Madre, the San Bernardino Mountains, and still southward to Palomar and Cuyamaca and the hinter-highlands of San Diego—throughout all the magnificent reach of the Coast Ranges, despite the depletion of some species, wild life yet is to be found "in God's plenty."

Of the life zones of California, as set forth by the scientists, most are represented in the Coast Ranges. The diversity of wild life to be readily observed is a pleasant feature of a sojourn in many parts of the mountains, though no one, even if lying in wait within a wild-life refuge or bird sanctuary, is likely to see a majority of the furred and feathered creatures. Many are nocturnal in their habits, and are observed in daylight only by rare chance. Many are, as one mountain man said, "wery wary" of humans—for cause.

Even a motorist, however, hurrying along hill-country roads will note

79

some of the wild life characteristic of the region, and a wanderer in the woods and mountains will soon come to know many of the typical animals and birds. Here "meeting the mammals," to use the inviting phrase of Victor Cahalane, is in many instances not difficult. They are perhaps best known to naturalists and to high-aspiring walkers, such as the members of the Sierra Club, who hike in the Coast Ranges as well as through the loftier Sierra Nevada.

Besides the hunters and anglers who frequent the far-reaching ranges (it is estimated that about a million hunting and fishing licenses will be issued next year in California), there are a great many who wander through the wilds armed with nothing more formidable than a trail map, a camera, or a field glass.

The fur-bearing animals which are trapped nowadays in California are taken mostly by some country schoolboys and ranch hands, by professional trappers for Government agencies, and by a few private trappers. In the pioneer times occasionally the fur brigades of the Hudson's Bay Company, as well as outfits led by venturesome American mountain men, penetrated the more northerly ranges for furs. Hostile Indians and grizzly bears beset their paths. Before these trappers and hunters, the parties of early explorers—Cabrillo, Drake, Vizcaíno, Portolá, Anza, Fages, Vancouver and many another stalwart captain, besides Junípero Serra, Lasuén and the Franciscans who traversed the rugged wilderness embracing today that national forest named for them Los Padres—made first wondering acquaintance with most of the beasts and birds now so familiar.

THE GREAT GRIZZLY AND OTHER BEARS

Over all the coastal highlands lingers the dominating memory of a mighty animal now no longer living, so far as is known—the California grizzly bear. Around San Luis Obispo the Spanish explorers in 1769 discovered "herds" of fierce bears, evidently monster grizzlies. To a bear-infested glen here they gave the name Los Osos, The Bears, which it still retains, and similar place names are scattered on the map all the way to Bear Buttes and Grizzly Bluff in Humboldt County, in California's northwest.

In the San Luis Obispo region and elsewhere the *vaqueros* of the Spanish and Mexican period hunted the *osos* from horseback, often with

lariats or lassos. Some of the captured monarchs were fated to be central figures in fierce bear-and-bull fights acclaimed noisily by the populace. Still stranger were the bear-and-burro fights. The grizzly won in these cruel contests, but the tough Mexican burros sometimes put up terrific battles with their hoofs and teeth.

George Nidever, famous mountain man and sea otter hunter, who turned bear hunter in that rugged San Luis Obispo region, recounted his adventures to one of Hubert Howe Bancroft's historian aides. Telling how he had killed forty-five grizzly bears there in the year 1837, Nidever pointed out that "the natives hunted them occasionally but, for their mode of hunting, with the *lasso,* required open ground, while the grizzly seldom left the thickets and timber." Nidever sometimes rode into the very midst of bands of grizzlies—once, "four full-grown bears" —though he says, "one of my rules was never to go into a thicket if I *knew* it contained a bear. I killed some very large ones, and one in particular whose skin I sold to one of the trading vessels. It was much larger than any bullock's hide they took on board." Altogether, Nidever figured that he had killed upward of two hundred grizzlies.

Several old-time accounts tell of grizzlies estimated to weigh as much as two thousand pounds, but Dr. E. Raymond Hall, who has explored the question with keen interest, thinks that twelve hundred pounds was about the maximum heft for the California grizzly. The captive "Monarch," a great grizzly seen by thousands (I was one, a mite among them), was in that weight class.

One of the hunter companions of Nidever, called Black Steward (his name was Allen Light, though he was dark-skinned, a Negro from a Boston ship, "The Pilgrim"), had a bloody encounter with a grizzly bear. "Black Steward wounded a deer and got off his horse to crawl up and finish it," recalled the old mountain man. "In passing through a clump of bushes a small she-bear jumped on him, and before he could defend himself, knocked him down. He was a strong, powerful man, and immediately grappled with the bear. They rolled over and over for several yards, the bear biting him very severely in several places, and tearing his coat in pieces.

"Watching a favorable opportunity, he attempted to draw his knife, when the bear bit him in the forearm, tearing out some of the cords. At this moment, hearing her cubs cry, she raised up on her hind legs, when

Black Steward seized his gun and shot her, breaking her back. He did not stop to finish her but made for camp. The bite in his arm was very bad, and he was scratched and bruised all over. Sparks (another hunter) went to the place next day and finding the bear still alive killed her. He said that for a space of over ten yards square the bushes were broken down and the ground torn up, where Black Steward had fought with the grizzly."

Some of the bears formerly called cinnamons were undoubtedly grizzlies. The golden bear, which is the totem of the University of California, must have been such, on the prowl in the old Peralta grant upon a parcel of which the Berkeley campus now lies outspread below Charter Hill and Grizzly Peak, sounding boards for the raucous "oski-wow-wow" varsity yell. The growl of the grizzly is heard in this land only in such college songs and cheers, sunk often to the "whispering oski."

Not even a hint of an echo of his growl comes down the winds, fluttering proudly the Bear Flag which, as California's official State flag, floats beside the national colors. In old Sonoma a hundred years ago, when the California Republic was born, "a man named Todd" (Bill Todd, said to be cousin to Mary Todd Lincoln) painted the crude semblance of a grizzly bear on that improvised banner of revolt; and we can envision him, as he spat a stream of amber tobacco juice into the plaza dust, explaining, "A bar allus stands his ground!"

Here, as too often elsewhere, eternal fame has been the sole reward for such valor. Today the coyote roams California as of yore, and his skulking ways imply a mean maxim, "I'd rather be a live coward than a dead hero." But, bravest of the brave, the California grizzly is no more.

Concerning the grizzly, editor Bret Harte wrote in 1868 when he chose the bear regardant, crossing a railroad track, to adorn the cover of the to-be-famous *Overland Monthly*, "There is much about your grizzly that is pleasant. In his placid moments, he has a stupid, good-natured tranquillity, like that of the hills in midsummer. I am satisfied that his unpleasant habit of scalping with his fore paw is the result of contact with the degraded aborigines, and the effect of bad example on the untutored ursine mind. Educated, he takes quite naturally to the pole, but has lost his ferocity, which is perhaps after all the most respectable thing about a barbarian. As a cub he is playful and boisterous, and I have often thought was not a bad symbol of our San Francisco

Black bear and cubs.

California mule deer. The sun lights the
"velvet" on the antlers. This coating drops
off in the mating season.

The condor is the largest flying
bird in the world.

Mountain quail are found along
the inner arid Coast Ranges.

A redwood forest north of Avenue of the Giants.

climate. Look at him well, for he is passing away. Fifty years, and he will be as extinct as the dodo or dinornis."

Yes, this noble and sagacious beast, the symbol chosen as most characteristic of their land by Californians, here is spoken of now only in the past tense. The California grizzly fought mightily against the intruding pioneers, against such renowned bear hunters as James Capen Adams and George Nidever and Nat Vise (for whom Visalia is named), and today it is probably extinct, in spite of tales of ghostly grizzlies seen in remote wilds of the Coast Ranges and the Sierra Nevada. Some of our choicest folklore and altitudinous tales relate to the California grizzly; but this king of beasts is legendary, vanished forever like the cave bear, the saber-toothed tiger, and the dire wolf which once roamed these Coast Ranges before it, as the Rancho La Brea pits at Los Angeles record in their asphalt depths.

Still, a report or a rumor of the grizzly's presence comes up now and again, as in a press dispatch from Santa Barbara in 1931 which told how a professional lion hunter, Charles Tant, was confronted by a twelve-hundred-pound grizzly bear on Narrow Horse Gulch Trail, how the grizzly knocked two of Tant's dogs senseless and then turned on the hunter, who fired at close range, fatally wounding the bear—assuredly one of the last of his tribe, if he was indeed a grizzly. Despite this story, Dr. Hall sets the time when the grizzly became extinct in California as 1925, or possibly as early as 1922.

Though up in the Siskiyous and in the northern Coast Ranges you will hear talk about black bears and brown bears and "cinnamangs," careful scientists rush forward to assure us that in California today all are variants of the same species, which these naturalists have agreed to name *black*.

Familiarity with the black bear has become rather general lately, not only in the national parks and national forests of the Sierra Nevada but also in the northern Coast Ranges, especially in and near the parks and refuges and reserves. It is not uncommon to gain sight of these bruins in many places, and nowadays even to approach them without *much* fear of loss of life or limb.

You cannot safely count on such short acquaintance, though, for when crossed the black bear can be an ugly customer. "Do not feed the bears" is an admonition still to be wisely heeded. In some spots, the big burlies

and their cubs repair to feeding grounds where they can be closely observed, for in these areas they have shed much of their shy wariness. But it has come to be realized that a panhandling bear at a garbage pit is scarcely a nobler creature than a monkey with a tin cup.

Bear stories are still heard in many an upland hamlet, and accounts of tragic encounters with these animals are not few. It is agreed that generally the black bear is not looking for trouble; undisturbed, it will not "go for" a human with felonious intent. But when desperately hungry, when young cubs are around, or when wounded or driven to bay, this bear will fight fiercely, taking up the battle with man where the grizzly left off. Though not as big as the grizzly, the black bear is powerful and intrepid, a formidable antagonist with teeth and claws. The traditional bear hug has been debunked.

It is estimated that in the Great Smokies black bears *may* be as numerous as in colonial times, but on this side of the continent, in the Coast Ranges, that is hardly the case. Still, from northern Sonoma County up into Oregon, wherever there are forests, usually some bears survive. You may note "bear sign" from the Gualala River to the Siskiyous and beyond.

A scattering few bears are in the San Bernardino Mountains and other southern ranges, though the names of Bear Valley, Big Bear Lake and Little Bear Lake give promise not abundantly fulfilled.

In the summer of 1945 it was reported that a State hunter with headquarters in Ukiah, Mendocino County, in the previous five years had killed 153 bears. He had also killed in this period 283 wildcats, 223 foxes, 2 mountain lions and 6 coyotes.

Enoch Percy French, famous guardian of the northern redwoods, recalls seeing in early times a troop of bears in the forested canyon of Ah Pah Creek, near the Klamath. "Must have been a score or more," reminisces Percy, "and they paraded by, below the place from which I watched." Not so rife nowadays, bears are still to be seen in Ah Pah and Blue Creek canyons, and throughout the Klamath River region, especially in the Orleans sector. In the rugged highlands above the south fork of the Trinity River bears are numerous, and hunters in season and guides with dogs take out parties of city sportsmen seeking this big game in "the last of the West," as some term it.

Hiram (Toppy) Ricks, late head of California's Fish and Game Com-

mission, a mighty hunter and renowned raconteur of tales of adventure by forest, flood, and field, told about an old bear which lately swam across Humboldt Bay in search of a wild berry thicket on the peninsula near the mill town of Samoa. Bruin failed to find this berry-patch paradise, most of it long since vanished, which he might have recalled—or mayhap he followed an ancestral trail.

These heavy berry-eaters, the black bears, have a sweet tooth—indeed, their teeth decay much like men's, probably as a result of their liking for honey and such. They have good taste, too, in sugary stuff, and to get it they will climb trees, swim broad waters, walk much more than a mountain mile.

The bear walks like a man, and he is usually a manly fellow in other ways than in his traction—that is, if he has to forage for himself and is not made a tramp bear by easy handouts.

Ursus appears to have a sense of humor. The play instinct in bears is one of their amiable traits of which anyone who watches them when at ease will soon become aware. Even the adults are sometimes amusing, and bear cubs are taught tricks and become tame, like the little grizzly Baby Sylvester in Bret Harte's story, who, however, as he grew in association with humans had in his eyes an expression of "intelligent distrust." These cubs are the candy-kids of the animal kingdom, for their love of sweets is proverbial.

When in autumn the salmon run up the rivers and creeks of California's northwestern coast to spawn, the bears forsake their berry eating and take up a diet of fish. Then they may be met in the wilds along the streams, such as those of the Klamath watershed.

VARIOUS DEER

In the northern redwood region, too, is the last native habitat in California of a large red deer, or wapiti, generally called the Roosevelt elk (Cervus roosevelti), which is the largest of its kind in all the world. Once abundant from the Golden Gate northward to British Columbia, it has dwindled to a few isolated herds. Especially notable is that in the Prairie Creek Redwoods State Park and near-by forests and hill land around Orick, extending over westward to the Pacific Ocean. Motorists along the Redwood Highway pause at Boyes Prairie, now often called Elk Prairie, near the Park headquarters, and gaze across

the barrier fence at the fine herd grazing in the meadow, against the dark background of lordly redwood trees, many of them towering three hundred feet above the open grassland. The elk can vault over those fences "like nobody's business," as the local folk say, but usually they attend to their own business of browsing, ruminating, and dozing.

When the bull elk are congregated in the prairie they look indeed like "animated hat racks," with branching and wide-spreading antlers. These great antlers, which the statuesque adult male elk carry, exceed in size and spread the antlers of any other species. In coloration these elk are comparable to the redwood boles amid which they roam. The rich brown color of the antlers, as contrasted with the paler color of the antlers of other forms, extends also to the hue of their coats.

It was through the patience and ingenuity of Warden C. L. Milne that the elk were toled into this prairie in considerable numbers—about a hundred are usually to be seen.

At times the bull elk are resentful of the intrusion of humans. Some of their guardians, even, have been treed until rescue parties arrived. Granpa, the patriarch of the herd at Boyes Prairie, has now departed. He had a formidable charge, and once chased a too-venturesome motion-picture photographer, who rolled under the rail fence to save himself from being gored.

Granpa was a magnificent animal, as those rescued motion-picture films and many a postcard still amply attest. His fellow bull elk are noble creatures, too. They fight with one another at times, and some have lost parts of their antlers in combat. The cows are more placid, as their name would imply, and those who behold the spotted calves are delighted at their gentle ways.

This herd of Roosevelt elk has been praised by such notables as Guy Emerson of the National Audubon Society, and Olaus Murie, of the Wilderness Society. The habitat in the redwoods and on the coastward slopes is being protected, with additions to the reserve in prospect. Even more interesting than to watch elk at the prairie is to come upon them in the forests' inner recesses, as along the James Irvine Trails in the Godwood Creek watershed, in a redwood environment which is jungle-like in its lush luxuriance of growth. Bears, too, yet wander here. How much of a real wilderness this Prairie Creek Redwoods State Park

still remains may be judged from the opinion expressed by Superintendent French that many of its eight thousand acres have *never* been touched by human foot, not even by a foot in Indian buckskin moccasin.

Here you are held within the spell of the redwoods, the great maroon-barked trees which are unique in this world. These majestic Sequoia sempervirens, which have stood for two thousand years, impart a sense of timelessness and peace to those who wander amid their solitudes. "They connect us, as by hand touch, with all the centuries they have known," in the eloquent words of Dr. John C. Merriam, a founder of the Save-the-Redwoods League.

Barely saved from extermination, too, are the tule elk which formerly roamed in vast herds California's Great Central Valley and its environing foothills, and tributary valleys such as the Livermore and Moraga valleys in Alameda County. Today the main surviving herd, comprising a few hundred animals, is in a State reserve near Buttonwillow, in Kern County.

Most familiar of the larger animals throughout the Coast Ranges from San Luis Obispo northward are the black-tailed deer, found in nearly every seaboard county, and especially abundant in Mendocino and Humboldt counties and in the highlands south of Monterey. You may see these graceful creatures on many a chaparral-clad hillside and in many a forest glade, grazing in the wilds, or scampering away from the highway as you pass along. These are mostly does and fawns; the bucks are more careful when they show themselves, even in parks and game reserves. From the slopes of Tamalpais, deer look down and across the bay to San Francisco; and they are common in the Livermore hills and the Mount Hamilton Range not far from Oakland.

Now deer are believed to be more plentiful in many parts of California than they were at the beginning of the present century. This is due partly to the purposeful reduction of the number of cougars and coyotes, which prey upon them. In earlier years, the cougars made away with more deer than the hunters.

Deer are the animals most hunted, and in season the ranges are sought by throngs of sportsmen. No does or fawns or spike bucks can be killed legally.

In Los Angeles County ranges and adjacent regions, southward into

Mexico, deer are not uncommon despite the proximity of metropolitan areas. These are mule deer, principally of two closely related kinds.

In 1850 the swift American antelope remained in coastal valleys and foothills, and excavated remains in ancient shell mounds reveal its former presence on the margin of San Francisco Bay, though it bounded and abounded mostly in the dry interior valleys and plains. The inordinate curiosity of the antelope made it easy prey for the Indians and for pioneer hunters, despite its fleetness of foot. Now it is never seen along the coast.

Bighorns—the wild mountain sheep—were observed by early Spanish explorers, but long ago these animals also disappeared from the coastland. Indeed, they are almost extinct in California, though a few wary ones linger on the precipitous slopes of Mount San Jacinto as well as in the highest Sierra, and in the southeastern desert ranges. The adult bighorn, one of the largest of American wild animals, is about twice the size of the domestic sheep, and the adult male has enormous curling horns. In the coast country today, the best you can do is to stand and admire the magnificent habitat group of the crag-climbing wild mountain sheep in North American Hall of the California Academy of Sciences, in Golden Gate Park, San Francisco—one of many such displays there, artistic triumphs which enlighten the public on present and past glories of our wild life population.

CATS

Fierce hunter of all the deer tribe, as has been observed, is the cougar, a big feline animal which also goes by sundry other names—California lion, mountain lion, American lion, painter, puma, are some of the aliases. It lurks in wooded regions of the coastal mountains at elevations between three and five thousand feet, rarely making thieving incursions on the lowlands. Because of this predator's raids on deer, and on sheep and other stock, a bounty is ever upon cougar scalps; and some of the hill folk help support themselves by collecting the grim trophies of this outlaw with a price upon his head.

"Found wherever deer are found," the cougar can be hunted at any time—best with a pack of dogs. Except when treed or trapped, it is very seldom seen, outside of wild animal collections, where it is indeed a sullen specimen. Considered an ornery creature by most mountain

dwellers, its slinking ways have given the cougar a reputation for cowardice, though it will fight pursuing dogs to the death.

Cougar kittens are sometimes kept as purring pets. Quite a bitter disputation has been carried on among sportsmen and in "safety-valve" columns of California newspapers as to whether the cougar "cries" or not. Several frequenters of the outdoors swear that this varmint at night may shriek, or cry like a baby—in fact, a slang name for the cougar *is* "baby."

Thrilling accounts are given of the prowess of Jay Bruce, for many years the State's official lion hunter; many in the pattern of the classic tale of Israel Putnam and the wolf. In the mountains south of Monterey, the stories run, Jay Bruce would go after a cougar even if it was hiding in a cave or den.

Jay Bruce in a motion-picture record of his exploits is seen climbing a tree and fighting it out with a huge cougar, barehanded. One of his closest calls came when he had treed a big male cougar after the slaughter of many sheep by the varmint. The cougar ran out high on the dead limb of a cedar, which broke just as Bruce was about to fire his revolver—he seldom carried a rifle. A dog closed with the lion in a fierce struggle on the ground, and as the hunter stooped close, trying to place his pistol near the lion without risk of hurting the dog, the wild animal saw him, at once let loose his hold on the dog, and sprang at Bruce "with paws that looked like tennis rackets equipped with grappling hooks," as he later said. So impetuous was the lion's drive that as Bruce fired he was thrown backward into a pool of water which chanced to be there. His head was below water, his pistol arm bent under him, his feet on the ground at the brink of the pool—and the lion on top of him. Bruce struggled desperately from that position to throw off the lion—and saw it fall dead just at that moment, the victim of his timely revolver shot.

Virtually every range has its Wildcat Canyon. One of the best-known, frequented by hikers (and still a few wildcats), is that back of Berkeley. The wildcat, bobcat, or red lynx, is found in the Coast Ranges from south to north. The Spaniards called these felines *gatos montéses*. From their abundance in the Santa Cruz Mountains above, the ridge and the canyon of Los Gatos—The Cats—received their name, later transferred to the pleasant community which looks out over the Santa Clara Valley.

Hunters who know the fierceness and vise-like grip of the cornered wildcat have termed it "a pair of jaws on two legs."

DON COYOTE AND ALL THE REST OF THE ANIMALS

Come upon sometimes even in daylight at unexpected turnings, coyotes frequent many coastal valleys and surrounding hills. Coyotes are yet numerous, though a bounty is paid on every pelt. About two thousand are caught each year in the coast counties. This wild canine is a streak, swift in flight, and generally thought of as a sneaking coward. Yet in Indian mythology, Coyote often is pictured as a hero, considered even as the "savior of mankind."

Geographic names galore remind us of the sometime presence of this sly fellow. Coyote, hamlet in the Santa Clara Valley; the isolated Coyote Hills, *cerros* on the Alameda County bayshore; Coyote Mesa, in Monterey County, and many others, are testimonies to the ubiquitous prairie wolf. The name here is usually pronounced in the old trisyllabic way— kī-ō′tē not kī′ōt, though the dictionary permits both variants.

Widely dispersed in the foothills and lower mountains, especially in the chaparral belt, the gray foxes are also numerous, but not so often seen because of the dense cover which they usually inhabit. Where traps are set, the gray fox is suspicious and cautious, but in remote regions it does not always greatly fear the approach of a man, sometimes merely stepping a few feet to one side of the trail till he has passed. Swifter than swift, the gray fox climbs trees, when pursued, and can even jump from limb to limb like a squirrel.

Less popular in the animal world than the poison oak in the vegetal world are the skunks, in striped and spotted varieties, which are fairly common in the Coast Ranges. The adult striped skunks are usually much larger than the spotted fellows. Shunned because of their mephitic odor and potentiality for malicious mischief, these animals are called by a number of humorous nicknames—sachet pussy, perfume merchant, essence peddler, wood pussy—but a skunk by any other name . . . !

Though they may smell to high heaven, the blue sky of California, often the four-footed skunks are really beautiful creatures, with black and white coats—"two-color paint jobs," in the lingo of facetious hill folk, some of whom keep young skunks, which may be deprived of their essences, as pets around their cabins. Thus it is possible to speak of

skunks with familiarity, though in the wild state they are mostly nocturnal in their habits.

A true arboreal mammal, the gray squirrel is large and beautiful, the proud possessor of a gracefully curved bushy tail, longer than its body. No wonder this gray squirrel is conspicuous and well-known, especially as it is active in full daylight, and all through the year.

In the pine woods of the Carmel region, as in the Point Lobos Reserve, you see gray squirrels scampering around, finding abundant food. Often they seize and carry fresh pine cones; and they are fond of acorns, too, which they often shell and eat in or near the oaks. Though sometimes they bark sharply and persistently to protest intrusion of humans, still they usually are friendly to "the poets and peasants" of Carmel.

On the coast, the Douglas squirrels range mostly in the woods of the northern counties. These lively little reddish rodents, celebrated in the writings of John Muir, must have inspired the proverb, "You can't keep a squirrel on the ground."

Those squirrels which hug terra firma are not so highly regarded. In coastal regions, ground squirrels are numerous on terrain clothed with low vegetation, with their vision unimpeded, and where scattered bushes and boulders serve as lookouts. They do not climb trees except sometimes when seeking food; their homes are in the ground. Sporadic efforts are made to exterminate these rodents, but they "come back" rapidly in certain areas.

Humorous little fellows, friendly almost always, are the chipmunks —the "greeters" of the woods. Everyone is familiar with them, in the vicinity of upland coniferous forests and chaparral areas, especially in Boreal habitats. Strangely, they are not found in a few regions favorable to their presence, such as the Mount Diablo country—apparently because that aloof monument mountain is isolated by belts of grassland which chipmunks could never contrive to cross.

When you observe chipmunks closely, and you can, for they are eminently companionable, you will be struck by their beautiful soft, striped fur. The pattern consists primarily of longitudinal light and dark stripes alternating on a ground color, ocherous or gray. There are five dark and four light dorsal stripes.

Slender and graceful, alert and alive, "chippy" (Tamias or "tammy," he is called by folk with scientific book learning) has large internal

cheek pouches for storage of foodstuffs. When filled, these give him a comical aspect, like a little hoodlum with his "chaw."

Long-legged and long-eared, the black-tailed jack rabbits are hares renowned for their burst of speed on the getaway and in flight, exceeding the celerity of the coyotes, even. Our view of the jack rabbit is usually on his precipitous take-off when startled in the field or chaparral, a departure often laughable in its alarm. "Long after he was out of sight, we could hear him whiz," recounted Mark Twain about a "long-eared chum" which he surprised in the sagebrush.

Undoubtedly those spiring ears account for the name, given by the pioneers, jackass rabbit. Some, however, have fancied that it may have been bestowed because "the kick of his powerful hind legs is like that of a mule." In other words, like many another, a jackass in more ways than one.

When frightened, the little wild cottontail rabbit is wont to remain still for a space, then to "beat it," scuttling through the brush. Mollie Cottontail is certainly a "cute bunny," as say the children, with whom she is a prime favorite. The fluffy white fur of the tail of this little gray rabbit accounts for the name commonly given.

Greatly reduced in numbers, beavers are not much seen, as they are aquatic in habits and mainly nocturnal—and in the lowlands mostly. They cut down trees, but here do not construct such elaborate dams as elsewhere.

Raccoons, porcupines, badgers, pine martens, fishers, minks, river otters, weasels, gophers, wood rats, field mice—these are some of the minor mammals to be met with occasionally, or rarely. Dog-and-badger fights were common "sport" in the '49 mining camps. With the miners the ring-tailed cats—or raccoon foxes—were popular as useful pets, which kept their cabins free from mice and pack rats.

The 'possum, brought here from the South, is found in the Berkeley hills, and now is widely distributed in central and southern California.

In the coastal ranges south of the Carmel River, the European wild boar has been introduced and is often hunted, as it is also on some of the mountainous Cabrillo Islands—the Channel Islands—off the coast of southern California. There, too, wild goats, probably descended from domestic goats taken from the mainland many years ago, are hunted.

The wild horses which once ran through the hills, many of them

escaped from the vast herds of Mission San Antonio, have now galloped
off the scene.

Like most American hill people, the natives of these California ranges
take elfish delight in stringing the stranger, notably the tenderfoot sport
from the big city. Tales are told of legendary critters that never existed
except in spoofing conversation around the campfire or the stove in general store or saloon—yarns about goofus, gazook, whoofet, ring-tailed
snorter, and the sidehill badger, that fabulous animal with legs longer
on one side than the other, to facilitate its progress along the slopes.
Copious and curious folklore is yet to be garnered throughout these
hills, from long-time settlers whose forebears came hither from the
Ozarks or were of the dusky aboriginal tribes—sometimes both. The Indian animal legends as collected and recorded by the ethnologists are
often dreary and humorless, but the stories of the descendants of the
Pikes, likely to be as broad as they are long, are racy with native fun
and folk wisdom.

From the sheer slopes of the Sierra Santa Lucia, fronting the ocean,
and from other such coastal ranges in California, you can look down as
from a balcony to the surf-washed rocks offshore where sea lions dis-
port. It is as good as a play, especially if you have your opera glasses
(or field glasses) along.

Some of the best vantage points are those two points which are named
for these amphibians—Point Lobos off San Francisco's Sutro Heights,
and cypress-crowned Point Lobos, "the greatest meeting of land and
water in the world," on the Carmel coast. *Lobos marinos*—sea wolves—is
the Spanish term. There are two species, the stellar and the California
sea lions.

The sea otter once was very numerous along California's coast, but its
soft and glossy fur came into such great demand that a century ago it
was almost exterminated here, mostly by Russian, American, and Indian hunters. A pair of sea otters was found in 1916 in the waters south of
Santa Catalina Island. Apparently they were the last, and book after
book referred to the sea otter as extinct in California.

Then in March, 1938, a herd of nearly one hundred sea otters was discovered on the coast at Bixby Creek, south of Carmel. Great excitement
prevailed at this find—"a dramatic Return from Nowhere," as C. M.
Goethe has described it. Now that they are among those present again,

these sea otters attract much attention, as they float offshore—often observed through glasses. Though they look small as viewed from the highway that notches the precipitous flank of the mountains, high above the surf and the kelp fields, actually the largest of them measure almost six feet from nose to tail.

It is hoped that the sea otters will survive so much notice—as to this herd, for years its security lay in obscurity.

Whales are sometimes seen spouting along the coast, and occasionally their bulky carcasses are cast up on the sands, and to leeward of them you can pause to get a good idea of their remarkable features. The California gray whale is the species which has yielded most of the oil to shore whalers, who were busy for years at such bases as San Diego, San Pedro, Monterey and Point Lobos, Trinidad, and many other places, carrying on a picturesque calling which long ago aspired to rival the rock oil industry as the nation's source of oil.

BIRDS OF THE MOUNTAINS

The wild life of California's coastal region, as represented by the mammals, has passed briefly in review through these pages, not two by two but in diverse array, as befits such a casual account. Of birds, too, there are numerous varieties, only some of the best-known of which can here be even noticed. To become truly familiar with them, it would be a delight for any lover of wild nature to go on bird walks through these ranges with the guidance of John Baker of the National Audubon Society, or Bert Harwell, so widely known for his bird mimicry ("the Audubon warbler," he has been called), or with William Finley, Harold Bryant, Laidlaw Williams, Jean Linsdale, Robert T. Orr, or some of the others deep in bird lore.

That knight of the nodding plume, the California quail—the valley quail—is officially the State bird, by vote of the legislature guided by a popular poll of school children in which, we are solemnly assured, the quail won going away, by a thumping majority of 42,593. This, however, was only after the meadow lark and the mockingbird (so-called), favorites of many, were ruled out of the running because they had been selected for primacy by other States.

The valley quail, despite the name, is found not only in the lowlands but also in the hill country and the lower mountains. Among other

places, it is plentiful in the Monterey region and the Mount Hamilton Range, and on the coast side of the Sierra Morena in San Mateo County, not far south of San Francisco. Just north of the hillside Berkeley home of this writer is wooded Codornices Canyon, where talkative coveys of quail still are in evidence, as is indeed fitting, for *codorniz* is Spanish for quail, and the name (in the plural) is applied to that canyon where the cheery little calls of these feathered folk yet are heard. Despite the depredations of house cats, quail roam all our neighborhood.

Handsome, truly, but a fine family man, is the male bird, with his black gorget, and black-edged brown feathers on his lower breast. The narrow crest of glossy black feathers curves forward above his head, bestowing an air of pride but not of arrogance. The male's wings, back, and upper breast are of slaty gray or bluish color; the female is brown-ish. Both parents are appealingly solicitous of the welfare of their young, and such youngsters are indeed worth watching. You will have plenty of opportunity to observe them if you stay still on the edge of the chaparral.

The mountain quail, larger birds, though their principal home is in the Sierra Nevada, are seen in the costal ranges northward from Sonoma and southward from Carmel. Another fine bird, a rarer relation, is the blue grouse, a native of California, found not only in the Sierra Nevada but also in Humboldt and Mendocino counties, in the northwestern part of the State.

Only second among the favorite Californian birds, according to that so-precise balloting among school children, is the California woodpecker. Other popular birds are the brown towhee, the thrasher, purple finch, red-shafted flicker, Anna's hummingbird, Bullock's oriole, green-backed goldfinch—in that order. The California condor was included, not because it is a well-known or well-beloved bird, but because of its great size and rarity.

The sparrow hawk, canyon wren, wren tit, road runner, Western king-bird, black-headed grosbeak, Western tanager, Audubon's warbler, water ouzel, russet-backed thrush, Western bluebird, and bush tit ranked high in the estimation of the children, who can be counted on to know birds, especially in the rural districts.

Among the most beautiful of California birds, surely, are the wood-peckers. A favorite resident is the California acorn-storing woodpecker,

found almost everywhere that oaks abound, where its familiar cry of "Jacob, Jacob" resounds. This foresighted bird riddles tree trunks, posts, and sometimes even wooden walls with holes into which acorns are driven and tamped. Mostly black, its wide white patches are seen in flight. The males have bright red crowns; the females display less red.

The woodpecker family has several representatives in the California Coast Ranges. One of the finest is the red-shafted flicker, displaying a flash of red from its wings' underside when seen in flight, which is characteristically undulating. Other such birds are the hairy and the downy woodpeckers—black and white, with markings of scarlet. Brilliant feathers of the woodpeckers long have been used by the Indians in ornamenting basketry, in headdresses and other barbaric adornments.

Fearless of humans, the California brown towhee, a well-known garden companion throughout the year, is as likely to be perched on a window sill as in the chaparral wilds. Its cousin, the spotted towhee, is more a bird of mark, but no more lovable.

In brushy areas, as well as in gardens, you will see and hear the California thrasher, a brownish bird with a white throat, from which rises a song of heart-filling melody.

As the house finch, or linnet, is among the commonest of birds in California, so also it is one of the most popular, except among some farmerfolk. Like it, but larger, is the California purple finch, a mountain resident which in winter comes to the lowlands and hillsides. The male bird displays a more purplish red than the house finch.

Smallest of the goldfinches, here, is the green-backed goldfinch, which nests often in Monterey cypresses or other dense-foliaged trees. Though often termed wild canary, because of its song and the yellow hues in its plumage, this little bird is not a canary. The male has a green back, a yellow body, and a tiny black cap atop his head. White wing patches usually adorn the black wings.

Do you love those airy jewel-like creatures, the hummers? Present all through the year, the tiny Anna's hummingbird is an ever-colorful adornment of wild gardens, as of gardens within walls, from the Mexican border northward to the San Francisco Bay region. Iridescent green above and grayish green below, the male Anna (maybe Andy would seem a more fitting name for *him*) sports a metallic rose-red gorget and cap.

A summer resident along the coastland north from Santa Barbara, especially in gulches and canyons, is the even tinier Allen's hummingbird, a green-backed bird, which in its migrations southward traverses the higher mountains, probably guided in its buzzing flight by the midsummer flowers abloom.

A two-time visitor each year, upon its far migrations, is the rufous hummingbird, with its fox-colored back and glistening, glowing, copper-red throat. It visits favorite melliferous flowers, such as those of native gooseberry and currant and manzanita, and the orange groves and peach orchards in blossomtimes.

The Bullock's oriole, closely akin to the celebrated Baltimore oriole and showing the relationship in the male's bright orange-and-black attire; the small sparrow hawk, a true falcon; the canyon wren, frequenter of rocky places, where its ringing whistle awakes double-talking echoes; the unique wren tit, with its tail pertly uptilted and aslant, longer than its brown-feathered body; the Western kingbird, of the flycatcher family; the conspicuous black-headed grosbeak, a friendly melodious bird ranging up to the highest coastal mountains, except in late fall and in winter; the Western tanager, the adult male representative black and yellow, with scarlet head, a summertime resident of foothills and mountains; the alert Audubon's warbler; the courageous water ouzel, the dipper, forever renowned because of the classic description by John Muir; the russet-backed thrush, midyear visitant in the coastland, from plains to upper mountain heights; the lovely Western bluebird, purplish blue with ruddy brown breast and flanks; the tiny bush tit—these are among the best-beloved birds on the list of favorites.

On the "official" list of characteristic Californian birds, too, but not chosen for beauty of plumage or form or song, is the road runner. We don't seem to see so many road runners along highways as in former years, possibly because they have no liking for running along a track in an atmosphere perhaps tainted with motor-exhaust gases. They are in the offing, though. Curious, long-necked and long-tailed birds which seldom fly, and then mostly downward, these "racers" can run very swiftly. An old Spanish name still used sometimes is *paisano*, that is, country fellow. The bird is also called chaparral cock and snake killer, but an older name used by the Spaniards, *correo de camino*, is not often heard nowadays.

Largest flying bird in America if not in the world, larger even than the condor of the Andes, is the California condor—which is threatened with extinction such as obliterated the California grizzly bear. Only a few of these great vultures, which attain a wingspread of eleven feet, still exist. They are protected by law, but are likely to vanish nevertheless. Scientific societies recently witnessed a showing of motion pictures of California condors nesting, but the exhibitors were rightly secretive about the location. In wild, isolated highlands from southern Monterey County southward, condors may survive—or that is the habitat usually assumed.

From San Francisco Bay south to Santa Barbara County the yellow-billed magpie is resident, from sea level to lower mountains, but mostly in valleys or upon hills of gentle contour. Though evidently somewhat neglected in the popularity balloting aforementioned, this is truly a characteristic native bird; and one who spoke with authority wrote, "If a single California bird can lay any great claim to a place in officialdom as the State bird, this one—the yellow-billed magpie—certainly has the right."

Among others which should by no means be neglected, either, are such birds as the Western meadow lark, with its sequence of liquid notes, beyond compare; the song sparrow, another exquisite musician; the ruby-crowned kinglet, almost as diminutive as the hummingbird; the golden-crowned sparrow and the white-crowned sparrow, and other pert passerine birds; that "merry jester," the Western mockingbird; and the orange-breasted Western robin (what a gathering of distinguished Westerners, this avian horde); the red-winged blackbird and the Brewer's blackbird; the long-tailed mourning dove; the chickadee; the cedar waxwing, black-masked bandit that raids berrybushes in winter; the noisy, saucy California jay of the foothills; the crested blue-fronted jay, usually of the higher country; that camp robber, the crow; raven; swift; swallow; hawk; eagle; owl; the band-tailed pigeon; the blue heron, the crane and other waders—a feathered multitude to be seen by wanderers in the California coast country.

Mention has been made of the place names which come from the Spanish names of animals and birds. The Pajaro Valley was named by the soldiers of Gaspar de Portolá on their northward march in 1769,

for a place where the Indians displayed a great stuffed bird (*pajaro*), probably an eagle. Above the Gabilan Range near San Juan Bautista rises Hawk Peak, also called Fremont Peak after the Pathfinder, who raised the American flag there. *Gavilán* or *gabilán* signifies hawk. Gaviota, on the Santa Barbara County coast, and the famous pass above, bear the name of the sea gull. *Alcatraz* means pelican.

Sea gulls still survive despite the decline of San Francisco Bay ferry-boats, which they follow in swarms. Few may have expected the boats to near extinction first. The fact is that the glaucous-winged gull, the Western gull, and others of their kind are numerous.

California brown pelicans caused an air alert along the central California coast during World War II when they got in the way of radar alarm devices—now it can be told. These strange birds can be observed closely at Point Lobos and elsewhere along the coast, often in ponderous flight. Satchelbills they are often called, and their huge bills, with great pouches below, opened the eyes of early explorers. "They have a vast craw, which in some hangs down like the leather bottles used in Peru for carrying water." They are to be distinguished from the white pelicans of inland ranges.

Though sportsmen are keenly aware of the diminution of upland game birds, the migratory waterfowl—mostly wild ducks—have increased greatly, so that now there are probably more than there were half a century ago. The varieties include mallard, canvasback, sprig (pintail), widgeon, spoolbill, teal, bluebill, and ruddy ducks, which appear on their migrations around bays and lagoons and marshes. Wild geese and black brant are also fairly numerous.

FISH OF THE STREAMS AND THE SEA

Fish of the coastland streams attract many anglers in season. In hundreds of mountain streams and lakes, the gamest of trout await the cast of fly or spinner. Bright-armored battlers are they, that really bend the rod as they strike. Among the principal varieties are rainbow, cutthroat, Loch Leven, brown, brook, and Dolly Varden trout.

Trout in riffle and pool, black bass in lake waters and river waters, striped bass in the bays, king salmon and other big game fish to lure deep-sea anglers—well, with all these, and countless of their iridescent kind, the sportsmen have lots of luck, most of it good!

Famous sport is fishing for the big leaping steelhead in the rivers of the redwood region. Every gamester in the northern streams gives a desperate battle, testing the skill of the angler to the utmost. Ranging mostly from six to fifteen pounds, fighting weight, the big steelhead sometimes runs even larger, up to thirty pounds. The steelhead is generally supposed to be a rainbow trout which has been to sea, though experts are not entirely agreed on this. Renowned among the steelhead fishing streams are the Eel River and the Klamath River. Along the lower Eel the fishing is done in large, quiet pools; and as at that season there is but little current, it is desirable that the sky be overcast and that there be enough wind to raise a ripple. Much of the fishing on the lower Eel is done from boats, especially at Fernbridge and Weymouth Pool, near Alton. In other pools the anglers wade, working out from the shallow side and casting toward the deep water. Fishing with flies and spinners prevails, though some trolling is done from boats.

The Klamath River is a larger stream than the Eel, and the steelhead run far up its course. They afford good sport throughout the season. While boats are used near the mouth of the river, most of the fishing in the Klamath is from the banks. Tod Powell, "the Woodsman," tells how it's done: "You wade out into the river with discretion, not getting into the heaviest water. When you cast, send your line across the stream and quartering down the current. The riffles are heavy—if they're not, then you are not fishing the best water for this particular fish—so use a fairly stout hook-fly."

Steelhead are found in virtually all northern California coast streams and in the lagoons at their mouths. Twice a year these game fish gather at the entrance to the streams, congregate in the lagoons, and, as the spring and fall rains heighten the waters and give entrance over the bars, they run far upstream. Ordinarily, the best fishing in the northern redwood region is in October, but it extends over several fall and winter months.

Like the steelhead, salmon are caught both in salt and fresh waters. The king salmon and other kinds of salmon abound in the large streams, and are also caught off the coast. In the autumn months the salmon run far up the rivers to spawn. Northern headquarters for salmon fishing are Requa and Klamath, on the Klamath River, where launches may be hired, with expert fishermen-guides—many of them Indians.

The Atlantic salmon is not to be regarded as a brother of the Pacific salmon, but is, rather, a close relative of the steelhead trout.

All who find zest in the hearty traditions of the sea, delight in the far-flung coastline of California—twelve hundred sparkling miles long it is, taking count of its major inlets and bays. At almost every little landing place, and at all the big ports, you will come upon picturesque fishing boats, engaged in that vast industry which brings sea food to the tables of the millions. Salmon, halibut, sole, barracuda, cod, whitefish, tuna, sardines, mackerel, sand dabs, flounders, smelt—it would soon leave us breathless to try to cry all the fish brought to the markets. More than 120 kinds of food fish are taken from Monterey Bay, where fish species of northern waters and southern waters meet.

Much visited is the Monterey fish harbor near the venerable Customs House, with its brightly-painted boats behind the breakwater and beside the old pier reaching seaward, with its famed fish restaurants possessed of the art of preparing to perfection the festive abalone. On the shoreside, fisherfolk in jerseys and oilskins and capacious sea boots come up from the boats, and often you see bronzed old fellows mending their nets or spreading them to dry.

Santa Cruz presents longshore scenes, too, that smack of the salt sea, as indeed do other coastal communities.

Sight-seers, multitudinous as the silver horde (especially on Thursdays), visit Fishermen's Wharf upon the San Francisco waterfront. Though the graceful lateen sails of former days have disappeared, interesting types among the Italian *pescatori* are reminiscent of olden times.

Best of all this is an activity in which even the casual traveler can participate, to enjoy glorious sport. You can learn about "big game" fishing at Avalon on Santa Catalina Island. You can arrange to go out with the fishing boats from Monterey Bay in the early morning and return at night; or anywhere along the coast hire a boat and tackle for a few hours' quiet recreation; or visit the barges offshore or the wharves lined with intent fishermen—and thus share in the abiding thrill which is inseparable from angling for the shining prizes in the lottery of the sea.

"As many there as ever were caught," some say—but. . . . Throughout its animal realm, ashore and afloat, the danger of depletion everywhere stares California in the face. Careful scientists and conserva-

tionists warn that abundance of certain species in certain localities does not always assure that they are beyond the danger of depletion. We cannot assume the security of any species.

As a conclusion to all this about wild life, I think of a related field and the words of the eminent Californian botanist, Dr. Willis Linn Jepson, who wrote, "Don't call the native flowers 'wild flowers.' It is often the humans that are wild."

FOOTHILLS

BY JUDY VAN DER VEER

*So much for the wild environment. You must under-
stand that no American range of mountains, except
the region of the Olympics, is more inhabited than
the Coast Ranges. Read this chapter to catch the
enthusiasm which one inhabitant has for her hills.
(R. P.)*

By May the rainy season is over. Wild grasses drop their seeds and begin to dry, the slopes turn yellow again, bright in the sunshine. Dryness intensifies the smell of sage and buckwheat and greasewood. It is the sweet smell of summer on the hills. Down in the valley fields, the oat hay is cut, and the valley smells of new hay and sun-dried grass.

Greenness is not all gone from the land. Along the sandy river beds the cottonwoods are shining green, and there are willows and sycamores and groups of dark live oaks. Hills that are thick with brush are somber green, looking almost black from a distance, and deerweed is still leafy on canyon sides. The hidden springs have small trees around them, and the late wild flowers are not minding the dryness at all.

My favorite mountain has two names. Some people call it El Capitan and some call it El Cajon Mountain. It stands at the head of our valley —a long stony mountain that is purpled with cloud shadows and reddened with sunsets. It is wildly beautiful, but it looks fit for nothing but the homes of eagles and ravens. Travelers scarcely believe me when I tell them that beyond its rocky rim there are grassy meadows and big oaks and flowing springs. That is the way this back country is. It turns its sun-worn face to you, and if you want to find its gentler qualities you have to search them out.

Several days a week, late last spring, my neighbor, Dave, and I rode up that mountain to look over the blacksmith's cattle and count the new calves. It was May in the lower hills, but up on the mountain it was still April. The oaks were bronze and lavender with tassels and new leaves—it is in spring that live oaks wear the colors you expect to see

105

on trees in fall. There were wild lilacs, little streams were flowing, and grass was green in meadows where the cattle grazed. In groups of five and six, the new calves rested in the grass; the very newest were still hidden, fawn-like, in leafy places. Will James has written more beautifully than anyone of Hereford calves, "their little white faces shining in the sun." Only some of these calves had smeared white faces, due to the influence of what Dave called that "motley-faced bull." The unexpected splotches of dark red gave the faces a piquant expression to me; but the woman who lives on the mountain and leases the range to our blacksmith remarked disgustedly, "Some of them cattle don't even look human."

But the calves, whether splotchy-faced or clean, were adorable with their dark solemn eyes and their petal-like ears, and I was glad I didn't own them. Selling the veal crop would not have made me happy. While Dave checked the yearlings, I kept tally of the calves, and as their numbers grew, Dave, who really loves cattle, kept remarking what a fine big check those calves would bring to our blacksmith. Of course ranchers look at things that way.

Dave was having fun taming down the blacksmith's herd. He would ride into a lazy group, dismount, talk to them. When he reached the point where he could dismount without all the cows getting up and running off, he felt that he had achieved something. For this mixed herd had been a wild bunch, hard to handle, and by driving them into the corral and letting them out again and herding them from meadow to meadow, Dave was making it easier to work them.

A bunch had drifted down into the rough country on the east side of the mountain; some of them were black polled Angus, and they grew wild and canny. For a time it looked as if a number of them would be forever lost.

They hid in the thick brush, they were careful about going for water, they sniffed the wind for signs of man. Every week end the blacksmith would gather up what riders he could find; they would camp on the trail of the strays and ride from sunrise to sunset through horse-killing country. They had enough extra horses to change mounts fairly often, and they fought those cows through the brush and over the rocky slopes, riding hard in places where a horse had to be nimble just to keep four hoofs under him. We have good horses in this country.

Our blacksmith, Tom La Madrid, is a cattleman who does not live on a ranch; he lives in a house behind his shop, and he leases what pastures he can for the cows. They lead a migratory existence: sometimes they live up on the old Featherstone Ranch beyond the reservation, sometimes they are down in the river valley. It is a hard way to keep cattle, but it is the way many ranchers have to work it. There are a couple of big cattlemen in this country who have managed to lease the best of the ranges; the others must hunt for what pasture they can find. One cow needs a lot of range, for with the ending of the rainy season there is no more feed growing, and there must be enough dry forage to last over half a year. Anyone who owns a little bunch of cattle has to be on the lookout for new pastures.

Because Tom is busy shoeing horses most of the time, he needs what help he can get with his cattle. Dave and I enjoyed riding up the mountain to see the cows on days when our own small herds weren't demanding our time. Cattle are fascinating creatures, and though I never seem to make much money on mine, and Dave worries about the way his herd doesn't pay, we don't seem able to enjoy life without having cows around.

Soon we knew every one of Tom's herd personally, and what their dispositions were like. Some of the young Herefords were not so meek as they looked. One time on the way to Featherstone one six-months-old heifer got tired and hot and cross. She lay down and refused to get up. I got off my horse to tail her up, and she bounded to her feet and knocked me down. Those things are surprising because range cows are supposed to fear and respect humans.

Whenever we rode among Tom's herd we looked for a heifer named Tamale, because we considered Tamale someone special. Tom had got her when she was about eight months old, and she acted as if she had never seen a human before. He branded her and turned her out with his herd in the river pasture, and the next day he couldn't find her. She was missing for six weeks, and Tom looked everywhere before he gave her up. Late one afternoon he came across her unexpectedly. She was stretched out in the sand by the water hole, and at first he thought she was dead. She was like a skeleton with hide on it, she scarcely breathed, and her eyes looked glazed.

Tom went home and got a shovel, planning to hit her on the head

and bury her there in the sand. But he didn't kill her, after all. He shoveled some sun-warmed sand over her because it was fall and the night was going to be cold, and the next morning he hurried to see if she still lived. She wasn't much more dead than she had been the night before, so he got his truck and hauled her home and dumped her out behind the shop. He piled hay around her for comfort, and he fed her a bottle of milk with some whiskey in it.

There were a lot of things wrong with her. One ankle was twisted and swollen; the brand hadn't healed and had become a sore full of maggots; from the way she breathed it seemed that she had pneumonia.

Tom cleaned out her sore, put hot packs on her ankle, fed her more milk and whiskey, and kept her warm. In a few days, instead of being stretched out flat, she was, as Tom said, "sitting up." Her legs were tucked under her in a natural position, and she moved her head and looked around, enjoyed her bottle of milk and whiskey, ate some rolled barley, and chewed on some hay.

In another week she was standing up, though very wobbly, and two weeks later she was out in pasture with the others. Tom said that that's the way Herefords are, you can't kill them. But I think it was more than that. Tamale had a strong spirit, a great will to live, and that's what pulled her through. We couldn't imagine where she had been or what had happened to her, but when we see her looking well and, incidentally, wild as ever, we have great faith in the ability of living things to keep alive. Remembering Tamale is a great help to us whenever any of our own cows become sick.

Most cattlemen will tell you that Herefords are the best rustlers, but Al Greenleaf, who lives further back in the mountains where winters are cold and springs bitter with harsh winds, will tell you that he has better luck with Holsteins. Holsteins are dairy cattle, not range cattle at all, but Al's black and white cows do a pretty good job of foraging for themselves. Because they are a heavy breed he can sell them for beef, and because they are dairy stock he can sell them for milk cows, so he has a double market. In the winter he plants oats for hay, in the summer he puts in corn. At any time of the year he is likely to be doing some buying and selling and trading of horses and cows.

He comes as near to being a real California rancher as any man I know. His grandfather was a New Englander who made the trip around

the Horn, came into San Diego Harbor, and never left this country. Al grew up with horses and cows, married a pretty school teacher from back East, raised three children, and lived on different ranches until he settled in the mountains. Sometimes he thinks longingly of some warm valley, but his wife, with a sparkle in her dark eyes, says firmly, "No, I like telling people that I live up in the mountains."

FOOTHILL FOLK AND FOOTHILL RANCHES

The people up in those mountains seem a little different from the people living in the lower hills. They seem more like real ranch folk. It is too far to go to town to a dance, so they have their own dances and their own musicians. When trouble comes they need each other. Because they are used to certain hardships they meet disaster bravely, and when a very bad thing happened to one family they met it in a way that made them seem heroic. Instead of accepting sympathy they went about comforting their friends. "This terrible thing that has happened to us," they said, and smiled. "Well, we'll make out somehow. Don't worry about us."

Of course all their friends did worry, and worried more when matters seemed to grow worse, but none of us dared show any signs of pity. When we came across any member of that family we had to smile and make a joke of some kind and pretend that all was well. And we felt ashamed to think that we had ever groused over our own small troubles, and we resolved to remember these people and try to find some of their courage when, some time or other, trouble would hit us hard.

Down in the lower hills there are more assorted kinds of people: there are old settlers, and there are people from the Middle West, and from way back East, and from the coast cities. Some speak with western drawls and some speak like Easterners and if any of them speak like Californians I don't know it because I don't know what Californians talk like. Some of these people make a living off the land with dairy cattle or range cattle or chickens or pigs or orange groves, and some of them work their own places and work out also, either on other ranches or on jobs in town.

We who live in the back country are a little sensitive about the word "ranch" because of the way we are laughed at by Texans. It is rather odd to read in the paper that a quarter-acre chicken ranch is for sale.

It amuses Texans to realize that every small piece of land outside the city limits is a ranch here in California. But these tiny plots of land are called ranches because once they were part of the large ranches—ranches so big that a man could ride from the mountains to the sea without his horse's hoofs once stepping off his own land. These were the old Spanish land grants, where the cattle could range as far as they liked, through fenceless valleys and over the hills, until they were as wild as the deer that grazed among them. These grants seem to have been laid out any old way—a line might run fifty miles from one cracked boulder to one lightning-split oak. Or a creek, that might be afflicted by flood and forced to alter its course, could be a boundary line. In later days surveyors were puzzled.

The old names still mark localities. I live on the old El Monte Grant. There is the Padre Barona Ranch, now an Indian reservation; there are San Luis Rey, Santa Margarita, the El Cajon Grant. . . . I love saying their names. Mesa Grande is a good one to roll on your tongue; El Capitan is grand.

The people who live on the little portions of the old big ranches have no easy time of it. Most of them plant oats in the fall and cut it for hay in the spring, and raise corn and alfalfa in summer. The dairymen have settled in the river valleys where water is not too far from the surface, and corn and alfalfa can be grown with little irrigating, sometimes with none. The river pastures and hills can be used for growing heifers; the cows themselves are seldom in pasture except in winter when barley has been planted for grazing.

Dairy cows have the best to eat, but a range cow leads a pleasanter life. The milk herds spend most of their lives in corrals with no shelter from winter rains and no shade in summer, and calves are taken away from them and tied in uncomfortable places. Some of the dairies are clean and comfortable, but few dairymen these days have time to keep things up. The milking barns must be spotless because no one knows when a dairy inspector may come, but for some reason the inspectors aren't interested in corrals, and during the rainy season cows wade udder-deep in muck.

I have worked for three different dairies, and my first two jobs were easy. It was spring, and I had left school, and my first job was taking a dairy herd to graze all day on an unfenced mesa. The cows and I and

my horse enjoyed it, and I received a dollar a day. The second job was
similar, only I received ten dollars a week. I held down the third job
last summer, and then I did some work for forty-five cents an hour and
learned what a hard and harassed life a dairyman leads, so my sympathy was partly transferred from the cows to the cows' owner.

The rancher I worked for had left cut oat hay out in the fields for
weeks because he couldn't get enough help to bring it in. He wanted to
get it off the fields so he could put in corn, and already it was growing
late for that. All morning we loaded and hauled hay; all the hot afternoon while I weeded watermelons, the rancher and his sons ran hay
through the chopper and had it blown up into the silos. It was put into
the silos for dry storage, not for silage; by the time the hay was gone,
the corn (with luck) should be ready to be chopped green for silage.
But there was so much to do! There were potatoes to be dug and
tomatoes to be weeded and fresh heifers to be brought in from pasture
(and their hidden calves found) and always the cows to be milked and
fed—fresh green feed to be cut for them, dairy meal to be served them,
baled alfalfa put out for them. There were calves to feed and barns to
clean and milking machines to be sterilized. There was a grove of orange
trees to be irrigated, there were apricots to pick, alfalfa fields to water,
hens to be cared for, pigs to feed. The poor man must have got up
every morning with a feeling of being weighted down by work to be
done. And no matter how hard he worked he never caught up, there
was always more and more to be done. He was one of the ones who
wanted the barns and corrals spotless, the cows and calves comfortable,
everything looking neat and pretty. He strove to make his sons and me
work hard, but he worked even harder himself. Things would go wrong
and drive him nearly to madness, and I could so appreciate his feelings
that I said I would write a book called *Why Ranchers Swear*. They certainly have enough to cuss about these days, with all sorts of foolish
rules and regulations, papers to be filled out, and the army keeping away
sons and hired help. It seems to me that a rancher who works as this
one does can never have time to sit back and look at his beautiful fields
and hill pastures and enjoy them. He must be thinking of fields to be
planted and fences to be repaired. I have heard that there are farms
back East where there comes a time when all is done. The crops are
harvested, the barns are tight against the weather, and the farmer is

freed of everything but feeding and milking. For the Californian, whether he raises oranges or garden truck or poultry or pigs or cattle, there never comes a time when he can take a good breathing spell, unless you count a short time in the fall just before the rains come to make grain fields fit for plowing. But about that time I guess he'd be getting in the last of the corn, or raking up another cutting of alfalfa.

EVERYBODY ENDS UP IN CALIFORNIA

California is to the other States what America is to the rest of the world—it is the place to which people come from everywhere, so that in these hills we have no regional types of people. But we could, I think, be divided into several classes. The backbone of us would be someone like Al Greenleaf, whose grandfather settled here in the early days. In the same class are the ranchers whose people came across the plains in covered wagons, and the descendants of those who hurried to California in the gold rush, and the fine people descended from old Mexican families. All these are the true Californians who fit into the life of these hills so well that you could never imagine them living anywhere else.

These people make you realize that California is only a short step ahead of its bright past. They are not old people. George Miller, who drove a stagecoach through our hills and up to the high mountain town of Julian, is only just past middle age. Al Greenleaf drove stage, too, and he is just starting his sixties. Wes Beadle is another young old-timer who will talk endlessly about the good days not so far back.

There is a second class of old-timer ranching in these hills. These are not the native Californians, but men who came here years ago. Most of them seem to have come from the Middle West. They have lived here so long and know the country so well that it is hard to believe they are not California-born, but they still talk as people talk back where they came from, and their mode of speech is more picturesque than that of the native Californian. After forty or fifty years of being Californians they still remember the way things are done back home, and, somehow, they sound a little homesick. They will tell you that life was hard on the farms of Nebraska and Kansas, but life is hard here too. They say that they came West dreaming of the ease of growing things in California, and learned that you don't reach up and pick golden oranges off trees wherever you happen to be. It all comes down to the

solid truth that living off the land is hard and disappointing work no matter where you are. When one of these men went to a doctor to find out what it was that had been ailing him, and learned that he had only a short time to live, he accepted it in much the same way that he had accepted crop failures. When I was talking to his wife about it, she said, "Well, it's just one more disappointment. It's the way life is, I guess. I'm used to bad things happening." There was no trace of self-pity in the way she said this. She was stating a fact, something she had noticed about life in the same way she had noticed certain things about weather and animals. When you've ranched through bad years and good, had crops wither and seen good cows die young, you know that life is like that.

Of course, there are some ranchers who have given up completely. In remote spots you find crumbling adobe walls; also, you find parts of wooden buildings left from a more recent time. In the brown hills you see a clump of green eucalyptus trees, or a couple of pepper trees, and you know that once a house was here. Sometimes you will find a sunken grave near a green tree, and you wonder whose bones these are and how long they've been here. In the spring you might find daffodils or small roses flowering by a sagging-roofed shack.

There are others who have given up, but don't seem to realize it. They sell some of their acres, raise grain in winter and corn in summer, have a cow or two, some pigs and chickens. They earn money by doing odd jobs—or by driving to the city each day to work. They do their chores in the cold early darkness, travel long miles to work, come home to do night chores, and go to bed. They are still ranchers.

There are some who once were cattlemen and were crowded off the range. I know one such man who raises turkeys for a living, but he still looks like a cattleman. No one thinks it out of place that he should come to town in high-heeled boots. For so many years he wore boots, Levis, and sombrero that he could not be comfortable in any other clothes. And he wouldn't look right.

THE INDIANS BELONG HERE

The people who belong to this hill country as no others ever can are the Indians and the Mexicans. An observing person can't wander half an hour in the hills without seeing where Indians have been. Their

small metates, those hollowed stones wherein they ground acorns, are gone because people can pick them up and carry them off. The smooth stones that fitted the hand are still scattered about, because most people don't see them. But the big metate stones, or mortar holes, are here for eternity. In a flat rock you will see as many as six or seven hollowed out, some old deep ones, some less worn. In back of our house there is a hollow boulder that forms a small cave, and there are these metates at the entrance. I have found small fragments of pottery in the cave, and someone else found arrowheads.

In the days before the missions California was a land of plenty, and the Indians had no need to think hard and be clever in order to live. The hills were full of game, the sea full of fish; in the fall the oaks dropped a plentiful harvest of acorns. Though I feel that our winters often are too cold, the Indians, being used to living outside, probably didn't suffer much. Life was easy, so why bestir themselves to create a lot of things they didn't need? Hardship makes primitive people develop a culture; our Indians had little need of inventing anything. They made what baskets and pottery they needed, and these were not without beauty. But the most beautiful things they made were arrowheads. I have seen them made of quartz, each arrowhead as lovely as a jewel. The only time our Indians showed a great deal of stupidity was when they allowed themselves to be enslaved during the days of the missions.

Now their descendants are living on the reservations, and the old ones have little love for us, though they are not given to expressing their feelings freely. Our nearest reservation is a beautiful high valley, the old Padre Barona Ranch. The Indians have not been there many years. They lived at the head of our El Monte Valley, but the city built a dam there and the El Capitan Indians had to become Barona Indians. The young ones didn't mind moving, the old ones didn't like it very much, but it was the dead ones who objected. They rested uneasily in their new graves, and sent up strange lights at night, and kept kicking up a fuss until the priest got around to saying services for the removal of the dead.

I have an Indian friend named Richard. He is nearly blind and looks older than he is, and because he can't see well, time is heavy on his hands, so he doesn't mind talking. He tells me that these California Indians are really Yuma Indians, that generations ago there was conflict in

Along Canoe Creek in the Garden Club of America area near Myers.

The vineyards of Lake County, California.

Vivid blue lupines covering the rolling hills of Southern California.

the tribe, and some of the Indians struck out for themselves and headed west across the desert. "Just like your story about the Pilgrims," he says.

At first I thought it impossible that a few Indians could travel across the trailless desert to the coastal hills, but, after all, Yuma Indians are desert Indians, and there are times of year when there is water in the desert. Richard says that there is similarity between the speech of the Yuma Indians and the mission Indians. He says that Indian talk is confusing, though, because, right here in this county, there are many different dialects. The people of one reservation will not talk exactly like the ones on a reservation a few miles away. Children are growing up with no knowledge of Indian language, and soon only the very old will remember tribal languages.

The older Indians feel that they have never had a square deal—promises have been made and broken. They talk about their "four corners"—lands promised to them with the "four corners laid out exact." The oldest ones say, "Yes, we will have our four corners, the four corners of our graves." I told Richard I'd like to write a book called *Four Corners*, and he thought it a good idea.

The Indians may seem very modern, but Richard says that in their hearts they have never given up the old gods. The Catholic religion does not fit in too badly with their ideas: church teachings and primitive beliefs are mixed together, seasoned with a goodly amount of superstition. They seem to take it all for granted, believing in God and the saints, believing in ghosts and magic.

Their *fiestas* are not very exciting. From the dry creek bed the Indians cut willow branches and build their little booths, *remudas*, around a square. There is a wooden platform in the middle, where there's sometimes a juke box and sometimes a real orchestra, and the young people dance modern dances. We go there and look at the Indians sitting about, and look at the kewpie dolls and the wheels of chance in *remudas*, that are like booths in a fair. There might be a small carnival contraption that goes round and round, on which we can have a ride for five cents. Or we can buy tamales and chile, soda pop and near beer. Officially, there are no alcoholic beverages on the reservation. But some of the people, both Indians and white, are very drunk.

The young Indian women dress in the latest style; the old women favor long, full, bright-colored skirts. The men, of course, wear Levis,

bright shirts, high-heeled boots, cowboy hats. Some of the Indians look very old, and there was one great-great-grandmother who danced at every *fiesta* until she died. When she was a hundred years old she still danced in the squaw dances.

The *fiesta* is primarily a harvest feast, a time of thanksgiving in late summer when the moon is full. But since our real harvesttime is in the spring, when the oat hay is cut, the *fiesta* must be a time of thankfulness for the corn harvest, and some years very little corn has been planted on the reservation. But August is the month of the corn moon, anyway. And *fiestas* are times when Indians go from one reservation to another and see all their friends. They have balky old cars with very worn tires, so there are numbers of cars broken down on roads between reservations at *fiesta* time. You see women waiting patiently while men struggle to patch and change a tire, or ponder over the puzzling vital parts under the hood. Sometimes they give up, and you see people sleeping in their stalled cars, waiting for someone to come and give them a push.

While we stand around at the *fiesta* hoping for tribal dances, the Indian children play like any children, the young people jive and jitterbug, the older ones enjoy themselves, sitting and talking to friends whom they haven't seen maybe since *fiesta* time last year. We grow bored and wish something would happen, but this *fiesta* is no entertainment for tourists; from the Indians' point of view plenty is happening. There are new babies to be admired, young married people to be congratulated. Finally most of the white people go home. If it were afternoon they could have watched the Indian boys play baseball, but it is night now and nothing happens.

Eight men get up a peon game. Under blankets the counters are passed back and forth; the eight men sit on the ground, four facing four. They sway back and forth and cultivate poker faces. Their women should stand in back and chant, the object of that being to confuse players on the other side, so they can't guess so well. This may go on until morning.

A long line of dancers may form, and there is chanting and stepping back and forth. It is a singing game, mainly for the women. It seems to be a matter of discovering which woman knows the most old songs.

When one song is ended, another is started, until nearly all have been sung, and only the old ones can keep remembering more.

Finally the old men light a little fire and dance solemnly around it, and it doesn't seem as if much is happening. But this is the thing to watch. For a man will put his hands and feet in flames and not be burned.

After *fiesta* time the Indians settle down for another year of day-to-day living. In September the school bus picks up the children and takes them to county grade schools and high schools. Some of the men work on ranches, some of them put in crops on the reservation. The reservation is like any small community; there are friendships between some families and quarrels between others. There are gossips and non-gossips, good people and bad, and children who are always wanting to go to the movies. Young girls demand permanent waves, boys plead for cars of their own.

MEXICANS ARE HAPPY PEOPLE

It is said that Mexicans are happy people, and this seems to be true. A Mexican is ready to laugh at almost anything, and he seems able to have a very good time whatever he is doing. In our part of the country there are prosperous Mexicans and very poor Mexicans, and I find it hard to believe that the poor and miserable can be so very happy.

A family of the poorest lived near us. The mother was thin and ill-looking, the father was not strong and could not keep a steady job, but the children seemed well and happy, and their numbers kept increasing. They lived in a dreary shack, and I used to wonder where they all found room to sleep. I think the children piled up in a corner somewhere, keeping warm together like a litter of puppies. One night I went past that shack on the way to phone a vet to come and take care of a sick colt. I thought I heard a woman scream. The next day I learned that, without the help of doctor or midwife, the Mexican woman had borne her ninth child. Later I heard that two days after the child was born the woman had gotten out of bed to do a washing. I felt shocked to realize that my colt had had a doctor's care for colic while a poor woman had had a baby with no help at all.

But this was an unusual case. I think most poor people go to the county hospital for their babies. As a rule the poorer Mexicans do not live

in squalor, for Mexicans are clean people, and they like a bit of garden by their doorway. And if a Mexican family has a good goat, it is a great help. A smart goat (and what goat isn't smart?) makes a wonderful playmate for the children, besides supplying milk to drink, and, once a year, furnishing kids to be eaten. When a poor Mexican has a goat to eat, he and his family do not eat alone. It is the occasion for a small feast, with friends and relatives invited to enjoy it.

These people have a way of making a party out of anything. During the days of the PWA, Pablo had a job as night watchman where a bridge was being constructed. He built a little fire in the sandy river bed and there, off and on throughout the summer nights, his friends and relatives came to sit by the fire and roast corn and eat watermelons and drink a little wine. They would sing, and I, riding by, thought it sounded beautiful.

I know of only one truly worthless Mexican. And he is charming. I asked him to work for me and he said that he had decided never to work again. "But how," I asked, "are you to get along? You've got to eat and have a place to sleep."

"Oh," he said, "it is easy. I have friends and I can borrow a quarter here and a dime there. It is much easier than working."

Most of the Mexicans I know are pleasant people who work as hard as anyone else, and live as well. The most noticeable difference between Mexicans and Americans is that Mexicans are unfailingly polite. Even their language is a far more gracious language than ours.

Around here people like Mexican help on ranches, and some of our best horsemen are Mexicans. The best blacksmith in the county comes of an old Mexican family, and he not only knows how to shoe a horse right, he knows all about horses and their innermost feelings.

When it comes to riding anything on four legs, no one can beat a Mexican boy named Alex who seems to have a magic way of feeling exactly what a colt is thinking, sometimes to such an extent that the colt himself seems astonished. Alex is unfailingly gentle and quiet, he doesn't even swear, and I've never seen him smoke a cigarette or take a swallow of whiskey. When he is having trouble, he merely sits himself down and cools off while he thinks about the colt. He doesn't have trouble often, but there were two horses he had trouble breaking because, no matter what he did, he couldn't keep them from running wildly. I met

him one time when he was on one of these animals. When the horse saw me, he dove into a thicket of bamboo. There were agitated rustlings and crashings, and presently Alex and his horse emerged, Alex miraculously still wearing his hat. "What happened?" he asked mildly. Once he got on a spoiled horse of ours and disappeared around a bend of the road. The horse started off bucking, and then ran, and we wondered when and where Alex would stop him. Five minutes later they returned. Alex was laughing, and the horse was the best behaved you ever saw—and the most surprised.

Alex loves to sing and play his guitar, and he loves his children. His little sons learned to ride before they could walk. A man who loves horses, music, and children is the sort who belongs in this beautiful hill country, so we hope Alex has lots of sons just like him.

BIRDS AND BEASTS

But the true owners of all these hills and valleys and tall mountains are the deer and the coyotes, the quail and doves and road runners, the brush rabbits and cottontails and jack rabbits, the kangaroo rats and field mice and pack rats, the possums and skunks and badgers, the mountain lions and bobcats and foxes, the eagles and hawks and buzzards and ravens, all the big and little singing birds, the ground squirrels and gophers, the snakes and lizards and horny toads, the little frogs that sing in damp places. . . . From time to time I meet some of the shyest of these, and we stare at each other in breathless amazement until the wild thing realizes that I am one of a deadly species. Man is the great killer, more deadly than the rattlesnake, more to be feared than anything else in creation. The deer and the coyote run from me and there's no way of telling them that this one human is no foe.

One burning summer day I searched through the canyons and looked for tracks by every small spring, hunting for two young bulls that had strayed. I rode far into the hills and looked under every clump of oaks, found all the bedding-down places where cattle like to rest, and finally came down a steep hill to a little unused road in the valley. My horse suddenly stopped and stared, and before me, not twenty feet away, a half-grown mountain lion was so intent on making a kill that he was unaware of my nearness. He crouched by the roadside ready to spring, his haunches moved tremulously, then he was a quick tawny curve as

he leaped across the road and caught a ground squirrel that screamed once, struggled, and was limp. It was beautiful, and I held my breath, hoping to see the young lion eat his meat. But my horse shook his head so the bit rattled, and the lion left his meal and bounded into the brush. I made a wide circle around the dead squirrel, thinking that if there was no scent of me or my horse the lion might come back to his food. I felt mean about intruding; at the same time I was delightfully excited because I had been privileged to see this thing. Though I am always sorry for little animals caught by big ones, I am glad, too, for the hungry one who gets the bite of meat. And there is the fact that if this land were free of all varmints, there would be an oversupply of rodents, and if ever all the coyotes and lions and bobcats were gone, I wouldn't want to live in these hills.

Coyotes are the most maligned animals. They are no more thieves or cowards than we are. We take life for food, and so do they. They are beautiful animals, and if they were not intelligent and crafty, they could not survive with the hand of man against them. Once I saw a male coyote being very brave. He stood on a boulder and barked to attract my attention while a smaller coyote slipped away through the brush to a safe hiding place. Only ten feet from me, the big coyote stood on his stone and watched and waited, and then leaped down and melted into the hillside coloring. People complain of coyotes destroying crops as well as making off with unprotected hens, but there are ways of keeping both hens and crops in safety. One way is not to kill all small animals yourself, but leave some rabbits and squirrels for the coyotes. Another way is to let your scent linger where you do not want the coyote to come. One farmer went out to his field every night and put his hand on each of his growing watermelons, and not one hungry coyote took a bite of one melon. (Though people came quietly one dark night and took some of the biggest melons from that field.)

I meet the deer when I ride into the hills to look for my heifers; sometime three or four does will bound up a hillside, sometimes a young buck will whistle like a playful horse, stare at me a minute, and go leaping off in that wonderful springy way of deer (and playing lambs).

In summer the cow trails are dusty in the hills, and in the morning I find the handlike track of badgers, and that is all of them I've ever seen. Possums I see quite often, and the skunks and civet cats are not

in the least bashful. It has been a long time since I have seen a fox, but surely there are some still about.

During this dry season the springs are very important, with narrow game trails leading to them from every direction. The secret springs are sweet cool spots among the summer hills. You find them in the canyons—I know of only one hillside spring: its source is under an overhanging boulder on a dry steep slope, just where you'd least expect to find water. It is the only spring I know that hasn't a little cottonwood by it. All the canyon springs are marked by bright green leaves, so you look down from a hill and see the shining green, and it's a good sight whether you are thirsty or not.

But nothing needs go thirsty in the hills. The cactus stores water, and from the plant called "hen and chickens" it is easy to extract moisture. All you need do is take a big bite of one of its leaves, and you have a mouthful of water.

My favorite spring is a stone basin under an oak tree. The water overflows into a small pool, and there my horse Pericles likes to stand and soak his feet. Grass is bright green around the water's edge, there are wild sunflowers waist-high, and I can enjoy sitting on the edge of the stone basin as long as Pericles wants to stand in the water. He dreams with eyes half shut, ears and lower lip relaxed, while red and green dragonflies zoom past his nose. Rippling shadows, reflected from the water, move over his gray belly. Polliwogs with golden flecks on them wiggle about his ankles. A snake can glide from one side of the pool to the other, and Pericles never sees it. Once when we came here I saw a field mouse swimming earnestly across the water. It is one of the oddest sights I've happened across, for why should a mouse be swimming when he could have walked around?

I don't know what I'd do without my cows to go hunting for in the hills. Cows always find the best places for resting on a summer day, and they make good trails up and down the hills and to the canyon springs. When you are looking for stray heifers you are alert, and when your eyes search the hillsides for the tawny hide of a Jersey heifer you are quite likely to spot deer or coyote. When I've located all the heifers after a day of exploring hillsides and canyons and small draws, it gives me the most satisfied feeling to be riding home when the late afternoon light is at the mellow stage, and little frogs are singing summer songs

by a hidden spring. A canyon wren will whip down the scale so that notes of music are like drops of water, and half of every hill will be in shadow.

SUMMER IS A GOOD TIME

Summer, in these hills, is a long golden dusty season, haunted by day by the calling of wild doves and the sharp whirring sounds of cicadas. The song of summer nights is the crying of killdeer over the dry river, the muted voice of the owl from the hill, and the call of poorwills sounding everywhere. The first hot day of summer is the Fourth of July, but early morning is not hot, and coolness comes when the afternoon shadow of the mountain drops over the valley. On hot afternoons we sit on our front porch and watch for that shadow to spread itself until it reaches a certain fence. Then it is time to do the evening milking and feeding.

I, who have no love of early rising, must admit that on a summer morning it isn't such a hardship to get up while stars are still over the hill's rim. My niece Wowser and I will do it for one reason, if there is to be a long cattle drive. The first time our blacksmith took his cattle to the high pastures on El Capitan, Wowser and I were up and had the cows milked before sunrise. Just as we were saddling our horses we heard the quick soft beat of many cloven hoofs, and the cattle, all excited, came trotting up our road. They swung their horned heads from side to side; saliva dripped from open mouths.

One rider went ahead to protect an unfenced watermelon patch, men rode on each side, one was behind. The cows had no need to be driven, only guided in the right direction, for they were in the mood for travel.

We fell in at the end of the procession, and, when the sun rose, it made the dust bright gold, so that the cattle moved dimly in a burnished haze, and their spread horns were shining. Never have I seen such beautiful animals as those, moving east into the sunlight.

Long before we reached the foot of the mountain, the herd settled down to slow plodding. The calves began to drag until they were in the rear ranks, their poor little noses crusted with dust, their tails limp with weariness. From time to time one of us would dismount and push a little one along for a while. There was a truck at the foot of the mountain road to pick up the most tired. Then the mothers of calves began

to worry and to voice their worry dismally, and all the long winding way up the mountain, the cows called, and from across a deep canyon echoes answered.

The narrow mountain road turns back on itself as it climbs, so we could look up to the next level, at the marching herd strung out in a brown-and-white design, a cloud of dust over it all. The hot part of the day had arrived, and we looked down through our dust cloud to the cool green river trees. The way to love and know trees is not to live in a wooded country. I feel stifled in the woodsiness of New England, where even the trees seem smothered with underbrush. Here our trees grow cleanly in separate clumps; they are there when you want them and not in the way when you want a clear view for half a hundred miles. From the mountain we could see miles of curving river marked by the green of willow and cottonwood and sycamore. We looked at valley and low hills and high mountains and the colors—bright green of valley alfalfa fields, yellow of foothills, darkness of the near mountains, and blue and purple and slate gray of the distant ones. To the west was a sun-struck flatness that was the Pacific, and far out were two islands, the color of the furthest mountains.

We plodded on through heat and dust, and two cows left the herd and went bolting straight down to a deep brushy canyon, and two riders took after them and lost them completely, while the rest of us worked to keep others from going the same way. They had smelled water down there.

High up, the road made its last turn, and the herd filed through an open gate. Before them were shade and water and grass.

We unsaddled horses and turned them loose to roll and graze. We sprawled under a live oak, and life was perfect there in the deep shade. I thought that of all wonderful trees the live oak is the best of all. It is the great and gracious tree of California and should be our State tree. If we have a State tree it probably is the redwood, which is a pity, because thousands of Californians (including myself) have never seen a redwood. The live oak spreads its dark branches in many places up and down the State; it makes the valleys soft and adds gentleness to hills. Life is so strong in the oak that after fire has burned its trunk and destroyed every leaf, it may still survive, though its coming back to life is a slow and patient process.

It is the very aridness of summer that makes it so interesting and beautiful. The dry season gives to these hills some of the same quality of mystery that the desert has. Because water isn't everywhere, each damp place is a treasure, each patch of growing green is of value. In certain valleys, underground streams supply enough moisture for roots, so that grass follows the way of an unseen watercourse, and happy is the cow who has such a spot in her pasture. The willows and cottonwoods and sycamores flourish where their roots find water; they are the trees that show you a good place to live.

The very hottest summer days are not hard to bear if you will be lazy as the cows and rest under a tree. Those days have certain sounds and certain smells that other days don't have. You can hear things stir with heat and dryness, and the sun-cooked chaparral has its fragrance intensified. Every living thing shares your feeling of wanting to find a cool spot. The heat is solid as a wall.

The first cool air of night is like a drink of water. The quail go to roost in their live oak, and sputter and quarrel and push each other. Nothing makes so much fuss as a covey of quail going to bed. By the time they are quiet, the earth is cooling, and then come the delicious damp green smells of the river bed.

Night climbs the hills slowly. Darkness moves upward from the valley floor; it is a long time before it reaches the last sunlit mountain top.

We saddle our horses and follow trails by the river willows. If a waning moon is to rise, we see its light on the high part of our mountain before we see the moon itself come over its hill. The stones on our mountain become so radiant that they seem to be lighted from within; our mountain stands out brightly while the valley floor is still deep in night. The moonlight moves down our mountain just as sunlight comes down it in the morning; light spreads slowly until the valley is bright gold.

We walk our horses and listen to the little sounds by the damp places, and we love to hear coyotes call into the night. A coyote has many different things to say and many ways of saying them.

Summer is a good time for being lazy and enjoying the night, but it is a time of worry, too. For when fire starts on a dry hill it is uncontrollable in a minute. Always in summer smoke hangs over the hills; there is scarcely a day when there is no fire. When we smell the first

faint whiff of smoke we rest uneasy. Sometimes a fire is so far away
that we know only that somewhere the hills are burning: the smoke may
be drifting into our valley from miles away. When a fire is anywhere
near, we can tell exactly where it is by the great black billowing funnel
of smoke. It is both beautiful and terrible, burning the greasewood with
fury, seeming to make oaks explode into flame. Twice we have had
fire come into our own pasture, and there were wild anxious times of
getting animals to a safe place.

South of the border, they let the fires burn on. Here we fight to stop
them, for no one knows how far a fire will go. Ranch houses and barns
and animals have been destroyed in our valley. Even when fire keeps
to the brushy hill, it is bad because not all the small animals can escape.
Some ranchers say it is good to have brush burned from the hills, for
the next rainy season will bring plentiful grass. There are others who
say that after fire there is too much erosion. But I notice that little time
is lost: even before it rains you see the new shoots coming up where
sumac burned.

After a fire the hills are very beautiful, for their structure is plain to
see. You see rock formations and crevices that were unnoticed before,
and you can travel anywhere without a trail. Just before night the black
hills are the color of ripe plums, soft and curved. When you ride over
them everything looks so strange that you have the feeling of being on
another planet. There is no distance at all between the hills and the first
stars, and strong is the feeling of you on this earth moving through
space.

Summer days are not all hot. There are the soft sweet days when a
fresh breeze comes in from the Pacific and there is an Indian-summer
haze over the hills. Then there are days when it almost rains. Over the
high mountains the clouds are dark, lightning flashes out, and thunder
rolls. Sometimes a few fat raindrops splash into our dusty valley, and
the sweet smell of wet dust is strong. We know that the mountains are
receiving good showers. Cuyamaca gathers all the clouds around its
peak, and then I believe what I have been told, that the word *cuyamaca*
means "no rain beyond." People on the desert side can look at those
clouds with no hope at all. Cuyamaca keeps that moisture, and there's
not one drop to fall on the vast dryness to the east.

As far as we are concerned, the seasons are neatly divided, three

months to each. June, July, and August are summer—August almost the best of all, with blue-shadowed cumulus clouds piling up like mountains. Corn is tall in the fields now, its leaves curled at noon, but fresh and crisp in the morning. Alfalfa likes hot weather when it is irrigated a lot, and the Bermuda grass makes good green pasture in damp places. Our horses graze and graze on our small strip of it, until it is cropped so short their noses get calloused.

FALL IS A BAD TIME

The first day of September comes with the crack of guns, and it is fall. The wild doves fly, piteously looking for a place to hide, and their children die in the nests. Fall is a bad time. When deer season comes, no Jersey cow or buckskin horse is safe in the hills, and the only thing that cheers me is that hunters frequently shoot each other. After the rainless summer the hills are like tinder, and when the hunters are about, there are more fires than ever.

Fall is so beautiful I wish I could appreciate it. But it is a time when pasture grass is scant, when deer and quail and doves are in danger, and I can't be happy. Fall is a hungry time. A few ranchers are careful not to overstock their pastures, and those have enough dry grass to last. But even then the feed is not very good; the sun has burned the strength out of it. Range cattle look their worst now, and it is time to put out cottonseed cake or corn stalks or hay. When you have to feed hay—especially if you've run out of the hay you've raised and have to buy feed—profits diminish swiftly. Some ranchers watch their herds closely and gather in all the weak cows to be fed, letting the hardier ones get by as best they can. But if a cow gets too poor, it takes a long time to build her up again. Every fall some old horses and cows starve to death.

Until the real cold comes, it is still fly time, so every scratch has to be watched for maggots, just as in summer. Cows have ticks in their ears and warbles on their backs, and the botflies pester the horses. I have noticed that if a horse or cow grows sick in the fall, it seems to be sicker than at any other time, and if an animal gets a barbed wire cut, it takes longer to heal.

Even the crisp bright days leave me unmoved. And the bad days, of which fall has many, leave me feeling that I would like to hibernate until spring. There seems little good about a day that starts out with

frost in the morning, and turns so hot by noon that it's hard to breathe, and becomes chilly with the first shadows. But that is nothing compared to the kind of day when an east wind blows from the desert, and harsh clouds of dust sweep down the valley. People's hair and horses' tails stand out wildly, and no living thing is comfortable. Sometimes that desert wind will scream about for three solid days. The orange leaves curl up, and not one grove looks capable of surviving. It might be good to go to bed and bury one's ears under blankets, except that sand has contrived to get in bed, too.

But the hottest, dryest fall day is beautiful, whether I like it or not. The dry air is so extremely clear that every hill and mountain has moved nearer; sunlight is very strong and shade is very black. It is at this time of year that the mountains color best: autumn leaves are pale compared to the colors of stony mountains when the sun goes down. El Capitan glows blood-red, changes to rose and lavender and purple, holds its color until there is no light left in the sky. Stars grow bigger and brighter than at any other time.

As soon as the sycamore trees turn rusty in our valley, we think it is time to ride up to the Padre Barona Reservation. That high valley is only a few miles away, but there is enough difference in altitude so that leaves are a brighter color. Up there the sycamores are pink and peach and pale gold. The willow leaves are like segments of orange.

From the last hill we look down into the reservation. The valley is broad and flat, the stubble grainfields are pale. The creek bed is a red and yellow ribbon, the live oaks are dark green. The hills beyond never look real at this time of year. There are low tan hills and tall tan mountains, and they look like stage scenery made of cardboard. Miles away the very highest peaks are dim blue.

We ride on through the reservation to the old Featherstone Ranch, where there are dark live oaks in meadows of gold grass. By a stone watering trough a windmill creaks lazily, and the horses dip their noses in the sweet water, and we gulp quantities of it from a rusted pipe. A windmill is a most pleasant thing, making a comfortable sound. We rest a long time in the golden meadow by the water, and then we feel we have to ride up Featherstone Canyon to look at more sycamore leaves, to see the metal of cottonwoods twinkling and turning in the least stir of air.

When we ride home, down Wildcat Canyon, we like the sun to be low and intense so that all the sycamore trees burn red, the cottonwoods burn gold. Our valley is below us in patterns of red and gold, and we forget the bad things about fall.

For fields to be planted, it is the time of waiting. Until rains come to soften the earth there is no use plowing. Nothing seems to be growing anywhere. In the hills the little springs, so nearly dry in late summer, come alive. The cold nights have brought water closer to the earth's surface. But that seems to be all that happens.

The oaks drop their acorns, and cows and horses and deer eat them. The Indian women make acorn mush, using the old metates and grinding stones. But they have a modern way of taking out the bitterness. Instead of soaking the acorns and changing the water, they put them in a little sack, attach the sack to a hydrant, turn on the water, and let it run and run until no bitter taste is left. The mush is nourishing, and tastes no worse than oatmeal.

There comes an intense longing for rain. The sun-baked earth is suffering, the dusty oak leaves are in need of washing, the hides of cattle would feel better for a good rain. Cows and horses are growing shaggy winter coats, but every fall calf and colt is born already wearing its heavy coat.

If it rains too early, there may not be another rain soon enough to keep the green sprouts growing. It is a sad sight to see the green grass come up and wither down again. Better to wait until November and the probability of steady rains.

But even then it may not rain. It is discouraging when fall seems to go on endlessly with no rain at all. Promises are made and broken. The sky will cloud, a wind will blow from the south, red-winged blackbirds will hold conventions—and the next day will be clear again.

Always the rains come, though. It is only a matter of waiting. Beautiful dark clouds fill the sky, the south wind blows damply, the blackbirds go mad again—and the rain comes lightly, letting the hard earth receive it slowly. Time for a swift downpour later, after the earth is softened so the water won't run off.

You can hear the earth drinking. The dust-buried seeds move, and in a day the land is lifting with new green grass.

This is the greatest of all things. After over half a year of drought, the

hills return to life. There is no smell like the smell of that first rain. Wet dust, wet sagebrush, wet brown grass, wet air, wet hides of cattle, wet leaves. The birds sing into the rain, and tree toads and frogs lift up their voices. The cows cavort, the horses run. The young bulls, born in the spring and unused to rain, paw the earth and bellow like their sires. The earth has turned to a new exciting season. It is the time of growth.

Tractors moan in the big fields. The feed stores are busy selling oat and barley seeds. The brown, turned earth is so fragrant that it seems you can taste its goodness. If cows get into a plowed field, they run and buck like horses, rub their heads in the earth, paw like bulls.

Our neighbor, who owns a dairy, seems to be plowing day and night. I think his sons work in shifts. If there is a moon the tractor goes far into the night. The fields must be seeded, ready for the next rain.

Now life comes with great fullness to the burned hills. I do not know where all the grass seeds come from. The grass is thick on the slopes where only heavy brush grew before. The hills that were black in summer are a brighter green than any other hills.

The metates catch the rain and become drinking and bathing places for birds. Water remains a long time in these hollowed stones, so if it does not rain again for a while, the birds need not worry.

It is fall, but it is like spring, too, with new growth everywhere. It seems that spring and fall are mixed together, new grass with colored leaves dropping on it.

SNOW ON THE MOUNTAINS

Winter is a cold, wet time. The grass grows slowly, frost is spread thick on clear mornings. The grain in the fields grows faster than the wild grasses. The pastures are green, but the short grass is scant and gives the animals no strength. Cold winds and heavy rains drive horses and cows into the shelter of canyons, rumps to the storm.

On clear nights people who have orange and lemon groves listen for frost warnings on the radio. They must go out and light heaters to keep the orchards warm. Raising California oranges is not only a matter of letting our famous sunshine do its work. It is a battle with frost and drought and insects and scale.

Officially we consider it winter when one morning we look up from

our frosty valley and see mountains white with snow. After it has rained in our valley and snowed in the mountains, there come mornings of clear coldness when you wonder how the shivering grass can stay alive. Sunset turns the snow red, and the stars shine glassily, and the cold is so intense that it has quieted the night. The cry of a coyote is sharp as ice.

But just as all summer days are not hot, all winter days are not cold. It can be warm in our valley even when the mountains wear snow. One warm winter day a friend and I looked up at Cuyamaca and saw no snow at all, so we decided to load two horses in a trailer, drive to the foot of the mountain trail, and ride up to the forestry lookout on Cuyamaca's high peak.

It was cold at the foot of the trail, a clean cold filled with the unfamiliar smell of pines. This high country was so different from our foothills that it was almost impossible to think that we had left home only an hour ago. We started up the trail through the pines, and squirrels scolded us—not our kind of ground squirrels, but furry squirrels that lived in trees. There was a sudden snap of twigs, and two deer disappeared into the forest.

We rode for ten minutes and came upon a patch of snow. The horses bent their heads, and lifted astonished cold noses, and turned their upper lips toward the sky. It was their first experience with snow, and had they known what lay ahead of them, they wouldn't have gone another step. We didn't know what was before us, either. Patches of snow became more numerous, and soon there was no bare ground at all. The unhappy horses had to walk in snow, and as we climbed higher the snow was deeper. Hoofs would punch through the crust, and the horses would flounder and plunge because it felt to them like boggy places in our hills. A wise old mountain horse would have plodded through the deep places, but our poor horses thought they had to scramble fast to keep from bogging. Their noses smoked and their hearts thumped.

Our hearts thumped, too, but from excitement, because of the unreal beauty of this new world. The snow was white in the sunshine and blue in the shade. The pines still held snow, and though we didn't feel any wind, there was a constant soughing in the upper branches.

We toiled so slowly up the steep and winding trail that when we rounded the last bend and found ourselves at the summit, the seeming suddenness of our arrival was overwhelming. All at once we were

in the sky, and we sat shivering on our shivering horses and looked at range after range of white mountains. We looked north to more mountains, south to Mexico, east to the pale desert, and west down to our own warm valley.

But always we looked at snow again. Mile after mile of whiteness. Slopes and meadows and valleys of snow. Mountains of snow.

From that day on I have not been able to think of the word winter without seeing again those endless, lonesome miles of snow. It was silent and lifeless, but I think that there was life, only unseen. Undoubtedly the mountains were full of animals, birds were in the trees, roots were alive. But all the time that we stood on that high place we saw no other warm living thing, only the pines, only the endless snow.

So that, in my mind, is winter.

Down here the rains grow more fierce as winter progresses. There comes a morning after a hard rain when we waken to the sound of roaring water. The creek is foaming down our canyon, into the lower pasture, on to the river, on to the sea. A thousand creeks are pounding through a thousand canyons, a billion tiny rivulets are pouring down the slopes to join the creeks. There are thundering cascades in the stony canyons, there are echoes in the hills.

The soaked grain fields are shining green, the hillsides are vivid. By now there are wild flowers, the lilac is almost ready to purple the hills. The whole tempo of the season is speeded up; it is hard to remember back to the waiting days of fall. Dark and powerful-looking clouds gather around the mountains, roll away and return, drop to the foothills and climb again.

The rains seem to be shouting to the oats in the fields, to the wild grasses in the hills, "Grow! Grow!" It is as if the driving rain were whipping things into life. The pasture grass has been short and without strength for too long; now it has its roots deep and firm. Now let it spread thick and grow tall: the range cattle have been hungry long enough.

Before El Capitan Dam was built there used to be bad floods; before San Vicente was built there used to be good little floods. El Capitan's overflow is piped to San Vicente, so we don't have the wonderful roaring river to maroon us for a few days. Being marooned used to be fun. We rode the horses along the dark river up to Walt Hartung's ranch

where a cable was rigged across the river. Big, good-natured Walt had a lovely time taking a cable ride across the water, going to town to buy provisions for us marooned ones. Walt knows all about this country and its good years and bad; he has lost money and made money and takes good and bad as they happen. I have never seen him in a hurry. When I meet him in town, he is never too busy to stop and talk a while. He knows every hill trail, every spring, every old mine. He lives right at the foot of El Capitan and is the one who has to go out at night and find the hikers from the city who have got themselves lost on the mountain.

I think he agrees with me that winters were more fun when we had our little floods. This country is being tamed a little too much. Walt thinks that anyone who wants everything to be easy and convenient ought to stay in town. He has all the scorn of the old-timer for the new-comer, but it is tempered with amusement. Walt can see the funny side of most anything.

But though our river can no longer run wild, it flows enough every winter so there are little pools left for summer; and the canyon creeks will never be subdued.

SPRING

One day you see bluebirds, and it is time for the sun to shine a little longer.

All at once the pastures look fine. No need to put out feed for the heifers and horses. Winter is nearly done.

Wild tobacco bushes have blue-green leaves and yellow blossoms; and colored hummingbirds hurry among them, just as in summer.

The air turns soft and sweet, bees make a great humming. Their owners no longer have to feed them sugar. The slopes are covered with wild flowers.

Sycamore branches are beaded with leaf buds; they shine like glass when the early sun comes through the fog. Pussy willows turn into catkins; pale yellow-green colors the trees by the river. The cotton-woods grow leaves so shining they always look wet. Brightest green of all are the new elderberry leaves. The live oaks are gentle pastel shades; the old leaves make room for new. Little golden tassels make the oaks seem to wear halos when the sun shines through them.

It is lilac time.

First the white lilac, then the blue, then the very deep purple that grows but one other place in the world. Lilac time, and the air like honey, so that the fact that we are alive and breathing is all that matters.

The road runner whimpers his love call over the hills, the cock quail calls "Get back there, get back there!" The calling of doves drifts through the valley; there's never a minute you don't hear it. The orioles and woodpeckers tell you it is spring, meadowlarks and linnets sing all day, and the mockingbird sings day and night. Swallows return to nest under our eaves, whether it is a saint's day or not. These are the birds who do not mind being around people. Back in the hills the canyon wrens and the rock wrens sing in the deep canyons and by the waterfalls and on the stony slopes. Eagles nest in the high wild places, and ravens quarrel with them.

The wild oats begin to ripen; they ripple like water in the wind. Wild mustard is sweet and yellow, wild radish is like a cloud low on the fields. The grain begins to head out.

Late rains are brightened with sunshine, rainbows span our valley.

All the horses and cows are fat and shining in their new spring coats. Foals frolic, calves sleep hidden in the deep grass. Ranching all at once seems easy.

When the sun is low you walk on shining grass and you see a halo around the shadow of your head. The horse and the dog that are with you wear halos, too, but you can't see theirs, and they can't see yours. For a magic time each living thing is holy, the blessing of spring is soft on the land.

Now the sheep come. I don't know where they have wintered, but one morning there are flocks of sheep on the unfenced mesas. There are Basque herders with them, and dogs, a few goats, and a burro. There are the piping voices of little lambs and the deep sad voices of old ewes. The wild grains are dry, and the sheep dogs go about shod in moccasins. Without their little shoes the dogs would not be able to walk: foxtails and bronco grass would work into their paws.

Cactus blossoms are like big yellow roses. The white spires of yucca candle the hills. Indian paintbrush is crimson; the lovely apricot-colored monkey flower starts its long season of blossoming. Everywhere there are more flowers than I can name.

It is the time of ripening, the time of harvest. Time for sheep to be shorn, time for hay to be cut, time for mares to be bred again.

And now, of all times, is the time to be in the hills. The trails that go into the hills are bordered with flowers, and the hills are filled with bird songs, and water makes a soft tinkling in the canyons. The wild torrents of early spring are gentled into brooks, and polliwogs are fat in the pools. We follow hill trails that are old and overgrown, and I think how odd it is that in the most remote hill place, you can almost always find some kind of trail. Ancient paths leading into the hills' hearts, game trails and Indian trails, and trails made by range cattle. A burro trail, half-lost, goes up the side of El Capitan to an old mine. One of our very best trails was a stagecoach road half a century ago.

We ride to a ridge and look at the low hills and the high hills and the far tall mountains. We look down on the ripening grain fields in the valley, green turning gold.

In another week the hills will be golden, too; this is the ending of the green time. But the flowering will go on; the flames of scarlet buglar against the rocks, the wild sunflowers in the canyons, the bright, sturdy conchal agua blossoming from dry earth.

No matter what season is ending, there is always more beauty to come.

FARM, ROCK, AND
VINE FOLK

BY IDWAL JONES

It would be wrong to think of the chapter you have just read as telling the whole story of the variety of life and people living among the Coast Ranges. Something of that variety is given you in this chapter, and yet more of the tale of human variety must be left for other chapters. (R. P.)

Toyon was a ranch in the Coast Range, sixty years away in time, but two hours by the watch, if one goes across the Carquinez Strait, with its fog and high-running tides, the sirens howling sonorously at the Punto de los Quatros Evangelistas. I always got to Toyon by night. With its ten farm-clearings, its duck swamps, and a square mile of timber, alive with coyotes and bobcats, it was the largest ranch in the county, and assuredly the wildest. Hardly less wild were the Portuguese tenants, a light-hearted and raucous tribe, mainly, who farmed well enough in a guerilla fashion, grew wheat and hay, and were fond of pig roasts, church festivals, and applejack.

I liked to get there on a wet night, the air full of oxygen, with smells of pine, tarweed, red earth, and eucalyptus balsam, and a storm dying out among the trees. Your foot crunched on pine cones, shards of eucalyptus bark, highly pungent, and dead leaves. That was the California night smell—the smell of the Coast Range in the rainy season.

Usually Ort Whitby, who looked after the crops for Toyon, met me with a lantern. He was a dry, thong-like Englishman under a big hat, with vest and watch chain, and shirt wrists unbuttoned. Ort never had anything to say. He had long ago become utterly Californian. He was also a silent agrophile, so earth-spelled that he would stand immobile for hours in a field, in smiting heat or in frost, gazing at the hills, or into space, as if mesmerized by earth currents and sound of insects and wind.

Ort, by nature distrustful, kept to himself, and slept in the harness room of the stable, a den packed with fusty gear and shelves of cob-webbed horse medicine and salves. Armed with some vague managerial

137

powers, I lived in the ranch house. It was built in solid New England style, at the time of the Civil War, handsome and gloomy inside, with poppy-head finials at the balustrade; and hidden in a cluster of immense blue gums, which kept it forever in deep shadow. It was also haunted, and therefore shunned by the Portuguese.

The grand seigneur of Toyon, Henri Ebeniste, bought and sold ranches and water fronts, and he had achieved a fortune that even in comparison with the wealth of the Comstock Lode barons was imposing. His hospitality was renowned, his taste in wines exquisite, his dinners ceremonial. In small matters he was sharp-set and greedy, and this earned him the dislike of his tenants, who, after some trouble at law, took to firing at him from behind trees as he rode past in his carriage. Then, daily, a loaded hay wagon left Toyon in the morning and returned at night, driven by Wong, the Chinese valet and coachman. Concealed in the hay was a large box, fitted up with a chair, wherein M'siew Henri rode comfortably, with cigar, newspaper, and hanging lamp.

After a month, he ended the grievance, threw a dinner for the tenants, and peace once more descended on Toyon. The seigneur's death even prompted some expressions of regret. He left a quarter million to Wong who, himself dying shortly after, bequeathed his fortune to an orphan asylum in China.

I used to help Ort haul out posts and fence wire to the tenants, the old agreement being that, for keeping the fences in repair, they got poisoned grain to rid the wheat fields of mice. Toward harvesttime, I saw that the fields were a heaving carpet of velvet. Yet we had trucked out enough poison to kill off all the mice on this edge of the planet. Hercules would have known better. The Portuguese, too, were wiser. They washed off all the arsenic, and with the grain fattened their lordly, black pigs. Their fences they let run down, anyway.

"How long have these mice been here?" I asked.

"About a hundred years," said Ort.

"Then these Portuguese don't need advice from me or anyone else."

Ort filled his pipe with chips from a slab of "eatin' tobacco." After the molasses in it began to bubble and splutter cosily, he grunted, "I could have told you as much when you came."

Toyon was fortunate in its tobacco. We got it free from Mr. Pereira, who grew it himself on the acres where he grew tomatoes for a cannery,

and also tobacco for his friends. The green leaves, wet with molasses, he pounded into a bored log with mallet and broomstick, to release them with an axe in the spring—a hard and gray lot of snakes, that we called "cobra head." Neophytes at first puff of it exhibited symptoms of snake bite and syncope, with spots before the eyes, and a profound dejection of spirits. It was not a very good tobacco—California is unable to grow fair tobacco, for lack of dew—but after the third bout one became immune, a devotee of the brand, and a frequent caller at the shack of the excellent Mr. Pereira. A vast, hulking man in red undershirt, with unbelted paunch, and the mustachios of a grenadier, he was a sluggard and lotus-eater, and no man had a kinder heart. He dozed blissfully in his arbor, read through cracked glasses, and played mildly on a tuba.

For him the great events of the year were the Sons of Portugal *festa*, and the annual ball of the Crab Fishermen's Protective Association, of which we were honorary members, because the ranch tomatoes went into sauce for tinned sardines. This ball was a dress-up affair, held at Fishermen's Wharf in San Francisco, and quite wonderful for its warm and unaffected gaiety. After the banquet of *gran galera* salad, bouillabaisse, enormous crabs caught that morning off the Golden Gate, and claret, the tables were upset, and the debris swept out, to leave the floor with a patina of oil and wine, almost as tacky to dance over as resin. Mr. Pereira slept through the ball, and slept all the way back to Toyon, but he was packed with enough recollections of that banquet to keep him in talk for the rest of the year.

Ort slept in his Sunday black suit, with tan shoes and silver watch. Years before, when he was asleep, a thief had tiptoed into the harness room and purloined his Sunday outfit. And Ort was not one to be caught napping twice.

I remember an advertisement I once read in the *California Swine Breeders' Friend:* "Wanted—a man to live on a farm. Must be sober, and have sympathy with pigs." Ort was sober, save perhaps on Sunday nights when he discoursed with Mr. Pereira over the applejack, which was deceptive, for within it lurked the guile and power of a land mine, but his sympathy was with dogs, and his secret favorite was Rink, an ornery hound, half Kerry beagle.

The trees about the ranch house and in the yard are Eucalyptus globulus, lifting their marmoreal columns, bluish-gray, to the heavens.

their high-lifted swatches of gun-metal foliage rustling in the zephyrs, casting down a shade grateful on hot days. They drop in the September winds clusters of their long, oily leaves, and pods, and the yard is matted with fronds. Thad Newlin, pensioner of Toyon, who was ninety, said these Australians had been planted at the close of the Civil War. He had a seat at the foot of his favorite blue gum, where he spent his last twenty years dreaming, he and his tree growing together like Philemon and Baucis.

Silva and three or four farmers I knew used to gather these pods, crush them as if they were juniper berries, steep them in a liqueur, or else distil them with a rough wine. The drink is called "eucalypsinthe" and it is palatable but strange, not very unlike some Cartosa aged in kegs of eucalyptus wood.

Everywhere in California the eucalyptus grows, in the Sierra foothills as well as on the Coast Range, where the tawny landscape, its curves and bronze planes shifting through a scale of tones in hazy sunlight, has fitted itself to the tree. Among the hundred and forty varieties are weird specimens—scorbutic and gaunt, their bark clattering in the wind, like gibbet relics. It was these medicine poles, "their system of radication a scandal this side the globe," that Norman Douglas had in mind when he tore into the eucalyptus in *Old Calabria*. A while after that he relented. A lady I knew at Cupertino sent him photographs of the double colonnade of blue gums about the hill farm where she lived with her pack of mastiffs, for she was dog-mad as well as dendrophile. They were truly admirable, her blue gums, of a remote and melancholy beauty, in starlight Cyclopean ghosts from the never-never land.

An exchange of letters, arboreal in theme, sprang up. Then more letters went back and forth, with such a drifting in of books, pictures, and manuscripts from Italy that the large upper chamber in this house amidst the blue gums was, when I saw it fifteen years ago, wholly filled.

I have heard Mr. Newlin say that the Reverend William Taylor often visited this corner of the Range, on the way up to Sacramento, to pluck brands from the burning. This black-bearded giant, who swung his arms and lustily sang and preached at street corners in San Francisco, came to the Coast Range in 1849, the year of the gold rush. "Auld Jawn" McLaren, who created Golden Gate Park, always believed it was Taylor who introduced these trees to California, sending to his wife, when he

was on a missionary trip in Australia, a pound of eucalyptus buds. She planted them in their garden, where they grew faster than the green bay tree. I once had a picture of this evangelist and a book of his sermons. Though his income was so small that when he built his home he had to chop down redwood timber, trim logs into shape with an adze, and haul them across the Bay in his rowboat, he buried more than a thousand paupers at his own expense, walking as the sole mourner, preaching for each a funeral sermon. Taylor had the true missionary fervor. Seventy years ago he went to Africa where he died, a bishop. He has long since receded into myth.

MEN OF THE LONG PIPE

So likewise has the Chinese butler and coachman, Wong, to whom riches were naught. The Chinese who settled in the Coast Range and there struck root never wandered far, and the native virtues abandoned the restless, the loose of foot. Wong for several years kept the road through Toyon in repair, crowning it with a split-log drag. All the great ranches saw to it that the roads were passable, with ruts not overdeep, or else a coach axle would break, and a load of passengers would have to be sheltered for days.

Kim Toy raises garden truck and a few chickens at the upper end of our township, where he has lived sixty years, in the same cabin, on a half-acre lot hidden by jacaranda trees. A faded sign reads "Kim Toy Rancho." Two or three days of toil a week keep the place up, and its owner in comfort. Pine cones keep him in fuel, he trades eggs for rice, and a small job of cobbling now and then pays for a monthly subscription to the Great Moon and Sun Lottery. Its tickets are covered with little pictures of ducks, eagles, herons, dogs, and suchlike fauna. If the ticket he sends back by mail has the right creature punched out, he gets a prize of money, and he spends it at once on a jar of *ng-ka-py*, which is very powerful, and tastes like mildewed burlap, but is a cheer to those of bushy eyebrows.

Kim Toy is seventy-eight, and is a Republican. He has a golden-moon face, is plump, and wears steel-frame spectacles. Everyone knows and likes him, and he knows everyone, back to their grandfathers. Amiable and benign, he is the eternal type of Chinese patriarch you read of in books, and find in every Coast Range village. When he sees friends, or

a bird perches on his gate, or a tabby cat shows up for a visit, his features are lost in the totality of a smile. He has, like most Chinese, a passion for cigars; they don't have to be very good cigars, so long as they are strong. Up to seventeen years ago he smoked a long pipe, like a chair leg, and then suddenly, nobody knows why, these pipes went out of fashion.

Once a year Kim Toy goes to his tong in San Francisco, where he attends a banquet and a ceremony for departed tong members, and himself bangs the cymbals in the orchestra when the mourning song for bachelors is played. When ships sail regularly to China again, their bones will be sent back to their ancestral villages. But not Kim Toy's, who was born in California, at Marysville.

Kim Toy also attends a service at a church in the Quarter, being a Presbyterian; an orphan asylum, to which he carries gifts; and a masonic lodge—of the White Lotus order, I think. And all these duties performed, with both ardor and serenity, he buys a jar of preserved ginger, a bale of cigars, extra strong, and rides home by the night bus, content: established, soul-braced, a citizen who has won for himself "the Crown of Life that forevermore lasteth."

If the younger generation draws wisdom from the same well as the older, and holds as fast to the values tried by five thousand years, it will be strong in the inward garrison, and indeed fortunate. I knew many such as Kim Toy, the farmer. Calling at the office of a lawyer in San Francisco some years ago, I found him giving a farewell tea to one of his clients, a Chinese rancher who had been a millionaire twice over until the crash, and now was returning to a town up on the Hoang-ho. All he had was the clothes he wore, a carpetbag, and his boat ticket. This man, fabulous in the Range, was seventy-three. He was gravely cheerful when we shook hands, and, escorted by one of his friends, a Chinese meatcutter, left for the docks.

"Only thing that perturbs him," remarked the lawyer, "is that a cousin of his father's, a blind priest of ninety, may be too old to recognize him. In about a year he should be back. There's a cabin in the Santa Lucia country he expects to settle in. The fishing is good around there."

Of his friend, the ambling meatcutter, I learned that he has a son who teaches Latin at a university, and a daughter who is an associate professor, and has written a treatise on paleontology.

I know of another Chinese, who lives on a tiny farm with a roomful of books, who has sought obscurity in the Coast Range, for he is eighty-six, and has much work to do. He was for decades one of the most influential spirits in the world, the man who planned the revolution in China, and is still head of the secret order that brought it about. All day and half the night, he works, dipping brush in ink block, writing on sheets of rice paper, a servant almost as old himself guarding the gate, though nobody ever comes up the lone mountain road, its quietness stirred only by the song of the crickets—which is silence made audible.

At Toyon I stayed from the end of one rainy season to the beginning of another, when I left, Ort Whitby taking me by the pick-up car to the road. The eucalyptus smell was pungent. It was dark night, and he waved a torch of newspaper to halt the bus. I climbed in.

"Thought you might like this," he said, giving me a farewell gift. On the ferryboat I opened the parcel. It was ten pounds of the Pride of Toyon, gray and tricky cobra head.

GOLD IN THEM CREEKS

Dove Canyon is up in Trinity, and it is an ancient mining camp like a hundred others; with a young-fatigued air, for it lives in the past and has an aspect always springlike. Before the old buildings are massive shade trees, a ruined hotel, before which sit and drowse white-bearded elders, with the shoulders, wrinkles, and innocent, mild look of hard-rock miners. The scenery is a lift from the backdrop of *The Girl of the Golden West*. Doves mourn in the blue gums. Far down in the canyon the creek bickers and swirls around black rocks. Vico Voynich, large and grizzled, with mustachios like a waterfall, runs the hotel and saloon, and has a smokehouse in which he cures goat meat. He is a Dalmatian —or was in childhood—and now is a Coast Range man. Since the mine shutdown by Governmental edict, he is Dove Canyon's leading citizen. He is a very good man, and sells you claret by the gallon, which he makes himself, and also discs of cheese which is sent up to him regularly from Tomales Bay. The admired Monterey jack cheese is peculiar to this stretch of the coast.

My brother, who came to Dove Canyon before I did, told me of his journey thither by motor stage, when he fell asleep and woke up with a start at midnight. So did the other passenger, a little old gentleman

with a goatee and periwinkle-blue eyes, who had boarded the stage at Marysville. Blue-eyes rose, leaned forward, and brought his umbrella down with a crash on the head of the driver, who himself woke and instantly stopped the bus. Right ahead, in dense fog, was an abyss, and here the road curved sharply around a precipice. The driver said nothing, nor did the little old gentleman, who opened a newspaper, lighted a cheroot, and settled back comfortably to read.

But I got to Dove Canyon in a flivver, riding with Ruler Button, who was a merchant and had a fine trade with all the old camps from Middle Eel and Yolla Bolly clear up to Weaverville. He was eloquent on mountains and rivers.

"You have traveled a lot, Mr. Button?" I asked.

"Quite a good deal, sir. I've traveled all my life. But I've never been outside of California."

Dad Dunnaway, a forty-niner from Mizzourah, used to dig around here, then he moved to Quartz Mountain, where I knew him when he was about ninety, a hobbling venerable with a sunburst of beard. He lived by himself in a shack, which he shared with a flock of hens that nested in the front room, a handy arrangement when it came to gathering eggs. He lived on chicken, fried eggs, and boiled dumplings—floury cannon balls that bent my three-tined fork when I once coped with them. On Sundays he went out with his rifle and shot a guinea hen down from the sycamore in his yard. This made an awful clamor in the sycamore, but the birds flourished mightily, and I don't know how many generations of them had roosted on its boughs.

Nights he sat by his stove, with a yellow tin box of Pedro tobacco on his knees, and he drew prodigiously on a brier, his head lost in a cloud of smoke. He had the prospector's knack of keeping up a steady draught on it, as if it were a blowpipe, and I have seen him burn clear through a cob pipe in fifteen minutes. Dad had a headful of queer and simple notions, among them the belief that the clerks at every big hotel in San Francisco would fall on his neck if he went in, and lodge him gratis in a front room, and send up newspapers and an armful of liquor. His last visit to the city was in 1880 or so, when he journeyed down to see Bernhardt. The play was in French, *L'Aiglon,* and after an hour of it, Dad left for the docks and took the first boat going up the Sacramento.

"She war fair, but there warn't no making her out. We had better shows up here in them days, like Parepy Rosa's, and little Emma Bishop."

That was going back a long way. Parepa Rosa, who smoked stogies and counted the change closely at the operas she staged hereabout, later went on to Milan and fame; and little Emma Bishop, with her Pre-Raphaelite neck, still lives in a novel of Du Maurier's, for she was the original of Trilby.

Dad Dunnaway was spare of talk, and it was mostly of rock, for he had been a miner all his grown-up life, starting at Grass Valley. One night, when the wind was howling among the pines like a thief, and the stove was glowing red, he was talking in scraps of that camp's young days. Something furry banged on the window screen, to cling with sharp talons and utter its cry.

"Them damn catty mounts is gittin' thick around hyar," he said balefully, without slackening the furnace-like draw on his pipe. " 'Tain't enough for 'em to take a hen, but they got to come in and get warm."

"In Grass Valley, I worked at the Northern Star. . . ."

He remembered Lola Montez. She used to sit at the gate of her cottage in Grass Valley, with her embroidery, and if an injured miner came by, she took him in, bound up his wounds, and had her coachman drive him home.

"The Countess, they called her. She war a fine-looking young widdy woman, and goodhearted, but there war wimmin in the camp that didn't have no good to say of her. She war very pale. There war wimmin that said she put on chalk, but didn't never put soap on her neck." Dad's beard parted with a deep chuckle. "The men was mashed up quite bad, too, some of 'em. But if they went in to rest up and have a slug of her French brandy—wal, sir, those miners never did hear the end of THAT from their ol' wimmin!"

'TISN'T WHAT YOU FIND THAT MATTERS

Of that mole-like strain bred to struggle and pit cunning against all the evil powers of darkness a mile underground, groping through on their backs in tunnel, drilling in tremendous heat, or propping up a cosmos of rock with a timber, was our patriarch. His eyes were childlike and candid, for he had lived long amidst dangers. Because the clink of steel on rock was music to him, he spent days at his hobby of tapping

at nuggets with drills and a minute hammer, chipping off the matrix, and releasing the gold that emerged exquisite and wraith-like, with the shapes of fan coral. He had the patience of a jade cutter. People from all along the Range brought him their pet nuggets to be cleared to filigree.

Most of the old hard rockmen, when the mines closed down, turned to sniping in the ravines, along the Trinity, or up Whiskey Creek. The best season is the end of spring, when you start out with blankets, pick and shovel, a pan, and supplies—a slab of pork, some Mexican red beans, flour, coffee, and tobacco. Then you follow the snow line, look for color, fill the pan with gravel, and wash it out at the creek. The snow then, melting, trickles in runnels that vein the red earth, dark as old wine, and not again in the year will the metal sparkle so brightly.

Petey Stevens, who is seventy-four, has been sniping along Whiskey Creek for the last two decades, and lays off in December and January to sit on the hotel porch at Weaverville and play dominoes. Summertime, two or three families will join up with him, live in tents, and snipe until fall. It is a pleasant way of life, outdoors, healthful for the youngsters, and the nights, even after the hottest days, are cool enough for three blankets.

One late spring, I slid down through the manzanita to visit Petey. He was sitting in shade, working his rocker, a pipe in his teeth. A cluster of tents was along the bank, and here and there an old car; it was quite a camp, with a dozen people in it, at least, and easygoing Petey was its hierarch. Dragonflies were darting about him; the air was scented with mint and juniper; catbirds were filling a toyon bush with their screams.

"There's not so many sniping this summer," said Petey. "They've gone down, all but a handful of them, to work in the war plants. Seems like there's always wars going on somewhere. But there's a couple of families here. And Mrs. Tandy, the widow, with her young 'uns."

Snipers hardly ever find much gold, and a dollar and a half is thought a good day's panning. Now and then a group of young men would take up a claim, install a long tom or a vanning table with engine, run barrowloads of dirt to them over planks, and work with furious energy two weeks or so, then vanish elsewhere. If they had profited greatly, they would have stayed, no doubt; but the intake was a pretty constant factor, not to be cracked. Petey, working with calm and the minimum of

toil—*festina lente*—with pan, or rocker at the most, earned a dollar and a half between sunrise and dusk, and throve.

"You're finding color, Petey?"

"A show. More'n that some days. I c'n tell you something. If I find pay dirt I stay and dig. There's some that lift a shovelful of dirt, then on up or down the crick. I tell these youngsters here if they see a man with a stake, he's stayed in one place. He's dug to grass roots, then up to his pants buttons, then over his head. He's got bacon, he's got terbaccy, he's got sense."

He pointed to the boulders in the creek. "There's not a boulder around here that hasn't been turned over twenty times since Andrew Jackson was President. The whole country from Oregon down was gone over with a fine-tooth comb. But we get along, and have a fine time at it, and next week you won't know what you'll find."

The name of Whiskey Creek commemorates a tragedy still a legend in these hills, and Petey indicated the site where it befell Amos Grimes, who came here from Shasta in 1852 with a string of pack burros, on the staunchest of which he had roped a keg of whiskey. It was a confidence misplaced, for on the high trail this animal grew unruly and fell into the creek.

"The burro swam in, but the keg was lost. That keg," added Petey, somberly, "was worth fifty burros."

Touch history around here, and you are pulled back ninety years, and plunged into excitements, killings, gold strikes, prodigies, internecine Chinese wars (all bloodless), lynchings, trials "mobly," huge buffooneries, and a spate of heady events—that stop short in the middle 1850's. The sky-rocking Aristophanic comedy was over, and with the fall of the curtain came quiet. But a society requires a dramatic and formative past, its Pierian spring, toward which, like Petey, it must turn in reflective moments and refresh itself.

It came on to rain. Lightning blinked through the gulch, with thunder at its heels, and the downpour clattered like bayonets. Petey caught up a sack of pine cones, and on we went to Mrs. Tandy's to stay until the gale howled itself out. In this tent, which had two smaller tents adjoining, and a wooden floor, quiet Mrs. Tandy served the group their dinner. Petey went out under a sack and returned with a demijohn of claret. Three snipers came in, and around the table we buckled down to Shasta

Sam, six points for a penny. The air was steamy from wet coats, and aromatic with apple pie just out of the oven, and rank tobacco. Mrs. Tandy began to iron shirts on a plank wrapped in newspapers, and a vapor lifted, redolent of linen, paper, and printing ink.

"Tell you where it gets real wet—down there on the gravel," she said. "We had a tent for the children to go to school in last year. We were quite a way from the camp, and the county sent books and papers and pencils. It rained, the water rose, and the children were regular cutups, yelling and playing tag. They wrassled the whole tent down on their heads and they had a time dragging the teacher out. The pore lady, she couldn't do nothing with them.

"Most of those children were from up Trinity, lumber folks, not cut out for sniping. They didn't stay long."

"That was the summer we run out the gold buyer," said Petey, dealing another round. "The pennyweight man!"

That visitor was a smiling, talkative man with a cigar. He placed a scale on the lid of his suitcase, and, after handing out cigars, announced his willingness to buy all the gold offered him. The snipers had always turned over their metal, in boxes or tins, marked with names, to Petey, who sold it at the assayer's, and brought back the money in the same containers, and so they told him.

"That's all right," the buyer said affably. "I'll buy any amount, by the pennyweight."

He laid a penny on one balance, and Mitch Hoyt emptied a phial of gold into the other, until the scale was in poise. Mrs. Tandy thought the pennyweight looked a bit sick and she went out and brought in her twelve-year-old Jimmy.

"What does a penny weigh?" she asked him.

"It's a pennyweight, the State around," smiled the buyer.

"A pennyweight," spoke up Jimmy, who had helped at the assay office one vacation, "a pennyweight is twenty-four grams. And a cent weighs forty-eight."

The buyer picked up scale and suitcase and trod straight out for the bridge, not once looking behind him. The snipers, gathered before the widow's tent, saw him knock on the wooden railing before he trudged on to his car.

"Jimmy's a wonder," said Petey, as, the rain over, we went out for a

look at the pan washings. "Jimmy's a world-beater. He's through high school now, and we figure on him going to Berkeley to study for engineer."

THE BLOOD-RED WINE

Rightly, the grape farms bask in the most charming parts of the Range, in sightly agglomerations of hill and dale. Below Santa Clara the spur, crowned with hill-top villages, has the drowsy, haze-washed beauty of the Apennines in summer. The villages lack yew groves, of course, and ruinous Temples of Jupiter; they are, perhaps, too modern, with gasoline stations, a dingy fountain-luncheonette, and a tourist camp; but in the sight of Heaven, I suppose, we are all tourists.

In Napa Valley, which is straight up from San Francisco Bay, I always make the rounds in tow of my cicerone, Eck Mosby, the Wine Institute's fieldman, whose parish all this delectable region is. Eck is a sort of circuit rider, Old Farmers' Almanac, and confidant of the winegrowers, small and large. A night ride with Eck, when you hang on grimly, jouncing like a pebble in a drum—and most especially when he is speeding over the back-canyon road to look into some rumor of phylloxera or Anaheim blight—well, that is an adventure. He drives, often, two hundred miles a day, and like another Mosby, that considerable guerilla, may sometimes bob up in three places at once. Eck is always on the verge of being explosively merry, but once I saw him in a state of alarm.

I had come to give an address before a group of vintners at a St. Helena hotel. Eck, as chairman, saw to the tables and the placing of the "representations." That's part of high etiquette in the valley. Every winegrower sends in two bottles of wine as "representation," whether he can come himself or not. Since I had half an hour on my hands, I strolled through St. Helena, the wine capital of California. The long hill behind it is low, orange-tawny, with a half-English air, its greenery dense, its oaks numerous and massive. In a book store I met an old customer who remarked that he had spoken twice with Robert Louis Stevenson here in 1880, at the *Star* newspaper office, and at Uncle Jake Schram's vineyard.

It was then that Eck broke in, aghast, in shirt sleeves.

"We've got fifty representations—a hundred bottles! And we can't find a corkscrew anywhere! This is terrible! Not packing one, are you?"

I was and I exhumed it, a silver, folding, bottle screw that had been given me by a cellarman foreman an hour before, in one of those bursts of kindliness so frequent among those who labor in vineyards. I suppose there is no moral in this episode, unless it be that the most famous wine town in the land harbors steady drinkers of coffee and tea.

Visitors do not much abound in St. Helena, which is off the main stream of travel, and, for all that it is attractively framed, is a village like many another in the State. They mostly go on, the visitors, to see the geysers at Calistoga, and the Stevenson haunts on Mount St. Helena.

Along the winding road, behind pollards and graystone wineries, ivy-hung, are the grape farms, where the vineyardists, of European and New England provenance, have lived since the Mexican days in their secluded world. The history of the vineyards is interwoven with the tale of the generations that lived in them. Winegrowing is not only a handi-craft of Noachian antiquity, complex and mysterious, depending on inherited skills, but also a way of life. Sound wine is a matter of in-tegrity. No maker of it vaunts the largeness of his vineyard, for he is aware that in wine goodness is never synonymous with quantity, and quality is only to be found in small parcels. In the tribunal of the craft, where wines are brought to judgment, some little grower, the master of three acres, may utter a decision from which there is no appeal.

The winegrower is a holdout from the rugged age of individualism. His conscience may be intractable, Calvinistic even, and harshly grim, but his reverence for the unaccountable quality makes him a romantic. One of the Napa Valley growers who also had a distillery was marched upon by an official, armed with full powers, who announced that he had come to affix more locks on the still.

"Do I understand that my honesty is brought into question?" thundered the distiller, who was, moreover, the soul of rectitude.

"There are new regulations to be complied with," said the official.

"Do I understand, sir," asked the owner, "that Washington questions my honesty?"

"It will question mine if I do not collect the last penny of spirits tax owed it by this distillery."

Reaching for an axe, the owner hacked the still and smashed the dials and tubing.

"I owe the Government nothing," he said, the liquor rising above his ankles. "And you need never come here again."

Alicante he would not touch, it was harsh and common; Chauche Noir and Rose of Peru were poor creatures; Mission and Gros Manzenc, which might flourish elsewhere, unworthy of this ridge. But no farmer, who hauled in a load of delicate Beclan or summit-grown Camay ever shook in his boots at the doorway; he was led into the office for words of praise, a cigar, and a beaker of that uplifting drink prevalent in the valley, half vermouth, half brandy, served chill enough to rattle your teeth.

Wine making, older than the Law and the Prophets, is of all man's arts the most primitive as well as the most complex. The grapevine can be as a besieged fortress, sapped by foes underground, breathed upon by malign influences, winged about by myriad bacteria, fatal as lance thrusts, no more visible than a breath. And, in the keg or the bottle, the cunningly built-up architecture of the wine may be wrecked in an hour by a spore, an adverse wind, or the trying heat. Wine is a living organism; whatever has life has its mysteries, and Pasteur himself, and all the oenological chemists after him, were never immune to influxes of wonder as they peered into the heart of a yeast spore, or listened to the stir of ferment in a vat, with systole and diastole, with rhythms of sound, as of a sea on a remote planet.

An old winegrower in the valley, one of the early Italian farmers, who recently died, for forty years made a claret for himself and his friends. A. Paganini, a simple and wise man, ignored both cabalism and science and cut to the heart of the matter. He filled a vat with grapes, Gamay for choice, and massively thumped them with the end of a log. No steamer or press for him, no frivolism, just a clean sycamore log and a vat. His intent was to match the wine he had been accustomed to in Tuscany. The sunlight was the same; the soil, the air, and some microorganisms were different. He thumped confidently in his chill stone cave, delaying fermentation by half a week, for a September day in Napa Valley can be smitingly hot. A. Paganini was a wine maker in the Theocritean style. To pound with that log and be dyed red with the splashings was for him a joyous, anachronistic rite; he came to grips with his materials and found, no doubt, an enrichment in this fusion of his life with the past. So utter a disregard of the illusions

labeled progress cannot but exact one's respect. Also, it was the manifestation of the ethos of a people and a craft.

Quite another example was Indian Jinny, who used to come to our mountain ranch years ago, a papoose on her back, and two older children afoot. The local tribe was well-fed and prosperous, but Jinny came dragging a sack of California acorns, which, if not poisonous, are acid in the extreme and raise hob with the insides of the unwary. This old Stone-Age lady was ninety at least. At the foot of a smoke-begrimed cliff she boiled water, threw in some pieces of rock, and cooked up the acorns. Then she and the small ones had a ritual meal. I think the rock was basalt, which contains magnesium, and neutralized the acid. This is a bit of chemistry so primordial that it antedates chain stores. Her tribe had known it for two thousand years. And Indian Jinny spooned that gruel plentifully down the throats of her descendants. She believed in every generation starting right from scratch.

Close to Yountville lived Pasquale, who had a hillside cave of the kind so frequent about St. Helena, and eight acres of vines, planted in quincuncial fashion, wheeling and fanning out handsomely over undulating ground. He was a stocky and active little Sicilian, in corduroys, always with a pruning shears in his belt and a cigar in his teeth, a withered black spike of a Toscano. His farm like himself had an air of happy prosperity. It was no ordinary vineyard. A half dozen connoisseurs devoutly hope that nobody will ever know of it but themselves, for Pasquale was no ordinary winegrower, but an experimenter who grew only the most difficult wines, Johannisberger and such. His mind was enterprising. He had studied viticulture at the University farm, and, until his father left him this farm, was a soil chemist, with his own laboratory. His favorite wine he grew on a rocky hill so barren that nothing but wild rosemary had flourished on it. But it was a wine that brought him medals; a wine dry, gun-flinty, with the faint odor of rock violets, and incomparable save for that grown in Livermore Valley, where the Saint-Emilion vine grown on a chalky slope has become something quite other. He pointed to a niche where a rack of bottles, in which the sunlight and fragrance of a forgotten summer lay entrapped, slept in the dark.

"There," said Pasquale. "Take a bottle—five bottles! *Vino e da bere!* Wine is only something to drink, and not something to write about."

He kept it in his long cave, where the temperature holds to its norm of fifty-eight degrees all the year round. He lit our way through this dungeon by a lantern atop a staff. "A Chinaman dug all this for my father. Limestone cuts like cheese, then hardens like concrete. Well, that Chinaman vanished, and later, when a skeleton was found up on that ridge, my father had it sent to the tong in San Francisco, and they shipped it all the way to some village beyond Foochow. Then, suddenly the Chinaman turned up again—he had gone broke in gambling— and went back to work here.

"The skeleton must have been of some drunken stranger, I think. When the last trumpet blows, that stranger is going to sit up puzzled, wondering how the devil he ever got to China."

Eastern syndicates have bought many of the large vineyards, but Pasquale—and half the vineyardists are of his stamp—will remain as free as a grizzly hunter. Nor will he be pressed to sell. The small proprietors are invaluable where they are, they set the key, and upon many of them is the cachet of prestige.

These local caves, dark and winding shadow worlds, their Gothic portals at the roadsides already stained and mantled with creepers, may a century hence show encrustings of legend, with myths of grotto-dwelling hermits, but they were cut only seventy years ago, the oldest of them, like the two-mile windings under the Beringer farm. That a tunnel collapsed in the earthquake of 1906 and sealed up a cache of wine, which has mellowed itself into prodigious value, is the one fable I unearthed. A belief in it still impels some old laborers to search on the hillside for signs of it and probe deep with iron rods. But the only damage wrought by that temblor was to shake down a portion of cave roof near the village, and bury a hogshead of sacramental wine that was dug out a decade later, not only unharmed, but improved.

"ENCHANTED CIGARETTES"

Fables of early vintners there are aplenty. The wine trade attracts personalities verging on the fabulous. Robert Louis Stevenson encountered most of them—three Jacobs: Messrs. Schram, Grimm, and Beringer, pioneers all from the Rhineland. But the Scot himself is the most legendary being hereabout. He wrote *Silverado Squatters* when he spent

his honeymoon summer here in 1880, often visiting the Schram homestead and its caves. Nowhere is the Stevenson cult so strong as in this
vicinity, taking in also San Francisco and Monterey. Pasquale had on
his shelf a battered copy of *Silverado Squatters* that had belonged to
his father, and a new one that was his own. This recounting of a honeymoon summer on Mount St. Helena, with its gallery of portraits all done
to the life, is better known than Holy Writ, and more piously quoted,
in this region, which no biographer of R.L.S. has ever visited. Glints of
his Silverado prose Anne Roller Issler, the Napa chronicler, has seen
reflected in the essays of the county school children and in the files of
the newspapers. For years, Mrs. Issler, with the fervor of the true
collector, has been labeling every vestige of R.L.S. and his Gipsy summer she could track down, stock and stone, drawing, photo, every
shadow of memory in the head of the oldest inhabitants. The second
impulse, or wave, of a legend, it is said, is stronger than the first.
Stevenson will soon become more of a local divinity than before, for the
efforts of Mrs. Issler and the small, shining band of his devotees, are
bringing about the creation of a memorial park and museum on sun-
drenched Mount St. Helena, where he lived with his family, his little
Davos press, and the dog that shook eternally in fear of rattlers.

There he worked over *Prince Otto* and *The Pavilion on the Links.*
The vista from the old mine top gave him scenes for the opening of
Olalla; and Spyglass Hill in *Treasure Island,* and its vegetation, for here
are the calycanthus, prospering nutmegs, and sweet bay trees, whose
perfume carries far on the night wind. Kelmar, the Jewish storekeeper
who had the ships' kettles—he was Moses Friedberg of Calistoga—and
most of the adult figures in *Silverado Squatters* are gone. But Charley
Crouch, whose father bought Stevenson's pony for him, is about. So
are Lawley, the toll collector, who was then a boy stage driver, and
Maggie Turner, who, in her leggy 'teens, remembered R.L.S. saying,
after a spell of coughing, "I brought this on myself: I went the pace."

Other winegrowing nooks there are, beyond the main roads, each fos-
tering its semidivinities, or legendary giants, of which the vineyard
country is prolific. Charles Wente had a hillside farm on white, pebbly
gravel. There his vines flourished, and as they achieved perfection he
so merged himself with them that he was lost in anonymity.

Ten wine merchants, whose exhibits had won the prizes at a State fair when the century was young, gathered at the Palace Hotel in San Francisco for dinner. "The first toast, gentlemen," said the chairman, rising at table, "will be to that little farmer in Livermore Valley. Every prize-winning bottle we have, he filled for us from his barrels."

The owner of a neighboring farm, though a pundit in viticulture, and a subtle judge of wines, was less of the recluse. James Concannon, enamored of grandeurs and state, heard on Aran Island, where he grew potatoes, that the Civil War was over. He sped to San Francisco, ped-dled books, then became a salesman for one of the most horrible of inventions, the rubber stamp, and grew rich. He was restless, he wan-dered far, but his heart was in his Livermore farm, which he planted to cuttings that he picked himself in Burgundy and Alsace. When the wine trade was dull, he dashed to Mexico to recoup. Mexicans had a passion for thumping paper with huge rubber stamps, all colors.

"Your capital, Señor Presidente," he told Porfirio Diaz, "strikes me as being in dire need of broom work and a hosing. It is dirtier than any I ever saw in Ireland."

"Then it must be cleaned up at once!" thundered Diaz. "I wish you'd show these fellows how to go about it."

The man from Aran and Livermore made a fortune cleaning up Mexico City—he had the Midas touch—and sank his gains into the vine-yard. He settled most of the valley with relatives from Donegal, built a larger house, installed his own bagpiper, and, devoting himself to religion, prayed in Gaelic, the one language, he explained, that could pierce Heaven. He left Livermore but once again, and at Diaz' insistence, to establish the largest vineyard in Mexico, at Celaya, and to show the peons how to tend vines. A troop of cavalry with lances and a brass band escorted him from hacienda to hacienda, this hot-gospeler of an Irishman, who orated as he pruned sample vines, and cast right and left showers of pamphlets in Spanish, from his own pen, on the com-plete art of grape husbandry. Today, sixty years after, Mexican workers from those haciendas are now in the Coast Range, tilling the vineyards, bringing in the harvests, as if they had lived nowhere else. Spanish has never been forgotten in the Coast Range, with its eucalyptus-scented smile, nor anywhere in it can any people seem alien.

A DEMIGOD THERE WAS

On the way up from St. Helena some ten summers ago I stopped in at Fountaingrove to visit with the Baron. In many ways this vineyard, near Luther Burbank's garden at Santa Rosa, is the quaintest and the most imposing of all in the State. Some of its towering wine casks are outdoors, buildings unto themselves, with hexagonal, spired roofs. There is a Louisa May Alcott mansion, with arbors, library, and a banquet hall elegant with candelabra and plaster festoons. This day of overpowering sunshine, with crickets twanging drowsily, and the vineyard tremulous under heat waves, no one was about. I made enquiries of a truckman on the road.

"The Baron? It's lunch time. You ought to find him down over there."

He pointed to the old stone winery that was hidden under a mantle of vines, and thither I went. Fifty workmen, at least, must have been sitting about the table between the rows of cool vats—all wearing the coarse white aprons vineyardists don in lieu of serviettes when they lunch in the winery. I climbed in among the rest. We might have been in some wine cave in Naples or Touraine, for all was in the pagan tradition of vintners who are never more hearty and festal than in the *vendemmia*, and the grape crop in Sonoma County this summer was prodigious. The food was helped from casseroles full of chicken, fish, *risotto*, mushrooms, and fennel with sauce.

Wine after wine, in rush-covered flasks, was passed around, clockwise. The toasts were running three to the minute. The master of Fountaingrove, who was eighty-four, gave toasts as well as he received them. Then, rose-ivory and benign, he hoisted his glass and rose, though he was no taller afoot than when seated, and gave a toast to the workmen, a quite long one, more like a speech. He said it in English first, and then for the older workmen in familiar, country Italian. It was a little address worth hearkening to, for the Baron had an exquisite taste in wines; he was an advisor to the State Viticultural Commission, a member of the wine jury at the Panama-Pacific Exposition, and the last survivor of the Brotherhood of the New Life, that in 1875 founded this vineyard.

That was the Baron Kanaye Nagasawa. His accent, even as he spoke in Italian, was a broad Scots.

At fourteen Nagasawa had been sent from a medieval home in Japan to cram up on the culture of Europe, about ten years after Commodore Perry's visit. He drifted to Scotland, with a volume of Burns and some personal effects in his valise, and wound up in Aberdeen, lodging with the town crier. In this bleak seaport he acquired a taste for porridge that never left him, a fancy for tweeds, a liking for Calvinistic sermons, and his education. After he had gone through the town schools, his funds ran out, and back he went to London, to work, and read Herbert Spencer.

From there he went to America, in the retinue of Thomas Lake Harris, apocalyptic poet, trance orator, and occultist, who founded a colony on Lake Erie. The colony—all persons of wealth, for in Harris visions of the New Jerusalem were not incompatible with a genius for monetary affairs—toiled with their hands. Artists and doctors dug trenches and chopped down trees. Laurence Oliphant, novelist, Member of Parliament, advisor to Lord Elgin, and one of the most brilliant of English diplomats, was told off to board trains at the Brocton station and peddle sandwiches and milk. His mother, Lady Oliphant, washed dishes in the kitchen. The Brotherhood of the New Life prospered—for Harris— and had its own mills and bank. Nagasawa was his secretary.

The next shift for Harris and the inner group was to Santa Rosa, where Nagasawa laid out the vineyard and built the mansion. The vineyard prospered like a banyan tree. For three years the faithful were content in this Utopia, but trouble grew, and Oliphant won a suit he had brought against Harris, whom he had regarded as an incarnation of the Deity. Harris, out of pocket $50,000, pronounced doom on the Oliphants, who were still in his thrall, and returned to his plans for the rehabilitation of the Cosmos and mankind.

Nagasawa took down his trance utterances, millions of words of "vast statement, Swedenborgian theophanies, Heavenly dithyrambs, and unveilings of Patmos," his pen for hours hurrying on without rest. "As a vitality—a one-twain from the Lord," Harris might cry out, after putting an ear to a fermenting vat, "has passed twice through the finer electro-vinous spirit in our winery, it is now being potentialized in the Joy Spirit . . . divine, produced in consecration to the Father-Mother."

Nagasawa found time to work among his plants, grafting, planting new varieties; and the Brotherhood throve, outwardly. Then sinister

forces pressed about the Utopia, with rumors of scandal, flights, rebellion, and Harris' daughter took her own life. Fountaingrove went in and out of courts, like a shuttlecock. The elders died off, Harris left for the outer world; in 1906 his life ended, closing the tale of the strangest pseudomystical colony in the United States. William James, brought up as a Swedenborgian in youth, gives space to him, perhaps overmuch, in his *Varieties of Religious Experience.*

The durable Nagasawa, who had decades before renounced allegiance to Nippon, became sole owner·of Fountaingrove, a sage and plant lover, who enjoyed the affectionate respect of Burbank and Professor Frederic Bioletti, the State Viticulturist. He did not outlive Prohibition, but the vines which for nearly sixty years he so piously tended "still their ancient ruby yield."

FOR MAN AND BEAST

It is conceivable that the Hotel Europa had once been thriving, but I think it must have been back when stagecoaches clattered over these piny Santa Cruz hills. Luigi owned the Hotel Europa, which ran itself; he sat·behind the bar and played dominoes until near suppertime, when he rustled up wood for the stove, and, after dining, read *La Voce del Popola* by a kerosene lamp until midnight. Luigi was a zoophile. Twenty dogs ambled in and out through the wreck of a screen door. Out under a peach tree was a pair of chained eagles, that pranced about, wings spread, doing a slow-motion gavotte as if on hot bricks. There was also a goat, and if a coyote howled in the forest at night, goat and dogs dashed out in hot pursuit.

A group of old-timers on the veranda cracked and nibbled pine nuts or smoked or dozed. The Hotel Europa had a garden, where Luigi dug when the mood seized him, and brought in garlic and lettuce for the Mexican woman who did the cooking. Antiquity and a great reasonableness of tariff were the charms of the Hotel Europa. You paid nothing for staying all night, or a week, or a month. Once I went right into the bunkhouse, picked out a room, propped up a rusty iron cot with a brick, and stayed five weeks. Luigi would have been shocked if you offered to pay; his reputation as a host would have been impugned. The food was tolerable, fleas were nonexistent, the air was healthful, the company

was often good, and the claret, brought from Wright's, on the next hill, was lively and cheap.

Luigi, before he became landlord of this pleasant hotel at the time of World War I, had done a little farm work, trucked for a bean farm, and helped in the kitchen at Tassajara Hot Springs. He often spoke with regret of the loss of a job when three strangers, in the Dry Era, built a formidable still in an abandoned tunnel a mile away down the creek. The boiler was set going, with Luigi, at the honorarium of five dollars a day, as watchman. It was drowsy work: the steady gazing at the thermometer was hypnotic, and he fell asleep. He was aroused by a mighty crackling. The apparatus was on fire, the pile of brown sugar, nearly two hundred sacks, bubbling like pitch. Smoke plumed majestically to the heavens, as from a volcano. Luigi hid out in Monterey for a week, and returned home, still shaken by the magnitude of the disaster.

"Everybody say, 'Aha, Luigi—you been fishing, ha?' Nobody know of a fire. Those three fellows, they did not show up again. That smoke scared them away—a thousand-dollar smoke, like Vesuvio!"

When that intrepid hiker, Spanish scholar, and pontophile—few experts are more learned than S. Griswold Morley in the study of covered bridges, and none more ardent in their collection—tramped jovially with his Basque walking stick into this sky tavern one week end, Luigi's joy was complete. At his board were no less than two professors from the University at Berkeley. Tony, the campus bootblack, was the other, and he basked, perhaps, in slightly higher esteem, for here he bought his quarterly cask of wine, and had a pigeonhole in the wall where he kept filed his private napkin.

Professor Morley has a list of some hundred taverns in the Coast Range, most of them as inaccessible as lairs of the gray-footed falcon. He gives three stars to Lombardi's, up on Putah Creek, where you sleep on the ground, and huge bullfrogs bellow all night like a herd of cattle. Lombardi sold you eggs and milk, otherwise you had to pack in your own grub, or depend on the trout that would leap at your Red Coachman before it flicked the water. "Is old Lombardi still alive?" he wrote me. "Can one still make his way there, and lay a bag beside Putah Creek? I'd like to go, but I haven't the gas." Though effective in pathos, the query must be rhetorical. If the professor wants to visit any of his

favored inns—and one must not be deluded by his triple stars, for they may only indicate that there is some ripe old native around, or a Basque who can appreciate the grain of his walking stick—he will get there somehow, if not by car, or by bicycle, then by grimping irons and rope.

Other haunts there are on this brow of the Santa Cruz Range, with its forest and blue-black shadows and hidden clearings. They are French pensions, mostly—an utter seclusion from the world, each with its small, rocky vineyard, herb garden, and bowling green; remote fragments of Vendée or the Alpes Maritimes; their clients usually French milliners, dry cleaners, bakers, or red-faced butchers, and their families.

Frequently the guests are merchants in a small way, often retired or out of health, who feel close enough to France in these wooded and lofty nooks: simple and thrifty folk, who ask little more than quietness and seclusion from the world, where they can sit in rustic chairs and read the *Courrier du Pacifique*, knit, play chess, and listen to the clink of the boules and its echo in the *bois rouges*. And these are haunts you discover only by chance.

I recall a night drive I once made with a young architect through these redwoods, on the way to a canyon in the Santa Lucias, where we were to hunt in the morning for a clump of incense trees. On the hill road the engine stopped with a cough. We got out to hunt for a gasoline station, not very hopefully, for it was almost midnight. After a few minutes we arrived at a gateway; we entered it, found ourselves in a graveyard, felt our way along to a small lodge, and knocked. Next moment we were inside, sitting with the caretaker and his wife, an elderly French couple in black, dining by lamplight on a casserole of hare, with a bottle of wine, salad, and a fresh loaf. Madame, in shawl and rusty bonnet, and her husband in smoking cap, were hospitable and talkative. They knew little English, and had been living in this graveyard for twenty years. We played dominoes until two in the morning, and M'sieu walked out with us toward the gate. It was now pitch-dark; he flashed a light on an old tomb, which he said was Spanish, pushed over the slab, bent, and pulled out a five-gallon tin.

"I keep that here for emergencies," he said, kindly. "And this is the first in I don't know how long. But a pleasant one! And now, if you are going to Hollister, you turn to the left, where the frogs are loud. *Bon soir!*"

ROSE-RED EARTH

That social, likely enough, was the Shrovetide jollity, winding up with a *cascaron* dance, in which all the minefolk took part; the august Mr. Randol, coattails flying, dancing with the furnaceman's daughter, and the timber foreman's wife with José, the velvet-jacketed teamster. The cascarons—each girl had her basket of these, eggshells filled with confetti—were cracked to slow music, and, as the tempo quickened, they were cracked on the heads of the dancers. All very quaint and regional, though a shade less idyllic when the cascarons began to yield face powder and bird shot.

New Almaden clung to its customs and innumerable festal observances for eighty years, up to the era of motorcars and the strenuous life. Its Mexican and Spanish ways of mining—when ore was carried in baskets up notched tree columns—vanished when the tin streamers from Cornwall came in, and excavation on the heroic scale, with timbering that rose boldly, fanning out under the roofs, upholding the mountain, made this quicksilver mine, with its galleries and a hundred miles of tunnel, the largest on the globe. It was twelve years ago when I knew it, in its dead time between wars; and no stranger gazing at the weed-grown top, with its drunken gallows hoist, might have guessed there was more in it than met the eye. It was a vast structure hacked out underground, a wide-spreading honeycomb, large as two Empire State Buildings, half a mile deep, and more than a century old.

It was a mine that since the Franciscan days has bred its own race. Some of its children have returned in these insecure times, but not Laurence Bulmore, though he does come here once a summer to visit the Casa Grande where he was brought up. He is a ferryboat engineer on San Francisco Bay, the *doyen* of those who make a cult of the New Almaden mine, especially the old workings, with their stalactites, bats, and legends of the "Tommy Knockers." He has old tunnel maps and account books in Spanish, and the spiked iron candlesticks of mine heads of renown, his father one of them.

"The miners," Mitch Shields told me on my visit, "have gone away a while. Up to Grass Valley, the younger ones. *That* camp is still running. With Spanish mercury coming, I think New Almaden won't last the year out."

About seventy-five years ago, Professor Wayland D. Hand, the folk-lorist, says, a Grass Valley priest had some regional gold cast into a bell and prophesied that wherever its tolling could be heard, there one would always find ore. And they did, until a Government whose voice was louder than the tolling put gold under a ban, and the miners came out of their diggings, stunned, and drifted elsewhere.

"Not me," said Mitch. "I wouldn't shovel any ore but cinnabar."

He is one of the old *mercureros*, a class apart, a special order of miners; a little touched in the joints, prone to rheumatism, and with few teeth, for mercury, a mystical element though it be, can do queer things to the digger. But like the alchemists, mercury miners are enamored of the jade. Mitch's real name is Joseph, but he changed it to Mitch because he had a brother who was also "Joseph."

"I was 'Joe' and my brother was 'Seph,' and my father's name was both. It runs in the family, 'Joseph.' It's been in the family a couple thousand years—which tells how long we've been mining tin in Corn-wall. That's where Joseph of Arimathaea came in a ship to get his tin. And the first song I learned was one I used to hear my father sing at the organ, 'Joseph, he was in the Tin Trade.'"

The old mine was once all but proper Cornish, and the "Cousin Jacks" had their own beliefs and customs. In the tunnels no one might whistle, nor on Innocents' Day and Good Friday do any work, but one drank beer and ate saffron cake. On Christmas, the mine horses were lifted out into the sunlight, to be thanked with a speech, and given presents of apples and sugar. Children were taught to speak up brightly to the mine-bound workmen they met on the road. Their "Good morning, sir," might very well be the last salutation a miner would hear.

Robins were sacred—except to small boys. To refer to a cat always as "Old Tailey," and a rat as a "peep" would baffle the devil, and thereby enhance luck. On meeting a snail, that miner was wise who propitiated "Bull horn" with a nubbin from his tallow candle.

"And my father," Mitch reflected, "called a smelter 'the Jews' house,' because they were the first to run smelters in Cornwall. We had other sayings. I can't think of any more; they've mostly died out now, here at Hollister, and the other mercury-digging places."

San Benito, with its pine tracts, bashed-up landscape, rocky and sun-

lit, odorous with false sage and little vineyards at the foot of the slopes, I have roved over in company with Mitch, who still prospects for quicksilver. He has a small retort where he "cooks" up cinnabar ore—a flask of quicksilver a month. The stuff is packed in iron bottles, like bombshells, weighing seventy-six and a half pounds when full. The "Almaden shape" has been standard the world over for a hundred years. "Empties" used to be quoted in the market columns as a staple, like sherry barrels. Mitch does a neat bit of trade in buying up an empty flask here and there, riding about in his flivver in quest of them.

"They last forever," he says. "But they've a way of dropping out, like razor blades. Only, they're handier. Saw off the round, and you've got a good prospector's mortar. Flasks are handy to flatten out pastry, for window weights, and to roll heavy machinery into place."

LIGHTS OUT

A flask will also make a dinner bell and throw out a din like a Tibetan gong. Mitch has sixteen of them strung on a wire for the ends of pure music. They are graduated with water, and after supper he may light his pipe, take a bolt, and knock out as on a xylophone a couple of Methodist hymns and "El Pajarito." The hymns he had heard, as a tow-headed child, his father play on the organ. "El Pajarito" he had learned at some Mexican fandango. Mitch had been a considerable stepper in his day.

We climbed that day to the ridge, where air came in salt from the Pacific, and pelicans—slatternly fowl, but beautiful in flight—trolled overhead in the stillness; and we went in to look at what was left of an old mine. It was a black rift, propped with broken trunks of fir, the walls dripping with seepage from cinnabar, and mercury a foot deep on the floor. There was a mousy odor of bats, and the wind blew out chill.

"There's plenty more around here. Like spots on a wildcat, more'n you can count. This one was pretty good—they took a lot of mercury from a gallery in there. A Spaniard was killed in there, and they put up a shrine to him and kept a candle burning before it."

The last memorial candle in the Coast Range guttered out in 1892. At the shrine of Nuestra Señora de la Guadalupe, deep in New Almaden, the votive candles burned for fifty years.

An old Spanish custom.

HEADLANDS IN
CALIFORNIA WRITING

BY JOHN WALTON CAUGHEY

Californian delights are measured in part by the people who have come to live in its hills and mountains. Many of these have been writers, and the relationship has been reciprocal: writers have distinguished California, but as an environmentalist your editor cannot but note that environment has inspired writing. (R. P.)

California's rich literature, like its history, is the heritage of the entire State. Yet there are many respects in which it belongs particularly to the district that is dominated by the Coast Ranges, a region so fundamentally Californian as seldom to be thought of as a section.

The bold headlands of this shore looked down on the beginnings of California; and today, of the eight and a half million residents currently estimated, probably eight million are to be found in the western half of the State, most of them clustered near the bases of the Coast Ranges. California is larger, but the major part of its political, agricultural, industrial, commercial, and social history must be written primarily in terms of this area where most of the landmarks are located, where most of the significant changes have occurred, where most of the population is now to be found, and where it has been through the entire span of history.

The true character of this varied and kaleidoscopic growth, the climax of the westward expansion of the American people, may be glimpsed in the writings of men and women who have understood its history and problems, its potentialities and beauty. Their literary achievements stand out splendidly, like the mountain headlands.

THE PRIMITIVES

Although seldom recognized as such, the first manifestations of literary talent in California were in the prehistoric period. These earliest craftsmen operated without printing presses and without even a system of writing. What they produced was therefore highly perishable, and it has come down to us only in fragmentary form and with the anonymity

customary in folk literature. Most of it is in the form of tales, usually centered around animal characters, whose thoughts and actions, however, are on the human plane. Some of these tales are merely diverting, but most have a substantial philosophical content. In idea and in execution they are considerably better than one would expect in view of the material backwardness of these first Californians. As an example I quote a tale collected and translated by Hugo Reid, an intimate and staunch friend of the Indians of the Los Angeles region.

The Coyote and the Water

A Coyote, which, like all the rest of his kin, considered himself as the most austere animal on the face of the earth, not even excepting man himself, came one day to the margin of a small river. Looking over the bank, on seeing the water run so slow, he addressed it in a cunning manner, "What say you to a race?" "Agreed to," answered the water very calmly. The Coyote ran at full speed along the bank until he could hardly stand from fatigue and on looking over the bank he saw the water running smoothly on.

He walked off with his tail between his legs and had something to reflect upon for many a day afterwards.

SPANISH ANNALS

Upon this scene of strictly oral literature the Spaniards at length introduced the art and the practice of writing. Of course it was not true that all the newcomers were literate. Most were not: none of Los Angeles' first citizens, for example, could so much as sign their names. But there was literacy among the Spaniards, and Spain's imperial system, furthermore, had developed a strong tradition of paper work. Her frontier agents were required not merely to perform, but also to file detailed written reports. This requirement applied to civil and military officers, such as Governor Portolá and Captain Anza. It applied doubly to the missionaries, who customarily reported both in their capacity as employees of the Government and as churchmen responsible to their superiors in the Franciscan order.

This writing bulks large and, because its purpose was to inform the authorities in Spain and New Spain, it consists primarily of matter-of-fact narrative of steps taken and problems encountered, and of descriptions of natives, climate, terrain, vegetation, and water supply, almost always

in terms of the potentialities for empire building in the Spanish style, through missions, presidios, pueblos, and ranchos.

The greater part of this voluminous writing has no more claim to classification as literature than do the outpourings of present-day bureaucrats. Scattered throughout, however, are a number of pieces that deserve a better rating. Frequently these writings derive part of their merit from the dramatic or significant exploits that they describe. *Fray* Juan Crespi's chronicle of the march of Portolá is an example. It is written with clarity and vigor, but a chief reason for regarding it as a classic is that it contains the earliest description of the Los Angeles Plain, an account of the first crossing of the Santa Lucia Range, and an on-the-spot story of the discovery of San Francisco Bay.

Similarly, *Fray* Pedro Font's *Complete Diary* would be prized, whatever its style; and the descriptions by Pedro Fages and José Longinos Martínez are treasured though they do not have much style. By common consent, however, the foremost writer of this epoch was the California Boswell, *Fray* Francisco Palóu.

Palóu had been left in charge in Lower California when the first missionaries came north. He followed with the reinforcement of 1772, was stationed at Carmel, then at Mission Dolores in San Francisco, and then once more at Carmel. For many years he was vice-president of the missions, and he succeeded to the presidency in 1784. Noteworthy though his missionary career was, he is known almost exclusively for his writings. These included countless letters, of which a sampling has been published, and two longer works. The first, entitled *Noticias de la Nueva California* (Historical Memoir of New California), was written during a ten-year period at Carmel and Dolores. It is a detailed history of early California and especially of the missions. In good part it records what Palóu had personally observed, and the primary character of this work is further augmented by liberal quotations of significant letters. It establishes Palóu as California's first comprehensive historian.

His other and more famous work is a biography of his life-long friend, *Fray* Junípero Serra, first president of the missions and securely established as California's most revered hero. This biography was actually written in Mexico, where it was published in 1787. It was the fruit, however, of long association in California, and it was based to a considerable extent on the earlier *Noticias*. We need not hesitate about claiming it as

a California item. Strictly speaking, Palóu was not so good a biographer as he had been a historian. He was exceedingly partial to his hero. He did not hesitate to color the narrative in his favor, and at times he inadvertently blackened the character of Serra's antagonists. Even apart from its bias the *Vida del Padre Serra* is not as accurate as the *Noticias*. Nevertheless, it found a publisher seventy years sooner and it has been far more widely read. Comparative brevity of course is on its side, but perhaps more fundamental is that in Serra, Palóu had an exceedingly compelling character, a vivid personality, a man of infinite devotion and determination, a great force in the establishment of this Spanish outpost, and, all in all, virtually the personification of the province in its initial period. It is appropriate indeed that the first real example of California letters should be this biography of Junípero Serra.

TRAVEL BOOKS

The clerical or military report persisted into the Mexican period as the most common species of writing. Then, as foreign contacts multiplied, a new type appeared. It, likewise, was almost purely narrative and descriptive, and usually it was highly personalized. One cardinal difference was that, whereas the older writers had been primarily servants of the Empire of Spain and the Church of Rome, the basic interest of the new writers was in commerce, modified occasionally by a bent toward pure science or an inclination to promote the expansion of the United States. As foreigners, furthermore, these travelers and traders were less prone to take for granted the specifically Spanish features of the period. Their writings, therefore, are not only good sources on otter hunting, fur trapping, the hide trade, and the rise of the foreign contingent, but also have special merit as records of early California customs. Interest or significance of content thus is a principal recommendation of the writings of such men as Perouse, Vancouver, Shaler, Duflot de Mofras, Wilkes, Robinson, Colton, and Bryant. To a considerable extent their works were read because they dealt with a land that was strange and far away. If they are read now, it is largely because that land has become important. In general the writing continued to be without artifice, featuring direct and unadorned recording of things seen and experienced.

Such simplicity, of course, does not preclude literary excellence. Sev-

eral of these writers did creditably well, and distinction was achieved by at least two, John C. Frémont and Richard Henry Dana.

Although he gave his work a cumbersome title and put it in the hands of the Government printer, Frémont, ably assisted by his "immortal wife," wrote with dash and verve about his dramatic exploits in the West. His story lost nothing in the telling, and it enchanted a wide circle of readers.

Dana also had a grand opportunity, for he was a pioneer in writing about a long sea voyage from the perspective of the ordinary seaman. Mere novelty, however, would not account for the continuing popularity of *Two Years Before the Mast,* nor for its frequent use in composition classes as a model of style. Here was literary craftsmanship of a high order.

GLINTS OF GOLD

Considering the fewness of the Californians and the backwardness of the province, it may seem that there had been in these parts a phenomenal urge to write. Discovery of gold intensified this impulse. The forty-niners sensed that they were embarking upon a great adventure, pregnant with consequence, and a sort of contagion spread among them of recording their experiences in journal, letters, essay, or reminiscence. Hundreds of such accounts exist in manuscript or in print, and additional examples are still coming to light.

Quantity production, alas, is no guaranty of quality; and these gold-rush journals run poorer than the earlier travel accounts, yet with exceptions to the prevailing mediocrity. Some of these exceptions were provided by seasoned writers who joined the rush in search of new materials for their writings. Bayard Taylor came by way of Panama on such a mission, and his *Eldorado, or Adventures in the Path of Empire* is adequate justification for the trip. With like intent Friederich Gerstäcker hurried out from Germany by way of Buenos Aires, the Andes, and Valparaiso. Besides writing up his travels, he did a series of dramatized sketches, which as recently as 1942 found their first publication in English. Carl Meyer, a German-writing Swiss, was another such visitor. He was an observer more than a participant in gold mining, and his travel sketches, though written with some license, are packed with good reporting. Meanwhile, Alonzo Delano was demonstrating that a

forthright narrative of experience on the overland route could make a capital book, and Louise Amelia Knapp Smith Clappe—"Dame Shirley," for short—was setting down in letters to her sister the classic description of life in the diggings.

For California the gold rush touched off a period of sudden and remarkable growth. In politics the consequence was the 1849 constitution, in the best American pattern, and prompt admission to statehood. In agriculture it meant a rapid conversion from hide production to a stress on beef and grain. There was a mushrooming of new businesses and industries, including banking, lumbering, tanning, and ironworking. With express lines, stages, river boats, and coastal steamers, the State quickly acquired its first public transportation.

As part of this lush growth, various forms of writing luxuriated. The forty-niners were flush; they were hungry for reading matter; they were remote, in fact, months removed from the eastern sources of supply; and their tastes were unconventional. The natural result was the development of a local catering to this market. It began in journalism, with a proliferation of newspapers in San Francisco, in the mining towns, and eventually all up and down the State, so that in the fifties and sixties California had more newspapers per capita than any other part of the world. These papers, furthermore, were untrammeled by the superstition that news reporting was their chief function. Editors took free license to color, slant, and individualize such news as they did print, and their columns were open, to a degree far in excess of current practice, to creative writing in the form of verse, stories, essays, and anecdote. The next easy step was the establishment of weeklies like the *Golden Era* and monthlies like the *Pioneer,* the *Californian,* and eventually the *Overland,* which were professedly literary. These journals were the backbone of California letters in the days of gold, not to the exclusion, however, of some indulgence in the production of books.

Rank in its growth, to a considerable degree undisciplined, rough-edged, and sometimes coarse, this exuberant flood of writing has proved rather resistant to analysis. Several appraisals have been attempted, none of which perfectly measures the forces that thus found expression. The difficulty is that paradoxes and contradictions are the rule. For example, this writing oftentimes lapses into crudities and coarseness, as in Mark Twain's Washoe Giant squibs from San Francisco, yet the con-

ventions of the period were fully observed. Bad taste was often present, but there was a scrupulous avoidance of the themes and the blunt Anglo-Saxon words that incite Bostonian censorship today. This writing had a provincial flavor, but the influences that the writers brought with them from New England, New York, England, and elsewhere are very much in evidence. Autobiographical impulses contended with a penchant for pen names. The preference was strongly for realism, yet exaggeration was almost the norm. The local scene and the immediate present supplied the favorite subject matter, and this suggests a sense of self-importance, yet a favorite literary form was to lampoon gold-rush California. This humorous bent was matched, furthermore, by frequent lapses into sentimentality. It all adds up to a distinctive literature, youthful and robust, not derivative from the earlier forms that had flourished in the area, but thoroughly true to the Argonaut social pattern.

In the long run Mark Twain and Bret Harte came to be reckoned the brightest stars in this particular galaxy. They rose, however, somewhat belatedly, and the miners' earlier favorites were men like Old Block, Squibob, Dogberry, Caxton, and Yellow Bird. Needless to say, these were pen names, then very much the fashion and, however else psychoanalysis may explain them, excellent specifics against timidity and inhibitions.

Alonzo Delano, or Old Block, began his writing career with a few sketches hesitantly submitted to the editor of a San Francisco paper. Encouraged by their success, he wrote others which ran in the *Pacific News* and the *Pioneer* and subsequently appeared in book form under such titles as *Pen-Knife Sketches* and *Old Block's Sketch Book.* Then he wrote a one-act play, *A Live Woman in the Mines;* and the Hogarthian pamphlet, *The Idle and Industrious Miner,* is sometimes ascribed to him. His genius was to write factually about the mines, stressing the seamy side of life in the diggings, doing full justice to the hardships and the disappointments, but at the same time pointing up the ludicrous aspects. The realism that he achieved was greatly appreciated by his California readers, who likewise enjoyed being made fun of. They also esteemed him because of his personal qualities, not least of which was his nose, famed as California's largest.

Prentice Mulford, who wrote as Dogberry, was likewise an experienced and disillusioned prospector. He had tried his hand at a number of

things, including schoolteaching and politics, before discovering his pen, and in his latter days he gained an eastern vogue as a mildly spiritualist philosopher. In California letters, however, he is memorable for a sheaf of sketches, amused and ironic, on the foibles of life in the mining area after the first great rush was over, but before the arrival of sedateness. His "Barney McBriar, the Shootist," forecasts and parodies Billy the Kid. The narratives of his campaign for office and of his tribulations as a schoolmaster, though written to amuse, are valuable social documents. So is his soliloquy on the culinary art in the mines. It begins: "I am a survivor of all the different eras of California amateur cookery," which he enumerates as the pork, bean, and flapjack era, the epoch of stewed dried apples, the pie period, the canned provision era, "fruitful in sardines and oysters," the latter "as destructive as cannister shot," and finally, a mouth-watering description of mountain cooking.

Mulford's sketches are more jocular than profound. His contemporaries liked them because of their genuineness, and by and large that is why they are readable today.

George H. Derby, a portly lieutenant assigned to topographical duty in gold-rush California was the most popular and probably the most significant of these early writers. His vein was the broadly humorous. Through heroic self-restraint he kept all levity out of his official reports, but it dominated almost everything else that he did.

He was an inveterate punster, many of his puns execrably bad, and many in the pattern of twists upon well-known sayings, such as "Great aches from little toe corns grow." He had a passion for off-color stories, and he was a constant perpetrator of practical jokes. Nothing was sacred. Before introducing his wife to his mother, he made each believe that the other was deaf. When left in charge of Judson Ames' San Diego *Herald*, he changed the sheet's politics. He even perpetrated a hoax on himself, killing off his alter ego, Squibob, at the height of popularity, and then having to start over again as John Phoenix.

Puns, off-color stories, and hoaxes are not ideal avenues toward immortality. And the practical joke has the drawback of never seeming as funny in retrospect as it did at the time. Some of his best efforts, furthermore, were dated. For example, his elaborate account of a survey for a railroad route through the heart of San Francisco, a salty burlesque on the military reconnaissances that were standard procedure in the fifties,

can be appreciated today only by antiquarians who are immersed in the nicer details of the early West. In his brief day he came near to being the nation's, as well as California's, favorite humorist. Thanks to George Stewart's recent biography and Francis Farquhar's reprinting of *Phoenixiana,* he is experiencing something of a revival, and he has been hailed as a polished and skillful workman, the founder of a new school of American humor, and a valuable corrective to the preceding style of depending on illiteracy and bad grammar as the mainstays of humor.

In charting literary history the overwhelming temptation is to concentrate on quality. An alternative approach is to look at what is read in quantity. On this basis attention is due two pamphlets of the fifties, John R. Ridge's *The Life and Adventures of Joaquin Murieta,* and Royal B. Stratton's *Captivity of the Oatman Girls.*

Stratton, a Yreka clergyman, interviewed Olive Oatman shortly after her ransom from the Mohaves. He did full justice to the harrowing story of the Apache attack on the emigrant train in which the Oatmans were traveling, the barbarity of the Apaches toward Olive and her sister, the kindlier treatment by the Mohaves, and the eventual rescue. As William B. Rice pointed out, Stratton and the California press in general had been scooped by the Los Angeles *Star,* which printed a long interview with Olive immediately after her release. Stratton's book, however, had two San Francisco printings in 1857, others in New York and Chicago, and sold thirty thousand copies within two years. In 1935, edited by Lindley Bynum, it circulated again as a Grabhorn imprint.

John R. Ridge, our other conspicuously successful pamphleteer, was more of a figure in California writing. As Yellow Bird, a translation of his Cherokee name, he contributed to the literary journals, and under his own name he submitted occasional poems, graceful and conventional. His story of Murieta's life appeared in 1854 and was pirated by the *California Police Gazette* five years later. Ridge doubtless considered it hack writing, for it is a dramatized biography containing a frank embroidering upon the available and attested facts. It is spirited in style and reinforced with Charles Nahl drawings that are full of dash. Into it Ridge poured an intensity of feeling that traces back to a tragedy of his childhood, when his father was assassinated in a vendetta rising out of the Cherokee removal. In writing about Murieta, Ridge apparently sublimated his own desire for revenge. He succeeded beyond his ex-

pectations. He elevated Murieta from a petty bandit to a folk hero, a California Robin Hood, and without substantial modification this interpretation is echoed by Bancroft, Hittell, Miller, and most subsequent writers. Herein is demonstration of the power of the pen.

In terms of letters the climax of the golden era was clearly with the establishment of the *Overland* in 1868 and its first few years of operation under the editorship of Francis Bret Harte. Harte used it as the vehicle for the best of his stories and verses. He drew to its columns practically every local writer of promise. He made the journal live up to its subtitle, which proclaimed that it was "devoted to the development of the country." The *Overland* carried numerous items that were frankly promotional. It embraced some that were placeless, but a larger number dealt specifically with the American West or the Pacific area. And in addition to its predilection for western subjects, the *Overland* had a vibrancy, a freshness, and aroma that were unmistakably western.

Another few years and the golden era was plainly at an end. No precise date marked its finish, and several of its literary figures, including Ina Coolbrith, Joaquin Miller, Charles W. Stoddard, and Ambrose Bierce, carried on lustily toward the end of the century or beyond, but somewhere in the seventies the curtain came down. The completion of the transcontinental railroad obviously had a hand in the matter. It not only carried away Harte, Twain, Mulford, and others; it also struck a blow at isolation, brought in eastern wares, publications included, more expeditiously than before, and sharply reduced the distinctiveness of California society. Other factors were at work in this same direction as frontier roughness tended to wear off, as prospecting gave way to more orthodox employment, and as time eroded the masculine and youthful imbalance of the California population.

WRITERS OF THE SECOND GENERATION

The generation that followed was far less glamorous than the bearded and red-shirted forty-niners. At the hands of the historians of politics, economics, and culture it has received far less attention. Nevertheless, the indexes of population, production, and wealth indicate that the material achievements of this second American generation bulk considerably larger than those of their predecessors. In literature also, although

they may have been less colorful, ebullient, and spontaneous, the writers of this middle epoch are an important contingent in the State's roster. In consonance with their epoch, they exhibited more diversification and more sophistication. The audience they had in mind was not exclusively Californian, but much that they did was closely tied to the region.

As the first example of this generation, consider Robert Louis Stevenson, Edinburgh-born, a traveler in Spain, and subsequently at home in Samoa, but briefly a Californian. To him we are indebted for a graphic account of an early journey across the continent in the hard-seated coaches of the Union Pacific and the more sumptuous palace cars of the Central Pacific. Next we find him a refugee from the fogs of Monterey and San Francisco, in a ramshackle cabin on the upper slopes of Mount St. Helena. His gratitude for the relief there obtained is expressed in a sensitive little volume, *The Silverado Squatters,* a cameo likeness of one segment of the Coast Ranges.

The scene of this little book (he begins) is on a high mountain. There are, indeed, many higher; there are many of nobler outline. It is no place of pilgrimage for the summary globe-trotter; but to one who lives upon its sides, Mount Saint Helena soon becomes a centre of interest. It is the Mont Blanc of one section of the California Coast Range, none of its near neighbours rising to one-half its altitude. It looks down upon much green, intricate country. It feeds in the spring-time many splashing brooks. From its summit you must have an excellent lesson of geography: seeing, to the south, San Francisco Bay, with Tamalpais on the one hand and Monte Diablo on the other; to the west and thirty miles away, the open ocean; eastward, across the corn-lands and thick tule swamps of Sacramento Valley, to where the Central Pacific railroad begins to climb the sides of the Sierras; and northward, for what I know, the white head of Shasta looking down on Oregon. Three counties, Napa County, Lake County, and Sonoma County, march across its cliffy shoulders.

To him the mountain was primarily an escape from the coastal dampness, yet one of the brightest spots in this volume is a picture of an early morning fog, rolling in from the sea, and inundating everything below him. As he describes it:

Napa Valley was gone; gone were all the lower slopes and woody foothills of the range; and in their place, not a thousand feet below me, rolled a great level ocean. It was as though I had gone to bed the night before, safe in a nook of inland mountains, and had awakened in a bay upon the coast. . . .

Far away were hilltops like little islands. I began to observe that this sea was not so level as at first sight it appeared to be. Away in the extreme south, a little hill of fog arose against the sky above the general surface, and as it had already caught the sun it shone on the horizon like the topsails of some giant ship. There were huge waves, stationary, as it seemed, like waves in a frozen sea; and yet, as I looked again, I was not sure but they were moving after all, with a slow and august advance. And while I was yet doubting, a promontory of the hills some four or five miles away, conspicuous by a bouquet of tall pines, was in a single instant overtaken and swallowed up. It reappeared in a little, with its pines, but this time on an islet, and only to be swallowed up once more and then for good. This set me looking nearer, and I saw that in every cove along the line of mountains the fog was being piled in higher and higher, as though by some wind that was inaudible to me. I could trace its progress, one pine tree first growing hazy and then disappearing after another; although sometimes there was none of this forerunning haze, but the whole opaque white ocean gave a start and swallowed a piece of mountain at a gulp. It was to flee these poisonous fogs that I had left the seaboard, and climbed so high among the mountains. And now, behold, here came the fog to besiege me in my chosen altitudes, and yet came so beautifully that my first thought was of welcome.

This one essay is a princely rental for Stevenson's brief sojourn in California. His sketches are among the finest in her literature: the descriptions of Calistoga, the "prospecting" of vintners trying out the land in experiments with one grape and another, the act of squatting, and the story of Silverado Mine. In appreciation, a movement is on foot to preserve Toll House, the rustic hostel, with its toll bar and acres of woods and streams as a State park in honor of this friendly visitor.

Nature writing was a constant temptation in California. For the earlier epoch, James M. Hutchings comes particularly to mind because of his passion for the Yosemite, but there were many others, including Benjamin P. Avery and Edward Rowland Sill, who naturalized chiefly in the environs of the Coast Ranges, and William C. Bartlett, whose favorite locale was the wooded district above the Napa and Sonoma Valleys. The Titans in this type of writing were, however, two men of the post gold-rush era, Clarence King and John Muir. Both made the Sierra Nevada their central theme. King won fame as an incomparable raconteur of mountaineering adventures. In casual conversation he poured forth the equivalent of a whole shelf of books, only one of which got

Sunshine in the Mill Creek redwoods.

On the way to Santa Barbara's annual fiesta, "Old Spanish Days."

An old Spanish house at San Juan Bautista.

actually onto paper, but this work, *Mountaineering in the Sierra Nevada*, is a model of its kind.

Muir was more deliberate about picking up his pen, but far more industrious in its use. A self-tutored naturalist, he arrived in California in 1868 and immediately posted off to the wilds of the interior to continue his lessons from nature. For the Yosemite and the Sierra, and later for other parts of California, he developed a boundless enthusiasm, which set his writings afire. Personal, highly figurative, and often mystical, they convey the intensity of his feeling. Yosemite and the Sierra were first in his affections, which, however, embraced Alaska and its glaciers, the gentler Contra Costa hills, and the redwoods of the Coast Range belt, where Muir Woods commemorates his name.

Meanwhile in southern California an equally zealous crusader had appeared. This was Helen Hunt Jackson, erstwhile writer of children's stories and sentimental romances. As a resident of Colorado and a visitor to California, she was stirred by the injustices dealt the Indians. As coauthor with Abbot Kinney she filed an official report on United States Indian policy, which she had previously stigmatized under the graphic title, *A Century of Dishonor*. Bidding for a wider hearing, she rewrote this theme as the novel *Ramona*, which attained immediate and lasting popularity and assisted considerably in salvaging mission Indian rights.

Concurrently in San Francisco sardonic and acerbic Ambrose Bierce was laying about with bitter witticism and crushing abuse. A Civil War veteran and a former watchman at the San Francisco mint, Bierce turned out a number of gripping war stories and chilling horror tales. His talent was greatest, however, in the acidulous retorts scattered through his column of "Prattle" in the San Francisco *Wasp* and then in Hearst's *Examiner*. He was as untrammeled as the gold-rush journalists. He was a self-elected scourge of the Southern Pacific, Hubert Howe Bancroft, and all amateur poets. It would be difficult to prove that his barbed shafts benefited society, but they were a tour de force, an epigrammatic feast, and one of the most brilliant literary exploits of the middle generation.

In journalism, Bierce's southern counterpart was doubtless Horace Bell of the *Porcupine*, whose *Reminiscences of a Ranger* in 1881 was Los Angeles' first real book. As intellectual arbiter, the parallel figure would be Charles F. Lummis. In showmanship Lummis equaled Joaquin Miller; as a protector of the Indians he surpassed Helen Hunt Jackson;

his zeal for acknowledgment of the Spanish heritage matched Muir's love of nature; his *Land of Sunshine* was as "devoted to the development of the country" as Bret Harte's *Overland*. As city editor of the Los Angeles *Times*, as city librarian, as father of the Landmarks Club, the Sequoyah League, and the Southwest Museum, he exerted a profound influence on the community. This was supplemented by an informal salon where his literary disciples foregathered, and by a series of books, *The Land of Poco Tiempo, The Spanish Pioneers, A Bronco Pegasus,* and *Flowers of Our Lost Romance*, reiterating and underlining his message about Spanish and Indian achievements and about the destiny of the Southwest. Among his followers Mary Austin was the most competent. Her *Land of Little Rain* and *The Flock* depict the hinterland of Owens Valley. Her *Isidro* is more believable than *Ramona*. Her translations from the Navajo carry out a Lummis interest.

In the closing decades of the nineteenth century the great power in California was the railroad. Although its primary concern was with revenues, land sales, and politics, it left its imprint on letters by prompting some writers and arousing others. Charles Nordhoff, Ben C. Truman, Lindley and Widney, B. F. Taylor, W. H. Bishop, and T. S. Van Dyke obliged with promotional brochures. Van Dyke found a better vein in his *Millionaires of a Day*, a delightful twitting of the realtors and their clients in southern California's boom of the eighties. For writing that was considerably more vigorous one would turn to the critics of the railroad, including Ambrose Bierce in his pugnacious column, Josiah Royce in *The Feud of Oakfield Creek*, and, more especially, Frank Norris in *The Octopus*.

Norris began as a romantic, turned to naturalism, and with *McTeague*, in 1899, took rank as Zola's most thoroughgoing American disciple. A study in character disintegration induced by economic pressure, *McTeague* is also a psychological study of sadism. In *The Octopus* and *The Pit*, Norris took a further step and appealed fervently for economic and social reform. Whatever this may have done to his work as literature, it enhanced its historical significance as a factor in the reform movement that culminated in the Lincoln-Roosevelt League.

As I measure it, he was the best California novelist of his day. Gertrude Atherton and Stewart Edward White might be nominated, but

their principal work came later. A closer competitor was Jack London.

London went along with and beyond Norris in his denunciation of the ills of society and the sins of capitalism. But because this theme was concentrated in two of his less-read works, *The Iron Heel* and *The Revolution,* he is most often recalled as the master storyteller of *The Call of the Wild* and *The Sea Wolf,* vivid in his characterizations, authentic in his settings, rapid in pace, spontaneous and vigorous.

By the canons of literary workmanship, London, Norris, Austin, Bierce, Stevenson, and several of these others were far more mature than the gold-rush writers. There is another respect also in which the second American generation had gone beyond the first, namely, in the realm of serious writing. Nonfiction occurred before the seventies, but almost always in the form of simple narration. In the subsequent epoch much more ambitious tasks were undertaken. Josiah Royce went to Harvard and became a famous philosopher. Thorstein Veblen sojourned for a time in Cedro Cottage at Stanford and excoriated the leisure class. Theodore H. Hittell produced a massive history of the State in four ponderous volumes. Still more impressive were Henry George's excursion into economic doctrine and his argumentative treatise, *Progress and Poverty,* and the thirty-nine volumes of Hubert Howe Bancroft's *Works,* setting forth in endless detail the history of the western half of North America from before Columbus to the 1880's. These projects rested on an economic and social structure advanced considerably beyond that of the gold-rush days.

THE MODERNS

In the modern era, roughly the period since the turn of the century, the San Francisco Fire, and World War I, particularly the war, California has experienced its greatest growth and, in some respects, its most thorough transformation. The automobile, the moving-picture industry, and airplane manufacture belong almost exclusively to this epoch, and other elements, like the oil industry, grew beyond recognition. With everything else on the increase, it is not surprising that the stream of writing widened. It also displayed far greater diversity. Hollywood, for example, has been a market for scenarios, a type of writing hitherto unpracticed, and has brought to California many distinguished writers, some of whom promptly naturalized themselves as Californians,

Will Rogers and Irvin Cobb, for example, while others proved totally resistant to such change.

Because this modern era is still in progress any estimate of its achievements must be provisional. In several fields, however, recent attainments are indisputably the best. Anthropological literature, for example, was produced more or less by accident as early visitors set down descriptions of the Indians, and then somewhat more systematically as Father Boscana, Hugo Reid, B. D. Wilson, Alexander Taylor, Stephen Powers, and Hubert Howe Bancroft recorded what they had been able to learn. Professional and scientific appraisals were delayed until the twentieth century, when A. L. Kroeber, Frederick W. Hodge, and their cohorts entered the field. In history writing, the indebtedness of the moderns to Hubert Howe Bancroft beclouds the issue, yet the ranks of living historians are so much larger, the scope of their studies so much broader, and their command of scientific method so much greater, that they clearly outrank the previous generations. In literature as a whole a similar generalization ought to be valid, and in the realm of what is usually called creative writing—verse, essay, short story, and novel—I believe the recent superiority is obvious.

In the first of these categories the gold-rush bards, including Edward Pollock, John R. Ridge, Charles Stoddard, Ina Coolbrith, Francis Bret Harte, and Joaquin Miller, had been succeeded by another school, headed by Edwin Markham, Herman Scheffauer, and George Sterling. Markham's *The Man with the Hoe* is the best-known, but by no means the best poem of this generation. Like Miller's *Columbus* it was better in idea than in execution. Sterling is the acknowledged master in this middle era, and he might have made a still greater reputation had he not elected suicide. The literary capital of the State was still at San Francisco but, in verse at least, was showing signs of migrating to Carmel. As the new century continued, other voices took over. They may be divided into three groups: a numerous and undistinguished substratum; a contingent of able and inspired writers headed by Hildegarde Flanner, Genevieve Taggard, Charles Erskine Scott Wood, and Sara Bard Field; and one poet of heroic stature, Robinson Jeffers.

Jeffers' poetry shows a marked influence of place. He acknowledges a large debt to "the magnificent unspoiled scenery" of the Monterey peninsula, to "the introverted and storm-twisted beauty of Point Lobos,"

to the rugged headlands jutting out into fog and ocean, and to "the savage beauty of canyon and sea-cliff." The pounding of the ocean on this rugged coast, the waves and spray, the gulls, hawks, the tortured cypress, the towering redwoods, these and a thousand other elements of the "Jeffers country" are the recurrent materials and symbols of his writing. Without them it would lose much of its force and character.

The essential difference between prose and poetry, so Jeffers contends, is that whereas prose deals with the ephemeral and transitory, poetry "must concern itself chiefly with permanent things and with the permanent aspects of life." With this division I do not completely agree, but the definition is a helpful key to an understanding of Jeffers' work. Universals are his chosen subject matter, particularly love and hate, revenge, remorse, and expiation. Even in his shorter poems, less morbid with murder, suffering, and incest, a steady seriousness of purpose dominates. In imagery and lyric quality they stand high, but their essence is their thought content. His longer narratives are in the nature of psychological analyses, involved, relentlessly pursued, and unswervingly pessimistic. Jeffers is not and will not be the people's poet, but if our civilization, as he has warned, proceeds to destroy itself, he will be ideally suited to compose its requiem.

In the shorter prose forms excellent performances include the unpretentious stories in Edwin Corle's *Mojave* and Max Miller's *I Cover the Waterfront* and the sketches, hovering between history and fiction, in Idwal Jones' *China Boy*. Wider acclaim has been won by William Saroyan and John Steinbeck. Saroyan's writing is at once introspective and exhibitionist. The effect is of artlessness, and much that he does seems utterly inconsequential, yet there are rewarding pieces of droll humor, revealing incident, and subtle characterization. Consult, for example, "The Pomegranate Trees."

The Pastures of Heaven and *Tortilla Flat* reveal Steinbeck in what, to me, is his best vein. The stories comprising these volumes are set just around the corner from Jeffers' favorite Big Sur locale. They feature characters as humble as his, but less abnormal, certainly under less severe strain, and apparently possessed, therefore, of a greater universality.

At other times Steinbeck has chosen the role of protagonist or crusader. *In Dubious Battle* is the most convincing, though *Of Mice and Men,*

The Grapes of Wrath, and *The Moon Is Down* gained far greater fame. *Cannery Row* crusades for an unexpected cause and class, has moments of inspired writing, but is marred by gross sentimentality and muddled thinking. Steinbeck, as intimated, has been only a part-time crusader. Therein he must yield to two inveterate jousters against evil, two and perhaps a third. Lincoln Steffens, one of the original muckrakers, recently departed, made reform his lifework and, the cynical would add, his livelihood. Upton Sinclair, with scores of volumes attacking corruption and special interest wherever he saw it, has been still more indefatigable. And Carey McWilliams, in a series of popular, book-length briefs, has persuasively argued the cause of the farm laborer and the racial minority. Together with Steinbeck they make a formidable quartet, which, if words could kill, would have completely routed the forces of darkness.

Novelists more innocent of social or political intent have likewise abounded. Arbitrarily, I pass over Zane Grey and the other architects of "westerns," the mystery writers such as Willard H. Wright and Erle Stanley Gardner, and the exponents of pure narrative, such as Kathleen Norris and Kathleen Winsor. Among the fabulously prolific and popular, Gertrude Atherton and Stewart Edward White must also be mentioned. Both have capitalized on California historical themes, the one with an eye to romance and the other with an eye to realism. Perhaps it is wishful thinking on my part, but I believe that White's *Gold, The Gray Dawn, The Rose Dawn,* and the "Long Rifle Series" are the more apt to endure.

Eleanor McKee, Scott O'Dell, Lillian Bos Ross, Edwin Corle, George Stewart, Robert Easton, Budd Schulberg, Hans Otto Storm, Jo Pagano, Frances Marion—California's living novelists are a long procession. Consensus places Steinbeck at the head, not for consistency, but for flashes of brilliance and for the most powerful novel yet to come out of the State. With this judgment I do not quarrel, nor with the nomination of White and Sinclair for file leaders. My personal preference, however, is for two quieter works, period pieces, if you will: one, Idwal Jones' *The Vineyard,* a saga of the guild craftsmanship in at least a portion of the State's wine industry, and the other, Oscar Lewis' *I Remember Christine,* a backward glance at the social structure of old San Francisco,

a mild debunking of some of the men who built the West, and incidentally a take-off on the practices of historians.

In the impressive totality of California writing, one persistent tendency stands out, and one unmistakable trend. The trend has been a steady improvement in the quality of literary output; the continuing factor, attention to the local scene. This latter observation runs counter to the opinion of the editor of a recent anthology, who remarks that until the last quarter century "California writers in general had not discovered their state and were not particularly interested in it." It is true that a good many writers domiciled in California have dealt with aberrant topics, more or less as Lew Wallace sat in the Governor's Palace in Santa Fe and wrote *Ben Hur*. Yet the most obvious connecting thread, from the earliest writers to the most recent, is a consciousness of the region and an attention to its literary implications. In newspaper writing as we move from Delano to Bierce to Will Rogers, in comprehensive histories from Palóu to Bancroft to Chapman and Cleland, in the novel from Harte to Norris to Steinbeck, and in verse from Miller to Sterling to Jeffers, the characteristic of improving quality is apparent, but no more so than that of awareness and vital interest in the California environment.

THE WILDERNESS
MOUNTAINS

BY LOIS CRISLER

Now we enter the dark realm of the Olympics. Now, in terms of those who insist that mountains must be mighty peaks that unbend above one in almost frightening proportions, we have achieved that requirement. This chapter tells eloquently of the mountain wilderness of the Olympics. (R. P.)

The Pacific Ocean has made the intensely characteristic quality of the Olympics. It pours its southeast trades against their western side to deluge them with the highest rainfall in the country—in places, 144 inches. Lower, the great rain forests are the response; higher, it is the association of clouds and moisture and mountains that is characteristic. The brightness, the freshness, the ceaseless shift of mist and shadow give their characteristic of wild secret playfulness to the Olympics. Camping in a river valley, you may waken in gray fog, only to see, beyond your breakfast campfire, the mists melting from sunny forested mountainsides above you. Camping up in mountain meadows you see the morning whiteness dissolve around dark crags and alpine clumps of fir, folding and unfolding in dreamlike glimpses. If you make high camp for the climb of Olympus in fog and rain, you stand a chance of seeing the Olympic fogscape at its grandest, of reaching the summit the next day when cumulus piles sail off in sunlight over hundreds of square miles of blue mountains and white peaks.

On the north side of the Olympics, within nine miles, you can go from tidelands and marine life to the arctic-alpine life zone at sixty-four hundred feet altitude on Mount Angeles. Not high as mountains go, the Olympics look high because they rise abruptly from a low coastal belt, not from a plateau. Partly because of the alliance of sea and mountains the glaciers begin on the Olympics at the elevation where they end on other mountains, and forests sweep up dark green almost to the bare rocks and snow.

These mountains are young historically. On account of their geo-

logically youthful ruggedness, their dense timber, and the fact that they are all but hemmed in by salt water, up in the extreme northwest tip of the United States, their main human history is less than sixty years old. The man is living who as a boy of sixteen first ventured into the interior from the north, exploring alone beyond the Bailey Range. The long-lived Indians out on the coast could have heard from their grandparents of the coming of the "King George men," the English, and the "Bostons," the American traders. They have their own tradition of the coming of the Spaniards before that.

In 1774 Juan Pérez, coasting up along "California," having glimpsed isolated snow peaks off in the interior, came in sight at last of what looked like a whole range of white mountains, the first range he had come to, floating on dark blue bases to his east. The highest peak he named ephemerally Santa Rosalia. The next year came more Spaniards, Bodega y Quadra and Bruno Heceta, and these tangled with the Indians. While the one landed to leave a cross, claiming the land for Spain, the other put out a short party near the mouth of the Hoh for water. The Spanish version is that the Indians gestured to trade for metal and then massacred the trusting Spaniards for the metal in their boats. The Indians tell rather of drunken adventurers who had not seen a woman for months.

Still the Olympics stood inviolate, the rivers tearing down, gray with alpine debris, the elk treading out trails as broad and beaten as wagon tracks, the cougar and deer and marten making a network of living creatures in the great forests and the mountain meadows.

It was three years later that Englishmen hove in sight of the Olympics. First came James Cook, better known for his South Seas explorations. Then on June 29, 1788, John Meares' vessel entered the strait of Juan de Fuca, sails set, bow cutting white, black Indian dugouts double-rowed by naked men following, a rock-walled island crowned by an Indian village on the lee side, and towering above the alien foliage of the madroña, the white of unknown mountains. Saints never crossed this Englishman's mind. "The home of the gods," he must have thought, for Meares named the highest peak Mount Olympus. That name stuck; the Spanish one lapsed. When Captain Vancouver's ship "Discovery" sailed into the strait in May, 1792, the men were coasting "the Olympics," with the

sense of unknown still waters and boundless forests, the wonder of un-recorded lands upon them.

Never did a land more virgin of myth wear a name from more elaborate mythology. There is a curious nakedness about the Olympics. The land is so alive, so speaking, that it almost articulates a mythology—around the slender white alders by clear black pools in the rain forests, or around a deer lick on the Elwha, where, between the brown rock and tree trunks, show far-off blue mountains. Not one of the old-world figures fits here—not djinn or dwarf, fairy or goddess: there is a tinge of fearfulness about all of those. The melancholy of that artifact, the Cheshire cat, belongs as little as the menace of the *loup-garou*. The pioneers' rollicking creatures fit better—the high-behind; the sidehill gouger; the wampus cat, that sheds his whiskers morning and night, black ones for night and white ones for day; and the ornithorhyncus, that builds his nest in the fog banks off Mount Olympus, out of the wampus cat's white whiskers. These are without the least trace of fear-fulness, creatures of people released into new land, confident of a great future.

First came the traders; then followed the hunters, the settlers, the "expeditions," and the climbers. The traders, like the Indians, stayed along the coast. The Indians considered it a sign of good sense to keep out of the mountains, rationalizing their lack of crampons, ice axes, and dark glasses with the myth of the thunderbird up in the mountains, who resented intrusion. Moreover, the Clallams, along the strait, were not very venturesome. They knew that if they fished more than a mile or so offshore, Indians from Vancouver Island might swoop down on them; they did not care to test whether there were similar hostile tribes in the mountains.

Bolder were the Quillayutes over on the Pacific, hunters, who canoed up the Hoh almost to the foot of the Cream Lake Basin, to slaughter elk on the side of the Hoh canyon, and dry the meat in drying sheds along the river. The hot springs up the Soleduck were visited, too. And ex-perienced hunters among the Indians were not afraid to go anywhere with a white man. Two Indians went on the first reported climb of Mount Olympus, in 1853, with two white men, Henry Cock and Colonel Ben-jamin Franklin Shaw, a redheaded giant of a woodsman who is reputed to have made the first attempt on Mount Rainier also, and only a month

later. Not much is known of the climb, which was unreported till 1907. If they made the top, it is extremely unlikely that they sorted out and climbed the highest peak rising from the confusing summit field. The two Indians, who took the white men up the Hoh by canoe, may have been Quillayutes.

The fifties were great climbing years in the Northwest as well as in England, where mountain climbing was becoming smart, and young Leslie Stephens was getting half the dons of Cambridge into the Alps during the vacations. Besides, the Americans were swiftly getting acquainted with the Oregon Territory, to which England had freshly yielded claim.

About 1853, too, the Hudson's Bay Company, snubbed out of Fort Nisqually on Puget Sound, from their new quarters in Victoria, on Vancouver Island, reached down a paw into the Olympics, sending in hunters, forty-niners from California who had followed the trail of gold to the Caribou, in northern British Columbia. Among those hunters were forest-skilled men with quiet steady eyes, full of experience and courage —men like John Sutherland and John Everett, who became settlers, too. Everett's son Billy was that first explorer beyond the Bailey Range. But he was just a boy; what he knew no one noticed. Even to the people of Washington Territory itself the interior of the Olympics was still a mystery.

THE MYTH OF THE CENTRAL VALLEY

The Olympic peninsula, a rough rectangle about seventy by seventy miles—nearly surrounded by the Pacific, the strait of Juan de Fuca on the north, and Puget Sound on the east—presents a white rampart against the sky from all three seaward sides. And by sea it was almost always approached, for to the south rolled lower hills bearing in those days a tremendous evergreen forest, of which only the giant stumps now remain. Hemmed in by water on three sides, by forests on four—forests that inspired a lyric phrase in the U. S. Coast Survey report for 1858: "the immeasurable sea of gigantic timber coming down to the very shores"—those white ramparts, though familiar in outline from the sea and from across the Sound, were unknown in person, proof of which was the general supposition that they were merely a coastal range guarding a vast central valley.

There were stories about that mythical valley: it was suitable for colonizing; there was a central lake—probably with subterranean outlets to the sea; there were coal and minerals; a fierce tribe of Indians inhabited it. It was a combination of Jules Verne, Stanley and Livingstone, and the new Yellowstone Park. "Washington has her great unknown land, like the interior of Africa," said the governor of the now newly made State to a reporter from the *Seattle Press* in 1889; twenty-five hundred square miles that had never "to the positive knowledge of old residents, been trodden by the foot of man—white or Indian."

"Here," said the *Press* grandiosely, "is an opportunity for some one to acquire fame by unveiling the mystery which wraps the land encircled by the snow-capped Olympic range." The era of the "expeditions" was launched. With equal dignity came an answering letter from a Scotsman, James Hellbal Christie: "It is no ambitious, untried youth who now writes you, but a man tried in all the vicissitudes of mountain, forest, and plain." However, there was the little matter of finances; perhaps some gentlemen of the Sound would care to assist. The gentlemen did, chiefly Mr. Bailey, publisher of the Seattle *Press*.

On December 8, 1889, Christie started from Port Angeles with four men and fifteen hundred pounds of supplies, including Winchester rifles, iron army kettles, and fifty pounds of colored fire to set off on peaks visible from Seattle. They were to ascend the mountains by way of the Elwha Pass, the object of their winter start being to get "over the first ranges and into the central valley ready for work when spring should open."

In their thirties were Christie, prospector and hunter, at the moment from Yakima, east of the Cascades; Charles Adams Barnes, topographer and historian of the party; John Crumback, a home-loving Canadian; and John Simms, a recently arrived Englishman, the oldest of the five. The youngest was a twenty-two-year-old cowboy also from Yakima —Christopher O'Connell Hayes, great-grandson of Daniel O'Connell, the Irish patriot. All five men had "an abundance of vim and manly vigor." They did indeed. They also had abundance of ignorance of conditions in the Olympics in winter. They were starting blind to cross unknown mountains in the dead of winter, without once touching a base of supplies. And what no one could possibly have foreseen was that they were facing "an extraordinary winter with an unheard-of mass of snow," fol-

lowed by avalanches and severe storms in the spring, as Henderson, the botanist, described it the following summer.

The first thing they did was to fall foul of the settlers. This *Press* party had a picture in their minds of the requirements of an expedition. The settlers along the coast were cagy old birds with a good deal of experience, in spite of the newness of the country. When the *Press* party wanted horses, the price tripled, and they had to go clear to Dungeness on the strait for a couple of mules, destined for trouble. Feeling that a boat was essential to a well-run expedition, they crashed straight westward to the Elwha River, their intended highway into the interior, ignoring or ignorant of the good trail angling to the river farther toward the mountains.

Along their own trail, through swamp and snow, they dragged green lumber, its corners worn off before they got it to the river. Working with incredible zeal, dreaming of the fabulous discoveries ahead, they constructed a thirty-foot boat, launched it on the swift narrow mountain stream, and christened it "Gertie." "Gertie" immediately sank. The *Press* party dragged her out, upheaved her in the snow, and kept a fire under her for days to dry her out. What the settlers and the half-breeds may have been thinking of the expedition was beneath their notice. Recaulked, repitched, and relaunched, the "Gertie" floated and the expedition started.

What with rapids and rocks, the men were wading in the icy water half the time, coaxing the "Gertie" up the Elwha. Without any visible embarrassment, they kept coming to the "last" cabin. At Indian Valley, confronted by the log jam the settlers used as a bridge, in order to get "Gertie" portaged, they threatened to cut out the jam. The settlers helped! Three or four miles farther the hard-working explorers wangled their boat before they got enough of her. She had done them one incalculable service, though; she had detained them for two months, keeping them out of the mountains in the heart of winter.

They still brimmed with ideas. When Christie now told each man to devise some conveyance to haul supplies, they flew to work to build travois and a two-man contraption they called a go-devil, which one man was to hold back so it would not go too fast. When all the rigs were ready and loaded, by the aid of crowbars they prodded the go-devil a hundred yards forward into the wilderness. Then the expedition soberly

came down to the two mules. On the Devil's Backbone just beyond the present Elwha ranger station, one mule went over the crag with a two-hundred-pound pack of flour and the colored fire. The men climbed down and got the flour; the colored fire they pitched over the cliff. They were learning.

Really beyond the last cabin now, they were blazing a trail into the wilderness, the famous Press Party Trail that was to become approximately the Elwha Trail, a thoroughfare into the mountains, along which, on certain old trees, can still be read their triple blaze, the line-tree mark of eastern surveyors. Often and carefully they blazed, marking a trail for colonists to follow to that central valley. In the winter range of the Olympic game now, in virgin country, their scouts cached an elk carcass on every log, meat for the advancing party. Deer trooped up the mountainside in bands of thirty or forty. Near a tributary stream one day, a wildcat over four feet long stepped out of the forest across the river and paused wonderingly to gaze at them. Beautiful, they noted, and shot it. The same day they shot a wolf, and from the two kills named Cat Creek and Wolf Creek.

Ahead of them were mountains and rivers and lakes to name—the Bailey Range for their sponsor, Press Valley for his paper, Mount Meany for his city editor; Mount Ferry for the governor; Mount Seattle, as the biggest mountain they could see; for themselves, the Hayes River, Crumback Creek, Mount Christie, and Mount Barnes; for friends, sweethearts, and wives, the Goldie and the Lillian, and Lakes Mary and Margaret. Their troubles with the settlers balked them on one point. Right now they thought they were already skirting under a spur of Mount Olympus. Strangely enough they were never even to detect Olympus on their whole trip. A decade later the mountain they mistook for Olympus was named Mount Carrie by Mr. Rixon for his wife. The settlers could have set them right.

The men were now entering a paradise that made them lyrical, a valley "peaceful, happy, covered with mammoth trees, through whose interlacing boughs gleamed the golden sunshine lighting up the long trailing vines, the creepers and mosses of many hues. The enclosing mountains rising steeply on every side were alive with game animals, tame in the happy ignorance of the gun. The river, here broad and rippling, teemed with salmon, and its deeper pools were filled with

trout." Pleased to hear what they thought was a geyser, they named this Geyser Valley. They could not quite locate the geyser, but they carefully charted its intervals. The sound, lasting eight seconds and coming about every four minutes, was like a ratchet on a cogwheel, accelerating to a blur, then abruptly ceasing. Strangers in Geyser Valley thirty years later heard motorboats instead of geysers, but in 1890 no one heard motorboats. The delusive sound is the drumming of the ruffed grouse.

They did not catch that deception, but the Olympic myth soon started to dissolve for them. Moving up the river, they did not realize that they were leaving the winter range of game. When they did get an elk now, they could boil the meat for hours without raising an atom of fat. Their starving dogs stole their last precious bacon. Their remaining mule, with no forage but stiff evergreen salal leaves and prickly, holly-like Oregon grape leaves, lay down exhausted and famished one morning and refused to go farther. They abandoned her, to live like the elk if she could. They had used their last coffee in Geyser Valley; other supplies were running low. They used pieces of blanket for socks under their worn shoes. The country, instead of opening out into a central valley, grew more rugged and wild, the snow deeper. Quietly, the five men had given up their dream of brilliant discoveries. They could have only the glory of being the first to cross and report on the interior of the Olympics. Even this they feared might be filched from them by "notoriety-seeking strangers," swiftly overhauling them, along their clear, slowly-made trail, and sweeping through to claim the victory of the first crossing.

There was just one thing the men wanted now—to get out of this country, hit the Quinault, which must lie to the southwest, and head for home. They had reached the Goldie, a tributary of the Elwha, flowing down from the southwest, at the head of which must lie the Quinault Divide. Christie and Barnes reconnoitered. It was as rough a part of the Olympics as they could have picked; the heavy spring snow was ava-lanching above timber line, and the two lonely men moved cautiously. Snow cornices hung out thirty to forty feet, "like a great wave curling over." When they gained a vantage point they saw ahead of them a sea of mountains "in no order." They were almost stunned. They were the first to learn that the Olympics are not a range, not a barricade around the margin of the peninsula, but clumps of mountains sticking

up like the fingers of one's hands, cut by canyons four or five thousand feet deep, slanting down to unseen rivers in their depths.

It was a hard lesson; the party had supplies for only twelve days, but the two men did pick out what seemed to be the watershed of the Quinault, "across a deep precipitous gorge rising to snowcapped, vapor-wreathed summits." They returned to camp; the party made up back packs, abandoned the last of their equipment, and set out cheerfully on snowshoes, "homeward bound!" At night they slept on ledges to be out of the snow. One night on a ledge so narrow they feared to fall off if they slept, Simms and Hayes sat up the whole night. After one comfortable camp on a bare, sunny ledge, fifteen by twenty feet, young Hayes in the morning inquired if they would mind if he just packed that ledge along.

When the men got to the top and realized that they were simply cutting a base line across a vast curve of the Elwha, after the first shock they took it in good humor. After all, it was the kind of mistake explorers cannot avoid. Their only food now was flour soup, one and a half quarts of flour to three gallons of water. Coming back empty-handed one noon from hunting, Hayes said he had at least seen rabbit tracks in the snow. "I'm going to polish up a club," he announced, "and see if I can't get some of those tracks for supper."

Early in May the five ragged, half-sick men and three starving dogs climbed in snow from the Elwha Valley into the Low Divide. Between the lakes they named Mary and Margaret, they plodded over a low hump that they knew was the divide. "Water flowing south is going to taste pretty good," said Hayes. But a more cheerful event was due. At the far end of the pass the dogs started a bear, fresh from hibernation. The men shot it and Christie decided right then to follow the Indian custom and camp by the kill. In fifteen minutes they had a fire and were frying slabs of bear fat. The men were inconceivably hungry for fat. They had lived on plain flour for a week and little besides flour for several weeks. Before that they had had plenty of meat but no fat for months, except a little dole from their precious bacon. This bear fat was pure white and soft as butter; seasoned with salt and its own peculiar favor, it tasted better than butter. The rest of the afternoon and evening the *Press* party sat by the fire keeping the frying pans going and drinking bear grease as fast as they could fry it out.

That bear changed their plans to the extent that, instead of starting

at once down the Quinault, they could do a little more exploring. The next day, through steep wet snow, Barnes started up Mount Seattle, to camp that night on a south ledge two thousand feet above the Low Divide. In the morning he climbed to the saddle, wondering if some unexpected range just beyond would cut off his view. A final step brought his head above the wedgelike saddle, "and the curtain rose from before the unknown region." Barnes accurately mapped and sketched, sleeping another night on his ledge. When he got back to camp hungry and "fresh out of" bear meat, he found the bear cleaned up, a second one killed, and the whole party beginning to look fat and sleek. Before he could tell a word of his trip, however, the dogs started another bear. Thanks to the two months' delay caused by building "Gertie," the boat, the famished *Press* party had arrived none too early at the Low Divide to connect with the dehibernating bears.

The surprising Olympics had one more surprise for them—the deep forests and, buried under them, the cleft canyons along the Quinault, down and up which they climbed with ropes. "Like exploring in a dark rat hole," said the homesick men gloomily. The Olympics had no fierce tribes, vast valleys to settle, freaks of nature to draw tourists. There were only rugged white mountains and deep forests down in whose silent, rotting undergrowth a few men seemed negligible. Sick to get out to where the busy "cooked-up doings" of human beings filled the days with the feeling that a person mattered, that there was something of importance leading to constant little climaxes, the men struggled down the Quinault and out to the world of newspapers and homes, with a story that they told honestly and temperately. They had done the best they could as explorers, even if they, as others in history, had not found what they expected.

THE LOST COPPER BOX

The ripples seethed up fast around the Olympics that summer of 1890: squatters, homesteaders, timber claimers, and prospectors were like the roily fans of water searching the beach ahead of the tide. Before the *Press* party story could be printed, another expedition, under Lieutenant Joseph P. O'Neil, was off to try to cross the Olympics from east to west. He received the *Press* party report, scornful of the time it had taken those men to get through the country. He had ten soldiers, packers,

mules, and the whole summer to travel in. His subordinates built a trail a mule could struggle over, up the Skokomish from Lake Cushman, across the divide, and down into the Quinault. His pack train rolled constantly, bringing new shoes and fresh supplies. The Board of Trade in Hoquiam volunteered to build the last thirty miles of trail for him. Still progress did not go so swiftly.

Lieutenant O'Neil's method was to send scouting parties up the rugged, nearly impassable creeks, hunting for a way ahead and mapping the country. Some of the men all but lost their lives from falls or famine, bucking the Olympic forest head-on, climbing up and down cliffs and snow, walking over the tops of eight-foot trees along cleavers, where the woodsmen, Indians, miners, and settlers over there on the east side —who slip negligibly in and out of the party's report—would probably have found pretty good going, without realizing how much skill and experience they were using, piecing together the ends of random elk trails.

Three outsiders from the Oregon Alpine Club who joined this autocratic expedition would have fitted better with the democratic, free and equal *Press* party. Each had a plan that was to be partly thwarted. Professor Henderson, the botanist, smiled afterward at his own glowing dream of new species, even new genera, as he said, "peeping out from the crevices of every succeeding mass of rocks, smiling down upon me from every cliff, or being crushed by every other step upon those green, sunny banks, which always border the perpetual snows." But after little over a month with the mule-dragging party, and still not far enough in from the coast, once crushed by Pleistocene glaciers, to find the few endemic species of these mountains, Henderson broke civilly with the lieutenant and came out, five hundred specimens on the back of his army mule; of these only one was an endemic: the low white alpine Spiraea that bears his name. And within a few weeks another exploring botanist was moving up that new trail, collecting, an energetic young fellow from Seattle, Charlie "Vancouver" Piper, who was to be the grandfather of botany in the Northwest.

Bretherton, the naturalist, and Linsley, the mineralogist, from the Oregon Alpine Club, fared worse than Henderson, for to their half-victory was added the scorn of the lieutenant. Their dream was the pioneer ascent of Mount Olympus, and they were packing a copper box

from the Alpine Club to mark the summit. It was the middle of September, late in the season for the Olympics, when Lieutenant O'Neil, now on the Quinault side, detailed a back-packing party with twenty-five days' provisions, led by Linsley, along with Bretherton and five soldiers, to find and climb Mount Olympus, blandly adding that they were also to explore the courses of the Hoh and the branches of the Quillayute, and meet him in Port Townsend, where the expedition had started.

Twelve days later the men were down at the mouth of the Queets River, instead of the Hoh or the Quillayute, their shoes worn out, their rations low; and one soldier, lost, had struggled out alone. It seems certain that they had climbed Olympus, but probably from the south, a part rarely if ever traversed. The copper box, containing the register with their names and a few trinkets, probably still rests on one of the jagged rocks on the south side of Mount Olympus, yet to be discovered by some exploring mountaineer. Lieutenant O'Neil did not, he wrote stiffly, "feel satisfied by the work done by them." He did not feel satisfied with the Olympics either. They were, he said, "absolutely unfit for any use except, perhaps, a national park, where elk and deer could be saved."

PIONEERS OF SEVERAL KINDS

The pivot of pioneering was swinging now from physical hardship on the frontier to daring on the social frontier. The last of the pioneers of nature followed the *Press* party accounts in the paper to the last frontier on the continent. Some of those pioneers are still living—barrel-chested Pa Huelsdonk, the "iron man of the Hoh," for instance, a man having a natural genius for pioneering, as another man might have for music. The odder, lonelier men who preceded them are gone—old bachelors in the forest. There was the man who toted his violin for company when he walked the trail from Indian Valley to Port Angeles for groceries once a month, sitting down against some fir trunk now and then to fill the lonely forest and the ears of surprised deer and cougar with reels and melodies that meant a whole world of people and ideas to him, and that vanished without an effect among the vast branches. There was the old fellow who wanted to raise chickens and pigeons, and foreseeing their tender interest to skunks, hawks, and wildcats, made two holes in his cabin, one high, one low, for them to enter. The

chickens roosted nightly on the foot of his bed and when they fell asleep, he turned them around to face the head of the bed. Lonely queer traceless little lives, but those of men who enjoyed the forest.

Back in Washington, D. C., pioneers of another kind were interested in the forests. For three hundred years, on an apparently inexhaustible continent, men had been killing everything that moved or lived its own life. Either it competed for their food or it was their food. That attitude was part of the old "pioneer spirit." The new pioneers were beginning to fight to hold onto the remnants of what had been hated and wasted. The continent had been choked with wilderness. Now wilderness was getting scarce. And wilderness is very valuable. Its chief values are intangible but as specifically useful as those of "trace" minerals in food. Under Gifford Pinchot a national forest commission was set up during Cleveland's administration. And presently the new pioneers came to the Olympics.

Meanwhile the *Press* party's "rat hole" was looking like the robbers' cave of Sesame to lumbermen who had gutted the forests of the East. And when Henry Gannett, Chief Geographer, showed up in the Olympics from Washington, D. C., to organize a survey for a national forest here, the Senator from Washington State growled in Congress with anxious anger, "Why in God's name do these scientific gentlemen from Harvard have to come out here and butt in on our affairs!"

Henry Gannett one clear spring day found two lean daredevil surveyors, Dodwell and Rixon, and with two aides for them, climbed Mount Ellinor, on the east side of the Olympics. In the vast silence up there the five men looked westward over a sea of white peaks, azure distances, blue-hazed canyons cloaked with shining virgin forest. Gannett turned to the men: "There's your work, boys. Go to it."

They went to it, working sixteen to eighteen hours a day, packing their aneroid barometer and dry-plate camera to peaks, triangulating, running compass lines out, covering six to eight miles a day, noting the kinds of timber, and estimating its gigantic stands. Ali Baba had got into the robbers' cave. In three years, they had made the original survey of twenty-four hundred of the ruggedest square miles in the country. And Jack McGlone, of their party, in 1899 had made the first recorded ascent of Mount Olympus.

It was as funny and characteristic in its way as the sourdoughs' pioneer

climb of Mount McKinley over a decade later. McGlone, a little short Irishman, was working under Rixon, and when not surveying, just looking the country over, they lapped up twenty to thirty miles a day. Camped one September day at the head of Press Valley, now known as the Elwha Basin, they had climbed up through the Dodwell-Rixon Pass into the Queets Basin, then to the Quinault Divide, a very fair day's work for rugged men, and when they had circled back to the rocks above Humes Glacier, on the flank of Mount Olympus, Rixon called it a day, and prepared to start the two-hour hike back to camp.

Mount Olympus, rising radiant and massive at their side, had preyed all day on McGlone's mind. McGlone had an appetite for mountains, and under many a wild peak he had observed with delusive casualness, "I'll just be going up there to have a look around." Before Rixon could turn around now, McGlone had squirreled down the rocks and out onto the glacier.

"Come back and I'll go with you tomorrow," Rixon yelled.

"Too much trouble now, to get up those rocks again," McGlone yelled back.

The Irishman did not know yet what trouble was. There is one peculiarity about this eastern approach to Mount Olympus that makes it a major climb though a little under eight thousand feet. There is a steep, icy drop of seven hundred feet to the Hoh Glacier, before the real ascent can start. Rixon, watching the little dark figure moving up the Humes Glacier toward the evening sunlight, hunting a way around crevasses, saw him vanish from sight, just at the moment McGlone must have been discovering that peculiarity. Doggedly he went on.

The sun had gone down into the Pacific when the little Irishman took his "look around," alone on the virgin East Peak of Mount Olympus. The silent snow fields below him were satiny in the evening light; white peaks rose in every direction; and, dim on the blue eastern horizon, floated the pure volcanic cones of the Cascades. McGlone tucked a piece of newspaper, brought for a more useful purpose, into a tin can, built a little cairn over it, then headed for the Elwha Basin and blankets at two in the morning.

This first ascent was unknown to northwest mountaineers, and for eight years that scrap of newspaper rested undisturbed.

Getting sixty-five members of the newly formed Mountaineers Club

of Seattle sixty miles into the wilderness, to Mount Olympus, in 1907, was first of all a job of trail building. Port Angeles came to the rescue. Diverse groups had rounded the long yellow spit that cleaves its deep still harbor from the blue strait, to float toward the wall of snow-topped mountains. Here, in 1865, had landed fifty war canoes with Neah Bay Indians in black bearskin robes, bearing red and blue blankets as gifts, for the wedding of a chieftain's son—men with their own ways of dealing with the dead and the living. Here, twenty years later, had landed a socialist colony, full of plans and traditions from Robert Owen and the Old World. There was an impetuous unanimity about the people of this town. When they jumped the military reservation, they jumped it "legally," that is, unanimously, in a Squatters' Association! When they ordered a drill, to tap what they hoped was coal, the whistle of the overdue steamer bearing the drill booped out as a politician was speaking in the opera house, and the whole crowd jumped for the door, leaving the embarrassed orator to wonder what in God's name he had said.

With the same unanimous financial zeal Port Angeles undertook to open a trail to the Elwha Basin for the Mountaineers. There was national publicity about this expedition for a proposed "first ascent" of Mount Olympus. Professors were going—to find new plants, new ore deposits. Who knew what might come of it? Impassively the Olympics waited. No one knew yet quite what to do with them; but there must be something. Port Angeles had the windfalls cut out of the old Press Party Trail up the Elwha and a new trail carried into the Elwha Basin.

The Mountaineers also had much to do. They bought pack horses, and for packers hired the Humes brothers, who had built a log cabin in Geyser Valley, the *Press* party's little paradise. By the first of June, pack trains were rolling up the Elwha, through the dim, level forest, with supplies to be cached in the basin: food that the wilderness bear would be too shy to molest; the 1907 version of mountaineering equipment— heavy blankets instead of sleeping bags, heavy canvas tents instead of hikers' tents. By July the personal dunnage of the climbers was going in.

Then, just a week before the Mountaineers were to start, one of those things happened to which there are always two sides; the ground was undercut from the Mountaineers' labors for a first ascent. Three men —Professor Herschel Parker, Belmore Browne, and a Mr. Clark—engaged one of the Humes brothers, a man innocent about "first ascents"

but familiar with the new trail, to guide them to the basin. The year before, Parker and Browne had made an attempt on Mount McKinley, led by Dr. Frederick Cook, who three months afterward, with only one attendant, returned to that mountain for the partial climb he claimed was complete, a deception that may have encouraged him later to claim discovery of the North Pole. With Will Humes as guide, Parker, Browne, and Clark ascended the Middle Peak of Mount Olympus, swept out again and, with what seemed to the Mountaineers indecent celerity, had an account in the papers of the "first ascent of Mount Olympus."

On August 12, 1907, L. A. Nelson, the leader of the Mountaineers, and two other men climbed the East or Sphinx Peak of Mount Olympus —in "four hours and five minutes from Hospital Camp"—to discover in a little cairn a can with the lone Irishman's unsigned scrap of newspaper dated 1899. "We salute the brave pioneers who climbed in 1899," wrote the Mountaineers on their record, not knowing who had made this original climb.

The next day L.A. led nine men and one woman, Anna Hubert, to Middle Peak, where they examined the record of the Parker-Browne climb. It ended with a doubtful admission that possibly a rock they saw to the west was higher. From the half mile of snow over the top of Olympus rise a number of rock peaks. Fog closed in as the party got down to the snow field; they scouted the confusing summit, the taste of cloud in their mouths. Three of them were up the black rock they took to be West Peak when the fog shifted to blue and there, a quarter of a mile away, rose the true summit of Mount Olympus. Within half an hour the Mountaineers were joyfully building a cairn on the hitherto unclimbed peak. They had won the game of first ascents after all.

A HIGH-RIGGER HITS OLYMPUS

One more first was left on Mount Olympus—the first ascent of all three main peaks in one day. Officially, this record went, in 1933, to Dixon, a postman on vacation, passing his time by hiking. *De facto*, it probably belongs to the maddest man to climb a mountain, Tom Newton, a high-rigger who became a legend even before his death. In 1920 he led three slick-shod, trembling youths over Olympus on a scouting trip for the Klahhanes, the Port Angeles mountaineering club. To Tom Newton everything on God's earth was expendable. It wasn't so much that he

was reckless as that he knew his own prodigious strength. He could jump twenty feet downward and light on a rock like a cat, a leap it would break your jaw to follow. Lithe, with flawless balance and rhythm, when he topped a hundred-and-fifty-foot fir for a spar tree and the severed fifty feet dropped off, leaving the tree lashing in rebound, Tom would leap to the cut end and ride it, standing free, swaying against the sky. On Sunday afternoon, when other loggers played black-jack for pastime, Tom, for his recreation, would springboard fifty feet up a fir tree.

When he tackled Olympus, he had something worth his skill at last. He climbed it like a high-rigger. The men back-packed in from the Hoh River side and made high camp in Glacier Meadow alongside the Blue Glacier. In the morning Tom led up the Snow Dome. Under a cornice he hooked his fingers over and raised his body. "Sure! This is a good place," he called; and reaching over, gave each young fellow a heave up, to a steep snow slope with no trace of purchase; then an upward boost.

They climbed West Peak, and Tom stood on his head on the cairn. It made the men dizzy. He romped across the snow field to Middle Peak and on to East Peak, his party panting after. What was down he took at a leap; what was up, at a stride. From East Peak, without an instant's pause Tom plunged over the side, so steep you couldn't see below the bulge, down toward the Hoh Glacier. His shout drifted back, "Come on!" So he was still alive. One by one the men sat down and whizzed out of sight. The one left alone on the peak was Herb Crisler, a boy from Georgia, who had never been in the mountains before. "You can't stay here and freeze to death," he thought. "This is it," and over he went. Tom's shout roared through the glittering rush, "Hey you, stand up there and jump that crevasse!" He made the six or eight foot leap and landed trembling, vowing in his heart if he ever got off this mountain alive, like an Indian he was through with white peaks. The thunderbird could have them. It was not mountaineering of course, but only Tom Newton's style, a high-rigger's bold delight in risk that skill could balance toward life.

Tom took the men down Hoh Glacier on a run, jumping crevasses and shouting as he went. It was a nightmare to follow him. They siwashed it on the rocks beside the glacier that night, by a little fire of gray sticks,

continually trading places by the fire during the night to keep warm. The next day the men toiled around to Glacier Meadow and their cache, but Tom included a side trip. He bounded up to Blizzard Pass and down to the Queets Basin to tell the Klahhanes not to bother, that he had climbed the mountain and there was but little left up there worth coming for.

THE OLYMPICS

Mount Olympus is the focus of the Olympics. In its glaciers, or headed toward them, the brief mighty rivers of the central Olympics hook their tendrils—the Hoh, the Elwha, the Queets, the Quinault—curving through valleys whose sides lift from two thousand feet at river bottom to a height of five or six thousand feet, within a mile and a half as the eagle flies. Sometimes these valley sides run in long ridges, rising here and there to monadnock peaks, as along the Bailey Range. Sometimes they are deeply cut by tributary streams into wild, low peaks to whose summits no trail leads.

From the top of Mount Olympus one overlooks a sea of peaks, falling away to the west in blue ridges, beyond which, rather high on the horizon, lies the band of odd blue that is the Pacific Ocean. To the south, also, the heights fall away in foothills, to a deltalike plain along the Pacific; but to the north and east rise white-topped mountains, not much lower than Olympus itself. Beyond them, the silver streak of the strait of Juan de Fuca is patched with islands. Through a gap to the east, one sees a bit of Puget Sound, and ranged along the eastern horizon beyond it, from north to south for two hundred miles, the scattered white volcanic cones of the Cascades. From this peak no towns or habitations are seen. It is a majestic alpine view of a vast wilderness.

Most of the main peaks of the Olympics are grouped either in a long, narrow reversed S, centered at the east side of the massif of Mount Olympus, or in a rough line along the east side of the peninsula. Near Mount Olympus, around the south hook of the reverse S, rise several of the usual main climbs—Mount Meany, Mount Seattle, Mount Christie, and lesser peaks. Over on the Puget Sound side rises a row of monadnocks including Mount Constance, Mount Ellinor, and the Brothers, the peaks whose outlines are familiar to the cities across the Sound, carving their western horizon. From between the bases of these peaks

a row of streams races down to Hood Canal, a long arm of Puget Sound —streams with walloping Indian names: Skokomish, Lilliwaup, Hamma Hamma, Duckabush, Dosewallips, Quilcene.

The rivers of the Olympics have to be short because the mountains they come from are close to the sea. They have to be mighty and many because the rainfall and snowfall on those mountains are heavy and when the Chinook comes—the snow-melting southwest wind—a lot of water has to get out of the mountains in a hurry. Overnight the Quillayute, a union of the Soleduck and Bogachiel, may rise twenty feet. There are no floods, partly because the rivers are rapid. They start off the mountains with a rush, making most of their drop in the first quick miles, then speeding through deep-carved canyons down to the ocean. Some are glacier-fed, some clear. A glacial stream is not a "water show" for campers, because of its gray detritus. It rises during sunny days, when the snow is melting at its source, and subsides during the night.

Although the annual precipitation is enormous, it is a case where "statistics and practicability are not consistent," according to the commander at the Quillayute navy airfield. Although five inches of rain may fall in twenty-four hours, the number of flying days is so high that during the war they were able to keep well up with their training schedule.

Old-timers remember when the Olympic glaciers descended low, some of them with overhanging snouts, from which blocks broke off in thunder; but they are rapidly receding. Some glacial basins are completely exposed. But snow fields still abound, on the north sides of ridges or mountains, which on their sunward side fall away in dry slopes or crags.

There is little parklike or meadow country along the tops of ridges, but recessed around the mountainsides are scores of alpine basins where elk range in the summer, if disturbed moving out of one basin over a ridge into another. They can keep up this basin changing for days.

As you look at the mountainsides from a distance, you see two kinds of marks it is well to avoid. One is the yellowish inverted V of earthen slides. These slides, as bare and sometimes as hard as ice, should be headed or else treated as hard-packed snow slopes. When deer hunters roamed the Olympics before the National Park Service took over, they wore down their gun stocks using them as ice axes, to jab steps across the slides. The other marking is areas of light green among the darker timber.

These are second growth, where burns or blowdowns have destroyed the original forest. Second-growth Douglas fir stands so dense and branchy for its first twenty years—from two thousand to twenty thousand trees to an acre—that it all but gives one claustrophobia to force one's way through. After that age it thins itself rapidly, down to the open forest a century or more old, where brown columns rise branch-free, only twenty to a hundred trees to the acre.

The dense cloak of evergreen forest over the rugged mountainsides deceives one into thinking the slope is smooth, though steep. But this forest often masks crags and precipitous slopes. You may start down off a ridge expecting an easy descent through open forest, only to run into slides or cliffs that force you to climb back and hunt some other way down.

SPRING IN THE HIGH COUNTRY

The changes of the seasons in these wilderness mountains are marked as much by changes among the animals as among the plants. Spring, up in the arctic-alpine zone, above five thousand feet, is urgent. Both plants and animals are on their marks, set to go the minute the snow releases them. In the false spring frequent in February, when high south slopes turn bare, the buttercups launch chunky buds, to bloom and bleach to white enamel under March snows, then bud again. And suddenly the small Olympic chipmunks are out from hibernation, racing, lustrous scraps of agility, after the months of impersonal whiteness.

The birds of the high country begin to return. Cawing inquisitively, Clark's nutcracker flashes like a small white airplane directly over your head. With shy boldness the soft-voiced camp robber, or Oregon jay, glides in on level wings for plunder. Through the alpine scrub move the gray-crowned rose finches. The heads of pine grosbeaks show rosy against the deep blue sky. Mated pairs of gentle horned larks run as if hand in hand to hollow their nests in the lee of a tuft of grass and sing their thin sweet song on some low rock till nine o'clock, under the vast pallor of the evening sky.

On the south talus slopes, near rocks, blooms the rosy douglasia, sometimes mistaken for heather. Delicate white blossoms of miner's lettuce follow the melting snow patches in concentric circles, till at last a drift of flowers substitutes for snow at the very center. The high meadows are

noisy with transient brooks, scoring bright dark streaks among fields of yellow glacier lilies, flooding the marmot dodge holes.

About the last of April or the first week in May, after the first warm night, up on the snow of the ridges one sees black spots, the mouths of tunnels, and, sitting beside them, dopey brown figures that squat or move gently around. The marmots have dehibernated.

Since the whistling marmots are animals you are likely to see and sure to hear, they deserve a closer look. Cousins of the woodchuck and squirrel, they are rodents larger than big tomcats, with the protective mingled colors of many mountain animals—gray, cream, light brown. Marmots look orange-tawny or a dim dried-grass color according to their surroundings. Since their hind quarters are definitely lighter than the front part of their bodies, they sometimes have a divided look. They can growl like puppies, mew and fuss like cats, but the sound that gives them their name, whistlers, is their warning signal, a clear bright peep, like a piercing whistle. That whistle has sounded human to many a person, from Dodwell and Rixon to the Mountaineers, who, waiting once in the fog on a snow field for signals from their scouts, began blindly to try to obey the marmot calls. I saw a grouse warned by a marmot just as a hawk was diving for him. Because the wild creatures take warning from the marmot's whistle, deer hunters systematically tried to exterminate them, killing hundreds before the National Park Service took over.

The marmot community goes into hibernation when the grass is sere and the high ridges waterless about the first of October. For seven months these little mountaineers sleep under the fields of smoking snow, but during the five months that they are out of hibernation they are the most romping and affectionate of animals. We have stood shaking with silent laughter watching two young ones boxing on the rounded lip of their burrow. Standing on their hind legs like bears, they waddled toward each other to clinch, then tumble, and roll over and over down the side of the hummock, which was already worn bare. That rolling appeared to be the cream of the romp. When they raced back up, one on each side, to begin all over, an old marmot, their mother perhaps, who had lain above, watching them, jumped down to stand and box too, then topple over for that furry roll.

One of the first things the marmot attends to on coming out of hibernation is establishing his grazing rights. But after a few squabbles

on that score, he lives peaceably, digging succulent roots and wild onions, nibbling the miner's lettuce and douglasia blossoms, and gathering hay to line his burrow, which is often shared with another marmot.

CHALLENGING SEASON

The glory of autumn in the high country is the huckleberry, glowing in great ruddy patches above timber on the mountainsides. The plants are only a few inches to a foot high, and the leaves are dull individually, but when back-lighted, their color glows flame-red or a warm blue-red so ardent that it is positively exciting. Now is harvesttime for the black bear. Here and there on the mountainsides you can spot the bear gathering huckleberries, storing up energy for the months of hibernation ahead. And now, too, the elk congregate in the high country.

The elk, or wapiti, the largest and stateliest deer in the world, are by all odds the handsomest animals you stand a chance of seeing in these mountains. They have three distinct color zones—chocolate-brown head and neck, cream-colored rump pad, like a fluffy apron, and on the body a neutral, variable-looking gray-cream. The bull is a lighter cream and strikingly handsome with his great crown of five-foot antlers, rough, cylindrical, brown, tapering to whitish points. The number of points shows the age of the bull up to five years, after which he carries about six points to the antler.

One would suppose with an impediment like those antlers a bull would get hung up in the tangle of second growth, where a man with even a small pack board can hardly make his way. But if you jump a bull in there he will go like the wind, his nose away up, his antlers laid back so they come down along his sides, plowing through the trees like the bow of a boat.

He sheds his antlers about April, a month or two later than do deer. In May sensitive blue-black balls appear, elongating into antlers under the fur. In June and July in remote mountain meadows you may come upon groups of young bachelors flocking by themselves, sometimes nearly a dozen in one group. When they are between you and the sun, their antlers, in the velvet, look as if furred with fire.

The hermit bull, whom old-timers believe to be a deposed king, likes to lie alone in the low-fanned fir on some rocky cleaver between the

Mount Olympus viewed from the Bogachiel-Hoh Divide. Near the summit is the White Glacier.

Storm King Mountain and Lake Crescent.

Mountains standing knee-deep in the Pacific near the Oregon coast.

northern and the southern winds, as if the commanding view consoled him.

The calves are born about the first of June, dappled like fawns. The place to find the herds of cows and calves in early summer is near water, on the gravel bars along the rivers, or by subalpine lakes. Your first sign of their presence may be the squealing of the calves, like a whole flock of shore birds. The elk have a convenient habit of parking all their calves together in the brush, with a couple of cows guarding them, while the rest of the cows take their afternoon siesta some distance away. If startled, the band of cows and the band of calves with their guardians run in the same direction but separately, a minute's interval between them. Very young, weak calves stay behind, in the lee of a log, but they are returned for later.

September and October are the climax of the year for the elk, when food is plentiful and they are congregating well up the rivers or in the high basins, far from their most dangerous enemy, man. September is the beginning of the challenging season, when the bulls join the herds, one as the king of the harem, while the young bachelors hang about, as close as they dare. At frequent intervals the old king runs them off to what he considers a safe distance. When a cow elk—less preoccupied than the bull—barks danger, and the herd clusters, sometimes so closely that you can hear the rustle and chafe of their sides, the old bull stands at the edge of his group ready for defense, trying to spot the danger. Then the young bulls slip closer, unchallenged.

The challenge or bugle is a keen whistle above a deep vibrating boom. The whistle carries far; you do not hear the powerful vibration unless you are fairly close. At night if you are camped in a remote basin, every time you waken in the starlight you may hear that thrillingly strange vibrato under the bugle, only a hundred yards away, where some bull stands in the darkness, answered at intervals by ringing whistles far and near, up on the mountainside. By day, owing to the contour of the basins, you can see as in an amphitheater, all the participants—bulls, alone, in pairs, or with herds, near the sparse alpine trees or groves, high and low on the mountainside. You often come upon an alpine fir stripped white, or a low cedar grove with the bark threshed to ribbons and the ground hooked and pawed where a bull has vented his fierceness as he answered distant challenges.

But this is merely bluff; for the first few weeks the bulls do not contact each other. Then in October, which is the rutting season, the kings have to fight to retain possession of their harems, not just once but perhaps several times. The fights may be to the death of both bulls if their antlers become locked. Contouring along the Bailey Range last October, we encountered a solitary bull with both antlers snapped off. On a high barren flat there was a glazed bluish-red pool of blood near trampled earth. A cow is sometimes gored to death, apparently by accident, during a fight. Sometimes neither bull is injured, and the defeated one moves off slowly, turning now and then to look back at the victorious king, who stands watching him, near the prize, the closely rounded-up herd.

Through this process of fights the weaklings are eliminated and the strength of the herd perpetuated. The reverse effect is achieved during the open seasons on elk, when the finest bulls are sought, and many wounded escape to die slowly. Whether the elk will survive or not is problematic. In 1937, when the herd was estimated at 6,000, special elk-hunting licenses—at five dollars each—were issued to 5,280 people; 811 elk were checked out legally, and two paid hunters were out for weeks afterward, seeking for wounded elk, to put them out of their misery.

The sawmills on the peninsula are overbuilt, and, according to the supervisor of the Olympic National Forest, the timber is being overcut by almost 400 per cent. So the mill operators exert continuous pressure to get possession of the stands of timber in the Olympic National Park, which are the last protected winter feeding grounds of the elk.

Twenty years ago there were many large bands, from a hundred up. When Billy Everett first looked down on the Cream Lake Basin, beyond the Bailey Range, he said, "The grass was knee deep and the meadow full of elk, some lying in the shallow margin of the lake. Elk were coming out of all the openings in the trees. There must have been a herd of three hundred. I thought it was the prettiest place I had ever seen."

Wild creatures complement their habitat. They belong in it. Without them, any wild place, no matter how beautiful, is a little flat and dull.

It is only poverty of experience that keeps people from knowing this fact. To a woodsman, wilderness gives an experience that is a complex of all the senses, and full of detail. One has to graduate from the attempt

to handle it merely as "scenery"—seeing it only vaguely, as composition and color. It is a total, of many strands, much more stimulating and exciting than "landscape."

You do not need to fear any of the wild creatures. There are not even any poisonous snakes in the Olympics. Not even the cougar, the big cat of the mountains, nine feet from tip to tip, will molest you, because he has plenty of game. This magnificent native predator is entitled to his living. It adds to the interest of the country to know that these big cats are prowling through it. It is the chance of a lifetime to see one, though; many an old woodsman has never seen a cougar unless it was treed by dogs. There is one cougar sign, however, that you may discover along the trail, and that is little heaps of earth pawed up at intervals of about a hundred yards, perhaps from pure playfulness and high spirits.

The climbers' group of the Mountaineers projects a technical guide to the Olympics. Until it is available, detailed information about climb routes can best be obtained through the club headquarters, 709 Pike Street, Seattle 1, Washington.

A WILDERNESS TRIP

The Olympics are not the wilderness, now, that they were fifty years ago. There are still white patches on the latest map, where contour lines have not been established. But the forests have been logged up to the margin of the national park, and logging in the rain forests leaves desolation. Still the cap of enchantment settles over your head when you start up the trail, and the silence closes in like velvet. Still the Olympics are satisfying to those who love wildness, not pretended, twenty yards off from a road, but real. Some of the trails and basins are regular highways for foot travelers now. But wilderness travel is possible in these wilderness mountains if you gain your elevation by trail and then take off across the mountains in the most typical and fascinating of Olympics trips—beyond the trails, with compass and map.

Of course there are many people who should not attempt it. You have to be able and reasonably skilled. Those who are, won't thank me to point out in detail the ways to go. Of course, too, you cannot rampage through with reckless wastage of an infinite supply, as in the old days when everything from forests to clams looked "inexhaustible." No longer

in the rain forests will you gather moss beds, rolling up the blanket of moss off the top of a log, peeling it down from a tree trunk, picking up a pillow of it from a stump, to make a dry haycock of moss for your bed in five minutes. It takes too long for that moss to reconstitute itself. You won't whack half a dozen low and ancient alpine firs to make a shelter. The white man must go light-foot now through the wilderness, taking with him what he needs and leaving no mark on the country. For thousands of people love wilderness. It is irreplaceable and scarce in these United States.

Again, those who can travel the wilderness way will need no advice on how. Back-packing skillfully is an art. If you don't know it, you need to learn it from a master. In general, there are two styles of back-packing: that of the man who won't do without anything, who takes it all along, saying he'd rather pack it than go without. He can pack it all right, but he can go only half as far, camping twice as often as the other style of back-packer, who keeps his weight down. Your pack-board is almost as important as your shoes. Above all, it must not drag the weight away from your back. A man can travel happily with a forty-pound pack, and up to twice that with diminishing joy. A woman travels easily with eighteen pounds. Twenty-five pounds is a good limit, but you can't keep some women from packing their forty.

The first day out is likely to be a long hard drag. You are gaining elevation. It is possible to get horses, however, to many of the good jumping-off places. Your back-pack can even be taken up and cached a day ahead of you. From there on you are on your own, and it's not going to be easy, but there's nothing else like it in the world.

Because it took us through the very heart of the Olympic wilderness, one autumn trip of ours might well close this chapter.

We left the trail by Oyster Lake, a shallow pool on the top of Appleton Ridge, five miles up from the Olympic Hot Springs. Scarlet huckleberry coated the steep side of the ridge ahead of us. Erratic game trails a few inches wide made imperceptible terraces around it, and along them, heavy with our full packs, we picked our way to a pass above Cat Creek, and contoured in to Cat Creek Basin.

It was a cloudy, dull evening but the basin glowed with color—the rose color of the huckleberry. In low green thickets as we entered, we had jumped groups of elk. Here in the basin itself two bulls were

challenging. One big pale cream-colored bull lay couched with majestic command on a shelf by a dark pointed clump of alpine fir, his herd grazing the fuchsia-colored slopes above him. At intervals he answered a vibrating bugle coming from near us, down on the floor of the basin. As we stood silently looking, the challenger, a brown-headed bull, stepped out of a clump of trees. He bugled and moved toward us, his antlers high. He stopped to challenge, first the king up on the hillside, then us, who were standing very still. He pawed, ripped up the ground with his antlers; his sides heaved with the quick fierce bark. Then he slowly advanced. I felt like running, but he got suspicious and turned, moving off slowly and proudly.

We struck Wildcat Ridge the next morning, a jagged cleaver with alpine fir fans flung over it. I stepped on their springy limbs and clung to the boughs, feeling blindly, over sheer space, for a place to get my foot down to the sharp rock. For an hour it was tough going with our heavy packs.

The worst place came near the other end of the cleaver, where Herb grabbed a long fir limb and swung across a steep, bare slope like a pendulum. He came back for my pack, and I launched out timidly, got astride of my alpenstock half way over, but clawed up onto the rock on the other side, trembling. The cleaver flattened to hold a muddy pool, a game wallow, by the bear and deer tracks, and on the grass near, under the low firs, I sprawled flat on my back to regain my nervous equilibrium.

From there around the bare southern flank of Mount Carrie, a seldom-climbed wilderness peak, seven thousand feet high, we contoured along game trails. Four thousand feet below us the Hoh River made a silvery scratch through its gray gravel bars. The dark-timbered ridges south of it rose into the white crests of Mount Olympus and Mount Tom, another peak rarely climbed. We had been following an elk "travel trail," which gave us in places very good footing, but it drifted down onto a ridge while we kept our elevation, running into one place so sheer, above a thousand-foot drop, that I lost my nerve for the second time and stuck to the mountainside like a postage stamp, till Herb, ahead and almost at a standstill himself, conceded, "Turn around. We'll try it lower."

Game trails are plainest where the choice of travel routes is the

scarcest. If they run out or seem to spread over the country in "feeding trails," the chances are that the going is fair anywhere along this strip. But you must be on the alert and try to pick up the travel trail when leaving this area to cross a rough strip. If you start across without a game trail, you are liable to get into very rough going or even get stuck.

When we broke around a "corner" of the mountainside into Eleven Bull Basin, the shallowest and briefest of shelves, we halted silently to watch a bear browsing just ahead of us, before we even noticed two more a little higher. We camped at Eleven Bull that night in the low black firs at the edge of the drop-off. I had laid my bag in a game trail, which made a slight cradle for me, and in the morning I heard a rustling beyond the foot of my bag. The head of a doe, her tall ears up, was looking at me over the bushes. It was probable that she had never seen a human being before. She vanished as I sat up, then came slipping back to peep and stare.

In sunshine we climbed out of the basin to head a rock gorge and hit a travel trail. Around the middle of a cliff that to me had looked impassable, it opened foot by foot as we advanced, getting us safely across. We were traveling above timber, and now from back of us and far below, a fog front moved in from the Pacific. We paused occasionally to watch it moving up the Hoh Valley toward us. Overhead the sun hazed and we were in a cool world between two cloud layers. Across the valley Mount Olympus and Mount Tom looked wild, white, and desolate above the bluish, timbered mountainsides. The wind from ahead of us and the undulating fog river moving up from behind were battling below us now. Suddenly the vapors sifted up through the tree-tops toward us, and in five minutes, chill and light-moving, had softly closed us in.

"Can you find the way?" I asked with anxiety. Herb traveled steadily ahead. In an hour the wind had won and the fog was drawing back toward the ocean. We passed bear and bucks, scores of elk, and a flock of pine grosbeaks.

About noon Herb stopped and looked a moment, then quietly drew back with a smile, turning to me. "There's your first view of Cream Lake," he said.

Beside a clump of alpine scrub I stood and looked silently down at the basin below and ahead of us. Seated at the base of a circle of moun-

tains, with Mount Ferry white beyond, and Mount Olympus off to the right, a great mountain basin opened out—the largest, the wildest I had seen in the Olympics. Far below us spread the "seat," a pale green valley marked with blue water channels. At its extreme edge, beside the drop-off, lay a spot of color, the creamy, glacial blue-green of Cream Lake itself. We jolted down the steep mountainside, foot below foot, till at last the descending skirts of the slope swept out in green, to the level shore of the lake. There we camped.

Flat on the ground in our bags that night, we looked up at the black spires of the firs against the stars. Every few minutes sounded the clear keen bugle of an elk, sometimes near, sometimes far.

We ascended the basin in the sunny morning, picking huckleberries as we went, my freshly washed spare shirt drying like a flag from my alpenstock. The third lake we came to lay cradled in clean white living rock. I stripped and went in. As I dried on a blue bandanna, big raindrops hit my bare back softly, falling from a momentary haze overhead.

To our right opened out a wide pass looking toward the shining Hoh Glacier on Mount Olympus. We bore to the left of the pass, contouring around the south side of Mount Ferry into a saddle, then heading southward over rock and snow toward Mount Olympus, along the crest of the Bailey Range. The wild region at the head of the Goldie spread far below the crags to our left, and jagged peaks and snow fields to our right.

There is one place where this spine of the Olympics widens a little, and the firs, centuries old, a few feet high, spread their dense skirts over its windward edge—a place where we could lay our eiderdown bags that night, pull the drawstrings snug around our necks, and fall asleep, to waken now and then under dense stars, in the profound stillness on this spit of land in the sky, with the void on each side and white mountains dim beyond.

We were near our goal now. The next day, over snow and dark jagged rock, we climbed up and down into swales along the very crest of the Bailey Range again, then up a rather wide snow field, to break over into the head of the Queets Basin. The basin did not open out suddenly, but in a succession of steep descents and little basins.

Camp that night was deeply satisfying. The toil and uncertainties of the trip were over; only the delight remained. There is an inimitable

delight about making camp in the wilderness. The problems presented all must and can be solved immediately—the wood show, the water show, the "bedroom." There is none of the circuitousness with which food and shelter are obtained in civilization.

We camped on a wide grassy spur under crags crowned by sharp-spired clumps of alpine fir, overlooking the Queets Basin, across which rose Mount Barnes and Mount Queets. Toward dawn I wakened sleepily. It was very still. Fog was studying what it could do: folding in, dim white, then falling away to let in a window of dark crag and swallow it again; or half disclosing a black, pointed fir, then veiling it. It was like watching preliminary studies for the creation of a world.

As we climbed away toward the Dodwell-Rixon Pass, the mists were dissolving against the blue sky and off the shining glacier; the huckle-berry brush shone crimson and translucent against the long sun just topping the ridge ahead. It was the Olympic symbiosis at its best. We dropped down the Elwha snow finger and out to our homeward trail. For six days we had not followed nor crossed a man-made trail nor seen a human being. Ah, wilderness!

TIMBER

BY THOMAS EMERSON RIPLEY

The real men of the mountains were not the alpinists who struggled to the peaks and then repaired to the city, but the lumbermen, tough, hard-hitting empire builders, men who fought the wilderness and who, on conquering, moved on to new conquests. (R. P.)

To one who has heard the haunting cry of "Timber-r-r!" echoing through the aisles of the forest of our great Northwest, followed by the crashing of the great tree as it comes to earth, there comes back the old dream of inexhaustible timber and the wealth to be extracted therefrom, all within reach of the easy skid road. And to the town-minded one who has sniffed the smell of the forest floor, deep with the humus of centuries, while at the same time his nostrils were assailed by the acrid smell of burning stumps on the hillside where his house is to stand, there comes again the rosy vision of a new and fair city, carved out of the wilderness and dipping its feet in the waters of Puget Sound; a young city, built, peopled, and run by young men and women, the spirit of destruction and creation going strong—destruction in the forest, creation in the town. The forest holds back settlement; the settlement pushes back the forest to make room for creative and destructive man. And, it must be said, to make room for the real estate salesman with his huge roll of blueprints, ushering in a high, wide, and handsome brand of speculation. All this was not so long in the past.

In the memory of many an old-timer, the pounding of hammers and the screech of saws on the main street of his chosen town make exhilarating music. The groves which were "God's first temples" are being shaped into uncouth false-fronted temples of saloon and market. Mud squirts up through the cracks of the loosely-planked roadway as horse-drawn loads of freshly sawed lumber rattle down the street. Here and there, the tap of trowel handle on scarcely dried brick gives promise of solidity and permanence. The chief preoccupation, however, is quick shelter from the "liquid sunshine" of Puget Sound.

East and West! The twain meet on the planked street. Japanese meet Bostonians. Native sons of California meet down-Easterners from the State o' Maine, asking, "What was your name back East?" Lumberjacks from the Saginaw, fresh from the skid roads and stepping high, meet Siwash Indians from their camp on the mud flats below the bluff.

Standing timber! Slathers of it! It covers the hillsides, already platted into town lots. It falls before axe and saw, leaving a melancholy waste of slashing, punctuated by blackened stumps, rarely less than eight feet high. And when the destruction is complete, the area is marked down on blueprints in town lots and the lots are labeled "improved" real estate.

Where the timber, axe-ripe, marches to the water's edge, lumberjacks are carrying on the gospel of "improvement." The forest bordering the shore line goes first. As the tree falls, buckers are ready to cut it into forty-foot logs. The hook tender yards them out, and, with a booming and a crashing, the log rushes down the fore-and-aft skidway. Boom! Splash! Another flooring log floats amid the debris of rafting.

Falling timber, rafts of logs, the clatter of the sawmill, boards, rustic, siding, shingles, fancy brackets for the porch on Nob Hill, plate glass for the new bank, red glass for the red-light district. Trainloads of loggers from the pineries of the Lake States, boatloads of eager newcomers from California, high-spirited Americans, low-minded Americans, the godly men and women and the bad men and the drunks, all coming to profit from the slashing of the timber and coming for the fun of building a new town. To the old-timer, it is a memory of a happy-go-lucky yesterday, of boundless faith in riches, limited only by a horizon which could not be seen through the forest.

A GLIMPSE INTO THE FOREST

There are few experiences of life more breath-taking than a first plunge off the beaten trail into the green jungle forest of our northwest coast. The giant trees, guarding within their tree-ringed hearts the secrets of many centuries of history, have been elbowing each other like men struggling for sustenance in an overpopulated area, competing with each other for one of the necessities of tree life, stretching themselves upward in their fight for the upper light. And as they fought for height, they have pruned themselves of their less useful members, their lower branches, till they stand clean and straight, affording to the

logger's enraptured gaze three, four, even five forty-foot logs, clear of limbs. The timber cruiser needs no X-ray machinery to see in a single tree a carload of clear lumber. To borrow a phrase, repeated *ad nauseam* in Hollywood: "It's thrilling! It's stupendous!! It's colossal!!!" In the language of the logger, "By the holy old skid road, that, Mister, is *timber!*"

The early logger little realized the extent of his timber empire. In a zone rarely more than a hundred miles in width and stretching from the strait of Juan de Fuca to the bay of San Francisco, an area no larger than the State of North Carolina, there is found almost one third of the standing timber of the United States today. Even when the whole continent was covered with the primeval forest, this was the greatest timber stand in the world, surpassing in stumpage, acre for acre, all other forests.

If you step off the comforting blazed trail, you will be wise to carry a compass and to know how to use it. And you will be wise to put a handful of tally sticks in your pocket. On second thought, you would be wiser to take along a seasoned timber cruiser and leave the compass and the tally to him. Alone, you won't go far into the jungle before a detour around a fallen giant throws your sense of direction all askew; and while trying to recapture it, you will forget to tally your paces; you will be lost in the midst of this awesome beauty, as lost as a soul wandering between the worlds. The mammoth Douglas firs, the stag-headed cedars, the hemlocks, tower above you to a height, sometimes, of three hundred feet. Below, you are in a tangle of head-high tropical-looking ferns, manzanita, vine maple. The sinister devil's-club reaches for you, poisonous as the very devil himself to the tenderfoot, but, like the wilderness about you, harmless to the lumberjack who knows how to stroke it the right way of its fur. In some regions, rhododendrons and foxglove, gay in their season, light up the somber density of the forest. Here and there one sees cascara, pulled over into arches by the bears in their hunger for the medicinal bark. Oregon grape, salal, and kinnikinnic carpet the forest floor and trip your confused feet. If the weatherman is kind (which is not too often, except in the dry months of the short summer) the sun manages to shoot his golden shafts of light through the lofty green armor to make a giant fairyland, fit for gigantic wood sprites. It is beautiful but dangerous.

In this forest the naturalist will find a wonderland of interest before

he has tallied his first fifty paces. And, being a naturalist and, therefore, a nature lover, he will stop and catch his breath in the midst of such prodigal beauty, before whipping out his notebook and getting busy on the record of what he sees. He will see, in the greatest abundance, the Douglas fir (which is not a fir at all), named Pseudotsuga Douglasii for David Douglas, that intrepid Scots botanist who discovered it more than a century ago. The botanical name is a tongue twister for a lumber-jack. If he bothers with the name at all, he translates it: "all same hem-lock," which is near enough. It is also called Douglas spruce. In the trade it goes, in California, by the worst of misnomers, Oregon pine— O.P. for short. It is one of the wonder trees of the world. There is a fine sample of the Douglas fir, selected by the British for its height and symmetry, serving as a flagstaff in Kew Gardens near London and carrying a very large and very defiant Union Jack two hundred and twenty feet above the earth. According to Colonel F. R. S. Balfour, a director of Kew Gardens and largely responsible for its erection, this spar, when felled, measured three hundred feet in height. And even this is probably an example of British understatement. It must be con-fessed, however, that this spar was felled in British Columbia. We have no monopoly of tall flagstaffs in our forests.

The naturalist will see among the Douglas firs great stands of cedar, from which the Indians hollowed out their great war canoes and their totem poles (and which, again, is not a cedar at all). And he will see, crowding in, as though to claim their own *Lebensraum,* a great assort-ment of the true firs, the grandis, that aristocrat among trees, the mag-nifica, the nobilis, the amabilis. The early logger called the latter two the noble and the lovely fir, which seem rather nice names to bestow upon such trees as these. About these true firs, the early logger knew little and cared less, as lumber trees. The cruiser lumped them all to-gether under the name of white, or silver, fir, trees for which, as a lum-berman, he had scant regard. The hemlock he hardly counted in the early cruises. One item sufficed: "Considerable hemlock."

THE TRAIL BLAZERS COME

The extent of this wealth of timber was known to a few, years before the Northern Pacific engineers struck pick into the resisting earth to grade the right of way over the Cascades. It was recorded in the notes

of Lewis and Clark and described in their report to President Jefferson.
The history-making captains wrote of the "excellent timber" with which
the "whole neighborhood" was clothed. The President must have wiped
his glasses to be sure he had read aright:

The first species (one of the true firs) grows to immense size and is commonly twenty-seven feet in circumference, six feet above the earth's surface.
They rise to a height of two hundred and thirty feet and one hundred and
twenty feet of that height without a limb. We have often found them thirty-
six feet in circumference. One of our party measured one and found it forty-
two feet in circumference at a point beyond the reach of an ordinary man.

Almost as David Douglas was exploring the region, Dr. John Mc-
Loughlin, the Hudson's Bay Company man, had the vision and the
courage to build the first sawmill on the Columbia River at Vancouver.
It was a water-powered affair, and one wonders how the homemade
contraption ever handled the huge logs which he must, perforce, have
cut, just to find room to swing his axe at the neighboring tree. A savage
country this, no country for a weakling. The logger and the city builder
alike had to have what it took to survive, physically and economically.
To quote D. W. Brogan, that perceptive Englishman who wrote *The
American Character*, "It took a high degree of pugnacity and a taste for
acquisition on a big scale." And again, "It took adaptability, toughness,
and, perhaps, not too sensitive a social and moral outlook." And it took a
lot more patience than the pioneers possessed, during the years between
McLoughlin's attack on the Columbia front and the big-time operations
which followed. As the years passed, impatient and restless fellows on
Puget Sound, holding fast to their dream of the coming of the railroad,
were mapping the tide flats, sounding the waters, and betting their all
on the location of the terminus of the dream railroad, not if but when
its engine should puff its way to tidewater. The railroad was coming;
sure, it was. A train of cars, running on two rails over the endless prairies
and the impassable mountains? Fantastic idea! But fantastic ideas were
ever part and parcel of the American spirit. It was exemplified by the
Reverend Samuel Parker, back in New England, who, with fine missionary zeal and confidence, wrote:

There would be no difficulty in the way of constructing a railroad from the
Atlantic to the Pacific ocean. There is no greater difficulty in the whole dis-

tance than has already been overcome in passing the Green Mountains between Boston and Albany; and probably the time may not be far distant when tours will be made across the continent as they have been made to Niagara Falls to see Nature's wonders.

But it took a long time for the dream to materialize in steel rails over the graded right of way. It was not until 1864 that President Lincoln put his signature to the charter which authorized the Northern Pacific. During the long years of grading and steel laying, the dream lured the pioneers, few and very far between at first, followed by more and then more. Like salmon fighting their way up the waters of the Stilaguamish River, they came, kingfish, middle-sized, and fingerlings.

Following McLoughlin's early mill venture at Vancouver, Henry Yesler laid the sills of his mill and, with them, the foundations of his dynasty, on the site where Seattle now stands. His memory is perpetuated by the name of a street, Yesler Way.

But to a good Commencement Bay booster, the more modest exploits of Nick Delin hold greater interest. Nick was a Swedish adventurer. Unlike his Viking ancestors, he wore his horns upon his palms. Blacksmith, rough-and-ready engineer, jackknife craftsman at all trades, he whacked at the door of his opportunity and demanded admission. He had thrashed his way around the Horn in the good ship "Edward Everett" and landed in California, which, apparently, he didn't much care for. After a look at the torn and unlovely gold diggings, he got a bad case of "Oregon fever," a honing for that vast territory stretching from the California line clear to the somewhat indeterminate southern boundary of British Columbia. "Fifty-four forty or fight!" It still rankled in the minds of the handful of Americans who had "occupied" the region of Oregon that President Polk had compromised with the British at the forty-ninth parallel. They wanted to roam clear to the southernmost tip of Russian Alaska. Nick accepted the compromise.

That "Japanee Current," now—he'd heard of that. Up against the west coast it flowed, bringing warm rains to all growing things on the coastal slopes and about the big inland sea called Puget Sound. The Indians called it by the outlandish name of *Whulge*, an onomatopoetic sort of name, but Nick probably hadn't learned that word. And there was a

mountain up there which the Indians called Tacoma, snow-clad and glistening with glaciers.

So he got as far as Tumwater, then to Portland, where there were several hundred people—too many for Nick. He journeyed forth again toward that "something lost beyond the ranges" and landed on Commencement Bay of Puget Sound, where dark green mountains were mirrored in dark green water, where the mists hung over the tops of the mountains, and where the cloud gods held possession.

At the mouth of Galliher's Creek, Nick Delin laid the foundations of the vast industry that was to develop about the spot. As he fashioned his water wheel, the Indians gathered about to wonder at the marvelous works of the white man. When the wheel began to turn, they shouted, *"Tyee! Hyas skookum!"* Nick knew that this was the Indian accolade and that he had been dubbed the big white man, superlatively smart. Having, perforce, to learn the most useful word in the Chinook jargon, Nick told them *"Klatawah!"* which means "Get the hell out of here" or "please make room," depending on the temper of the speaker and the inflection of his voice. Legend has it that Nick was a kindly soul and that, with friendly words and gentle shoves, he moved the crowd out of harm's way. Anyway, the Indians seemed to have liked Nick. A short Indian war soon followed. Nick retired for a space to Fort Steilacoum which lay across the peninsula. When he returned, no bit of plank was found to have been disturbed. Pretty nice, this consideration on the part of old Chief Shilwhaylton, for the red men were covetous of board and batten to take the place of pole and bark for their houses.

One can imagine Nick, surveying the wealth of his new domain, planting his two feet on the damp earth, and speaking his wisdom: "If a feller got good board, comes alwis some feller wants to build house. Look! planty room hare for build house." One can see him leaning against a giant fir, measuring its neighbor with his eye, and waving a comprehensive arm to embrace it all. "Planty room hare; planty board too."

His cockeyed logic is the only logic which can explain the birth and growth of American cities. A complete reverse it is of the logic of older civilizations where cities were born of necessities, military, industrial, agricultural—and evolved or stagnated as circumstances dictated. The

American has hewn his townsite out of the wilderness, cocksure that with "planty room" and "planty board," with, perhaps, a harbor thrown in, the men following the covered wagon would beat a path, and the railroad engineer would grade a right of way to the open door of his fiat city.

So Nick dreamed of a village, in the fullness of time, clustering about his little mill, needing boards and battens. And, since rail transportation was only in the dream stage, he probably dreamed of a tangle of masts and spars, silhouetted against the evening sky, with decks and holds below, waiting for his cargo. California's gold diggers needed more and more lumber, and already cargoes of fir and cedar had found their way around the Horn to the lumber-hungry East—yes, and to the Orient, where, as the logger put it, "Them fellers is livin' in paper houses and need our lumber *bad.*"

From his first log cabin, in every direction Nick saw beautiful timber covering the hillsides, down to the water's edge. Plenty of it for California, New England, and the benighted Orient. "Inexhaustible" was the word.

In the north, one good Swede always draws another. Pete Anderson turned up. Pete became head faller, second faller, swamper, and bucker, all rolled into one. Steve Judson stepped in with the jobs, if not the titles, of rigging slinger, hook tender, bullwhacker and hump durgin man, his humble yoke of oxen doing duty in place of the donkey engine which came later. He snaked the logs out from the tangle of fallen timber to the little head saw. In truth, it was the *only* saw.

Gertrude Meller, a fine, upstanding, and tempting girl, appeared at the camp. Following the covered wagon, she had trekked all the weary way across the plains, toiled over the fearsome Natchez Pass, and forded sixty-eight river crossings. No wonder Nick looked with ardor at Gertrude. Small wonder that Gertrude looked with favor upon Nick and the promise of a cozy cabin, a patch of "garden sass," and a chicken coop. They "stood up" before a Justice of the Peace in Steilacoum and the knot was well and truly tied. The first family life began on Commencement Bay. On scheduled time, a girl baby came, the first white child to be born on the site of the future Tacoma.

Nick Delin was the prototype of the small loggers who first dared

tackle the big trees. He and his like broke the ground for the inrush of the big fellows from the exhausted forests of Maine and the Lake States.

THE TYEES COME

Compared with the bigger things that were in the making, Nick Delin's clattering little mill didn't make much of a dent in the development of the lumber industry. He was only one of the pioneers, and being a pioneer is mostly its one and its only reward. His job was to carve a home out of the wilderness, to raise a family, and to become an American pioneer ancestor. In that, he did a good job. As for fame, he had first a gulch and then a street named for him—and he didn't name either of them himself. It is generally the followers of the pioneer who garner the titles and emoluments of pathfinders and empire builders. While his modest little mill was transforming the "round stuff" into boards, the big tyees were coming.

Pope and Talbot, having laid waste the country about Machias, Maine, came to let the light into the swamp, and they cut a wide swathe. Henry Yesler's cookhouse on the site of Seattle expanded along with Yesler's power and influence. Yesler's heart was knit unto the dream of making Seattle, in the shortest possible time, a city to rival great Babylon itself. In the meantime, he was content to tell his rivals in the budding city of Tacoma to go jump in the bay. For two decades these two towns, competitors for importance, ran neck and neck under the whip and spur of the American passion for crowded population. They shouted, they boasted, they lied, and at each decennial taking of the census, each padded the census figures with a right royal will. In this contest Yesler won, and his name is still green in the memory of the old-timer, while Tacoma, settling contentedly into second place, says wisely, "Who *wants* to live in an overcrowded city anyway?"

"Puget Sound," said a cynical old logger, "is a large body of water completely surrounded by men who know exactly what they want." It was timber they wanted, and they went after it, tooth, nail, and cant hook. The acquisition of large bodies of standing timber presented no insurmountable difficulties. To get a quarter section, you had to be the head of a family and be twenty-one years of age. Then you had to be a citizen of this beneficent country or, if not a citizen, you could declare

and register your intention to become one. Thus equipped, a homestead claim of 160 acres was yours, almost for the asking. Clear an acre, build a cabin that looked more or less (generally less) like a home, putter about it for a bit, and lo! a timber "chance" was yours, on which stood, perhaps, ten million feet of the finest timber on earth. If you fudged a bit on your qualifications, nobody much cared. Troublesome questions were not asked. There was plenty of the stuff left. If a straw entryman, perhaps a sailor, turned up to file his claim, he could sell his rights for enough to get all perfumed up for a frolic on the skid road of the nearest town, and then ship for parts unknown. Ha! ha! It was a hell of a joke on somebody, but nobody asked on whom. And so big baronies of standing timber were staked off by some of the big fellows of the timber realm. It was only later that troublesome consciences came, to bedevil the public and spoil the fun.

The Northern Pacific engineers crept across the prairies and hacked their way up the eastern slopes of the Cascades toward Stampede Pass. The pass acquired its name when the whole crew of swampers quailed at the prospect ahead, quit work, and *stampeded*, leaving only one youngster on the job. He was not a quitter. The young humorist lettered a sign on a bit of board: "Stampede Pass." Nailing it to a tree, he stuck to his post till a new crew came. They switchbacked the grade over the pass. The first train puffed itself up and slid itself down on screaming brakes to tidewater at the elected terminus at Tacoma. Puget Sound made whoopee.

Today the old-timer may travel over the mountains with no sense of climbing up-up-up and plunging down-down-down; no sense of altitude and, worse luck, no sense of adventure. He can only squint his nostalgic eyes from a lower level at the heights the old switchback scaled, and beat his breast in regret that the old breed, extinct now, has been succeeded by another whose job seems to be to ride the rails in safety, comfortably ensconced in an overstuffed, overheated chair car. " 'Farewell, Romance!' the cave men said," and each succeeding generation has repeated it, all oblivious of the romance that unfolds about it.

With the completion of the Stampede tunnel a short time later, the loggers knew that the great era of railroad building was on. Eastern markets were opened up and the demands of the railroads themselves

were insatiable. All the trees that the loggers could cut down and all the lumber that the mills could saw were wanted, and in a hurry. The demand, like the standing timber, was "inexhaustible."

THE OLYMPIC PENINSULA

While the shore line of Puget Sound was being denuded of its forest cover, the Olympic Peninsula stood, dark and mysterious. The Olympic timber empire stretches from the strait of Juan de Fuca in the north to the Chehalis River in the south; its western boundary is the Pacific Ocean, its eastern, Puget Sound. It was a forbidding area in the early days, a rugged country, a challenge to the courage of the early logger, an irresistible invitation to his logger's instinct. From the lower reaches the mountains rise, not to surpassing altitudes—only something over eight thousand feet. But, owing to their northern latitude, the snow on their summits is eternal. Here, timber line is found at five to seven thousand feet. At timber line, one meets Alaska cedar, alpine hemlock, and alpine fir, wind-tortured, lightning-riven, and snow-burdened—a tangled scrub.

At lower altitudes, these same species straighten up, take on normal shapes, crowding, slim and glistening, about the sopping, flowering meadows. At still lower altitudes, they are joined or displaced by different sorts of trees. There is a sprinkling of the beautiful Idaho white pine, much like its eastern counterpart. And there is western hemlock, putting in its gracious appearance at this zone, along with the well-named "noble" and the "lovely" fir. Much of this mountain forest is still in its virgin state and, insofar as it is included in the Olympic National Park, it will ever remain so.

At lower altitudes still, other species enter into the picture. Now, for the first time, we meet the Douglas fir. And here grows the mighty canoe cedar, from which the first loggers split off shakes for the roof and rived long boards for the siding of their bunkhouse, cookhouse, and commissary. (And if there is anything more heartening to see than the skill and rapidity of the man with the "frow," or more musical than the zing, zing, zing as the shapely shakes fall from the bolt, the old-timer has yet to see and hear it.) There is timber for all tastes—Sitka spruce, the giant of the forest, without whose best cuts many of the American,

British, and French airmen would have lacked planes in World War I; the Nootka cypress, looking like giant municipal Christmas trees, with their down-sweeping boughs trimmed with their own dripping foliage and pretty cones.

Lovely lakes, rushing streams in which trout abound, all the delights of the sportsman or the nature lover are now within easy access of one who cares to see. Crescent Lake, until recent days so hidden between the mountains, can now be reached by a motor road which runs through miles of forest, with green vistas ahead and the fleeting memory of green loveliness behind. In the memory of the old-timer, it was an adventure to come upon this gem among lakes. Lake Cushman, another shining gem of an older day, now the source of Tacoma's water supply, used to be journey's end of a more or less hazardous trip, first by pack horse and later by a road that could be negotiated by the motorist who had not grown dependent on six-lane highways. It is almost too easy now, except for those for whom the spirit and the opportunity for adventure are lacking. Here the Skokomish tumbled from dark pool to dark pool, with white water between. (The deep pools were *skookumchuck* and the white water *tumwater* to the Indians.) The Satsop, the Quinault, a dozen streams with haunting names find their way to the sea.

At Cushman there lived William T. Putnam, a graduate of Trinity College in Hartford. Heaven knows why he took up his homestead claim in this wilderness—perhaps it was to "get away from it all." If that was his wish, his wish was gratified. The memory of Put's hospitality still lives with the few who came to cast for trout in the Skokomish, to sleep in his blankets at the Inn, which, inevitably, his place became, and to taste the pungency of Put's philosophy.

Sol Simpson from Quebec peered into this dark forest and found it good. With his cruiser's eye, he could measure the quantity and the quality of the timber from the water's edge. With his logger's eye, he could estimate the men and equipment required for the job. He brought along his lumberjacks. They brought along their tin pants, their calked boots, and their peavies, to turn logs the like of which no peavy had ever turned. And they brought logger's traditions, their logger's thirst and their logger's he-man hunger for the skid road and all that it offered. They looked, and it is safe to say that they said, as jacks have said ever

since King Solomon's loggers laid low the cedars of Lebanon, "By God!
It takes a man strong in the back and weak in the head to do this job."

BULLS, BEANS, AND BUGS

The logging of the early days was largely a matter of letting the light
into the forest by the b'guess and b'god method. The good "chance" lay
close at hand where there was an easy downgrade. Only the big and
choice logs found their way to the mills. Economic compulsions dictated then as they do today. If it cost more to get a log to the mill than
the log would yield in the market, it was left in the woods to be burned
with the slashing. And at the tail of every mill there was a mounting
pile of gray ashes, sending a pall of smoke heavenward to proclaim the
destruction of riches unheeded and uncounted. "Give us those big old-
growth flooring logs," said the millman, and in turn the buyer said,
"Give us the vertical-grain stuff. Send the slash-grain to the burner." And
then the oft-repeated slogan, "The best is none too good for us." From
the head faller in the woods to the grader at the tail of the mill, it was
a case of "high-balling," speed 'er up, and to hell with the waste. There's
plenty of the stuff left. Yes, and there's a city to build, needing room
where the trees now stand and lumber which the same trees would
yield.

Bull strength and awkwardness were brought to the job; literally bull
strength, for the only motive power thought applicable to the job was
a long string of oxen, driven by the first authentic boss of the camp, the
bullwhacker. He was a rugged individual, armed with a goad with a
sharpened spike in the end and a variety of profanity that has been
equaled nowhere on earth, since, as they used to say, "Puget dug the
sound." An imposing string of oxen dragged a turn of logs along what
is now, perhaps, the street where perfume and lingerie are sold—and a
heartening sight it was. The bullwhacker yielded precedence only to
the big boss of all the works, the "bull of the woods" as he was called
on the Saginaw. For a brief period he carried this title in our Northwest. He was a tough customer, able and willing to maintain his authority with any weapons at hand or on foot—preferably the latter. If
his authority was questioned, he could jump at the recalcitrant logger
with both feet and thus "put the calks to him." Those calks were wicked
instruments. The bindle stiff who got gay with the boss was a lucky boy

if he lived with the wish to fight another day. The big boss was a rocket-propelled producer.

But even a half dozen yoke of oxen found difficulty, and anyway they were all too slow. Many ingenious fellows were dreaming of the use of steam. The donkey engine evolved. It was a crude affair at first, but it served. A line horse, a canny beast who knew the danger of a whipping cable, dragged the line out to the yarding crew where the hook tender, the heir apparent of the bullwhacker, made ready for the strain; the whistle punk yanked his line, and the spool tender at the donkey gave it the works. The donkey engine huffed and puffed, and the log came crashing from the yard, carrying with it every growing thing that stood in its path. To the thoughtful, its path was a highroad of desolation, but to the high-balling boss it was a noble sight. Once yarded out, the logs were hooked up, end to end, and the turn was dragged over the skid road to the boom or to the millpond.

The early logging camps of the Northwest, though a step up from the camps of the Maine woods and the rivers of the Lake States, were, in truth, rough and tough enough. A log and shake bunkhouse contained a double tier of bunks, in which straw supplied the place of mattresses. A potbellied stove stood in the middle, giving out its fervent heat. The place was steamy from the wet socks, long-legged drawers, and Mackinaw coats which hung about the stove in the vain hope of drying. Each logger packed his own blankets, heavy, and smelling very high, at least in the memory of one, then a neophyte in the logging game. Having experienced one remembered night in borrowed blankets, rich with the aroma of sweat and "snoose," he provided himself for his next visit to camp with a pair of thin cotton blankets to fold like sheets between his nose and the too-rich smell of the loggers' equipment. It worked beautifully. As he left camp the next morning, he explained to the questioning boss that he had a touch of rheumatism and had been told that the cotton might ward off an attack. He rolled his cotton blankets and put them for safekeeping on a rafter overhead. "Just keep these till I come back," he said. "Sure," said the boss of the woods. On the occasion of his next visit, he asked for his cotton specific. "Well, now," said the boss, "I been havin' a tech o' rheumatism myself. I been sleepin' in them things ever since you was here, but they don't seem to be a-helpin' of me, fur's I can see."

The cookhouse boasted a fine range at one end of the kitchen, where the cook presided. Well-separated from these sacred precincts, long trestle tables, covered with oilcloth, occupied the big room. After the men had straddled the benches and wolfed their grub, the flunkey hustled up and down the tables, picking up each dish, whanging it edgewise on the table, and thus emptying its left-over contents onto the oilcloth. Then, with a huge garbage bucket on his arm, he swept the leavings of two kinds of meat, beans, and "pie, cake, an' puddin'." Of these items there was no lack. As a final housewifely gesture, he brought in a bucket of suds, with which he sloshed the oilcloth clean.

Good men came to the camp where the biggest variety of the best foods was served. *Hiu muckamuck* (lots of food) meant steady crews. And it took lots of food to generate steam in the boilers of men for the heartbreaking work in the woods.

The commissary, where the timekeeper presided, sold all the items needed by the well-dressed logger and much for his insides as well. "Snoose," or chewing snuff, was a major item. The way to any well-run camp could be traced by the little yellow tins, empty and thrown aside. Another item was a row of bottles of Lydia Pinkham's Compound. A spoonful taken after a wet day in the woods lifted the heart, which was, perhaps, after all, one of the organs which Lydia considered when she made up her compound. Calked boots, tin pants, suspenders, socks, plug and smoking tobacco, and a limited but fascinating variety of other things were for sale—which seemed to take on a value they never could have had when displayed in a city department store. The commissary was a pleasant place in which to pass the time of day, but the lumberjack was not encouraged to loiter there. If he found time on his hands, he could squat on his hunkers outside the cookhouse and swap his bawdy stories there.

Much is remembered of the tough, hard-boiled character of the early days when the first swampers tackled these forests, and the old-timer heaves many a sigh over the dear, dead days and the passing of a great race. It is to be doubted, however, that the present-day logger casts many nostalgic backward looks. In truth, it *was* a great race, and in truth it still *is* a great race—tough, fearless, openhanded, and wonderfully skillful at the trade. It is not likely that the early logger acquired his "strength through joy," though he may well have acquired much joy

through strength. He had a well-developed sense of histrionics, as the onlooker could see as he watched the high and lofty antics of a good loader who was perfectly conscious of the eye of the admiring city slicker. He was a good man and he didn't care who knew it. It was always a marvel how he could stand the pace from early dawn till dark. It was a case of work while the light lasted, for the boss measured time not by the discreet ticking of the clock but by the hours of daylight. Before the cold gray dawn, the flunkey banged the gong (sometimes a circular saw, and sometimes a big triangle, made by the blacksmith) and routed the logger out from the luxury of his straw and into the woods in time for the first lick of work when the half-light of morning enabled him to see. He came back to his bug-infested luxury when the light failed and not before, scrubbed his face and hands, slicked his hair, and straddled his bench for the big feed. He was not allowed to linger over the delights of the table. Conversation was limited to "Pass me some o' *that* kind." Fifteen minutes were enough to satisfy his Gargantuan appetite, after which he could have the whole darkening evening before tumbling into his blankets by the light of a lantern.

Small wonder that Saginaw Red, tired in body and cantankerous in spirit, demanded his time, rolled his blankets, and hit the trail for the town, where he could blow his wages on whatever diversions the skid road afforded. The boss, an experienced psychologist of the woods, let him go, knowing that when once his blood was cooled and his spirit chastened he would return. Red was no Beau Brummell of the woods. His Mackinaw coat hung with the fringes of torn fabric, his tin pants were out at the seat, and his underwear, what there was of it, wouldn't stand washing. In consequence, he just didn't wash it. Time after time, as he loaded his jeans with his wages, the boss sent him down the trail with his parting fatherly advice, "Now, Red, before you go a-roarin' around, go and get yourself some new pants and a boiled shirt (the badge of the logger on holiday) and some new drawers." Red, his heart big with good resolutions, promised. And he kept his promise. He did fit himself out with fine new logger's raiment, and then proceeded to his more pressing business at bar and brothel. With the willing help of his boy and girl friends, he blew what was left of his three months' pay in one wild burst of enthusiasm, recovered his old clothes, turned up at the saloon, and shoved all his new glad raiment over the bar in pay-

ment for the means of one more gaudy night. He hit the trail back to camp, a good and amenable logger.

PUBLIC CONSCIENCE BEGINS ITS PRICKING

It is not surprising that this riotous crew, driven by the big boss, whose compelling ambition was to turn his timber holdings into cash before taxes on his standing timber ate him up, life a literally scorched earth as it passed. It must be said, however, that neither the big boss nor the lumberjack looked at the destruction without vague prickings of conscience. These prickings found expression, but they were quieted as best they might be by the reflection that the big trees were mature, already overripe, in fact, and if not turned now to the uses of man, they would shortly die, fall, and rot in the woods, as had uncounted billions of feet in centuries past. This was true, but in harvesting the mature trees the logger had, perforce, to shut his eye to the destruction of the potential billions of feet of young timber which stood in the path of the hook tender. There was another comforting thought, often expressed, but totally untrue at the time: *the annual growth equals or exceeds the cut.* (Though untrue in the nineties, the theory approaches truth today.) And if a budding social consciousness disturbed the sleep too much, one could always fall back on the theory that clean cutting opened up the country to agriculture and, thus, to the greater good of mankind. There is truth in this conception, too, as one may see in the good earth and the fat barns as one spins north on the broad highway from Puget Sound to the Canadian line. It was comforting to the timber owner when he sold a forty, or perhaps a quarter section of logged-off land to a farsighted Swede and watched him as he bent his back to the job of clearing the slashing, acre by acre, putting in a patch of clover, turning loose first one cow and then another to browse between the stumps, which had to be removed by bull strength and what powder the courageous fellow could buy. Fertile little oases these, which grew, as the years sped, to fruitful farms.

Thus the logger eased his conscience with the thought that God, Nature, and Economic Forces would save the nation's timber supply and make the coast logger rich in the process.

But the Jeremiahs of Washington were more vocal. Gifford Pinchot, an ardent conservationist, was predicting the total exhaustion of our

timber supply in an alarmingly short span of years. To the logger, the word "conservation" was a dictionary word. As for the title "forester," it seemed to have been brought into our vocabulary by Pinchot himself. In his days at Yale, he had announced to his bemused classmates, "I'm going to be a *forester*." The boys hooted. What the hell *was* a forester, anyway? Gifford knew the answer. He became not only *a* forester, but a *national* forester. And so zealous a national forester did he become that he got himself fired by President Taft for too much competence.

Surveys of the nation's timber resources resulted in alarming prophecies of early exhaustion in the eastern and southern States, a prospect that brought little regret to the coast lumbermen. They wagged their heads in all seriousness. "They've wasted their substance back there," they said. "Now they've got to come to us for their lumber." They tore into the timber with renewed zest.

A crop of young foresters was graduated from the Yale and other forestry schools. The loggers on the coast pictured them as romantic young crusaders, clad in Lincoln green, ranging the forests, telling the rugged old lumberman how to do his job. Chop down the timber and save it at the same time?

"Huh! It's damfoolishness," they said.

"*He* never had to meet a pay roll," they said.

"Anyway, it's *un-American*," they said.

And truly, in view of their old-time "cut-out-and-get-out" policy, the latter was an understatement. But the young foresters persisted, like so many Johnny Appleseeds.

Conservation presented puzzling problems. The very vastness and ruggedness of the terrain presented what seemed to be insurmountable difficulties, both in saving the young trees and in planting new seedlings. The latter idea seemed to be one huge joke. As for selective logging, that is, the taking of the old-growth and overripe trees and leaving space and light for the more rapid growth of the younger trees, while the area about them was reseeded—the notion sounded all right, but with the old-fashioned ground-lead method of logging, the old-growth log demanded right of way over every living thing in its path. The idea of taking your power to the tree instead of hauling the tree to the power had not dawned, nor could it dawn, till the internal combustion engine had been developed into the tractor, the bulldozer, and the big truck.

But the destruction of our timber by the hand of man was as nothing compared with what was lost each year by forest fires. In early July, clouds gave way to the lovely rain-washed blue that is the peculiar reward of patience to the webfoot who has seen the winter through. The Puget Sounder lifted his eyes to the glistening slopes of Mount Rainier, turned his gaze eastward to the jagged backdrop of the Cascades and westward to Mount Ellinor and Mount Olympus. He worshiped the mountains as Puget Sounders still worship them. But the vision was short-lived. The mountains drew a veil of smoke across their faces. "Forest fires," said the habituated old-timer. He shook his head. "Seems kind-a too bad to see all that timber burning, but—" and he turned his attention to other things. After all, there was little that could be done about it, and the fire didn't *always* ruin the timber, if you got at it quick and logged off the burned area before the borers got into it. It was with a sort of resignation as to an inevitable act of God that the destruction of such valuable acres was viewed.

A stroke of lightning was an act of God, wasn't it? But those forester fellows figured that a fire started by lightning was a rare phenomenon. Act of God, hell! You couldn't blame God for a campfire left uncovered, or for the burning stub of Bull Durham tossed into that dry underbrush. It was mighty dry, that brush; like tinder it was. And a donkey engine or a geared locomotive shot a power of sparks from their stacks. Something *could* be done about it after all. And, little by little, something *was* done about it. Spark arresters became necessary parts of equipment on donkey engines and logging locomotives. Careless campers and smokers found themselves unpopular citizens. Forest rangers took to watching for incipient blazes and dealing with them before they got out of hand. Thus the beginnings of the present vast, co-operative, and efficient system of fire prevention were made.

A DEPRESSION AND A RECOVERY

The gay nineties found things going as merry as the whanging of the gong by the flunkey at the cookhouse door. Holdings were increased, bigger mills were built, hopes grew higher as the burning waste piles mounted. How could the loggers suspect the gathering of economic forces thousands of miles across land and sea, forces which could touch and blight their hopes? But the great house of Baring in London failed.

London called on New York, and New York began to quake. New York called on Chicago and points west. A bank failed. It toppled onto another and it, in turn, toppled onto another. And as they fell, like the proverbial row of blocks, they always seemed to fall westward toward our little world of the coast which, heavily indebted, was least able to withstand the strain. The panic of '93 was on, and to the timberman of the coast it seemed as though the vortex of the storm centered about his operations. To one who remembers the coast in those black days, all subsequent depressions seem to be just that: depressions. About Puget Sound it was a depression that left a hole in time itself.

> So that there was neither hammer nor axe,
> nor any tool of iron heard.

Building stopped dead, so no lumber was wanted; sawmills shut down, so no logs were wanted; logging camps shut down, so no loggers were wanted. There being no value left, money, as a measure of value, evaporated. It was then that Mr. Dooley suggested his famous economic nostrum. "Whiskey," he said, "is the only steady medium of exchange: two slugs for a quarter."

It was then that the humble clam came into its own. On the beaches there was "equality of opportunity for all"—opportunity to dig. For miles around, driftwood fires lighted the evenings, announcing clambakes for all. For the less gregarious there were clams at home—raw clams, stewed clams, baked clams, and "babes in their blankets." An old song comes to memory, sung, it was said, to the tune of "Rosin the Bow." No one ever seemed to have heard that tune, however. There were many stanzas, two of which come back:

> I tried to get out of the country,
> But poverty forced me to stay
> Until I became an old settler,
> Then nothing could drive me away.

> No longer the slave of ambition,
> I laugh at the world and its shams,
> As I think of my pleasant condition,
> Surrounded by acres of clams.

But it was a young man's country. They took it and they battled it and they weathered it. As one young hopeful put it, "By golly! We've saved 10 per cent of our banks, anyway." But another, an older and therefore less hopeful timberman, who had expanded and hoped for more expansion, when approached by a hopeful salesman with a defunct sawmill for sale for five thousand dollars, shook his head. "My God!" he said. "If I had five thousand dollars, what the hell would I want with a sawmill?"

A millman wandered about the sad streets of his town, looking for orders. He had to be content with an order for a wheelbarrow load of number three boards, with which to board up the windows of a deserted house whose owner had found the cash for a ticket back East.

Carroll D. Wright, our first Commissioner of Labor, made his first annual report to Congress. It didn't help a bit to raise the spirits of a despondent country: ". . . It is true that the discovery of new processes of manufacture will undoubtedly continue, but it will not leave room for marked extension, such as has been witnessed during the last fifty years, or afford remunerative employment of the vast amount of capital which has been created during that period." Poor old capitalism! And poor old individual initiative! Its death knell sounded fifty odd years ago.

It fell on deaf ears. A panacea was wanted. William Jennings Bryan found one, and the "crown-of-thorns-and-cross-of-gold" campaign tore the country apart. A campaign song ran:

> McKinley in the White House,
> Bryan on the fence,
> Tryin' to make a dollar
> Out-a thirty-nine cents.

McKinley, conducting his campaign from the front porch of his house in Canton, Ohio, was elected. Recovery was signalized by the modern marvel of electricity. As the newspaper stories went, a connection was made between Washington and a moribund manufacturing plant out in St. Louis. The newly elected Republican president pushed a button while the country held its breath. It *worked*—and the idle plant was galvanized into activity. The Republican goldbugs, from the Atlantic to the Pacific, gave three cheers. They quoted: "The way to resume, is to *resume*." The recovery was on. The faller found his way to the tall timber and

mounted his springboard; the hook tender found his voice; the heartening sound of the donkey engine's whistle sounded through the forest;
the skid greaser greased his skids.

IMPROVEMENT IN LOGGING AND CONSERVATION

"Conservation of our natural resources." For many years the forward-
looking had been repeating the phrase, but little had been done about
it. Now, the idea gained ground. New ideas of cheaper and less waste-
ful methods of logging were hatching in the Northwest. Someone
thought up the idea of the high lead, by which the end of the log could
be lifted above the tangle of obstacles in its path as it was dragged from
the ministrations of the hook tender. It was a daring innovation. It called
for a fellow with a new kind of strength and daring, a fellow who could
climb a spar tree, perhaps two hundred and fifty feet high, chopping
off limbs as he climbed, and then with axe and saw cut off the top. That
kind of fellow was not to be found in every camp. But, as Brisbane used
to say, "What man can imagine, he can do." The courageous fellow was
found; a new forest job came into being; the high-climber came into his
own. He dug his spurs into the treacherous bark, hitched his steel rope
about the tree, and wriggled his way up. Unlike his brother aerialist of
the circus, he wore no tights. Instead, he carried axe and saw dangling
from his belt, and a Bull Durham tobacco tag dangling from his shirt
pocket. Inching his way up to a dizzy height, he made the undercut and
then sawed his way through till the top began to tremble, then sway;
and finally, with a roar of cracking fibers, it crashed to earth. That moment called for all the high-climber's strength and nerve, as his perch
vibrated in a wide arc under the impact of the falling top. He braced
himself for the shock, while the tenderfoot watcher from below caught
his breath and hid his face in his hands.

The high lead worked like a charm. But why not lift the whole log
and thus keep clear and save all the young growth? That would be a big
step in the process of taking the timber and saving it at the same time.
That meant topping and guying two trees, between which a very heavy
connecting cable was stretched, along which a complicated bit of machinery on wheels could run. Now the great log could be lifted bodily
and carried through the unresisting air to the landing. All this was a vast
improvement over the old ground lead. It was fast; it saved power; it

made it possible to yard in the timber across hill and dale; and it saved the young growth from destruction. But it was a very expensive rig, and only the logger with a large holding and a plethoric purse could afford to risk so much capital. The answer to this problem came with the development of the tractor, the bulldozer, and the big truck. The old-timer rubs his eyes as he sees huge trucks running rapidly along the paved highway, carrying loads of logs which would have made respectable railroad flat-car loads. Perhaps these are the "Gyppo" loggers of which he has heard. This new kind of logger can bring his power to the tree instead of hauling the tree to the distant power. He found his useful place when the demand for spruce for airplane construction suddenly put the whole coast on its toes. This wonderful spruce is frequently found in more or less isolated patches, too small for the big-time capital to go after. The logger with the truck can swamp his way into these tracts, move his power to the tree, and snake it out with a minimum of damage.

Prodded from without by Washington and from within by an uneasy social and economic conscience, the loggers of the coast awakened to the value of what the earlier operators had slashed so ruthlessly. The term "forest management" took on significance. The forester was not such a godawful visionary after all. His high-flown theories, some of them at least, might mean long-term investment in the business of logging. The forester began to exchange commodities with the logger. He brought his vision to the logger, and the logger, in turn, taught the forester something of the practical application of the vision to the business of "harvesting" the timber. Perhaps the forester needed the faith of the logger and the logger needed the faith of the forester, each to bolster up his faith in himself. Between faith and works, the forester has come into his own. "Forest management" has become a respected and important part of the business of using our timber resources while saving and reproducing them.

PEOPLE OF THE OREGON COAST RANGE

BY ARCHIE BINNS

Do not look here and in the following chapter for a history of settlement of the Coast Ranges of Oregon and Washington. Rather you will find therein the quality of men and the lives they run, told by one who is at once master in the art of understanding human nature and the tenor of the mountain ways, and master at telling stories. (R. P.)

From the beginning, the earth's rotation circulated things from Asia to the northwest coast of America. The gigantic action still goes on, bringing the winds and tides and flotsam of Asia to the timeless Oregon shore. In almost every house there, one finds hollow globes of bubble-flecked glass, ranging from the size of an orange to more than the size of a basketball. These bubbles have been arriving for as long as the Japanese have been using them for floats on their fishing nets. Recently a few large globes of purple-red glass have drifted across and into the shops of curio dealers, who offer them as floats from the private fishing nets of Emperor Hirohito. The emperor upwind may be grooming himself for a new occupation, but more likely the red floats were used to warn wartime traffic of the presence of nets.

The easterly circulation is in the air as well as in the sea. During the war, watchers on the Oregon coast saw other bubbles drifting out of the west—white bubbles so high in the substratosphere that balloons appeared the size of golf balls.

In earliest times there was an easterly drift of peoples across Asia and wild Siberia and across narrow Bering Strait or a now-submerged land bridge to North America. From Alaska the drift continued southeast and south, and the Coast Range region was populated in the process. Whatever the storm or ferment that caused this overflow from Asia, it seems to have ended in times so distant that the Indians eventually had no memory or traditions of their homeland in Asia.

During the occupancy of the Indians the coast region of Oregon had a relatively static and homogeneous population. But the great circula-

tion system of the rotating earth still washed its shore and occasionally there was a straw in the wind that blew from Asia: silent as something in a dream, a lost and battered junk would drift into the breakers and lurch up the beach. When the Indians waded out between the breakers, they found the yellow-skinned crew dead or feeble from starvation. They learned no secrets from the dead, and whatever they learned from the occasional survivor was absorbed into their culture, much as meteors become a part of the earth on which they fall, losing all ties with the distant regions from which they came.

Before the end of the sixteenth century, there were shadows and echoes of western exploration in the misty Pacific. In the spring of 1579, Indians on the southern Oregon shore saw Sir Francis Drake's "Golden Hind," a dim, fantastic shape, ghosting through drifting fog. It was on this voyage that Drake named the region "New Albion," or New England; but his description fits nothing that ever was seen in that latitude on land or sea. In summer, through "stinking fog and Arctic cold," he reported "a low, naked coast covered with snow." Perhaps he saw sand dunes, and the rest was the chill of fog working on his imagination.

In that same neighborhood of time, *Acapulco* galleons were carrying treasure from Manila to Mexico, and the eastward drift of weather brought tribute to the feet of the Oregon mountains. Thirty-odd miles below the mouth of the Columbia River, a large vessel drove ashore on the sandspit that shelters Nehalem Bay. According to the Indians, all the crew had light complexions except one, whose skin was black. There were twenty men, and when they found there was no hope of getting the ship off the beach, they accepted the Indians' hospitality and built huts on shore. One of the things they brought from the ship was a heavy chest, which they wished to bury; but they were not satisfied with the low, almost featureless Nehalem shore. Five miles to the north was a high, bare mountain, with the Pacific forever charging and bursting against its western base—an unforgettable landmark, visible for many leagues at sea. The sailors carried their chest to the southwest side, where the mountain rose from a little meadow. Elk were feeding on the grassy slopes that went up toward the sky, and when the castaways saw them they cried, *"Carne!"* which is Spanish for "meat." From then, according to the Indians, the mountain was called Neacarne, "the place of the meat," which has been corrupted into Neahkahnie.

Near the foot of the mountain the sailors dug a pit into which they lowered the chest. Then they butchered the black-skinned man, put his body on the chest, filled the pit, and went back to live with the Indians—but not for long.

One of the habits of the castaways was to ignore marital arrangements and take their pick of women. When they refused to learn the ways of civilization, their hosts surrounded the huts and exterminated them, and peace descended upon Nehalem. The castaways were buried on the shore where they had been betrayed by their arrogance; the dead Negro slept on the mysterious chest at the foot of the mountain; the Indians, who feared places of burial, avoided the spot and in time forgot its location.

Long afterward, white settlers of Nehalem heard the Indian legends of the ship and the buried chest. The ship was still there, with its teakwood frames sticking up out of the sand, and in the meadow at the foot of Neahkahnie Mountain they found a large rock carved with European symbols: crosses, the letter *W*, and *DE* followed by a row of dots above an arrow that pointed toward the mountain. Near-by was a smaller rock with other symbols and an arrow pointing toward the larger rock. It took little imagination to deduce that the long-buried chest held treasure and that the carving on the larger rock was a code for locating it.

Few people can resist the idea of a treasure hunt, and enough have tried at Neahkahnie. None of them found the treasure, but old age found Pat Smith of Manzanita at the end of forty years' search. Lynn Wood, a Portland streetcar conductor, and his father drove a shaft into the side of the mountain, and they found death when it caved in on them. The chest is still concealed somewhere about Neahkahnie Mountain—if there ever was a chest—and the treasure rock is still there, in the tall grass behind a garage. Anyone so inclined may consider its obscure instructions and follow the direction of the arrow that points toward golden wealth, or old age, or sudden death.

Part of the treasure ship's cargo had been cakes of beeswax and candles. Occasionally the sea brought some of them to the surface. In 1813 Alexander Henry of the Northwest Company, visiting the site of Astoria, wrote in his *Journal:* "The old Clatsop chief arrived with salmon; with him a man with extraordinarily dark red hair, supposed to be an offspring of the ship wrecked within a few miles of the entrance of this

river many years ago. Great quantities of beeswax continue to be dug out of the sand near this spot, and the Indians bring it to trade with us." The following year he observed: "They bring us frequently lumps of beeswax fresh out of the sand which they collect on the coast to the south, where the Spanish ship was cast away some years ago and the crew all murdered by natives." Late that century learned men proved to their own satisfaction that the wax was of mineral origin from a natural outcropping. Their declaration was so emphatic that no one seems to have commented on the cleverness of nature who had stamped trademarks on the cakes of wax and made some of it in the shape of candles supplied with wicks. Hopeful money was sunk into an oil well where the skeleton of a derrick is now being covered by sand dunes. Later, more learned men proved scientifically that the substance was beeswax, and their analysis proved that its source was the region from which the *Acapulco* galleons sailed.

Near the end of the eighteenth century the tide of western trade and exploration swept along the Oregon coast. Ships of all the maritime nations sailed by in quest of the sea otter, or lay to while they sent boats ashore to slaughter the fabulous animals or trade with the Indians for their skins. In 1792 Captain Robert Gray entered the River of the West, which he named the Columbia, and thereafter the water-borne fur traffic flowed along the west and north sides of the coastal mountains. Early in the nineteenth century, Hudson's Bay men and their Canadian Indian trappers filtered down the Willamette Valley, on the east side of the Coast Range, and through the passes of the mountains. The world of the Indians was changing, but so far it was almost without pain. The fur brigades had no hunger for land or wish to alter the ways of the inhabitants.

GOLD IN THE HILLS

In the 1840's a new and irresistible tide set in from the East, a tide of American migration, streaming over the Oregon Trail, sweeping along the Willamette, populating the valley as it went, and filtering into the valleys of the Coast Range. For a while after the discovery of gold on the Sacramento some of the westward migration was diverted to the south. Americans poured into the gold fields of California, and they

continued to pour into the Willamette Valley, and presently they joined hands by land.

Messrs. James Cluggage and John R. Poole saw the possibilities of the tie-up and established a pack train between Yreka, California, and the rich Willamette Valley. The dusty trail had an unexpected golden by-path. One afternoon in the summer of 1851 Cluggage and Poole rested their mules in the Rogue River Valley, near the present site of Jacksonville. Two young men who were camped near-by confided that they had found traces of gold in the neighborhood, and Cluggage strolled into a gulch to investigate. He dug with his bowie knife and found nuggets which made him and his partner change their plans. They staked claims and made the usual attempt to keep it a secret. But miners smelled the new gold all the way from California, and by 1852 the stampede north made an undying column of dust from the Sacramento to the Rogue River. By 1853 the lonely camping place in the foothills had become the second largest city in Oregon: Jacksonville, with a population of ten thousand men and four white women. On Jackson Creek and in Rich Gulch the rockers and sluice boxes were busy every daylight hour. In 1860 the stage road was opened from Sacramento to Portland, and through the following years there rolled an increasing flood of wheeled traffic: ponderous freight wagons drawn by eight yoke of oxen; trains of Marietta wagons, each drawn by six spans of horses, with the bell team drawing the lead wagon. The silver laughter of the bells was the music of that road of dust and mud and sweat and curses and rumbling wheels, and it was useful as well as beautiful. On the mountain roads there were only occasional places wide enough for two wagons to pass, and when bullwhackers or teamsters heard the bright warning of bells they halted at the first passing place while the towering Marietta wagons went lurching by in the deep tide of dust. After the wagons came loaded pack mules, single file, in a column a quarter of a mile long. Twice a day the great red-and-yellow stagecoaches swept by, drawn by splendid matched horses, packed with bearded and dirty California miners, frock-coated gamblers, and travel-stained businessmen with dust-filmed silk hats. In the coaches and wagons and on horseback and on foot, there were men of half the races of the earth, coming to exploit or build. No one could have recorded who they all were, where they came from and what they did in Oregon, and what became of them. An impossible task,

but Peter Britt came nearer accomplishing it than anyone had a right to expect.

Peter Britt was born in the village of Wallenstadt in the Swiss Alps. He began painting when he was big enough to hold a brush, and by his teens he was an accomplished artist. Then science produced the miracle of the daguerreotype, and young Peter bought one of the first outfits and learned its mysteries. In 1844 the Britt family sailed for America, and from New York they traveled west to Highland, Illinois. For six years Peter Britt made daguerreotypes of Illinois pioneers. Then, in the spring of 1852, he bought a Colt five-shooter and a double-barreled weapon that was half rifle and half shotgun—and he set out on the Oregon Trail. His party looked like an excursion—four young men on horseback, with a wagon for supplies. They took eight months to loaf across the Great Plains and the Rockies. Once a party of Sioux Indians swept down from a ridge and raced their ponies in a narrowing circle around the young travelers. The others wanted to kill as many Indians as they could before they died, but Peter argued them into waiting. When the Indians tired of their merry-go-round they galloped up and spread a blanket. Peter threw in some hardtack; the Indians gathered it up and galloped away.

When the young men arrived in Portland, the gold rush was roaring through southern Oregon, hungry for supplies, and Peter Britt became a packer on the trail that led across the wild Siskiyous. But Peter was an artist, and in 1854 he built a log cabin in Jacksonville and put up a sign: "GALLERY." Here he began recording in daguerreotypes the pageant of gold-rush days. He also kept up with advancing science. When photography was perfected he bought equipment for the new process. He met a girl he had known in Switzerland, and they were married. In 1862 Peter Britt built a house at the edge of town, an imposing frame house with a tower. On the top floor was the photograph gallery with a big square skylight in the roof. Around the house the Britts planted their garden: flowers and hedges and young apple and walnut and orange trees and little Italian cypresses. And there their three children grew up.

When Cluggage dug in Rich Gulch with his bowie knife, Jacksonville sprang up around him. When the gold gave out, the town became quieter and smaller. The railroad passed it by in favor of Medford, six miles

away, and that city drew in the trade of the rich Rogue River Valley. Jacksonville was left with its memories and echoes of great days.

Today Jacksonville is a ghost town where people continue to live— seven hundred where there were once ten thousand. People are there because it is a pleasant place, and because motor transportation makes possible a town without industries. Men drive to work at logging camps back in the hills and to sawmills in the valley around prosperous Medford. In the town there is the feeling of enough room and not too much hurry along streets shaded by great oak and walnut and locust trees. The buildings of the past are there because there is no crowding present to demand their place. Boy Scouts and the Grange meet in the great brick courthouse of the eighties that has stood empty since Medford became the county seat. The shell of the old brick building which was the United States Hotel still stands on California Avenue, but a sign over the entrance says, "MUSEUM, admission 10c." The curator of the museum looks as if he might have driven the stage in the days of Jacksonville's rough-and-ready glory. He sits with his cronies on a bench across the street; when he sees museum customers hesitating in front of the ghost hotel he crosses over to show them the hodgepodge of relics from old days. He labeled some of the articles himself; in one case a crumbling skeleton is marked, "A Good Old Indian," preserving the attitude of the past along with its bones.

Farther up the street fortunes in nuggets and gold dust once poured into Beekman's Bank. The square, one-story, wooden building is still there on the corner with its sign: "C. C. Beekman, Wells Fargo Agent." There is a notice over the cashier's window, "Bank Closed," and the clock is stopped at four. Everything remains as it was. The iron door of the stone vault is closed, and for two generations the fire has been out of the stove in Beekman's private office. The gold scales wait on the counter worn by elbows and sacks of nuggets and dust, and old placards look down from the walls: "WELLS FARGO & CO., Express Office. Reasonable Rates on Freight and Treasure." "WELLS FARGO & CO., Drafts on Union Bank, London." "Gold Dust Shipped to the Atlantic States and Insured." "WELLS FARGO & CO., Drafts on Paris." "Gold Dust Accepted for Coinage, U. S. Mint."

Peter Britt's house stands on the hill at the edge of town, almost buried under vines that run up the cupola and overhang the one-word sign:

"GALLERY." The garden he planted has grown up around the house like the garden where Beauty slept. The boxwood hedge is ten feet high; the little palm he brought from California looks into the upper windows; the dark Italian cypresses are seventy-foot spires, and the English walnut tree is an airy world for the birds. In the house, which sleeps among the foliage and green shadows, Emil Britt and his sister keep faith with the past and preserve the memory of their father and his work. Emil, white-haired, handsome, and soft-voiced, more European gentleman than Oregon pioneer, shows visitors about. On the table are the textbooks of his youth. His father was from the German-speaking part of Switzerland, and most of the art books are in German. Peter's children studied with tutors.

On the top floor is the gallery, under the great skylight. Here on its tripod, ready for use, is Peter Britt's daguerreotype camera, a solid, lensed box of wood, built to last forever. Here are the adjustable headrests with iron jaws that fitted the sitter's skull and held him rigid for the half hour while light made its slow impression on the plate. Here, where it was used for the last time half a century ago, is the camera for photographs, massive on its heavy tripod. Across the room is the background which Peter Britt used in the eighties: a painted terrace with an awning, and potted palms at the head of a stone stairway leading down to a lake flecked with white sails.

This still place seems far away from the roaring days of Oregon's gold rush, but the historic faces of the past are here. The faces of men and women who made and marred the history of southern Oregon look out from the walls and up from the glass cases: California miners and young ladies from New York and Illinois; the gambler, and the nun, and the Indian chief; the sailor who jumped his ship, and the young clergyman who came to save souls; the actress from San Francisco, with the daringly short skirt and painted toenails; the solid businessman, and the young Indian woman in her beaded buckskin dress and cap.

PERSONAL PORTRAITS

To know who these people were and what they did is to know the history of southwestern Oregon.

Portrait of a gambler, in a frock coat and wide, flat-brimmed black hat. His drooping black mustache would do for melodrama, and his sneer

gives the look of muttering, "Foiled!" *He found plenty of games and dust in early Jacksonville, but here miners didn't react the way they did beside the Sacramento. One of his gambler friends, observing that Jacksonville needed livening up, shot the first miner he met, just for the hell of it. Jacksonville had no government or law, but the citizens held a mass meeting and elected an alcalde. It was the idea of a miner who had lived in California under Spanish rule. The alcalde was a judge elected by the people, and as soon as he was elected, he heard the evidence against the gambler. When he had heard it, he said, "Swing!" And the gambler was swung from the limb of an oak tree. Later, a miner tried to do his partner out of a fortune because he had been too sick to help work the claim, and the alcalde upheld him. But the citizens shouted, "Outrage!" and they elected a supreme alcalde who reversed the decision. It's an odd sort of place where they hang murderers pronto, and even injustices are corrected.* So the gambler stands for his portrait, uneasily, with his hat on, ready to get out of town if the miners of Jacksonville develop any more odd quirks.

Daguerreotype of a young lady, seated, with her hands in the lap of her dark dress, with its demure white collar and cuffs, her hair parted above her sober face and swept back over her ears in the style of the 1850's. The composition is beautiful, and the smooth-toned portrait has the quality of a painting from an age when girls were made to fit a subdued pattern of gentility. You seem to have fitted the pattern very well, young lady, and now you are committed to it forever. But didn't you have moments of revolt against the dead pattern laid down in a living world?

She was Olive Oatman, one-time resident of Jacksonville. Yes, there were definite ideas of conduct and deportment in those days, but history was boisterous, and rough winds sometimes fluttered the pages of Godey's Lady's Book. *That faint smudge on Miss Oatman's firm chin? The daguerreotype has dimmed a little, but with a magnifying glass you can see the smudge separate into three tattooed lines. . . .*

When Olive Oatman was a child on the Oregon Trail, the wagon train was attacked by Indians, her parents killed, and she was made a captive. She became a legend of the plains—a white girl growing up among the wild Apaches. Eventually she was ransomed by carpenter Grinnell of Fort Yuma, who had heard of her brother's search for her, and rela-

tives brought her to Jacksonville—an athletic and copper-tanned young woman, with three lines tattooed on her chin.

In Jacksonville Miss Oatman brushed up on English and she even learned a few words of French. She memorized one of Pope's poems, and she attended worship in the first Protestant church in southern Oregon. She was taught knitting and embroidery, and she was taken to quilting parties and church socials; she went to the dressmaker, and she sat for her daguerreotype in Peter Britt's log-house gallery. While she did these things, the Apaches were out in the sun and wind and rain, raiding their enemies, riding over the desert, camping under the stars.

Miss Oatman did not discuss her two lives until she was a young lady, schooled in the ways of civilization. Then she said to her foster family: "This world is wide and beautiful—and white people shut themselves up in prisons of their own making. This is a world of great silences and great music of rivers and weather and wind. White people do not let themselves hear the silences—or the music. All they hear is their own noise. This world and the sun and moon and stars were made for people with bodies and souls. White people are ashamed of their bodies and they ought to be ashamed of what they have done to their souls. I am going back to people who live in the world."

Factual historians say that Olive Oatman thought better of going back to the Apaches; instead, she went to Albany, New York, where she finished her education. In 1863 she was touring the eastern States, lecturing on the Indians, and afterward she married and went to live in Texas.

Portrait of a Chinese miner in a high-collared jacket and a bell-shaped cap, with a queue down his back.

Miners in that far corner of the earth liked to send pictures to the folks at home. It didn't make much difference whether the home was in Pennsylvania or Shantung Province. There were Chinese miners in the stampede to Jacksonville, and some of them stayed to work the worked-out mines. They made a living, but how good a living no one knew. When they were asked how much they made, their stock reply was, "Two-bitty day." Recently unearthed records show that Chinese miners sent millions of dollars home from the Oregon mountains.

Photograph of a pioneer businesswoman, with a stout frame, firm upholstery, rugged, cheery face, and an eye for business.

In the eighties, at the time of the photograph, she was Madame Holt. Before that she had a French name, but she traded it for Holt and a brickkiln. Madame De Raboen was a hearty soul, good-natured without a drink and better-natured with one—and a good businesswoman all the time. She ran the Franco-American Hotel, and miners with dust paid handsomely for accommodations. Those who were broke were never turned away hungry. The Franco-American was more tradition than building, and when it burned Madame yearned for something grand made of brick. Brick cost more than she could pay in cash, so she married Mr. Holt, the brickmason, and he became her willing helper. He mined clay and burned bricks, and built the United States Hotel to her order. Before it was done, President Hayes was touring the West, and he wired for accommodations. The President of the United States was just the class of guest Madame Holt had visualized for her new hotel, and her only regret was that the right people had heard of it too soon. But she was the master of situations, and when the presidential party arrived, they were shown into a handsome suite, smelling of new plaster and rich with new furniture, mirrors and rugs and paintings. The bill for the night was $200, and the President declared it was an outrage. Madame said, "Yesterday this suite was an empty shell, and look at it now. A miracle takes hard work, and $200 is a small charge." The President agreed with her and even praised one of the paintings. That was a mistake. It was a life-size portrait of the Madame, which was a lot of picture. She immediately presented him with the painting, and when he demurred, she had her Chinese houseboy crate it and load it on board his stage. Detractors say that the embarrassed President had the thing unloaded at Salem and put in dead storage, but Madame Holt knew otherwise. When people admired the photograph taken by Peter Britt, Madame would say, "It is a nice little thing, but not in the class with my portrait which hangs in the White House."

Early photograph of a Rogue River Indian chief, with long, unbraided hair, and a muzzle-loading rifle on his shoulder. The chief's somber, enduring face turned sideways to show his rugged profile.

The Indians of this region were not always somber. The French Canadians of the fur brigades found them high-spirited and full of mischief. Because of that, they called them "Les Coquins," and they

named the river "La Rivière aux Coquins," which the English translated into Rogue River.

The Indians had their own word for "rogue," and they applied it to white men who stormed into their country, uprooting the earth, cutting down the trees, killing their game, and misusing their women. In 1855, from California to Canada, there were sporadic attacks on the invaders. Around Jacksonville the Rogues sometimes picked off a white man whom they did not like. Then the miners would put down their picks and shovels, take up their rifles, and raid the nearest Indian camp, where they found only the women and children at home. After a few such sorties, the miners began seizing likely-looking young Indian women. From that the Rogues assumed that women were no longer noncombatants, and unlucky white women were killed or taken captive. One day two young Indian boys wandered into Jacksonville, wide-eyed at the great encampment of the white men. Someone decided the two were spies, and half an hour later a mob hung them from a tree. From that the Rogues assumed that children were also combatants, and the war continued on a still lower plane.

From the gallery you can see Table Mountain, low at this side and level as its name, and dropping off out there in a high, sheer cliff. According to local tradition, a handful of Rogues made their last stand up there against an army of miners and settlers who forced the trail on this side and stormed up the mountain. When the warriors saw that they were trapped, they retreated to the edge of the cliff and jumped into space. They were the first Americans, but their traditions were Asiatic.

UNYIELDING FRONTIER

West of the rich valley, famous for its pears, the Rogue River snakes through the Siskiyous and empties into the Pacific at Gold Beach. In past times it mingled particles of gold with its silt, and there was placer mining on the beach. Gold is supposed to be the most enduring of metals, but it melted away like snow, and the citizens of that region turned their attention to raising sheep and cattle, which could be driven to market over rough mountain trails. The only transportation was an occasional small sailing vessel that put into the shallow mouth of the Rogue River, which became shallower after a while. The sailing vessels stopped coming, and the steamship and the railroad never came. Curry County was

shaped by isolation that was only cracked at the edge when the Coast Highway was built through.

On the west side of Gold Beach the Pacific breaks on the low, flat sandy shore with a sound like rolling drums; on the east it is crowded by the Siskiyous—wooded mountains broken by high, grassy patches and penetrated by green valleys. In summer, under a white daytime moon, the rough mountains and green valleys look like the land of the Lotus Eaters. But the people of the region have learned self-sufficiency with isolation and they have no particular fondness for Greek poetry or Greeks or any "foreigners," which includes people from other States and other parts of Oregon. Newcomers are called "Johnny-come-late-lies," and they are apt to be out of step with the citizens who like things as they are. Of late years Gold Beach has had an invasion of Johnny-come-latelies, and reactionary old-timers blame them for the fact that Gold Beach has become an incorporated town. As the county seat of Curry County, Gold Beach, unincorporated, enjoyed the benefits of sheriff and jail and courthouse without cost. Now there will be taxes to pay. There will also be improvements—and more taxes. The sentiments of the reactionaries were summed up a few years ago by a county official. When a Johnny-come-lately suggested the town could be improved, the old man said, "Listen, I was born here and grew up here, and I like things the way they are. Anyone who doesn't like them can get to hell out of here."

The atmosphere of the region is insidious. An outsider, annoyed by its stubborn independence, begins blueprinting changes—and realizes with a start that the annoyances of the place are part of its rugged charm. Who would delete the Mad Hatter's tea party from *Alice in Wonderland*? And who, on second thought, would abolish the Dragon Restaurant for a colorless chain lunchroom? The Dragon is one of the few eating places at Gold Beach, and at almost every meal it is the scene of some diverting crisis. As the customer enters he is greeted by a sign: "We reserve the right to refuse service to anyone." The sign means what it says. Recently, while some customers were trying to get in during the noon hour, the door was closed in their faces and held shut by a young waitress who shouted, "You can't come in, you can't come in! The cook doesn't want to cook any more!" And the customer is not always right. Down the street during the war was an equally independent but more

helpful place of business. It advertised fishing tackle, live bait, and fishing licenses. The store was closed indefinitely, but a supplementary sign in the window read: "No more tackle until after the war. You can catch your own bait. Get your fishing license at the Courthouse."

The settlements and farms of Curry County are for those who like the last frontier and want it to stay, and for those who like each other's company. Beyond the settlements and farms are the rough, forested mountains for those who like to live beyond the frontier and who prefer their own company.

Kurt Miller, a powerful, reticent man of thirty with a love of the woods, built a cabin back on Wildhorse Mountain; he pastured a few cattle in the open glades and hunted in the wilderness, where game wardens never bothered him. He was there at fifty, still powerful, and more taciturn. Now and then he drove a steer down the mountain trails to Gold Beach and exchanged it for cash, and he packed in his supplies. At eighty Kurt was still there. On rare occasions he came into Gold Beach, keen-eyed and shaggy and stooped, and as fiercely independent as an aging grizzly. Now and then someone from town paid a visit to the old man on Wildhorse Mountain. If Kurt liked him, he was treated to a meal of venison and biscuits and coffee. If Kurt did not like his looks, the visitor was glad to get down the trail alive. His friends soon learned to announce themselves from a distance.

Kurt was on Wildhorse Mountain when he was well in his eighties and he is still there, but no one knows where. Once, when he had not been down for a long time, his friends went up to investigate. The shack was unoccupied, Kurt's rifle was missing, and his dogs were running wild in the woods. They never found him.

Curry County, Oregon, has known isolation, but it is doubtful if there are any isolated places left in the world, or any backwaters that do not feel the tide of events. For better and worse, Curry County is a part of Europe and Asia and everywhere else. Just now, Gold Beach is in the thick of its second gold rush, which stems from Holland and Japan. The Nazis broke the Holland dikes and let the sea cover the bulb beds, and the Japanese have alienated themselves from flowers. There has been a scarcity of bulbs for forcing. Scarcest and most profitable of all were the dwarf Easter lilies. The lilies flourish between the toes of land which the Siskiyous dabble in the Pacific. In misty little valleys around

Gold Beach and in the town, ranks of green-uniformed lilies stand with their white trumpets to their lips, blowing the last call to fortune. You could hear it, except for the drumming of the surf that marches in from Asia. Some people have heard it, and you can get it from them, second hand, in stories that have the sound of all gold rushes: land that citizens could have bought once for a dollar and a half an acre now sells for a thousand. Mr. Dodge laughed when his wife wanted to take up lily culture, but she persisted and put in a third of an acre— and realized thirty-five thousand dollars the first season. Now Mr. Dodge has given up his business to spray and cultivate lilies. No, the Dodges didn't take all their thirty-five thousand in cash; they saved some of the bulbs to pyramid their fortune. . . . Mr. Curry has a few acres of lilies in little valley patches scattered from the edge of the beach to the foot of the mountains, and the last time he added up the profits he expected in one season, they came to two hundred thousand dollars.

The big money is in the bulb, which divides and quadruples into many bulbs, and the scales on the stems turn into more bulbs. Looked at the right way, each lily is like a Standard Oil Company dissolving itself into many profitable companies. Bulbs are the thing! But while producing them, the lily produces blossoms that may sell for as high as twenty-five cents a trumpet. A plant may have one or half a dozen, and florists are eager for them. Gold Beach ships lily blossoms as far as Chicago.

The gold rush is on! In the misty little valleys ranks of green-uniformed lilies stand with white trumpets to their lips. The throats of the trumpets are gold, and they are blowing the last call to fortune. You could hear the trumpets except for the louder drumming of the surf that marches in from Asia. You hear them a little anyway: New York is calling for bulbs; Chicago is calling for more blossoms; the fortunes of Gold Beach are shaped by events in Holland and Japan.

MRS. BLAKE TAKES THE MAIL BOAT

Gold Beach is beside the mouth of the Rogue River. Agness, thirty-two miles back in the mountains, is the head of navigation and the last outpost. The mail boat runs between the two settlements, carrying incidental passengers and freight.

Mrs. Blake, who lives near Agness, has come down the river on a

shopping trip and she puts up at the Gold Beach Hotel. In the evening she sits in the new lobby of the old hotel, where there are people. Behind its plate-glass window the unfinished lobby is bare enough: two sofas and a few chairs standing on the newly laid linoleum. But the patient and soft-spoken proprietor is triumphant. When the hotel was new, in a moment of indulgence, he rented the lower floor to a druggist, and he had to wait fourteen years to get it back. The drugstore moved out a few days ago, and the hotel is coming into its own.

In the lobby there is talk of lily culture, and talk of the jack salmon that are beginning to strike in the jaws of the river. Someone timed them: in ten minutes the half-dozen fishermen who were out hooked five salmon and landed four of them. Two young women travelers are going to Agness in the mail boat. They confide the fact anxiously, having heard stories of the perilous run up the rapids. . . . Two strangers join the talking circle—a lean, roughly-dressed man of sixty, with a humorous, wry face, and a blond young woman, soft-voiced and confident and daintily dressed. They talk about themselves and their work. They are part of the roving crew that mends the roads of southwestern Oregon. The man is a foreman, and the dainty blonde a "grease monkey." She is also a "cream puff" because she once ran from a bear. There are other women in the road gang, truck drivers and "gravel-hack" drivers, and they live in their own trailers or put up at what hotels they can find. No, the war had nothing to do with it; the road gang was coeducational before the war. The foreman is feeling good because he has a document which entitles his crew to breakfast. The Dragon Restaurant didn't want to be bothered, and the foreman had to get a court order compelling the place to serve meals at a reasonable hour. Farther south, in the Pistol River region, the foreman had less luck during the gasoline shortage. The neighborhood was a closed corporation, with everyone interrelated, and the gas-station operator served only his relatives. The road crew had to make an eighty-mile round trip to California for gasoline so they could repair the highway in front of the clannish gas pump. . . .

In the morning the little hotel lobby is sociable again. The road menders have had their court-order breakfast and have gone to work. But the tourists are there, waiting for the mail-boat car; Mrs. Blake is there with her purchases, and the unshaven proprietor is there, talking with sleepy geniality. Two of his guests were taking the 2:00 A.M. bus

to San Francisco; he had to set his alarm clock to wake him early, so he could wake his guests. A sport fisherman had come in on the bus to take the room which had just been vacated, and one way and another there hadn't been much sleep.

At nine Captain Elliott of the mail boat arrives; the travelers pile into his car and are driven to the river landing where other passengers are waiting. There are over twenty of them, which means two boats. The boats are lying beside the little dock, with their engines warming up—slender, half-decked craft, thirty-odd feet long, with powerful eight-cylinder motors. The freight and mail sacks are on board, the passengers climb into the thwartship seats, and the boats cast off. Each boat has a crew of one, who stands at the high steering wheel behind the roaring motor; if he didn't see all he could, the boat would never reach Agness.

On one side of the river there are naked hills which the Indians burned over for centuries; on the other side the hills have been protected from fire in recent times and already they are shaggy with timber. Between the bare hills and the forested ones, the boats drive up the swift river, between half-sunken snags and a clay bank close enough to be touched with a yardstick. Buzzards and sea gulls soar overhead, and cranes stand solemnly on long legs. Ahead, a willow stake that marks a turn in the channel has sprouted small branches and leaves. (Mrs. Blake recalls that a navigation stake once grew into a big tree out in the river. It was there for years, until the flotsam of a winter flood battered it down.)

The first boat reaches the leafy stake, turns, and drives across the river, straight for a gravel bar, and the second boat follows. In the middle, the gravel bar is cut by a channel ten feet wide, and the boats roar through, with their keels pounding and grinding over the gravel. They swing and labor up the slope of broken water on a riffle, and rumble through quieter waters. A big crane swoops down toward the second boat, as if he meant to strafe it—then zooms away with a derisive squawk, his straight legs parallel behind him. A sea gull has just landed a fish on a rock ashore and he stands by, sulkily, while five buzzards eat it for him, smirking hypocritically. Nature has decreed that they eat only dead things, and they use it as an excuse for making the gulls do their fishing.

There is white water ahead, and the first boat lurches out of it, unexpectedly, and makes a forced landing against the bank. By the time the second boat comes up, Captain Elliott has removed the bent pro-

peller which he holds against a boulder and beats into shape with a much-used hammer. The situation is in hand, and the second boat lurches up the steep riffle, with its engine laboring like a truck on a heavy grade and the keel striking rock now and then. Mrs. Blake recalls the earlier mail boat, with a one-lung engine and a Rogue Indian boatman who steered with his feet while he helped his craft up the riffles with a pole.

Above the riffle the tourists exclaim over a spotted fawn swimming in a deep pool, while a doe watches anxiously from a rock. In a reach as smooth as green glass, the repaired first boat dashes alongside, and Captain Elliott hands Mrs. Blake a piece of mail which he has just sorted, a letter from Sears and Roebuck. The first boat takes the lead again while passengers kid Mrs. Blake about her special delivery.

The second boat has mail for Lobster Creek. The boatman has to back into the awkward landing, with passengers catching the tops of small willows and helping pull the boat in. (Picking up the mail on the way down-river is easier. Each landing has a long pole extending over the water, with a device that releases the mail sack when it is snatched by the boatman. At Lobster Creek the mail sack holder is made of snap clothespins, but settlers of another school of thought use rattraps.) The boatman hands the mail-order packages to a waiting settler, poles the boat into the clear, and gets under power. The boat drives past a tilted hayfield peppered with black stumps; past shores heavily wooded with fir and maple and alder and bay and madroña and spruce and smoke bush, with bloom that really looks like blue wood smoke; and it passes cliffs where azaleas grow and bloom on shelves of bare rock.

Ahead is Hawkins Landing. Some of the passengers comment on the group of comfortable buildings on the hill and ask the name of the village. Mrs. Blake is amused. That is no village; it is only a farm. The Hawkins are Rogue Indians, and they need all the buildings for themselves and their stock, and for visiting relatives and their saddle horses. Yes, there are more Indians than whites on the river. Some of them run a fishing resort, but most of them do some farming and raise beef cattle, and they make out at least as well as their white neighbors.

No one is in sight at Hawkins Landing, only a big red collie coming down to the beach. With perfect timing, he and the boat reach the landing float at the same moment. The boatman reaches out the mail sack,

which the dog takes in his mouth. The boat roars on up the river, and the dog starts up the hill with the mail. His name is "Tarzan," and he has been meeting the mail boat for years—with one temperamental interlude. The first boats he met were painted red, and the boats are red now. But one season they were given a coat of white paint, and Tarzan would have nothing to do with them. The next season, when the boats were painted red again, Tarzan met the first boat, and he has been collecting the mail ever since.

The boat drives on up the river, lurches around boulders in a narrow, crooked channel, and labors up the roaring slopes of riffles. A passenger asks Mrs. Blake how she likes to make this trip every time she goes shopping. This is nothing, she says, and she points to bleached drift logs and the wreckage of a boat hanging up in the trees seventy feet above the river. Once in a winter flood, when the river was up there, she and her husband came down to Gold Beach in the mail boat—at night, with the maniac river full of drift logs and big trees it had torn from the mountainsides. Having started, there was no turning back, and it had been touch and go in the dark and the hellish din of water and crashing logs. No, she hadn't been afraid. Captain Elliott wouldn't have started down if he hadn't thought they could make it.

The second boat runs alongside a gravel bar, where a thin, somberly dressed settler waits for the boatman to throw him his bundle of mail. The settler smiles and calls in a cultured foreign voice, "I thank you for the package last night," and the boat rumbles on up the river. He is Louis Grass, a Yugoslav, who is said to have a fine collection of degrees from European universities—anyone who hears him discourse can well believe it. Louis is in his seventies, although he doesn't look it, and he lives by doing a little hunting and trapping. He came to the Rogue River years ago to forget the fevered Old World in this cool silence.

Close to the channel a small herd of goats plays on the rocks in happy exile. Tan and white goat shapes stand out against the dark shore with symbolic clearness. The goats belong to people on the other side of the river. But they ate the garden and were ferried over here where they do no harm or good. Last year the goats adopted an orphan fawn and treated it as nicely as their own kids; but other beings are less considerate and the fawn has disappeared.

Beyond is Benson's Landing. You can see their house and fields on

that hill, a mile back from the river. The Bensons like privacy, and they have lived there for three generations without cutting a road to the river. There is just a narrow trail, and they come to meet the mail boat with a saddle horse or pack horse, depending upon whether they expect mail or freight. There is freight this time, but evidently they expected only mail. Benson and his son-in-law wait on the shore with a fine saddle horse. The boat pulls up beside the landing and the boatman hands the heavy boxes to the tall man with bright eyes and leather-tanned face. While the smaller man is checking them, the horse wheels and starts back toward the hills. The tall man goes in pursuit and brings him back. As the boat rumbles up the river the tourists dispute about which man was which. Most of them agree that the son-in-law was the tall man who lifted the freight ashore and pursued the horse so nimbly. No, that was the father-in-law, who is somewhere in his nineties.

This is Copper Canyon, in the shadow of somber cliffs. Here the water really piles up in flood season. By measurement, the river has risen as much as thirty-nine feet in thirty hours. Up there, scratched into the face of the cliff, is Copper Canyon Trail for the hardy. It comes in above Painted Rock Creek and turns along the shoulder of the cliff where it meets the river. Mrs. Blake has been over the trail three times, without getting used to it. Each time, she crawled on her stomach, vomiting into the abyss below. From that tiny gravel bar, between the foot of the cliff and the sounding river, they picked up Indian Jim last year, very dead. He had hurtled down from the trail above, but it is still disputed whether he fell or was thrown.

Copper Canyon is gone like a dream and the boats rumble in tandem past wilderness shores and lodges owned by California millionaires. You might think people who choose this wild place should have their heads examined, but the examiners come here, too. That lodge is owned by Portland brain surgeons.

There's Crooked Riffle, with white water coming down its ramp like a zigzag of lightning. The landing is at the edge of the "zig," and the boat pulls alongside and stops in white water while the mail is handed to the caretaker. Then the motor roars and the boat labors up the slope of the "zig," wrenches around sharply into the "zag," and climbs to level, quieter waters.

At the end of their trip the boats are docked by running ashore along-

side a steep gravel beach, and the passengers scramble out. This is Agness, they are told, but they do not see anything except the Rogue River going away downstream to mountains that are incredibly purple, the gravel beach at their feet, and the wooded shore above them. The settlement is up there, behind the trees, what there is of it: the idyllic inn, a decaying log house that was once the Federal Building, the post office-store, the grammar school, and a few houses. But they all have their stories—the stories of people. Amaziah Aubrey, from California, was the first postmaster, and the settlement of Agness was named for his daughter Agnes. (Some postal authority added the extra "s" and Agnes' own father couldn't get it removed.) A later postmaster was the son of General Tom Rilea. Postmaster Rilea grew up in the roar of Chicago and he found peace at the last outpost on the Rogue River. He said he would never again go in sight of smoke from a factory chimney or within sound of a train whistle, and he never did. He lived up here for forty years and he is buried up here.

NOT EVERYBODY ENDS UP IN CALIFORNIA

Other people who have known cities have come up here to something they considered better. Like Arthur Dorn, who comes to the store for his mail and for supplies which he packs up to his home on the mountain. He was a brilliant criminal lawyer in Los Angeles. Now he translates from Sanskrit and writes delightful letters to his friends about his few mountain neighbors. Among his favorites is Johnny Fry, who is one of the world's most generous men. Johnny sends word that the great platinum meteor is still buried in the side of Brushy Mountain: anyone interested can come and get it. The platinum meteor is the one that fell the night in 1857 when the Volunteers were going home from the Rogue Indian War. (The geology department of the State University verifies the meteor, but suggests that it is nickel and not platinum.)

Learned men come up by choice, but children are at a disadvantage here. There is no high school, and children for the upper grades are sent down-river to Gold Beach, where the State pays their board for the school term. But the one-room grade school has its moments, and conflicting races and views have boiled in that little melting pot. During the war there was trouble with children of Jehovah's witnesses who

refused to salute the flag. They and their parents battled the school to a draw. Then the Rogue River Indian boys lost their patience and made the Witnesses salute the flag, kneeling. To be sure, their grand-parents had killed and been killed by American settlers; but the boys are Americans and their older brothers were fighting in Europe and on the islands of the Pacific.

Superpatriotism can hurt what it defends, and self-sufficiency has its dangers but it also has its rugged virtues. During the war some four hundred young men of Curry County served in the armed forces. While citizens in other places were still debating over what the GIs would come home to, the people of Curry County faced their boys' future in the tradition of the pioneers. They acquired and subdivided and laid out farms, stocked them, and repaired old buildings or put up new ones. Their answer to the problem was not a theory but the fact of security and something better than the boys had known before.

THE FRIENDLY LAND

Young men from other wars have come home to Oregon, and others have come there by ways so indirect that their stories read like novels.

Albert Matson was a Swedish sailor who spent twenty years at sea and had adventures. Early in the American Civil War, he left a ship in New York and enlisted in the Union Navy. He did not have much to learn about ships and the sea, and before long he found himself with the fleet that blockaded Cape Fear, Virginia. The setup was like this: nature laid a thick fog bank off the coast; Union ships patrolled the inner side, and British ships with supplies for the Confederates lay out-side, waiting their chance to slip through. When watchful waiting grew monotonous, the Union commander would call for volunteers to drum up business. A dozen tars would put on Confederate uniforms and row through the fog bank to the blockade-runners lying outside. "Ahoy, there! The damn Yankees have mined the harbor, but we can pilot you in blindfold, Suh. Let's get under sail while their patrol boats are gone!" If the ruse worked, the blockade-runner piled on sail and drove through the fog bank into bright sunshine that gleamed on the guns of the wait-ing Union fleet. If the ruse was detected, the volunteers never came back.

It was a good life to Albert Matson, the Swede who had been reborn an

American sailor with a cutlass in his hand. He helped trap three block-ade-runners and might have trapped more if his ship hadn't been or-dered to the California coast. While she was on the way around Cape Horn, Lee surrendered, and the crew was mustered out at San Francisco.

Albert Matson had helped his new country through a war, and he spent the last of his pay celebrating the peace. Then he took the first shore job that offered. It was in the redwood country of northern Cali-fornia. Swedes are supposed to be born loggers, but Matson knew bet-ter than that, and he knew still better after a season in the giant woods, and he told amusing stories of a sailor s struggles with a crosscut saw. He returned to the sailors' boardinghouse in San Francisco, knowing that the chances favored a long sea voyage, with or without his consent, but he went back because he didn't have anywhere else to go.

At the boardinghouse, the keeper told Matson that the internal revenue men were after him; he didn't know why. That was before the days of income taxes, but still the sailor didn't like the sound of it, and he felt inclined to ship out on the first vessel that offered. He thought it over for a day, then spruced up and went to face the music.

At the revenue office an official shook hands with Matson and pre-sented him with four thousand dollars in cash. The sailor knew it was a mistake, but when he demurred, the official mentioned ships' names with a familiar sound. Matson remembered them: blockade-runners he had helped lure through a fog bank into the arms of the Union fleet. Quite so, and this four thousand dollars was his share of the prize money. It was his, and it was real.

Sudden fortune is strong drink to some men, but it was black coffee to Matson. He went out of the office, a man of purpose. On the way to his boardinghouse he bought a Prince Albert coat and everything that went with it. A week later he was a gentlemanly passenger on board a ship bound for Sweden. A few months more, and he was back in the home from which he had started twenty years before. But the world had changed, and Albert Matson had changed. Now he was a man of purpose, with an adopted country on the other side of the Atlantic. He stayed only long enough to marry the girl of his choice, and they sailed for New York.

Matson had promised to show his bride a thrilling world, and he did. The Union Pacific had just been completed; young Mrs. Matson was

one of the first women to see the brave new continent from a train window. There were blue-uniformed soldiers on the train, with their rifles always at hand. Sometimes the car filled with powder smoke as the soldiers exchanged shots with the Indians, and sometimes the train stopped while they piled out and fought a pitched battle. Sometimes the train paused in a sea of grass and flowers, and the soldiers in blue stood guard in the spring sunshine while the crew replaced ties which the Indians had burned.

It was a fabulous wedding trip across a thrilling land, but when the Matsons reached San Francisco, Albert felt anxious. Four thousand dollars don't last forever, and he had to make a living. He had a mate's papers, but there was his bride, and he didn't want to go to sea again. After a while there was nothing else for it; he called on Captain Frank Simpson, who had shipping interests. "I need a job," he said, "but I don't want to go deepwater. I have a young wife who is a stranger in this country, and she doesn't know the language. She shouldn't be alone for too long. If I could get a coastwise ship. . . "

Captain Simpson said, "The sea's no place for you, Matson. Take the schooner "Gotena" to North Bend—that's on Coos Bay, Oregon. Take your wife along and go ashore at North Bend. My brother, who runs the sawmill, will have a job waiting for you. Stay ashore and raise a family, and God bless you."

Concerning North Bend, the pioneer historian, Dodge, observed:

It is on a Northeastern point of land that seems to have been formed by nature to enable pioneer mill men to inaugurate the most substantial and prominent saw mill and ship yard on the coast. Beside the mill and yard, there are elegant dwellings and cozy cottages and one store only for trading. The whole area is owned by the Simpsons. . . . They have strenuously forbidden the sale of intoxicants or immoral practices on the premises.

The Simpsons, you may gather, were paternalistic. Albert Matson worked in the mill for several years, then moved to the little settlement of Marshfield, on the south side of Coos Bay. There the Matsons lived the rest of their able and good lives, and there their sons grew up.

The Coos Bay region was opened for settlement in 1855, and pioneers began drifting in. It was a rich region, difficult to manage. Around the great bay, at the foot of the mountains, the flat land and water inter-

penetrated: mud flats and rivers and creeks and sloughs segmented by beaver dams, and all the solid ground was heavily timbered. There was little room to grow food, but it was already growing everywhere. The maze of waters was full of fish of every kind, and its surface was alive with ducks and geese in season; the beaches were packed with clams, and the woods were full of game: grouse and deer and elk and bears. The pioneers ate well while they slowly hacked clearings out of the woods, and settlements began to appear. The first settlement was on the peninsula that protects the bay: Empire City, founded by P. B. Marple, who led a party over the mountains from Jacksonville, with Indian guides. Lockhart settled at what became North Bend, but it didn't amount to much until the Simpsons built their sawmill. Marshfield was the scene of a land fraud so devious that it took settlers twenty years to establish claim to their property.

About this time California had more felons than she could use. One batch of freed convicts was loaded in a ship and sent north to Coos Bay, where they were put ashore at Empire City. There were two score of them, and settlers immediately dubbed them the "Forty Thieves." The inhabitants were thinly scattered about the complex waterways, but they were united by a spirit of realistic tolerance, touched with humor. Without their knowing it, the Forty Thieves were on silent trial. When poultry vanished at the edge of the deep woods, and clothing disappeared from cabins, there was no outcry. The settlers seemed strangely unobservant. It was strange, too, how soon the culprits left the community, and how smoothly. They couldn't even analyze how it happened. No one had done much of anything, but maybe everyone had some part in greasing the skids under them.

Some of the Forty stayed and made good with the help of their neighbors. Today few people remember who came to Coos Bay in the convict ship and who came of his own accord. Old-timers make it a point of honor to forget, but they say that some of their finest citizens were numbered among the Forty and their descendants.

From the beginning, Coos Bay has been one of the fortunate regions of the earth, and it suffered no long period of isolation. Early in its settlement, lumber schooners from San Francisco kept it in touch with the world. California contributed citizens and it also contributed land. The water-front streets of the present city of Coos Bay were once mud

flats, and they were filled in with the ballast of lumber schooners—gravel from San Francisco's Telegraph Hill. When the lumber trade declined, coal was mined and shipped, and the railroad came in the eighties.

Nature and history have been kind to the Coos Bay region, and old-timers say that even the beavers were philosophical. Many of the settlers lived up the sloughs that were segmented by beaver dams, and traveled by boat. When a settler went to town he had to break through one barrier after another, and while he was rowing away from the dam he had just broken, he saw the beavers appear and survey the damage, then go quietly to work on repairs. When the settler returned up the slough, all the dams had been mended, and he had to break through them again. Although the old-timers do not mention it, their accounts suggest that they, too, were tolerant. And so were the Coos Bay Indians. They had been generous and hospitable from the beginning, and they did not join in the Indian War. Dodge, the historian, says it was because the Coos Bay settlers bought their land from the Indians. Old-timers agree that this is partly true: some of their forebears bought the land, but never paid for it. But the gesture was appreciated by the natives, whose ambitions were always modest. Their attitude is portrayed in a story from early Marshfield. In Ferry's Tavern, Squirrel Whiskey was the favorite drink of Indians and whites. On one occasion it was so much favored that the supply ran out. When an old Indian came in and ordered Squirrel Whiskey, Ferry said, "It's all gone, but you can have Old Crow." The Indian declined it as too much. "I don't want to fly," he explained, "only hop around."

So much for the men of old on the west side of the mountains. What about the children of today on the east side of the Coast Range?

LONELY VALLEYS

Sheila is a little girl with dark hair and blue eyes, who lives on a farm near beautiful Lookingglass Valley. She sometimes visits around Kings Valley where her grandparents and her uncles and aunts and cousins have big farms. They raise hay and grain and walnuts and fruit; they are very busy at harvesttime, and busy enough the rest of the year—and nearly always happy.

The valley where Sheila lives is beautiful with things seen and unseen.

The river that flows through the valley is guarded by tall trees; you can't see it until you are there, but from the house you can hear the big riffle, like the laughing voices of people bathing behind the screen of trees. On this side of the river there is pasture land, with big oak trees for shade, and there are different-colored fields of hay and grain, with dark fruit trees growing in some of the fence rows. In the evening you can see deer jumping lightly over the fence into the meadow, and in the daytime great trucks with trailers go pounding by along the county road in traveling clouds of dust that almost hide the logs they carry. Around the valley there are smooth, steep mountains, bare except for grass and dark columns of trees that push up the draws or march over the head of an otherwise bald hill. In the spring the mountains are tender green, and in summer they are tawny, except when there are distant forest fires, and then they are pale gold, dreaming of a blue world. By moonlight they are gold, with the dark mystery of trees that have crept into the bosom of their valleys. The farm, too, has its dark mysteries, like the swamp beyond the grove of oaks. There a former tenant executed his wife and daughter with a rifle.

This part of the valley is not too productive of children. There are none on the adjoining farms, but there are nice grown-ups. Like Joe Rockwell. If the tractor breaks down, or someone's cattle get into a field, or a passing motorist starts a grass fire, Joe seems to get the message and he appears from nowhere; Joe, dark and slight and quietly helpful, is there until the crisis has passed. Sheila's father has never been able to get Joe to accept pay and he has never been able to hire him for work in the harvest or anything else. When Joe's own crops are ready, as likely as not, he goes fishing or hunting, or visiting distant relatives. And Joe's brother, Harry, is always too busy on his farm to work for others. Harry is the freak of the family and he is called "the working Rockwell," to distinguish him from all other Rockwells.

And there are Shorty and Bess who have a little farm on the hill. Shorty is called that because he is the short one of the family. He is six-feet-five, and his brother is six-feet-seven. Shorty helps with the harvest, and he is good with all things about farming and farm machinery, and he has his own way of talking. When he doesn't think too much of a piece of land, he shakes his head as if he were sorry, and says, "That field's so poor a jack rabbit has to pack a sandwich across it."

If someone drives along the county road, going very fast, Shorty says, "He's going like the tails of hell!" And if the tractor or combine breaks down, he looks at it reproachfully, as if it shouldn't have done that, and he says, "The son-of-a-vehicle!" Shorty is mostly quiet-moving, with a voice that tells you everything is going the way it was meant to, but when a bee buzzes around or a grasshopper lands on him, he jumps and slaps at it and says, "Gehistacutis!" He explains, "I don't like insects and all troublesome things." And sometimes he looks fierce when a little girl pesters him too much. He says, "I'll put you in my back pocket and *sit* on you!" Or he says, "I'll put my big foot on you and *squash* you like a bug!" But he never does.

Shorty has eyes for Indian things, and things of long ago. In the river, where other people see nothing but gravel, Shorty can see the shape of things. He reaches down into the water and brings up flint arrowheads and spearheads. When he is plowing, he sometimes stops the tractor and goes back to a round patch of blackened earth that someone else wouldn't have noticed. He studies the soil and says, "The Indians built a campfire here." When he and Sheila's father cut down a big tree, Shorty puts on his glasses and looks at the stump as if he were reading a book. He counts the rings until he comes to one that is partly black, and he says, "The Indians burned this land over ninety-seven years ago." He counts to another ring that was touched by fire, and says, "They burned it over a hundred and twelve years ago; they were here then." Sometimes he reads from a stump that the Indians were there three hundred years ago, and he points to the grassy mountains with dark wooded draws. "Those mountains are bald because the Indians kept burning them over, but they aren't as bald as they used to be; every year I see those trees creeping farther up the draws and spreading out on the mountains."

Shorty used to study how things happened all over America. That was when he had an itching foot. He would leave home, maybe without knowing he was doing it, and find a train going somewhere. He would ride the rods to Lincoln, Nebraska, or Chicago or Tampa, Florida, and find out what people were like and what they were thinking on the great plains and beside the Great Lakes and on the Gulf of Mexico. After a while he would come home and work until his foot began to itch again.

That was during a previous marriage. Now his foot doesn't itch any

Salmon fishing in Rogue River near Grants Pass, Oregon.

Smoketree Forest, Southern California.

Children of Solvang, the all-Danish village.

The Palomino breed is California's pride. Note the tooled leather and silver-studded equipment.

more, or if it does he doesn't notice. When he and Bess were married, they decided to have a farm of their own. They had to have money first, but it was a good time to earn money. They went to Portland and worked in a shipyard. Shorty was a coppersmith and Bess a sheet-metal worker. They earned money fast and made a game of saving it. They found a little old house near the river for ten dollars a month, and they didn't buy anything they didn't need. When they had enough, they came back to the valley and bought a farm and built a barn and fixed up the house.

In her way, Bess is as nice as Shorty, and she understands things. Sometimes when the men are putting a new piece of machinery together and it won't come out right, Bess looks it over and tells them how it should go. She is a good cook and a good car driver. She works hard, but she finds time to visit and talk about people and things and she has a way of telling stories. Sometimes she tells about the shipyard in winter, where she worked in a cold shed. It was a dreadful place except for a kind old Norwegian blacksmith. If the shed got very cold, he would put a slab of steel in the forge and, when it was red-hot, he would put it near Bess's feet, and that part of the story was very comforting. When the slab of steel was cooler, she would stand on it, with the last of the heat coming up through the soles of her shoes—and then the old black-smith would put it in the fire again.

Bess notices and remembers, and she is full of all kinds of information. Oregon, she says, has an old law forbidding anyone to cross a skunk with a rabbit. The law doesn't say why, but maybe it's to keep people from breeding secret weapons. Imagine the rumpus that could be raised by an animal with the speed of a jack rabbit and the fire power of a skunk! The law also forbids crossing a skunk with a cat. Maybe a precaution against fifth columnists; the resulting "scat" or "kunk" might be taken to a patriotic bosom by mistake.

Mr. Rogers, who drives the school bus, reads books and is very serious, and keeps his opinions to himself. Most of the neighborhood excitement comes from taking sides about things that happen. Like when a girl marries before she is fifteen, or when there is a disagreement between the Smiths, who raise horses farther back in the mountains. When things like that happen, all the neighbors take sides and argue about who is right and who is wrong. Except Mr. Rogers.

In the morning, Mr. Rogers takes the children to school, and in the

afternoon he takes them home. He has no children of his own, but when he is driving the bus they are all his children.

Sheila is too young for school, but Mr. Rogers doesn't forget her. If she is standing alone at the gate at going-home time, he stops and lifts her up into the bus. She rides proudly with the others, and when Mr. Rogers lifts her down at her own gate, he says, "I hope you had a good day at school." Sheila already knows what school should mean, and she has the feeling of belonging.

INGENUITY AND WHEELS

The story of the Oregon Coast Range is the story of pioneering in isolation and the coming of transportation. Most of the region was settled in the fifties, and to some parts reliable transportation came almost immediately. Others are still waiting, and still others waited until recent times. And the longest wait was not always for the place farthest from a center of civilization.

The Tillamook region is only fifty miles from the mouth of the Columbia River, and only seventy miles from Portland by land. But the railroad did not come to Tillamook until 1911. For sixty years the story of the neighborhood was the story of pioneer ingenuity struggling with transportation difficulties, or getting along without transportation. Joe Champion was the first white settler: he arrived in April, 1851. He came from the Columbia River in an open whaleboat, with companions who sailed back and left him to lead a Robinson Crusoe life on the shore of the bay. Champion took up his abode in a hollow cedar stump while he felled trees and split shakes for a cabin, and he stayed to see other settlers arrive and the wilderness become Tillamook County. He was the first clerk of the county.

R. P. S. Lamberson came the hard way from the Willamette Valley, over the wild Coast Range mountains. On Mount Hebo, where the going was roughest, he carved his name and the year, 1855, on his grindstone, and left it beside the mountain trail. He settled in the southern part of the county and became a prosperous farmer, but he never went back for his grindstone. A forest ranger found it a few years ago, with his name and date still clearly legible. The stone had been waiting there all the years that Lamberson lived in Tillamook County; but once in a lifetime is enough to cross Mount Hebo with your possessions.

When John Ward brought his family to Tillamook in 1892, transportation had improved only slightly. Supplies that reached the region came, intermittently, by a small steamer, and in good weather by freight wagons over the mountains, on roads that were still terrible. After the supplies reached the store, there was the problem of getting them home. The Ward homestead was ten miles from the nearest store, and the trail was too narrow even for a pack horse. Mr. G. H. Ward, John's son, who still lives in Tillamook, recalls carrying two-hundred-pound barrels of flour on his back along the ten-mile trail. In the 1890's, most of America was buying ready-made cloth, but one of the elder Ward's most useful creations was a spinning wheel. In order to make the wheel he first had to make a turning lathe, and lathe tools out of old files. The wheel was made of five kinds of native wood, with home-tanned cowhide for a belt, and bushings made of rounds of elk horn.

Pioneer ingenuity did well with the few supplies that reached Tillamook and the materials already at hand, but it had more difficulty with what it produced. The heavy rainfall on rich meadowlands produced luxuriant grass, and cows responded with milk that was more yellow than white. Tillamook was a natural dairy country and Portland, only a hundred and fifty miles away by water, was an eager market. The Tillamook farmers made butter that never needed artificial coloring, packed it in tubs, and sent it off to market in the little steamer "Elmore." In distance, market was less than a day from the wonderful meadows of Tillamook, but the eastward drift of weather across the Pacific had endowed Tillamook Harbor with a bar, and the Columbia River with another. Sometimes the little "Elmore" remained bar-bound for ten days, in sight of the meadows, with the butter in her hold growing older; and when the weather finally relented and let her go to sea, it might change its mind again and keep her bar-bound outside the Columbia for another week or ten days. Sometimes it took the "Elmore" three weeks to make the hundred-and-fifty-mile trip to Portland, and she arrived with rancid butter that was sold for skid grease, and the farmer got nothing but a freight bill. Some of the dairy farmers went on gambling; others gave up and tried something else.

The railroad came in 1911, with sure and fast transportation to waiting markets. But only a limited amount of milk and butter was shipped out by rail. In the long interim American and Swiss dairymen had dis-

covered that the milk which made such remarkable butter made even more remarkable cheese. Tillamook cheese has become the most famous brand in the West. It is now shipped by rail, but it was designed to defy time in the hold of the little "Elmore" as she waited patiently inside Tillamook bar or rolled for long days outside the roaring bar of the Columbia.

If the railroad is no longer as essential to Tillamook dairying as it once had seemed, it and motor highways have at least added to the comfort of life. Before 1911, traveling salesmen arriving in Tillamook inquired anxiously about ways of getting out and they were told, "There is the 'Elmore' by sea and the rockaway stage over the mountains. Whichever you take, you will wish you had taken the other."

The Tillamook region has had its double triumph over circumstances and that triumph is nicely reflected in the attitude of its people, who are healthily in tune with the present while preserving a genial attitude toward the past. This attitude expresses itself in the Tillamook County Historical Museum—a museum with a sense of humor. There, among a wealth of pioneer and Indian relics, one can see the spinning wheel which John Ward made for his wife; the autographed grindstone which Lamberson left on Mount Hebo; Phil Sheridan's sword, once possessed by the Indians—notched and fire-blackened, having served them as a fire poker; a model of the sturdy little "Sue H. Elmore" that got the butter through to Portland, sweet or rancid; and a great block of beeswax from the Nehalem treasure ship. The exhibits are brought up to date with a synthetic, puncture-proof tire of solid wood, made by a pioneer who couldn't get satisfaction from his ration board. Slightly earlier improvisations date from Prohibition days: a copper wash boiler converted into a still and a teakettle with a coil to produce liquor for a small family.

An example of pioneer ingenuity that deserves a place in a museum, though it isn't here, is the first powerboat used on the Umpqua River. It was a true hay burner and it presented problems unknown to the modern engineer. The works consisted of a treadmill connected to paddle wheels; and two oxen produced the power by climbing toward a manger of hay that was just out of reach. On her trial trip the treadmill jammed, and the boat drifted down the river while its inventor sweated. He cleared the mechanism at last, but there was no answering clatter of the treadmill, and the boat continued to drift down the river, with spec-

tators' guffaws growing fainter in the distance. The oxen had eaten all the hay and their incentive was gone.

Changing transportation has changed the habits of people and it has changed the people themselves. No other factor has brought about as much change as the internal-combustion engine, and perhaps the greatest changes have been in logging and loggers. In days when logging was done by oxen and by steam, loggers were a separate race; the logging camp was relatively static and the bunkhouse was its heart. Today the industry has gone democratic, and loggers and logs rub elbows with other people and other traffic in town and on the highways. Trailer-trucks with immense logs confound visiting drivers on mountain and coastal highways; or the trucks thunder by, empty except for their trailers, which they carry pickaback, with the trail elevated like the barrel of a big gun. And the spar tree, which used to be synonymous with the logging camp, is the common landmark of a western Oregon town—because the logs are brought into town by truck, and at the spar tree by a siding they are loaded on railroad cars for the last lap of their journey to the sawmill.

In the woods gasoline and Diesel engines have largely replaced steam, and gone is the "crummy" car that used to bring loggers into town on Saturday night. Gone, too, is the bunkhouse where loggers made their own entertainment, gambling for tobacco or telling Paul Bunyan yarns or dancing with each other to the music of a fiddle, with their calked boots raising a storm of dust and splinters.

Modern loggers drive their own cars, the married ones commuting to work from their small farms or homes, and the unmarried ones from hotels in town. They like the impersonal freedom of hotels and shun rooms in private homes. If most of the loggers' picturesqueness is gone, they like it better that way. No one paid them for being colorful.

Sometimes it is still possible to recognize the loggers' tracks. In the little Nehalem Hotel you see a narrow, deep-bitten trail of calk-marks across the lobby floor. It curves past the stove and into the dim hall like a trail through the woods. Except for their telltale tracks you might not be aware that loggers lived in that quiet place.

On the street on Sundays and holidays you see loggers with their families; they are easily recognized because their wives have their hair permanented, and wives and daughters are particularly well-dressed.

Having done well by their families, the loggers dress for comfort. They wear slouch hats and are averse to buttoned shirt collars and neckties, and their clean overalls are sagged off or rolled up well above the tops of their elastic-sided slippers. These smooth-shaven and domesticated loggers accomplish more than their hairy predecessors did, but they are less of the woods because they do not live in the woods; they only work there. Outside of work hours, their interests are in their homes and in farming, and sometimes in flying or politics, and in fishing and hunting; in the fall it is the aim of every married logger to bring home an elk or at least a big buck deer for the frozen-food locker.

In Oregon, as elsewhere, man is a generally sociable animal; but wherever there are lonely places there are occasional men who live there by preference and have no quarrel with their environment. A lifetime of isolated living is no tax on their sanity, but their very adaptability can make them seem odd to the outsider.

There was the little blue-eyed mountain man who showed up at the office of one of the local museums in Oregon. He was there to get an exhibit which his late older brother had lent the museum some forty years earlier. He said he was ninety-three, but the curator couldn't believe a man could get that dirty in ninety-three years. Actually, he was ninety-seven.

The old man had a receipt which proved the loan to the museum, and when he was asked if his brother had willed him his property, he said, "We'd always agreed that the one who lived longest would get the ten acres." As the survivor, he was awarded his brother's museum pieces, and out of gratitude he imparted a secret he had learned in the mountains. It was something that beat the fanciest washing machine, and it didn't wear out clothes. All it required was two shirts: while you wore one you had the other airing outdoors. At the end of the week you changed shirts. The old man kept two shirts going that way for years, and the shirt he put on was always cleaner than the one he had taken off.

The brothers had agreed that the one who lived longer would inherit the ten acres and the two-room cabin, but the survivor hadn't claimed his inheritance immediately. Tom died early in the winter, with the trail snowed in. So Joe put the corpse in the unheated room of the cabin, and there it kept very well. Joe lived all winter in the other room, and when the trail thawed out in the spring, he loaded the corpse on a pack

horse and took it to town for burial. Joe said that the last sharing of the cabin hadn't bothered him: Tom had never talked much, anyway.

When loneliness and isolation are imposed from the outside, the results are not always so placid.

Not long ago a self-appointed reporter went out to get the story on a shooting in the northern part of the Coast Range. The last ten miles were over a mountain road, ripped by the wheels of trucks, and at the end of the road was a logging camp. In a cabin the reporter found a four-year-old boy wailing over the body of a donkey puncher who had been his father, and down the road was one isolated farm. The farmer was in custody for the shooting, and the farm was being run by his seven beautiful daughters. (The reporter saw and counted them, and there were seven, all dazzlingly beautiful.)

The donkey puncher and his wife and child had once lived in the cabin as peaceful neighbors of the farm family. Then the wife succumbed to loneliness and boredom, and left for parts more civilized. The donkey puncher stayed with his work and looked after the child as well as he could. It was more than a full-time job, but something was missing—and the donkey puncher gravitated toward the seven beautiful girls down the road. The farmer disapproved and ordered him to keep away, but the lure was too great. One incident led to another, and ended with the shooting.

Outside the big woods of the logging country, Oregon has other trees that have affected people's lives. One of them is the myrtle, which grows only in the Holy Land and in southwestern Oregon. It is a slow-growing tree, with a straight column of a trunk and a rounded dome of glossy foliage. In spring and early summer, when the sun shines on the new leaves, every tree is outlined by a mysterious halo of light. The myrtle is a tree of classical beauty, but it was only a trial to the men who cleared the fields of southwestern Oregon. It was a job to fell one of the trees, and when the wood was seasoned, it could not be cut at all; it only broke the axes of the pioneers. So they developed a technique of felling the trees, cutting them up while they were green, and burning them. Millions of feet of one of the world's rarest woods went up in those expensive bonfires.

Toward the end of the century, when many of the trees had been destroyed, some people decided there might be another approach to the

myrtle. In addition to being as hard as rock and eternally durable, the wood had beautiful colors: soft gray shading into softer yellow and incredible orange, and rich brown shading toward black. A few local artisans began working the stubborn and beautiful wood. Like the trees themselves, the demand for the wood grew slowly. Around 1910, the artisans were still struggling when Jack London made a trip along the Oregon coast. London was at the height of his fame and affluence, and when he saw the myrtlewood he ordered an entire suite of furniture made from it. The publicity established the myrtlewood industry, but it did little for aesthetics. The artisans were mostly local carpenters who learned more about how the timber could be worked than what should be made of it. The most practical method was to turn it on a lathe, sharpening the lathe tool every few minutes. Lathe work suggested bowls and vases, and the models were not always good. Even now, some makers still turn out copies of crockery mixing bowls, nesting rim and all. There are also bowls of graceful design and proportions, worthy of their material. When you find a really beautiful object of myrtlewood, as likely as not, it reflects the influence of Bob Harbison of Coquille.

Coquille is the county seat of Coos County. In sight of the myrtle trees on the hills, the Coast Highway dips inland to the town, and Highway 42 winds east through the mountains. To the south are the Siskiyous, continuing the Coast Range and uncrossed by any highway for 140 miles. The traffic of the Coast Highway and the highway east rolls through the town: motorcars and busses to California, logging trucks with big logs, and lumber trucks with trailers stacked with fragrant Port Orford cedar. Coquille is a traffic hub, close to the Siskiyou wilderness, yet it manages to be one of the most quietly charming and civilized towns in the West. There one may see symbolic things. Sometimes a young Oregonian rides down from the hills, still triumphing over the motor manufacturers. Tall and long-legged, in blue jeans and Spanish cowboy hat, he rides down the main street on a humpbacked Brahma steer.

Bob Harbison grew up in Coquille, in sight of the haloed myrtle trees on the hills of the Coast Range. He admired the myrtles because he had an eye for beauty, but they did not figure in his plans. He studied archi-

tecture at the State University and was graduated into the great depression. He designed the municipal building of Coquille, and after that there was a long holiday for architects and builders. Bob had a young wife and two children, and he supported them by carving statues for schools, under the auspices of the WPA. The proceeds bought necessities, but left nothing for toys or adult entertainment. Bob tried to solve the double problem by making toys for the children, and in his spare time he cut animals out of myrtle and Port Orford cedar. Mrs. Harbison encouraged the pastime, but as fast as the animals were made she took them away; when she had a sizable collection she exhibited them in the family florist shop. The aim was to encourage people to buy flowers, but instead they demanded the animals. When the confusion was finally resolved, Bob Harbison no longer had any spare time: he was busy carving animals and turning myrtlewood bowls for his customers.

Today the Harbisons live in their own house at the edge of Coquille. At the back of the house is the modern woodworking shop where Bob tries to catch up on orders from stores in Washington and Oregon and California. He has ten years of good work behind him and he is independent; but he and his wife are so youthful and enthusiastic you would never guess it.

Along the way, Bob has transmuted myrtlewood bowls from copies of kitchen crockery to objects of art, but he has not been able to do as much for the artistic taste of his customers. The animals he produces to their order are literal ones: skunks with painted stripes and dogs with painted noses and eyes and shaggy coats that defeat the color and grain of the wood. They are good of their kind, but one can't help being a little disappointed in popular taste.

If the visitor shows his disappointment, Bob brings out something he has done for his own satisfaction. It may be the Harbison Colt, in even-textured Port Orford cedar. A year or so of time has given the wood the patina of old gold, but the colt has the breath-taking freshness of a bud at the moment of opening. It is more than a long-legged foal: it is the essence of all young things—colt and baby and bud. The Harbison Colt is something the Greeks would have understood, and Walt Disney might envy, but Bob's regular customers are suspicious of stylized and tender simplicity. It doesn't have hair and it doesn't smell like a colt. The few that have been made have gone slowly, but those that have

been taken are gone permanently. No one who cared enough to buy one of them would ever part with it.

The colt is put away, and Bob Harbison goes back to turning a bowl out of a dark myrtlewood burl that was three centuries in the growing. The lathe tool cuts smoothly through the years implicit in the grain of wood. And beyond the windows, there are haloes of light on the trees still growing on the smooth hills; the traffic of Highway 42 rolls in from the east to blend with the traffic of the Coast Highway; the tall young Oregonian from the hills rides by on his humpbacked Brahma steer; and a glistening air liner slips through the sky. Here, as elsewhere, the present is never found in its pure form: it is always a mixture of the past and future.

PEOPLE OF THE
WASHINGTON COAST RANGE

BY ARCHIE BINNS

The State has her great unknown land like the interior of Africa. The country shut in by the mountains has never, to positive knowledge, been trodden by foot of man. . . . The Indians never penetrated it, for their traditions say it is inhabited by a very fierce tribe, which none of the coast tribes dare molest. . . . White men, too, have only vague accounts of any man having ever passed through this country. . . .

The most generally accepted theory in regard to this country is that it consists of great valleys stretching from the inward slopes of the mountains to a great central basin. . . . Although the country around has abundant rain and clouds constantly hang over the mountain tops, the streams flowing towards the four points of the compass rise only on the outward slopes of the range, none appearing to drain the great area shut in by the mountains. . . . It must have a subterranean outlet.

$\mathbf{T}$his romantic and alarming account was not written in the Middle Ages to keep would-be Columbuses at home; it was written in 1890 for *The Northwest Magazine* as a description of the Olympic Peninsula of the State of Washington; and it was read with approval in Seattle, where the forty-three thousand inhabitants could look across Puget Sound to the snow-capped mountains which enclosed the land of unknown tribes and unexplored valleys and subterranean rivers.

The magazine overstated its case, but there are still untrodden areas in the Olympics; and while an increasing number of people lived within sight of those mountains, the ocean side of the peninsula was an undiscovered land for most of them until the opening of the Loop Highway in 1931. As for settlement, relatively few white men have cared to match themselves against the isolated, practically harborless coast, the jungle-like rain forests, and the rain—up to twelve feet a year. Indian inhabitants still outnumber the whites, and it is essentially an Indian coast.

During wholly Indian times this coast was a place of superb seamen and of violent deeds. There were six main tribes: from north to south, the Makah, Ozette, Quillayute, Hoh, Queet and Quinault; five of the tribes still endure. The Ozettes have disappeared, not through acts of white men but due to their relatively peaceful character on a warlike coast. To the north, in the Cape Flattery region, were the big, fierce Makah, and to the south were the numerous and pugnacious Quillayutes. The two tribes had been at war with each other for so long that they had forgotten the cause of their disagreement, but they continued to

raid each other's camps, sometimes with fleets of a hundred canoes. On the way they stopped to try their weapons on the Ozettes, and on the way back they stopped again to celebrate victory or avenge defeat.

But even the peaceful Ozettes were capable of biting the foot that stepped on them. On one occasion a squall drove a fleet of Quillayute canoes into open Ozette Bay, and the warriors had to land to keep from being swamped. The long-suffering Ozettes welcomed them with a great feast and built up the fires in their split-cedar houses. A handful of them stayed to wait on their guests, while the others walked around in the open air to keep themselves awake and alert. That night, when the glutted Quillayutes were asleep in the overly-warm houses, the Ozettes clubbed them to death. They dragged the bodies to the beach, laid them in a long row, and disemboweled them. Then they cut off their heads and stuck them up on poles.

Thereafter there were no direct attacks from their neighbors, but continual sniping wore the tribe down to one family, and the last survivor went to live with the Makah. He was Jim Hunter, who lived at Neah Bay. Jim had no trouble with the Makah after his adoption, and he also successfully adopted the ways of the white man. He secured the mail contract from Port Angeles to the Pacific and carried the mail in his dugout canoe to Pysht, Clallam Bay, Neah Bay, and Tatoosh Island. Later he had a succession of small steam vessels, and his last was a seventy-foot Diesel-powered craft. Jim lived to be something of a capitalist at Neah Bay: in addition to his maritime ventures he operated a garage, a gas-service station, and a dance hall. Sometimes, traveling in his fine, Diesel-powered "Hunter IV," Jim used to recall the days when the Makah went out into the open Pacific in their dugout canoes and killed whales. They used bone-tipped lances, ropes of chewed cedar bark, and floats of sealskins. Driving a lance home required maneuvering the canoe to within six feet of the whale and afterward being dragged on a wild ride through the Pacific. When the whale could no longer dive because of the accumulation of lances with floats attached, it was stabbed time after time until it died of loss of blood. Sometimes a whale would give up all resistance and allow itself to be guided into Neah Bay. The whale's moans of pain sounded very much like those of a human being. It was a cruel killing, but the Indians had no quicker method.

The whale was brought home on an incoming tide and beached with the assistance of the entire village. When the tide went out, men and squaws joined in stripping blubber and cutting whale meat. Some of the blubber was rendered into oil and some of it smoked like bacon and stacked up like cordwood.

That was the kind of thing recalled by Jim Hunter, who had bridged the gap between the Stone Age and Diesel power. In 1931 he saw Neah Bay linked with the outside world by road, whereupon he built his garage and gas station. Two years later, on Makah Day, he did what is expected of a wealthy Indian and gave a potlatch. The feast consisted of pots of stew for the entire village.

Makah Day is still celebrated by auto-driving Indians in gaudy modern clothes, the girls with permanented hair and generous make-up. In keeping with the times, the chief event of the day is a baseball game between two tribes. In the evening there are the old dances: the Bear Dance with one of the performers dressed as a bear; the ancient *Hamatse*, that deals with ritualistic cannibalism and links the Makah with the northern Nootkas—the Wild Man now wears a woman's bathing suit under his strips of red-cedar bark—and the Horse Dance. This is performed by men with paper horses' heads and tails, and women dancers with whips who drive the horses about in time with the drumming.

In their changing world the Makah no longer hunt whales but they fish for halibut from their canoes, with twelve hooks on a line and the arms of devilfish for bait. When they catch a dogfish they move to another location, not out of superstition but because they have learned by experience that the two kinds of fish do not run together.

A more debatable practice is followed by the Yugoslav captain of one of the Diesel purse-seiners fishing out of Neah Bay. When some other craft is the high boat and his own luck has been poor, he slips out at night and cuts a small piece from the lucky net and sews it into his own. The old captain also takes the weather personally. Going out of the harbor he stands on the exposed flying bridge, and if spray blows in his face he gets argumentative with God. "Is that right?" he asks. "What have I done that you should throw water in my face?"

In varying degrees, the Indians have adopted the white man's way of doing things. Also in varying degrees, the white men who settled on the rugged coast adopted the Indian's way of life. In the case of Otto

Strom, the white man was sometimes in the unique position of having to follow the white man's idea of what the Indian should do.

Otto and John Strom came to America from Sweden in 1887 and gravitated to the Pacific Coast by way of Colorado and Idaho. While they were in Coeur d'Alene they learned from real estate salesmen that Grays Harbor City was about to become the metropolis of the Pacific Northwest. John spent his savings on lots selected from a map, and Otto fell in love with the description of the cool green climate and with the salesman's picture of a beautiful big sawmill.

The brothers hurried to Grays Harbor to get in on the ground floor of the new city—but the floor hadn't been built, and neither had the sawmill. But there were mills and canneries at the twin towns of Aberdeen and Hoquiam. John, who was a property owner, stayed while his brother headed up the coast along Indian trails through the wilderness.

Otto found what he was looking for between the thundering Pacific and the southwest side of Mount Olympus, where the cloud-laden winds from the ocean are chilled by the mountains and drop on the western slope in prodigal rain and snow. There the great Hoh River flowed to the Pacific through what appeared to be a cool tropical jungle—the rain forests of gigantic fir and spruce and big-leaved maple festooned with hanging moss, with giant ferns growing up out of the deep moss which covered the ground.

Near the mouth of the Hoh River, Otto Strom found people to his liking: the Indians, quiet and resourceful and hospitable, good fishermen and great boatmen, living in their split-cedar houses and their dugout canoes. Otto settled among them—the first white settler on the Hoh River. He lived among the Indians, fished and hunted with them, and learned their way of life. In turn, he taught them the useful things he knew. The reservation had a neglected forge and anvil, and Otto, who was a passable blacksmith, gave the Indians a working introduction to the Iron Age. Afterward he said, "I had a lot of experiences with Indians . . . all of them were pleasant. I treated the Indians well and they treated me good. They liked some of the things I would do for them, and I did a lot that made them happy."

Otto's informal adoption by the Indians was a mutual gain, but it sometimes put him in an odd position with white authority.

A few days after Christmas, 1890, the Pacific brought the Indian coast

a present in the form of a beautiful new French sailing ship, "Louis XIII."
She missed the entrance to the strait of Juan de Fuca, crashed on the
outlying rocks, and was driven onto the beach at the mouth of the Hoh
River. Thirty years earlier, when another ship was wrecked there, the
Indians had dumped silver dollars on the beach and saved the useful
chests which had contained them, and they jettisoned flour and saved
the sacks for clothing. On this occasion, an Aberdeen man bought the
wreck and hired eight men from the reservation to salvage the materials
on board. Otto was one of the eight. The most important salvage on the
unlucky "Louis" was thirty thousand yards of new sails, worth a dollar
a yard. The men boarded the wreck and began hauling out the new
canvas in the sail locker. The first sail they moved uncovered a promising
keg. One of the Indians broached it and pronounced the contents good.
Otto had a taste and said it was cognac, and the others sampled it and
decided they liked cognac. While the sampling was going on, Dr. Cox,
the Indian Agent, came on board, and the sight of the happy, sampling
eight made him very angry. They must stop at once, he said, and remove
the liquor from the wreck. Other barrels of cognac were found and
brought ashore. The doctor then knocked in their heads, let the liquor
run down the village street, and saved the barrels.

As punishment for drinking, the seven Indians and the Swede were
ordered to cut four cords of wood each, and they were forbidden to
board the "Louis" again. While they did their penance, a southwesterly
wind and heavy sea pounded the ship to pieces and all the salvage was
lost.

That was life on the reservation during a bad moment. There were
also good days and years, and Otto Strom became an Indian—if a Swede
can become an Indian. In the summer of 1895 he was married, Indian
style, to Mary Fisher, a handsome Indian widow, and in 1900 they were
legally married. Otto was adopted into his wife's tribe, thereby becoming a Quinault, and he moved to their reservation, thirty miles south.
The Indian Service accepted the adoption, and Otto received reservation land and a fishing allotment.

Taholah was the capital of the Quinault Reservation, a village of shake
houses, with a log Government building and a log schoolhouse. Otto
fished and drove team, did blacksmithing and worked on the roads, and
he went on with the exchange of white and native culture. When his

three little half-Indian daughters were at play in the village street they talked the Quinault language, at school they spoke English, and at home they alternated. Otto served on the school board for fourteen years, and he helped build up the Taholah community, as he had helped at Hoh. His marriage lasted thirty-five years, until Mary's death in 1931.

Otto Strom had a good life on the Indian coast. About the only complaint he ever voiced was the fact that he had been the first white settler on the Hoh River, while everyone gave the credit to John Huelsdonk. Both Otto and John were important men in the region, but when it came to catching the popular imagination, who could compete with the "Iron Man of Hoh?"

THE IRON MAN OF HOH

John Huelsdonk was just old enough to vote when he arrived from Iowa, and while he was still in his twenties he became a legend: the Iron Man of Hoh. The feat was accomplished by settling in one of the most inaccessible spots in the West and applying himself to his own affairs. John's choice of a homestead was on the upper Hoh River, deep in the rugged jumble of the Olympic Mountains. Neither white men nor Indians lived up there, and the only company were elk and cougars and deer and bears, and the near-by peak of Mount Olympus. Once a forest ranger met John Huelsdonk on the trail, walking home from the store at Forks. John was carrying his purchases on his back, and the most conspicuous one was a large kitchen stove. The forest ranger blinked and asked, "Isn't that pretty heavy?" John shrugged his great shoulders, and something bounced inside the stove. "It isn't the stove," he explained, "but that sack of flour in the oven keeps banging around." He went on up the twenty-two mile trail to his cabin, with the ninety-eight-pound sack joggling in the iron belly of his load; and by the time the story had been told a few times John Huelsdonk had become the Iron Man of Hoh. Long ago John became thoroughly sick of the story, but before he stopped commenting on it altogether, he observed that in the course of time he had carried a number of stoves along with other freight, and that particular event had left no impression on his mind. One trip did stand out—a thirty-mile walk with a load of parcels post and mail, and what turned out to be two broken ribs.

Stories about the Iron Man of Hoh often exaggerate his size. One

of his daughters, Lena Huelsdonk Fletcher states, "My father was a big man in his prime, weighing two hundred pounds or more, and proportioned as sculptors like to depict old Thor of the Norsemen or Jupiter of the Greeks and Romans, and all muscle. He always left the impression of great size with everyone who saw him, where many other larger men would not do so."

Those who knew the Iron Man in his prime agree that he was a magnificent specimen, and he was fortunate in his choice of a wife. Mrs. Huelsdonk was a big, able woman with a good disposition and an uncomplicated love of the wilderness. Everything she wanted was there: her husband and children, and their big log house; the river for fish and the woods for game. For travel, there was the mountain trail, and the dugout canoe on the river. Not that the Huelsdonks felt any great need to travel. In forty-five years each of them made one trip to the outside world: John to Aberdeen, seventy miles away, and Mrs. Huelsdonk to Seattle, which was slightly farther. That was in 1909, and it took a World's Fair and a great deal of persuasion for her to make the trip. When she was asked how she liked the fair, she said it was wonderful and added fervently, "If I ever get back home I'll never leave it again!"

The Huelsdonks had their own civilization, and discerning people came to see them. They lived at Spruce, Washington, and they were Spruce. The traveler who arrived at the ferry landing on the far side of the Hoh River found a big steer's horn chained to a spruce tree. He blew a blast on the horn, and waited. Presently a young woman came out of the house or woods on the far side of the river—a handsome young Amazon, barefoot, in a short skirt, with her thick hair over her shoulders. She launched a dugout canoe with one shove of her powerful arms, took up her paddle, and the ferry was in motion. The younger generation of Huelsdonks were all girls, four of them, and they were all good woodsmen and good boatmen.

When the visitor had been ferried across the Hoh and entered the big room of the log house, he was in Spruce, with the essential elements of civilization around him: defense and communications and supply and heating; the post office was in one corner; in another, an arsenal of rifles and shotguns; in the third, barrels of supplies, with smoked hams and bacon and jerky hanging from the rafters; and in the fourth corner, the big cookstove on which Mrs. Huelsdonk cooked wonderful meals.

And the Iron Man of Hoh might come in from cougar hunting: a big, unassuming, bearded man with an axe in his belt, and a Winchester rifle carried lightly in one immense hand.

John Huelsdonk will be remembered for the stove, but he did other things more significant. One of them was to re-enact the story of civilization by upsetting the balance of nature with one hand and putting props under it with the other. The only neighbors with whom he had a quarrel were the cougars that infested the Hoh Valley, and he waged continuous warfare against them. He estimated that in one year a cougar kills upwards of a hundred elk, and in the course of time he killed between two and three hundred of the great cats. As a result, game that had been relatively scarce in early days became more plentiful each year. In a letter, Lena Huelsdonk describes the aftermath: "When white men had done in the predators, game increased enormously and became a veritable plague to itself, destroying its own abundant feed and ending in starvation and disease." When the Iron Man saw what was happening he began catching elk calves and carrying them home. There his daughters fed them by hand and nursed them back to strength, and presently they were sent to parks and zoos in the outside world.

If John Huelsdonk had been a native he might have considered that the elk had shared their valley with the predators from the beginning of time without being exterminated. But he was a warm-hearted, civilized man, and when he stumbled through the thickets with a big elk calf in his arms, he was truly carrying the White Man's Burden which he had taken over from Nature, who had more experience. Nature knew that the cougars that were the enemies of weak and unwary individuals were essential to the well-being of the elk race.

It was the Iron Man's lot to carry heavy burdens over mountain trails. In later years, when trails were being built in the Olympics, there was a demand for packers to take supplies to the crews working higher up. A hundred-pound pack was a full load for the steep trails; the Iron Man of Hoh was no longer young, and he had been partly crippled in a logging accident, but he regularly carried two hundred-pound packs—thereby earning money twice as fast as the younger packers. It was not done out of greed or bravado, but because he was putting four daughters through college, and ready money was scarce. The Huelsdonks valued

education; and while their valley was isolated, it was not remote; the world was just beyond the mountains.

The Olympic trails led to college; they were also the forerunner of the Olympic National Park, created in 1939 and enlarged in 1940 to take in most of the great peninsula. The idea of this great national monument was to preserve forever the wild life and the mountain wilderness which the Huelsdonks loved. The boundary of the park enclosed their homestead, and there were no provisions in the plans for splendid specimens of humanity. For a time it appeared that the family would have to go, but they had courage and friends, and they had caught the imagination of a State. They still live on the homestead, the Iron Man at the age of seventy-nine and his wife eighty-one. A daughter and son-in-law have taken over the farming in recent years, but the old pioneers are still active and they have not tired of the mountains.

THE LUMBER COAST

The Indian coast of the Olympic Peninsula was settled late, and then only sketchily, by white men, and it is still a frontier. The east side of the peninsula is a different story. Bordered by Puget Sound, and penetrated for seventy miles by the great waterway of Hood Canal, and crowded to the water's edge with valuable timber, the sheltered side was a scene of early settlement and of gigantic lumbering industries that declined with the cutting of the timber.

On the northeast corner of the peninsula is Port Townsend, a sleepy town with a population of less than five thousand—too small for its aging brick buildings. A pulp mill and Fort Worden provide pay rolls, and the town is usually the site of some Government operation. The story is told, and denied, that when Mayor Bertha Landis of Seattle expelled the prostitutes from her city, they migrated to Port Townsend. There local women promptly brought pressure on the town government and had the intruders expelled. The women's committee was still congratulating itself when it had a call from a business organization spokesman. "How could you?" he wailed. "Look what you've done: you've spoiled Port Townsend's first business boom in fifty years!"

Port Townsend is a quiet, homey place with a past. In the eighties and nineties its harbor was filled with sailing ships of the maritime nations of the world; Indians in rakish dugout canoes paddled from ship to ship,

sight-seeing and trading; and white side-wheel and stern-wheel steamers shuttled between the docks and all the ports of Puget Sound. Ashore, the water front was crowded with the sailors of the world: Americans, Moors, French, Chinese, English, Portuguese, Greeks, Germans, Japanese, Norwegians, and Spaniards.

That was when Port Townsend claimed to be the third port of entry in the United States, second only to New York and San Francisco. For those windjammer days its location was strategic: at the junction of the strait of Juan de Fuca and Puget Sound, it was the closest-in port where sailing ships could depend on wind. Owners found it thrifty to pay off their crews at Port Townsend, tow to their destination on the Sound, and pick up another crew on the way out. Ashore, for the sailors' money, there were saloons and brothels and honky-tonks and sailors' boardinghouses, and during the earlier days a squaw dance house, known as the "Madhouse," which specialized in "blue ruin" whiskey. Where there was hesitancy about shipping out, there were persuasive crimps, and places of business with trap doors to the beach below.

The sailing ships that paused at Port Townsend were bound to or from the great lumber mills of the Olympic Peninsula region: Port Discovery, Port Ludlow, Port Gamble, Port Blakeley, and others. The Port Discovery and Port Gamble mills were established in 1853, and Port Ludlow still earlier, and for a while the peninsula mill towns were of more commercial importance than Seattle, across Puget Sound.

Of all the great early-day sawmills, the Port Gamble mill is the only one left in operation, and the community shows little of accumulated benefits from the wealth it has produced. After ninety-odd years the population of the town is five hundred. When the mill is running at capacity, it employs about the same number of men, drawn from the town and the Clallam Indian village of Teekalet at the entrance to the bay. The village is older than the town, and it does not live up to its name, "Brightness of the Noonday Sun." The people of Port Gamble are quiet, like the town, and they seem indifferent to the ugliness of much of the place—drab barracks and cabins in treeless yards that are parched in summer and muddy in winter. Those are the newer quarters for employees, traditionless and ugly. On the original main street there are trim New England houses built by the Popes and Talbots for mill of-

ficials. Along the street are big elms grown from slips brought around the Horn from East Machias, Maine. Port Gamble stands still while the local timber supply declines—and the trees of New England grow taller along the quiet street.

The other early mills are gone, and their towns have turned their interests to other things, or declined toward the vanishing point. Port Ludlow, once the capital of the Pope and Talbot lumber empire, is a ferry landing and a handful of houses. (Most of the New England houses were ferried across the Sound, shortly before the beginning of the recent war, to shelter defense workers.) The people who remain in the houses that are left give the impression of being without roots—as they are, in a fragment of a town without industry or resources.

If archaeologists ever excavate the site of the Port Discovery mill, they may be rewarded by finding the record of an historical event carved on one of the foundation stones. The inscription will state that Captain George Vancouver of His Majesty's Navy landed at that spot on May 7, 1792. His sojourn in the bay is a matter of history, and according to tradition his landing was recorded on a large rock. In 1853, when the sawmill was being laid out close by, the builders blasted the historic rock for foundation stones, and if the inscription survived it is now buried under the remains of the mill.

At present, magnificent Discovery Bay does not have an enterprise of importance or a settlement large enough to be called a town. Its wooded shores are broken only here and there by a village or farm or cabin camp or cluster of beach houses. At moments and places its wild idyllic shores belie its name; it has the feeling of being still undiscovered.

On the east side of the bay, the only named place for a dozen miles is Chevy Chase Inn, run by Miss Chase on her father's original homestead. The heart of the Inn is the house built in the seventies, and its lawn is shaded by tall seedling cherry trees. (When Mr. Chase was first there a nurseryman from Olympia went around the bays and inlets in a big Indian canoe loaded with budded and grafted fruit trees. The settlers bought so eagerly that the supply ran out before he reached Discovery Bay. The small fruit on the trees at Chevy Chase annually reproach his memory for passing off seedlings on later customers.)

The old Inn never advertises, and never needs to: the same people come there year after year, and children who were once brought there

by their parents now bring their children. The grounds of the Inn are between the golf course and the beach, and to the north a trail follows above the shore through idyllic woods interfiltrated by seedling cherry trees. They mark the course of earlier guests who strolled along the trail, eating the small sweet fruit and throwing the pits away.

The Inn is a place of simple pleasures that have stood the test of time, and the restful tone of the place is set by its hostess. Miss Chase, in her seventies, is a charming lady who likes people, but with quiet reserve. She was always that way: when she was a girl and a young lady on the homestead, she rarely went to town or to parties. The farm and the beautiful bay were enough, and she had no urge to be anywhere else. She stayed there and never married, and when she inherited the place, she began operating it as an inn.

Miss Chase never went out to look for excitement, but when you stay long enough in one place, it is likely to come to you. It was back in the last century when the Canadian Pacific Railroad was building through British Columbia, and a paymaster ran off with a pay roll of English gold.

Piecing together the stories of Indians, the paymaster apparently reached the entrance to Discovery Bay with a heavy box. There he dismissed boatmen and boat, and hired local Indians to take him south into the bay. On the shore of the Chase homestead he dismissed the Indians, and when they paddled away he was standing on the beach with the box which was too heavy for him to carry far.

That evening the paymaster appeared in Port Townsend, without the box, and boarded the steamer for Tacoma. He immediately went to his stateroom and stayed there until the steamer was docking. When he went above at the last moment, he found that he was not at Tacoma, but Victoria, B. C., and the Canadian police were waiting for him on the dock. The captain had recognized him and made the unscheduled run to the Canadian port.

At his trial the paymaster declined to tell what had become of the pay roll. He served his time in the penitentiary, where he developed consumption, and when he was released he went directly to the home of a brother in Texas, where he died.

Quite possibly the money was buried on the shore north of the Inn, but it has never been found. For years, when Mr. Chase went along

the shore he carried a crowbar, and at likely-looking places he drove it into the beach or the higher ground in the woods. But the sullen earth never responded with the ring of English gold.

Only once did Miss Chase think of personally looking for the treasure. That was years afterward, when some circumstance made her think she knew its exact location. She went secretly to the spot with a shovel, but when she was about to dig, she glimpsed the new hired man who had followed her and was watching from the woods. So she dug up a little tree which she carried home and planted in the garden. On second thought, it was just what she wanted. She already had what she needed, and she never went back to look for the paymaster's gold.

Port Madison, Bainbridge Island, on the west side of Puget Sound, is a village of commuters' homes and the summer homes of Seattle people, and yacht clubs sometimes have a rendezvous in its sheltered toy harbor. Port Madison is a pleasant little place, but it was once a leading industrial center of Puget Sound. California gold, buying lumber for San Francisco houses, gave the port an early start, and a peaceful one. In 1855, when the village of Seattle, across the Sound, was besieged by Indians, Meigs' big steam sawmill was operating full blast at Port Madison. However, out of deference to history, the mill crew knocked off early that day, got out their rifles and rowed to the defense of the infant city. Later, on winter mornings and evenings of their twelve-hour day, the mill and shipyard and foundry crews worked by electric light while gas-lit Seattle looked enviously across the water at the lights reflected in the sky.

Good things came to Port Madison, and official civilization came in 1861 when it was chosen as the county seat of Kitsap County. Until then the prospering town had managed pleasantly without court or jail or police force, but when it assumed the dignity of a county seat, one of its citizens became the sheriff, and a local builder began work on the courthouse and jail. The new order puzzled the children of Port Madison, where people had settled disagreements in a spirit of reasonableness, and they asked, "But who's going to be arrested? Who's going to be tried in the courthouse? Who's going to be put in the jail?"

The new order was also puzzling to some of the adults. People had always trusted the local builder: when he said that a building would cost about so much, it always did, and he made a good job of it. But

when he offered to build the courthouse and jail for "about so much," his old friend, the new County Commissioner, said he would have to bid an exact amount, and stick to it. The builder put in his bid, which was accepted, and he was given the blueprints which he was to follow exactly.

The builder saw things that could have been improved, but he followed the stock plans to the letter, sometimes pestered by the children, who asked, "Who's going to be tried in the courthouse? Who's going to be put in jail?" When he had finished, he asked for his money.

Kitsap County's new courthouse-jail was a good job as far as it went, but something was missing: the front entrance stood six feet above the ground, and there was no way of getting in except with a ladder. The resident County Commissioner demanded steps, and the builder hauled out the blueprints and proved that none had been called for. The plans assumed a flat earth, and the courthouse was on sloping ground. If other people could be legalistic, so could the builder!

It was a technical victory, but the builder's former friend had the last word: the county would not pay for the edifice until there was some way of getting in. The builder was equally stubborn in refusing to provide what was not called for in the plans. As months went by and the economic pinch increased, he brooded over the injustice of people who got legalistic and then changed the rules. One evening he hailed the Commissioner from across the street and gave him a blast from a shotgun. The sheriff then arrested him and locked him in the jail he had built, and he was tried in the new courthouse. The incident answered all the children's questions, and it proved that the building had been provided in the nick of time.

APPLES OF HESPERIDES

West of Puget Sound, Hood Canal opens a broad waterway into the Olympic Peninsula. For fifty miles it follows the foot of the mountains, then turns back in a northeasterly direction for twenty miles more. Hood Canal once had big sawmills and big logging operations; Union City, population 165, was once a boom town of stores and saloons built overnight, and tents pitched on land that sold for a thousand dollars an acre. That was when the Union Pacific started to extend its road to Port Townsend. The panic of 1893 began the day the construction gangs

arrived, and the same week they departed forever. Port Townsend never recovered from that blow, but Hood Canal has something enduring and stubborn in its dreamy calm.

The Canal has been the scene of gently stubborn events. There, in early days, a rumor was overtaken and silenced. A young schoolteacher went horseback riding with a married man. It was an innocent and casual happening, but the girl's brothers, twenty miles away, heard the tongues wagging. They got out their rifles and went to the starting point of the rumor. From there the brothers traveled in a widening semicircle, from house to house and farm to farm; hat in one hand and rifle in the other, they requested that the inhabitants stop talking about their sister. Days afterward they came to a frontier which the rumor had not reached, and they turned home. There was no more gossip.

Today the Hood Canal shore is a place of cabin camps, children's summer camps, huckleberry woods where the Indians come each fall, steep wooded shores with the highway notched close to the water's edge, and unambitious, rich meadowlands at the mouths of rivers. Over the land and the hazy blue reach of water there is the haunting sweet silence which the first explorers noticed and which has never been broken.

The Canal is a place to escape from cities and towns, and there is no need to be afraid of the few names that appear on the map of the region. There is Brinnon: a post office-store and gas pump; a deserted house among tall grass and orchard trees; and the Balches' miniature farm and modern white house. The Balches are Brinnon, and they work together or take turns in the post office-store and at the gas pump: Mr. Balch and Mrs. Balch and their capable young daughters—the dark one and the one with blond braids. When the children are not at school or helping in the store, there is the garden to look after, the rabbits to feed, and usually a litter of puppies to play with. On Sunday there is church; on Saturday evening there may be a dance in a near-by community; and sometimes there is a clamming expedition near the mouth of the Dosewallips River. On the river delta there are rich farms; beyond the farms the beach is half a mile wide; in the shallow water at its edge, seals go snorting by, and extreme low tides uncover the smooth periscope ends of geoducks.

In August the Clallam Indians come from the strait of Juan de Fuca,

as they have done for centuries of Augusts, only now they come in cars. They camp on the shore and catch dog salmon, which they smoke for winter. In the fall they pick huckleberries, which they smoke lightly to keep insects away, and dry in the sun. After that the Clallams go home for the winter dances.

On the highway just south of Balches' store an old sign reads, "Ferry to Seabeck," but anyone who takes the side road misses the ferry by years. The slip is in quiet ruins, and it is a long time since the boats ran. Half a mile south a narrow gravel road descends to Pleasant Harbor.

The right way to reach Pleasant Harbor is by boat. The Canal is usually perfect in summer, and even in the late fall it is sometimes possible to cruise comfortably in shirt sleeves on water that reflects patches of snow on the mountains. Pleasant Harbor is an ideal stopping place. You sail through a deep and narrow entrance into a little oval bay, green with reflected trees, and let the anchor go in six fathoms of clear, land-locked water. The only house on shore is a deserted one in the woods at the far end, but at the harbor entrance there are traces of habitation. On the east side, in a tiny clearing at the edge of steep woods, there is one apple tree, loaded with golden apples in the fall. On the west side, just outside the entrance, the gravel road comes down to an open grove, with grass and huckleberry bushes under big trees, the remains of a garden, and an apple tree with golden apples, like a reflection of the one on the other side. For years there stood here a deserted cabin and two sheds, familiar landmarks that weathered only a little from year to year. One fall the cabin and the sheds pooled their resources and grouped themselves into an attractive three-room building, with blue wood-smoke rising from the chimney. A cruising family, coming to investigate, was greeted by a welcoming shout from a ruddy-faced man in his late seventies. "Come on over," he shouted, "you're welcome! What do you think of the house? I did it with a car jack and a couple of rollers, and that girl of mine."

His name was Maxwell, and he had prospered in Oregon until the depression had caught up with him in his old age. He had lost his property, and then a long illness and a series of operations had taken the last of his savings. There was nothing left but his car and an old blue trailer. So he and Mrs. Maxwell decided to go pioneering again. They traveled

north until they happened on the security of Pleasant Harbor. The absentee owner gave them permission to live there, and they were digging in. Maxwell said, "The last house I lived in cost me twenty thousand dollars; this one didn't cost me a cent, and it's more fun!" He was properly proud of his accomplishments and of his wife. "That girl of mine is a fisherman," he said. "She's caught a hundred and thirty salmon this season, not counting trout and other fish."

"That girl of mine" was a sturdy woman of more than eighty, with a wise, wrinkled face and a cultivated voice. She wore riding breeches and walked with a slight limp. Mrs. Maxwell had grown up on the Canadian plains in the days of buffaloes and Indians. She had practically lived in the saddle, but gentility had decreed a sidesaddle, with her right knee hooked over a horn, and the wear had permanently damaged her leg. "People are more sensible now," she observed. "I wear riding breeches all the time, but that doesn't help my knee."

Mr. Maxwell was proud of his wife's fishing, but he didn't think a woman past eighty should have to row a heavy sixteen-foot boat while trolling. "It's too hard work for that girl of mine," he said. "When I get round to it, I'm going to build a power boat for her." He had other plans, like terracing the hillside above the house and putting in a real garden. Mrs. Maxwell encouraged the enthusiastic plans and worked valiantly with what they had.

The next year they were more comfortable. The sidehill had been terraced, and Mrs. Maxwell was cultivating a flower and vegetable garden and experimenting with plant vitamins. On sawhorses under the fir trees, Mr. Maxwell was building the power boat. He had never built a boat before, but he was doing a good job. By the following spring, the boat had been launched and powered with a small inboard motor. It was a good, seaworthy boat, complete even to mystifying oblongs of copper screening tacked to the gunwales at three-foot intervals. Steering his boat toward the fishing grounds, Mr. Maxwell explained, "They're for striking matches. Nobody's going to scratch up the side of my boat!"

The Maxwells lived off the land and the water and used their pension for improvements; they fished, gathered oysters, dug clams, and worked in the garden—a good and busy life. In the summer of 1943 they were gone. On the point where their house had stood nothing remained but charcoal and ashes and twisted metal. One of Maxwell's gadgets had

gone back on him: an oil burner he rigged for the stove had flared back and set fire to the dry old house; it went up so fast the old couple just got out with their lives. All they had left were the old car and the trailer with which they had started. They moved to Five Corners, near Port Townsend, where they had been planning to go anyway because of Mr. Maxwell's health. Habitués of Pleasant Harbor remember affectionately the deserted cabin and the sheds that drew themselves together into a home where valiant people defied age and misfortune and did the things they wanted to do, up to the flaming end.

THE FAR INLETS

South of Hood Canal the farthest, riverlike inlets of Puget Sound penetrate the Olympic Peninsula: Hammersley Inlet, Skookum Inlet, Totten Inlet, known locally as Oyster Bay, Eld Inlet, known as Mud Bay, and Budd Inlet, which achieves importance by having Olympia at its southern end. At the western end of Hammersley Inlet is Shelton, a logging and sawmill town of under four thousand. Otherwise, the radiating southern inlets do not have a settlement large enough to be called a village. They are the scene of generally small farms, small logging operations, and oystering; and their inhabitants are a good cross-section of America.

Among the younger generation a rather large proportion has gone in for higher education, and a still larger proportion has had a look at far corners of the earth; a number of the earlier ones went to Alaska in boats of their own building. There was a high degree of resourcefulness and ingenuity among those who went—and among those who stayed at home. There was Fred Blakely who lived on Pickering Passage; he could change himself into a bear so effectively that his own dogs went baying after him through the woods. He did it once in the presence of witnesses, but it gave him such a fellow feeling for bears that he never hunted them again.

On that occasion Fred had a new pack of dogs he wanted to train for bear hunting. When one of his neighbors killed a large black bear, Fred borrowed the skin and went to work on his plan. He tied up his dogs, and with his wife's help sewed himself up inside the skin. Then he ambled off into the woods. At the appointed time Mrs. Blakely turned

the dogs loose; they had already smelled bear and were going wild, and they picked up the trail in a flash. When Fred heard them baying after him through the woods, he climbed into a dead tree, just as a bear would have done, and waited. A few minutes more and the dogs came to the end of the trail and raved around the foot of the tree. When Fred was sure the lesson had sunk in, he started to be himself again. But he was sewed into his skin so well that he couldn't get at the stitching with his unaccustomed claws.

He was wondering what to try next when something grazed his snout and thudded into the tree, and he heard the crack of a high-powered rifle. Then another bullet thudded into the tree close to his left hind foot. A second rifle crashed, and a bullet from the first thudded into the wood near his left forepaw. Fred let go and fell a dozen feet to the ground, where the dogs pounced on him. When the hunters came up their quarry was underneath the pack; they were afraid to shoot for fear of killing one of the dogs, so they contented themselves with an occasional blow with a rifle butt. The bear made almost human muffled sounds, then it shouted, "For God's sake, get these dogs off me!" The hunters were so surprised by the miracle of a talking bear that they drove off the dogs and helped Fred change back into a battered version of a man.

That one lesson made keen bear dogs of Fred Blakely's pack, and soon afterward they treed a bear on their own account; but Fred didn't go to the house for his rifle; he only looked at the worried old he-bear and thought, "There but by the grace of God am I."

Traditionally the pioneers were a separate race of people, peculiarly endowed to withstand the hardships of the frontier. Actually they were all kinds of people, many of them better suited to an easier life. Among those specially endowed for pioneering was Mrs. Callow, who spent her last twenty years in Shelton. Mrs. Callow was a large, comfortable woman with a placid face, a fine-grained, civilized mind, and a great many friends. Even in her later years she was so unscarred by life that a stranger would never have taken her for a pioneer. When she was a young woman, she had been left a widow with seven redheaded children and an isolated farm on Skookum Inlet.

Other pioneer women with husbands and fewer children wondered

how Mrs. Callow had managed, but she made it sound simple and pleasant. They all worked hard, but the mother managed to keep work from being a burden. The children had their duties, but they also had their rights. As soon as they were big enough to carry firearms, they were allowed rifles or shotguns; and when they were caught up on farm work, they were allowed a day's hunting in the woods—seven redheaded boys and girls in overalls. The hazards of young people hunting grayed a lot of pioneer hair, but Mrs. Callow observed that she had good, careful children, instructed in the use of firearms. She never worried about them, except once.

That occasion had started, like many others, with the children cleaning and oiling their firearms on Friday evening for a Saturday of hunting in an abandoned logging works. The mother slept soundly, but she woke up in the morning with an overpowering premonition that one of the children would be shot that day. She could not shake it off; her mind kept shouting at her that the children must not go. But she had given permission and she mustn't ruin their day with an attack of nerves. So she kissed them good-by and tried to go about her work.

She knew the children would not be home until near dusk, but in the early afternoon she went out to the field they would cross on their way home and listened for them. It was warm, still weather, with blue haze hanging over the field and the woods, and the smell of distant, burning evergreens in the air. All she heard was the dry sound of grasshoppers in the stubble at her feet. She went back to the house, but her mind kept shouting of disaster, and half a dozen times during the afternoon she returned to the field, where she heard nothing but the grasshoppers and was aware of nothing but the haunting melancholy of the autumn air and her own overpowering premonition.

She was there in the warm dusk and she heard the voices of the children, happy and confident, as she wished them to be. She saw them come out of the woods, carrying their rifles and shotguns, and loaded with game. She counted them and there were seven. "Thank God!" she breathed. Just then the children saw her and hurried forward, the tall girl in the lead holding up a bunch of grouse. Hurrying up from the rear of the procession, one of the boys stumbled, and his rifle flashed and roared. The tall girl dropped the grouse and crumpled up.

In the Olympic National Park.

Sea fog on Sonoma's coast.

Snow fields of Mount Frazier.

When the mother reached her, one of the boys had already checked the bleeding, but he was spattered with blood. The bullet had gone through the wrist, close to the bone, and severed the artery. They were seventeen miles from the nearest doctor!

The worst had happened, and the mother's calm returned. In a few minutes they were all in the big skiff: the mother in the stern with the wounded girl, four of the children rowing, and two others waiting their turn. The mother had a lantern and her husband's fat silver watch; at twenty-minute intervals she eased the tourniquet on the girl's arm, trying for the delicate balance between having her bleed to death and losing her arm through lack of circulation.

The children rowed splendidly, four at a time, with the two odd ones keeping a lookout in the bow. They had started on an ebbing tide and the boat raced with the current out of the narrow inlet into wider Oyster Bay. They pulled swiftly past Windy Point, close to the bluff, in the dark. They rounded Steamboat Island in rough water, with the muttering of confused tides in their ears, and headed through Squaxin Passage, past Hope Island. It was then late at night, and they were as many miles away from Olympia as when they had started. But they were at the hub of the radiating inlets, and they could head for their destination at last. They pulled past Cushman Point and headed for the distant lights of Olympia, but almost as soon as they turned, they met the tide coming out of Eld Inlet and Budd Inlet, and they had to fight their way south, with the blisters on their hands wearing away to raw flesh. They rowed endlessly in silence, with the mother gauging the passing of time and flowing of blood, and the children who had been resting changing places with the most exhausted rowers. The same tide that had helped them on their way now held them back. After a while it stood still, and the boat gained speed, and the lights of town began to shine clearly. Past midnight, they came alongside the float in Olympia in a final burst of speed, and the young rowers collapsed over their oars.

At Olympia a doctor stitched the cut artery. The other children's hands healed, and none of them was the worse for the experience. One of the redheaded boys may even have profited by trying to find the last ounce of sustained speed that could be got out of flesh and blood

and wooden oars. He was "Rusty" Callow, who later developed championship crews at the University of Washington and became the most famous rowing coach in America.

THE RACE OF CITIES

At forty-seven degrees North, Grays Harbor drives a wedge into the Washington coast, fourteen miles wide and eighteen long. From the point of the wedge the Chehalis River extends like a crack across the Coast Range region, dividing the Olympic Peninsula from the Willapa Hills to the south.

In the spring of 1792, before his discovery of the Columbia River, Captain Robert Gray sailed into the great forest-walled bay without successfully waking it. When he sailed away Grays Harbor slept, almost forgotten, for another seventy-five years.

When it was time for the first white pioneer on Grays Harbor, history appears to have been explicit about the type—an Irishman from the neighborhood of New York City, with experience in the California gold fields, and in search of pasture for cattle.

William O'Leary had the qualifications: he was from Cork, Ireland, by way of New York, and California, where he had prospected unsuccessfully, and he was looking for a place where he could raise beef cattle. So, in 1848, history sent him down the Chehalis River to Grays Harbor in a dugout canoe, and a storm forced him to land at the mouth of a creek in what is now South Aberdeen. O'Leary accepted it as an omen, and there he built his cabin and planted the seed potatoes which he had bought from a Hudson's Bay post.

So far everything had gone very well, but William O'Leary had his potato patch; the waters were full of fish, and the woods were so full of elk and deer that there seemed no need for cattle. O'Leary lived beside the creek for the next fifty-three years without building a city or even taking a wife.

After O'Leary had lived his happy hermit's life for nine years, history made a second attempt. This time it selected Samuel Benn, an Irishman from Brooklyn, who had worked in the California gold fields and who was in search of pasture for beef cattle. Samuel Benn came down the Chehalis River to its junction with the Wishkah, or "Stinking" River,

and there he built his cabin and lived in solitude for years. And there the parallel ends.

Where O'Leary had dreamed of raising cattle, Benn raised cattle and drove them up along the Chehalis River to market in Olympia. While he lived in solitude he dreamed of a city on his claim, and when he visited Puget Sound he talked about the rich timber and fish resources of Grays Harbor.

Presently settlers drifted in, though not to Samuel Benn's immediate neighborhood. One handful settled near the mouth of the Hoquiam River, four miles to the west; others went to Chehalis Point, at the entrance to the harbor, and took up claims at the edge of the Pacific; and still others stopped short of Grays Harbor, on the Chehalis River.

In 1861, Grays Harbor County was created out of the northern half of Pacific County; Samuel Benn was elected sheriff, and Scammons, on the Chehalis River, was voted the county seat and rechristened Montesano. Altogether there were seventy-four votes cast in a county as big as the State of Delaware. Votes were scarce in those days, and when court convened at Chehalis, in the adjoining county, the judge could not always find enough men to serve on the jury. He solved the problem by having the prisoners sit on each other's juries; it worked very well and there was no swapping of leniencies. The prisoners were all honorable men who tried each other fairly, and all went to jail together.

In Grays Harbor County the race between cities swayed back and forth. Montesano had the county seat, but Chehalis Point had the school, and Montesano people with children had to move there for the school year, or board their children. Chehalis Point was a strong contender, and presently it had the first wedding in the new county: before breakfast on a chilly morning in 1862, Justice of the Peace Patterson Luark united in marriage Sheriff Samuel Benn and Martha Redman, of Melbourne. Benn had lived alone for five years, and when he brought his bride home to his cabin beside the Wishkah River she was the first citizen for the metropolis he had dreamed.

Soon after the ceremony at Chehalis Point, the second wedding in the county took place at the village of Hoquiam. The wedding presents were a cow, a calf, a little dog, household linen and bedding, and a deed to sixty acres of land. The gifts were practical, and the ceremony was enlivened by the presence of a naked little boy carrying a bow and

arrows. He had wandered in from the near-by Indian camp, and any resemblance to anyone mythological was purely accidental.

In the summer of 1863 Chehalis Point had a new triumph—a visit from Territorial Governor William Pickering, accompanied by the Superintendent of Indian Affairs and the Surveyor General. Justice of the Peace Patterson Luark was the welcoming committee, and Citizen Williams supplied transportation in his wagon. The Governor expressed a desire to see the lighthouse on the point, and they drove over the smooth sand toward the thundering Pacific. Williams felt the intoxication of the big event and the Squirrel Whiskey he had drunk, and fate put a long-horned Spanish cow on the beach. Williams whipped up his horses and dashed in pursuit, with the distinguished guests hanging on for their lives. The cow veered sharply and the horses veered after her, upsetting the wagon—and Governor and Superintendent and Surveyor General and Justice of the Peace and driver went rolling in the sand. It may have been an omen that Chehalis Point would lose in the race of young cities.

At the mouth of the Wishkah, city building progressed slowly. In 1878, after twenty-one years, there was just enough settlement to have a school, but that same year Samuel Benn obtained an industry for his city.

Benn's daughter, Mrs. Wappenstein, who still lives in the family's old house in Aberdeen, recalls the event. The children were in school when someone brought the news that the big event was happening. School was dismissed, and the children ran down to the shore in time to see the arrival of Industry. It came before a fresh westerly breeze, in the form of a big schooner with white sails. Close to the waving children it stormed by; off Sam Benn's Point it rounded up into the wind, and the anchor was let go with a roar of cable chain that echoed from the woods.

The new industry was a salmon cannery, directed by George Hume of Scotland and named the Aberdeen Packing Plant for the home of Scotch stockholders. Samuel Benn named his community Aberdeen, for its first industry.

The following year, the schooner "Kate and Ann" started plying between Grays Harbor and the Columbia River; two years later, logging camps started on the lower Chehalis; and the year after that, in 1882,

machinery for the first sawmill was unloaded at Hoquiam, consigned to George H. Simpson. The following year saw a rush for timber claims on Grays Harbor; the magnitude of the scramble can be judged by one of its by-products. The *Chehalis Valley Chronicle* was founded to advertise notice of application and of final proof on claims, and in ten months the owners realized a twenty-four hundred per cent profit.

Near the end of the timber-rush year, Samuel Benn platted a hundred acres of his claim which straddled the Wishkah; the following year, he sold a millsite on the east side of the river to A. J. West, a Michigan lumberman; and the year after he sold a millsite on the west side to Captain John Weatherwax, another Michigan lumberman. Then he sold two more millsites, one on each side of the river. Samuel Benn, who had lived in solitude and dreamed of a city, saw two settlements building on his claim. In 1888 he saw the settlements join in the incorporated town of Aberdeen. He platted an additional three hundred acres, and in the next two years the population jumped from eight hundred to nine thousand, and he saw a forest of ships' masts along the Wishkah. The telegraph and the railway came, and Grays Harbor pioneering was over.

At present there is the feeling that pioneering must lead to splendid things. In the Grays Harbor country it led to a great deal that was not splendid. The scramble for timber wealth reached its peak early in the present century, with high-powered logging equipment and "highball" methods that took an appalling toll of human lives; the towns of Aberdeen and Hoquiam, which grew until they met, had more than their share of ugliness, and in 1912, when the loggers demanded $2.50 for an eight-hour day, a citizens' committee silenced them with pick handles, and civil authorities closed their hiring hall. In the next turbulent twenty-odd years the temper of citizens changed, and in 1935, when the National Guard was called out to protect the operation of mills during a strike, thousands of citizens marched in protest and held a stormy demonstration. The history of the Grays Harbor region leaves the feeling that something was missing between the brave early days and the present. Perhaps it was a definition of the American way of life and a plan for achieving it.

Samuel Benn lived to see Aberdeen much as it is today, and he was pardonably proud of having twenty thousand neighbors on the claim

where he had once lived in solitude. But his fondest recollections were of the times when Olympia was his nearest market, and he went to town twice a year. He died in 1936, at the age of one hundred and three.

Big-time physical pioneering is over in the Grays Harbor country, but there have been throwbacks to earlier times. In 1936, after the fruit harvest in the Chehalis Valley, migratory pickers from the Dust Bowl discovered the Pacific and camped on its shore. And they considered the destiny of America while living on clams which they dug from the beach.

South of the entrance to Grays Harbor, within sound of the Pacific, pioneering continues on a diminished scale. On what was recently wasteland, thickets of buckbrush disappear, the flat peat bogs are drained and scalped; weedless lawns of cranberry bushes appear, and trim white houses replace unpainted cabins. The Finns are the modern pioneers at Grayland, conquering the stubborn land and nursing the cranberries that grew wild on their native bogs in the old country. Here the cultivation is intensive, and two acres is a full-time job for a man and wife. It is also a living, and after a few good years the couple may be able to build a comfortable home.

Cranberry culture has developed special equipment, such as cars running on tracks over the bogs and carrying far-reaching pipes for spraying. There is also a super-vacuum cleaner for picking the berries, and growers have experimented with an airplane motor and propeller for driving away fog. But even with modern equipment, it is hard work in perpetual dampness; rheumatism is the common industrial disease, and some of the enterprising have worked themselves to death at a comparatively early age. But it is a living, and an industry which the Finns understand, and they make no mystery of it. When Carl Johnson of Grayland was asked the secret of his success, he said, "To grow cranberries you need strong wimmens."

The Finns of Grayland are like other Finnish-Americans, who become less distinguishable from Americans of other stock with the passing of each generation; but they continue a few old-country traditions like steam baths with water poured over hot rocks, and a cedar branch to whip up the circulation of blood. On Midsummer Day, the twenty-fourth of June, they put on native costumes and celebrate all night with bonfires and folk dances and old songs. At Christmas lutefisk takes the

place of turkey, and on New Year's Day the Graylanders gather in their community hall for the annual soothsaying. As each in turn pours a ladle of melted lead into a cauldron, the stillness of the hall is broken by the explosive hiss of molten metal in water; a puff of steam rises and drifts away, and the learned men of the colony read the pattern in which the metal has congealed and prophesy what is in store for the pourer for the coming year.

NOSTALGIC SHORE

Early in World War II an invasion of the Washington coast was a definite possibility. One likely beachhead was Grays Harbor, funneling to a level highway that leads to the cities of Puget Sound. According to local fishermen, the choice of the beachhead was indicated shortly before Pearl Harbor by a strange epidemic among Japanese citizens of fishing out of Aberdeen and Hoquiam. They forgot the familiar channels and blundered their boats ashore on every likely and unlikely sandspit and flat. As fishermen, the captains had a right to their expressed embarrassment, but what is bad for a salmon troller might be good for a landing barge.

The other probable beachhead was Willapa Harbor, beginning a dozen miles south of Grays Harbor and extending to within five miles of the Columbia River. Willapa, once Shoalwater Bay, opens to a twenty-five-mile width inside the entrance, and its eighty miles of water front are ringed by a highway with connections south to the Columbia, north to Grays Harbor and Puget Sound, and east through the moderate Willapa Hills to the traffic hub of Chehalis, with highway connections to everywhere.

For most of the soldiers sent to the defense of Willapa Harbor, it was only a name until they disembarked, although it is one of the earliest-settled regions in the State. They found the shores of the bay a nostalgic place of quiet, wooded headlands, herds of cattle in calm-toned, diked meadows that suggest Holland, river mouths and sloughs and lonely beaches around a vast expanse of blue water that diminished with the ebbing tide and uncovered oyster beds that stretched as far as the eye could follow.

The largest settlement directly on Willapa Harbor is South Bend, county seat of Pacific County, with a population of eighteen hundred,

and a blend of the frontier and mellowed civilization. One of the important places in town is Semphill's Drugstore, "where they know everything about everything." Service at one restaurant has taken a turn for the better because, as the proprietress explained, her "daughter's husband's sister's husband's mother" has come to work in the kitchen. The weekly South Bend *Journal* advertises itself as having the "Largest Circulation in Pacific County of Any Paper on Earth," and it has other distinctions. While metropolitan dailies ignore people who spend their time looking down into excavations and up at buildings under construction, Editor Hazeltine has organized these forward-looking citizens into the Bystanders Club. (During the depression, when the WPA was putting up useful buildings, the Bystanders had their clubroom in an unfinished privy, and their words of wisdom and deliberations were faithfully recorded in the *Journal*.)

On the peninsula southwest of South Bend is the settlement of Bay Center, with an oyster cannery and shell-crushing plant on which the population of two hundred depends. Bay Center is a village of mostly old houses, tall shade trees, and streets that are unpaved broad paths without enough traffic to generate mud or dust. You walk on them with a feeling of coming home, and with a realization that the pavements of civilization rob you of something in taking away your contact with the earth.

The mixed white and Indian population of Bay Center is a clue to local history. Another clue is the fine old Chinese willowware dishes in some of the part-Indian homes.

Beginning in 1849, California gold sent ships north along the Pacific coast in quest of necessities and luxuries for San Francisco—lumber and shingles and ice and oysters. Superior oysters in quantity were found on Shoalwater Bay, now Willapa Harbor. The oyster industry began in 1850, followed by the shipping of lumber. The region had its nostalgic quality then, and occasionally sailors from oyster schooners or lumber ships deserted to settle down with Indian girls, and some of the deep-water sailors brought china from China. The Indian girls became devoted wives and careful housekeepers, and ancient dishes continue in the families of their descendants while collectors coax in vain.

Bay Center has never gone in heavily for "Culture" or higher education, but one of the colorful spots is the town library. Mrs. Clark is

the librarian, and the library is on the old homestead. Off the unpaved street, in the garden around the house built in the seventies, brightly-painted wooden birds sit on stakes, and painted wooden sunflowers and roses and lilies compete with the flowers of nature. The public library is in the dining room of the house, but since the demands on it are not heavy, Mrs. Clark is likely to be found in her upstairs studio, among the fumes of paint and turpentine. She is a brisk, bright woman of Pennsylvania descent, with an urge toward beauty. A self-taught artist, she paints and sculps, but her principal work stems from local industry. With selected clusters of big Pacific oystershells and additions of plastic wood and paint, she makes up souvenir ash trays and book ends, and swans and ducks and flowers. Her mother did the same kind of work before her, and she covered the walls and ceilings of some of the rooms with landscapes and carefully-done vines and flowers. One of her most successful creations is a fire screen of wire netting, decorated with graceful sprays of dogwood blossoms made from Economy jar tops. After her mother's work and some splendid hooked rugs, Mrs. Clark's chief pride is a deck light from the schooner "Jessie Nickerson," wrecked on the Willapa Bar. That was long ago, but such things can still happen. There was the steam schooner "Trinidad," in 1939. She left Raymond with a cargo of lumber and struck on the bar in heavy weather. While she was pounding to pieces, the Coast Guard rescued twenty of the crew; the other two had been washed overboard during the night.

It was a sad event, that brought a different kind of sadness to one of the citizens of Bay Center. Two days before, he had bought lumber for a new house, and he stood disconsolately beside the pile as his neighbors went by with truckloads and carloads of lumber salvaged from the sea.

One of Bay Center's leading citizens is Bert Walther, superintendent of the oyster company. Bert is big and broad and slow-spoken, and modest about his achievements. Other oystermen say that Bert can take an oyster dredge to any designated bed in the great bay and set it within ten feet of the boundary line, even if the markers have been washed away. But Bert prefers to talk about hunting, or the Army.

One of Bert's favorite subjects is the army that guarded Willapa Harbor from invasion during the war. Bert's son served with distinction in the Pacific, and Bert considers the American Army the best in the world;

but Willapa Harbor is quite a place when you know it, and even more when you don't: a setting for a Comedy of Errors. . . . There was the young ex-civilian officer who tried to read the mysterious code flashed from a moving light on the beach. The dashes he took down on a pad refused to make sense, and there were no dots. He appealed to his sergeant, who could only tell him it wasn't Morse code. Then Bert came in with local knowledge. "That isn't any code," he explained. "It's Grandpa Wright going to his boat with a lantern by his side, and his walking legs make it flash on and off." . . . Then there were the two Brooklyn boys who shot it out with two prowlers. They were on night patrol, and the trail along the shore divided, one fork rising toward a headland, and the other descending to the beach. So one boy took the high road and one took the low road, agreeing to stop at a designated point. The one on the beach overshot the mark—and was fired on by a sniper in the woods. He returned the fire, and kept on shooting until his ammunition was gone. Then he started back to camp for more. Where the trails joined he met his partner, also going back for more ammunition.

And there were the saboteurs who did too good a job. . . . That was the time the defenders of Willapa Harbor divided up into teams and fought a sham battle, the defending Green Army against the invading Purple Army. Well, the Purple invaders were doing all right until they were infiltrated by Green Army saboteurs who offered to show them a way of cutting around the defenders and falling on them from the rear—or giving them the slip and going on with the invasion of America. The Purples fell into the trap and followed the saboteurs along an old logging road that came to an end. From there they stepped off into the wilderness—and were missing for two days. All of them got back alive, but there were casualties that included two broken legs. And nobody was any sorrier than the saboteurs who had lost themselves along with the enemy.

But the most alarming incident of the Willapa War happened to a civilian. He was on the shore at dusk when he saw soldiers with rifles coming along the beach. He knew there were patrols and thought no more about it until the soldiers were close enough for him to see their faces. They all had Japanese faces, and then he saw the emblem of the Rising Sun on their shoulders! Well, he didn't wait to see anything more;

he just high-tailed into military headquarters, shouting that the invasion had started, and the Japs were in possession of the beach! That time the soldier had the laugh on the civilian. He hadn't seen either Japanese or Rising Suns: he had seen Japanese-American members of the Sunset Division who were there to defend their country. Their officers had absolute faith that they would have made a good job of it, too, if there had been an invasion.

THE GEOLOGICAL STORY

BY DANIEL E. WILLARD

Logically, we should place the geological story first, raising our bastion from some primordial sea. Then we should tell the story of plant covering and the coming of the animals, all this before the story of the Spanish fathers and their missions. But until the lay reader has learned some place geography, some variety of landscape, he or she is not ready to understand the geology. (R. P.)

All the ranges of the Coast Range system have a common origin in that they were all formed by upheaval and they all have a common core, or base, of granitic rock. A mountain is not merely a large hill; nor is a hill a miniature mountain. A hill, generally speaking, is a result of wearing away, or erosion. A mountain is primarily the result of upheaval of the crust of the earth. The Coast Ranges have all been formed by upheaval.

The western margin of the continent has been severely rent and broken by mountain upheavals. Time is long in geology. Mountain ranges, the ancestors of the present ranges, have been upheaved and worn down to plains, the plains covered by the sea, and finally the ranges as we see them today have been uplifted and are now being worn down before our eyes. There is evidence that the ranges of the Pacific coast are being slowly uplifted today. There is no question that they are being worn down by erosion.

It is the wearing down that interests us, for it is thus that the peaks become rugged and the slopes become dissected into gullies and canyons. It is in the mountain valleys that history has been made. In the valleys are vineyards, orchards, gardens, broad fields, and the homes of men. On the hills are fine building sites, and flowers bloom in the gorges. If erosion had not been at work, there had been no hills and no gorges. Had the mountains not been uplifted, there had been no erosion. So when we dash our feet against the granite rocks on the mountain slopes, or as we scale the peaks, let us give thanks that great earth-interior masses of molten rock, called "batholiths," were driven upward from

earth's depths and caused the mountains to be uplifted. We salute with joy the rough hard granite which forms the core of the mountains and which greets the eye and bumps our feet, for it has determined the form of the coast and directed the trends of human progress.

Let us journey over the ranges over which the Spanish padres laboriously traveled. We may not follow their footsteps, but we shall see the same mountains, gaze at the same peaks, cross (or try to cross) the same gullies and rocky ridges, and if not with the same spiritual zeal, at least with as great enjoyment of this rugged mountain land.

ACROSS THE PENINSULAR RANGE

Between the Pacific Ocean at San Diego on the west and the Imperial Valley and the famed Salton Sea on the east lies an immense mountain block, the Peninsular Range. This is a continuation of the Coast Range system, and extends throughout the length of the Peninsula of Lower California (how much farther under the sea is not known). The mountainous plateau extends one hundred miles north in the State of California, descending at the north to the broad plain about Riverside and the Perris Plain. Originally the region was a broad flat plain not much above sea level. It was uplifted as a vast block, raised higher on the eastern side on the line of a "fault," or break in the earth's crust, and rotated or tilted toward the west.

Not only has the block as a whole been uplifted and rotated, but the block has been shattered by many faults, or fractures. Flat-topped blocks stand out higher and higher toward the east from the coast at San Diego. A ride over this mountain range is one to be remembered. The keen eye of the sojourner who crosses it will observe that the rise eastward from the coastal plain is marked by a series of stairlike steps, each step toward the east higher than the preceding one. The higher peaks and ridges rise from one thousand to twenty-five hundred feet above the little canyons and valleys around their immediate bases. Each successive little valley is higher than the one immediately preceding it. The journey eastward across the range is literally going up stairs! The elevated blocks are segments of the original plain, each cut off by faults and uplifted.

The mountain plateau reaches its highest elevation in the Laguna Mountains, Cuyama Peak being 5,880 feet above sea level. The eastern

and higher side of the mountain plateau is cut off abruptly by a great fault wall, the southern extension of the Elsinore fault, a sheer wall of rock descending abruptly to the low plain of the Colorado Desert. The eastern side of the great block has been uplifted to the height of nearly a mile above sea level, and the block has been rolled or tilted toward the west so that its western side is below sea level. (Mission Bay is the drowned valley of San Diego River.) The fault wall on the east is steep and rugged, cut by deep gullies.

The descent from Monument Peak in the Laguna Mountains to the floor of the desert valley at the foot of the "scarp," or cliff, is forty-five hundred feet in four or five miles. The view from Cuyama Peak is an impressive one: far to the north rise Mounts San Jacinto and San Bernardino; to the east the dazzling white plain of the Colorado Desert; to the south the Republic of Mexico; to the west the broad blue of the Pacific Ocean. Near-by, spreads out the top of the mountain plateau "like an angry Ocean of knobby peaks, with short ridges running in every direction, with numerous gorges and canyons from 500 to 1,500 feet deep."

The descent to the desert plain to the east from the crest of this mountain block calls for skill on the part of the driver and calm nerves on the part of all. No advice from the back seat is permissible. A scream at a hairpin turn may be fatal. Carrizo Gorge, fifteen miles north of the international boundary, is followed by the railroad but not by the highway. There is scant room for the railroad. The highway leads by Smugglers' Cave near the boundary line (hurry by!); then turn north and see the rocks in Boulder Park at the foot of Mount Jacumba.

THE COLORADO DESERT LIES BEYOND

Now on the desert plain, stop and take a drink at Coyote Wells (you will probably be thirsty) and, if interested in what has happened to the forests that once thrived in this now arid country, turn south and visit the petrified forest near the Mexican line. At Coyote Wells a small stream crosses the highway. This stream has eroded a gorge in the soft sedimentary rocks which is appropriately called Painted Gorge from the variegated colors of the rocks.

North of Coyote Wells rise the Carrizo Mountains (called also Coyote Mountains). In the flanks of these mountains are coral reefs, fossil relics

of myriads of polyps that once thrived in great numbers, or great masses, in the (Tertiary) seas that once covered this region. These mountains are noted for the occurrence of fossils in great numbers, not only of corals but of sea urchins, mollusks, and snails or conchs (Gastropoda). The shells, or their casts, have weathered out of the rocks and strew the slopes in great profusion. These fossil beds can be reached from the old stage road between Carrizo and Plaster City, fifteen miles.

The vast, broad plain of the Imperial Valley is the floor of the sunken basin of the Colorado Desert. This is a segment of the earth's crust which was depressed probably at the time when the Great Peninsular Range block was broken and uplifted. Superstition, Carrizo, and Black Mountains are outliers of the Peninsular Range extending into the valley.

Travertine Rock marks the high water stage of the ancient larger Salton Sea, called Lake Cahuilla. The granite rocks of the Santa Rosa Mountains projected half a mile into Lake Cahuilla from the eastern end of the range. The rock was named from the deposit upon the rocks of travertine (calcium carbonate) from the waves of the ancient lake. The beach line of the ancient lake is 40 feet above sea level and 315 feet above the present surface of Salton Sea.

North of Travertine Rock is the famed sub-sea level Coachella Valley (*coachella* means heat) and here are Indio (-22 feet) and Mecca (-197 feet), home of "Asiatic" (Deglet Noor) dates. Mecca's "wailing wall" is the high fault wall of the mountain range. Here is desert, the most abject, where horned toads, greasewood, and cacti represent nature's effort to maintain biologic life; nevertheless palms, figs, and 119 varieties of dates are produced in commercial quantities (as testify the fruit stands and grocery stores of the east). Water that dashed down rocky gorges in near-by mountains—only to sink in the porous soil of the desert, to be recovered by pumping or from springs which rise to the surface by hydrostatic pressure—is the magic that transforms the otherwise parched and barren desert into a veritable modern Garden of Eden.

Salton Sea occupies the lowest part of the sunken basin of the Colorado Desert, at the foot of the great fault wall. The bottom of the basin, the Sink, is more than five hundred feet below the level of the sea. It was a dry salt bed before the Colorado River broke from its banks and inundated the valley. Evaporation from the water surface has been

determined to be at the rate of one hundred and thirteen inches per annum, whereas the annual precipitation is less than three inches.

The basin is surrounded by rugged mountains, all deeply gashed by gorges and canyons cut by torrential streams which follow seasonal downpours. These streams dash out upon porous deltas at their mouths, when they flow at all, and the waters rapidly sink and disappear below the surface. It is these ground waters, seeping into the central basin, that prevent the quick desiccation of the basin. The bottom of the basin was at one time a salt bed and will probably be one again.

The fault wall of the Peninsular Mountain plateau and the slopes of Mount San Jacinto to the north are serrated by canyons and gorges. These are dry during much of the year. During "seasonal" rains, which often are in the form of cloudbursts, these canyons and gorges, minia-ture valleys, carry torrential floods. Notable among the many is Palm Canyon, below the mouth of which is the famed "Capital of the Desert," Palm Springs, where artists, theatrical stars, scenario writers, and every-day travelers (who have the price) are wont to assemble. This canyon has its beginning high on Santa Rosa Peak, in the cluster of mountains of this name, the southern extension of the San Jacinto Range. The canyon is twenty-five miles in length. Occupying the bed of the canyon for several miles is a natural forest of California fan palms, which has been described (rightly, we think) as one of the most enchanting in the United States.

The mountain slopes are the desert's western wall—the mountain plateau's eastern fault wall—a troubled wilderness of bare slopes, tree-less hogbacks, and dry, rock-bound canyons, gorges, and gullies. This, the Sierra Madre de California of the early Spaniards, is a wild region, this wonderland of southern California, scantily watered, uninhabited, unvisited—except by a herdsman in search of strayed cattle, or a science lover who has the temerity to seek out the secrets of nature in unknown places, or the foolhardy adventurer who wants to get somewhere where no one has been before.

The story is authentically told of a zealous mountain climber whose ambition was to scale a peak which had long defied all climbers, and which (he thought) no one had ever reached. The climb was little short of impossible. When there was no further foothold (or handhold) he cut notches in the hard rocks with a chisel to make further ascent

possible, at the imminent risk of death by falling. All day he toiled. He reached the top in time to see the setting sun kiss the surrounding mountaintops. He had accomplished the hitherto (supposedly) impossible. He had scaled the peak which had defied many ambitious climbers—and lo! in a crevice in the rocks was a rusted fragment of tin, relic of a grocery store which had contained the lunch of someone who had been there before!

THE SAN JACINTO RANGE IS MONARCH OF THE SOUTH

Standing high above the desert plain are the San Jacinto Mountains, one of the most stupendous and majestic mountain ranges of southern California and of the Coast Range system. The core of the range is granite. Through this hard granite rock, above which are sedimentary rocks, a boring fifteen feet in diameter has been made to carry water from the Colorado River to the city of Los Angeles.

The range is cut off on three sides by faults. A sunken valley separates the San Bernardino Range from the San Jacinto Range. It is thought that the two ranges may once have been continuous and may have been separated in the earth disturbance by which the San Andreas fault came into being. The cold barren peak of the San Jacinto Range reaches more than two miles into the clouds. The tourist will look up and long to scale the top, but he had better make the climb in imagination only. It is not that the peak has never been touched by the foot of man, but its slopes are terrific. On the north slope Snow Creek descends four thousand feet in a mile of the stream's descent. On the northwest side the slope falls twenty-five hundred feet in as many feet of horizontal distance. Torrential streams have notched deep narrow canyons with precipitous walls in the mountainsides. To climb up is impossible. To attempt to go down is to fall—to death.

If the visitor longs to climb to the top of the mountain, near the top (if he gets there) he will find a flat tableland, a segment of the plain which was uplifted with the rising of the mountain. This flat surface was carried up intact nearly two miles. It is the sloping sides of the mountain that are vigorously eroded. The top of the mountain is the last to be eroded. From a distance, as from the plain surrounding the mountain, the top looks to be a peak. The flat plain, however, is there.

The flat plain is large enough and nearly level enough for a base-

ball diamond. But if the ball should be driven beyond the limits of the diamond and fall over the rim of the plain it would indeed be a "lost ball." It would be hazardous to attempt to recover it.

If a tight-rope were imagined stretched from the top of San Jacinto to the top of Toro Peak twenty-five miles south in the Santa Rosa group, a panoramic survey would embrace most of southern California: it would reach over the Pacific Ocean on the west; over the ten-thousand foot plateau of Santa Catalina in Lower California; over the Gulf of California on the south; over the broad sandy sweep of the Colorado Delta to the mouth of the Colorado River on the southeast; and far over the Mohave Desert on the northeast. At the foot of the mountain is the Devil's Garden on the broad plain of the Coachilla Desert, where the giant barrel cactus abounds, and more species of cactus grow than are known in any other locality in the Colorado Desert. Near-by is the terrific jungle of huge boulders at the mouth of Mission Creek, many of whose boulders weigh many tons. Twenty-nine Palms, claimed to be the only true oasis in all the desert, with palm trees seventy to eighty feet high, is only a few miles away. On the north extends the San Bernardino Range. The crag-flecked Perris Plain (where sweet potatoes of the finest quality are grown extensively) is beyond. Let the imagination have full sway, but do not attempt to walk the tight-rope or to climb to the peak of either mountain.

There is valid geologic evidence that the uplifting of the San Jacinto Range to its present height occurred in very recent geologic time. Evidence that the uprising of the mountain may be still in progress is seen in the earthquake tremors which a few years ago violently shook the villages of San Jacinto and Hemet. This is known to have been caused by earth movements along the San Jacinto fault. Evidence that earth conditions that are associated with mountain building are still existent is apparent along the line of the San Andreas fault. Mud volcanoes occur along the line of the fault through Imperial Valley. A group of mud volcanoes and boiling pools is a few miles northwest of the city of Imperial. Near these is a row of knobs of obsidian (volcanic glass), pumice, scoriaceous lava, and tuff. A group of nearly perfect cones, with little craters at their tops, existed before the region was flooded by the breaking of the Colorado River from its banks in 1904-1905. Along with these were hot mud pools and craters emitting gases. A more extensive series

of mud craters and geysers occurs along the shore of Volcanic Lake, south of the international boundary.

In the stratified rocks of San Jacinto fossil forms are found by which the age of the rocks is determined. The rocks of the Coast Ranges have been the burial places of many species of animals and of many plants. The sea bottom has been the tomb of myriads of minute organisms (diatoms) whose tiny skeletons have furnished the material for thousands of feet of shale rock, and from whose small bodies have come the oil of many "gusher" oil wells. In the rocks of San Jacinto's sides oysters and other marine forms of life have found their final resting place. Far from the waves of the ocean, in the flanks of the mountains, where rain seldom falls and temperatures go far up into three figures Fahrenheit, oyster beds galore await the call of the scientist, of the interested traveler, or indeed of the hungry tourist (though he cannot eat them, for they have been in cold—stone—storage for probably ten million years). But they are there in great numbers and beautiful to behold. Let the traveler not be discouraged because of hunger. Palm Springs, with spacious and elaborate hotels, is on the plain of the desert near-by, near the mouth of Palm Canyon at the base of the range.

THE SAN BERNARDINO RANGE AN UPLIFTED BLOCK

The San Bernardino Range is a vast fault block eighty miles in length and thirty miles in width, extending in a southeasterly direction across southern California. The block is cut off on all sides by faults. The surface is that of an old worn-down landscape, an old plain uplifted intact, with rounded hills, hummocks, and ridges. The fault which bounds the block on the north is abrupt. At its foot lies the Mohave Desert. The southern boundary is the San Andreas fault, which runs through San Gorgonio Pass. At the western end, the range is cut off abruptly in Cajon Pass, through which also runs the San Andreas fault. The southern slope of the range is dissected by many stream gorges, at the mouths of which are sandy and gravelly deltas, or "washes." On these sandy plains are many fine citrus orchards.

San Gorgonio Pass lies along the southern side of the range which separates the San Bernardino and San Jacinto Ranges. This pass was discovered by W. P. Blake in 1853, and was hailed as the much-sought acces-

sible route for a railroad between Los Angeles and the interior of the continent. The discovery of the pass determined the construction of the Southern Pacific Railroad. Blake and his party entered the pass from the west, and joyfully proclaimed: "Here at last is discovered the greatest break through the western cordilleras leading from the slopes of Los Angeles and the Pacific coast into the interior wilderness."

High on San Bernardino plateau are two outstanding peaks, San Gorgonio (11,485 feet) and San Bernardino (10,500 feet). These peaks are remnants of a very ancient landscape. A flat-topped ridge extends between the two peaks, and beyond to Cajon Pass. To the north lies a flat plain at about the level of the top of the ridge. This is an ancient plain that was originally uplifted in the upheaval of the mountain range. This ancient plain is four to five thousand feet above the rolling hummocky plain and the broad valleys and meadows of the main mountaintop. On the lower plain rest Bear Lake and Arrowhead Lake, six to seven thousand feet above sea level.

On the summit of San Gorgonio Peak are knobs of granite boulders carved by wind-driven sand and long-continued weathering into fantastic shapes, pinnacles of granite boulders resembling crude monuments of masonry, one huge block resting upon another. High upon the mountain, patches of snow linger throughout the year. Well-defined "cirques," glacially gouged valley heads, and glacial deposits, "moraines," give evidence of ice action. A typical cirque occurs on the northeast side of the mountain, and, below, a well-defined moraine lies across the valley of Whitewater River. A large moraine lies across the valley of the south fork of Santa Ana River, on the northwest side of the mountain. Five semicircular moraines cross the canyon of Hathaway Creek on the northwest slope. Viewed from below, these moraines present a bold front of jumbled boulders, many of great size.

A wrinkle or fold in the rocks, related to the uplifting of the San Jacinto and San Bernardino Mountains, extends from the west end of San Gorgonio Pass south and west to the fault wall of the San Bernardino Range, separating the San Gabriel Valley on the west from the San Bernardino Basin on the east. This is commonly called the Bunker Hill Dike, though it is not a dike at all but an uplifted fold in the rocks. This fold acts as a dam over which the Santa Ana River passes. The

depression east of the fold, or "dike," is called the San Bernardino Basin. This basin is very deep, a sunken valley, and is filled with detritus washed from the mountains. Such a basin, saturated with water, was called by the Spaniards a "*ciénaga*," a name that is still retained. The city of San Bernardino is located on this *ciénaga*.

At the eastern end of this uplifted fold, west of Beaumont and the head of the pass, the rocks are soft and easily broken up, and have been eroded by streams to a very rough badland type of topography. In the rock formations of the badlands are found a great array of fossil remains of animals that once roamed these plains. Animals that have long since disappeared from the earth lived and thrived in the then sub-tropical climate. Among them were droves of small light-limbed horses (Pliohippus), several species of camels, antelopes, deer, pigs, and four-tusked elephants. In the forests lived saber-toothed cats, ground sloths, wolves, and bears of great size.

High on the six-thousand-foot fault wall that overlooks the city of San Bernardino, the Rim-of-the-World Highway leads from the basin where the city stands to Arrowhead Lake on the mountaintop and, beyond, twenty-five miles to Bear Lake. The construction of this highway was an engineering achievement. Through Cajon Canyon, where sandstone rock, metamorphosed to quartzite, has been eroded into massive columns, sharp pinnacles, and boulders of tremendous size, the highway has been toenailed into the steep rock wall and winds with many hairpin turns to an elevation above six thousand feet. Those who have screamy nerves should not undertake the ride either up or down unless they close their eyes. It is an enjoyable ride with a skillful driver and a sound car—if no one on the back seat gets excited. At the top, royal entertainment at comfortable hostelries awaits. If the day is clear the view over the vast plain below is one to be remembered. It is dotted with orchards of citrus and other fruits, and vineyards, the very thought of which brings visions of cheer and thirst to the palate.

THE SAN GABRIEL RANGE

One of the most rough and rugged ranges of the Coast Range system is the San Gabriel. The rocks exposed at the surface are broken and intermixed in great confusion, forming a heterogeneous mixture of crystalline limestone, schists, and quartzites, which have been invaded

by intrusive granites and other igneous rocks, all forming a most complicated mass. Dikes cut sharply through all the formations. The rough surface of the range is in marked contrast with the generally flat, smooth surface of the San Bernardino mountaintop.

The San Gabriel Range is a block of the earth's crust fifty miles in length and twenty-five miles in width, broken from the surrounding rocks by faults. The great block is itself broken into many smaller blocks by faults. These minor faulted blocks were uplifted to different heights, and thus the surface of the range is broken into higher and lower segments, capped often by peaks and ridges. The surface is exceedingly broken, being cut by streams into canyons and V-shaped gorges to depths of a few hundred to several thousand feet. It is an almost inaccessible region, for the most part untrodden by the foot of man, though but a few miles from the great population center of Los Angeles. The region is one to be visited only by the intrepid and courageous. There is abundant room for summer cottages amid high scenic ridges and peaks in romantic surroundings, but a location on a hill may be dangerous because of violent windstorms, and the approach is rough and jagged. Location in a gorge or canyon is hazardous. A sudden downpour may send a raging torrent, carrying huge rocks, gravel, and sand, sweeping all in its way. The tourist, sight-seer, or hunter need carry his rations and wear heavy boots.

At the eastern end of the San Gabriel Range is Cajon Pass, by which the range is separated from the San Bernardino Range. Through Cajon Pass runs the San Andreas fault, which breaks the State of California in two, for hundreds of miles. It is thought that the San Gabriel and San Bernardino Ranges may originally have been one. The structure of the rocks in the vicinity of Cajon Pass suggests that a great convulsion of the earth occurred by which the rocks were wrenched apart a distance of fifteen to twenty-five miles. The two ranges are now separated by the gap of Cajon Pass. At the western end of the range is Newhall Pass, through which runs a fault which separates the San Gabriel from the Santa Susana Range.

The San Gabriel Range is divided, almost throughout its length, by a structural valley into two north and south parallel ridges or ranges. The highest peak of the northern range is San Antonio, locally called Old Baldy (10,800 feet). The highest peak of the southern range is Cuca-

monga (8,911 feet). The structural valley is occupied by two streams flowing in opposite directions, the east and west forks of San Gabriel River. The two streams meet head-on near the center of the range. Neither can make the other back up and run uphill! So the two streams compromise and, together, turn at right angles and dash down the mountainside. In their rage they have cut a deep gorge, a steep-walled canyon in hard, metamorphosed sedimentary and igneous rocks. Through this canyon, in times of heavy rains or melting snows, passes a torrential stream. The river flows *across* the San Gabriel Valley out upon the plain south and west of Azusa. Here the flood waters spread out, forming what is called the San Gabriel "wash."

The southern slope of the San Gabriel Range is the Sierra Madre fault. The fault wall is steep and rugged. At the foot of the fault wall lies the San Gabriel Valley, a sunken basin, or "graben," that was depressed (probably) at the time of the uplifting of the range. The bottom of the basin is one thousand feet below the valley floor, as has been determined by borings.

A drive over the foothill route from San Bernardino to Los Angeles or Pasadena is a fascinating one to the nature lover. The high fault wall of the mountain range overhangs. Cucamonga and Old Baldy occasionally come into view. The floor of this sunken valley is a succession of deltas, or sand plains, formed by the streams that debouche from the mountain range. At the mouths of the canyons cones or deltas have been built and spread out as fans until they coalesce into a nearly continuous plain. The route affords a fine near view of the mountains. Citrus orchards, grape vineyards, hot-dog stands, wine refectories, gasoline filling stations, and other "filling stations," divert the attention from the great fault scarp of the mountain range, but the ride will be exhilarating and enjoyed by all lovers of nature. North of Fontana and Etiwanda are Day and Deer Canyons. Cucamonga Peak frowns from high on the range upon the delta at the mouth of its canyon on which vineyards yield wine to cause a smile. Upland and Claremont are on the alluvial fan or delta of San Antonio Creek, which pours out of Icehouse Canyon from the foot of Old Baldy. San Dimas wash and the fan of Dalton Canyon are crossed east of Azusa. The valley of San Gabriel River, from far up in the mountain range, crosses San Gabriel Valley at nearly right angles.

In these canyons are many fine sites for summer cottages, recreation camps, and country residences. All is fine eleven months and twenty days of the year. However, during a few days—it may be less than ten— terrific destruction may occur. The boulder-strewn deltas at the mouths of the canyons tell of torrential floods. In times of heavy rains or melting snows the destructive power of the streams is tremendous. Huge blocks weighing many tons crash to the plain below. Woe betide the cottage, camp, or residence that is within the stroke of the mighty current. Remember the formula, $P = V^6$.

Drive out a few miles from Pasadena and behold the fine orchards, vineyards, and beautiful homes. Then, suddenly, here is a vast field of boulders, gravel, and sand. A fine highway, bridges of solid masonry (if they have not been washed out by floods), and a view of the mountains and valley, seldom equaled and never excelled, lie ahead. Why is this not a good place to build a cottage or permanent residence? Here are plenty of stones for walls and building. But beware! The broad plain is a waste of rocks. In a few days when a flood of water has descended from the mountains, the area becomes a vast surging field of rushing, raging water.

A RANGE UPLIFTED AND DEPRESSED

The Santa Ana Range extends forty miles south from the hills about Los Angeles. Its crest is about twenty-five miles from, and parallel with, the Pacific coast. The range is an uplifted block having a core of granite, the block uplifted higher on the eastern side and rotated toward the west. The eastern side is very steep, cut off by the Elsinore fault. The range increases in altitude from north to south, culminating in Santiago Peak at 5,680 feet. The block has been alternately uplifted and depressed below sea level several times. This is shown by the occurrence of marine sediments in successive formations on the top of the range and on the western slope. Finally, a tremendous disturbance occurred in which the range was uplifted to approximately its present height. Whether this was the final disturbance of this region the future will determine. Crustal earth movements along the San Andreas, Inglewood, and Elsinore faults have occurred in historically recent time. Whether the mountain crest is still being uplifted is not known with certainty. The mountain range is young geologically. The Elsinore fault, which bounds

the range on the eastern (uplifted) side, was one of the controlling factors in the origin of this mountain range. Recent earthquake tremors at the villages of Hemet and San Jacinto were caused by movement along fault lines in this region.

The deep-lying intruded granite of the intruded batholith is exposed at the surface on the top of the range and in gullies on the slopes. The eastern slope, the fault wall, is steep and precipitous. A highway has been constructed across the range west from Lake Elsinore to San Juan Canyon. Much of the high part of the range is so rugged as to be reached with difficulty even on foot, and many slopes are practically impassable. East from the crest of the range, down the fault scarp, the descent to Elsinore Valley is very abrupt. The high crest of the range has been much rasped and eroded by wind and weather, and the ancient intruded magma, long cooled and crystallized to hard granite, is exposed at the surface. Granite and metamorphic rocks have been broken into blocks, many of which show crushing and polishing ("slickensiding") due to the fault movement. Immense granite blocks (of the batholith) project above the surface as huge boulders.

From a lookout high on the wall of the fault scarp the view over the Elsinore Valley is one to inspire gods and men. In back (west) rises the rugged granite wall, huge blocks projecting hard against the highway; east lies the deep valley (a sunken basin, or "graben") in which lies Lake Elsinore; and beyond spreads the broad Perris Plain with rugged granite crags projecting above the surface. The Palms-to-Pines Highway has been hewed from the hard rock wall at enormous expense, and winds circuitously toward the mountain crest. No lover of nature, no one who sees beyond the rocks he looks at, can fail of the keenest enjoyment of the panoramic view from a mountain lookout on the fault wall of the eastern slope of the Santa Ana Range. Lookout stations are strategically located as the highway loops around the heads of deep canyons and gorges. The Palms-to-Pines Highway leads across the range to the fine old mission at San Juan Capistrano—well worth a visit—where the calendar is regulated by the return of the swallows on a day in March each year.

RIVERS CROSS A MOUNTAIN RANGE

The Santa Ana River crosses the mountain range through a narrow steep-walled canyon. It is thought that the river was there before the

mountain range was uplifted, and kept on its course while the range was being uplifted, and so cut the mountain range in two. The river with great persistence cut its channel into the hard rocks. The stream behaves in a manner that in man-made affairs would be called courageous. It starts with great vigor and high velocity in the San Bernardino Mountains. Its swift current is employed to generate electric power at three locations on its upper course. In the San Bernardino Valley its waters are diverted to canals for irrigation and municipal purposes; water which seeps through the porous soil from the irrigation ditches rises in springs and flowing wells, or is pumped with power of the river's own generating higher upstream to irrigate lower lands. A dike, or fold in the rocks, which crosses the valley, acts as a dam above which water collects and finally goes over in a trickling current, from which it is again diverted for irrigation purposes. The seepage water from the ditches is still again recovered by pumping for further irrigation by the river's own electric power. And finally it ends its labors by cutting the hard rocks in the canyon through the mountain range, at last spreading out on the coastal plain and disappearing in the Pacific Ocean to rest from its sevenfold labors—the water literally used seven times.

Still the story of the river is not fully told. Its persistence is further demonstrated in its progress toward the sea. In its course it has picked up gravel and sand from the porous soils. In seasons of melting snows or heavy rains the stream is a raging torrent. Not only gravel and sand are transported, but boulders of great size are moved. When the floods have subsided, the river's bed appears as a broad pavement of boulders, gravel, and sand. During the summer season but little water trickles over the dam. Much of the summer season the stream bed is dry—on the surface. Deep in the gravel and sand, and below the boulders, water still moves till it rises to the surface over the solid bedrock floor, when it continues to cut its channel through the canyon. Above the canyon, the pavement of boulders, gravel, and sand is on top, dry. The water is down below. In short the river is upside down, the bottom on top!

The broad, boulder-strewn river bed extends to gravelly terraces formed by side-cutting of the stream. A monument on a terrace at the south end of the bridge which crosses the Santa Ana River near the

east end of the canyon marks the place where the first public school in California was opened in 1867.

MOUNTAIN DOME PARENT OF LOS ANGELES BASIN

The Santa Monica Range extends in an east-west direction, parallel with the ocean coast northwest of the city of Los Angeles. The range is an uplifted arch, or long dome. At the eastern end the range is crossed by Los Angeles River through a sag, or "pass," in the mountain ridge. This ridge forms a connection of the Santa Monica Range with the Repetto and Puente Hills, which in turn are regarded as the northern end of the Santa Ana Range. Cahuenga Pass is a notch in the eastern end of the range which afforded a way across the mountain range from the Los Angeles Basin to the San Fernando Valley, *El Camino Real* traversed by the mission fathers between Mexico and San Francisco.

The core of the Santa Monica Range is granite. The surface is rough and rugged from long weathering and erosion of streams. The western end of the range is nominally at the ocean shore. The range, however, extends far into and under the Pacific Ocean. Santa Catalina and other islands of the group lying off the coast are parts of the range that project above the surface of the sea. It is thought that the high mountainous islands may be the tops of upfaulted blocks, and that the depressed ocean floor between the islands and the mainland may be downfaulted blocks. The western end of the land range is much broken by faults.

A BIT OF DRY, HARD GEOLOGY

What is now the Santa Monica Range of mountains was at one time a flat plain covered by the sea. On the flat bottom of the sea, muds were deposited and in time became shale rock. Later the region was uplifted by intrusion of a vast mass of molten rock, and the sedimentary formations were uplifted, forming a roof over the intruding mass. The uplifted shales were changed by metamorphism to slates and schists. The intruding molten rock, long since cooled and crystallized, which forms the core of the range, is known as Hollywood granite. After the intrusion of the batholith, the region stood as a land surface, a vast anticlinical fold, and so continued until it was worn down by erosion and weathering to a low plain not much above sea level. This second low plain sank

and was covered by the sea. Gravel and sand were deposited on a shallow sea bottom to a great thickness—approximately five thousand feet. Earth disturbances and volcanic activity followed, and the formation which had been deposited and had become rock strata, was crumpled, folded, and faulted, and the whole region was uplifted into a dome-like ridge or arch. This elevated land remained for a long time, eroded by streams and weathered by frost, heat, wind, and rain. In time (a long time) the region was again worn down to a low flat plain with streams meandering widely over the worn-down surface. Again the land sank and was again covered by the sea. In the seas swarmed great numbers of minute organisms known as diatoms, remains of which (tiny microscopic shells), together with volcanic ash thrown out from nearby volcanoes and silt or fine mud swept into the sea by streams, make up the formations deposited upon the sea bottom during this epoch. After the deposition of a vast amount of diatomaceous remains, volcanic ash, and muds, the sea again retired, and again a great anticlinical arch or ridge was uplifted. The region henceforth remained land for a long time, and erosion went on till much of the deposit of diatomaceous shale, muds, and volcanic ash had been removed. The region continued to be worn down by streams and weathering until the land became reduced nearly to base-level. Finally the region was uplifted as an arched ridge or long anticlinical dome approximately to its present height. Since the final upheaval of the range, streams have cut deep canyons, and the present rugged topography has been developed.

The Los Angeles Basin is bounded on the north by the Santa Monica Range. Deep below the surface of the basin are strata of gravel, sand, and shale, derived from erosion of the Santa Monica Mountains, having the enormous thickness of eleven thousand feet, or more than two miles. In these sands are vast pools of petroleum, the occurrence of which is thought to be due to distillation of oil from innumerable bodies of diatoms, or microscopic plants. The fracturing (faulting) of the rocks made it possible for oil, distilled by heat and pressure from myriad bodies of diatoms, to be drained from where it was formed and to accumulate in the tops of folds or domes. The Los Angeles Basin, between the Santa Monica Range and the Santa Ana Range, is marked by many domes, anticlines; and folds of the basin are elongated low hills. Baldwin Hills (Inglewood), Dominguez Hill, and Signal Hill (Long Beach)

are examples of such hills. Elysian Park Hills, in the northern Los Angeles Basin, is an elongated dome. So, also, are the Newport-Inglewood-Beverly-Hills uplift and the Coyote uplift. These and adjoining lesser folds contain seventeen oil fields. The larger oil pools are along fractures or fault lines.

At Hancock Park in the Salt Lake oil field, on Wilshire Boulevard, seven miles west of the business center of Los Angeles, are the famed tar pits of Rancho la Brea. These are pools or seepages of petroleum tar or pitchlike oil which oozes from the ground, probably through faults or joints in the rocks. The pools are famed for the relics of animals and plants that have been recovered from the asphaltum or oil tar. Between four and five hundred species of animal remains, and many fragments of trees, seeds, and leaves of plants have been recovered, many of species that no longer live upon the earth. Beds of skulls, teeth, and bones have been exhumed, and trunks of trees, seeds, and leaves so perfectly preserved that the minute tissues can be distinguished.

Specimens of skulls and other bones of large cats, bears, wolves, and other flesh-eating animals now extinct have been found, and from these it has been possible to restore the complete skeletons of these animals. Remains also of huge mastodons, mammoths, elephants, camels, and deer have been exhumed, showing that these animals, many of which no longer roam the earth, lived in Pleistocene time on what is now the plain of the basin of Los Angeles. The locality is unique in all the world. At no other single place has so great a number of fossil vertebrate relics been recovered. It is related that in a mass of less than four cubic yards there were counted more than fifty heads of the dire wolf, thirty skulls of the saber-toothed cat, and many remains of bison, horse, sloth, coyote, and birds, and even of reptiles, amphibia, and insects.

Of the cat family the sabertooth, now extinct, occurs in great numbers. The great lionlike cat, Felix atrox, larger than any of the large living cats (lion, tiger, leopard) of Eurasia, heads the list as the most formidable predaceous animal, remains of which have been found. Among the bears the short-faced bear (Tremarcotherium) was the largest flesh-eating mammal found in these deposits. This bear was of large size, resembling the Kodiak bear of Alaska. The species is now extinct (let us give thanks).

Among the plant-eating animals were many of the bison family, larger than the living North American buffalo, many of the horse family, ground sloths, camels, antelopes, elephants, mastodons, and deer. The elephants and mammoths were larger than the mastodons and exceeded in size the elephants living today. Approximately seventy-five types of birds have been discovered, among these many now entirely extinct. Remains of eagles, owls, crows, and magpies occur in great numbers.

OIL FIELDS IN SOUTHERN CALIFORNIA

Far south in California the Coast Ranges meet in a sort of focus of mountain ranges, a mountainous plateau. The San Rafael Mountains form a rough group in the plateau. Southeast from Newhall Pass extends the San Gabriel Range. West from Newhall Pass is the Santa Susana Range, an uplifted fault block of sedimentary formations cut off by faults from the surrounding formations. The Santa Ynez Range, another uplifted block of sedimentary formations, parallels and overlooks the Pacific Ocean, rising abruptly from the coastal terrace. To the northeast the San Emigdio Range forms a connecting link between the Coast Ranges and the Sierra Nevada. The Santa Lucia Range extends from the mountain plateau far north, standing boldly against the ocean coast.

The Santa Maria oil field extends from the coast of Santa Barbara County far east to the Simi Hills, Barnsdale, and other oil fields. The field embraces a series of east-west rock folds, or anticlines, of the Monterey formation, one of the leading oil-producing districts of the west.

Most of the oil (petroleum) in California comes from the Monterey formation. The Santa Maria oil district is one of long sinuous folds, or anticlines, in Monterey shales, and it is on the axes of these folds that the productive wells are located. Oil, being lighter than water, rises under pressure into the tops of the folds. One of the largest oil fields in California is located on the Ventura Avenue anticline in the Santa Susana Range in this geologic formation. It extends west from the valley of Santa Clara River in Ventura County, and its crest passes into or under the ocean at Sea Cliff. The Rincon oil field is located on this fold, and is partly on shore and partly under the sea. In 1910, after a geological survey of the ocean floor, a long pier was built and wells drilled under the water. On Oak Ridge, the western extension of the Santa

Susana Range, an anticlinal fold, a series of oil fields is located. One of these is the South Mountain field. This field is one of the most picturesque in California, an example of rugged badland type of landscape in which the soft friable rocks have been eroded by running water into jagged peaks and ridges separated by almost impassable gullies and canyons. Locations for a number of derricks were so inaccessible that all materials for drilling were transported to them by inclined railways.

The ultimate source of oil (petroleum) has been the subject of much study by geologists, and the problem is still not fully solved. In the Pacific coast region the Monterey shale has been pretty definitely demonstrated to be the source of oil from the microscopically small bodies of diatom plants. These tiny bodies have existed in great numbers in the geologic past, as is shown by the occurrence of rock formations made up largely or entirely of the minute shells of these tiny plant bodies.

It was long a question whether these minute organisms were plants or animals, but since it has been determined by specialists in biology that the tiny living bodies give off (exhale) oxygen and absorb carbon dioxide, they have thus established their place in the vegetable kingdom. In their bodies they "manufacture" oil by synthesis of carbon from carbon dioxide with hydrogen. This, strange as it may seem, is the supposed source of oil which is derived from the Monterey shale.

At the foot of the mountain slope near the Pacific coast, at Lompoc, in southwestern Santa Barbara County, California, is what is probably the world's greatest deposit of diatomaceous rock. The formation is of Miocene (Tertiary) age, the Monterey formation. The deposit embraces an area of approximately five square miles, with a depth as great as 1,400 feet. The formation consists of almost absolutely pure diatomaceous shells. According to expert report, a cubic inch of the rock contains from 20 to 75 million diatom shells. The fossil shells vary greatly in size, shape, and markings. The oil from these microscopic shells, stored in these tiny bodies as a food supply, has been distilled away. The rock, almost chemically pure, is quarried and used in the manufacture of a great variety of useful commercial articles.

Diatoms reproduce in myriad numbers. The dead shells settle upon the sea bottom, forming deep sea ooze. Diatomaceous deposits are widespread in the Monterey formation. Diatoms abound in great numbers in the seas and in lakes and pools of quiet water practically everywhere,

and numbers of tiny bodies of a great variety of shapes and sizes, but all microscopically small, may be seen by placing under a microscope a drop of water from a stagnant pool, lake, or quiet stream. The variety of shapes and markings of the shells is most fascinating, and between eight thousand and ten thousand different forms of diatoms have been identified.

AN OUTSTANDING COAST RANGE

The Santa Lucia Range is one of the most prominent of the Coast Range system. For more than a hundred miles it dominates the coast of California. Throughout much of this distance the range rises abruptly from the Pacific Ocean, and many observers regard it as forming the most picturesque portion of the California coast. It terminates in Point Pinos, south of Monterey Bay. Far to the southeast the range blends with the Diablo Range, and finally merges into the irregular mountain plateau in northeastern Santa Barbara County.

San Luis Obispo (Bishop of St. Louis) is at the foot of the slope of the Santa Lucia Range, on the plain of the San Luis Valley. This was a Mission station on the *Camino Real*. The Mission building, constructed by Father Junípero Serra and the *padres* in 1772, is still standing.

The elevation of the railroad station at San Luis Obispo is 240 feet. The summit of the Santa Lucia Range is crossed by the railroad through a tunnel 3,616 feet in length, at an elevation of 1,570 feet. Thus the railroad climbs 1,330 feet in a straight-line distance of six miles, winding a circuitous way of more than double the distance, passing through six tunnels. The long tunnel at the summit (Cuesta Pass) is nearly six hundred feet above the Salinas Valley, to which the railroad descends. The padres crossed the mountain range through Paso Robles Gorge, by which the Salinas River passes from the upper valley to the lower main valley. The highway follows the course of the Salinas River through Paso Robles Canyon.

A striking geologic feature near San Luis Obispo is a row of eight hills, four northwest and four southeast of the city, which are the cones of extinct volcanoes which broke through the sedimentary rocks of the region, poured forth lava, and strewed volcanic ash upon the surrounding lands. Whether these volcanoes are permanently "dead" or whether they will again become active remains to be seen!

West of the Santa Lucia Range, and parallel with it, is the San Luis Range, separated from the main range by the broad flat plain of the San Luis and Los Osos Valleys. This range projects into the Pacific Ocean in the form of a broad and prominent highland or promontory. The San Luis and Los Osos Valleys together form a continuous basin twenty miles in length. This is not a valley of erosion but a structural basin lying between the Santa Lucia and San Luis Ranges. San Luis Obispo and Pismo Creeks start high on the slope of the Santa Lucia Range and descend through rocky gorges to the plain of San Luis Valley, across which they meander; then flow through rock gorges cut in or through the San Luis Range. They are antecedent streams. Their courses were established before the San Luis Range was uplifted. As the mountain range was uplifted, the streams continued cutting down their channels as the obstruction slowly arose across their courses.

An outstanding feature of the Santa Lucia Range is one that is a result of mountain activities rather than of the mountain itself. Mountains are the foster parents of rivers. Salinas River is a product of the mountains, and its history is definitely associated with the mountains. The river has persistently fought the mountains in the effort to maintain its course. The mountains have made the river possible by supplying water with which the river has ceaselessly sought to make its way through the mountains themselves.

Salinas River starts 150 miles from its mouth high on Santa Lucia Peak. It flows through a valley which is not of its own making, a graben. The valley does not extend to the ocean or offer an outlet for the river. So the river cuts across a range of hills through a deep gorge. This steep-walled gorge, the Paso Robles (Pass of the Oaks) offered a passageway, *El Camino Real,* through the rugged land for the intrepid mission fathers en route between Mexico and San Francisco in days now long gone by.

The river gets down from the high valley through the pass to another sunken basin, larger and longer, and having a broad flat bottom which the river seemingly might have followed but does not. The valley extends for a hundred miles in a northwest-southeast direction and would seem to offer a highway for the river. The river curiously turns away from the flat, nearly level floor of the valley and makes its way through hard granite rocks of the Gabilan Range.

The river is called by geologists a superimposed stream: that is, the region of the Gabilan Mountains sank and was covered by the sea, and the mountains were deeply buried beneath sea sediments. In the lapse of time, the sea bottom was upraised, and the soft friable formation which had been deposited became dry land. Rains fell and streams developed. What is now the Salinas River became established. All land surfaces above sea level are worn away by wind, rain, frost, and heat. The new landscape was slowly worn down. The beds of rivers are always lower than the surrounding land. As the landscape was worn down, the river bed was lowered. In time the river cut down its bed till it encountered the hard granite of the buried mountains. As the granite rock was reached, it was chiseled by sand carried by the stream, and the channel was lowered into the hard rocks. Today the river flows through a granite-walled canyon with walls six to seven hundred feet high and nearly vertical. The river flows through this granite canyon for six or seven miles and, about three miles northeast of Santa Margarita, returns to the flat plain from which it had turned away.

THE PINNACLES, CHALONE PEAK, AND THE GABILAN MOUNTAINS

In the Gabilan Mountains a volcanic disturbance occurred millions of years ago, the marks of which appear today in one of the most unique regions of all the Coast Ranges. This remarkable district has been wisely established as Pinnacles National Monument. The entrance to the Monument is on the west side of the Gabilan Range.

En route between Los Angeles and San Francisco, northbound, turn off the highway at King City and drive thirty-five miles; or southbound, leave Highway 101 two miles south of Gilroy and drive through Hollister to the west side of the Gabilan Range. The checking station is on State Highway 25, about one mile from Monument Headquarters in Bear Gulch. (An annual automobile license fee of fifty cents a car is payable at the checking station on the first entrance.)

The Monument is about three by five miles in extent. In an area of about two square miles volcanoes long ago burst forth in vehement eruptions, and nature has since been constantly repairing the damage and changing the scene by persistent action of streams, wind, and weather. Those who are geologically minded and all zealous mountain climbers will find joy and exhilaration in the High Peaks Trail to the

Pinnacles and the Chalone Peak Trail, though both are somewhat strenuous. All visitors will want to take the Cave Trail in Bear Gulch. There need be no fear that the big rock over the cave (which is estimated to weigh more than fifty thousand tons) will fall. It has been there a long time. The huge blocks that have fallen from the cliffs and form the walls of deep canyons are quite stationary! The circuitous High Peaks Trail is about three miles air-line, but it will be several times the distance the way you will go, and the distance that your head will travel up and down as you stumble along the path may be left to a mathematician to compute. If you are an enthusiastic climber and your heart action is good, you will enjoy it. The trail to the southern part of the Monument leads over Chalone Peak, the summit of which is 3,287 feet above sea level. If your nerve is equally good you will want to walk over this trail, three miles air-line (again a good deal more the way you will go).

The geology of the region may not interest the average visitor. Its scenery will. About fifteen or twenty million years ago, volcanic activity of great intensity occurred, and the region was violently blasted. Lavas burst forth from volcanic craters. Volcanic ash and rock fragments were hurled into the air. In the long time since that terrible period, running water, wind, and weather have been constantly at work. Chalone Creek has carried away the volcanic debris from the eastern side of the old volcano. Beds of volcanic deposits, thousands of feet in thickness, remain on the western slope, carved fantastically into pinnacles, caves, and canyons. In the rocks of Chalone Peak are marble and other crystalline rocks, said to be older than any others in the Coast Ranges.

In Stone Canyon, in the Gabilan Range, there is coal in rocks of Tertiary age, authoritatively reported to be the best in California. Beds of coal range in thickness to as much as sixteen feet. The greater part of the coal output of the State during the past few years has come from the Stone Canyon mine.

A quicksilver mine, officially stated to have produced more of this metal than any other mine in the United States, is located in the foothills of the Santa Cruz Range fourteen miles by paved highway from San Jose—the New Almaden mine. One of the oldest in America, it has been in continuous operation since 1824 and has produced metal of a

value of more than eighty million dollars. It is reported to be exceeded in production at present by the New Idria mine in southern San Benito County.

Before the appearance of the Spaniards, the Indians utilized the cinnabar ore from the old mine for red pigment with which to paint their bodies. The ore was dug from a cave in the mountainside. Year by year the cave reached deeper and deeper into the mountain, and, as the Indians did not know how to timber their rough tunnel, the earth and rocks above crashed down, and the tragedy that occurred was discovered years afterward when Spaniards reopened the cave and came upon a group of skeletons, remains of Indians who had been trapped and had died there. In 1777, when the Spanish padres built the Mission Santa Clara, they learned from friendly Indians of this red earth that made red paint, and it was used in adorning the mission.

VIEW FROM MOUNT HAMILTON

On Mount Hamilton in the Diablo Range stands the great Lick Observatory, at an elevation of 4,209 feet, thirteen miles from San Jose. It is reached by a paved highway that winds the ascent in about double the air-line distance. The location is an admirable one, and the great telescope and accessories are a splendid monument to the donor, James Lick. The high altitude, and an unobstructed view over a radius of one hundred miles, and clear skies six or seven months of the year, are of great advantage.

From the top of Mount Hamilton a cloudless day brings into view the broad fields of lettuce about Salinas and Watsonville where John Steinbeck's Joad family drove their dilapidated Ford and worked on the mile-long lettuce rows. Following *El Camino Real* north of Pajaro Gap, the view extends over what were broad open plains when the padres of old journeyed toward San Francisco; now far-spread fields of vegetables, fruits, and vineyards. It is mountains that concern us now, but there cannot be mountains without valleys. Here in these fertile valleys are grown 95 per cent of all the lettuce seed used in the gardens of the United States, nearly all the radish seed that is planted in gardens all the way to the Atlantic coast, and 75 per cent of all the onion seed used in the United States. Farther north, near Hollister, are the old San Juan Bautista Mission, built by the padres in 1797, and an

old pear orchard, planted soon after the building of the mission, from which fruit may still be gathered in season.

MT. DIABLO IS A VOLCANIC PLUG

An outstanding feature of the Coast Ranges in central California is Mount Diablo, twenty miles east of San Francisco Bay. Rising from near sea level to an elevation of nearly four thousand feet (3,849 feet), Mount Diablo is a conspicuous landscape feature. The conical mass of the mountain is the culminating feature of the Diablo Range. The range extends far south as one of the parallel ranges of the Coast Range system. South of Tracy, the range is called the San Jose, and, still farther south, it merges with the Gabilan Range. From Tracy north to Sulphur Springs Mountain, beyond Carquinez Strait, the range is uplifted into a distinct fold. At the apex, or highest point of the fold, an upheaval of tremendous proportions occurred which forced a segment or block of the earth's crust upward under the overlying sedimentary formations. The rocks were uplifted, bent, overturned, and metamorphosed. These rocks have been removed by erosion, along with much of the top of the upheaved block. It is estimated that more than twenty thousand feet, or five miles, in thickness of sedimentary rocks have been removed from what is now the peak of Mount Diablo. The central mass of the mountain is what is called a "plug" of igneous and metamorphic rocks four miles in diameter. The uplifted plug is cut off on all sides by faults. The highest peak of the mountain is the eroded surface of the uplifted plug. What is called Mount Diablo is a mass of igneous and metamorphic rocks fifteen square miles in area. The central peak is what remains of the upheaved plug. The uplifted sedimentary rocks that surround the peak stand at various angles, often in a vertical position. A ride to the top of the mountain is one to be remembered. The view from the top is exceptionally fine. The rocks of the mountain are mantled with soil, but in eroded gullies and roadside cuts the rocks are exposed.

MOUNTAINS NORTH OF SAN FRANCISCO

North of San Francisco the mountains are rough and rugged. From these mountains sedimentary rocks totaling five to six miles in thickness, which were deposited when the region was below sea level, have been removed by erosion. Volcanic outbursts in the past have been

many and violent. Craters on mountaintops have become meadows and cultivated fields. The slopes of the mountains have been much eroded and are marked by sharp gullies and broad valleys. The fertile valleys were sought out in the early days by settlers for cattle ranches and farms.

Mount St. Helena poured forth from its crater lava which overwhelmed and buried a forest of redwood trees. The lava ejected from the volcano contained the mineral silica, and, as the tissues of the fallen trunks decayed, the minute structure of the wood was replaced particle by particle, so that the "petrified log" is the original tree trunk perfectly preserved in stone. A trunk called "Queen of the Forest" is eighty feet long and twelve feet in mean diameter. Another trunk, "The Monarch," is one hundred and twenty feet long with a mean diameter of eight feet. Another log near-by is sixty feet long and nine feet in diameter. The petrified forest is near the main Redwood Highway between Santa Rosa and Calistoga, northwest of St. Helena.

In far northwestern California and southwestern Oregon the famed Redwoods (Sequoia sempervirens) still thrive, the world's tallest and most majestic trees. The Redwoods are adopted children of the mountains, and so intimately related and associated with the mountains that they form a part of the geological story. In the geologic past the Redwoods thrived over a wide range in North America, parts of Asia and Europe, and the Arctic Islands. The hospitable (or inhospitable) climatic conditions afforded by the mountains have given asylum to this once widespread species, now extinct except for these forests of the far northwest coast. Adopted and saved from extinction by the mountains, which afforded the needed conditions of cool climate, heavy rains and fog-laden skies, these trees belong to the mountain picture.

At the apex of Howell Mountain is a crater of great size. The bowl of the crater is filled with lava, now cooled, the surface of which has become fertile soil. In the midst of this crater, surrounded by a large and productive farm, is located a great institution, Pacific Union College, operated by the Adventist Church. In the community center are a church, and mercantile and industrial plants, including a bookbindery that does work for libraries throughout the United States. The central features of the community are a college of liberal arts and a large sanitarium and infirmary. The department of music in the college would do credit to Boston or any other city. No tea, coffee, tobacco, or whiskey is sold at the

community store, as these articles are doctrinally considered unnecessary and therefore to be eschewed.

A few miles north of St. Helena is a mountain of volcanic glass. When forced up from the depths of the earth, the mass was boiling hot. The molten mass was forced upward under a great thickness of sedimentary rocks and was not poured out upon the surface. The molten mass slowly cooled. During the lapse of time, the overlying uplifted sedimentary rocks were removed by erosion, and now a vast mountain of glass, called obsidian, remains to tell of a once-great earth disturbance.

THE KLAMATH MOUNTAINS ARE AN ORPHAN RANGE

On the California-Oregon boundary line, an irregular and confused group of mountain ranges is collectively known as the Klamath Mountains. The group is a sort of orphan in the family of western mountain ranges. The irregular arrangement of the ranges raises a question as to the geologic relation of the several ranges to the Coast and Cascade systems. The ranges of this complex group, which are without definite order or relation, are thought to be not all of the same age, not all simultaneously uplifted. The ranges may be classed into two main systems, which probably represent two or more periods of upheaval. The two systems cross each other nearly at right angles. The most conspicuous ranges, the Rogue River, Siskiyou, Scott, and Trinity, have a generally east-west trend while the Salmon River Range and a number of lesser ranges have a generally northerly direction. The east-west ranges are thought to represent an earlier upheaval.

All the larger valleys of the Klamath Mountain region are structural valleys, basins entirely surrounded by mountain ranges. Almost without exception, the streams which drain these valleys cross one or more ranges, into which they have eroded narrow gorges and canyons. Klamath River flows out of the Shasta Valley through mountainous country for nearly a hundred miles. In its course it crosses the axis of the Salmon River Range through a rocky gorge. Scott Valley, a nearly level plain two hundred square miles in area, is drained by a stream which passes through a canyon more than twenty miles in length and so narrow as to be almost impracticable for a wagon road to follow. In places the walls of the canyon rise precipitously for more than a thousand feet.

The explanation of this remarkable drainage is that these outflowing streams are antecedent lines of drainage. There is no drainage eastward from these mountains. In late Tertiary time the westward drainage was established probably much as now, though the stream channels were not so deep. The later uplifting of the north-south ranges was across the lines of drainage of the established streams. As the mountains were slowly uplifted, the streams continued in their courses, thereby cutting the gorges and canyons. The drainage of the Klamath Mountain valleys, which lie to the east of the high mountain ranges, furnishes a most unique example of antecedent drainage.

Among the complexities of the Klamath Mountains is the outpouring of volcanic lavas. The waters of the Klamath lakes were originally carried to the ocean by way of Rogue River. Faulting of the rocks and the outpouring of lavas, one or both, changed the drainage of these lakes. Their waters now reach the ocean by the circuitous winding course of Klamath River.

The Rogue River Range at its western end fronts upon the Pacific Ocean. Its general direction is east-west rather than north-northwest. It thus lies athwart the line of the Coast Range system. It extends as a great fold far to the east across the State of Oregon, crossing the axis of the Cascade Range. There seems reasonable ground for the conclusion that the Rogue River Range is older than the mountains to the north and south. That there have been more than one mountain upheaval in the region of the Klamath Mountains appears established. If the Rogue River Range was uplifted earlier, and the Coast Ranges are younger, still the Coast Range system maintains its continuity to the north and south in the several north-south ranges which were later uplifted.

THE COAST RANGE IN OREGON

North from the Klamath Mountains in Oregon a rough and rugged region bears the euphonious name of Umpqua Mountains. In Oregon the Coast Range is an irregular series of maturely dissected hills and ridges. The main range extends somewhat brokenly across the State from the Rogue River Range to the Columbia River, forming the divide between the Willamette River valley on the east and the Pacific Ocean on the west. The range is officially called the Coast Range. The main

divide is generally parallel with and about thirty miles from the coast. No less than thirteen mountain peaks between Rogue River and the Columbia River have heights officially measured as ranging from about three thousand to 4,297 feet, the height of Mount Bolivar.

The Columbia River cuts the mountain range to near sea level, as do the Nehalem, Yaquina, Siuslaw, and Umpqua Rivers. Their courses were established before the uplifting of the mountains, and the streams have continued in their courses during the slow uprising of the mountains.

The coast of Oregon is uniformly straight, lying almost due north and south. There are no harbors of importance and only a narrow coastal plain. There are small bays and sandy beaches which furnish fine summer resorts and recreation camp sites. The hills and mountains, dissected by erosion into rough peaks and crags with deep gullies, crowd close upon the sea. Coastal lakes have been formed by the drowning of the mouths of streams on the western slopes of the mountains. The combined effect of bars, spits, and dunes has produced delightful bodies of water near the coast. The largest of these is Siltcoos Lake, which is several miles long.

On the Oregon coast stands Tillamook Head, a bold rock promontory which the Coast Range thrusts out defiantly against the waves and tides of the Pacific. Farther north is another rocky headland near Sugar Loaf Mountain. On these cliffs the waves beat. Here is the factory in which wave-worn pebbles are made. On the Pacific coast glacial ice pushed far south in the State of Washington, but not in Oregon. West of Portland is Astoria, where John Jacob Astor bartered with the Indians for furs. Seaside, a favorite resort, is farther south, where a sandy beach invites children (of all ages up to ninety) to wade in the surf and bathe in the sand! A rocky promontory near Sugar Loaf Mountain tells how "the rugged rocks become wave-worn pebbles."

Along the beach the sand becomes coarser toward the south. Presently there is no longer sand, but gravel. The pebbles become larger farther on, then small and larger cobbles, soon boulders too large to lift. The boulders become larger and now reach a size of many tons' weight. And here is the rock promontory, a nose of the Coast Range pushing into the sea. Huge blocks, as large as houses, have been broken from the cliff. Returning to Seaside, all sizes of broken rock from immense

blocks to boulders, cobbles, pebbles, and fine sand, all wave-worn, are seen in succession.

The coastal mountains of California supply the explanation of wave-worn pebbles. This is the way the Coast Range mountains stand up against the waves of the battling ocean, and the way the ocean fights to overcome the land. This is the way the rugged rocks have, during the ages, become wave-worn pebbles. This is the way that myriad millions of rounded pebbles have been formed, that make up the conglomerate formations, the "pudding stones" of the earth. The finest displays of wave-worn pebbles this writer has ever seen are at Encinitas and Ocean-side on the California coast between Los Angeles and San Diego.

OLYMPIC NATIONAL PARK

The Olympic Peninsula in northwestern Washington is one of the most rugged, wild, and fantastic regions of all the Coast Ranges—or of any other mountains. The region has been little trodden by the foot of man. In this scenic wilderness an area of 835,000 acres has been wisely set apart as a national park, a wilderness empire rich with evergreen forest. The unspoiled primeval wilderness is being preserved as America's "last frontier." The park occupies the heart of the Olympic Peninsula.

Mount Olympus, 8,100 feet above sea, is snow-clad throughout the year. Too high, too cold, and too bare of soil on the heights, trees grow upon its sides to about two thirds of its height. All the mountain heights are barren, but the valleys and the slopes are densely forested. The mountain peaks form no definite range but are scattered without pattern across the park.

Within the park are numerous glaciers having a combined area of twenty square miles. Blue Glacier, one of the largest in the park, is a tremendous jungle of ice, broken into cascades forming an impassable field, grand to look upon and dangerous to step on. Heart Lake nestles high among the lofty peaks. White Glacier is a broad snow field near the summit of Mount Olympus. Mountain of the Gods, near Mount Olympus, is a mass of impassable crags with snow-ice filling the intervening gullied spaces. Hoh and Jeffries Glaciers extend down the slopes halfway from the highest peaks to sea level. Cirques, the starting places of glaciers, greet the eye from every vantage point of observation. Among

spectacular peaks in deep-winding canyons and gullies, trees find a protecting foothold, and avalanche lilies bloom in profuse abundance on favorable slopes.

Around the coast of the peninsula, wave-cut terraces show the labors of the ocean in the ceaseless warfare against the land. Wave-cut cliffs and rocky offshore flats show the incessant wearing of the waves upon the rock shores. Perpetual snow clings on the slopes of the high peaks, relics of the vastly greater avalanche of snow and ice of the glacial period. The effects of former glaciation are apparent far down the slopes —moraines, polished rock surfaces, tarns, and boulder-laden beds of clay.

During the glacial period, when the great continental ice sheet pushed its way south from the great cordilleran ice center, ice met ice, the continental ice sheet meeting that from the Olympic center. Ice from the Olympic center pushed far into the Puget Sound Basin before the oncoming of the cordilleran ice from the north. The Olympic ice left its mark in the deposit of pebbles of Olympic rocks, but was overwhelmed later by the invasion of the northern ice. A boulder several feet in diameter was carried by the Olympic ice far into the Puget Sound Basin and landed on a sea cliff on Hood Canal. Later it fell down the cliff forty feet without breaking, but was demolished at last by the waves. The character of this rock and that of pebbles found in the earth near-by show that the drift came from the Olympic region. The occurrence of granitic boulders (from the north), unlike rocks from the Olympic region far up on the northern Olympic slopes, shows that the northern (cordilleran) ice dominated the Puget Sound Valley and pushed far up the Olympics.

The geologic history of the Olympic Peninsula is little known. Placer gold has been washed in gullies eroded by streams along the coastal margins and in gulches far inland. The occurrence of gold suggests subterranean uprising. All the known gold of the world has been traced, so far as it has been traced at all, directly or indirectly to origin deep in the earth. The intrusion of igneous rocks and the highly metamorphosed sedimentary rocks of the range show upheaval of highly heated matter from earth's depths. Important mineral veins, which owe their occurrence to igneous activity, many of which have been discovered in this region, are evidence of subterranean uprising of highly heated molten

matter. The peninsula is a vast, uplifted dome which, it is thought, may be still rising. That orogenic (mountain-building) movement is still taking place seems possible. That such movements have occurred in recent geologic time is evidenced by the very gently folded and tilted clays, sands, and gravels in the vicinity of Port Angeles.

Between the Olympic Peninsula in northwestern Washington and Vancouver Island in British Columbia lies the strait of Juan de Fuca. The great Coast Range system continues for a thousand miles to the St. Elias Range in Alaska, and dominates in magnificent grandeur the western coast of British Columbia.

The Coast Range system of mountains, which borders the western coast of the North American continent is not the highest of the mountain ranges of the world, and not the oldest. It is among the youngest, the longest, and, considering its narrow width, the most persistent of the mountain ranges of the continent. Whether or not the system is geologically continuous with the mountains of Alaska, or whether the ranges continue beneath the sea beyond the southern tip of the Peninsula of Lower California, the Coast Ranges are unique among the mountain ranges of the world in the varied complexities of the surface, the high peaks, and the peaks partly or entirely submerged beneath the sea. The ranges form the western wall of the continent, standing boldly and high against the sea, young in the family of mountains and, from geologic evidence, thought to be still rising. The story of the Coast Ranges has not been fully told. When their history and the processes of their building are more fully known the chapter which shall reveal their full history will be a volume of great size and of fascinating interest.

CLIMATIC TRANSITIONS
AND CONTRASTS

BY RICHARD JOEL RUSSELL

Residents from Puget Sound to the Gulf of California will be surprised that I place climate last. Always in their conversation climate bears a higher priority, and its justified virtues are so stressed as at times to make the Easterner skeptical. Here is the statistical and exact truth of the climate of the West Coast, most of which is extremely pleasant and all of which is an interesting experience. And, though last, here are some of the most pertinent and informative facts about the Coast Ranges. (R. P.)

If you were to ask a resident of coastal Washington whether it rained much in his neighborhood he might well reply, "Is it raining now?" If you answer in the affirmative he will immediately inform you that it rains a great deal. To a negative opinion he is likely to state that the rainfall is moderate, or even light. He knows that it is far rainier a short distance back in the hills, on the seaward face of the high Olympics, or in the still higher Cascades. The truth of the matter is that the coastal lowland is a region of comparatively gentle, drizzling, misty rains, notable for long duration rather than intensity.

Broad sheets of grayish and black cloud hang low over the Washington coast much of the time. Sunshine penetrates them considerably less than half of the time the sun is above the horizon. Dense fog occurs on an average of one day in nine.

North Head, near the mouth of the Columbia River, has an annual rainfall of less than 50 inches, but it is divided among more than half of the days of the year. As elsewhere along the Pacific coast of the United States, winter is the wettest season. North of the Columbia three quarters of the year's rain comes between the first of October and the end of March. The normal rainfall for each summer month is likely to be little more than one inch, but during individual years even a July or August may have its quota exceeded by 500 per cent or so. There are eight rainy days during a typical July or August, twenty-two in December or January.

Temperatures are remarkably uniform along this damp coast. The annual average of 50°F.* at North Head results from 43° for the three

* All temperatures are Fahrenheit.

winter months, 48° for spring, 57° for summer, and 53° for fall. Winter is thus the season of greater wetness, rather than a distinctly cold time of year. On less than one day of the typical year does the mercury descend below 32°, or climb above 90°. At Tatoosh Island, northwest-ernmost point of the United States, the recorded temperature has never been lower than 7°, nor above 88°.

From one day to the next the change in average temperature in the northland is less than 2°; a change of 10° is experienced on fewer than four days of the typical year. During the warmest hour of the ordinary winter day the temperature will be almost 50° and during the coldest hour of night, about 39°. In summer these values approximate 60° and 53°. These are extremely monotonous temperatures. The forecast, "continued cool and cloudy," is correct most of the time. To find winter temperatures as low as those of New York City one would have to go northward along the coast well into southern Alaska, or eastward a comparatively few miles to an elevation in excess of 2,000 feet, in the Cascades.

Winds are the transporters of weather. The bracing climate that ruddies complexions in western Washington really originates to the west, over the cold North Pacific. Air that has spent days, or even weeks, over the ocean becomes moist and cool. In winter it moves across coastal Washington with an average velocity in excess of 15 miles per hour, a speed that emphasizes its dampness and chill. The summer velocity is about two thirds as great.

In striking contrast to this "west coast marine climate" is the "conti-nental climate" of the interior, where annual precipitation is lower, with summer the wettest season of the year, where seasonal temperature con-trasts are extreme, and where nights are ordinarily much colder than early afternoons.

Western Washington is fully exposed to marine influences, but the Cascades and other mountains to the east protect it from air that has become dry and cold as a result of lingering in the continental interior. Air is heated by descent. If forced down 5,000 feet the temperature rise will be about 25°. Heating decreases weight to such a degree that even the coldest continental air is unable to descend for many thousands of feet. The Coast Ranges are sheltered by the Cascades in winter.

The storms of western Washington are mainly strong winds or heavy rains. Abrupt changes in weather, so common in many parts of the United States, are practically unknown in the extreme Northwest. Tornadoes, violent squalls, and thunder storms are foreign to coastal Washington. Hail is almost unknown. Strong winds occur now and then but they build up gradually. The most violent are likely to be the tail ends of typhoons that failed to "blow themselves out" in crossing from the Philippines.

Raininess and overcast are emphasized on the seaward slopes of the Washington Coast Ranges. A rather broad belt receives more than 100 inches per year, and it appears likely that the rainiest place in the United States is some point, as yet not precisely identified, up on the western slopes of the Olympics. Records in excess of 150 inches are fairly common.* Individual months from October to March are subject to more than 20 inches of rain. A similar wetness characterizes higher elevations in the British Isles, where climatic conditions resemble those of western Washington. Ben Nevis, in Scotland, has an annual rainfall of 150 inches, Glencoe 185, and Llyn Llydaw, in northern Wales, 206, which makes it the wettest known place in Europe.

Many persons dislike a place where changes in weather are so feeble from day to day or season to season, but one of the most pleasant things about the climate of the Pacific Coast Ranges is its geographical variety. A few miles may bring one into an entirely different scene. Not far from the rainy west side of the Olympics are such places as Port Angeles, where the annual rainfall is but 27 inches, or Port Townsend, where it is less than 20. We must not jump to the conclusion that these places experience Mediterranean sunshine. Fogs and clouds drift in along the strait of Juan de Fuca to keep skies overcast over four fifths of the time in December and over one third of the time in July. Summer temperatures are about those of North Head, and winters are slightly colder —a mild touch of climatic continentalism. Interior valleys to the south have considerably more sunshine, notably less rainfall, and somewhat greater seasonal and daily temperature contrasts than places directly exposed to oceanic winds. Less than 50 miles back from the coast,

---

* Various figures for greatest rainfall in the Olympics have been given in this volume. Actually exact figures are not known.

thermometers climb above 100° on occasional summer days and drop
to more than 10° below zero during record freezes.

THE BIG SNOWS ARE TO THE EAST

Snow forms only a small proportion of the annual precipitation in
the coastal hills of Washington. Places at lower elevations are likely to
get less than 10 inches per year and it doesn't remain on the ground
for many hours. The somewhat colder winters a few miles back from
the coast increase snowfall to 20 inches or more at similar elevations.
The winter blanket is heavy toward the summits of the Olympics but the
country of excessive snows lies to the east, in the Cascades, where Mount
Baker Lodge, at an elevation of 4,177 feet, averages 478 inches per year
and Paradise Inn, at 5,500 feet, on the side of Mount Rainier, 587 inches.
During the winter of 1916-1917 a total fall of 790 inches was recorded
at the latter place, with some of the record missing because the snow
gauges had not been set up soon enough to catch the early flurries of the
fall. On April 2, 1917, the ground was still blanketed by over 27 feet
of snow.

It is characteristic that snow in the Pacific Coast Ranges is "wet," because it falls at comparatively high temperatures. A column of wet
snow about 10 inches high will melt into an inch of water. The "dry" snow
of continental interiors may run in a ratio of 20:1, or even 25:1, between
snow and melt-water thickness. Dry low-temperature snow is powdery,
so that it drifts freely down-wind. Wet snow clings to everything it
touches. It is more picturesque while falling because it comes down in
larger flakes. It is more scenic on the surface because it covers all
trees in typical Christmas-card tradition. Residents in the low valleys,
who are likely to regret that their snows disappear so soon after falling,
commonly make trips back into the hills and mountains to enjoy the
novelty of winter sports.

Climates similar to those of western Washington extend southward
along the Coast Ranges well into California. The belt of excessively
heavy precipitation includes west-facing fronts of several ranges in the
north but narrows across Oregon to the width of the seaward face of
the first hill or mountain barrier toward the Pacific. Rainfall decreases
southward toward San Francisco, even in the most exposed locations.
Glenora, about 40 miles west of Portland and 20 from the coast, has an

average rainfall of nearly 130 inches per year, and had over 167 in 1896. During an extremely wet December, 1917, almost 53 inches fell. Monumental, a much higher place, at an elevation of 2,750 feet, just south of the Oregon boundary, has an average of 109 inches, and had over 153 in 1909. Helen Mine, at approximately the same elevation, but hardly 60 miles north of San Francisco, averages over 86 inches. In 1909 it received nearly 137 inches, approximately 72 of which fell in January.

The number of rainy days per year also decreases southward. Along the Oregon Coast it exceeds 200 at some places but toward the California boundary the average is closer to 150; at Eureka 120, and at Point Reyes, close to San Francisco, it is 77.

Summer is more emphatically the dry season southward. Eureka has 48 rainy days in the typical winter and but 9 during the three summer months combined. The chances are better than 15 to 1 that it will not rain on any particular day in July or August. At Point Reyes there are 37 rainy days in winter and but 3 in summer, the average for July and August combined being 1.

STRAW-HAT SEASON, WITH OVERCOATS

Cool summer climates extend along the entire west coast of the United States. The warmest month has an average temperature of 54.6° at Tatoosh Island, Washington. The following warmest-month temperatures are arranged in order from north to south: Newport, Oregon, 57.2; Gold Beach, Oregon, 57.9; Crescent City, California, 58.6; Eureka, 56.3; Point Reyes, 56.3; San Francisco, 61.3; Monterey, 62.1; Santa Barbara, 66.8; San Pedro (Los Angeles), 67.2; Oceanside, 69.5; Point Loma (San Diego), 67.9. These warmest-month temperatures occur during July only at one of the places listed, Tatoosh Island. Elsewhere the climax of summer is delayed to August, or in the vicinity of San Francisco to September. San Francisco is ordinarily the coolest major city in the United States during July and August. Hardly a night occurs when one ventures forth without a topcoat. During many July and August days one sees straw hats, in deference to summer, worn in combination with overcoats, demanded by bodily comfort. Only the unwise leave the sweltering East without packing heavy clothing for a summer on the Pacific coast.

Winds from the ocean create the cool summer belt because they bring low temperature both from the water and from drift-in fog. While the official number of days with "dense fog," as shown in Weather Bureau records, decreases from 51 per year at Eureka to 19 at San Francisco and 20 at San Diego, the number of foggy days in the ordinary sense of the expression is far higher. The July and August sun has difficulty penetrating a "high fog" to shine on San Francisco earlier than ten in the morning. In late afternoon the daily sea breeze ordinarily manages to drift in a sea fog heavy enough to require the lighting of many automobile headlights. Cool summers in some parts of the earth are the result of a rainy season, but in the fog belt along the Pacific coast they are largely the product of dry-season sea fog.

It is fascinating to watch the afternoon sea fog pour into valleys along the coast, especially through the Golden Gate into San Francisco Bay and its marginal lowlands. From a point of vantage on the Berkeley Hills, the woolly mass looks a good deal like a torrential river surging ahead violently through the narrows and spreading broadly where confining hills widen out. In less than half an hour after breaking through the Golden Gate the fog may have crossed the bay and started banking against the foot of the hills to the east. Within another half hour it may cover the entire northern part of the bay and have thickened to a depth of several hundred feet, so that higher hills rise above its billowy surface like so many islands. High on Mount Tamalpais the sun shines 95 per cent of possible hours during July and 93 per cent in August, while below, in San Francisco, the sunshine percentages are reduced to 69 and 63. In the south near San Diego a similar contrast has dictated the location of Palomar Observatory.

In the most exposed places along the rather chilly and windy coast north of Point Conception the landscape is barren. A few ostrich-like pine and cypress trees here and there defy the wind and fog, especially in the vicinity of Monterey. Their limbs are streamlined landward as a result of "wind shear." Bracken, grass, berries, lupine, and other hardy plants hug the ground. A belt suitable chiefly for dairying and the cultivation of certain highly specialized crops, such as artichokes, beans, and peas, follows coastal lowlands.

Ridge faces and summits are scarred by numerous "balds" or "barrens." Trees nest in sheltered valleys, laurels and live oaks being the most

numerous, and redwoods the most stately. The latitudinal range of the latter is between the Santa Lucia Range and the Oregon line. Farther north are rhododendrons, lusty enough to attain individual heights of as much as 40 feet. In early May their blossoms rival those of Cornwall or Devon. Vegetation is somewhat greener in rainy January than in rainless, but damp, July and August.

THE INTERIOR IS DIFFERENT

The climatic contrast between coast and interior is more and more emphasized southward along the Pacific Coast Ranges. On July afternoons when the temperature at Brookings, on the coast, is below 65°, the mercury stands above 90° in Rogue River Valley, about 60 miles away. The temperature during the coldest hour of typical January nights at Brookings is above 39°, whereas at Grants Pass in the valley to the east it is below freezing. Brookings has never recorded a temperature much below 20°, but in Rogue River Valley the coldest records are zero and lower. There is a corresponding decrease in precipitation. Brookings averages over 70 inches, spread out over 122 days, whereas Grants Pass has but 29.6, on 100 days. Snowfall is about six times as heavy at the inland station, but values are trifling, because Brookings receives only about an inch in the average year. At an elevation of 2,100 feet and about 25 miles inland, Happy Home has an annual snowfall of over 132 inches.

Foresters call the particular assemblage of trees that originally covered much of the Coast Range belt of Washington and Oregon the Douglas fir forest. The stands of those tall and picturesque trees are nearly pure in many areas. Along the immediate coast they are less common. Hardy pines face the chilly breezes from the ocean at lower elevations. Western red cedar, hemlock, Sitka spruce, and other trees enrich the forest of the next zone back. Toward higher summits the stands are more typically Sitka spruce, alpine firs, and hemlock. In southern Oregon, Port Orford cedar and myrtle form conspicuous elements in the sylvan scene.

Into this forested region came Finns and other northern Europeans. Many lingered awhile in the Lake States, where they picked up the lore of Paul Bunyan. Their labors have resulted in deforestation which is apace with that of other parts of the humid western States. Where

the virgin timber has been removed, alders gain prompt foothold, spreading from their typical stream-side environment to become the second growth on the slopes above. Oats, other forage crops and cereals, and fruit trees are cultivated on cleared lowlands.

The contrast between coast and interior climates was clearly emphasized in the pristine forests of southern Oregon. Western yellow pines and incense cedars were dominant east of the first main summits.

In the valleys today are fields of hops and extensive orchards, which, in addition to their world-famous pears, produce walnuts and many times as many prunes as the better-known Santa Clara Valley, below San Francisco. Many valleys are so dry that fields require irrigation, a strange contrast to the bleak surf-pounded coast not over 40 or 50 miles away! Little wonder that the more prosperous valley inhabitants have beach houses to which they hope to retreat during the summer. To a western Oregonian the annual fortnight when temperatures rise above 90° is oppressive heat. The magnetic attraction of fried clams, barbecued crab, halibut, and other sea food, the lure of mountain trout in rippling streams, or steelhead in coastal lagoons—help draw him to the cooler coast.

Behind the fog-belt redwood forest of the California coast is an even more emphatic contrast than that between coast and interior in southern Oregon. Originally the northern redwood forest was one of the densest timber stands in the world. Many an acre has yielded over 2.5 million board feet; single trees yield as many as 480,000. Today a few large redwood groves have been preserved, but generally this forest is now in various stages of second growth. It takes somewhat more than a century for redwoods to attain size sufficient to tempt the logger. For decades the forest will be mainly a region of young trees. Dairies and farms of various sorts have taken over only the flatter ground.

The silence is impressive among dense redwoods. Thimbleberries, bracken, and other plants hug a surface little molested by animal life. Visibility is restricted by fog much of the time, but here and there a shaft of sunshine manages to break through atmospheric and vegetational canopies to emphasize the contrast between the light greens of the undergrowth and the dark, somber greens and tans of the trees above. Amateurs have underexposed many miles of film, trying to record the scene.

A few miles back from the fog belt, in a much drier climate, are sugar pines, incense cedars, red and white firs. Still farther back, the lowlands are grassy or covered with scrubby vegetation, adjusted to summer drought so severe that forest will not grow.

The climatic contrast between sides of the northern California Coast Ranges is well displayed in a comparison between Crescent City and Yreka, some eighty miles inland. The coastal station receives over 74 inches of rain on 110 days of the average year, whereas the inland point gets but 17.3 inches, on 78 days. No temperature of less than 23° has ever been recorded at Crescent City, while at Yreka the record low temperature is —7°. During the average warmest hour of the warmest month the temperature is below 68° on the coast, and above 91° inland. The coldest hour of January days averages about 39° at Crescent City and but 23.7° at Yreka. The interior climate is quite continental as compared with that of the coast, but from the standpoint of southeastern Wyoming, in the same latitude, even Yreka is decidedly marine.

The Oregon Douglas fir forest penetrates only into the higher mountains north of the Klamath River in California. The redwood forest displaces it along the coastal fog belt and a yellow pine-incense cedar forest occupies territory to the east of the first main ridges behind the coast. Douglas fir and several kinds of true fir are abundant in wetter parts of the yellow pine-incense cedar forest. Eastward and southward, toward drier territory, the yellow pine prevails. Here and there an isolated valley flat is altogether too dry for forest. Manzanita and other shrubs flank its sides and grass covers its floor. During winter months valleys are green, in early spring they burst forth with multicolored wild flowers, but in summer they dry out to the yellows and browns so characteristic of "Mediterranean" landscapes to the south.

This climatic summary of the northern coast ranges may be concluded with a comparison between two stations not far north of San Francisco. Point Reyes, on the coast, has about 10 more days of rain per year than Santa Rosa, about 20 miles inland. Each has an annual rainfall of about 30 inches, with about an even chance each year that there will be one rainy day between the first of July and the end of August. The lowest temperatures on record are 30° on the coast and 15° inland, the highest, 98° and 109°. The average mean maximum temperature of the warmest month is 61° at Point Reyes and almost 82° at Santa Rosa, while the

average coldest hour in January is 45.1° on the coast and 35.7° inland. September is the warmest month at Point Reyes. August is slightly the warmest at Santa Rosa. The seasonal range between coldest and warmest months at Point Reyes is only 6.8°, the smallest in the United States.

The interior valleys north of San Francisco Bay are notable not only for their excellent orchard fruits, but especially for the quality of their wines. The same variations that roughly correspond to latitude in Europe are exhibited in California. In southern California are grown grapes that yield the equivalents of Algerian and Spanish wines, in the San Joaquin Valley Tokays and other grapes that produce the sweet wines of central, and the drier parts of southern, Europe. In Napa Valley and north beyond Cloverdale are the grapes capable of making the delicate dry wines of eastern and northern France and western Germany. In a climate similar to that of Normandy, in the hills west of Petaluma, are cheese factories engaged in equaling, or bettering, the finest Camembert of Europe.

TRANSITIONAL CENTRAL CALIFORNIA

San Francisco Bay is the most significant natural boundary in the Pacific Coast Ranges. Forests dominate most rolling country to the north. Southward dense stands of timber are confined mainly to basins and individual valleys. Chaparral is the predominant vegetational cover of slopes in the southern Coast Ranges. This distribution of native vegetation is largely a reflection of climatic conditions. To the south is the land of truly hot, dry summers, less abundant rainfall, almost total absence of snow at lower elevations, irrigation, inadequate municipal water supplies within easy reach, and landscape features commonly regarded as being typically Californian. There is little mystery as to why the Russians worked southward along the coast only as far as Fort Ross, less than 70 miles from San Francisco, or as to why the Spanish missions stopped just north of the bay. Each group had come to the end of territory to which it was accustomed and where it knew how to make a living. The sharpest boundary between different kinds of insects in the Coast Ranges is also the Golden Gate.

The bleak fog belt extends southward, well past San Francisco, and few swim with comfort in the Pacific north of Point Conception. Some excellent redwood stands occur in the Santa Cruz Mountains and a few

in the Santa Lucia Range, south of Monterey Bay, but these are only outliers of the main forest belt to the north. Lumbering has been little more than a short-lived novelty south of the bay, not the main support of a large population, as has been the case northward to the Canadian border.

The southern Coast Ranges recall the climates of Mediterranean Europe and the northwestern coast of Africa. They are climatically far removed from the British Isles type of territory in Washington and Oregon. Here, for about half the year is a land of yellowish, dried-grass hills; shrubs with small leaves, grayish and resinous in many cases, in order to withstand summer drought; trees that spread broadly along the ground to shade with tender care the surface above their roots, so that it may not yield moisture excessively to evaporation—and other characteristics of the macchie, maqui, or garigue of southern Europe.

To a person who has spent his life in the vicinity of San Francisco Bay, rain is something that comes with cold weather. The rainy season is winter, when days are chilly. Rainless days may be warm and sunny. The experience of rain during hot, sultry weather, such as occurs in the Middle West, is unknown. It is difficult to convince a native of this region that summer is generally the time of maximum rainfall in most parts of the earth, and that his climatic conditions are duplicated elsewhere only around certain shores of the Mediterranean, and in four small west-coast areas in the southern hemisphere.

In combined area these regions of "Mediterranean climate" are minute as compared to the extent of the continents yet they produce most of the dried fruit of commerce, a large proportion of the world's wine output, an important share of all garden vegetables, all olives, and a considerable share of all citrus products. They are not only suited to growing practically all nontropical fruits but, what is even more important, they have a dependable dry season for their harvesting and preservation. Wherever sufficient water exists for irrigation the naturally fertile soils of Mediterranean flats are potential garden spots. In the absence of near-by hills or mountains, irrigation may be impossible, in which case the summer desiccation of unwatered land may be so intense that it is rendered fit for little else than meager pasturage.

There is more diversity of landscape within sixty miles or so of San Francisco than across the widths of many important nations. Varied

topography is the fundamental causal factor. Many sharply differen-
tiated climatic and vegetational landscapes readily catch the eye. From
bracken and berries on the coast, chilled by the afternoon wind and fog
of July and August, the distance is not far to sheltered, grassy valleys
with clear skies and intense, dry heat. During the warmest part of the
typical July day the temperature is less than 70° in San Francisco, but
over at Antioch, about thirty-five miles away, it is 91.4°. The annual rainfall drops from over 22 to less than 12.5 inches between these same places.
Less than fifty miles to the south, at Boulder Creek, the rainfall is in
excess of 55 inches, at an elevation of 470 feet. There is no Weather
Bureau information as to the amount toward surrounding summits, but
it is certainly well over 60 inches. From the dense forest of huge redwoods in Big Basin, not far from Boulder Creek, to the barren short-grass
hills near Antioch is a landscape change more striking than that between
the longleaf pine forests of easternmost Texas and the buffalo grass of
the Texas Panhandle.

DWARF FORESTS FACE NORTH

In no other region is the contrast so great between vegetation on
opposite sides of even small hills. Typically the south slopes, exposed
almost vertically to the rays of noonday summer sunshine, are baked
and parched as a result of intense evaporation. The green of winter
changes to the yellowish brown of summer early in the warm season.
Few trees have the courage to dispute territory with short grasses.
Children bring out their grass sleds in May. Dense chaparral or forest,
depending on the availability of water, covers north slopes. Where
rainfall is heaviest the forest may be a local grove of redwoods, as is the
case at several places in the hills east of San Francisco Bay, at near-by
Muir Woods to the north, or in the Santa Cruz Mountains to the south.
More commonly the trees are evergreen laurels and oaks, red-barked
madroñas, or scrubby pines. Here and there is a novelty, such as the
unique grove of Santa Lucia fir in southern Monterey County. Along
streams are slender alders, supple willows, and patchy-barked sycamores.

On drier north slopes the predominant growth is the "dwarf forest," or
chaparral, comprised mainly of shrubs with stiff, thorny branches and

small leaves. Chamiso, a tiny-leaved greasewood, several types of wild lilac, manzanita, and many other plants generally grouped as "brush" by the natives, form the assemblage.

Protection from vertical sunshine and relatively low rates of evaporation explain the vegetational cloaks of the northward slopes of hills. Trees do much to preserve the soil moisture that favors their presence. Most of them hug the ground quite closely, spreading a broad, evergreen canopy that keeps sunshine from reaching the ground above their roots. This "squat structure" is also typical of trees in other regions of Mediterranean climate, as are the vegetational contrasts between north and south slopes.

Each successive range back from the coast is ordinarily drier than the one in front of it. Redwoods hardly get foothold anywhere to the east of the first, main rows of hills. Forests are limited to higher and higher elevations toward the San Joaquin Valley, and many of the easternmost ranges are almost treeless. The valleys between ranges share in this rain-shadow effect. Many are so dry that their climate is classified as "arid steppe," the kind of place where only short grass and low shrubs grow wild.

At Santa Cruz the annual rainfall amounts to nearly 27 inches. At Laurel, within the mountains, at an elevation of 910 feet, it is almost 51 inches. In the lower end of San Francisco Bay Valley, at San Jose, it is but 14.5. Though Lick Observatory, east of San Jose, has an elevation of 4,209 feet, the rainfall amounts to only 29 inches. No records are available for other places in the Mount Hamilton and other ranges eastward, but at Newman, on the western side of the San Joaquin Valley, in the same latitude, the rainfall is but 10.24 inches. This is the typical transition eastward, from the fog belt of the coast to the arid valley of the interior. The warmest hour of the typical July day at Newman has a temperature of 97.3°, which is 22.5° above that at Santa Cruz, less than sixty-five miles away.

MEDITERRANEAN SOUTHERN COAST RANGES

Southward along the Coast Ranges annual precipitation diminishes in amount and summer drought becomes more and more intense. Landscape patterns follow a convergence of rainfall belts toward the coast.

Scenes typical of the easternmost ridges along the Sacramento Valley, north of San Francisco Bay, occur centrally in the Coast Range belt near San Francisco and reach the coast itself at Point Conception. Each ridge intercepts moisture enough to emphasize rain, shadow conditions eastward. The initial moisture burden of the winds lessens southward. Toward Point Conception a climatic traverse resembles the one given above, but omits the Santa Cruz end and reaches Newman conditions short of the San Joaquin Valley.

A cross section back from the coast of the Santa Lucia Range, south of Monterey Bay, includes Big Sur, with 35.77 inches of rain, at an elevation of 300 feet. No records have been kept toward the higher summits, but the vegetation suggests a belt with over 50 inches. At 1,050 feet, on the slopes toward Salinas Valley, Abbotts records 19.66 inches. Within the valley, King City, at 331 feet, has but 10.57 inches. Priest Valley, at 2,400 feet, somewhat similar to the Lick Observatory location on the section east from Santa Cruz, gets 19.32 inches. Coalinga, on the western side of the San Joaquin Valley, at an elevation of 663 feet, has an annual precipitation of 6.55 inches, an amount low enough to establish the surrounding territory as climatic desert. All of these places approximate the same parallel of latitude, and the distance from one end of the line to the other is less than eighty miles.

The temperatures of two valley stations less than 45 miles apart along the Big Sur-Coalinga line present interesting contrasts. The average July temperature at King City in Salinas Valley is 68°, whereas at Coalinga in the San Joaquin it is 82°. During the warmest hour of July days the average at Coalinga is over 102°, but at King City is only 86.7°. A resident of Coalinga will experience an average temperature of 62° each night during July, while in King City the thermometer drops somewhat below 50°. Only a resident of the fog belt or of the northern Coast Ranges would consider July a hot month at King City. Everyone will agree about the daytime heat of Coalinga, but most residents of the United States would regard the nights as from cool to chilly, even in midsummer. The maximum temperature ever recorded at King City is 110°, that at Coalinga, 120°. The respective minima are 18° and 11°. Hot summer drought renders all ridges east of King City comparatively barren and arid, whereas those to the west have moderately large

areas of forest and abundant chaparral. Toward Coalinga the vegetation is that of the desert.

South of San Luis Obispo, where general trends of ridges and valleys change from being roughly parallel to the coast to about east-west, the vegetational contrast between north and south slopes is even more accentuated than to the north. South slopes are especially barren. North slopes bear scattered forests or mantles of dense chaparral.

The valley mouths of the east-west Coast Ranges ordinarily widen, funnel-like, toward oceanic winds. Fog drifts up valley floors far more easily than across transverse ridges. The upvalley invasions vary from day to day with the general result that landscapes change progressively from being similar to those of fog-belt lowlands near the coast, through various inland valley types, to fogless desert toward valley heads.

Places near the coast experience remarkably uniform temperatures. The range at Santa Maria, between extreme months, is only from 64° in August to 50° in January. On the typical August afternoon the maximum temperature is 74.7°, not quite as warm as in September, after the season of maximum sea fog has passed. During the typical August night the thermometer drops to 52.6°. During drier September, it drops to 50.9°. Farther inland, out of the fogs, the warmest month shifts back to July, and temperature ranges of all types broaden considerably. At Bakersfield, in the San Joaquin Valley, the warmest hour of all July days averages slightly more than 100°, the coolest 63.6°. The ordinary temperature difference between coldest and warmest parts of the day, during the warmest month of the year increases from 22.1° at Santa Maria to 36.6° at Bakersfield.

COAST RANGE DESERT?

There are several different meanings of the word "desert." The original meaning is uninhabited, or deserted, with the implication of being uninhabitable. The desert of northern Africa was the closest and best known example to Europeans, so "uninhabitable because of lack of sufficient water supply" became the most common meaning of the word. Later on people began to speak of polar deserts and other kinds of deserts when blank spots appeared on world-population maps. To the botanist a desert became a region characterized by plants adapted to

extreme drought. In the most striking cases the environment is so unfavorable that there are practically no plants at all. The climatologist has still another concept of dry desert, one based on such factors as amount of precipitation, season of maximum rainfall, rate of evaporation, and temperature. His definition of desert is mathematical.

For a given temperature and season of maximum rainfall, a place is classified as desert by a climatologist if the total precipitation fails to attain some critical value. Generally speaking, the more humid boundary of desert climate in the United States has an annual rainfall of 10 inches or less. The amount is smaller in colder climates, where evaporation is less rapid, and is increased by an inch or more in hotter climates, because of intense evaporation. If the season of maximum rainfall is winter, moisture is more effective in promoting plant growth. Evaporation is less capable of parching the ground during the growing season than in a region of summer rainfall. A cool region of winter rainfall may escape classification as desert even though the annual rainfall be below 8 inches or even less.

There are many who dispute the identification of desert within the Pacific Coast Ranges, or even in the San Joaquin Valley to the east. The mean annual precipitation at Bakersfield is but 5.54 inches, and numerous other San Joaquin Valley stations record less than 6 inches per year. With a mean annual temperature of 64.6°, a record of that sort is to be regarded as severe desert, from the climatic viewpoint. While temperature and precipitation records are lacking, so that factual proof is unobtainable, the vegetation and general appearance of the lower parts of ranges lying just west of the southern half of the San Joaquin Valley certainly are those of the desert. Farther west and at higher elevations are the short grasslands of the somewhat less arid climatic "steppe." Only on higher ridges or in valleys toward the coast are the chaparral, forest, and other natural plant associations of nonarid climates.

The inland heads of longer valleys between San Luis Obispo and Point Conception are intensely hot in summer, despite the fact that their mouths are cooled by chilly ocean breezes. Spring and summer drought burns off the previous winter's scanty bunch grass. Low shrubs and other plants drought-resistant enough to remain alive during half a

dozen or more rainless months face daily temperatures commonly exceeding 100°. Sheep range widely in such territory in search of palatable foliage.

CLIMATIC VARIETY IN SOUTHERN CALIFORNIA

The climate most commonly associated with southern California in the minds of many people is restricted to the lowlands of a rather narrow belt along the east-west coast near Santa Barbara and southeastward, toward San Diego. In large measure it depends on the configuration of the coast. In part it is the result of an irregular oceanic platform, with many submerged basins and ridges, the summits of which rise as islands. The famous Catalina is one of these. Others somewhat less well-known are the large Santa Barbara, Santa Cruz, and Santa Rosa Islands, and several smaller bits of land extending west to San Miguel and south to San Clemente. The irregular barrier system of this submerged platform concentrates currents along definite channels in some places and provides basins for relatively stagnant water elsewhere. Near-shore waters, on the whole, tend to warm up more in summer than do waters northward, beyond Point Conception. Surf bathing is comparatively pleasant along the beaches during a month or two in summer and actually comfortable in sheltered bays. The summer winds from these waters are neither so chilly nor so foggy as those striking San Francisco and other places to the north.

On the immediate coast of southern California air temperatures are moderate enough. The yearly range runs from 54° in January to between 64° and 70° in July. The average January day attains a high of about 60° and a low of from 41° to 48°. In August the range is from nearly 80° in early afternoon to as low as 57° just before sunrise. Most places have experienced temperatures above 100° and as low as 21°, but Point Loma, Oxnard, and several other coastal points have never recorded a thermometer reading below 28°. The precipitation varies from over 18 inches at Santa Barbara to less than 10 at several places, Point Loma (San Diego) having slightly over 11 inches per year. January is the rainiest month in all of southern California. The three summer months combined rarely record over 0.2 inch. About 85 per cent of the annual precipitation occurs between the first of November and the end of March.

The effects of relief and inland position on precipitation are shown strikingly along a line extending northward from San Pedro to the Mohave Desert. At an elevation of 10 feet, San Pedro receives but 10.66 inches per year. Los Angeles (338 feet) has an annual rainfall of 14.95 inches, Pasadena (805 feet) 18.17 inches. Sierra Madre, at the base of steep mountain slopes, gets 23.67 inches, at an elevation of 1,100 feet. Lowe Observatory, somewhat over half the distance up the seaward face of the Sierra Madre (3,420 feet) has an annual rainfall of 26.74 inches; and Mount Wilson, 5,850 feet, on one of the summit peaks, gets 31.20 inches. Across the range, even though 3,400 feet above sea level, Llano has a total precipitation of but 6.41 inches. Barstow, farther out in the desert, has a rainfall of 4.10 inches. The distance from San Pedro to Mount Wilson is 40 miles and that to Llano is less than 60.

A similar section, about 75 miles long, takes us from Oceanside, where at 60 feet the rainfall is 12.87 inches, past Nellie (5,000 feet) with 47.97 inches, down to Oak Grove (2,751 feet) with 17.02 inches, and Indio (22 feet below sea level) where the annual rainfall is but 3.00 inches. From steppe, or dry Mediterranean vegetation near the coast, one climbs up to magnificent forest, on the San Jacinto Range, and then descends through various shades of steppe into extreme desert on a trip from Oceanside to Indio. The average July night cools off to 57.4° at Nellie but stays more than 20° warmer than that at Indio. During the average afternoon of the warmest month the temperature at Nellie is less than 84°, but at Indio it is 106.5°. For four consecutive months the typical early afternoon temperature is in excess of 100°. Once the mercury ascended to 125°, which is 25° higher than any temperature ever recorded at Nellie. The extreme minimum has been 16° for the desert station and 9° for the mountain. The famous resort of Palm Springs, a few miles from Indio, boasts of its 42° January nights and 69° afternoons, rather than its average July day, with a maximum temperature of 107.4°. Even then, however, a drop to less than 73° can be expected before sunrise.

Many laughs are heard over the radio about southern California rainfall. During more than half a century the average number of days with measurable rainfall at Los Angeles has been 53 per year. Of these 18 occur during the three winter months and 12 in the spring. The average has been 1.0 for the three summer months combined. During

the driest year on record the rainfall amounted to but 2.0 inches, and during the wettest, 51.2. Typically it is about 15 inches. The sun shines 72 per cent of all hours possible, the brightest months occurring during fall, when the percentage rises to 77; and the most overcast is spring, with 66 per cent. Snow and hail are practically unknown, and only two thunderstorms are heard annually. On 13 days of the typical year the mercury will rise above 90° and less than once will it sink below freezing. Not over three dense fogs may be expected during any month of the year, but such days add up to a total of 27 for the whole 12 months, summer and early fall being somewhat foggier than January.

San Diego is considerably drier than Los Angeles, the average precipitation being 9.6 inches, with but 27.5 for the maximum year on record. The sun shines slightly fewer hours per year, but dense fogs are not quite so frequent, the average per year being twenty. The temperatures are slightly lower, the average summer day being about 8° cooler than in Los Angeles and the average winter day about 3° cooler. Once the thermometer descended to 28° at Los Angeles and to 25° at San Diego, but during the typical year the mercury neither tops 90° nor drops below 32° at the latter place.

WINTER MAY FIND TREES BEING HEATED

Citrus trees are readily killed by low temperature. Individual types differ greatly in resistance, but a short drop to 22° is likely to be fatal, and an hour or more below 28° may ruin the season's crop. In general, lemons are the first to be affected, so the lemon zone is close to the coast, where freezes are the least frequent and least likely to be severe. Behind them are the more hardy oranges, many of which are on low hills—rather than along valleys—which provide drainage ways for cold air on still winter nights. Kumquats and grapefruit are relatively resistant and for that reason are crowded back to less favorable sites, inland.

The general practice of orchard heating provides artificial temperatures for the trees during the frosty nights of winter, but it is not necessary to light the fire pots every year. When pots are spaced so that each tree has its own heater the temperature can be kept high enough to save crops and trees, except those in the most exposed situations.

Santa Barbara, San Fernando, and Pomona have each experienced temperatures as low as 23°. In slightly higher territory, such as at Sierra

Madre, where the minimum has been 28°, and Yorba Linda, with 26°, oranges are relatively safe, year after year. Toward the edge of the citrus belt are such critical low-temperature records as from 18° to 20° at Azusa, Claremont, and Redlands. The last possibilities for safety, even with heaters, lie not far away.

About the citrus belt is a zone of deciduous fruits, where apples, cherries, apricots, and peaches are raised. Here a trace of snow or an occasional temperature drop to 15° or lower is to be expected during some winters. Uncleared hills are locally clothed with chaparral, and groves of trees line ravines and the sides of streams. The citrus belt below in uncleared condition was mainly a grassland. Farther upslope are pines, in some places densely enough distributed to be dignified by the name forest.

NAKED SLOPES ARE STEEP

Steep, southern California mountain slopes are a novelty to most visitors. In part they are a result of geological history. The region is one of growing mountain ranges, a fact now and then emphasized to residents by an earthquake. Steep slopes are also a product of the climate. One looks in vain for the gently rounded contours of New England's Berkshire Hills anywhere in the arid Southwest. The typical mountain ranges of the desert rise abruptly from definite bases. Their slopes are steep and summits are likely to be knife-edged. Drainage ways are steep-sided. Closely spaced ravines lead to deeply engraved canyons. All such surface features are the earmarks of rapid erosion on slopes not adequately protected by vegetation or resistant layers of soil. In climates too dry for forest or uninterrupted grassland development, most surfaces are covered by rock fragments, rather than true soil. Rapid runoff, even from extremely infrequent rains, is a powerful agent of erosion on barren, comparatively soil-free slopes. In a well-watered region slopes are likely to be clothed with dense vegetation which helps form a protective sod or a soil layer extremely resistant to ordinary erosional attack. Rates of erosion on slopes and summits are not much faster than those on flats. Few deep canyons are formed, and hills are gently rounded. The coastward hills and ranges of southern California are somewhat more rounded in outline than those farther inland, where the climate is truly arid. Jaggedness of outline finds optimum development in the desert.

The naked details of erosion suggest, and the ravages of floods appear to confirm, the idea that deserts and other arid places are subject to terrific cloudbursts. One looks in vain for proof of this in actual weather records. The heaviest rainfall intensities on earth occur in the places that ordinarily get the most precipitation. The showers of the desert are modest in comparison. Actual cloudbursts ordinarily accomplish comparatively little erosion because their energies are spent on surfaces well prepared to drain off surplus waters. The major exceptions to this rule occur in some mountains where steep slopes set the stage for a spectacular surface change now and then. Though desert rains are not heavy, they commonly cause great floods and leave deep, fresh scars on the face of nature, time after time. Railroad service may be suspended occasionally across the valley bottoms of some rainy region because flood waters have backed up across the tracks, but in deserts schedules are upset and service is interrupted time after time by actual washouts, where long stretches of track are swept away. Highway engineers well know that the arroyos of the Southwest had better be crossed by dipping roadways rather than bridges, because they are more readily repaired after rains. There are probably many times as many miles of protective levees along the roads and railroads of the southwestern deserts than in the lower Mississippi Valley. That the desert has its terrific floods is well known. That they result from heavy rainfall is an unwarranted conclusion. Floods occur because runoff is rapid, which, in turn, is the natural consequence of vegetational sparcity, the absence of soils and litter cover, and the steepness of slopes.

The Los Angeles River has been the butt of many a joke. Like the arroyo of the desert, it carries little or no water most of the time, and also like the desert stream, one should never minimize its potentialities in time of fury. The Montrose Flood of 1934 was a particularly severe tantrum vented by a few of its minor upstream branches. On this occasion a chaparral fire had stripped the steep slopes above Glendale of their meager plant protection. Rains somewhat over a month later caused a flood that claimed several lives and ruined several hundred houses. Boulders weighing as much as 32 tons were carried over a mile beyond canyon mouths, and those approximating a ton twice as far. No fewer than 700,000 cubic yards of sand, gravel, and boulders were deposited on streets, over yards, and even within crushed houses that lay in the path

of the flood. Yet this devastation resulted from rainfall that fell at a rate of less than 1⅓ inches per hour, 10 inches during any consecutive 12 hours, or 14 inches per day. In the Carolinas, Georgia, Louisiana, and other rainy places such rates of precipitation are relatively common. There are many places between coastal Texas and New York that have experienced 20-inch rainfall days without serious damage or striking topographic results. Places in the Philippines, India, and the Hawaiian Islands have received over 40 inches a day. The term "cloudburst" implies a rate of about 4 inches per hour. A station in Virginia once received over 9.25 inches in 30 minutes and one in Pennsylvania recorded 23 inches in 4 hours. The Los Angeles River and other streams along the coast toward the Mexican boundary, though generally dormant, are now and then awakened abruptly by floodwaters because they serve a territory semiarid to arid climatically. Their headwaters lie where run off is practically unchecked.

SUMMITS ARE WHITE AT TIMES

Southern California would lose much of its scenic attraction were not Old Baldy and other peaks now and then covered with snow. Bright oranges dotting brilliant green foliage in the foreground, framed by the angularity of semiarid slopes, and capped by high, glistening snow-covered peaks are an unforgettable scene. The possibility of skiing after only a short drive up some excellent highway from a place enjoying delightful spring or even mild summer weather is something that attracts thousands of persons, time and time again, to the mountains. In no other place having an average January temperature of 55° do so many people own winter-sport outfits, and have so many automobiles been equipped with racks for carrying skis.

At Bear Valley Dam, some 20 miles air-line from San Bernardino, at an elevation of 6,700 feet, the annual snowfall amounts to over 117 inches. During at least one year, each month from December to March received over 40 inches, and from November to April over 20. At times the snowfall has exceeded 50 inches in February or March. The typical afternoon in San Bernardino attains a temperature of 66° in January and above 70° in March.

Mount Wilson, about 18 miles from the heart of Los Angeles, has an average snowfall in excess of 50 inches, and in some years gets more

than double that amount. At Squirrel Inn, less than 13 miles from San Bernardino, the 1929-1930 snowfall amounted to nearly 200 inches. Not far back from San Diego the annual snowfall is ordinarily 30 inches and more, Cuyamaca, at 4,677 feet, having received 150 inches one winter.

The Coast Ranges of southern California have even greater climatic variety than those to the north. Their oceanic margins have a touch of the chill and overcast so well developed upcoast, but with far less precipitation and actual dampness. Their seaward faces exhibit vegetational and climatic zonation starting from rather mild types of arid landscapes at lower elevations to fairly well-developed forests near summits. Interior valleys are typically arid, with intensely hot summer days but moderate to cool nights. Toward the interior the annual precipitation is so small that severe desert occurs. From a few places near Palm Springs one may look up to sheltered ravines on the sides of San Jacinto, even on the hottest summer day, and see the residue of last winter's snow. In a region so varied climatically, there is little wonder that Hollywood finds it possible, within a few miles of its studios, to film scenes from all parts of the world, from the quiet of the Arctic waste to the shifting sands of the Sahara.

Here ends the volume, but here is no end to the delights of the Pacific Coast Ranges. No volume of the "American Mountain Series" has told or will tell of such variety of human kind and human experience. In no other ranges in the United States are there so many kinds of intimacies and adjustments between men and their environments. If this volume does not finish the story, the logical sequel for the reader is to become voyager by motor, pack train, or on foot. May I admonish you to take that trip not hastily, but leisurely, enjoying to the utmost the delights of each day and each valley or peak.

R.P.

MAPS

OF THE PACIFIC COAST RANGES

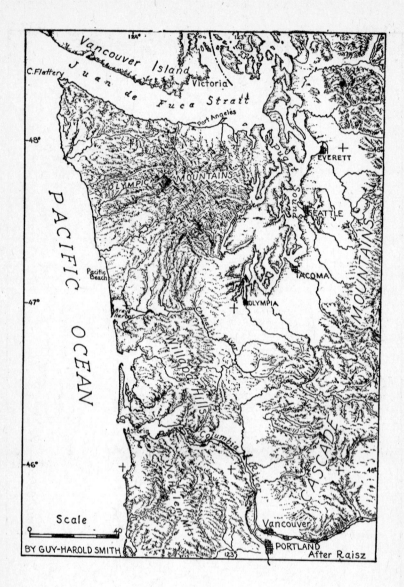

PACIFIC OCEAN

Columbia River
PORTLAND
Mt. Hood

COLUMBIA PLATEAU

-45°   45°

Cape Lookout

Wilson River

Nestucca River

South Yamhill River

North Yamhill River

Valley

Salem

CASCADE MOUNTAINS

Seal Rock

Albany
Corvallis

Alsea River

Willamette

COAST RANGE

-44°   44°

Eugene

Siuslaw River

Umpqua River

Calapooya Mts.

Cape Arago

Coos River

Coquille River

Roseburg

CASCADE

BASIN AND RANGE PROVINCE

-43°   43°

Cape Blanco

Sugar Loaf

Rogue River

Illinois River

Crater Lake

Rocks

Siskiyou Mts.

Upper Klamath Lake

Scale

0   40

BY GUY-HAROLD SMITH   123°   After Ratsz

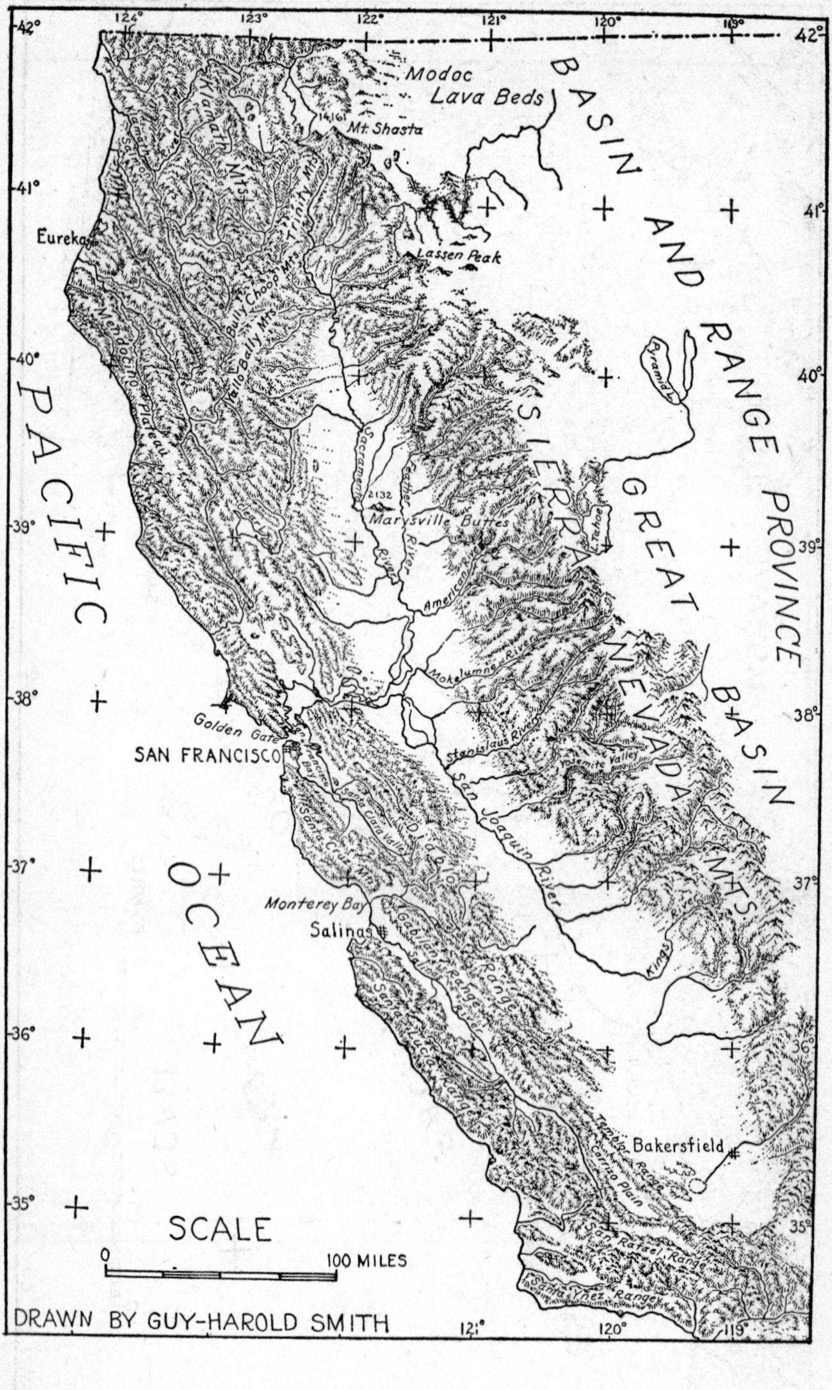
Modoc
Lava Beds
Mt. Shasta
14161
BASIN AND RANGE PROVINCE
Klamath Mts.
Trinity Mts.
Eureka
Lassen Peak
Bully Choop Mts.
Yollo Bolly Mts.
Mendocino Plateau
Pyramid L.
PACIFIC OCEAN
SIERRA NEVADA MTS.
GREAT BASIN
Sacramento River
Feather River
2132
Marysville Buttes
Tahoe
American River
Mokelumne River
Golden Gate
SAN FRANCISCO
Stanislaus River
Yosemite Valley
San Joaquin River
Santa Clara Valley
Santa Cruz Mts.
Diablo
Monterey Bay
Salinas
Gabilan Range
Salinas River
Santa Lucia Range
Kings River
Bakersfield
Temblor Range
Carrizo Plain
San Rafael Range
Santa Ynez Range
SCALE
0
100 MILES
DRAWN BY GUY-HAROLD SMITH

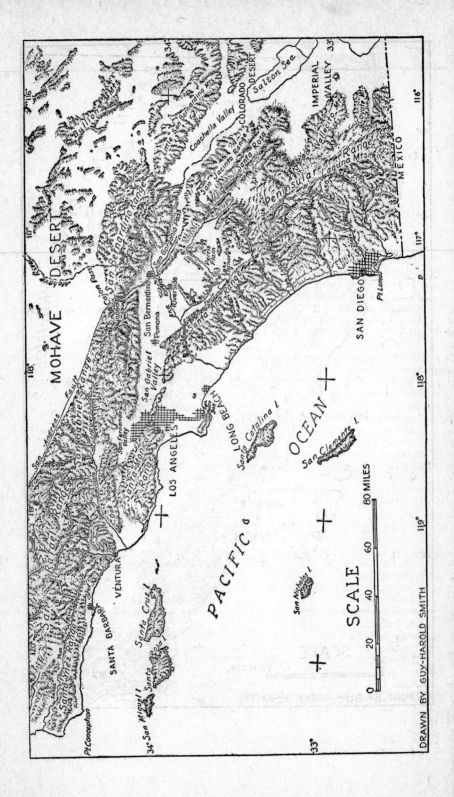

DRAWN BY GUY·HAROLD SMITH

INDEX

387

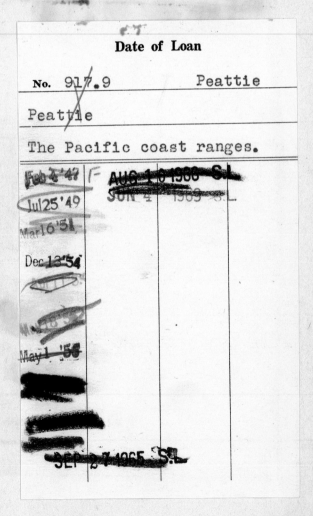

Date of Loan

No. 917.9 Peattie

Peattie

The Pacific coast ranges.

Feb 7 '47	F	AUG 10 1966 S.L.
Jul 25 '49		JUN 4 1969 S.L.
Mar 16 '51		
Dec 13 '54		
May 1 '56		

SEP 27 1965 S.L.